Reiser rt46

ALSO BY GEORGE BUSH

Looking Forward: The George Bush Story
(with Victor Gold)

ALSO BY BRENT SCOWCROFT

*Defending Peace and Freedom: Toward Strategic Stability
in the Year 2000* (editor)
Military Service in the United States

A WORLD TRANSFORMED

A WORLD TRANSFORMED

*by George Bush
and Brent Scowcroft*

ALFRED A. KNOPF

NEW YORK

1998

THIS IS A BORZOI BOOK
PUBLISHED BY ALFRED A. KNOPF, INC.

Copyright © 1998 by
George Bush and Brent Scowcroft

A list of photographic credits will be found
following the index.

Library of Congress Cataloging-in-Publication Data

Bush, George.
A world transformed / by George Bush and
Brent Scowcroft. — 1st ed.
p.   cm.
ISBN 0-679-43248-5 (alk. paper)
1. United States—Foreign relations—1989–1993.
2. Bush, George, 1924–   . 3. Scowcroft, Brent.
I. Scowcroft, Brent.   II. Title.
E881.B86   1998
327.73′009′049—dc21   98-13499
CIP

Manufactured in the United States of America
First Edition

GEORGE BUSH

To my understanding and beloved family, especially Barbara, and to the superb team that was at my side

BRENT SCOWCROFT

To Jackie and Karen, the lights of my life

CONTENTS

16 pages of illustrations will be found following page 272

ACKNOWLEDGMENTS

This book is the product of a lot of work by many people. The two of us started off thinking we would research and write the whole thing by ourselves. After all, we had lived through the momentous events we were describing and analyzing, and it was our efforts and their results that we were setting forth. But it quickly turned out that we, individually and collectively, did not remember as much as we had hoped, and what we did remember had gaps. That notwithstanding, our first draft of chapter one was over 400 pages long.

Our cry for help was answered by James McCall, who had been doing similar work for Paul Nitze. James was an invaluable addition to our writing team. He rapidly tamed and reorganized the project, and was adept not only at research, writing, and editing—helping us shape the substance of the book—but also at working between two authors a thousand miles apart. In addition, James made sense of the thousands of boxes of documents and papers stored in College Station, Texas, awaiting the opening of the Bush Presidential Library. He was able to identify, uncover, or track down the materials that found their way into the book. He has a fine instinct for history and brought a valuable perspective, not warped by having been a participant in the events. We are deeply indebted to James.

Our editor at Knopf, Ashbel Green, has been the soul of patience, wisdom, and understanding. He has been there when we needed him, and hasn't looked over our shoulders when we required time to work things out for ourselves. We could not have asked for a better mix of help and forbearance. Closer to home, Jean Becker and Virginia Lampley managed the two of us, kept the communications lines open and productive, and prodded us whenever our enthusiasm waned. They were wise judges and counselors on every aspect of this project, unfailing and unflagging in their efforts, even when we were more than a little grumpy. Attorney Terri Lacy was responsible for putting us together with Knopf, negotiating the contract, and worrying about all legal aspects. She took a sizable burden off our shoulders. Arnold Kanter was instrumental in many ways. He helped define the scope and method of the manuscript. He was the first to explore ways to utilize the raw archives and has been a constant source of advice as we progressed.

Our appreciation as well goes to Don Wilson, director of the Bush Presidential Library Foundation, and to Dave Alsobrook, director of the Bush Presidential Library itself. Our special thanks go to Warren Finch, Mary Finch, Gary Foulk, Kathleen Dillon, and Jimmie Purvis, the National Archives team in College Station. Despite the difficult conditions their temporary quarters imposed on them, they were unfailingly courteous and helpful in ferreting out the precise documents and photos we required.

In putting together some of the major themes of the book, we were greatly assisted by Richard Haass and Condoleezza Rice, who traveled to Houston and Kennebunkport, respectively, for lengthy sessions discussing the raw materials of the text and refreshing our memory of details and events. Both have reviewed the manuscript as well, and provided useful comments and suggestions. We wish to thank them and others who were willing to devote time and energy to reading all or portions of the manuscript: Bob Blackwill, Dick Cheney, Bob Gates, Bill Hyland, John Karaagac, former Prime Minister Brian Mulroney, Kevin Nealer, Doug Paal, Richard North Patterson, Paul Wolfowitz, Philip Zelikow, and Bob Zoellick. Still others helped us locate materials and check facts, such as Richard Greco and Suzie Peake. There are countless people who assisted in ways too numerous to mention; we are eternally grateful. Then there are those who really did the work we describe, laboring anonymously in the trenches—military, political, and diplomatic—to bring to a successful conclusion this unique piece of history. Without their tireless efforts, there would have been no such history and thus no book.

Finally, there are our wives, Barbara and Jackie, who stood by our sides through the interminable hours in the making of this story and the almost as interminable hours in the writing of it. While Barbara likes to remind us that we began our book at the same time she did hers, without her quiet inspiration and encouragement—and Jackie's while she was here—these pages would not exist.

—*George Bush and Brent Scowcroft*
January 1998

INTRODUCTION

Some of the most dramatic and epochal events of the twentieth century took place during the short period of 1989 to 1991, events grouped broadly under the umbrella of the conclusion of the last great confrontation of the century—the Cold War. This book is our personal account of those developments. What follows is not a memoir or history of the Bush Administration, or even of its foreign policy. We prefer to leave history to the historians. Instead, our account is meant to offer insight into the decisions that shaped the character of a new world.

So much happened during our four years on watch that a single volume could never adequately cover it all. Our conclusion was that to discuss everything would be to discuss nothing: we would be forced either to write a multivolume work of many thousands of pages (which, for a time, seemed our fate), or to be content with a superficial summary. We chose to focus on the most important events of the years 1989–1991—the end of the Cold War, upheaval in China, Desert Storm, the collapse of the Soviet Union, and the emergence of the United States as the preeminent power.

Narrowing our scope was a difficult decision, for we were forced to leave out far more than we could include. We have omitted the changes in Latin America, and the operation in Panama, as well as the renewal of the Middle East peace process. We also do not cover the events of the last year of the Administration, such as the conflicts in Somalia and Bosnia. Most conspicuously absent is arms control, which we deal with only in passing. While arms control remained a central issue of US-Soviet relations (and had been for years the primary if not the only area of political dialogue between the powers), the subject is excruciatingly complex and of contemporary concern only to the experts. We elected not to inflict the details on the reader. Finally, we touch on domestic issues only where they inextricably interacted with foreign affairs, and then simply to mention that interaction, primarily as it related to Congress. In so limiting our topic, we felt we could produce something a little different—more personal and in greater depth—about the truly historic developments which were packed into three brief years. We wanted to give the reader a chance to revisit these crucial policies and policymaking challenges as they were seen at the White House by the two of us.

The book is written largely in the first person, but in three voices. We each give our own perspective on events and decisions (in passages identified by our names), and reflect on and interpret their significance. In the background runs a narrative, written in the first person plural (and presented in this typeface), providing some of the context and a thread of continuity for what transpired. The narrative "we" represents the two of us and, more broadly, the Administration. We generally restricted our individual contributions to what each of us saw, thought, or experienced directly, leaving the rest of the story to the narrative voice. We are not "experts" or scholars on the Soviet Union, the Middle East, or Germany, and we don't pretend to offer the final word on events. The narrative represents the "big picture," not a definitive history. It does not attempt to cover the monumental efforts of the National Security Council, State Department, and Defense Department staffs as they planned and implemented policies and decisions at the White House.

We have reconstructed our story with care and it rests almost entirely on the original (primary) sources. We have drawn deeply on the materials preserved in the Bush Presidential Library at Texas A & M (among them thousands of original NSC documents), the President's personal diary, notes, and letters, and other direct sources. With a few small exceptions, where we have had difficulty tracking down items, nothing is drawn from memory, apart from anecdotes. There are no created quotations, no second- (or third-) hand conversations. Not that the material was without its problems. We relied heavily on "memcons"—memorandums of conversations—covering discussions on the phone and in person. These are the records of conversations taken down by staff members physically present for that purpose. Though mostly excellent, reliable, and nearly verbatim, these records are not always complete. Sometimes a staffer was asked a question, a translator lagged behind, or several people spoke at once, leaving a gap. In many cases, one or both of us took our own notes, which we have used in addition to the record of the official notetaker. Brent Scowcroft was nearly always the US notetaker for "one-on-one" discussions between President Bush and foreign leaders. This makes us confident that the content is correct, if not always complete.

We have avoided virtually all the "secondary" sources, histories of the events, which are sometimes inaccurate (and, frankly, on occasion disturbingly "inventive") because the original records were not yet available to the authors. We did, however, make use of the research of Philip

Zelikow and Condoleezza Rice, who have preceded us in the production of their excellent book, *Germany Unified and Europe Transformed.* Both were present for much of what they describe. They also had access to original materials in the United States and overseas. For these reasons, we have leaned on their research to refresh our memories in some cases dealing with German unification.

Because most of the documents we consulted remain closed to scholars, we have not used footnotes. Most of the sources for passages are in any event self-evident—for example, a conversation with Canadian prime minister Brian Mulroney on a particular date. The President's diary is a different matter. On an episodic basis he kept record of his thoughts, which was never meant to be (and is not) either all-inclusive or an official record of his life. Portions have been included in the book, but these do not represent a larger work meant for publication—or for scholars. In a few cases, the language may have been altered slightly, solely for clarity.

The Bush Administration reached a national goal sought since the early 1950s, for which many patriotic Americans had given their lives, and which was brought closer during the Ronald Reagan years: freedom for Eastern Europe and the end to a mortal threat to the United States. What Harry S Truman's containment policy and succeeding administrations had cultivated, we were able to bring to final fruition. Did we see what was coming when we entered office? No, we did not, nor could we have planned it. The world we encountered in January 1989 was the familiar bipolar one of superpower rivalry, if no longer of total confrontation. Yet, in only three years—historically only a moment—the Cold War was over. While there were dramatic moments, epitomized by the opening of the Berlin Wall, perhaps the most important story is that they came largely *without* great drama. Eastern Europe threw off Soviet domination, Germany united, and the Soviet Union dissolved, all without significant bloodshed. Tragically, lives were lost in the turmoil within some of these countries, particularly in the Soviet republics, but none were claimed in the greatest change in the strategic balance since the end of World War I. In a sense, these years concluded nearly three quarters of a century of upheaval, the tides of totalitarianism, world wars, and nuclear standoff. Their hallmark was a peaceful, if sometimes awkward, superpower cooperation, symbolized in the response to the first post–Cold War crisis—the Iraqi invasion of Kuwait. That moment marked the threshold of an era of possibility and hope.

The long-run framework of Bush foreign policy was very deliberate: encouraging, guiding, and managing change without provoking backlash and crackdown. In the short run, the practical effort included as well a certain amount of seat-of-the-pants planning and diplomacy. At a time when personalities and relationships made a significant difference to the course of history, the international leadership, East and West, found it could work generally in cooperation to sort out the tough issues—on Germany, on Iraq, on the future of Europe. The great forces in action could have led to world catastrophe, but with down-and-dirty, hands-on participation, we molded it so there were no losers, only winners, furthering stability and long-term relations for the sake of peace. We eluded the shadow of another Versailles. Paralyzing suspicion had given way to growing trust; confrontation to collaboration. What we describe here are the people, events, and changes as we knew and experienced them—and America's role in transforming a world.

A WORLD TRANSFORMED

CHAPTER I

Past and Prologue

GEORGE BUSH

As the ferry carrying Mikhail Gorbachev slowly approached the Coast Guard station at Governors Island through the gray waters of New York harbor, a feeling of tense expectation spread across the waiting knots of US and Soviet officials. The arrival field had been largely cleared of spectators, and Coast Guardsmen and their families peered from windows, eagerly waiting to glimpse the Soviet leader as he stepped out onto the island. It was a crisp December 7, 1988, and I was looking forward to seeing Gorbachev, who had just finished a major address to the United Nations General Assembly—one filled with far-reaching arms control proposals. He was on his way to meet with President Ronald Reagan for a brief summit, which had been tacked on to the tail end of his visit to New York.

To tell the truth, I was a bit uncomfortable. As the first sitting vice president to be elected president since Martin Van Buren, I was in the awkward position of having to weigh my present role against my future one. I was only the president-elect, a few weeks away from my own inauguration and not yet setting policy. At the same time, I realized Gorbachev was anxious to know what direction I planned to take regarding the Soviet Union. It was a balancing act I had tried to maintain since the November election. I had to be careful to separate my own plans from those of President Reagan, who, after all, was still in charge and who had been extraordinarily considerate and kind to me for eight years. I tried to avoid anything that might give the appearance of undermining his authority, such as meeting separately with foreign leaders. I was determined to be a supportive vice president, one who had been—and would continue to be—loyal to his president.

I first met Gorbachev on March 13, 1985, when I was in Moscow rep-

resenting President Reagan and the United States at the funeral of
his predecessor as Soviet general secretary, Konstantin Chernenko. In
the early 1980s, the Soviets had worked their way through a series of
leaders—from Leonid Brezhnev to Yuri Andropov to Chernenko—and
I had flown to Moscow for the funeral of each. I think it was Jim Baker
who came up with the slogan for me "You die, I'll fly" to describe these
trips. Though necessarily somber events, I found them useful opportunities. State funerals allow world leaders to hold brief talks. In addition,
these occasions gave us the chance to eye the new man in charge. With
the high mortality rate in the top position at the Kremlin during that period, we had little first-hand knowledge of the personalities of the Soviet
leaders—just as we were adjusting to one, he was dead.

After the Chernenko funeral, our delegation, which included Secretary of State George Shultz, was ushered into the inevitably stiff and
formal setting of a high-ceilinged, opulent official Kremlin receiving
room, where we were greeted by Gorbachev. I recorded my first impressions of him in a cable I sent to President Reagan. The language reflects
both the time and the suspicions of the Cold War, but I think, in retrospect, that the substance hinted (if perhaps unwittingly) at what was
to come:

> Gorbachev will package the Soviet line for Western consumption
> much more effectively than any (I repeat any) of his predecessors. He
> has a disarming smile, warm eyes, and an engaging way of making an
> unpleasant point and then bouncing back to establish real communica-
> tion with his interlocutors.
>
> He can be very firm. Example: When I raised the human rights
> question with specificity, he interrupted my presentation to come back
> with the same rhetorical excess we have heard before. Quote "Within
> the borders of the US you don't respect human rights" or [referring to
> African-Americans], "you brutally repress their rights." But along with
> this the following: "We will be prepared to think it over" and "Let's
> appoint rapporteurs and discuss it." The gist being as follows—"don't
> lecture us on human rights, don't attack socialism but let's each take our
> case to discussion!"

Looking at these words years later, they were almost a prescription
for the way US-Soviet relations would unfold in the years to come. We
would talk through problems, not allow them to block progress. But
there were other signs of change as well, although perhaps we did not
pick up on them in 1985. At the end of our meeting, Shultz made a
superb presentation in which he told Gorbachev that Reagan wanted to
be personally engaged with the Soviet leader. He did it with great genu-

ineness and warmth. And it was clear from Gorbachev's response, even in translation, that he was offering the same kind of man-to-man sincerity. Perhaps this would not be a leader who would simply hide behind the same old rhetoric, as had his predecessors.

I subsequently developed a good feel for Gorbachev during his summit visit to Washington in December 1987. When I saw him at the Soviet embassy, we discussed the forthcoming US presidential race. I'm sure he had no desire to involve himself in an American election, but I had the impression he would not be unhappy if I won. I suppose he expected there would be some predictability and continuity from the Reagan Administration—in arms control, in working together on regional matters, in encouraging the Soviets toward openness and reform.

I told Gorbachev not to be concerned about the "empty cannons of rhetoric" he would hear booming during the campaign, and explained what the expression meant. It was a phrase Chinese leaders, I think Mao Zedong especially, had used years before to describe their propaganda criticizing the United States. Don't worry about excessive bombast, they would say; look at deeds and actions instead. I said that the upcoming presidential campaign would be filled with strong, hard-line statements from all kinds of sources about US-Soviet relations. He should not take them too seriously. I also told him I was willing to think anew about the future relationship between our countries.

One incident that day showed me Gorbachev the skilled politician at work. We were to go from the Soviet embassy to the White House in the same motorcade, and he was running a little late, although it didn't seem to concern him. He impulsively asked me to get into his "tank" (armored limousine) and ride with him. As we drove along, the crowds were enormous—Americans waiting to catch a glimpse of him. At one point I told him that I wished he had time to stop and speak to people, and that he would be well received. A minute later, the limo screeched to a halt, Gorbachev having commanded the driver to pull over: Secret Service agents from both the Soviet Union and the United States rushed to get into position as he plunged into a surprised and responsive crowd of onlookers, shaking hands and greeting them all in Russian. It was an amazing sight, and it was like a shot of adrenaline to him. He got back into the car visibly uplifted by the warm reception.

Later on during that visit I also learned something of what his wife Raisa was like when I was seated next to her at the reciprocal dinner given by Gorbachev for Reagan at the Soviet embassy. The evening wore on and on with ceremonies, formalities, and toasts. After an excellent meal at which we all ate too much, a large Russian opera singer appeared at the far end of the dining room. She was very talented, but not very pretty—I think that statement could stand any objective test. In an effort to inject a little levity into what was a rather somber evening, I leaned over to Raisa as the singer started her final song and said, "I think I'm falling in love." Raisa paused and looked at me in a serious way. "You'd better not," she replied sternly, "remember Gary Hart!" She had obviously been well briefed on the troubles the former senator had endured during the Democratic presidential primaries. I looked in her eyes to see if she was kidding; but no, I think she was serious.

Now, a year later at Governors Island, I was meeting Gorbachev in my new role and in the middle of a Soviet propaganda offensive. By this time he had captured the imagination of the entire world and was perhaps its most popular statesman. His address that day at the UN had been dramatic in both content and delivery, and it was obvious he loved the gamesmanship that went with an appearance there. It was an encouraging speech. Gorbachev had said that the threat or use of force should no longer be an instrument of foreign policy. He had promised to shift Soviet military doctrine to a more defensive stance and would unilaterally reduce their armed forces by 500,000 in two years—which, given their total size, was small but a good start. He also announced that several armored divisions would be withdrawn from Czechoslovakia, Hungary, and East Germany by 1991 and disbanded. I was looking forward to hearing what he would add when he spoke to the President.

A broadly smiling Gorbachev emerged from the ferry waving, dressed in a smartly tailored gray suit and a serious red tie. Shortly after President Reagan greeted him, I somewhat self-consciously joined them dockside and soon we ducked inside one of the buildings. With only a month and a half to go in his term, this would be Reagan's farewell meeting with a man he had come to respect and for whom he felt genuine fondness and friendship. Reagan had brought the US-Soviet relationship a long way forward. He had dispelled the myth that he opposed absolutely everything to do with the Soviet Union, and the Soviet leaders no longer looked upon him as an unreconstructed Cold Warrior.

Our discussion was a strange one, a blend of the old and the new. I spoke infrequently. At one point, Reagan asked me if I had anything I wanted to add. I said I hoped to build on what he had achieved in US-Soviet relations. We would need a little time to review the issues, but what had been accomplished could not be reversed. Gorbachev said he understood. It seemed to him that prospects for our relations were good. There was a lot that he and I could do together, and he urged that I think about the possibilities.

Wanting to avoid specifics, I pledged general continuity with Reagan's policies toward the Soviet Union. I told Gorbachev I would be putting together a new team. I had no intention of stalling things, but I naturally wanted to formulate my own national security policies. Our group would have people in it who hoped to move the relationship forward, and if we could get a break on Nicaragua (where the Soviets were pouring in aid), it would help in arms control and in everything else. He did not respond, nor did he offer anything in the way of his own vision for the future of US-Soviet relations—just some vague general references that he hoped things would continue as they had been.

Sitting in on the Soviet side was Anatoly Dobrynin, a man I knew well and liked. He had been ambassador to the United States for over twenty years and was now a special assistant to Gorbachev. During a break, Gorbachev came over to me and said that if I wanted to get any special messages passed along to him in confidence I should use Anatoly. Given the fact that Foreign Minister Eduard Shevardnadze, Central Committee Secretary Alexander Yakovlev, the current ambassador, Yuri Dubinin, and others were in attendance, I was surprised that Gorbachev had designated Dobrynin as the approved "back channel." In retrospect, I think he was signaling to me his eagerness to move forward in Soviet-American relations, and his desire for close contact with me as president. It was a good sign.

During the meeting Gorbachev bristled only once. It is easy to tell when he gets a little mad. His eyes sparkle and he turns red, with his mouth firmly set, and he kind of shrugs. Later on, when I got to know him much better, I felt he would deliberately throw a little anger into a statement to more passionately make a point. But at the Governors Island meeting, he genuinely flared up when Reagan innocently asked him about progress in reform and perestroika ("restructuring"). Gorbachev, with some real feeling, replied, "Have *you* completed all the reforms you need to complete?" I think he had misinterpreted the question as a criticism, because after we talked about our desire to see reform succeed he calmed down considerably and his good humor returned.

There is resentment on the part of many foreign leaders when they deal with the United States, a notion that we arrogantly consider ourselves perfect while they still have far to go. Indeed, we often do seem to lecture and confront other nations publicly on issues such as human rights. For that reason I went out of my way to be careful in questioning foreign leaders or diplomats about their countries' internal affairs. I had no hesitancy in telling them of our commitment to human rights, but I tried to avoid becoming the pedantic lecturer. In this case, Gorbachev seemed to believe that Reagan was speaking for certain Western "elements," as he called them, who hoped that his reforms would fail and the Soviet Union would fall into chaos and stagnation.

Gorbachev's visit was cut short the next day by the news of a terrible earthquake which had ripped Armenia. It had killed at least 50,000 and left half a million homeless. In its aftermath there was great tragedy, and for the first time since World War II, the Soviet Union permitted foreign assistance. AmeriCares, a wonderful relief organization started by my grade-school classmate Bob Macauley, a truly compassionate man, planned to send a plane loaded with medical supplies to Yerevan. Macauley called to see if any member of the Bush family would like to make the flight. He felt that such a gesture would mean a great deal to the Russian people.

Our son Jeb and his twelve-year-old son, George P., signed up — even though it meant being away from home at Christmas. They did their job helping to unload the plane, and then were whisked away from the area by a welcoming team. They toured a hospital and later said their Christmas prayers in a small chapel. Both my boys cried, overcome by what they had seen. Later on, Gorbachev was to tell me, and Shevardnadze Jim Baker, that when the Bushes — father and son — wept, it sent a strong signal across the entire Soviet Union that America genuinely cared about their suffering. It reflected an important new tone in our attitudes about each other as peoples.

The day after the Governors Island summit, I sat down with Brent Scowcroft, my national security advisor–designate, at the vice president's house at the Naval Observatory in Washington. I told him I wanted to come up with something dramatic to move the relationship with Moscow forward—not just responding to Gorbachev's latest ideas, but something bold and innovative, which would reaffirm American leadership in shaping the international agenda. Gorbachev was presenting us with an enormous opportunity to make fundamental changes. Although I could not foresee the dramatic shifts that would take place during the next four years, I did believe that, given Gorbachev's commitment to reform and to better relations with the United States, we had a chance for some significant breakthroughs, particularly in arms control.

There was a practical political need to react to Gorbachev's overtures as well. Although his troop cuts did not significantly affect Soviet superiority in conventional forces, I knew his proposals would appeal to Europeans, particularly the Germans. Gorbachev was very popular in Europe, where there was a kind of euphoria in the air. His speech increased the pressure on our incoming Administration to get moving, to match him with offers of our own. I did not want to be seen as lagging behind Gorbachev with nit-picking, foot-dragging responses. Yet I certainly did not want to make a foolish or short-sighted move either.

I was probably less suspicious of Gorbachev than were others in my incoming team. I thought, as Prime Minister Margaret Thatcher had once said about him, that this was a man I could work with. I knew him well enough already to feel he was sincere in his desire to change the Soviet Union and superpower relations. Gorbachev was, and is, a very proud Russian. He has convictions. I believed he was so committed to reforming his country and its foreign policy that he could not, and would not, retreat from the revolution he had set into motion. I never subscribed to the view, so prominent among some Soviet experts, that he would immediately test us with something provocative to see how the new Administration would respond. I did, however, think he was carefully watching to see if we would veer off to a harder line than Reagan had taken at the end of his Administration.

Looking back at the evolution of my relationship with Gorbachev, I'm struck by how it reflected the changes in US-Soviet relations in the last days of the Cold War. We started out in the 1980s with formal meetings such as I have described, addressing each other stiffly as "Mr. Chairman" and "Mr. Vice President" (then "Mr. President") and ended in the early 1990s with informal and genuinely friendly conversations between "Mikhail" and "George." (Barbara and Raisa experienced much the same evolution in their own relationship.) That growing confidence in each other became very important and helped each of us in reaching difficult and, at the time, controversial decisions. I felt I could trust him, and I think he felt he could trust the West at this time of deepest, and ultimately final, crisis for the Soviet Union. Had the dynamics between us, and other leaders, been different, the changes we saw might have been more painful than they were. Not that there would have been war, but the character of a unified Germany, or the path to arms and troop reductions — to say nothing of the handling of the Persian Gulf War — would undoubtedly have been different, and our world perhaps less secure.

One contrast between our relationship and those that preceded it was the amount of contact I had with Gorbachev. I probably had more interaction with him than my combined predecessors did with their Soviet counterparts. I liked the personal contact with Mikhail—I liked *him*. How many American presidents could say that about the leader of the Soviet Union? Roosevelt or Truman saying that about Stalin? Kennedy about Khrushchev? Nixon about Brezhnev? I know President Reagan felt warmly about Gorbachev too—a feeling genuinely reciprocated—but he did not have the opportunities to work as closely with him as I did. Gorbachev and I found we could sit down and just talk. We could go around the world on issues. I thought I had a feel for his heartbeat. Openness and candor replaced the automatic suspicions of the past. It was a stark contrast to the dark decades of Cold War we were leaving behind.

It was indeed a remarkable change in the superpower relationship we had known over the previous fifty years, during which US foreign policy had been largely defined by the Soviet-American confrontation. The Cold War, and a predictable preoccupation with national security, altered how Americans viewed the world and how we set our domestic and foreign policy priorities. Moscow and Washington were locked in a competition that reached throughout the globe and penetrated every aspect of international politics. Third World civil wars, the division of Europe, and the gridlock of the United Nations were all part of the prolonged struggle.

The history of those years was littered with near-collisions between these two giants or their proxies in what had become essentially a bipolar world: Berlin (over and over), Korea, the Cuban Missile Crisis, Vietnam, Ethiopia, Afghanistan, Nicaragua, and an ongoing arms race. The Soviet-American engagement was a complex entanglement, one, we quickly learned, that required patience and a sense of balance to manage well. All the changes that would come to pass in Europe during the Bush Administration played out in this adversarial context, from the revolutions of 1989 to German unification, the Baltic crises, the reformation of NATO, and, finally, the collapse of the Soviet Union itself.

This environment of suspicion and rivalry had fostered, at best, uneasy relations between our countries. Throughout most of the Cold War there was little direct communication between Moscow and Washington, except on matters of security and arms control. The two powers held fundamentally incompatible views of society, government, and man's relationship to them. The Soviet Union was, in philosophy and action, committed to the proposition that the two systems could not permanently coexist. These differences were not mere intellectual disagreement couched in the rhetoric of debate. While the animosity between these former wartime allies stemmed from the ideological elements of the competition, the urgency of the political situation flowed from its serious national security implications. For the first time, the United States faced a foe capable of striking it anywhere, inflicting immeasurable loss of life, damage, and misery on the American people virtually at a moment's notice. The oceans, behind which for generations we had felt secure, were no barrier to nuclear attack. The USSR was a mortal threat to us and to our friends and allies, who looked to us to ensure their own political independence. The United States was, after all, the only nation with both the will and the resources to confront the Soviet Union around the world. We took up that responsibility and that leadership.

Since the 1950s, the central tenet of US foreign policy and security strategy had been to "contain" the Soviet Union and communist domination and influence. The intent was to stop Moscow from extending its control, in the hope that Soviet communism would ultimately be transformed into something less threatening. By the late 1960s, the raw confrontational character of containment was infused with the idea of détente. Its basic assumption for the United States was that the two systems and superpowers were going to exist side by side for the indefinite future. Therefore, the focus of our policy should be to reduce the potential for conflict by seeking to ameliorate tensions and to increase areas for cooperation. In practice, however, enduring rivalry and suspicion proved too much for détente. Unable significantly to modify the attitudes and behavior of the Soviet Union, it finally collapsed with the Soviet invasion of Afghanistan in 1979.

When Reagan assumed office, American policy took a sharp turn back toward confrontation. Initially, the Reagan Administration, at least in part, perceived the Soviet Union as the "Evil Empire" portrayed in its rhetoric. Détente was replaced with the notion of bringing down the USSR over the long term, exerting economic and political pressure to encourage its eventual collapse. Reagan's strategy was to deal with the Soviets from a position of renewed strength, and he focused on a defense buildup in order to exert leverage on them, rather than relying simply on negotiations. There were no summits in the early Reagan years, as the United States rebuilt its defenses and modernized its nuclear forces. By 1984–1985, however, with the buildup well underway, the rhetoric was beginning to soften, and the arrival of Gorbachev and his reforms in 1985 helped accelerate this change. To the consternation of many of his hardline subordinates, Reagan liked Gorbachev and came to believe that the Soviet leader's commitment to reform was genuine. He moved from simply exerting pressure to entertaining the possibility of a changed Soviet Union, to doing business with them; he even began to speak of the end of the Cold War.

BRENT SCOWCROFT

While I was, in general, a strong supporter of the Reagan Soviet policy, I was quietly critical of some aspects of its execution. It was my sense that the "Evil Empire" rhetoric had been excessive. It tended to frighten our allies and make support of American leadership of the West more difficult. That harsh period was then followed, rather rapidly, by another extreme, marked by what I considered an unwarranted assumption that the changes in Soviet attitudes and rhetoric, or perhaps the accession of Gorbachev to power, signaled the end of the forty-year confrontation between East and West.

The Reagan Administration's willingness to declare an end to the Cold War, without taking into consideration what that would require, disturbed me. The bristling battle lines were still in place, along with a complex strategic nuclear and conventional weapons balance. Nuclear weapons were, for me, an indispensable element in the US strategy of keeping the Soviets at bay, a compensation for their enormous superiority in conventional forces. I was therefore concerned by the implications at the 1986 Reykjavik summit that we might be willing to reduce, or even eliminate, that compensation independent of a real reduction in Soviet conventional capabilities. It appeared that the Reagan Administration had disregarded the strategic aspects of arms control, placing emphasis on reductions as a goal in itself. It had, I believed, rushed to judgment about the direction the Soviet Union was heading.

As we began our own planning about new approaches, I felt that the stakes were far too high for us to operate on the basis of wishful thinking. As a country, we had in an earlier period mistaken a twist in the road for a basic change in direction and I was determined that we should err on the side of prudence. I had a reputation for being cautious—a charge to which I plead guilty. I believe that one should try to change the direction of the great Ship of State only with care, because changes, once made, are inordinately hard to reverse. This was the great downside of the détente of the early 1970s. Because of its political attractiveness, what was in practice a purely tactical maneuver assumed—in the popular mind—the character of a permanent strategic change in the US-Soviet relationship, a mistake for which we paid heavily for some years. The discipline, toughness, and costs of the Cold War no longer seemed necessary, and US determination to contain the Soviet Union began to flag. As a result, at least in part, Moscow became more aggressive in areas such as Ethiopia, Angola, and Afghanistan. It took the harshness and determination of the Reagan Administration, at considerable budgetary expense, to restore a realistic perspective. Given the costly consequences of the détente experience, I did not want us to be responsible for a repeat performance. The real question was: were we once again mistaking a tactical shift in the Soviet Union for a fundamental transformation of the relationship? The answer depended heavily on Gorbachev, what he was up to and how it would be received inside the Soviet empire.

I was suspicious of Gorbachev's motives and skeptical of his prospects. There was no doubt he was a new phenomenon. Following a period in the 1970s when the United States seemed to be faltering and the Soviets were confidently talking about a permanent change in the "correlation of forces" (the measurement by which, under their ideology, they judged whether the time was ripe to move offensively), things began to turn sour for them. The last several years of a semi-senile Brezhnev, followed by a fatally ill Andropov and a weak and sickly Chernenko, amounted to a half dozen or more years of almost total stagnation. In contrast, the United States, under President Reagan, experienced a dramatic rejuvenation. Add to these parallel developments a deteriorating Soviet economy and the result was, by the time of Chernenko's death, a consensus in the Politburo that strong leadership, capable of making drastic changes, was essential. In choosing Gorbachev, the old men of the Politburo clearly did not think they were selecting someone who would overturn the system, but one who could get it back on track. Gorbachev's hard-nosed reputation, and the character of the chief sponsors of his rise through the ranks, seemed to confirm their choice. The fundamental question was, were they all wrong? In 1989, I didn't think that was likely.

To oversimplify, I believed that Gorbachev's goal was to restore dynamism to a socialist political and economic system and revitalize the Soviet Union domestically and internationally to compete with the West. To me, especially before 1990, this made Gorbachev potentially more dangerous than his predecessors, each of whom, through some aggressive move, had saved the West from the dangers of its own wishful thinking about the Soviet Union before it was too late. In the 1960s, the Soviet strategic nuclear building program destroyed our assumption that their goals were simply the attainment of a modest—or matching—assured nuclear destruction capability. Likewise, in the 1970s, our hopes that SALT I had essentially stopped Soviet strategic modernization in its tracks were dashed by the emergence of new and more advanced missiles. The occupation of Afghanistan in 1979 ended notions of more moderate Soviet goals in the Third World. These are but examples of the Soviet leaders periodically hitting us between the eyes to remind us of their aggressive ambitions.

Gorbachev was different. He was attempting to kill us with kindness, rather than bluster. He was saying the sorts of things we wanted to hear, making numerous seductive proposals to seize and maintain the propaganda high ground in the battle for international public opinion. The unilateral force reduction initiatives contained in his December United Nations address had little military significance, but the speech struck a responsive chord among many and won him much approbation, putting the West on the psychological defensive. Everyone was tired of the Cold War, and even leaders such as British prime minister Margaret Thatcher were now declaring it over. My fear was that Gorbachev could talk us into disarming without the Soviet Union having to do anything fundamental to its own military structure and that, in a decade or so, we could face a more serious threat than ever before.

In short, I thought Gorbachev remained a communist, committed to a socialist future for the Soviet Union. Through glasnost ("openness") and perestroika ("restructuring") he sought to revitalize the USSR and strengthen its economy. He was not basically interested in political reform for its own sake but rather as a means to deal with those in the Party who were blocking his economic changes.

Gorbachev hoped, and probably believed, that he could bring the inefficient economy of the USSR close to the level of the West by the year 2000. It was never clear, however, that he really understood what fundamental economic reform required, nor how far he was willing or able to accept Western methods. Just how much could the existing Soviet system be readjusted to accommodate the changes Gorbachev had in mind? It was difficult to grasp the extent and depth of the problems it faced. As it turned out, the situation was far worse than anyone—either inside the USSR or abroad—ever imagined.

Glasnost gradually began to reveal the extent of the problems, only some of which were known or suspected in the West. Vast sections of centralized industry and agriculture were under the control of Party leaders who ran them as private fiefdoms, diverting money to their own pockets and falsifying production figures to meet inflated quotas. The distribution system was poor, with crops left rotting in rural areas while the urban population endured shortages and empty grocery shelves. Fuel scarcity during the legendary Russian winters meant inadequate heat for much of the population—despite the fact that the Soviet Union had immense oil fields and huge coal reserves. In the face of these difficulties, by 1989 Gorbachev was looking to the West for desperately needed economic and technological help to shore up the crumbling Soviet economy and smooth the effect of the reforms he was getting underway.

As daunting as the obstacles may have appeared, there was an even greater challenge—gaining Communist Party support for reform. While a government administrative structure existed and wielded authority, in truth the Party and its apparatus were ultimately in charge of the State. The Party selected the State's leadership in the name of the people, and it was from this basis, as general secretary of the Communist Party, that Gorbachev drew his power and authority. Gorbachev's economic changes faced tremendous resistance arising from ideology, the politics of bureaucracy and corruption, and plain ignorance and prejudice about market economics. His efforts to overhaul the Soviet system helped spark crisis, both through the threats it posed to entrenched institutional Party and bureaucratic interests and the opportunities it offered for outsiders to the establishment to assert themselves—liberals, dissidents, and nationalists in every republic. Reform openly divided both the Party and the Soviet policy-making process—and the powerful interest groups of the military and industry.

BRENT SCOWCROFT

Gorbachev had not counted on the resistance of the Soviet system to his reforms. He began with a relatively straightforward program to improve worker productivity and campaigned against drunkenness, absenteeism, and corruption. He also sought to replace the rule of terror with the positive incentive of an increase in the quality and quantity of consumer products. In my opinion, faced with his inability to get the Party behind these changes, Gorbachev instituted democratic reforms as a way to threaten the recalcitrant apparatchiks with elections, opposing them with people who supported his programs. His policy of glasnost was, no doubt, sincerely intended to remove the Stalinist horrors from the system, but he also used it to apply pressure to the Party bureaucracy by exposing their depredations. He was trying to save the system, not destroy it.

Still, as long as Gorbachev was doing our work—moving things in our direction—I agreed with George Bush that he deserved a carefully cooperative response. But being cautious and wary did not mean I didn't want to make bold moves. I believed strongly that it was now time for innovative thinking and a fundamental review of the basics of American strategy toward the Soviet Union. There were two main areas of the relationship which to me warranted far-reaching moves, ones that would restore the initiative to us and also advance our interests. The first was in Eastern Europe, where nascent moves toward reform might provide us an opportunity to capitalize on the "new thinking" within the Soviet Union in order to loosen Moscow's grip on its satellites. The second was nuclear and conventional arms control—where we would inherit the ongoing strategic arms control negotiations, with the goal of concluding a

START treaty, and faced upcoming negotiations as well on conventional forces. I thought these were opportunities for dramatic cuts to not only strengthen strategic stability but also reduce the conventional forces Moscow relied on to control Eastern Europe. We would have to become familiar with the excruciating intricacies of the US and Soviet positions on the issues involved. More fundamentally, we would have to review whether the existing US positions reflected our own philosophy (which we had not yet established) especially about what a START treaty should accomplish, and find the best way to take advantage of the new possibilities unfolding in Eastern Europe.

GEORGE BUSH

As I prepared for the presidency late that fall, I thought about the people I wanted to fill the senior posts in the new Administration, those who would bear major responsibility for tackling these questions. I was fortunate to have served under three Republican presidents—Richard Nixon, Gerald Ford, and Ronald Reagan. I had observed Lyndon Johnson when I was a congressman, and later, from afar, Jimmy Carter. Through their experiences I came to understand how foreign affairs and national security policy-making should function, how to work with Congress, and the challenges of the presidency itself.

I learned the most about the presidency from Ronald Reagan. I did not really know Reagan when he asked me to be on his 1980 ticket, but one of the joys of my life is that I soon got to know him well. He was an example of how you can be a strong leader yet still be a kind and gentle man, something I spoke of as a goal for the nation. He had a few firm principles that guided him and that he repeated over and over again. Everyone knew where he stood on issues such as taxes and the Soviet Union. I marveled at the way he could take complicated problems and then, in penetrating but simple terms, explain his views to the American people.

Reagan demonstrated that leadership need not be equated with a flamboyant style. Some can lead with rhetoric, with great speeches, while others lead by character and example. I never felt comfortable with flowery phrases dreamed up by a speechwriter. I felt that people could see through it if I tried to act the great historical scholar or use extravagant language. I once asked Reagan at one of our private weekly meetings how he managed to get through some of the very emotional speeches he gave. I was thinking of the words he delivered near Omaha Beach in Normandy as he paid tribute to those who had died there. He told me that after he crafted the remarks he would go over them time and time again so that the emotion he felt would be somewhat diminished. By doing this, he found he could deliver the words with meaning, but without breaking down in the middle of them. I never mastered that art. I choked up too easily.

Even if I could not express it as well as Reagan, I knew what I hoped for our country and for the world. I wanted to tackle the big problems facing us, such as lingering superpower confrontation. I was determined to do what I could to make the world a better, safer place, where people would no longer fear imminent nuclear war. Although certainly no expert on the technicalities of arms control, I wanted to reduce nuclear weapons in a way that would not diminish our deterrent capability. It was difficult for me to give dramatic speeches on my vision for the nation. I was certain that results, solid results that would lead to a more peaceful world, would be far better than trying to convince people through rhetoric.

I, too, had my own guiding principles and values. Everything I learned from history, from my father, Prescott Bush, everything I valued from my service in the US Navy reinforced the words "duty, honor, country." I believe one's duty is to serve the country. This can mean not only military service, especially in time of war, but also appointive or elective office. I think it is important to put something back into the system—to get in the arena, not simply to carp and criticize from the sidelines. Honor and integrity also are both very dear to me. Vietnam and Watergate had created an adversarial sense of cynicism among many in the press, who seemed convinced that all public servants could be bought or were incapable of telling the truth, that all were unethical in one way or another. The result was that every rumor is pursued no matter what the truth, no matter how hurtful to innocent parties. Given this climate, I felt it was important that my Administration try not only to have but also demonstrate clearly the highest possible standards. I believe we succeeded and that our Administration was made up of people who respected the offices they held. I know I made mistakes in my years of public service, but when historians review the Bush years, I hope they conclude that I served with honor and integrity.

Besides examples of presidential leadership such as Reagan's, my predecessors offered insights into how the machinery of foreign policy and national security should work. I intended to be a "hands-on" president. I wanted the key foreign policy players to know that I was going to involve myself in many of the details of defense, international trade, and foreign affairs policies, yet I would not try to master all the details and complexities of policy matters. I planned to learn enough so I could

make informed decisions without micromanaging. I would rely heavily
on department experts and, in the final analysis, on my cabinet secretaries and the national security advisor for more studied advice. A president must surround himself with strong people and then not be afraid to
delegate.

At the same time, strong individuals can lead to some practical
problems in making and implementing decisions. I had witnessed the
inevitable personality conflicts and turf disputes that would spring up
between cabinet members, advisors, and departments. I was determined
to make our decision-making structure and procedures in the new Administration so well defined that we would minimize the chances of such
problems. While the secretary of state is the president's chief action officer and source of foreign policy advice, I envisioned a special role for the
national security advisor, who is the manager of the National Security
Council.* I needed an honest broker who would objectively present to
the president the views of the various cabinet officers across the spectrum. If the national security advisor commanded the proper respect, he
could resolve many of these inevitable clashes. Thus, I wanted very special and trusted people in these two key policy posts.

My choice for secretary of state was what we call in golf a "gimmie."
James Baker and I went back a long, long way. In 1959, when Barbara and
I made the 492-mile move from Midland to Houston, Jim became one of
my very best friends in our new home town—and our wives were best
friends too. Jim was there when the political bug bit me in the early
1960s. He was at my side when, after two terms, I left the House of Representatives in 1970 to run for the Senate the second time. I was beaten
by Lloyd Bentsen, but Jim helped me a great deal in that race and in
many subsequent campaigns. From our political collaboration, and from
many other contacts, including sports, I knew that Jim was competitive
and tough. I also saw him face great personal adversity with strength
when his first wife died of cancer. I was with him at her bedside, and I was
at his shoulder when her suffering finally ended. In whatever he does, Jim
is a real fighter and he goes the extra mile. This quality was proved again
and again in those endless meetings around the world and in putting
together the coalition that fought in Desert Storm. Jim also was, and is,
a tough trader and a strong negotiator; I knew he would always tell me
directly and forcefully how he felt on various matters.

*The National Security Council has four statutory members: the president, vice president, sec-
retary of state, and secretary of defense. The director of Central Intelligence and the chairman
of the Joint Chiefs of Staff, as statutory advisors, and the national security advisor also attend
NSC meetings.

I also knew that I wanted Brent Scowcroft, another trusted friend, to be my national security advisor. I had worked closely with Brent when he had the position under President Ford and I was director of Central Intelligence (DCI), as well as when I was vice president and he served on various boards and commissions. Thinking that, having already served in the job, he might prefer a different post, I briefly toyed with the idea of persuading him to accept Defense or the CIA. But the more I thought about it, the more convinced I became that putting Brent in the national security advisor job was best for me and for the nation. His reputation, based on his deep knowledge of foreign policy matters and his prior experience, was such that there could be no doubt he was the perfect honest broker I wanted. He would not try to run over the heads of cabinet members, or cut them off from contact with the president, yet I also knew he would give me his own experienced views on whatever problem might arise. In selecting him, I would also send a signal to my cabinet and to outside observers that the NSC's function was to be critical in the decision-making process. There was one additional dimension. I came into office with a vision of the world I wanted to see, but I had no fixed "ten-point plan." Brent more than made up for my failings in arms control and defense matters. He fit the bill perfectly. He was someone who would hit the ground running.

BRENT SCOWCROFT

On Sunday morning, November 20, 1988, President-elect Bush asked me to come to the vice president's residence at the Naval Observatory for a cup of coffee. When I arrived, I found Jim Baker there as well.

I considered George Bush a good friend, someone I knew well and admired enormously. We had met when I first came to the White House in 1972 as military assistant to President Nixon and he was US ambassador to the United Nations. Our contacts through the end of the Nixon Administration were pretty much limited to cabinet meetings. In 1974, however, when I was deputy to Henry Kissinger in his national security advisor role, President Ford appointed Bush chief of the US Liaison Office in China—the second person to hold the position. The Liaison Office was established in 1972 following Nixon's trip to China and remained the form of US representation in China until the United States and the People's Republic established diplomatic relations in 1979. Since the early days of the Ford Administration, we had frequent interaction, although when Bush went to China it was, of course, mostly by cable or telephone.

It was during his days at the CIA that we developed a close relationship.

We had a standing joke—at his expense—that he was our barometer of crises, though not because he was DCI. He would frequently visit his family's summer home in Kennebunkport, Maine, for the weekend, and he would always call to inform me he was going. There seemed to develop an uncanny coincidence between his absence from Washington and the eruption of crises. So, whenever he told me he was heading for Maine, I would wonder aloud to him where the inevitable crisis was going to break out.

My background with Jim Baker was more casual. We had known each other since 1975, but the relationship was mostly a bantering one. The banter centered on how we two had tried to deal with Ford's mishap in the 1976 campaign, when, in the San Francisco debate with Carter, he declared that Poland was not dominated by the Soviet Union. That was a traumatic experience. My heart sank into my shoes when I heard him say it, but at the "stand-up" interviews we gave the press immediately after the debate, there were no questions about Poland. I was momentarily encouraged, thinking perhaps we had dodged a bullet. However, by the time we got back to the hotel, what looked like the entire press corps had gathered, demanding an explanation. Baker, as campaign chairman, and I, as national security advisor, were tossed to the wolves. The very first question was how many Soviet army divisions were stationed in Poland. The two of us perspired heavily as we explained what Ford meant to say. It was a tough evening, but it was a bonding experience.

On this cold Sunday morning thirteen years later, President-elect Bush, Baker, and I went into a small study behind the living room, where there was a fire crackling in the fireplace. With very little preliminary exchange, the President-elect asked me to be his national security advisor. The offer came as a total surprise, although I had considered the possibility that I might be invited to join the new Administration. The previous June, he and I had discussed foreign policy strategy and how that ought to appear in his campaign, and I had offered to help in any way I might be useful, without any expectation of a "reward." Given a choice, I probably would have preferred to be secretary of defense, principally because I had already served as national security advisor. However, I was aware of John Tower's aspirations for Defense and, with no hesitation, I said yes to the offer. I considered George Bush the personification of the qualities a president should possess and I was honored and excited to be offered the opportunity to work closely with him.

GEORGE BUSH

Another important member of the foreign policy team is the director of Central Intelligence. Here, too, I was certain about what I wanted, for as Ford's DCI I learned the proper role for the director in the national security structure. He is not, and should not be, a policy-maker or implementer, and should remain above politics, dealing solely in intelligence. The only exception to that role, I feel, concerned covert action as part of a specific policy decision. I never asked to be accorded cabinet rank and I felt strongly that the DCI should not even attend cabinet meetings unless they related to foreign and national security policy. When the subject shifted from foreign policy to, say, agricultural policy, I would get up and leave the room. For these reasons, when I became president I decided not to put the DCI in the cabinet.

I also believed that the DCI appointment should not be considered in the same light as other presidential selections. Automatically replacing the director in each new administration would tend to politicize what essentially is a career service that is supposed to be beyond politics. Treating the DCI just as presidents usually treat the chairman of the Joint Chiefs of Staff—as continuing through changes in administration—is, under all but the most unusual circumstances, a good formulation. The CIA job should, in my opinion, go to a career employee or to someone instantly compatible with the intelligence community. When Ford named me DCI, I had to work hard to overcome the understandable concern about bringing politics into the agency. I wanted my own choice to send a positive signal to the intelligence professionals. That proved easy. William Webster, who had served with distinction on the federal bench in St. Louis and then as head of the FBI and DCI under Reagan, was serving very well indeed. He had stayed out of politics in both positions. I asked him to remain, confident that he would have the respect of whoever made up our national security team. I was never disappointed in that decision.

Choosing a secretary of defense proved more complicated. Former senator John Tower topped my list. John was an old and loyal friend I had known more than twenty-five years in and out of Texas politics. He was a very strong leader of the Senate Armed Services Committee, and time and again I had watched him fight for a sound defense policy backed by sound defense budgets. I was certain about Tower's knowledge of the subject of defense, but I had some slight reservations. I wanted to be sure in my own mind that this strong-willed individual would be in harmony with the new national security team. Although some regarded him as an uncompromising hard-liner, those of us who had worked with him knew him to be far more reasonable and accommodating than his public persona suggested.

When I nominated Tower, I had no idea that the confirmation process would deteriorate, and how hurtful and humiliating it would become for

John and his family. It also would adversely affect the desire of many good people to serve in Washington. Historically, members of Congress, or former members, are treated with respect, almost deference, by their peers. I was certain, with Tower's long service in the Senate, that he would go through the process easily. I probably knew John better than most of his Senate colleagues did. I had never seen him fail to perform his duties or live up to challenges. The rumors and ugliness that attended the Senate action on Tower were a disgrace. While I did not take the eventual defeat of the Tower nomination on March 9 as a personal one, I sympathized deeply with John and his family. I am proud that I stayed with him until the bitter end. He was a good man. Like anyone, he had shortcomings, but none so glaring that he did not deserve my loyalty, my standing by him when the going got downright tough.

With the Tower nomination shot down in a blaze of partisanship, I moved quickly to find a new, first-class replacement. The lack of a defense secretary had paralyzed policy work at the Pentagon for the first weeks of the Administration, so we had to have someone who would sail through the confirmation process, ideally a member of Congress. I still thought that Brent would be wonderful in the job, but I already knew I needed him badly as national security advisor. I soon decided that Dick Cheney would be ideal, provided he could be talked into leaving Congress and his position of leadership there.

Cheney had not chaired a major committee dealing with national security, as had Tower, but as part of the Republican House leadership and as a ranking member on the Select Committee on Intelligence, he had a sound knowledge of defense matters. Furthermore, he had been President Ford's chief of staff and knew how policy was made. He had a reputation for integrity and for standing up for principles and, at the same time, for getting along with people. He was strong, tough, and fair. I was confident that as secretary of defense he would be skilled and effective at dealing with both the Senate and House, where he was well liked and widely respected. Less than forty-eight hours after the Tower vote, I offered Dick the job, and he immediately accepted. As I hoped, he was quickly confirmed, and like Brent he hit the ground running.

BRENT SCOWCROFT

I was delighted with the selection of Cheney, whom I had known since the early days of the Ford Administration when he became deputy to Chief of Staff Donald Rumsfeld. Then, in the grand shuffle of October 1975, Cheney was made chief of staff at the same time I became national security advisor and George Bush came back from China to head the CIA. Dick and I worked closely together. He was solid, no-nonsense, and practical, with no ego to get in the way of the business at hand. His approach encouraged cooperation from everyone. Following the Ford Administration and after Cheney entered Congress, I helped get him involved in study group activities related to arms control and other strategic issues. The result was that Dick had far more detailed knowledge of defense issues than was evident from his formal committee assignments.

GEORGE BUSH

The other national security principal is the chairman of the Joint Chiefs of Staff. The term of office of the chairman is fixed by law at two years, and Admiral William Crowe was just past the halfway point. As he is primarily an advisor, not a policymaker, I viewed the chairman as a career officer and above the usual political pressures. I was impressed with Bill, and retained him. He gave us strong support until he retired at the end of September 1989.

When Crowe announced he would be leaving, Cheney suggested I appoint Colin Powell to replace him. I first got to know Colin when he was national security advisor to President Reagan. He was easy to like, and easy for all to get along with. We soon became friends. He has a great sense of humor, which got us through a lot of tense times. But while Colin was an excellent choice, I was concerned on two accounts. First, I worried about elevating him too fast, about jumping him, a junior four-star general, ahead of other very qualified senior officers. Then I wondered whether it was actually the right step for Colin at this stage of his service. Perhaps a senior command might be better. He was young enough to serve as chairman later. Cheney was adamant—and persuasive. Needless to say, I never regretted my decision to appoint him.

Colin came on board on October 1, in the middle of the continuing crisis over Panama's stolen election and, within a few days, a coup attempt against its dictator, Manuel Noriega, by a member of his own security guard. Later, in December, I watched him during the sensitive planning for the operation to save American lives, bring Noriega to justice, and restore Panamanian democracy. When he briefed me, I found there was something about the quiet, efficient way he laid everything out and answered questions that reduced my fears and gave me great confidence. I admired his thoroughness, and above all his concern for his troops—something that came through again and again in planning for Desert Storm and during our humanitarian operations in Somalia.

BRENT SCOWCROFT

I first met Colin when he was serving as executive officer to Defense Secretary Caspar Weinberger, although our contact at that time was fleeting. Our paths next crossed shortly after he became deputy to National Security Advisor Frank Carlucci, when we shared a podium at the National War College discussing the NSC system. I was impressed at that time with his management views and the orderliness of his mind. That impression was reinforced during the transition to the Bush Administration, when I replaced him as NSC advisor. The replacement was managed with great ease, as a simple, low-key shift of responsibility. He had in mind exactly what I wanted to know and I, having been in the job before, gained insight into his views about foreign policy and national security, which I found broadly compatible with my own. I did worry whether his appointment, as a very new and young four-star, would cause problems regarding his acceptance by the military, especially given his "White House connections." I need not have worried; there was nary a ripple. Powell was unfailingly imperturbable, even when the situation or the conversation became tense. He managed brilliantly the sometimes awkward relationship between the secretary of defense and the chairman in NSC discussions with the president, serving as an NSC principal alongside his own immediate boss.

GEORGE BUSH

Two other important individuals, though involved mainly in domestic policy, contributed to our foreign policy team—Vice President Dan Quayle and Chief of Staff John Sununu. Both were bright and very interested in arms control, and over the years their advice would prove extraordinarily helpful.

While choosing the right people at the top is important, giving them leeway in picking their associates is vital as well. Jim Baker had told me that he wanted Lawrence Eagleburger as his deputy secretary of state. I was enthusiastic about the idea. Larry was a distinguished and outstanding career Foreign Service officer. He had a great deal of practical experience—having served abroad as an ambassador and in key State Department positions in the Ford and Reagan administrations.

BRENT SCOWCROFT

Baker and I spoke about his selection of a deputy. He mentioned several people, including Eagleburger, and asked what I thought. I told him there was no one else, in my judgment, as qualified as Eagleburger. I had been somewhat surprised when Baker first mentioned his name.

Larry and I were extremely close, both personally and professionally, and we both had a long association with Henry Kissinger. Baker could have been uneasy about the possible implications of such a situation. I think it showed great strength of character that he swept all the negative possibilities aside and went for the best man. I was—and still am—impressed by his taking that step. The addition of Larry tremendously facilitated and improved the business of national security policy-making and execution.

Like Baker, I was also selecting my own staff. The NSC staff is small and it is my philosophy that people should join it with the expectation that they will be working incessantly and under constant pressure. When they feel they can no longer sustain the pace, it is time for them to move on. It is essential that each member carry his or her full load. I believe that good personnel can make even a poor organizational structure work, but that even a good structure cannot compensate for poor personnel.

My top priority was selecting a deputy. I needed an alter ego, someone who had broad substantive background, knew the NSC system, understood how the executive branch operated, and, last but most important, had the confidence of the President. I directed my focus to Robert Gates, deputy director of the CIA. I had brought Gates into the NSC as a junior staffer during the Ford Administration. He also had served on the NSC during the Carter Administration and thus knew the business well from the perspectives of different presidents. Bob had been nominated by President Reagan to be DCI at an extraordinarily young age. Immediately he had become enmeshed, unfairly, in the Iran-Contra net. At a time of great national emotion, Gates, rather than persisting in order to vindicate himself (something accomplished by his confirmation as DCI in 1991), had the courage to withdraw so as not to risk embarrassing his president. President-elect Bush, of course, knew him, and when I raised Bob's name, gave his enthusiastic endorsement.

The team the President had selected proved a close one. Most had served together before, and brought enormous experience to the Administration. There was a deep camaraderie among us as well. I think this quality set apart the Bush Administration from any other I knew, and certainly from those in which I served. These were strong personalities, yet egos did not get in the way of the nation's business. A genuine sense of humor made jokes and respectful kidding part of the daily routine, and eased even the most difficult crises. It was an informal—but, at the same time, deadly serious—crowd. This was also true within my NSC staff. Although most had not worked together in the past, their bonds became tight at the beginning of the Administration as we tackled the review

process, and a good-natured humor developed among us. I soon felt—
and still feel—an affection for each of them.

GEORGE BUSH

As January arrived and the inauguration approached, I saw Brent
nearly every day for what we called "look-ahead" sessions. He came up to
Camp David (which President Reagan would generously allow me to use
when he wasn't there) on January 2 to talk about the opportunities and
challenges ahead of us. In that relaxed setting, especially during the
course of long walks through the snowy woods around the camp perimeter, we ruminated on the Soviet Union, arms control, and a general
policy review. We were not trying to reach any conclusions, only spell out
what was needed and set up our priorities. I was eager to get moving.

Soon thereafter, on January 9, I had a long talk about the Soviet Union
with Henry Kissinger, John Sununu, Jim Baker, and Brent. I have great
respect for Henry's knowledge of history and for his analysis. He spoke of
a need for a grand design and, though he was too polite to say it, it was
clear that he felt we lacked a broad strategic concept in our approach to
Europe and the Soviet Union. Kissinger was also pushing to set up a
separate informal channel with Moscow, something other administrations had used, perhaps with himself as the contact. I was wary. I wanted
to be sure we did not pass the wrong signals to Moscow, with some in our
Administration saying one thing while others were conducting secret
negotiations that might be sending out contradictory signals. Although
helpful, back channels can leave critical people in the dark on either a
forthcoming policy decision or the details of some conversation between
the President and a foreign leader.

While I hesitated to use anyone as a formal back channel, I had left the
possibility open when Gorbachev at Governors Island had designated
Dobrynin to fill the role. I did take advantage of Kissinger's upcoming
trip to Moscow to send along a personal note to Gorbachev. I thanked
him for the attention given to Jeb and my grandson during their visit to
Armenia. I also underscored the remarks I had made to him during the
UN visit and explained that the new team would have to take some time
to reflect on the central issues of the Soviet-American relationship—
particularly arms control. I thought it was also important to lift our dialogue beyond simply arms control matters to the important issues of the
larger relationship we wanted to create.

BRENT SCOWCROFT

I agreed with Kissinger. I was a strong proponent of back channels as
a means to bypass the bureaucracies on both sides and a way to ensure

instant contact with Gorbachev. But Dobrynin, whom Gorbachev had already tapped, came closer to filling both those requirements than did Kissinger. In January, Baker and I met with Dobrynin at Baker's house in order to exchange views and discuss what arrangements would be needed. As it turned out, the channel did not really bear fruit, despite a number of efforts on my part in succeeding months to use it. Dobrynin became ill early on, and perhaps being out of circulation at a time of personnel changes in the Soviet Union had reduced or eliminated his access to Gorbachev. I regret that we lost an informal avenue of communication like those which served us so well with the British, French, and Germans.

A few days after his return from Moscow, Kissinger sent us a detailed and fascinating account of his extensive talks with the Soviet leadership and offered us an insight into Gorbachev's thoughts. The Soviet leader said he welcomed a confidential dialogue with the Administration and added that he took the fact that the President-elect had approached him even before the inauguration as a sign of good faith and a serious commitment to a dialogue.

Gorbachev told Kissinger there would be no Soviet pressure regarding START, but he thought the political dialogue could begin as early as March. He outlined a number of international problems, especially in Europe. "My view is that we should keep an eye on Germany and by that I mean both Germanies," he said. "We must not do anything to unsettle Europe into a crisis." He did not elaborate. As for Eastern European reform efforts, life was bringing certain changes no one could stop, and that applied as well to Western Europe. But both sides should be careful not to threaten each other's security. That was the spirit in which he would approach the dialogue.

Gorbachev dictated a reply for Kissinger to take back to Washington: "I am ready to begin an exchange of views taking into account the need to harmonize our policies in international matters. I greatly appreciate the message, especially that a confidential channel has been opened even at this early stage." From the tone and content of the message, it seemed clear that he wanted to establish a positive atmosphere and was ready to pick up immediately from where the Reagan Administration had left off.

Kissinger wrote in his report that, as he got up to leave, Gorbachev grew pensive. "I lead a strange country," he had told him. "I am trying to take my people in a direction they do not understand and many do not want to go. When I became general secretary, I thought that by now perestroika would be completed. Instead, the economic reform has just begun. But one thing is sure—whatever happens to perestroika, this country will never be the same again." Kissinger asked him how, as a product of the old system, he could be so determined to change its premises. "It was easy to see what was wrong," said Gorbachev. "What is harder is to find out what works. But I need a long period of peace." Kissinger concluded that the Soviet president was treading water with perestroika, and that he was looking to foreign policy as a way out. He also believed Gorbachev was willing to pay a reasonable price to that end.

CHAPTER 2

From Theory to Practice

GEORGE BUSH

The Oval Office itself is not that large, but it has a special atmosphere about it. Even as I left the presidency, I had the same feeling of awe and reverence for the room as when I first entered it in earlier administrations. It is a symbol of the institution of the presidency itself, with an almost overwhelming aura of history. I could feel the presence of the long line of presidents preceding me, a feeling reinforced by my own pleasure in reading American history and learning about events that had taken place in the room where I was sitting. That sense of presence could also be inhibiting at times. For example, whenever someone would think, well I'm going in there and tell this guy how he ought to do it, somehow, once inside, his knees would go wobbly. That was good in some ways, and it reminded everyone, including me, that something larger than all of us was at work. It helped us keep our perspective.

I enjoyed working in that room. I could look out the window and watch the grandchildren playing. Sometimes my dog Ranger, dripping wet from the rain, would straggle to the door begging to get inside. In the fall and winter there would always be a fire in the fireplace, which gave the room a warm cheerfulness. Just off the office was a much smaller private study or office, a cubbyhole really, where I could go with a couple of people to speak in a more informal, relaxed setting when we needed one. It was an inner sanctum for me. There was also a small dining room, which opened on to a garden, where I would often have lunch with guests. Alongside was a tiny kitchen, where Domingo Quicho would whip up a meal for us. Domingo was an institution at the White House and had worked there since the Kennedy Administration. He was a very special friend to me (he now has one of Millie's puppies). It was this welcoming, family environment that made the White House more than a place of work and responsibility, and made the duties of office easier.

In the days after the inauguration, we immediately began to establish routines and procedures. One important fixture was the 8:00 am national security meeting in the Oval Office, at which the CIA briefed me on the latest developments around the world. It had two parts. The first portion was the intelligence briefing, at which I was joined by Brent, Bob Gates, usually John Sununu, and, once or twice a week, Bill Webster. A CIA officer would bring in the President's Daily Brief (PDB), which was a written rundown of important intelligence reports and analysis put together during the night and small hours of the morning. I made it a point from day one to read the PDB in the presence of a CIA briefer and either Brent or his deputy. This way I could task the briefers to bring in more information on a certain matter or, when the reading would bring to mind policy matters, ask Brent to follow up on an item of interest. The CIA officers would write down my questions; in a day or so, I would get an answer or an elaboration.

Knowing of my interest in the oft-berated but essential clandestine service, Webster would occasionally ask to bring along some individual who had risked his or her life to gather critically important intelligence. I found those sessions fascinating, and I was always impressed with the courage, the patriotism, and the professionalism of those who served in the Directorate of Operations. I have great respect for the people who devote their lives to the intelligence field. They never get recognition and never get to sit at the head table, but they are among the most dedicated Americans I know. There was always a danger that they or any one of their comrades would be killed because of their cover being blown by people I consider traitors; but they continue to serve with honor.

BRENT SCOWCROFT

After the CIA briefing, the second part of the national security meeting would begin. The Vice President, already briefed separately by a different CIA team, would arrive and I would go over pertinent events of the day, items where the President's guidance was needed, and anything else requiring discussion. The President, who by this time usually had scanned at least seven newspapers and the White House News Summary, would frequently have questions or comments from his reading, and would raise issues of current concern or pursue other subjects that might be on his mind.

I was mindful of questions which arose during the Iran-Contra investigations about "process" in these daily meetings, questions implying that this was the venue for secret, irregular decisions "slipped by" the President without the knowledge of others who should have been informed.

Therefore, I was careful not to try to use them to seek decisions involving other national security departments or agencies. If the President indicated a policy direction he wished to take, I made sure that others concerned were advised so they could provide any comments they might wish to make. In addition, I established the procedure of having Gates attend the meeting as well, to take notes and serve as a check on the proper interpretation of communications which might have taken place, something I extended to formal NSC meetings as well. While I almost invariably met with the President at other times during the day, these early-morning discussions were an invaluable instrument for the shaping of foreign policy.

The Tower Board, which had investigated the Iran-Contra affair, had made numerous recommendations for changes in the organization and procedures of the National Security Council. Most of that portion of the report had been written by me, and I had discussed its findings with Frank Carlucci and Colin Powell when each in turn became national security advisor. As a result, virtually all of the Board's recommendations had already been implemented and the NSC was operating well and with great integrity. The major organizational change I wanted to make in NSC operations had nothing to do with Iran-Contra (which I thought had been largely a function of the people involved). I was eager to add a "principals' committee," which would be the NSC without the President and Vice President. I thought this could help clarify issues and positions among the principals before the issues were taken to the President. It could save him considerable time, and time, I believed, was his most valuable commodity. I included such a committee in the draft directive on NSC structure and practice that I circulated to Baker and Tower shortly after the inauguration. There was no objection from either of them. The committee proved extremely valuable.

There was one area where I wished to make a significant change in my own manner of operating—congressional relations. Since the national security advisor does not testify before the Congress, that relationship is informal. In the Ford Administration, I had tended not to give it top priority. I subsequently decided that was a mistake. The Congress is crucial in so many ways to the success of foreign policy, and, at the other end, the leverage to be gained by involving someone like the national security advisor, with such close proximity to the president, should not be wasted.

Therefore, as I put together the NSC staff, one of my first moves was to ask Virginia Lampley to assume congressional liaison responsibilities. She always knew instinctively when and whom I should call, and kept

Congress at the forefront of my thoughts, with constant advice for tailoring what we were doing to enhance its receptivity. Ginny coordinated the interagency legislative process with just the right mix of diplomacy and iron fist and ensured, more often than not, that the Administration spoke on the Hill with one voice on national security issues. Her personality and understanding of my priorities made her a natural hub for other directors in sounding out ideas before they came forward. The result was that I relied on her a great deal in matters far beyond her congressional responsibilities.

GEORGE BUSH

Like any new administration, we went through the drill on access to the president. It was very hard to strike the right balance between what I wanted to know and what I needed to or should know. Working out the procedure was painful. As vice president, I had loved the direct outreach and personal contact possible, but now Sununu understandably wanted to keep me from being inundated or too busy on the wrong things or overwhelmed with details. I missed reading all the materials that had come across my desk as DCI or even as vice president. I envied past presidents of a slower era, who had tons of time to read and write. I did not wish to undermine Sununu's well-crafted system: there had to be some controls. I relied heavily on Brent to sort out the flow of national security papers and who should see what.

BRENT SCOWCROFT

One organizational question was attendance at formal NSC meetings. President Reagan had designated a number of additional individuals beyond its statutory membership and advisors to join discussions. But because this was such a sought-after privilege, any exceptions tended to open the floodgates to additional requests. The President and I both wanted to keep numbers to the minimum necessary to transact the particular business at hand, both to facilitate frank and open dialogue and to reduce the likelihood of leaks. Attendance was not simply a matter of substance, however. There were some who seemed to feel that if they were left out, it would show that they had no clout with the Oval Office.

The President instructed that, at a minimum, whenever important issues of relevance to a particular department or agency head were discussed, he wanted that individual present. He also believed Marlin Fitzwater, his press secretary, in whom he had great confidence, should normally be there. This was more complicated. It was important that Fitzwater be aware of what was happening but, at the same time, not be embarrassed by having to refuse to discuss with the press issues that he would know about but which were too sensitive for disclosure. Marlin said he could handle any such problem, and he did—with great skill. John Sununu also had to know what was going on and was therefore on hand. While there were complaints from time to time, we were able to keep the situation manageable.

GEORGE BUSH

Not that everyone always made it through NSC and cabinet meetings they attended. Often members would be racked with jet lag or had been up half the night struggling with a crisis. Despite valiant efforts to remain awake, they would sometimes fail. Brent worked the longest hours of anyone in the White House. He'd labor into the night, then go home to run, eat a light dinner, and get a few hours' sleep. As a result, from time to time—well, maybe a lot—Brent would doze off in meetings. Perhaps *fall sound asleep* is a better description. He had it down to an art of style and form. He'd sleep solidly for a few seconds, then awaken as though he hadn't missed a beat of the discussion. We marveled at this ability to cat-nap and at what became known as the "recovery factor." This might consist of waking up and immediately writing something, anything, on a pad, or a vigorous nod of approval as the speaker made what *might* have been a telling point, although Brent hadn't heard a word of the presentation.

Brent's sleep-and-recovery performance was so outstanding that in the first year of the Administration I named an award in his honor. *The Scowcroft Award for Somnolent Excellence* was presented at an annual festive dinner for the cabinet. Various cabinet members would, during the course of the season, observe the performance of contestants who they felt merited nomination for the prize, although the nominees did not need to be cabinet members themselves.

A secret, one-man "ranking committee" subjectively evaluated the contestants on soundness of sleep-and-recovery techniques, for which competitors developed all kinds of resourceful methods to take attention away from the nap itself, and from the fact that they had no clue as to what was going on around them. While the first award clearly belonged to Brent, who walked—snored—away with it, after that it became slightly more difficult to choose. Some of the contestants earned the respect of the committee for the length of their challenges, or for the diverse nature and originality of their recoveries. Every once in a while a contender, clearly oblivious to the deep and prestigious honor of the award, would protest that he or she had not been asleep—just something caught in the eye, or the effects of a cold. The committee could not be bought off. It kept copious notes of the nominees' performances, which were then secured in a computer file.

Here are just a few entries from May 1991, demonstrating the quality both of the challenges and of the committee's intelligence-gathering capabilities:

MAY 8

A fine challenge by John Sununu. At our regular 8 AM meeting, John dropped off to sleep at precisely 8:16 AM. He followed this by snoozing a little in the Cabinet Room with some "fast track" legislators—a modest challenge, however.

MAY 15

General Scowcroft and John Sununu announced that I had made a challenge for the award while Jessye Norman was singing during the State dinner for Queen Elizabeth. Confident of my innocence, I discussed the matter with Barbara, who confirmed I was never out of it. Brent's alleged witness was daughter Doro; but when contacted, Doro defended her father against this ludicrous charge. Though this entry is now part of the "Scowcroft File," it is really so fallacious a charge that it shouldn't have been brought up. Oddly enough, Her Majesty mounted a minor challenge on May 16 as we returned from the Orioles baseball game, but it was night, 4:00 AM London time—no entry there.

MAY 31

At a private lunch with [Chairman of the USSR Supreme Soviet Yevgeny] Primakov and me in my private dining room, Brent himself showed promise. After a chocolate chip cookie, make that two, his eyes began to glaze over. It cannot be fairly said that he slept, but Primakov noted the challenge and smiled at me. He knew. But that's not all. At a follow up meeting with our delegation that went to the Soviet Union, Brent mounted a serious challenge. A sterling performance, but regrettably not a winner.

It's 2:00 PM in the Cabinet Room—about 12 people are there. Brent is three down from me (maybe two).

He drops off.

He recovers nicely, nodding vigorously in assent when his seat mate to the left made a telling point. . . .

Several times the eyes were totally closed—several earned points here. Several recoveries were carried off with aplomb. It was only near the end of the meeting (2:48 PM) that he leaned forward, his head moving on to his arm, the elbow was on the table.

[Bob] Zoellick speaks again. Scowcroft makes yet another great recovery and nods vigorously as Zoellick spoke of some complicated facet of the agricultural credits situation.

At 2:51 PM, the head was all the way down, elbow gone, now, head 4½ inches from the table. Criticism—the eyes were not *tightly* closed.

Dick Cheney was the eventual winner of the second annual award, excelling in what the citation itself called "the most important category— 'soundness of sleep.' " Perhaps he summed it up best in his acceptance speech: "I am honored," he said, "but I truly don't deserve this award." He did, though.

Once the NSC system was up (awake) and running, Brent acted as my national security and foreign policy manager. I was very much a believer that if you had confidence in your people, if they come together and agree, their common solution will probably prevail and work best. Brent tried to reduce the issues to the point where he and I, and perhaps Jim Baker or Dick Cheney, could sort out any remaining problems. Sometimes cabinet members might still have deep differences of opinion, or rival departments would feel strongly about an issue. Brent always made sure the views of every "player" were understood by him and by me. If he could not resolve the impasse separately, then the principals would sort it out with me. Even then Brent would have to knock heads before he let them in my door. He took a lot of the pressure off me by keeping an open, honest approach to the NSC job. He was one of the reasons why we had a really cohesive and sound policy-making process: key decisions were well vetted ahead of time. It was an imperfect system at times, but it worked.

To preserve Brent's brokering role, I was careful to make sure that he was informed and that he was not taken by surprise, especially on substantive, important decisions. Brent would generally be in the room if I was ever talking to Jim or Dick on a matter of significance. There may have been occasions, especially during our busier months dealing with German reunification or Desert Storm, when Jim would brief me alone or by phone or cable and I'd give him a go-ahead, but I never failed to inform Brent or share material with him. Usually, any request to get me on the phone regarding security or foreign policy would come through Brent anyway.

Brent and Jim did get moderately crosswise, but very rarely. Jim worried that he might be excluded from a decision that affected his department. As a former chief of staff, he knew how a strong-willed presidential advisor, if backed by the president, can easily isolate a cabinet member. It is probably accurate to say that the NSC staff and Brent were also concerned about what State might be up to. We tried very hard, and I think successfully, to keep all the participants informed and eliminate personality clashes which could undermine policy-making as well as effective diplomacy.

BRENT SCOWCROFT

The first "test" of our "crisis management process" began on the first working day of the Administration, Monday, January 23. The Secret Service quietly informed me that a mysterious large box from the Soviet Union had been delivered to the White House. There was no identifying information whatever on it, and a call to the Soviet embassy drew a complete blank. The Secret Service, exercising every precaution, mobilized its bomb disposal unit, removed the box to a safe place, and carefully opened it. Inside was a colorfully decorated, five-hundred-pound cake, now somewhat the worse for wear. Someone had gone to a great deal of trouble, but who?

I assigned the cake to Gates, who logically made Condoleezza Rice, the NSC Soviet director,* chief detective in tracking down its origin. Diligent sleuthing revealed that the cake had been baked for the President by a collective in a Soviet town (the name of which I forget) in honor of his inauguration. It was a very thoughtful gesture and the President was touched. He suggested that a picture of it be taken, if possible with members of his family standing beside it. He would then send the photograph with a note to the collective, and the cake itself could perhaps be given to a local charity. All this took days, and, by the time the arrangements had been made, the rats in the Secret Service warehouse had had a field day. The donation-to-charity idea had to be abandoned. However, some— by now probably dismantled—bakers' collective has a picture of its cake with a personal note of thanks from the President. This first encounter demonstrated that our crisis-management system needed some improvement.

---

*I had chosen Condi because she had extensive knowledge of Soviet history and politics, great objective balance in evaluating what was going on, and a penetrating mind with an affinity for strategy and conceptualization. She also had served as a fellow with the Joint Chiefs of Staff and was therefore conversant and up to date with military affairs. She was charming and affable, but could be tough as nails when the situation required.

. . .

In those opening days we launched our strategic reviews reexamining existing policy and goals by region, with reviews of arms control as well. They would take time to complete, but we wanted quickly to put our own stamp on policy. This was a new and different administration, something the press did not seem to understand. We needed this opportunity to determine what direction we wanted to take, rather than simply accepting what we had inherited. Dealing with Moscow and the changes in the Soviet Union was obviously our first priority, and with it getting ahead of the ferment in Eastern Europe.

Developments and opportunities inside the Warsaw Pact formed the backdrop to our initial thinking about the Soviet Union. Unrest was rising in Central and Eastern Europe, in a kind of two-steps-forward, one-step-back manner (or occasionally vice versa). Over the years, a pattern had emerged in the region: repression, a gradual buildup of resentment, then an explosion, followed by another round of repression. But now there were new twists: Gorbachev had given reformers there new hope. Soviet self-absorption had led to a sort of benign neglect of its European satellites. Perestroika and the easing of Moscow's control were allowing the Central and East Europeans to assert more control over their own affairs and to move away from the authoritarian political systems and centralized economies of the past. The result was a general, if uneven, bubbling up of political challenges to the existing regimes.

I thought Poland was the most likely to take the lead toward liberalization. The situation there had never really stabilized after the 1981 crisis and the subsequent declaration of martial law. Pope John Paul II, a man whom the President and I greatly respected, and the Catholic Church itself were providing quiet inspiration in the move for greater freedom. Solidarity, the dissident, unsanctioned labor union, was in near-constant confrontation with the government. By 1989, however, there were positive signs of substantive change. Warsaw approved laws encouraging private enterprise and foreign business operations. In an extraordinary turn of events, General Wojciech Jaruzelski, who had symbolized military crackdown in the early 1980s, and other leaders threatened to resign to force adoption of a resolution which would open the way to the legalization of Solidarity.

After long confrontation with the union, the Polish government was at last indicating some willingness to give it a share of parliamentary power in return for its support of the regime's economic programs. Roundtable talks were set up to discuss its political participation. From our perspective, this process might be one on which we could capitalize and which at

least appeared to be in our interest to encourage. The very fact of meetings between the government and the principal opposition was a dramatic development. It was brought about by the desperate economic
situation and the apparent feeling of the government that there was nowhere else to turn. Big Brother in Moscow would not bail them out of
this one.

I also saw promise in Hungary. In November 1988, the government
had announced a plan to legalize non-communist political parties and
unveiled an extensive reform program, including a new constitution for
1990. Reformer Miklós Németh was appointed premier and, in early
January, legislation assuring freedom of assembly was adopted. Then
there was Czechoslovakia. The Czechs, cautious by nature, were still
somewhat demoralized by the harsh events of 1968 and the invasion by
Warsaw Pact forces. Police were repressing unauthorized demonstrations and raiding the homes of opposition leaders, and in January they
arrested the dissident leader Vaclav Havel. On the other hand, the government allowed, for the first time, large demonstrations by independent
organizations on the fortieth anniversary of the Universal Declaration of
Human Rights. Lagging well behind these three were East Germany,
Romania, and Bulgaria.

I thought that this changing atmosphere warranted a shift in the priority of US attention away from our relations with the Soviet Union,
which were focused almost entirely on arms control, to Eastern Europe.
Emphasizing Eastern Europe would also remind everyone that the fundamental structure of the Cold War was still in place and Soviet troops
still occupied Eastern Europe. My line of thinking had two main elements. The first would be an attempt through agreements on conventional force reductions to get the Soviet Army out, or at least drastically
reduce its stifling presence. That would create a better environment for
political evolution there. The second would be to revise our strategy for
treating individual East European states.

For years the United States had given preferred treatment to those
Soviet satellites showing the most independence from Soviet political
direction or control over their foreign policies. That emphasis had made
good sense in creating complications for a still adversarial Soviet Union.
Under that policy, Romania, one of the most Stalinist of these states, had
become a favorite of the United States. If we were to foster a more cooperative relationship with the Soviet Union, I thought we should replace
that strategy with one that would give preferential treatment to those
satellites which were the most vigorous in undertaking internal political
and economic reforms. This would further encourage the governments
of Eastern Europe toward reform, with the hope of reaching our long-

term goal of freeing the region as a whole. Such a change in policy would, because of dictator Nicolae Ceausescu's brutal totalitarian grip on the country, move Romania from first place to last in US attention.

GEORGE BUSH

I agreed with Brent that Gorbachev's new emphasis on reform might allow us to influence the situation in Eastern Europe, but I wanted to be careful. The traumatic uprisings in East Germany in 1953, Hungary in 1956, and Czechoslovakia in 1968 were constantly on my mind through these tumultuous months. I did not want to encourage a course of events which might turn violent and get out of hand and which we then couldn't—or wouldn't—support, leaving people stranded at the barricades. I hoped to encourage liberalization as rapid as possible without provoking an internal crackdown—as had happened in Poland in 1981—or a Soviet backlash. The problem was figuring out exactly where that line was and what was likely to be seen by the Soviets as provocative.

BRENT SCOWCROFT

One of the complicating factors in determining what might constitute a sustainable rate of change was Gorbachev's apparent strategy in Eastern Europe. He was encouraging reform there and, in some respects, he could be considered a *de facto* ally. He seemed motivated by an interest in being able to point to progress there as a prod to recalcitrants inside the Soviet Union who were standing in the way of his own reforms. I thought Gorbachev did not understand the true nature of the situation in Eastern Europe. He appeared to be trying to cultivate a number of "little Gorbachevs" who would have popular support and thus represent a positive and permanent improvement in the region. What he apparently failed to realize was that the Communist regimes, whatever their complexion, were an imposition from the outside and would be overthrown as soon as the opportunity presented itself.

Gorbachev's domestic policy also had to be considered. What was the internal situation in the Soviet Union? What were his relations with the conservatives, and what was his staying power? These questions further complicated an already complex calculation, adding to the difficulty of assessing a tolerable pace of reform, and they remained at the forefront of every policy decision related to Eastern Europe.

GEORGE BUSH

While the formal internal NSC review on the Soviet Union was under way, I also sought other expert views. Jack Matlock, our ambassador to Moscow, first appointed by Reagan and a long-time Soviet observer, offered long, detailed, and helpful cables. I also told Brent to organize gatherings with outside scholars, and met with the first group in early February up in Kennebunkport—meeting in our master bedroom, which was about the only heated room in the house. Although the opinions varied, I found their input helpful in thinking more about what might happen next in the Soviet Union. From this point on I asked for similar discussions on every major foreign policy issue.

BRENT SCOWCROFT

The formal report from the strategic review on the Soviet Union (NSR-3) was on the President's desk on March 14. It was disappointing— mainly a "big picture" document, short on detail and substance, without the kind of specific and imaginative initiatives needed to set US-Soviet relations on a productive path. Because of its shortcomings, we worked instead with a "think piece" on Gorbachev's policies and intentions, drafted by an NSC team headed by Condoleezza Rice.

Condi's memo laid out the premises that I believed should guide the development of an overall strategy for US-Soviet relations, and it evolved into a four-part approach for coping with Gorbachev. First, we should work on the domestic side to strengthen the image of America's foreign policy as driven by clear objectives. We could not meet Gorbachev head on if we did not appear confident about our purposes and agenda. Second, we needed to send a clear signal that relations with our allies were our first priority. It would be important to underscore the credibility of NATO's nuclear deterrent through modernization. In addition, the alliance would soon require a political strategy for the upcoming conventional arms reduction talks and where we wanted them to lead. We also would have to prepare carefully for bilateral arms control, including START, which was closely watched by the world community. If we performed competently in arms control, alliance confidence in our ability to manage the broader relationship would soar.

Third, after our review of policy, we might undertake initiatives with Eastern Europe. Since the Eastern Europeans were taking advantage of Gorbachev's invitation to exercise greater control over their own affairs, the region had become a potential weak link in the solidarity of the Soviet bloc. Our best tool would be the promise of economic assistance. Fourth, and finally, was regional stability. Recent developments in Afghanistan and southern Africa had raised hopes that US-Soviet cooperation would spur agreements in other parts of the world. We had to work aggressively to promote regional stability, aware that the Soviet Union could be an important asset in some but not all places. Central America was one such exception. There the Kremlin had shown no signs of abating its support for communist military activities.

The memo picked up on one intriguing possibility that Matlock, among others, had begun to suggest: that we might have leverage over Moscow because of its need for Western economic resources and know-how. In a supporting memo at the time, Condi reminded us that the Soviet Union was in the midst of domestic turmoil and was looking to the outside world for ideas and resources to rebuild its failing system. It appeared we might be able to take advantage of that situation to make dramatic progress across the entire US-Soviet agenda. This was, as she pointed out, an argument for setting our sights literally on transforming the behavior of the Soviet Union at home and abroad. It was both an ambitious goal and a distinct and positive departure for US policy. This four-part strategy became our blueprint for crafting policy toward the Soviet Union in the early days of the Administration. It would, however, require extensive revision—alongside some improvisation—as changes in Eastern Europe began to unfold rapidly through the coming months.

After what seemed an eternity, but was actually less than six weeks since they had been commissioned, the results of the other strategic reviews on Eastern Europe (NSR-4) and Western Europe (NSR-5, emphasizing the planned unification of 1992—what became the Maastricht Treaty), were beginning to emerge.* Discussion on Eastern Europe was scheduled for an NSC meeting on March 30. As I started to prepare, however, it became apparent that we should not begin our top-level debates on the direction of policy with only a portion of what was a closely interconnected whole. I asked the President to delay the meeting on Eastern Europe in order that we could first have a session covering all of Europe. I also raised another idea. Even this early in the Administration, it was becoming apparent to me that a full-blown NSC gathering was not always the place for a no-holds-barred discussion among the President's top advisors. Some might be inhibited from expressing themselves frankly with staff present and the constant possibility of leaks. I suggested that this opening session take place informally, in the Oval Office, and with only a select group present, in this case Quayle, Baker, Cheney, myself, Eagleburger, Gates, and Sununu. The President liked

---

*Heading up my European team at the NSC was Robert Blackwill, a Foreign Service officer who had been in the process of leaving government service for academia. I had known him for nearly twenty years, though not well. He had a reputation for brilliance, laced with irascibility. He was a forward-looking original thinker who reveled in finding ways to take advantage of the rapidly changing European scene to fashion strategies which would advance American interests and move us toward a new international structure.

the suggestion, and it worked. This marked the beginning of a new pattern for top-level meetings (the "core group") during the rest of the Administration. While we continued to hold formal NSC meetings, an informal group became the rule rather than the exception for practical decision-making.

At the opening of the discussion, Scowcroft reviewed the issues before us. American postwar policy toward Europe and the Soviet Union had been successful. The USSR had been contained for four decades and Western Europe had prospered. We were, however, in for a period of rapid change as East-West confrontation waned.

A central question was the stability of the Soviet Union. Whatever Gorbachev had in mind, he was setting in motion forces with unknown consequences—unknown even to him. Keeping in mind that the country was, and would remain, a massive military power, there were at least three aspects to what was transpiring. One was economic reforms. Were we facing a generation of turmoil and paralysis, whether these changes succeeded or failed? Another was the political reform process. Would it produce a life of its own or would it end in more repression? The third was nationality. Would the struggle between nationalist groups and the central political authority become an imperial battle?

As for Eastern Europe, it had long been the Soviet security zone, and the instability there was assuming explosive proportions. What was the US objective there? Was Eastern Europe only a tool to get at the Soviet Union, or did we want to emphasize it for its own sake?

Finally there was the question of potential European unification. Were we looking at a potential new superpower in Western Europe? There had always been some US ambivalence about the prospect of European unity. It was not clear whether the implications of European integration and unification were good or bad for the United States. A European pillar might make NATO more efficient. Could it also be a substitute for US forces?

We had also to consider the effects of the nationalism reawakening in the East. The Russian Revolution of 1917, and then the rise of Stalin and the ascent of Nazi Germany in the 1930s, had frozen the process of the restructuring of Eastern Europe following the collapse of the Austro-Hungarian Empire after World War I. It appeared that we were witnessing the incipient collapse there of Soviet domination—the successor in many ways to Austria-Hungary. What did the breakup mean for us, and was it in our interest? Would the instability and nationalism prior to World War I, for example, recur? Had there been permanent modifications to the political processes of these countries which made national-ism irrelevant? Although in Western Europe the notion of nationalist conflict was passé, it was too soon to tell whether political evolution in Eastern Europe since 1945 had moved at an equal pace in places like Yugoslavia, Hungary, or Romania, where there were long-standing ethnic tensions and separatist pressures.

The Soviet occupation of Eastern Europe had led to huge numbers of troops facing one another across the Iron Curtain. There had been, how-ever, another major underlying reason for the military forces in Central Europe—a divided Germany, the result of World War II and prolonged by the Cold War confrontation. Its potential reunification as Moscow's con-trol ebbed had serious implications, both for the Soviet Union and for southeastern Europe. Would a unified Europe as set out in the Maas-tricht Treaty preclude all these prospective problems and dangers?

In the debate that followed, there was unanimity that we should change our strategy toward Eastern Europe along the lines raised during the transition: We would focus on encouraging moves toward reform and getting Soviet troops reduced or removed, but our initiatives must be bold ones. Scowcroft pointed out that the United States was losing the battle with Gorbachev over influencing the direction of Europe. The Soviet leader was preaching that the Cold War was over and we should be dismantling its structures (although he said little about the future of Soviet forces in Europe). If we looked as if we were just dragging our feet, the Europeans would cease to follow and the Soviets would seize the international agenda. The President agreed that Gorbachev had under-mined US leadership, and he wanted to go to the NATO summit in May with a series of bold proposals that would put us out in front.

BRENT SCOWCROFT

I introduced a version of an initiative I had first made to the Presi-dent during the transition: the withdrawal of both US and Soviet ground forces in Central Europe. It made military sense because NATO minus most of its US troops was better off than the Warsaw Pact without Soviet troops. But, primarily, such a move would reduce the smothering pres-ence of Soviet forces in Central Europe—one of our goals.

Dick Cheney looked stunned, and replied that it was too early to con-sider such a fundamental move. We should wait to see what happened in the Soviet Union. He suggested that, instead, we challenge Gorbachev to a public accounting of defense expenditures, à la glasnost. Jim Baker chimed in with his own proposal, also first raised during the transition, for the elimination of all tanks on both sides. Unlike troops, he argued,

removing tanks was easily reversible, and we should do nothing permanent yet. Baker's idea missed my main point. Certainly we were seeking
to make an ambitious move to regain the initiative with Gorbachev. But I
thought the principal goal should be to try to lift the Kremlin's military
boot from the necks of the East Europeans. The Soviets did not need
tanks to dominate Eastern Europe. The President closed the meeting
by saying, in a resigned tone, "If we don't regain the lead, things will fall
apart."

It was our first general strategy meeting, and it was important in several respects. There was consensus on encouraging reform and liberalization in Eastern Europe at the fastest sustainable rate. The only dissent
came later from Treasury, not on the issue of grand strategy but on the
narrower matter of rewards for progress in economic reforms. The President also had made it abundantly clear that he wanted far-reaching
initiatives. Since neither Cheney's nor Baker's received support, troop
withdrawal was all we had before us. While my suggestion was too extreme, we eventually adopted a greatly reduced version of it.

The discussion revealed the differences between the advisors on the
broad philosophical question of how to deal with the swiftly moving
events in Europe and the Soviet Union. Cheney was the most skeptical,
holding the view that the changes were primarily cosmetic and we should
essentially do nothing. Gates' views were similar. He believed that Gorbachev was unlikely to succeed in reforming the Soviet Union or that the
process was likely to be reversed. Baker was the most optimistic about the
Soviets, an inclination which became strongly reinforced as he got to
know Foreign Minister Eduard Shevardnadze better.

GEORGE BUSH

As I look back on Brent's presentation that day, his inclusion of German reunification sticks out; at the time none of us could predict its
imminence. My own thoughts were focused on putting the United States
back out in front, leading the West as we tackled the challenges in Eastern Europe and the Soviet Union. We had to regain the initiative if we
hoped to encourage stability in Eastern Europe as it changed. Things
there were happening very quickly, and the longer we waited or remained
passive, the less we could affect the outcome. Our immediate policy
options regarding reform in individual Soviet bloc countries were limited, for there was little we could do directly to influence the pace of
change. We could not incite revolt, for that would probably provoke
another wave of violent suppression and all the progress of recent years
would be lost. Brent's general approach about fostering an *environment*

which would encourage positive change—getting Soviet troops out—made a lot of sense to me. I realized, however, we would have to consult our allies frequently and carefully to explain our aims and strategy in reducing our troop presence, and that would be a complex process.

I liked the uninhibited and informal debate the "core group" stirred up, which was why I approved using the gatherings more often in the future. I was stimulated by the ideas going back and forth between Cheney, Baker, and Scowcroft. We were moving in the right direction with the innovative suggestions they were tossing around. American leadership required proposals that would have broad appeal in the alliance—and beyond. This discussion was evidence to me that I was getting the best thinking possible on what to do. But I was impatient to develop practical policies from these ideas. We had work to do.

BRENT SCOWCROFT

While we had spoken of conventional arms reductions in Europe as part of the NSC discussion, nuclear arms control was a separate and complicated topic of our reviews. After all, it had been the guts of our policy toward the Soviets for twenty years. Up to now, negotiations on the subject had been carried out more or less in a political vacuum, because the relations between the two countries were fairly confrontational. A paradox evolved as adversaries tried to cooperate on this thorny subject. We had managed this anomaly by separating arms control from the political relationship and handling it as a technical military question. I think a bit of that tendency carried over into the Bush Administration, where some continued to consider arms control a self-contained subject. The habit of thought persisted even as arms control evolved from something carried out in isolation into a vehicle of dialogue and cooperation in the overall improving US-Soviet relationship. At the outset, however, given the importance of arms control for US security and US-Soviet relations, I wanted us to think through our positions until we were comfortable with the direction we were taking. As we reviewed arms control policy, I leaned heavily on my senior director for arms control and policy, Arnold Kanter. In addition to having an incredibly analytical mind, Arnie was a true strategic thinker, which, in my experience, is a rarity. He knew the arms control field, but never let its thick trees obscure the forest of our strategic goals.

I was convinced that the primary objective of arms control should be stability, not reductions for their own sake. We should above all seek to avoid a situation in which one or both sides feared that if it did not use its nuclear weapons first they would be destroyed or, conversely, that if it did use its weapons first it would achieve a decisive advantage. This kind of instability was dangerous because it encouraged escalation of any crisis between the two sides into total conflict. It was, therefore, what arms control should first seek to eliminate. These were important issues, and it would take time to sort them out. To provide that time, we delayed discussion with the Soviets on arms control until June.

Related to arms control was the question of a US-Soviet summit. Even during the transition, the press had been speculating about an early meeting, a speculation tinged with obvious advocacy. There were definitely advantages to an early summit. It could capture the popular imagination and get us off to a flashy start. An unstructured exchange of views between the two leaders had its merits also. But, on balance, I was firmly opposed to a meeting which had not been meticulously prepared and at which no concrete achievements would be concluded.

To me, it was almost an article of faith that poorly prepared or cosmetic summits were dangerous, in that they almost invariably furthered Soviet objectives. Unless there were substantive accomplishments, such as in arms control, the Soviets would be able to capitalize on the one outcome left—the good feelings generated by the meeting. They would use the resulting euphoria to undermine Western resolve, and a sense of complacency would encourage some to believe the United States could relax its vigilance. The Soviets in general and Gorbachev in particular were masters at creating these enervating atmospheres. Gorbachev's UN speech had established, with a largely rhetorical flourish, a heady atmosphere of optimism. He could exploit an early meeting with a new president as evidence to declare the Cold War over without providing substantive actions from a "new" Soviet Union. Under the circumstances which prevailed, I believed an early summit would only abet the current Soviet propaganda campaign.

If we were to be the stage props for the dispensation of more euphoria, I felt we at least should be able to derive some specific benefits from it. That would require considerable time and much hard work. While I was probably one of the principal opponents of an early summit, there was actually little debate within the Administration on the issue. Jim Baker held the same view I did, though perhaps not so strongly. I had the definite impression that the President wanted to sit down with Gorbachev at an early date. He did not press the idea, but he periodically came back to the issue as the months passed.

Over the spring of 1989, critics complained of the slowness of the review process, expecting that we would simply carry on the policies we

had inherited from the Reagan Administration. Almost daily the press asked when the reviews would be completed and speculated that they were producing nothing of value. Stories began to appear in March that they were a cover for the fact that the Administration had no philosophy, design, or strategy, and was drifting. It was also true, however, that the reviews were a convenient excuse for us to use, since we were not yet ready to reveal our strategy publicly. At the same time, charges that we lacked "vision" were hurting us, and would make it much more difficult to get our strategy reported seriously when we did announce it.

Now that we were coming to grips with the major issues of strategy and policy, it was time to begin thinking of a program for unveiling our strategic framework. Two matters of timing influenced the way we would publicize the new policies, one a requirement and the other an opportunity. A successful conclusion to the ongoing Polish roundtable talks between the government and Solidarity would require an American response, and we could use the occasion as a springboard to launch a new US policy of encouraging reform in the governments of Eastern and Central Europe. A broader opportunity to publicize our plans came in the form of college graduation time—commencement addresses were handy opportunities to announce policy. We decided that President Bush would lay out his strategy toward Europe and the Soviet Union in four speeches: one each for Eastern Europe, Western Europe, the Soviet Union, and defense and arms control.

We had followed the progress of the Polish roundtable closely and anxiously, since its failure would make announcement of a departure for our East European policy awkward if not impossible. The talks frequently were rocky: extremists in both camps denounced and demonstrated against them. About halfway through the projected six weeks of negotiations, Moscow rendered its own judgment. On March 1, it allowed the publication of a long and very positive interview with Lech Walesa, the Solidarity leader who had heretofore been regularly denounced in the Soviet press. This development was also encouraging because it meant we might have significant leeway to provide assistance to Poland without unduly provoking the Soviets.

The discussions dragged on past six weeks. Finally, on April 5, the roundtable reached an agreement, one which marked a profound change in the Polish political system. Solidarity was legalized, a new and powerful office of president was created, as was a new 100-seat senate. The opposition would be permitted to compete for the Senate, and for 161 of the 460 seats in the existing Sejm, or parliament. We were delighted with the outcome—so delighted that we sent Marlin Fitzwater into the White

House briefing room to welcome the agreement even before it was officially announced in Warsaw. Unknown to us, the negotiators had decided
to take a break for dinner before making public their success. No one
seemed to notice our error.

This historic agreement, signed two days later, signified the end of
the Polish Communist Party's forty-five-year monopoly on power. It now
appeared certain that Poland was moving toward autonomous political
development outside communist control, and the process required the
support and encouragement of the United States. We had an ideal peg on
which to hang a new policy toward Eastern Europe. The question was
when and how we would announce it.

BRENT SCOWCROFT

Since it was only April, the speech on Eastern European policy would
have to be made prior to the commencement season. The White House
planners cast about for an appropriate venue. They hit upon the town of
Hamtramck, Michigan, a Detroit enclave and a natural for the speech. Its
hallmark was patriotism, it had a high concentration of families with ties
to Eastern Europe, particularly Poland, and it had lots of Reagan Democrat blue-collar workers. It was the right place to talk about change inside
the Soviet Union and our aspirations for Poland's freedom.

We had three tasks before us as we fashioned the speech. The first
two dealt with the policy itself: clarifying it and then establishing what
kind of assistance we could offer the Eastern European countries which
responded to it. The third was purely bureaucratic but, in its own way,
critical: who would write the speech? Formulating the outline of the new
policy was straightforward, since we had decided to make change in Eastern Europe an end in itself, not simply an instrument for use against the
Soviet Union. The practical effect was that we would be looking more
at internal political and economic reforms of these states and less at
their foreign policy behavior as the criteria for US support. This change
reflected our view of the most likely course of events in the Soviet empire: a gradual loosening of bonds with Moscow and an increasing tolerance for deviation from Leninist-Stalinist dogmatism.

The questions of the nature, amount, and circumstances of any assistance we would be prepared to give to the struggling economies of Eastern Europe were more difficult. Condi Rice scoured the executive branch
for programs which we could tap for aid to Poland and other Eastern
European states. Budgets were extremely tight everywhere, and the huge
federal deficit cast a pall over any additional spending. But the sharpest
controversy was over defining when aid to Eastern Europe would be

appropriate. In an NSC meeting on April 4, Treasury Secretary Nicholas Brady argued that there should be rewards only for economic, not political, reform. He pointed to the experience of the 1970s, when the US poured funds into Poland in response to changes in its political behavior. There had been no economic reform that could make good use of the money, which consequently was squandered. Poland ended up no better off and heavily in debt. Baker and I argued that the policy this time was different, based not simply on distance from the Soviet Union but on real political strides toward an open society, of which economic reform was an integral part. The dispute was emotional and irreconcilable. It took President Bush to break the impasse.

GEORGE BUSH

It was not easy to choose between Nick's and Brent's positions. Nick properly put forward the argument for being cautious and not throwing good money after bad. Funds were tight, and the deficit tied our hands. Part of our limitation was of my own doing. I had imposed a rule that we could not commit funds to a new program without taking them from elsewhere in the budget, so we had to be very careful in proposing plans that would require large amounts of spending. Dick Darman, director of the Office of Management and Budget, was constantly reminding me that we had no blank checks. He was very bright and imaginative, and his sound advice on our limitations was always on my mind throughout our four years.

On the other hand, Brent and Jim recognized that, while Poland's credit was not good, we had to help the dramatic changes underway there. I was convinced that we simply had to encourage Poland with substance; rhetoric would do little to guarantee their movement toward greater political change and openness. Although the economic conditions in Eastern Europe were so bad that the usefulness of aid might be limited, we had to try. I directed that I wanted to see aid proposals—I hoped that, in a pinch, Darman could find money.

BRENT SCOWCROFT

We still had to decide who would write the President's speech. The question sparked a controversy which remained unsettled through the life of the Administration. It was a good example of the exasperation which could surround the preparation of a presidential address. I had assumed that, for national security policy speeches, the NSC would be responsible for the first draft. This seemed logical because it was critical to get the substance exactly right. Its message was designed not just for

Americans but also for an international audience. After the content was right, the draft could then be given to the speechwriters for smoothing out the language, putting it in the President's style, adding catchy phrasing and other touches designed to turn good substance into a great speech.

The speechwriters did not see it that way. In their opinion, they were not simply technicians but professionals, perfectly competent to get the substance right as well as the style. Their preference was a conference with the appropriate NSC people to discuss content and the general approach, following which they would produce the first—and, of course, all subsequent—drafts. They maintained that not only was it an affront to suggest they were not able to get the content down correctly, but that the NSC invariably wrote in an academic and "heavy" style, which was too difficult to fix.

At the heart of the controversy was a bureaucratic fact of life, that the author of a first draft had, generally speaking, the preponderant influence on the final product. John Sununu, who supervised the speechwriters, generally supported their position, in large part, I believe, because they were his people and because he thought the President would be helped by more dramatic rhetoric. The White House staff secretary, Jim Cicconi, sought to arbitrate the dispute. However, since he had a strong personal interest in foreign policy and felt, not without justification, that he possessed considerable writing skills, he had a stake in keeping the composing process open so as to influence the product.

Compounding the problem, for me, was my belief that the White House speechwriters, with some exceptions, did not compose what I considered particularly good speeches. Their texts seemed to be marked by a choppy political-campaign style, designed for applause at rallies but hardly befitting a serious discussion of important policy issues. In this particular case, Condi and the chief speechwriter, Mark Davis, together provided the first draft, but the practice varied from speech to speech. We tried the conference process, but found that, from the NSC perspective, no matter how detailed the discussion on what the substance should be and how it should be articulated, the speechwriter seemed to believe he knew best what the policy should be. The situation was better or worse, depending in part on the particular writer involved, but there were instances of competing NSC and speechwriter drafts.

On significant addresses, the President frequently became involved early, and the NSC position on substance would almost invariably be adopted. He would rework the text until it reflected the exact content and tone he wanted. The nuances in his editing reflected not only the depth of his understanding but also his belief in the importance of the message and the way it was expressed. The process itself, however, was never clarified to my satisfaction. It remained a major irritant, with a negative impact on the quality of many of the President's foreign policy speeches throughout the Administration.

GEORGE BUSH

I could sympathize with our writers, for they did not get enough time with me and I was the first to recognize that my delivery was not great, but the Hamtramck speech was one instance when I was involved from the outset. I worked on the content, and on my delivery, at Camp David the weekend before I was supposed to give it. There were a number of points I wished to make and several issues to avoid. For example, I wanted to respond to a comment Gorbachev had made at Governors Island back in December. I asked that a statement be inserted specifically denying that some quarters in the United States hoped to see glasnost and perestroika fail and declaring that there should be no doubt that we saluted the changes made so far and encouraged reform. I also wanted to eliminate a passage reading that "some regimes are testing the limits of Soviet tolerance" and to insert language giving some credit to Jaruzelski for what was happening in Poland. I also reworked the words, the kind of fiddling I always like to do and which sometimes drives speechwriters crazy.

The final text did the job we wanted, and President Bush spoke with feeling on April 17 at the Hamtramck City Hall. To recognize the reforms underway in Poland and encourage further steps toward a market economy, he announced some specific trade and financial measures. We would seek to give Poland access to tariff relief, propose to our friends and allies a rescheduling of its debt, ask Congress to allow the Overseas Private Investment Corporation (OPIC) to operate there, support International Finance Corporation loans, encourage the International Monetary Fund to work out with Poland sound, market-oriented economic policies, promote debt for equity swaps, and offer negotiations for a business agreement detailing cooperation between US firms and Polish private businesses. If Poland's experiment succeeded, he declared, other countries might follow. While we would still make policy distinctions among the nations of Eastern Europe, Poland offered two lessons. First, there could be no progress without significant political and economic liberalization. Second, help from the West would come in concert with liberalization. The long shopping list of incentives for reform laid out in

the speech made embarrassingly obvious our lack of resources to provide real rewards for Eastern Europe. While it was a start, any serious
observer would see that the response was not really enough to address
the magnitude of the problem facing the economies of Eastern Europe.

GEORGE BUSH

Hamtramck decked itself out in festival manner, with American flags
in every window, and smaller ones in what seemed every hand. Emotions
ran high, and the enthusiastic audience listened intently as I unveiled our
program. It was a colorful and sympathetic crowd especially interested in
Solidarity, which was formally recognized the very day I spoke. I enjoyed
rounding out my visit with a wonderful lunch of Polish food in a local
restaurant. This was small-town ethnic America at its best. There was a
footnote to the visit, however. Far in the back of the crowd was an armed
assassin who had come to kill me. He had been deterred from getting
close by the metal detectors. After the speech, he went on to Washington, where, lying in wait, he tried to intercept me at two different restau-
rants that Barbara and I occasionally visited. Fortunately, we never went
out while he was waiting. He left town, only to be apprehended on the
West Coast, where he confessed.

BRENT SCOWCROFT

We had taken our first major step on Eastern Europe. It was only a
beginning, but it was a crucial move to try to capitalize on the signs of
thaw in the communist states of Europe and to steer events in productive
directions, but at a speed Moscow could accept. It was a serious effort to
address the central questions of the Cold War. Although this was the
President's first foreign policy address, in the US the speech merited
scarcely a glance. Admittedly, part of the problem was that we had not
done much advance work with the press, but Washington reporters
apparently were of the opinion that if we had anything really serious to
say, we wouldn't be saying it in Hamtramck.

That certainly was not the reception in Europe and the Soviet Union,
where the speech was given careful coverage. The East European press
divided according to the positions the various regimes took on the issues
of reform and the attractiveness of sharing in assistance from the United
States. Thus the Polish and Hungarian responses were cautiously positive, Bulgaria was ambivalent, Czechoslovakia and East Germany were
negative, and Romania was silent. The Soviet reaction was mixed. *Pravda*
was generally favorable, singling out for approval the President's positive
appraisal of Soviet reforms and the prospects for improved US-Soviet

relations. Moscow's international radio was more critical, declaring that the speech on the whole had a confrontational character and suggesting that the President had clearly relapsed into the doctrine of rolling back communism in Eastern Europe. It argued that any attempt to question the historical choice made by the Eastern European countries following World War II would inevitably bring about a return to the Cold War.

Publicizing our plans for future policy toward the Soviet Union took a little longer. Disappointed in the strategic review process, I had the NSC staff draft a decision memorandum for the President based primarily on our assessment of where we ought to be going, including ideas stemming from the earlier memos from Rice and others. The strategy recognized that new and different breezes were blowing in the Soviet Union, and challenged the Soviets to demonstrate by their actions their commitment to the principles they were beginning to enunciate. It was not dramatic, but it laid out a fundamental transformation of our relationship with Moscow. We announced the strategy in the President's May 12 commencement speech at Texas A&M University in College Station.

Much of the Texas speech reflected the language of the NSC memos: The United States would move beyond containment of Soviet expansionism; we would seek the integration of the Soviet Union into the community of nations; we would make a commitment to match Soviet moves toward greater openness and responsible behavior with moves of our own. Ultimately, our objective would be to welcome the Soviet Union back into the world order, but Moscow would have to demonstrate its sincerity:

> The Soviet Union says that it seeks to make peace with the world and criticizes its own postwar policies. These are words we can only applaud, but a new relationship cannot be simply declared by Moscow or bestowed by others; it must be earned. It must be earned because promises are never enough.

The Soviets would have to take positive steps, such as reducing their conventional forces, permitting self-determination for all Eastern Europe (tearing down the Iron Curtain), working with the West to effect practical measures for the diplomatic resolution of regional disputes around the world, achieving lasting political pluralism and respect for human rights, and lastly, joining with the United States in addressing global problems such as drug-trafficking and the environment.

To focus attention on the new policy, and help the American people better understand what we were trying to accomplish, we included in the address a proposal suggested to the President a few days earlier by Canadian prime minister Brian Mulroney: that we resurrect Open Skies. This idea had been first introduced in the Eisenhower Administration and would allow unarmed surveillance aircraft to fly over the territory of each country. We proposed expanding it to include the territory of the allies of both the United States and the Soviet Union.

BRENT SCOWCROFT

To me, the Open Skies proposal smacked of gimmickry, and would wrongly give the impression that we did not have the brain power to think of something innovative and had to reach back thirty years for an idea. After all, we now had satellites to do such surveillance work. I lost the argument, because I was unable to come up with anything better.

GEORGE BUSH

I didn't feel that Open Skies was such a bad idea—it looked like a no-lose proposition from our side. Gorbachev, committed to glasnost, would find it hard from a public-relations standpoint to reject it. It was old hat, but given the new openness offensive by Gorbachev, I thought we had a lot to gain. I knew there would be some hand-wringing in Defense about what could be overflown here in the United States, but I did not feel it would amount to much. Our country is so open already that I believed the Soviets would gain little additional knowledge about us. In contrast, I thought they would have some problems with unrestricted overflights of their territory. If Gorbachev could agree to it, we would only benefit—we had much to learn about the Soviet Union.

The President's speech at Boston University on May 21 was the third in the series. This was an unusual commencement, in that French president François Mitterrand also spoke. The two presidents traveled together to Boston from their meetings in Kennebunkport* and gave a joint press conference afterward. Although the Boston address was principally about Europe, President Bush emphasized our tempered optimism in dealing with the Soviets, applauding the positive changes they were making, but underscoring that while the change in the Soviet Union was dramatic, it was far from complete. They still had a formidable military machine, and we would put a high priority on negotiating a less

*See Chapter 3, pages 75–78.

millitarized Europe. We wanted "a real peace, a peace of shared optimism," he told the students, "not a peace of armed camps."

BRENT SCOWCROFT

President Bush delivered the final speech of the four at the Coast Guard Academy on May 24. Preparing this address turned out to be far more complicated than had been the case with its predecessors. Given its close proximity to the address at Texas A&M, we had relatively little time to work on it. The first drafts were done by the White House writers with limited NSC input. The President brusquely rejected the proposed draft as too bellicose. He was tired of criticism casting him as stuck in a Cold War rut. He felt the draft was bombastic, hard-line, and full of "macho" Cold War expressions that did not ring true to him. As a result of his dissatisfaction, I worked through the night before the speech revising it with the writers.

As befitted the venue, the text dealt with military strategy and arms control for the 1990s, spelling out that we intended to keep an effective nuclear deterrent but would seek an approach to arms reduction that would permit stability at the lowest number of weapons we considered prudent. The President outlined the substance of our strategic review on arms policy, but now put arms control in the context of the changes in the Soviet Union and the need to seize every opportunity to build a more stable relationship with Moscow across the board, not simply in military power. The INF* treaty and Gorbachev's pledge for unilateral reductions in conventional forces offered an opportunity to remove the threat of war from Europe altogether. In keeping with his speech in Texas, the President called on the Soviet Union to follow through on its promises, move away from an offensive military strategy, and transform the Warsaw Pact into a defensive alliance mirroring NATO. The speech got a good reception by the audience. Some in the press still thought it somewhat hard-line, but it delivered in understandable fashion our concept of the modifications in military and arms control strategy needed to take advantage of the rapidly changing security landscape.

The Coast Guard Academy speech completed the public exposition of our new strategy toward the cockpit of East-West confrontation. It was cautious and prudent, an appropriate policy in a period of turbulence and rapid change, but it proved surprisingly durable and established a valuable framework for the conduct of policy. We were shifting policy

---

*Intermediate-range nuclear forces.

from the old and narrow focus on strategic arms control to a wider dialogue designed to reduce the threat of war and bring real peace— including progress in Eastern Europe, CFE (conventional forces in Europe), and regional issues. All this was aimed at encouraging a "re-formed" Soviet Union, ready to play a trustworthy role in the community of nations—one far less threatening to the United States and its allies.

CHAPTER 3

Leading the Alliance

BRENT SCOWCROFT

As we established our new policies, we had a full platter of practical demands before us. We had to prepare for the NATO summit in Brussels at the end of May, followed by a G-7* economic summit in July. While most NATO summits were fairly routine, this one had a higher profile than usual. It was the fortieth anniversary of the alliance, and the flurry of dramatic arms reduction announcements Gorbachev had set forth in his December UN speech had put it—and us—on the political defensive.

Two immediate and related challenges faced NATO, and changes in East-West relations affected perceptions of both. The first was the start of scheduled talks for reducing conventional (non-nuclear) forces in Europe (CFE). The second, and more controversial, was alliance policy on short-range nuclear forces (SNF): their modernization and whether and when to negotiate reductions in these forces. While the issues were critical to NATO, they were dry and undramatic—and the timing could not have been worse. Gorbachev was delivering well-publicized speeches about peace and democracy in Eastern Europe, yet here we were, dourly debating tanks and missiles in the West. The sense of eased superpower tensions, coupled with Gorbachev's intense public relations campaign, prompted some European political leaders to question the need for sub-stantial defense spending—and, especially in Germany, to reopen the emotional issue of whether to retain our remaining nuclear forces on the continent. There were doubts about US priorities at a time when the Soviets seemed to have moved beyond the Cold War. It would be a night-mare of diplomacy to get the Germans to even discuss these matters, and to bring the alliance to full agreement on solutions.

*The "Group of Seven"—the leading industrial democracies in the world.

Resolving CFE and SNF was an urgent practical necessity, even if the political environment was hostile. Both President Bush and I strongly believed that NATO needed modern nuclear forces, a view shared throughout the Administration and a long-standing US policy. These forces were essential to offset the conventional superiority of the Warsaw Pact— which remained a danger. This was the "official" alliance position as well as that of the United States and Britain, but the NATO stance masked a growing division with West Germany. There, public resistance to nuclear forces was particularly sharp, and Chancellor Helmut Kohl faced a major domestic political problem over these weapons.

Because they had a range of under 300 miles, short-range missiles almost certainly would be directed against targets inside Germany, East or West. West Germans thus felt singled out as the venue of any nuclear attack. The strong and well-organized anti-nuclear movement in the Federal Republic mobilized in vocal opposition to modernization, calling instead for elimination of the remaining weapons (88 launchers— as opposed to about 1,400 for the Soviets). Under pressure from West Germany, NATO in June 1987 already had agreed to delay any decision on modernization until it developed a "comprehensive concept" for the integration of alliance strategy and arms control policy. That plan was supposed to be completed in time for consideration at the NATO summit in May. However, facing such a hot political issue and cooling support for the government, Kohl and his coalition partner, Foreign Minister Hans-Dietrich Genscher of the Free Democratic Party, hoped to have a decision further delayed, until after the German general elections in 1990.

On the other side, and speaking for most of the alliance, were the United States and Britain, which maintained that NATO could neither reduce the numbers of nuclear weapons nor halt modernization until we had successfully redressed the Warsaw Pact's superiority in conventional forces, achieving some general balance. In addition, Soviet force reduction was important to us because it was part of our plan to get the occupying Soviet Army out of Eastern Europe and allow liberalization to flourish without the threat of a crackdown. NATO members, by and large, agreed that talks on conventional forces would have to precede negotiations on nuclear ones, but several believed it important to concede to German domestic political requirements on deferring modernization of the missiles.

We sympathized with Kohl's dilemma, especially because we wanted to do what we could to strengthen him politically. We preferred his leadership to that of the opposition Social Democrats, who had moved left since the days when they were led by Helmut Schmidt. They now supported the elimination of nuclear forces, and their traditional views on foreign and defense policy we saw as accommodating the Soviets. Part of the current problem appeared to be willingness among some groups in West Germany, especially the Social Democrats and the Green Party, to accept at face value much of Gorbachev's rhetoric about arms reductions. Both President Bush and Prime Minister Thatcher wanted proof of Soviet conventional military cuts before we agreed to alter NATO's bulwark.

On January 14, the two alliances had agreed to the mandate for conventional forces negotiations, which were to take place within the framework of the CSCE (Conference on Security and Cooperation in Europe)* process. We had inherited an alliance position, presented by Baker at the opening round on March 6 in Vienna, that called for unequal reductions by NATO and the Warsaw Pact to establish an equal level of forces, at about 5–10 percent below current NATO totals. The alliance proposal was immediately and widely criticized as insufficient and unimaginative, since it required very little of NATO and a great deal of the Pact (decreases of over 50 percent in each category). The Warsaw Pact accepted that approach, however, and Shevardnadze, who presented the Pact proposals, advocated even deeper slashes on both sides.

Shevardnadze's proposals were something of a pleasant surprise. There had been speculation that Moscow might unveil a dramatic initiative designed to embarrass NATO. Yet the apparent Soviet willingness, even eagerness, to proceed to deeper cuts than the NATO position outlined, or than the alliance seemed ready to contemplate, added new fuel to criticism that the Bush Administration was stuck in the Cold War and unresponsive to the opportunities the Soviets seemed to offer. Congressman Les Aspin, chairman of the House Armed Services Committee, accused NATO of lacking a vision of a new security arrangement for the end of the century, with the result that "we look like a bunch of bean counters and Gorbachev looks like a guy who wants a different relationship in Europe." Far from taking the initiative away from Gorbachev, the NATO proposal had accentuated our problems, putting us even more on the defensive.

The debate over short-range nuclear weapons, however, rocked the alliance for the next few months, and it would require patient diplomacy to build a consensus for agreement before the NATO summit. We needed to demonstrate that a determined NATO was taking the initiative—

*Launched at Helsinki in 1975 as a forum for East-West security issues.

reassuring the public that the West, not Gorbachev, would show the way to Europe's future. The NATO allies were still far apart, and there were strong-willed personalities on both sides. While President Bush and Prime Minister Thatcher were as one on the substance of the issues, Thatcher was unyielding on any changes that might weaken NATO defenses. In contrast, Chancellor Kohl was determined at least to delay modernization and to begin talks to reduce the missiles. It would require an even stronger will to bring the sides together. From our perspective, resolving the differences in time for the summit, and doing so in a way which would strengthen NATO unity and put us out in front of Gorbachev, presented the first test of President Bush's alliance leadership.

GEORGE BUSH

I always have believed that the United States bears a disproportionate responsibility for peace in Europe and an obligation to lead NATO. In the 1930s, we learned the hard way that it was a mistake to withdraw into isolation after World War I. We watched as Europe struggled with fascism, but were drawn inevitably into battle to restore its freedom. When the Cold War began, Western Europe became the front line against a Soviet threat, and our allies depended on the United States to point the direction for NATO; the American president was to lead the way.

I believed that personal contact would be an important part of our approach to both diplomacy and leadership of the alliance and elsewhere. Some feel emphasis on personal relationships between leaders is unimportant or unnecessary. Henry Kissinger once argued to me that these are no substitutes for deep national interests. He pointed out that the leader of one country is not going to change a policy because he likes another leader. I suppose there is a danger that one can be naively lulled into complacency if one expects friendships will cause the other party to do things your way, but I thought that danger was remote. For me, personal diplomacy and leadership went hand in hand.

There are actually commonsense reasons for an American president to build relationships with his opposites. If a foreign leader knows the character and the heartbeat of the president (and vice versa), there is apt to be far less miscalculation on either side. Personal relationships may not overcome tough issues dividing two sides, but they can provide enough goodwill to avoid some misunderstandings. This knowledge helps a president formulate and adjust policies that can bring other leaders along to his own point of view. It can make the difference between suspicion and giving each other the benefit of the doubt—and room to maneuver on a difficult political issue.

I planned to use personal contact as a way to show foreign leaders that the United States was interested and involved with them, not aloof. If a president delegates too much high-level diplomacy to subordinates, he conveys the impression of indifference toward foreign leaders, or even arrogance. Every chief of state and head of government has pride in his country and should be treated with dignity and respect, and that must include consulting with them. While most countries already respect the United States, they want to know and trust that the United States also has great respect for them, for their ways, and for their sovereignty. It is important to make gestures that signal we value their point of view. The more contact you make the better, particularly if there are common problems you have to work out together. If you have the confidence of someone, confidence built through personal contacts, you can get a lot more done. You can't develop or earn this mutual trust and respect unless you deliberately work at it. I was fortunate; I had known many of the current foreign leaders for years, often before they took office, and that would help strengthen trust.

BRENT SCOWCROFT

President Bush invested an enormous amount of time in personal diplomacy, and, in my opinion, it was indispensable to the success of our foreign policy. His direct relationship with his counterparts had a tremendous effect upon them—most were immensely flattered. They would no longer be strangers, having only occasional formal contact. The President called his principal allies and friends often, frequently not with any particular issue in mind but just to chat and exchange views on how things were going in general. Some, such as his friend Dutch prime minister Ruud Lubbers, and Egyptian president Hosni Mubarak, became reliable and valued sounding boards of trends and views. Almost every day there would be such calls, sometimes just short ones to check up on something, but often long, detailed conversations. He enjoyed this task he had set himself and probably spoke with foreign leaders more often than his four or five predecessors combined. The contact meant that foreign leaders knew him on a personal basis, knew what his basic values were, and, therefore, were predisposed to respond favorably when he called to ask for support. As a result, foreign leaders tended to be there when we needed them, often only because they knew, understood, and empathized from having spoken with him on so many occasions.

Those leaders less crucial to US policy were also the object of the President's attention. By the end of 1989, for example, he had called virtually every head of government in Latin America. The practical results could be seen when we sent troops into Panama in December to restore democratic rule. Traditionally, such action would have provoked a firestorm of outrage from Latin American leaders sensitive to foreign, especially Yankee, intervention. The fact that these leaders knew George Bush, and understood his goals and what kind of man he was, resulted in a very muted and quite inconsequential opposition to the Panama operation.

Personal diplomacy paralleled traditional diplomatic processes and greatly reinforced them. Using the State and Defense Departments as the regular channels and augmenting them by presidential telephone calls made a powerful combination in rallying support for US policies. Foreign ministries had their own ways of viewing issues, sometimes quite different from those of their current head of state or government. The Quai d'Orsay (foreign ministry) in France, for example, had a reputation with the State Department as adversarial and obstinate. It was enormously helpful to Jim Baker that the various foreign ministries knew that, if they were disposed to be negative or simply drag their feet on an issue, they might receive an inquiry from their head of government— stimulated by a Bush phone call. This approach gave our friends the sense that we had done our homework, spoke with one voice, and were sincerely consulting with them as we formulated policy.

GEORGE BUSH

A good example of the value to me of personal relationships with foreign leaders was Brian Mulroney, the prime minister of Canada. He was a particular asset, both as a friend and as a source of policy advice. We had become close during the 1980s, when he became prime minister and I was vice president. I found him easy to talk to, gregarious, and possessed of a great sense of humor. He has a contagious twinkle in his eye, and he genuinely means it when he says, "Glad to see you." Of all the foreign leaders I have met, none has a greater interest in world affairs than Brian. When I first became president, he counseled me on dealing with many of our colleagues, and he rightly felt free to give advice at any time. I found it was always sound and offered in a direct, straightforward manner that I liked. He was well informed and well briefed, but he was a good listener too. Brian became an important part of my own policy process and we would talk frequently on the phone or in person—he often flew down for dinner. I could talk to him in confidence and I also knew he would accurately convey my thoughts to other leaders. At one point I asked him to explain to Gorbachev the domestic pressure I was under regarding Lithuania. I felt very comfortable asking this, and it did not hurt him to have Gorbachev know that Brian and I were talking about these matters—personally, without bureaucracy or other advisors. With his fluent French (and Canada's historic link to France), Brian also had a close relationship with François Mitterrand, and he could offer insights on François' thinking and concerns.

Brian demonstrated that it was possible to be both a strong leader for Canada and a true friend of the United States. When we had disputes on trade or environmental issues, he never backed away from placing Canada's interests first. But even when we had differences over policy, our personal relationship helped us talk about them frankly, and allowed us to try to solve them privately, without public posturing.

On February 11, Brian and I met in Ottawa for what turned into a typical brainstorming session, this time on policy toward the Soviet Union. As we sat with Jim Baker, Brent, Canadian secretary of state for external affairs Joe Clark and others, Brian asked about my plans for NATO. I told him that before we could negotiate successfully with the Soviets, we had to get our individual and collective acts together—and reinforce alliance solidarity. I was particularly worried about Germany. Brian asked whether, as part of an effort to counter Gorbachev's public relations offensive, a presidential trip to Eastern Europe might help. If I went armed with a comprehensive plan for dealing with the area, and a sense of how to use the symbolism involved, it could be quite a public relations coup of our own—and not necessarily bad for Gorbachev. I thought a trip was a great idea. It would remind people of the true differences between the Soviet Union and the West. "We need to make more of our strengths," I said, "the fact that we are the proponents of democracy, human rights, and free economies." As Clark reminded us, however, West Germany (the heart of NATO and where the bulk of our forces were based) was still the key in the public relations war, and the West was losing there.

Germany became the main battleground for countering Gorbachev's propaganda efforts in Europe. His December United Nations speech had further inflamed the issue of short-range nuclear missiles there and would make it more difficult to persuade the German public of the need for an early decision on modernization. It also increased the German government's eagerness for early negotiations to reduce the weapons. Bonn argued that such talks would demonstrate how the West wanted to take advantage of the new environment. Furthermore, if NATO refused to negotiate, the alliance would appear as reluctant to part with the

Cold War—and Bonn darkly hinted that this might undermine the governing coalition.

GEORGE BUSH

The Germans were becoming increasingly insistent and inflexible, both about starting nuclear arms control negotiations and about postponing missile modernization, without waiting until we had handled conventional forces. For me, and particularly for Margaret Thatcher, these were matters on which the Germans were heading in the wrong direction and on which compromise could be dangerous. Ever since I had known Helmut Kohl, I had thought him to be friendly to the United States and a firm believer in NATO solidarity. But I realized his political problems might tempt him to break ranks with the alliance. As Vice President, I had visited him when I went to Europe to help sell the controversial deployment of intermediate-range Pershing II missiles and had witnessed the ugly demonstrations against them. The modernization problem was particularly troublesome, but one I thought we could help him with. If the alliance had a good, strong position, it could give Kohl some cover for accommodation. I doubted that the German people would expect him to turn his back on the rest of NATO.

Kohl's Christian Democratic Union (CDU), and its sister party the Christian Socialist Union (CSU), governed the Federal Republic in coalition with the Free Democrats (FDP), led by Genscher. For this reason, Kohl often lacked the freedom to take positions on controversial issues that split the electorate. He had constantly to consult with his partners and read the domestic political tea leaves, lest he lose his thin parliamentary majority and with it the chancellorship. The FDP had produced just such a result a few years earlier when it defected from the coalition of Kohl's predecessor, the Social Democrats' (SPD) Helmut Schmidt. Genscher had also been foreign minister under Schmidt and was an influential voice in his own right.

I was confident that Helmut would prevail. Up to this point he was the consummate politician, perhaps the most skilled I have seen, and I admire him. No matter how down he appears in the polls (he typically runs very far behind in the run-up to an election), or how often his critics or the pundits have declared him politically dead, he has always sprung back. His political instincts have always seemed infallible. He has survived not by following but by understanding and anticipating his opposition, taking their views into consideration. He is always informed and alert to the machinations of the opposition, yet, in the final analysis, he leads from his own convictions. When push came to shove, I always found he tried to come through for the United States and the alliance.

A huge, affable man, Helmut seems at times like an enormous bear. He loves a good joke. I used to tease him about Petra Kelly, the German-American firebrand who became a strong anti-Kohl leader of the Green Party—protesting, pushing, speaking out, hectoring the Christian Democrats in every way possible. Once, as vice president, I had been Helmut's guest at Krefeld, where we celebrated the early emigration of Germans to America. Back then the Greens were very militant, not just the tree-hugging environmentalists the name evoked, and during the ceremonies they took part in demonstrations against US nuclear forces in Europe. Afterward, Kelly crashed a luncheon Kohl gave for me. As she pushed her way toward the head table, before she was intercepted by security, I turned to Helmut and innocently asked, "Is your attachment to Petra emotional or is it a physical attraction?" I thought he was going to die laughing.

BRENT SCOWCROFT

If we were to head off an alliance split over the nuclear question, we had to get the conventional forces talks underway. Once we knew what the conventional balance was going to be—and if good-faith reductions had begun—we would have the elements necessary for determining what nuclear forces we needed and thus a basis for undertaking the negotiations on them that the Germans wanted. Eliminating them remained completely unacceptable under any circumstances. As for modernization, while an early decision was not vital, it would serve to underscore the determination of the alliance to retain the capability necessary for deterrence or defense. I thought postponement could dangerously exacerbate the growing sentiment in Europe that no further defense efforts were required. The Soviets were in general retreat precisely because of our strong and resolute policies over the years. We should not abandon those policies at the point of victory. Then there was our Congress. It was becoming increasingly grumpy about spending money on tactical nuclear modernization, especially if there was no guarantee the Europeans would accept the weapons.

On February 10, the day before Baker was to arrive in Bonn on his maiden "get acquainted" trip through Europe, Kohl formally called on the alliance to postpone until 1991 or 1992 a decision regarding modernizing NATO's short-range nuclear forces. He pointed out that the existing system would not require replacement until 1995 or 1996, so a decision could easily be deferred until after 1990—beyond the West German elections. This was an unpleasant surprise. The request appeared to be an effort to deflect any attempts by Baker to persuade the Germans to agree to a specific statement in support of the principle of modernization. This inauspicious prelude to the Baker visit was confirmed during his time there. Kohl even toughened his position somewhat. Not only did he reiterate his call for deferral of a decision on modernization, at least until after the elections, but he also urged that NATO open negotiations with Moscow on reducing short-range nuclear forces—without waiting until we had resolved the central question of conventional force levels. Genscher took it a step further. In a radio interview on February 14, he questioned the need to proceed with the modernization of nuclear forces at all, in light of the promised Soviet arms cuts.

Kohl seemed to be reacting to the deteriorating political support for his coalition, with the nuclear issue an important focal point for the opposition Social Democrats. The *Christian Science Monitor* reported on April 5 that a poll showed nearly two-thirds of West Germans wanted Kohl to step down. In mid-April, he shuffled his cabinet and became more and more insistent about early negotiations, fueling the debate in the alliance.

GEORGE BUSH

In an attempt to deal with the problem directly, I spoke with Kohl and suggested he come to Camp David or to Washington for an informal talk, just to sort out the issues. Helmut insisted that coalition problems prevented him from traveling, but offered to send his advisor Horst Teltschik, Brent's counterpart in Bonn. That was fine with me, for Teltschik had Kohl's confidence. Helmut promised that a visit would be arranged soon, but in the end no meeting took place. Teltschik's repeated cancellations led me to conclude not only that Kohl was under increasing pressure to delay a decision on modernization and support early negotiations with Moscow, but also that he believed he was not in a position to enter discussions with us, for fear he might be seen by the German public to be compromising. I was becoming frustrated with his evasiveness. We had to fashion some sort of resolution if we were to build a consensus by the time of the NATO summit.

On April 12, I met with NATO Secretary General Manfred Wörner, a former minister of defense under Kohl and a prominent CDU politician. He urged that I work to keep the growing nuclear debate from spoiling the upcoming anniversary NATO summit, and reminded me that it was time to set a new direction for the alliance. "We are in a historic situation," he said, "and although we are successful, public perception is that Gorbachev is driving history." Manfred suggested that we now concentrate on the alliance's political message, not simply try to challenge Moscow with arms control proposals. NATO should point the way toward the future and project itself as a source of stability and security in a time of political change. "The United States should not expect others to deliver much," he warned. "They are waiting for the Americans." Manfred was right, it was up to me to both find a solution to the SNF—one that would unify the allies before the summit—and frame a new direction for the alliance.

A few days later, British foreign secretary Geoffrey Howe arrived in Washington to go over the problem. He repeated Margaret Thatcher's strong opposition to negotiations—a point she had made to me in our first conversation after my inauguration. I shared some of her concerns. Once we began talks, public pressure to get rid of all the missiles would grow well before we could take steps to fix the conventional balance. Howe passed along Margaret's basic message: the United States should stand down and let her work the problem out with Kohl. I was not willing to do that, in part because of our belief that the Thatcher-Kohl relationship was not smooth. Furthermore, she was even more unyielding than we, and far more emotional about the dangers of compromise. I did not see these as ingredients for finding common ground with Helmut. I think Margaret was unsure about how I planned to lead NATO and she took strong public positions on SNF, perhaps reasoning that this would make it more difficult for me to compromise with the Germans. I also expect she still wanted to speak for the special US-British relationship, as she had with Ronald Reagan. But I was determined that the President of the United States must lead the alliance.

BRENT SCOWCROFT

Mindful of German political problems, the NATO defense ministers met on April 20, and drafted a communiqué that, while pledging to retain "flexible nuclear forces across the entire spectrum" and keep them up to date, essentially accepted the German request to postpone a decision on modernization until after 1990. Less than a day after this conciliatory gesture, Bonn dropped a bombshell. We learned through a leak to the press that the ruling coalition had voted to support holding immediate East-West negotiations on reducing short-range nuclear weapons. The leak seemed deliberate, an attempt to manipulate public pressure on NATO to adopt the German position rather than pursue the question through confidential diplomacy.

GEORGE BUSH

I was annoyed with this unilateral move. I thought it an example of how *not* to conduct alliance business. When I spoke with Helmut the next day, he explained that the coalition had been working on the nuclear question and had now sent up an internal consensus paper on the issue. He promised to forward it within the hour, and asked that I see Genscher and his new defense minister, Gerhard Stoltenberg, when they arrived the following Monday to meet with Baker, Cheney, and Scowcroft. It would allow him to say that Germany was consulting with its friends on the subject—implying that the German position was still under debate—and he wanted some credit at home for at least making the proposal, even if it was not adopted.

I told Helmut I understood his situation and I did not wish to meddle, but he should have discussed SNF with us before such decisions were made—and were made public. I did not want Bonn to present us with a *fait accompli*. "It also means no leaks, which only tend to lock one into a position," I added firmly. He blamed the leaks on his three-party coalition, which left much room for such problems. It would be difficult to keep things solely between us anyway. He would still have to talk to the other allies when the NATO ministers presented their paper as a basis for discussions, and there was no way to prevent people from disclosing its contents, or keeping the debate from becoming public.

"That's not the problem," I replied. "The problem is that a firm FRG [West German] position [on behalf of] the alliance should not be taken in advance. We have to have some openness to discuss our differences and work out a mutually agreed position. We have to get it sorted out *now*, so we can have a successful NATO summit without any wedges into what is now very good alliance solidarity."

Margaret Thatcher shared my irritation and worries about the German tactics. The next day I told her about my effort to persuade Kohl to consult in advance, and my concern about his lack of cooperation. I thought the existing alliance pledge to keep the systems up to date should suffice and realistically was the most we could probably expect to get from the Germans. Specific decisions on deployment could wait until 1991.

Margaret vented her own annoyance. She thought the German position reflected Genscher's views, not Kohl's, and that he, Genscher, was using the proposals as a device to win acceptance for them. In fact, she suggested it was possible that Kohl was relying on the United States and Britain to block Genscher's efforts. NATO was not Germany, she said, and we could not have Bonn dictating to the alliance. In the last resort, if we could together stand firm for NATO, Kohl could not depart from his American and British allies. The consequences would be "too horrific." It was up to Washington and London to "rescue" the alliance, she argued. We must be firm with Germany; they were wrong to make their position public. She volunteered to make her own stance public, but as NATO's, not her own.

The message coming out of the summit could not be that there was no spine among the allies, Margaret declared. It would mean failure. There could be no question, no question, she repeated, of negotiations on SNF. "The Germans know full well that flexible response depends on SNF and that therefore these forces have to be kept up to date," she said heatedly. "The Germans agree that we need a mix of nuclear and conventional forces in Europe, but they deny this principle by their position on specific weapons. That is not Kohl. It is Genscher trying to run the alliance with his five percent of the German electorate."

Still, Margaret acknowledged that we could defer a decision on deployment of modernized missiles at this summit and that a delay was the best compromise we could get. "What is important is agreement between the US and Britain," she said, "because without those two countries there would be no NATO." She asked if we could at least go public with our telephone call, to show that the United States and Britain were cooperating on dealing with the Germans. I said I had asked Kohl not to go public, and had extracted a commitment from him that there would be no *fait accompli*. I preferred to wait until after the talks with the Germans in Washington before we said anything. We would deal privately and in good faith with the Germans when they came.

This conversation was vintage Thatcher, strong and principled. It reflected the friction she felt with the Germans—and the importance of my effort to find a balanced approach to Kohl's recalcitrance. I had admired Margaret's strength many times over the years. I first met her in Houston back in 1977, when I was asked to introduce her at an English Speaking Union event. She was not yet prime minister, and I was not in public office at the time. I was greatly impressed with her speaking ability. Later, as vice president, I saw a great deal of her when I traveled to London and on each of her visits to the United States. Margaret and I became good friends. I regret that we never were quite as close as she had been to Ronald Reagan.

Margaret had a genuine respect and affection for Reagan. While Reagan usually set the tone at international meetings, he often seemed to turn the rest of the discussion over to Thatcher, letting her speak for the two of them. She enjoyed talking on their joint behalf, frequently saying "Ron and I feel." I kept in mind the importance of the US-British relationship and was determined to work closely with Margaret, but I had to speak for myself. When we had differences we would iron them out. In her memoirs, she makes reference to a need on my part to assert myself. I think her perception stemmed from my decision early on that there could be only one spokesman for the United States. I know she understood this, but it was a change from the past and from the added authority with which she had been able to speak.

Margaret was never without an opinion, forcefully stated. I saw why she became such a strong leader. She was assertive and never reluctant to speak out or to differ with others. Where Mitterrand used to couch his arguments with references to the lessons of history, Thatcher was more inclined strongly and bluntly to state her position without worrying about niceties. She was strong, but not rude. She was also well briefed, and knowledgeable—very much the expert in arms control. I valued her wisdom and insight, especially in handling Europe and NATO. I learned from her, as I did from Reagan, the value of adherence to principle, and I respected her toughness and her total self-confidence. She did not suffer fools gladly and I never found that she warmed to humor. She didn't have the light personal touch that Brian Mulroney, John Major, or Helmut Kohl had. Certainly Gorbachev and Yeltsin had more humor, more levity than Thatcher.

Margaret never hid her considerable affection for the United States, nor the importance she placed on relations between our countries. She worked hard to keep the "special" relationship intact. She did not want our countries to drift apart in international forums, and if that meant some compromise on her part, she was willing to give us the benefit of the doubt. I was very grateful to her for that. Clearly troubled about European integration, she saw the United States as her most important ally and, indeed, friend. I believe she thought of us also as a counter-weight to what she feared was growing French-German cooperation. She did not completely trust the Europeans.

BRENT SCOWCROFT

Like Thatcher's, my reaction to the German move was not a happy one. The atmosphere was already a bit tense, and having the Germans make a unilateral decision on an issue of such multilateral concern—and then send a traveling road show to sell it—did not help. Baker, Cheney, and I met with the two German ministers on April 24, but the mood was anything but conciliatory and, although several proposals were raised (including unilaterally reducing our short-range forces while challenging the Soviets to cut to our levels), we got nowhere. The situation was threatening to develop into a major crisis in the alliance.

The impasse between the US and German positions drew increasing criticism inside Washington. Senator Sam Nunn, chairman of the Senate

Armed Services Committee, suggested that NATO was shooting itself in the foot and said he saw no strategy at all to deal with the US-German split. Paul Nitze, just retired senior government arms control advisor, warned that the United States was in danger of being isolated within the alliance by its refusal to negotiate. He declared that it would be politically impossible for West Germany to agree to modernize short-range missiles without a decision to negotiate with the Warsaw Pact. The public perception thus was—accurately—that we were unwilling to negotiate on SNF, but also—inaccurately—that we were not sure what we wanted to do. We wanted to delay negotiations on nuclear forces until the conventional forces balance was addressed. The problem was to help Kohl find a way to say yes to this approach without severe political damage—or compromising NATO's fundamental security needs.

GEORGE BUSH

Kohl called me again on May 5 to discuss the situation. I told him I was annoyed that our private differences were becoming public ones—I was trying to work with him for a harmonious summit. He pledged he would do his best to achieve a compromise in time for the summit, and he felt the chances were good. I wasn't so sure. Although he had said two days before in Rome that he saw no problem in linking talks on missiles with the conventional arms talk, I still hadn't heard anything about first seeing concrete conventional force reductions. We were going round and round and I saw no progress. I still hoped that direct, frank discussion between Helmut and me would create an opening for consensus on substance and avoid a disaster at the summit.

The Soviets took full advantage of the dissension within NATO. In Moscow on May 11, Baker found himself deliberately upstaged when Gorbachev, with Baker standing at his side, announced a planned withdrawal of 500 short-range nuclear warheads from Eastern Europe (which still left the Soviets far more than we had). Kohl and Genscher welcomed the Soviet move, and Genscher noted that it strengthened Bonn's commitment to seek early SNF negotiations. West German and other European officials charged informally to the press that Washington had once again allowed Moscow to dominate events.

BRENT SCOWCROFT

On May 17, Stoltenberg was back in Washington for two days of talks. He met primarily with Dick Cheney, but I joined them for lunch. It was shrewd of Kohl to send Stoltenberg alone. He was much more sympathetic than Genscher to the US position and recently had criticized the foreign minister for mishandling the issue. The German stance was that NATO should agree to SNF talks as soon as the Soviets showed they were serious about deep cuts in conventional forces, specifically an agreement to equal levels of tanks. There was, however, no mention of waiting for the cuts to take place before negotiating on the missiles.

Stoltenberg also raised an earlier proposal to refer to a study group the issue of linking the separate talks on conventional and nuclear forces. It essentially endorsed early negotiations, the only issue being when to hold them, not whether. I thought that putting the issue off to a study group would get the alliance through the summit without a confrontation, but it was basically a postponement, allowing the matter to continue to fester. Other than accepting the principle of negotiations, I doubted that the proposal would be much help to Kohl. While he finally appeared to be moving in the right direction, we could not accept the German initiatives as they stood.

In the meantime we had been developing our own linkage position, which included the provision that SNF talks could not begin until a treaty on reduction of conventional arms was completed and its implementation underway—putting conventional force reductions clearly out front. Our plan also required agreement that some short-range nuclear forces would remain after the negotiations. We were convinced this approach would permit the Germans to claim a substantial achievement. It appeared that this was the case. On May 21, Kohl's press spokesman, Hans Klein, told reporters that the West Germans saw our offers as the basis for agreement, but that "the solution is not yet completed."

Thatcher was not happy with our new proposal, particularly because we had not consulted with her beforehand. As she explained in her memoirs, she still wanted a definitive statement of alliance support for nuclear forces and modernization. She preferred no negotiations at all, she later wrote. "And, if there had to be any, I wanted tougher conditions than those in the American text. Above all, there must be no fudged language on the 'third zero' [eliminating short-range nuclear systems]."*

Although we prided ourselves on consulting our allies, there were a few exceptions to the rule. The truth of the matter was that we knew what Thatcher's reaction would be and had decided not to say anything ahead of time. We believed we had to make this gesture to the Germans, that it did far more good than harm, and, had we consulted the British, it would have been very awkward to proceed over their strong objections.

We had hoped to have the short-range nuclear forces issue behind us

---

*Margaret Thatcher, *The Downing Street Years* (New York: HarperCollins, 1993), p. 788.

before the NATO summit, now only two weeks away, but it was becoming apparent that was not to be. We would have to resolve the disagreements at the summit itself, in a way that did not destroy the celebratory aspects of the meeting. Our proposal was useful but probably inadequate, by itself, to solve the alliance division. We needed a supporting move in the conventional forces negotiations. Developing a new initiative might encourage the Germans to accept our position on short-range nuclear missiles. It might also help still the rising chorus of charges that we lacked vision and were reluctant to let go of the Cold War. The question was how to get it done.

I was still convinced we had to make a bold initiative to reassert leadership, to regain control of the international agenda and to reunify and bolster NATO. Any proposal also had to be substantive enough to dismiss speculation that we were merely offering symbolic cuts in order to take some of the heat off us. Yet this was not a case of politics prevailing over strategic need. There was no question that further US reductions in NATO were inevitable. Moreover, any proposal we made would require larger cuts in Soviet forces than in our own, and would therefore actually improve, not erode, the balance. My old idea for really deep cuts had been molded to reflect just these requirements and had the added attraction that it would reduce the muscle behind Soviet influence in Eastern Europe. I had continued to bring up the need for a new conventional forces proposal in our meetings, to keep it on the agenda. That proved superfluous, for the President wanted to act.

GEORGE BUSH
In the weeks since our original CFE proposal had fallen flat, I became impatient because I had not seen any dramatic ideas from our arms control experts. Various staff papers floated up the system outlining a few options, but nothing suggesting the deep slashes I wanted. After wading through numerous briefing papers, and after some talks with Brent and Dick Cheney, I proposed a 25 percent cut in the roughly 320,000 US troops in NATO forces, with a Soviet decrease to an equal number. I thought this was large enough to show we were serious and committed to responding to the positive changes we were seeing in the policies of the Soviet Union. I called a meeting on May 19, up in Kennebunkport, with Dick, Brent, Admiral Crowe, and others to present my ideas. Crowe reacted with alarm. He declared that reductions of that dimension would force a drastic change in NATO strategy. After a long debate, I asked him to go back to the Joint Chiefs of Staff to figure out just how deeply we could slash without disrupting the alliance.

The JCS were unenthusiastic about cuts of any size, but when I made plain to Crowe that I was determined, they came back with a proposal to trim 30,000 troops, or about 10 percent. That did not seem to me to be much of a reduction, but I was reluctant to ignore the unanimous advice of the Joint Chiefs. Generally speaking, I wanted proposals that the executive made on the use of force or arms control to have their unequivocal support if at all possible. I was determined not to bulldoze the military into silence or drag them into agreement. In this case, had I not sternly prodded, the Pentagon might not have come forward with anything at all. Crowe did agree that the reductions would be taken in combat forces (as opposed to support troops), which were about half the total troop strength. That allowed us to recast the arithmetic to claim a more respectable 20 percent reduction, by virtue of excluding the noncombat element.

BRENT SCOWCROFT

We also proposed that the timetable for reaching agreement on conventional forces be moved up from two years to between six to twelve months, and the actual time for reductions be changed from 1997 to 1992–93. This shorter timeline would probably make it much easier for the Germans to agree to delay short-range nuclear forces negotiations until we were certain conventional force reductions were taking place. This was a significant package. We hoped it would solve the political problem within the alliance and demonstrate both to the Soviets and the Europeans that we were serious, forward-looking, and prepared to take some risks to move East-West relations to a new plane.

GEORGE BUSH

In the midst of the alliance turmoil on force reductions, I took time out to play host to François Mitterrand on May 20–21. It would be our first meeting since a luncheon in Tokyo at the time of Emperor Hirohito's funeral in February. I had invited him to Kennebunkport specifically to give US-French relations a fresh start, for in recent years they had been under some strain. There was often friction between the State Department and the Quai d'Orsay, but some officials in the Reagan Administration felt that Mitterrand, too, was difficult. Frankly, they disliked him and felt freer to speak out against him because he and Reagan were not close. I wanted to change this, and a private, quiet weekend in Kennebunkport could provide the opportunity.

Camp David and Kennebunkport were perfect settings in which to hold relaxed conversations. At Camp David it was the quiet mountain setting, the trees, the trails, the movies, and the varied sports activities that contributed to frank conversation and the chance to get to know guests on a personal basis. At our home in Maine, it was the salt air and the seafood, the waves pounding against the rocks, fishing or careening over the Atlantic coastal waters in my twenty-eight-foot speedboat, the *Fidelity*. People loved meeting at the White House, but those encounters were more formal and less conducive to a candid exchange of views.

When I mentioned the idea, Barbara thought I'd lost it. Everyone expected the worst. Here was the formal and composed president of France coming to our most informal home. Furthermore, Mitterrand was not an athlete, and the usual ancillary activities at Kennebunkport—fishing, tennis, golf, boating, horseshoes—were likely to have little attraction for him. As the time approached, a large French advance squad appeared to inspect the facilities and, like our own counterparts, they had many requirements. Barbara and I had decided to put the Mitterrands in my mother's bungalow, which is a separate, smaller building at Walker's Point next to our own house. We soon feared, however, that the arrangements might not be suitable.

As Barbara has recounted in her own book, the little wooden bungalow was about seventy years old and, apart from some additions about thirty years before and seasonal cleanings, nothing had been done to it. Our daughter Doro took the French team through the house and showed them where the Mitterrands would be sleeping. Since it was still spring, and we were just opening up the house for the year, it looked a bit dirty and felt damp. Worse, my mother's hospital bed was in place, looking, in Barbara's words, "a little shabby." Doro told the dubious French not to worry, that we would be getting a new, larger bed for their president. Doro said the most embarrassing moment occurred when she showed them the bathroom, where there was a riser on the toilet seat. Barbara organized and led a thorough cleaning team, who worked day and night for several days to get the bungalow and the main house in shape for the visit. The riser was removed, an acceptable new bed was brought in, special phone lines were installed, and our little cottage nervously awaited our famous visitor. In the end, we should not have worried at all. Mitterrand liked the setting and, as he told me when I called on him in Paris in June 1995, he enjoyed the family atmosphere.

I had known Mitterrand for some time. When François was first elected in 1981, President Reagan asked me to go to Paris to assure him of our desire for close relations. Reagan was concerned about Mitterrand's announced determination to place Communists in his government. I remember clearly Mitterrand telling me he would put a few

Communists in ministries which would not be of major importance. "In a period of five years the Communist vote will be cut from fourteen percent to seven percent." I got the distinct feeling from that meeting, and from subsequent ones, that Mitterrand felt we were unduly obsessed with communism, and that we categorized all Communists as aggressive Stalinists. State was skeptical that his tactics would have the intended effect, believing he was being duped by the Communists. But Mitterrand was proved right. The Communist vote in France was cut in half over the years 1977–87.

I had developed a friendship with Mitterrand by the time I came to office, but not nearly as close as when I left. I wondered at first whether he suspected that I, a conservative, would be more sympathetic to the Gaullists than to him. He knew I was friends with, and had genuine respect for, one of his rivals, Jacques Chirac, then the mayor of Paris. But I found my relationship with Mitterrand interesting and rewarding.

I liked the way François made decisions. When I would call him about difficult problems, he would give me a straight answer. He told me what he was going to do; then he went ahead and did it. I also enjoyed listening to his historical analyses. At gatherings of heads of state, he loved to explain with examples how history could help us interpret current events. He had a quiet sense of humor and a glint in his eye that showed a warmth he was not publicly known for.

During the Reagan years, protocol and formalities seemed a stumbling block for relations. The French and US presidents, being heads of state, have a different protocol standing than their other G-7 colleagues—that is, a president outranks a premier. Their respective staffs developed a strong rivalry advancing the precedence of their presidents at international meetings. I did not care about all that, and if I could defer to Mitterrand on some matter of protocol, I was happy to. In my mind it did not diminish the United States to do so. He was older, he had been in office longer than I, so why not be respectful? My view is, if you have differences, be firm about them, but do not get caught up on "standing" or protocol rank. Mitterrand treated me with unfailing courtesy. The goodwill did not penetrate all the way through the two governments, but we worked at it and we didn't let the differences get out of control. I always enjoyed my time with this sage French leader, whose domestic socialist policies were contrary to my own views but who proved to be a dependable ally and a friend.

At Kennebunkport, François and I discussed NATO's problems over force reductions. A few days before, he had backed the US-British position that the alliance should wait to see progress on balancing conventional forces before negotiating on missiles. I explained our strategy for linking conventional and nuclear force talks and winning over the Germans. I noted that Thatcher wanted no change in our current position, but that it was necessary to try to find a way to help Helmut Kohl without letting NATO drift.

François believed that even though personally Kohl was close to the United States, he was driven by public opinion that rejected nuclear weapons in Germany. "There are many factors," he added, "but Gorbachev's popularity is a major one. Also there is World War II, Germany's destruction, the Communists, the neutralists, the Greens, and the 'realists.' " Although there was no policy agreement, these groups had formed an informal common front to say no. "This has led to an idealistic stand denouncing nuclear weapons and suggesting that there could be a Soviet-German agreement leading to reunification," he said. "This is a dream, since the Europeans and the Soviets have long feared German expansion. German expansionism dates back to the twelfth century and the Teutonic Knights in the Soviet mind; they are deeply suspicious."

Although he was a friend of the German socialists, said François, it was very difficult to reason with them in the NATO framework. He would rather work with Kohl and we should support him. "Speaking with full candor," he said, the problem was the antagonism between Kohl and Thatcher. "He calls her 'that woman,' " he confided. Thatcher was also irritated by the Franco-German axis. "For centuries Great Britain has worked to prevent continental alliances. This is still in Great Britain's subconscious."

"Nevertheless," he continued, "it is important to consider what we want in Brussels, technically speaking. The Soviet request is for a third 'zero.'* Given the current situation, this is unacceptable because of Soviet superiority in conventional, chemical, and nuclear forces. A third zero would not enhance the equilibrium. Kohl agrees, but he cannot say much. So he says, 'Let's negotiate.' We should help him save face. He agrees to reject a third zero; that is why we must first reduce conventional forces." The need to modernize was not so urgent—it could wait until 1992.

Following up on his remark on the topic, I asked François what he thought about German reunification.

"As long as the Soviet Union is strong, it will never happen," he predicted. "Since 1917 the Soviets have had a major hang-up about encirclement. Since their Civil War, they have had a siege mentality. Now

---

*The two sides had eliminated medium- and intermediate-range missiles. Eliminating short-range missiles would make a third zero.

they have Eastern European problems, Baltic problems, etc. They won't take a chance on reunification."

"How would you answer questions on reunification?" I asked.

"If the German people wished it, I would not oppose it," he said, "but not enough has changed since World War II to permit it." He did not see it happening within the next ten to fifteen years. "But the Soviets will never yield on the German problem," he added. "Gorbachev is very happy that East Germany is the most reactionary [of their satellites]."

"Can Gorbachev control the situation?" I asked. "Poland and Hungary are moving."

"Things might change one day, in the longer span of history," he acknowledged. However, he did not see the Germans pushing for reunification yet. Either that step or German acquisition of nuclear weapons would constitute a *casus belli*.

François did not want to go out on the *Fidelity*, so we took an afternoon walk through the woods, accompanied by his wife, Danielle. Maine never looked more beautiful. I am convinced this relaxed and friendly visit helped establish a deep trust between us, one that in the years to come would allow him to give us the benefit of the doubt when we differed.

BRENT SCOWCROFT

The Kennebunkport meeting was the President's personal style of diplomacy at its finest. The relationship established over this weekend played a great role in the way some of the momentous events of the next three years worked out. Despite deep differences on occasion, this personal rapport was able, in most instances, to allow sufficient cooperation for resolving issues satisfactorily. Only a few matters, such as the Uruguay Round of GATT and some aspects of the future of NATO, resisted even the magic of George Bush and Kennebunkport. As to the stalemate over SNF negotiations, Mitterrand seemed to think that Kohl was backed into a corner and needed a way out, one which would preserve as much political face as possible. I hoped that the President's strong new CFE proposal, plus the shortened timetable for final agreement on the cuts, would give him his opening to agree to delay talks on the missiles.

Joining us at Kennebunkport was Jacques Attali, my counterpart at the Elysée. Attali was not an attractive figure to most who knew him in Washington. He was widely thought to be brilliant, arrogant, intolerant and generally anti-American. I found him to be extremely intelligent, very well grounded in history, self-confident—even opinionated—with a formidable command of English. We had lively exchanges of views on a variety of foreign affairs issues, sometimes agreeing, sometimes disagreeing. To the disbelief of most of my colleagues, we hit it off well together and that began a very good association. He had a close relationship with President Mitterrand and seemed to know Mitterrand's thinking and to share his perspectives. He did have a sharp way about him and, if not anti-American, had something of a condescending attitude about America. Nevertheless, he was always stimulating and I thoroughly enjoyed our relationship.

Attali left after about a year and was replaced by Admiral Jacques Lanxade, who had been a junior member of the Mitterrand Elysée staff. He was a much more kindred spirit than Attali and more in tune with my notions of European-American strategic and military relations. He did not have Attali's relationship with Mitterrand, and the way the Elysée was structured resulted in Lanxade not being my exact counterpart. His office was actually across the street from the president's. When our direct line was installed, the French instrument was placed immediately outside Mitterrand's office, with the result that I had to warn Lanxade when I was going to call in order to give him time to cross the street. The procedure tended to negate all but the security advantages of the direct line.

Notwithstanding these obstacles, we developed an excellent mutual understanding. There was one event later, during Desert Storm, that greatly strengthened the bond between us and, I think, between the two presidents. One evening about six o'clock, Lanxade was in my office. We were deep in conversation when my private line from the President rang. It was Mrs. Bush, asking if I wanted to join her and the President for dinner at a local Chinese restaurant. I asked when they were leaving. "Now!" she replied. Trying to communicate without embarrassing my guest, I said I was in the middle of an appointment and could not get away. Five minutes later, the phone rang again. "Is your guest Admiral Lanxade?" she asked. When I replied "yes," she said "Bring him!" So Jacques and I piled in the motorcade with the Bushes and sped off to suburban Virginia and an excellent dinner. This was something beyond the Admiral's wildest imagination, something hard to conceive of in Paris, something typical of the Bushes.

It had taken a long time to reach internal agreement within the Administration over the new CFE proposal, and we now found ourselves approaching the end of May and the NATO summit. In order to maximize the potential effect of our conventional forces package, we had developed

it in great secrecy, with only limited involvement of our top staff and without early consultation with our NATO allies. The latter were completely in the dark—largely because we thought this was an important proposal coming at a crucial moment in history, and should therefore be kept as intact as possible. If we sent it through the usual NATO bureaucracies there would be too many opportunities to chip away at its content and water it down—not to mention the risk of leaks. But it would be counterproductive to spring it on our allies at the summit without warning. Providing them at least a couple of days to evaluate the proposal beforehand would be an essential courtesy. The press was already building up negative expectations, predicting the summit would be unproductive and a failed test of presidential leadership. We wanted to deliver the proposal quietly and give the allied leaders a chance to consider it before they read about it in the papers. It was also important that we explain our strategy, in order to increase the chances of garnering allied support in the NATO debate that would take place.

To accomplish all this, and to underscore the importance we placed on solving the impasse, we hit on the scheme of sending Larry Eagleburger and Bob Gates around Europe to explain the package to the heads of government of Britain, France, West Germany, and Italy. Eagleburger and Gates got a highly favorable reception everywhere they went, except London. Thatcher gave them a warm personal welcome, later affectionately dubbing them "Tweedle Dum and Tweedle Dee," but was cool to the proposal. She began and ended the discussion with the words, "I am very wary." She was unhappy that the proposal was being made on such short notice, and that certain reductions in equipment contained in it would encourage Gorbachev to attempt try to reopen other areas of the package. However unhappy she was, she closed the meeting with a telling comment: "If the President wants it, of course we will do it."

BRENT SCOWCROFT

On May 26, we departed for the NATO summit, traveling via Italy. We chose that route not only because we wanted to brief the Italians more fully on our proposals but also because, given the fact that we would be in Europe on Memorial Day, it would be important to visit a US military cemetery. Italy was an excellent choice. No president had gone to a cemetery there and it was a chance to commemorate one of the less celebrated, but painful and difficult, episodes of World War II, the landing at Anzio. It turned out to be a great choice. The American cemetery at Nettuno was beautiful, meticulously cared for by dedicated

Italian workers. The service was touching, the weather magnificent. We departed filled with a sense of patriotism and of profound gratitude, and sorrow, for all those who lay there having given their last full measure of devotion to their country. It was comforting that their graves were lovingly cared for in such a beautiful place.

Following the standard round of meetings, dinners, and discussions about our proposals—which the Italians agreed to support—we departed for Brussels. We were all very conscious how much was resting on the outcome of the summit. Could we shore up the German ruling coalition? Would we be able to bring Britain and West Germany to a compromise? Would we emerge with the President as the clear and decisive leader of the alliance? Could we get out in front of Gorbachev and turn around the sharply negative image the press had drawn of the performance and even the capability of the President and the Administration in foreign policy?

The beginning of the summit was not auspicious. At the crowded and noisy preliminary coffee for heads of government and foreign ministers, Thatcher was unhappy and apprehensive. Despite her reassuring closing arguments to Eagleburger and Gates, she privately repeated to the President the concerns she had laid out to them. She continued the discussion even as we walked into the meeting room, where she and President Bush were seated side by side.

In the formal session, the President detailed our four-point proposal: First, lock in the Warsaw Pact acceptance of the proposed NATO ceilings on each side's tanks, armored personnel carriers, and artillery. All the reduced equipment would be destroyed. Second, expand our NATO proposal to reduce to 15 percent below current NATO levels various types of helicopters and combat aircraft. Third, lower combat manpower to create a ceiling in US and Soviet forces in Europe of 275,000 each. This would require the Soviets to decrease their forces by about 325,000 (compared to the 30,000 cut by the United States). Fourth, accelerate the timetable for reaching an agreement to within six months to a year and conclude reductions by 1992 or 1993.

The outcome of the ensuing debate was reassuring. The proposal was strong, and the way we had previewed it, especially for the principal members, generated a number of speeches in support. The mood of the leaders was upbeat. Even Thatcher greeted the proposal warmly, and round one of the struggle, on conventional forces, was a complete success. The initial Soviet reaction was favorable as well. In his first formal comments, Gorbachev said he received the initiative "with satisfaction" and added that it was "a serious and specific response" to Warsaw Pact proposals. It might allow us to reach agreement much earlier than previously thought, he added.

Solving the disagreement over nuclear forces proved more difficult. The experts, who had been negotiating the issue while the heads of government discussed our conventional forces proposal, had made no progress at all. The alliance leaders decided in the late afternoon that to move things along, talks should be elevated to the foreign-minister level. The discussions quickly bogged down. The ministers had planned a big banquet together, but passed the word to cancel the affair and send in some sandwiches. Their deliberations continued into the night.

GEORGE BUSH

The dinner for heads of state and government was a little tense as we waited for word from the foreign ministers' negotiations. I sat down next to Margaret, who immediately lectured me. "We must not give in on this," she said. "You're not going to give in, are you?" Our host, Manfred Wörner, tried to get discussions going by calling on those who had not been heard from during the day to speak on the subjects from the afternoon meetings. From time to time he reported on progress from the ministers' discussions. I was not optimistic they could arrive at a deal and, if they did, whether it would be one that Margaret could accept. About midnight, long after dinner, Jim Baker phoned with a formulation. Once implementation of conventional force reductions was underway, the United States, in consultation with the allies concerned, was prepared to enter into negotiations to achieve a partial reduction (but not elimination) of American and Soviet land-based nuclear missile forces of shorter range to equal and verifiable levels. I was not sure if Margaret would buy this, but Jim predicted she would. I asked him to check with Brent. He called back and said that Brent was for it. I told him to go ahead with it, be enthusiastic, and hope it can be sold to the British.

At about two in the morning, after hours of sometimes acrimonious debate, some brilliant negotiating by Baker, and masterful management by Dutch foreign minister Hans van den Broek, who chaired the meeting, the ministers reached agreement. Our strategy of using our conventional forces proposal to encourage a deal over the nuclear forces problem worked. The West Germans admitted the discussions had been very difficult and pointed out that the conventional forces proposal helped them accept conditions on the nuclear forces negotiations which they had previously rejected. The next morning, when we assembled again at the conference, Margaret waxed enthusiastic. I suspect she did not want to be separated from the United States, and her advisors were telling her that the language was acceptable. I was grateful for her support on this critical deal.

BRENT SCOWCROFT

The NATO summit was a resounding success. An almost euphoric atmosphere surrounded Wörner's press conference. The press had to admit that we had turned the entire situation around. While we subsequently had a great many difficulties with reporters on specific issues, they never returned to their theme of the spring—that we had no vision, and no strategy but drift.

We went directly to Bonn to visit Kohl, who was positively ebullient. He embraced the President with a huge hug, and it was as if the tensions and difficulties of the past weeks had never been. When the two met the press in the garden after a chat in the Chancellery, Kohl said that the summit was "the best kind of birthday present" NATO could have, and "a fantastic result" to all the travail. It was quite a reversal of the crisis atmosphere which had pervaded both Washington and Bonn.

West Germany had elections for the European Community parliament and important local ones in Rhineland-Palatinate and Saarland coming up on June 18. It was not by accident, therefore, that Kohl conspicuously took us down the Rhine river aboard a large cruise ship. This was for him a campaign trip to highlight US-German relations and show off his great friend. It was a memorable day, culminating with the President delivering a major address to a packed house at the Rheingoldhalle in the historic city of Mainz.

This speech was a capstone of the unfolding of our strategy for relations with Europe and the Soviet Union, but with a German accent. One of the topics that concerned us was the sensitive issue of German reunification. We had not yet formulated a detailed position on the subject, nor had we discussed it with the Germans. The original text mentioned it, but I was concerned about unnecessarily stimulating German nationalism and took it out.

President Bush delivered a thoughtful speech which was warmly received. He spoke on the theme of the future of Europe, called for the destruction of the Berlin Wall and an end to the division of the continent. For the occasion, we had coined the phrase "a Europe whole and free" and, unlike "beyond containment," it did manage to achieve a bit of resonance. Another phrase, however, later caused a bit of unintended disquiet for Thatcher. The President referred to the United States and the Federal Republic as "partners in leadership." Thatcher took this as a challenge to the special relationship between the United States and Britain.

In truth, she need not have worried. The expression had no exclusionary intent and was meant only for flourish and encouragement.

GEORGE BUSH

From Germany, I flew to London for a meeting with Margaret Thatcher on June 1. This was our first extended face-to-face conversation. It was a fascinating discussion, and its relaxed atmosphere was a welcome contrast to the worries of the past weeks, especially the NATO meeting, when she had been very much on edge. Margaret and I compared notes on the situation in various places around the world—from economic reform and nationalism in the Soviet Union to the Middle East and South Africa. She was well-informed and insightful, and I discovered, as I was so often to find, that our thoughts on these matters were quite similar.

BRENT SCOWCROFT

Charles Powell, my opposite in the British government, joined me as notetaker at this private meeting. I cannot remember when I first became acquainted with Charles, but I knew him slightly when our Administration began. We quickly established a close personal relationship that became an important asset in the months ahead. Our communications technicians had undertaken the task of providing direct, secure lines to my counterparts in London, Paris, and Bonn. The London connection was the first to be installed and, when it was completed, all either one of us had to do was push a button and lift the receiver to have the phone ring on the other's desk. It allowed frequent, easy conversations in which we would explore the thinking of our principals on various issues as a first step in molding policies on which we could easily cooperate.

Charles was a wise, low-key individual, with a penchant for stating matters in the most felicitous way. That was little more than sugar coating, however, in the tenacious pursuit of British interests. We soon learned how to explore in a comfortable, offhand manner the limits of the flexibility we felt our principals would have on various issues. He was important to our policy-making. I became thoroughly convinced that he was the only serious influence on Thatcher's views on foreign policy. He was close to her, had uncanny insights into her thinking, and, even given her powerful personality, could be very persuasive. To me, the association with Powell and the way it facilitated US-British cooperation were the embodiment of the famous special relationship.

London concluded a tense and frustrating period for us, but firmly established the President's credentials and leadership. Augmenting the efforts of State and Defense with direct personal contact, the President had bridged the considerable and complex differences between Thatcher and Kohl. Through consensus-building and consultation, he pushed through a dramatic conventional forces proposal. It would be some time before a CFE agreement could be concluded (November of 1990), but the first steps toward reducing the Soviet Army in Eastern Europe had been taken. We had preserved NATO's defense strategy and reinvigorated the alliance. It was a tired but happy team who climbed aboard Air Force One.

CHAPTER 4

Untying a Knot

No sooner had we returned from the NATO trip than a long-simmering crisis exploded in Asia. On June 3–4, Chinese troops stormed Tiananmen Square in Beijing, ruthlessly dispersing what remained of tens of thousands of demonstrators who had been occupying it for more than a month. The shock and brutality of the action produced waves of protest around the world. The outrage in the United States was especially sharp and widespread. The upheaval had its catalyst in the death on April 15 of Hu Yaobang, former general secretary of the Communist Party, who had been removed from office in 1987 on grounds of what amounted to excessive liberalism.

In the 1980s, China's paramount leader, Deng Xiaoping, had embarked on a new economic reform effort. To many observers, both inside the country and out, this appeared to be a move toward liberalization, but at no time was he offering fundamental political change. The Party remained the authority for the political system. Yet Deng's changes alarmed some of the hard-liners and Old Guard within the Party, and a struggle ensued between those who backed market reforms and greater openness and those who demanded orthodoxy and retention of absolute political control by the Party. Encouraged by Deng's actions, students began demonstrations in 1986 and 1987, supporting further, deeper reforms. The display of dissent gave hard-liners an opportunity to oust Hu Yaobang, who had appeared to be Deng's choice to succeed him. He was replaced by Zhao Ziyang, himself a reformist.

To mourn the death of Hu, whom many considered a sincere reformer, thousands of students marched to Tiananmen Square, a central intersection of Beijing, the symbolic heart of the capital and often the site of China's national celebrations. Many of Beijing's most important buildings sit near or alongside the square, including the Great Hall of the People, the Forbidden City, and Zhongnanhai, the compound in which many of the People's Republic's most senior leaders live. It was as if thousands of people had appeared opposite the White House. The students presented the government with a list of demands, including increased democratic freedoms, a crackdown on corruption, and political reforms—but also practical improvements in university living conditions. They were careful to acknowledge the authority of the Party and the impracticality of trying to adopt American-style democracy in China. The official reaction was harsh. The police tried to break up the demonstrations, and beat students, while Deng attacked them in a speech for conspiring to create turmoil—a speech which was adapted into a widely disseminated editorial on April 26, declaring the students to be dangerously "counter-revolutionary." The students, who saw themselves as patriotic and promoting democracy, were furious. They soon turned from mourning Hu to protesting the government. But the hard-line response had also created divisions among the authorities. Zhao, who at first appeared to support the editorial, began to push for a more conciliatory tone. On May 4, the symbolically important anniversary of the 1919 student campaign for democracy against the old republican government, a much larger demonstration erupted—with tens of thousands pouring into the square. In an address that same day, Zhao described the students as patriotic and their grievances as "reasonable." The speech had a calming effect, and some people began to leave.

Because of the upcoming state visit of Mikhail Gorbachev on May 15, the first by a Soviet general secretary since the Sino-Soviet break some three decades earlier, Western television crews were already setting up their cameras and covered events in the square as they progressed. The students were emboldened by the international attention and by speculation among Western observers that the protests would open the path to greater democracy. On the eve of Gorbachev's arrival, several hundred began a hunger strike in Tiananmen Square. In an attempt to head off a major loss of face, moderate government officials met with the student leaders and tried to persuade them to leave, but to no avail. On the day Gorbachev arrived, the crowd in the square (and along the motorcade routes) was so great that the arrival ceremony had to be held at the airport, and other planned events had to be canceled. Within days, there were nearly a million demonstrators. The foreign press seemed to all but ignore Gorbachev and focused on the drama then unfolding.

Since a major focal point of the visit was to be the showpiece of the regime, the Great Hall of the People on Tiananmen Square, Western television cameras were at an excellent vantage point from which to cover the demonstrations. They showed in detail the paralysis caused by the occupation of the square. This was a serious loss of face to the government in front of their Soviet guest—and a world audience. At the same time, demonstrations began to spring up in provincial capitals. The Chinese government seemed frozen by the bold action of the protesters, or at least divided over whether to use force. For some time, no serious efforts were taken to dislodge the crowds. Even the security forces brought in to maintain order were seen fraternizing with students, or sitting in rows along the sides of the square.

As Gorbachev left Beijing for Shanghai on May 18, the Chinese leadership picked up their postponed battle over how to respond. Zhao insisted that the government take action to meet the student demands for reforms, while Deng and the hard-liners refused to budge. Zhao was seen visiting hunger strikers in hospitals that morning, and in the afternoon, in a heated television meeting, Premier Li Peng argued with student representatives in the Great Hall of the People. Li lectured them about the chaos the demonstrations were causing and declared that the government could not sit by.

Apparently, the leadership struggle reached its peak by the morning of May 19, when Zhao, unwilling to endorse the use of force, was stripped of all power, retaining only his title as general secretary. But he returned to Tiananmen and made one last appeal to the students to leave the square. The student leaders responded by ending the hunger strike and exhorting the demonstrators to tone down their rhetoric to avoid directly attacking the government. The next day Li announced the government's imposition of martial law. Security forces were withdrawn and local People's Liberation Army (PLA) troops were brought in. Thousands of Beijing residents blocked the soldiers from approaching the square, and by the end of the day more had taken to the streets to defy martial law itself, demanding the resignations of both Li and Deng. Many soldiers and officers appeared to be unwilling to use force against their fellow citizens. The commander of the 38th Army, based in Beijing, resigned, and more than a hundred officers signed a letter pleading against violence.

As the confrontation with the government continued, many participants became discouraged and began to drift away. On May 27, some student leaders called for an end to the occupation, but still insisted that they would continue to hold large-scale demonstrations to press for greater democracy and the resignation of Li Peng. On May 30, they erected what became a symbol of the protests, a thirty-three-foot statue of the "Goddess of Democracy" (bearing a striking resemblance to the Statue of Liberty), which was placed to face the giant portrait of Mao over the gate to the Forbidden City. By the first days of June only a few thousand people still occupied the ramshackle camp in Tiananmen. On the night of June 2, unarmed troops tried to march on the square but were driven back by thousands of citizens. The next night, tanks and troops from reliable units far from Beijing shot their way into the square, bloodily and mercilessly clearing it.

GEORGE BUSH

I had been watching the events in China with considerable apprehension, but the brutality of the final crackdown after weeks of comparative toleration caught me by surprise. On Sunday, June 4, I was at Kennebunkport for the weekend after our European trip. I immediately called Jim Lilley, since April our ambassador in Beijing. Jim reported that all was calm that Monday morning, Beijing time, but he was worried about the safety of American students at the university. I headed down to Washington, where, on Monday morning, Jim Baker, Brent, and I began to consider how best to respond.

The first and obvious point was to show that we considered the military crackdown to be unacceptable and to frame a public statement. I wanted a measured response, one aimed at those who had pushed for and implemented the use of force: the hard-liners and the Army. I didn't want to punish the Chinese people for the acts of their government. I believed that the commercial contacts between our countries had helped lead to the quest for more freedom. If people have commercial incentives, whether it's in China or in other totalitarian systems, the move to democracy becomes inexorable. For this reason I wanted to avoid cutting off the entire commercial relationship. Instead, I decided to suspend military sales and contacts. It was important that the Chinese leaders know we could not continue business as usual and that the People's Liberation Army realize that we wanted to see restraint. What I certainly did not want to do was completely break the relationship we had worked so hard to build since 1972. We had to remain involved, engaged with the Chinese government, if we were to have any influence or leverage to work for restraint and cooperation, let alone for human rights and democracy. While angry rhetoric might be temporarily satisfying to some, I believed it would deeply hurt our efforts in the long term. The Chinese are extremely sensitive to anything that might be interpreted as interference in their internal affairs, the legacy of many decades of damaging foreign intrusion. This was not simply a matter of wishing others to mind their own business. For this understandably proud, ancient, and inward-looking people, foreign criticism (from peoples they still perceived as "barbarians" and colonialists untutored in Chinese ways) was an affront, and measures taken against them a return to the coercions of the past.

We discussed appropriate language for a statement and decided on a list of retaliatory measures, and I went to the press briefing room to announce them. They included suspension of all government-to-government sales and commercial exports of weapons, suspension of visits between US and Chinese military leaders, and sympathetic review of requests by Chinese students in the United States to extend their stays. We would also offer humanitarian and medical assistance through the Red Cross to those injured during the assault.*

I felt confident we were taking the right steps. I had a keen personal interest in China and I thought I understood it reasonably well, enough to closely direct our policy toward it. My experience dated from my days as UN ambassador, and, although I had worked to preserve Taiwan's position at the UN under the Nixon "Dual Representation" policy, I tried hard to develop a good relationship with the PRC's first permanent UN representative, Huang Hua. I also met its foreign minister at the time, Qiao Guan-hua. But it was my time as chief of the United States Liaison Office in Beijing that gave me a deep and lasting appreciation of this extraordinary people, who make up a fifth of the world's population. When, in 1974, Gerald Ford had offered me a choice of ambassadorships, mentioning both Paris and London as possibilities, I asked him if he would send me to China—the big new challenge. Our relationship with this important country was just beginning and we did not have an embassy yet in Beijing: Richard Nixon had only reestablished contacts in 1972, when our countries set up liaison offices in each other's capitals. Formal diplomatic relations and embassies would have to wait until 1979.

I spent over a year in China and tried to get to know the leaders and people as well as I could. Our diplomacy with Beijing at that time was very active and, while Secretary of State Henry Kissinger conducted much of it, the job was fascinating and kept me busy. We were building a relationship with a country with which we had had no contact for over two decades and we were very much feeling our way. Barbara and I tried to widen our contacts in every fashion. We bought bicycles and went about town as the Chinese themselves do. I created as many excuses as possible to invite Chinese to functions, and I attended the national-day celebrations held by other countries. But high-level contacts were few

---

*The United States was the first major government to impose sanctions on China after Tiananmen.

and far between, all tightly controlled from the top. The only two times I met Chairman Mao Zedong were when Ford visited, and earlier when Kissinger had. At the Ford meeting, Mao asked, "Why does this ambassador not call on me?" Our experts all thought that was only a courtesy, but later I was told by two people close to Mao that "Chairman Mao would never say that unless he was serious, and had you called you would definitely have seen him." I have regretted that, and I also regret that I never met the legendary Zhou Enlai, perhaps the most respected of all Chinese leaders.

BRENT SCOWCROFT

During the presidential transition we contemplated the possibility of a visit to China in the early weeks of the Administration, and especially after one was announced for Gorbachev. We wanted very much to meet with the Chinese leaders to review and enhance Sino-American relations before Gorbachev had a chance to speak with them. We anticipated that he might attempt a rapprochement between Moscow and Beijing, and would have liked to be certain it did not come at our expense. There was no way, however, to justify a trip to China in the first quarter of the first year of the President's term. Important though such a meeting would be, I had all but given up on it when, on January 7, 1989, Emperor Hirohito of Japan died. In purely diplomatic terms, this sad human event gave us the required opening. The funeral was scheduled for February 24.

The President's attendance was a matter of great significance to the Japanese. His decision to go, despite some objections stemming from the Emperor's role in World War II, was also instrumental in the decisions of other world leaders to participate. The bonus of the trip was the opportunity it gave us to stop in Beijing for strategic discussions well before Gorbachev. It was too short notice for a full state visit, with all the preparation and protocol that would require. Instead, we quickly arranged for a "working visit" and talks with the senior leadership, including Deng Xiaoping, Li Peng, and Zhao Ziyang. This trip made President Bush the first American president to travel to Asia before Europe—a sign of priorities for the new era.

GEORGE BUSH

On the evening of our arrival in Beijing on February 25, I met with President Yang Shangkun. He assured me that future Chinese relations with the Soviet Union would not be as in the 1950s. There would be no military alliance or relationship. "We will on no account imperil the interests of any third country in improving relations with the Soviet

Union," he added. "In a word, we must watch the deeds of Mr. Gorbachev and not just listen to his words." Later, over the formal welcoming banquet co-hosted by Yang and Li Peng in the Great Hall of the People, we spoke about the prospects for perestroika. Both Yang and Li hoped Gorbachev would succeed, but Yang predicted it would be at least ten years before the Soviets saw any results, because it had taken China that long to get as far as it had.

The next morning I had a formal meeting with Li Peng, along with Vice Premier Wu Xueqian, and Foreign Minister Qian Qichen in the Xinjiang room of the Great Hall. Like Yang, Li emphasized that the upcoming Gorbachev visit was part of China's effort to normalize relations with the Soviet Union, but they were not seeking an alliance. "To be frank, to what extent the Soviet Union changes its policy we will have to wait and see," he said. He thought there was a possibility that the Soviets would have to cut back their defense expenditures in order to develop their economy. That should only help relax world tensions. "But the Soviet Union is encountering enormous difficulties in implementing perestroika. We feel that [these] have occurred because the Soviet people have not gained any practical benefits from perestroika, there has been more rhetoric than benefits, so the people are not enthusiastic. . . . For a time, the Soviets emphasized economic reform, but now they are emphasizing political reform and the process of democratization. The latter may suit the taste of the United States. However, the effect of the latter approach may be rather limited and may provoke ethnic problems in the Soviet Union. At best, it may only arouse the enthusiasm of the intellectuals for perestroika. In my view, the Soviet Union should mainly concentrate on the economic problems of the country."

As for relations with the United States, he hoped to accomplish more in the economic area, increasing US investment. But he warned against Americans trying to influence China's policies. "To be more blunt, this smacks of interference in China's internal affairs, and we are not happy about it," he said. "Of course, in the past, the problems came mainly not from the US government, but from various walks and circles including members of Congress and others who make trouble for us on this or that question. . . . We would be even more unhappy if this were raised to the level where there was interference by government officials. We have no business to interfere if the US observes developments in China from its own point of view, but if it tries to impose this view on us, we will oppose this." He thanked us for American support of China's reforms, but hoped we would also support their view that to improve the domestic economic environment required a strong central government. "We hope to see the continuation of a good friend in the development of relations between our two countries, so I particularly stress the above points," he continued. "As old friends, I feel we can talk in this very frank way. With others, I might not approach the question in this manner."

Almost immediately following the discussion with Li Peng I met with Deng Xiaoping, China's aging leader and a veteran of the Party's struggle to power. Deng was a fascinating personality. I had first met him when I headed the Liaison Office and Ford and Kissinger each visited. At those meetings, Deng sat several seats away from Mao. He kept leaning forward, putting his hand to his ear better to hear what was being said, listening hard to keep from being left out.

Deng was a diminutive figure, with asymmetrical features and a hyper-active way about him. A chain smoker, he would light one cigarette from the butt of the previous one. One of his hallmarks was an ever-present brass spittoon—which he used with great skill. In the Chinese setting for discussions, overstuffed chairs are arranged in a U-shape, with the par-ticipants at the center of the U, side by side and facing in the same direc-tion. With such an arrangement, it is possible to have a discussion where the principals face straight ahead and rarely actually look at each other. Not so with Deng. He would twist to face his interlocutor, maintaining eye contact and speaking directly and forcefully to his counterpart. He had an intense demeanor and talked with a bluntness that left no doubt about his meaning. When Barbara and I prepared to leave China in 1975, he gave us a luncheon. Inasmuch as China did not have formal diplomatic relations with the United States, it was the talk of the diplomatic commu-nity. As we ate he joked with me about going back to head the CIA, ask-ing, "Have you been practicing your spying here in China?" After Jimmy Carter was elected, and I was out of government, Deng came to the United States and at one point stopped in Houston. When I called on him, he greeted me warmly as a friend.

After I was nominated to the vice-presidency, Ronald Reagan asked me to go to China to reassure Deng that, despite having mentioned it in a campaign speech, he did not believe in two Chinas, and that he would honor the Shanghai Communiqué—which declared, in effect, that there was but one China. Joined by his top foreign policy team, Deng listened carefully as I explained that Reagan's statement had been taken out of context. Just as I was finishing, a door opened and a message was passed down the line of advisors until it reached Deng. On reading it, he looked puzzled and annoyed. "He did it again!" he announced. "Ronald Reagan has again referred to 'two Chinas' in a speech!" I talked fast and got out of there. Later on, Reagan was to demonstrate that, though his long affection for Taiwan remained, he was not about to do violence to the Shanghai Communiqué. After I became president, I would joke with Deng and others about the embarrassing incident. When Deng called me a *lao pengyou*, an old friend of China, I felt the phrase was not just the usual flattery, but a recognition that I understood the importance of the US-China relationship and the need to keep it on track. I will always have great respect for the positive changes this strong leader, who had his own ups and downs, brought to China.

At our meeting in 1989, Deng wanted mostly to talk about the Sino-Soviet relationship. He too assured me that Gorbachev's trip was not meant to signal a renewal of an old alliance against the United States. "So far, I don't know how many gifts he will bring," he said, shaking his head. "I don't even know what will happen regarding Vietnamese troop withdrawal from Cambodia." Deng recalled my own time and interest in China, and said that this visit was a good sign for the future. We might not see eye to eye on everything, but he hoped for a new pattern in US-Chinese relations. It would not be a strategic association, he acknowledged, but one of mutual trust in which we could minimize the problems between us. Deng then began a fascinating account of his own view of Sino-Soviet relations. It was a rare insight into his thoughts, and I was pleased he felt comfortable enough to share them with us and that he wanted the US to understand his intentions.

"China, like the United States, is improving its relationship with the Soviet Union," he began. However, just as a great many problems existed between the Americans and the Soviets, the same held true between Beijing and Moscow. "As a matter of fact, China and the Soviet Union cut off contact in 1963," he reminded me. "A good twenty-five years have elapsed since then. Sino-US relations were cut off in 1949 and resumed in 1972 . . . that was sixteen years ago. We have continued to make progress . . ." If the talks with Gorbachev proved to be successful, and relations were normalized, what would then follow? "Personally, I think it is still an unknown quantity," he said, answering his own question. "The fact is, there are many accumulated problems. What's more, they have deep historical roots. The Chinese people pay great attention to history. In China, it is a question of China's having been subjected to humiliation and invasion by foreign powers interfering in its internal affairs. This went on for a hundred and fifty years, from the outbreak of the Opium War in 1840. In that century and a half, foreign powers inflicted great losses on the Chinese people. But taken together, there were two countries that did the most damage. The first is Japan, and the other is Czarist Russia and the Soviet Union. In terms of who

got the most tangible benefits from these wars with China, it was
Czarist Russia and the Soviet Union. Japan did the most damage. Tens of
millions of lives were lost, and the damage is incalculable in financial
terms. However, in the end Japan didn't get any Chinese territory. In
terms of territorial questions between China and Japan, there is only the
Diaoyutai Islands. . . . We've proposed to shelve this problem for the
time being. . . .

"The situation is different with respect to Czarist Russia and the Soviet Union," he continued. "What the Soviets gained after World War II
was Chinese territory—more than three million square kilometers. . . .
I would like to add that one of the results of the Yalta Conference held
by the Soviet Union, Great Britain, and the United States at the end
of World War II was to divide up China. . . . This matter was mainly
between the US and the Soviet Union. However, because Chiang Kai-
shek was defeated in China, the United States did not gain anything. I am
speaking historically and I am not trying to offend you."

"You are not offending me," I said. "I don't like Yalta either. In retrospect, Yalta didn't turn out so well. It pledged free elections for Eastern
Europe, and they still haven't occurred."

"Yalta not only severed Outer Mongolia from China, but also brought
the northeastern part of China into the Soviet sphere," he went on.
"After the founding of the People's Republic of China, our first demands
to the Soviet Union were to recover Chinese sovereignty over the
Changchun Railway and Port Arthur. Only then was PRC authority in
northeastern China confirmed. . . . We raised the question of Outer
Mongolia, but the Soviets didn't respond.

"At present, the Soviet Union has an anti-Stalin campaign. But after
the founding of the PRC, Stalin did some good things for China. He
helped us with economic development. For example, there were a hundred and fifty-six industrial projects. Soviet experts also genuinely had
the intention of helping us. However, after Khrushchev came to power,
he scrapped several hundred Sino-Soviet contracts overnight. What's
more, Khrushchev's strategy, besides trying to counter the US and others, was to encircle China. All along the Sino-Soviet border, in the west
and the east, the Soviet Union stationed one million men and deployed
about one-third of all its nuclear missiles.

"Mr. President, you are my friend. I hope you will look at the map to
see what happened after the Soviet Union severed Outer Mongolia from
China. What kind of strategic situation did we find ourselves in? Those
over fifty in China remember that the shape of China was like a maple
leaf. Now, if you look at a map, you see a huge chunk of the north cut

away. . . . The strategic situation I have mentioned is very unfavorable for China. . . . This encirclement has continued from the Khrushchev period through Brezhnev to the present.

"On the northern and western borders of China the Soviets have massive numbers of troops and missiles. India was added and then Vietnam.* Now the Soviets have military air transit rights over North Korea, which allow them to connect to Cam Ranh Bay [in Vietnam]. Their planes can now conduct air reconnaissance over China. How can China not feel that the greatest threat comes from the Soviet Union? That's why we're addressing the questions of the normalization of Sino-Soviet relations. We have raised various obstacles to be removed; the danger posed to China by encirclement must be removed.

"It is precisely because of the above that China in the time of Chairman Mao and Premier Zhou Enlai paid attention to the development of its relations with the United States, Western Europe, and Japan. I have said all this to show that it was from a consideration of China's own interest that China came to this strategic decision. It was not a question of playing 'cards' against each other, and it was not a question of expediency. I have explained this passage in history to give people a clear point of departure to understand China's foreign policy and economic development. In the last few years, we haven't done a good job in educating young people in China. They don't understand this point. We have started to pay attention to this problem, but it will be difficult to show immediate results.

"Just now I said we're not clear what will happen after Gorbachev comes to Beijing. The most important question is whether the Soviets will dismantle their encirclement of China. In this regard, Afghanistan and Cambodia are the most important questions. We share a border with Afghanistan, although it's very short. Another question is what should be the basis for Sino-Soviet normalization? Because of this past history, can anyone really [say] that China and the Soviet Union will restore close relations, similar to what they were in the 1950s? No, this cannot be done. . . ."

That day I also met with Zhao Ziyang, who told me economic reform was irreversible in China. The Chinese people supported it, but were probably not prepared mentally for the extent of the difficulties and complexities. A few were claiming that it was too difficult and they should go back to old ways. There was also a small number saying that the

---

*A reference to Soviet support of these countries, with both of which China has had tensions and clashes.

economic troubles were occurring because China lagged in political reform. They wanted a multiparty parliamentary system—a Western political system. These people might be few, he added, but they were vocal and active. "Let's put aside the ideological question entirely," he said. "The above proposition does not tally with the realities of China. If it is carried out, chaos will result, and reform will be disrupted.

"Some press people in the West and the United States feel warmly toward those in China who advocate a Western political system and have great interest in them," he continued. ". . . In our view, if there are Americans who support those Chinese people who are opposed to the current policies of [our] government, they will hurt reform as well as Sino-US friendship. Mr. President, you know that it is the Chinese government and people who are promoting reform in the light of actual conditions in China. It is not these others. [You] know well China's history and its realities . . . I hope the US government will pay attention to this question for the sake of Sino-US friendship, the stability of China, and the success of reform."

In speaking frankly about China's internal and foreign policy challenges, the Chinese leaders had shown that they were serious about developing a practical relationship with the United States, one in which we could at least air our differences and talk about them. I hoped that a real level of trust was developing. Not that we would always agree, even about the nature of the problems between us or their solution, but I wanted them to see that we were not interested in lecturing and rhetoric. These would inevitably lead to perceptions of loss of face over "interference" and unnecessarily complicate relations. Instead, I hoped to foster openness and discussion about the meat of problems between us and encourage positive action. We could not look the other way when it came to human rights or political reforms, as Li Peng and Zhao Ziyang seemed to ask, but we could make plain our views in terms of encouraging their strides of progress (which were many since the death of Mao) rather than unleashing an endless barrage of public criticism. I understood that strong words and direct views were best exchanged between us privately, as in this visit, not in press statements and angry speeches.

I had left Beijing optimistic that we had laid some important groundwork for a productive period in our diplomatic relations, despite the threats of turbulence in China's domestic affairs. Now, just a few months later, the tragic events of Tiananmen, events which began with some hope of a peaceful resolution, seriously damaged our hard-won gains. I glumly began to fear that we might quickly find ourselves back at the point we had been in 1972. Tiananmen shattered much of the goodwill

China had earned in the West. To many it appeared that reform was merely a sham, and that China was still the dictatorship it had always been. I believed otherwise. Based on what I had seen over the previous fourteen years, I thought China was slowly changing and that the forces of reform that had been building were still strong. We had seen glimpses of them during the six weeks of Tiananmen before the hard-liners reasserted themselves. The question for me was how to condemn what we saw as wrong and react appropriately while also remaining engaged with China, even if the relationship must now be "on hold." I knew the feeling of outrage in the United States was increasing. In the days ahead, as the Chinese government began to track down the student leaders of the demonstrations, there probably would be rising pressure for stronger action.

DIARY, JUNE 5

[Representative Steve] Solarz on the left and [Senator Jesse] Helms on the right want us to move much more radically. Helms has always detested this relationship, and Solarz [, who wants me to recall our Ambassador,] is the guy who wants to overthrow no matter who's involved. He's the kind of guy that was delighted about the overthrow of the Shah, not worrying about what follows on.*

I talked to Nixon at 8:00 AM, and he was saying, "don't disrupt the relationship. What's happened has been handled badly and is deplorable, but take a look at the long haul." I told him I was not going to recall [Ambassador] Lilley, and he thought that was good. He doesn't think we should stop our trade [and should do] something symbolic, but we must have a good relationship in the long run . . . and that is what I will try to do while denouncing the violence and abuse of power . . . The reports from China are still crazy. . . . There are rumors that "Li Peng has been shot," and rumors that "Deng was dead." All of this tells me to be cautious, and be calm.

BRENT SCOWCROFT

Later in the morning of June 5, we arranged a meeting with Chinese students studying in the United States, to symbolize our solidarity. There was a previously scheduled session that afternoon with the congressional bipartisan leadership, to allow President Bush to review his just-

---

*I was to change my views on Solarz when, in 1990, he was influential in rallying support for the use of force against Saddam.

completed European trip. He used the occasion to denounce the Chinese actions and outline the steps already taken in response. The leadership supported his cautious approach—on this occasion even Helms.

The President was unwilling to leave our response completely negative. He wanted to communicate with the Chinese leaders, both so as not to sever contact at such a crucial time and to try to explain to them the enormity, in the eyes of the world, of what they had done. I strongly agreed, arguing that we had too much invested in the China situation to throw it away with one stroke. After some discussion, he decided to phone Deng, an extraordinary measure in that direct calls to senior Chinese leaders were something we had never attempted before. But he was unable to get through.

A complicated situation was made worse when a well-known dissident, Fang Lizhi, a highly regarded astrophysicist, appeared at the US embassy in Beijing asking for refuge. Fang had been a vocal critic of the government for some time. During our February trip, then-Ambassador Winston Lord had invited Fang to our banquet for the Chinese leadership, irritating our guests, as it turned out: the Chinese authorities intercepted him en route and prevented him from attending. Fang had also been at Tiananmen Square and fled the crackdown. The Chinese were furious. They demanded that we hand him over to them and threatened to seize him. But we could not give him up, knowing that he would be imprisoned—or worse.

DIARY, JUNE 10

Dissident Fang is in our embassy, and it turns out his wife may have been supported by unfriendly elements, and this will make the Chinese even more outraged. We had no choice but to take him in, but it's going to be a real stick in the eye to the Chinese.

At the press conference, I pointed out we weren't sure who was in charge, but then yesterday—the day after the press conference—Deng and Li Peng . . . reappeared, and the stories are [that] all the hard-liners are in charge. China needs to make a clear statement about reform, and going forward. It would be good if they could make some statement of regret about what happened; but they seem to be circling the wagons, going after students, and showing pictures of soldiers that were abused . . . I want to preserve the relationship, but I must also make clear that the US cannot condone this kind of human rights brutality. You have the networks, led principally by Dan Rather, pitching everything with the highest emotional content and driving to . . . almost break relations with China, and that I don't want.

Since the President was unable to reach Deng, Baker called in the Chinese ambassador, Han Xu, twice: on June 7 to express our displeasure with what had happened and to arrange the evacuation of Americans, and on June 10 to try to find a solution to Fang's predicament, perhaps letting him leave the country. The situation regarding Fang quickly turned into an impasse. It appeared that the Chinese did not want him to leave the embassy, fearing that if he did go abroad, he would feel free to criticize China again. If he were sent to jail, the world would condemn Beijing. So Fang remained where he was, and the Chinese posted security forces and police in the vicinity of the embassy.

GEORGE BUSH

I was frustrated when the Chinese rebuffed my attempt to talk things out directly. We had acted on the right side of the human rights issue and had taken the lead in imposing sanctions, encouraging our friends and allies to join us. But I was unwilling to leave the issue there. If I couldn't talk to Deng, I decided I would explain by letter how I felt and suggest the possibility of an emissary, to try to get the relationship back on track, however gradually. I wanted a letter straight from my heart, so I composed it myself:

> I write this letter with a heavy heart. I wish there were some way to discuss this matter in person, but regrettably that is not the case. First, I write in a spirit of genuine friendship, this letter coming as I'm sure you know from one who believes with a passion that good relations between the United States and China are in the fundamental interests of both countries. . . .
> Secondly, I write as one who has great respect for what you personally have done for the people of China and to help your great country move forward. There is enormous irony in the fact that you who yourself have suffered several reversals in your quest to bring reform and openness to China are now facing a situation fraught with so much anxiety.
> I recall your telling me the last time we met that you were in essence phasing out of the day-to-day management of your great country. But I also recall your unforgettable words about the need for good relations with the West, your concerns about "encirclement" and those who had done great harm to China, and your commitment to keeping China moving forward. By writing you I am not trying to bypass any individual leader of China. I am simply writing as a friend, a genuine "lao pengyou."

It is with this in mind that I write you asking for your help in preserving this relationship that we both think is very important. I have tried very hard not to inject myself into China's internal affairs. I have tried very hard not to appear to be dictating in any way to China about how it should manage its internal crisis. I am respectful of the differences in our two societies and in our two systems.

I have great reverence for Chinese history, culture and tradition. You have given much to the development of world civilization. But I ask you as well to remember the principles on which my young country was founded. Those principles are democracy and freedom—freedom of speech, freedom of assemblage, freedom from arbitrary authority. It is reverence for those principles which inevitably affects the way Americans view and react to events in other countries. It is not a reaction of arrogance or of a desire to force others to our beliefs but of simple faith in the enduring value of those principles and their universal applicability.

And that leads directly to the fundamental problem. The early days of the student demonstration, and indeed, the early treatment of the students by the Chinese Army, captured the imagination of the entire world. The wonder of TV brought the details of the events in Tiananmen Square into the homes of people not just in "Western" countries but world-wide. The early tolerance that was shown, the restraint and the generous handling of the demonstrations, won world-wide respect for China's leadership. Thoughtful people all over the world tried to understand and sympathize with the enormous problems being faced by those required to keep order; and, indeed, they saw with admiration the manifestation of policy which reflected the leaders' words: "The Army loves the people." The world cheered when Chinese leaders were seen patiently meeting with students, even though there were "sit ins" and even though disorder did interfere with normal functions.

I will leave what followed to the history books, but again, with their own eyes the people of the world saw the turmoil and the bloodshed with which the demonstrations were ended. Various countries reacted in various ways. Based on the principles I have described above, the actions that I took as President of the United States could not be avoided. As you know, the clamor for stronger action remains intense. I have resisted that clamor, making clear that I did not want to see destroyed this relationship that you and I have worked hard to build. I explained to the American people that I did not want to unfairly burden the Chinese people through economic sanctions.

There is also the matter of Fang Lizhi. The minute I heard Fang was in our Embassy, I knew there would be a high-profile wedge driven between us. Fang was not encouraged to come to our Embassy, but under our widely-accepted interpretation of international law we could not refuse him admittance.

. . . We cannot now put Fang out of the Embassy without some assurance that he will not be in physical danger. Similar cases elsewhere in the world have been resolved over long periods of time or through the government quietly permitting departure through expulsion. I simply want to assure you that we want this difficult matter resolved in a way which is satisfactory to you and does not violate our commitment to our basic principles. When there are difficulties between friends, as now, we must find a way to talk them out . . .

I have thought of asking you to receive a special emissary who could speak with total candor to you representing my heartfelt convictions on these matters. If you feel such an emissary could be helpful, please let me know and we will work cooperatively to see that his mission is kept in total confidence. I have insisted that all departments of the US government be guided in their statements and actions from my guidance in the White House. Sometimes in an open system such as ours it is impossible to control all leaks; but on this particular letter there are no copies, not one, outside of my own personal file.

. . . I send you this letter with great respect and deep concern. We must not let this important relationship suffer further. Please help me keep it strong. Any statement that could be made from China that drew from earlier statements about peacefully resolving further disputes with protesters would be very well received here. Any clemency that could be shown the student demonstrators would be applauded worldwide. We must not let the aftermath of the tragic recent events undermine a vital relationship patiently built up over the past seventeen years. I would, of course, welcome a personal reply to this letter. This matter is too important to be left to our bureaucracies.

I gave the letter to Brent, and only he, Jim, and John Sununu read it. I hoped that its openness, and the prior personal warmth between Deng and me, would make some difference in reestablishing communication. There had to be some way of getting the Chinese leadership to *listen* to us. It was the best hope to begin to resolve the situation, and perhaps gain some influence with the Chinese in the hopes of preventing further tragedy.

DIARY, JUNE 20

. . . I'm sending signals to China that we want the relationship to stay intact, but it's hard when they're executing people, and we have to respond. We've got to stand for what this country believes in — human rights, right for peaceful protests, etc. They killed three guys yesterday who allegedly burned a train in Shanghai, but I hope they won't go after all the student organizers in Beijing with the same brutality. Dissident Fang is making things much worse and Fang's son showed up at a hearing under the patronage of Jesse Helms—stupid—and it just makes things worse.

It's the morning of Wednesday, June 21. I told Brent Scowcroft that I wanted to [ask] Han Xu if he felt [sending an emissary] was worth doing. I went to a meeting . . . and during that hour, Brent talked to Han Xu [who] said he wanted to come over. So within a couple of minutes of Brent having set the appointment up—and without me even knowing about it because he had not had time to get back to me—we got a press inquiry saying, is the President going to meet with Han Xu? *Absolutely unbelievable.* I walked down to Brent's office to talk about it, and Patty Presock* was the only one who had some inkling of it; but the next thing she knew, she got a call from Brent's office, and it was overheard, apparently, by the press office. A *terrible* situation. So we immediately canceled the meeting. We cannot have a meeting like this in public—it just escalates our concern or attention to the matter.

BRENT SCOWCROFT

It was soon clear that the best way to get the message to Deng was to deliver it directly to Ambassador Han Xu myself. I had first met Han in December 1971, when I arrived in Beijing as a part of the team setting up the visit of President Nixon, less than ten days after I had arrived at the White House. Han was then vice director of protocol in the Foreign Ministry and he was standing at the bottom of the steps as we got off the aircraft. He was literally the first Chinese Communist official I met. Since that time, Han was stationed in Washington for long periods— he held the same position in Washington that President Bush had in China—and we became good friends. He was a fine person in every way. He was completely dedicated to his job and, as far as I knew, to his regime, but he was a strong supporter of a close US-China relationship.

When I approached the Chinese embassy that morning, it became graphically apparent that it had been the target of demonstrations by taunting crowds. A six-foot replica of the Goddess of Democracy, which had been erected in Tiananmen Square, had been placed in the tiny park in front of the embassy. A dummy of Deng was there as well, hanged in effigy. Banks of flowers and dozens of posters were arrayed around the square. The flowers were now dead, the statue was tattered, and posters were scattered everywhere. It was not a pretty sight. When I reported

---

*Deputy Assistant to the President Patty Presock had my total trust and confidence.

this to the President, he requested that the Secret Service Uniformed Division do an immediate cleanup.

I gave Han the letter and explained that President Bush wanted to communicate directly to Deng but in total privacy. Han said he could do that and said he was enthusiastic about the emissary idea.

DIARY

It's June 24th. . . . much to our surprise, on Thursday—less than 24 hours later—we got back a personal response [from Deng]. He accepts my idea of a personal emissary. [The question is, "who?"] Jim Baker does not want to be undermined, so I thought of a lot of alternatives: Kissinger and Nixon—too high profile, and too much propensity for leakage, though both would be very good; [John] Holdridge* or other ambassadors—not enough standing; and Jim Lilley—no good, because of the dissident, Fang. I don't want to embarrass Lilley by leaving him out to dry, but I don't want to undermine Baker's running foreign policy. I want to get the best expert who knows Deng—and that is Scowcroft. So on Saturday morning, I proposed to Brent that it be him and Eagleburger, and he's agreeable; I called Baker, and he's agreeable; and so we'll have a meeting on Sunday afternoon.

The plan at this point is to have an over-the-top flight in an unmarked plane going into some Chinese base. It's highly sensitive. China is blasting the United States for interfering in their internal affairs, and we are criticizing China, though not as vociferously as most in the Congress would like me to do. This has been a very delicate matter—how to handle this relationship. China is back on track a little with the Soviets, and they could indeed come back in much stronger if we move unilaterally against them and cut them off from the west. Deng still worries about "encirclement," and so do I.

The dissident [Fang] matter is horrible. There was a little squib in intelligence that they might condemn him and kick him out [of the country], and that would be the best answer right now . . . So far, we're getting reasonable marks for the way we're handling it, and good support from Broomfield, Foley and Lee Hamilton. The Senate is in a little more disarray, and Lloyd Bentsen told me today that he wants to help. It's highly complex, and yet, I'm determined to try and preserve this relationship—cool the rhetoric. I feel deeply offended by what China has done with the students and the others

*Deputy chief of mission when I was in China in 1974–75.

who courageously stood their ground. And I'm upset that Zhao Ziyang has been kicked out.* But I remembered his lecture to us on reform and "caution." I take this whole relationship very personally, and I want to handle it [that way].

BRENT SCOWCROFT

I almost certainly knew Deng better than any of my colleagues. In addition to the February trip with President Bush, I had met Deng in 1975, when President Ford visited China. I next saw him in 1981, again with Ford. At that time, Deng had a private lunch just for the two of us, during which he railed against the North Vietnamese. I told him that we Americans had held the same views about the North Vietnamese for years and it was too bad the Chinese hadn't realized much earlier the problems with them. Deng averred the correctness of Chinese policy during the Vietnam War, but added that, if the United States and China had not been estranged at that time, it might have been different.

The other reason I was chosen, I assumed, was because Baker, as a Cabinet officer, would not have been able to make a non-public trip away from the eyes of the press. I was pleased that Larry Eagleburger was to go as well. Not only was he invaluable to me, but his presence also precluded the possibility that the national security advisor was "going operational" and ensured that State was kept informed.

Larry and I set off from Andrews Air Force Base, accompanied only by Florence Gantt, my secretary, at 5:00 am on June 30.† We traveled on a C-141, a military cargo plane in which had been installed what was euphemistically called a portable "comfort pallet," a huge box containing bunks and a place to sit. We adopted so unusual a means of travel because that aircraft could be refueled in the air, avoiding the need to land anywhere along the route. The flight plan listed our official destination as Okinawa, but we would amend that on the way. The Air Force markings on the plane had been removed and the pilots and crew were instructed to begin the flight in military uniforms but to change to civilian clothes before we arrived. We were told later that our mission was known by so few in China that no one thought to tell the military air defense units. The defense forces apparently called President Yang Shangkun, to report

*On June 24, Zhao was removed as general secretary. He was replaced by Jiang Zemin.
†Florence Gantt had been Colin Powell's secretary and I asked her to continue as mine. Flo had been on Kissinger's secretarial staff when I first came to the NSC. I had worked closely with her and appreciated her work style and bright personality. She was unbelievably effective and still cheerful after more than twenty years in that pressure cooker. She was an institution in the White House, and everyone loved her.

an unidentified aircraft entering Chinese airspace near Shanghai and ask whether they should shoot it down. Fortunately for us, the call went right through and Yang advised them it was a very important mission and they should hold their fire.

After what seemed like an endless time in the air, we landed at Beijing at about 1:00 pm on July 1. The Chinese parked the aircraft behind the old terminal building (used by Nixon in 1972) so it would not be seen and we went directly to the Diaoyutai State Guest House. The next morning we were taken to the Great Hall of the People. Deng Xiaoping greeted us warmly and we posed for photos—by his own photographer, he assured us, and only for the archives (the photographer turned out to be the son of President Yang). Joining us were Li Peng, Vice Premier Wu Xueqian, and Foreign Minister Qian Qichen.

Deng began the meeting with a long monologue. "The reason I have chosen President Bush as my friend is because since the inception of my contact with him I found that his words are rather trustworthy," he said. "He doesn't say much in terms of empty words or words which are insincere. So that's why even before your general election I expressed the hope that he would be elected as President . . . However, he was not all that lucky because shortly after he assumed the office . . . turmoil broke out in China. This was an earthshaking event and it is very unfortunate that the United States is too deeply involved in it . . . We have been feeling since the outset of these events more than two months ago that the various aspects of US foreign policy have actually cornered China. That's the feeling of us here . . . because the aim of the counterrevolutionary rebellion was to overthrow the People's Republic of China and our socialist system. If they should succeed in obtaining that aim the world would be a different one. To be frank, this could even lead to war."

He argued that much of what was being said about the events at Tiananmen had been rumors, with exaggerations about the numbers killed. If a country were to formulate its policy on the basis of such rumors, he warned, that government would suffer a great deal. Congress, he said, had taken action against China on the basis of such rumors. "Indeed, Sino-US relations are in a very delicate state and you can even say that they are in a dangerous state. Such actions are leading to the breakup of the relationship." He took the fact that the President had sent us as a wise and cool-headed action. "It seems that there is still hope to maintain our originally good relations," he added. "I believe that is the hope of President Bush. It is also the hope shared by me. However, a question of this nature cannot be solved by two persons from the perspective of being friends."

The cause of the differences between our countries was not because China had offended or impinged upon US interests, he argued. It was the United States which on a large scale had impinged upon Chinese interests and had injured Chinese dignity. "With regard to how to resolve the issue, there is a Chinese proverb—'it is up to the person who tied the knot to untie it.' Our hope is that in its future course of action the United States will seek to untie the knot." It was up to the United States to cease adding fuel to the fire. He added that Beijing had not finished putting down the counterrevolutionary leaders. "China will persist in punishing those instigators of the rebellion and its behind-the-scenes boss* in accordance with Chinese laws. China will by no means waver in its resolution of this kind. Otherwise how can the PRC continue to exist?" He told me they would never allow outsiders to interfere in their internal affairs, no matter what the consequences. He added that he had not wanted to come to discuss these things, but since I was here he wanted to see me. "Just now I have told you my personal feelings on this matter and I hope you will convey my feelings to my friend, President Bush. Please convey the following . . . that no matter what should be the outcome of the discussions between our two governments on this issue, if he would continue to treat me as his friend I would also like to do that." He would leave it to Premier Li Peng to decide how to handle future discussions.

I reminded Deng that our countries had come far since the Shanghai Communiqué. "We represent two different cultures, backgrounds, and perceptions . . . ," I said. "There have been many ups and downs in the relationship but, on the whole, it has been a steadily deepening one. Not only because it responded to the basic interests of both sides, but because we respect the diversity between our two societies." Both sides had benefitted from the relationship, strategically with respect to the Soviet Union, and with respect to the stability that our relationship has brought to the world as a whole. We had benefitted economically as well. Our bilateral trade had grown from almost nothing to over ten billion dollars a year. "Finally it should be noted that the American people have strongly supported the improvement in our ties," I said. "As those ties have developed so has our admiration for the Chinese people and the efforts of the Chinese government to encourage economic reform . . ."

It had been onto this bilateral climate of deepening cooperation and growing sympathy that the events of Tiananmen Square had imposed themselves, I continued. "What the American people perceived in the demonstrations they saw—rightly or wrongly—was an expression of

*This cryptic reference was never clarified.

values which represent their most cherished beliefs, stemming from the American Revolution. . . . We, like you, hold deeply to the tenets of our own struggle for independence. Our whole national experience, beginning with our revolution, has been a struggle to expand the boundaries of freedom as we define that term. We fought our revolution to establish freedom of speech, freedom to assemble, freedom from arbitrary authority. These beliefs represent American tradition and culture. Americans, naturally and inevitably, respond emotionally when they see these values promoted elsewhere.

"How the Chinese government determines it must deal with those of its citizens involved in the recent events in China is, as you have so eloquently said, a wholly internal affair of China," I said. "However, how the United States government and the American people view that activity is, equally, an internal affair of the American people . . . It is an obvious fact that Chinese actions in pursuit of solutions to the recent problems of wholly internal concern to the People's Republic have produced a popular reaction that is based on and reflects our own beliefs and traditions. It has therefore produced its own internal reaction, which is real and with which the President must cope. That is the crux of the problem President Bush now faces.

"The President shares the feelings of the American people with regard to the recent events in China, but he also believes deeply in preserving the relationship between our two countries. He wants to manage events in a way which will assure a healthy relationship over time. That has not been easy. It has not thus far been without cost, and it could, depending on events, become impossible for him. The actions taken by the Chinese government to deal with the demonstrators have produced demands by the American people and the United States Congress to take steps of our own to demonstrate our disagreement with those actions.

"President Bush has taken certain steps he believes both necessary and appropriate under the circumstances. You have protested these actions of his, while the Congress and much of the US press have attacked him for not acting strongly enough." Three days before, the House of Representatives had voted to impose stiffer sanctions on China by a vote of 418-0.* "The President will continue to oppose such legislation, but the magnitude of the vote illustrates the political realities with which he has to cope. Even his veto authority is powerless against such unanimity.

---

*On June 28, the House attached an amendment to a foreign aid bill imposing additional economic sanctions on China. Even though the measure was fairly mild (heading off a more restrictive bill introduced by Senator Helms), and simply restricted OPIC and other investment assistance for Beijing, we objected to the interference in foreign policy although the President did not veto the bill. The Senate followed on July 14 with a similar bill and a vote of 81-10.

"The President is very sensitive to Chinese concerns regarding the actions he must take to preserve control over the course of events in the United States, but he is not omnipotent in his ability to control such events. [This ability] would, beyond a doubt, be strengthened were the Chinese leaders likewise to try to be sensitive—as you proceed over the coming days and weeks—to the reality that what you do and the way you do it will have a major impact on opinion in the United States and throughout the Western world." I concluded by saying I had brought no prescriptions as to what ought to follow, only to explain our point of view.

Deng said he hoped that the United States and its people would understand one point. "I think that one must understand history; we have won the victory represented by the founding of the People's Republic of China by fighting a twenty-two-year war with the cost of more than twenty million lives, a war fought by the Chinese people under the leadership of the Communist Party; and if one were to add the three-year war to assist Korea against US aggression then it would be a twenty-five-year effort. The second thing is that people must come to understand that China is an independent country, which means no interference by foreigners. . . . There is no force whatsoever that can substitute for the People's Republic of China represented by the Communist Party of China. This is not an empty word. It is something which has been proven and tested over several decades of experience." He did not agree with much of what I had said. "With regard to concluding this unhappy episode in the relations between China and the United States, let me just repeat that we have to see what kind of actions the United States will take." With those words, he left the discussion.

Li Peng said he recognized the differences in our cultures and traditional values. The concern of the Americans could not be denied. "What we disagree with is the effort to affect policy of other countries by way of American government and views," he said. He did not believe the US would succeed in such an effort when it came to China, and it should avoid operating on the basis of rumors instead of facts. "It is an old saying in China that emotion is no substitute for policy," he intoned. He was convinced that we did not have a clear picture of what had been happening, or accurate information. He insisted that the death toll given in the West was wrong; it was not 1,000 or in the tens of thousands but 310 or so, and the number included members of the PLA as well, and that only 36 Beijing students had died. They were trying to prepare a list of names, but it was difficult because some had come from the provinces. He also wanted to point out that they had not acted until after 48 days of turmoil—April 15 to June 3.

Li then gave his perception of the events at Tiananmen. The demonstrations had plunged Beijing into anarchy, something no government could tolerate. The demonstrators had occupied the square, the largest in the world, and attempted to storm Xinhua Gate. They had cut off access to the square, set up roadblocks, stopped civilian and government vehicles, and issued travel permits. This was no peace-loving demonstration, he argued. In the United States the authorities would have decided where the demonstration could take place. He began to recount what had happened in America during the 1960s, and how the US had suppressed protests. The Chinese were trying to maintain social stability, just as any other government would. The demonstrators had tried to overthrow the government and the Party leadership. Punishment would be meted out in accordance with the law to those organizers and parties in the rebellion and those who committed treason. Not all would receive death sentences. He blamed the problems on Zhao for his leniency, and for "failing to educate the youth."

As we ended this difficult session, it was clear to me that the clash of cultures had created a wide divide between us. The resentment by the Chinese of foreign "interference" was omnipresent. They were focused on security and stability. We were interested in freedom and human rights. The purpose of my trip, however, was not negotiations—there was nothing yet to negotiate—but an effort to keep open the lines of communication with a people inclined to isolate themselves and whose long experience with foreigners had engendered xenophobia. Both sides had been frank and open. We had aired our differences and listened to each other, but we still had a distance to go before we bridged the gap. It appeared to me that both sides were determined not to let Tiananmen obliterate the relationship.

As we sat down to lunch, I attempted to continue our conversation. With a wave of his hand, Li said both sides understood each other's position. "Let us talk of something else." There followed a discussion of developments in various regions around the world and their implications, both in general and for China and the United States. I had long felt it was important to keep China engaged in a strategic dialogue regarding world affairs, and this was a welcome opportunity to do so.

It had been, from my perspective, a most useful trip. We had conveyed the message on behalf of the President of the gravity, for the United States, of what the Chinese had done, but also underscored for them, beneath all the turmoil and torment, how important the President thought the relationship was to the national interests of the United States. In recent years we have been told several times by Chinese from different walks of life how crucial that trip and that gesture were to the Chinese, both in the regime and to those who had supported the demonstrations. For me, it was a great example of the President's instinct and touch on the important issues of foreign policy. Looking back on the meetings, I think this was a case in which personal relationships had cultivated a degree of trust by each side in the motives of the other—at least keeping open a door, as the President had hoped, even if we did not agree on how to move on.

GEORGE BUSH

Brent and Larry carried off the trip beautifully, and Brent was up in Maine briefing me on July 3, the day after his return. So far our effort to keep the discussion with the Chinese discreet was holding. With China heavy on my mind, I flew to Eastern Europe.

DIARY

It's now July 9th, and we're three hours out on our way to Poland. Down below is a bright blue Atlantic that you can see forever, and the gleaming blue and silver engines on Air Force One are over my right shoulder . . . China still worries me. We see nothing that I really want China to do in order to solve the existing problem of strained relations, and I don't think any other Western country does. I think they're glad I'm holding the line. They can be out front with more rhetorical overkill, but I will continue to try and hold the line, though I am uneasy about my ability to keep this relationship on track. As long as China tries to say there was no massacre in Tiananmen Square, no lives lost except for the lives of Chinese soldiers, then the matter will not be quiet.

CHAPTER 5

Radishes

Even though a visit to Eastern Europe had been tacked onto our trip to Paris and the G-7 summit, it eclipsed these in importance. President Bush's presence would be a highly visible way to underscore and call attention to our new policy, and an opportunity to take the propaganda initiative from Gorbachev. We would show American backing for reform efforts in Eastern Europe—and the Western vision of the future.

Poland and Hungary were ideal candidates for stops. They fit the political and economic reform criteria for US support the President had outlined at Hamtramck and stood in sharp contrast to the rest of Eastern Europe. Poland in particular was taking a courageous lead in reform and was wriggling loose from Moscow's grip. Hungary was not far behind. It had been dismantling its fences with Austria since May 2—tearing open part of the Iron Curtain. The removal of the fences was to have even greater significance later in the year for fleeing East Germans. But there was a special and emotional appeal for President Bush to return to Poland, which he had visited as vice president in 1987. That trip had helped legitimize and invigorate the struggling reform movement in the eyes of the Polish people and the world, when, after speaking to General Wojciech Jaruzelski, he had brought the leaders of Solidarity to the US embassy for historic discussions. Another visit would allow him again to offer American help and encouragement at a time of difficult transition.

Since the roundtable accords on April 7, the pace of political events had quickened. The Poles held elections on June 4 for their National Assembly and Solidarity made a virtual clean sweep. The accords had reserved 65 percent of the seats in the Sejm for the Communists, but Solidarity won every one of the 161 available. It also took 99 of the 100 seats in the Senate, where none were reserved. It was a remarkable outcome, one which surpassed even the most optimistic projections. The unexpected results complicated the process of electing a president.

The new president was to be chosen by majority vote of the National Assembly, and elections were tentatively set for July 6, three days before President Bush was to arrive. The Communists now lacked a majority, and neither Solidarity nor the Peasant and Democratic parties indicated a willingness to support Jaruzelski. Faced with the possibility of defeat, Jaruzelski, for whom the post was basically created, declared he would not be a candidate. He instead proposed General Czeslaw Kiszczak, the interior minister who had been the government's negotiator in the round-table deliberations and who was well respected by Solidarity. According to the terms of the accords, Lech Walesa was not permitted to stand for president, and the Solidarity leadership, not wishing to assume the post until the country was fully democratic, urged the union to support either Jaruzelski or Kiszczak. But popular backing for these symbols of the Communist regime and the military crackdown of 1981 was thin. The stalemate over a candidate prompted the government on July 5 to postpone the election until after President Bush's visit, which meant he would encounter a confused political situation. His official host would be Jaruzelski, as chairman of the State Council, but the General would be without authority as the head of the new political system.

BRENT SCOWCROFT

Crafting an appropriate response to the remarkable transformation taking place in Poland and, in less dramatic fashion, Hungary, was one of the most formidable problems we faced in preparing for the trip. Poland had enormous budget deficits, mounting inflation, sinking productivity, excessive foreign indebtedness, and poor public morale. Warsaw was informally suggesting that it needed $10 billion in assistance over the next three years. Without a doubt, the country qualified for help under the terms of US policy, and Polish-American groups were calling on us to recognize its strides in reform with substantial aid. But our dilemma had not changed: there was no money available, and, at a practical level, most of the economic effort had to come from the Poles themselves. There was one positive consideration on the horizon—the G-7 summit. Because of the intense interest of Western Europe in the East, we could propose to spread the burden of economic response to East European needs. The days were over when the United States could pick up the check for everything: a new Marshall Plan was not possible. Our resources had shrunk and our major allies and partners knew that our huge deficit was a detriment to their own economic growth. With the summit coming after our trip to Poland and Hungary, we could tell those governments truthfully that we could not give them the details of an aid program before we consulted our allies.

With these constraints in mind, we fashioned a package which included a proposal to reschedule Poland's $39 billion foreign debt, a request to the World Bank for $325 million in new loans, and $100 million in US funds "to capitalize and invigorate the Polish private sector." From a political standpoint, the package was embarrassingly meager. Although no amount of economic assistance reasonably available would have made a substantial difference to the Polish economy or its reform, what the Polish people did need was the sense that the United States was standing beside them as they faced the economic sacrifices which lay ahead. I thought our package was inadequate to send that message.

As Poland struggled its way into and through political and economic transition, Gorbachev was cutting a wide swath through Europe that spring and summer. He made highly publicized trips to West Germany on June 12, France on July 4, and a Warsaw Pact meeting in Bucharest on July 7–8, which ended the day before we were to arrive in the Polish capital. On his visit to the Federal Republic, Gorbachev had been mobbed by Germans supporting his rhetorical positions on deep reductions or elimination of nuclear weapons.

BRENT SCOWCROFT

In a major address before the Council of Europe at Strasbourg on July 6, Gorbachev offered immediate cuts in short-range nuclear missiles if NATO was willing to negotiate, with the ultimate goal of eliminating these weapons. Such a proposal, coming as it did on the heels of the NATO formulation on this issue, was clearly designed to create mischief within NATO and to reopen wounds which had only with difficulty been closed at the recent summit. Sallies such as this convinced me that we were right in moving cautiously with respect to Gorbachev. At least at this point, he certainly did not seem to be behaving as a wholly post–Cold War Soviet leader.

In the same speech, Gorbachev sketched out, probably with deliberate vagueness, his vision of a "common European home." He ruled out the threat or use of force between alliances or within them. Saying that "any interference in domestic affairs and any attempts to restrict the sovereignty of states—friends, allies, or any others—are inadmissible," he implicitly renounced the Brezhnev Doctrine, which claimed the Soviet right to prevent any attempt to leave the socialist camp. He hinted that Moscow would not intervene in the political changes in Hungary and Poland. Gorbachev also suggested that the states which had drafted the

Helsinki Final Act in 1975 meet again to develop a design for a new Europe, in which "the only battlefield will be markets open for trade and minds open to ideas." But his speech contained some troubling signs as well. One was his warning against any attempts to end the division of Europe by overcoming socialism. That, he said, would be "a course toward confrontation, if not worse." Despite graphic indications to the contrary in both Poland and Hungary, Gorbachev continued to express a belief in a socialist future for Eastern Europe. Another problem was his refusal, even after being pressed, to denounce the Chinese repression in Tiananmen Square. It was perhaps a sign of efforts to mend fences with China, but it might also be interpreted as a reminder that the Soviets still had the means to suppress dissent among their satellites.

In Bucharest, the Warsaw Pact affirmed Gorbachev's veiled rejection of the Brezhnev Doctrine. The Pact now openly asserted that members could determine their own pace of reform. However, it could not completely paper over a growing division in their ranks, with the political "heresy" being practiced by reformist Poland and Hungary strongly criticized by still reactionary Czechoslovakia, Romania, and East Germany.

GEORGE BUSH

The popularity of Gorbachev's new proposals in Western Europe made my trip to Eastern Europe imperative in order to offset the appeal of his message — that the West need not wait for concrete actions by the Soviet Union before lowering its guard and military preparedness. The visit, however, was intended primarily to encourage reformers there, yet I had to be cautious about what I said and did. The almost open quarrel in the Warsaw Pact demonstrated the delicacy of the situation. We had an obligation to be a responsible catalyst, where possible, for democratic change in Eastern Europe. We could support freedom and democracy, but we had to do so in a way that would not make us appear to be gloating over Gorbachev's political problems with Party hard-liners as he moved away from the iron-fisted policies of his predecessors. I was not going to back off my principles because it might offend Gorbachev. But hot rhetoric would needlessly antagonize the militant elements within the Soviet Union and the Pact, and might cause them to rise up against these changes and perhaps against their perpetrator, Gorbachev.

The Soviets feared that my trip to Eastern Europe was intended to foment unrest, or might stimulate it unintentionally. Far from having such designs, I shared some of their concerns. If massive crowds gathered, intent on showing their opposition to Soviet dominance, things could get out of control. An enthusiastic reception could erupt into a violent riot against the regime, with devastating effects on the growing sense of optimism and progress which was beginning to sweep the region. For these reasons, we restricted scheduled events with large crowds to one in Gdańsk, where Lech Walesa could be expected to keep things under control, and one at our arrival in Budapest.

BRENT SCOWCROFT

We landed at Warsaw's Okecie Airport at about 10:00 pm on a warm, humid summer evening to a formal arrival ceremony. There were no spectators, only a large official welcoming party, including not only General Jaruzelski but also representatives of Solidarity. Following an exchange of speeches by the President and Jaruzelski, and a performance by a goose-stepping military band and color guard, we left the airport for downtown Warsaw. The road was lined with relaxed and friendly well-wishers, waving flags and flashing the Solidarity "V" salute. Given the heat of the evening, some of the people were probably out on the streets simply to escape what must have been oppressive temperatures in their homes. We found out what that was like when we got to the hotel. It was a modern structure, adequately appointed, but the air-conditioning system was not even close to the demands of the weather. The inside temperature was definitely worse than that outdoors and, with windows not designed to open, we had a real problem. I finally managed to get a window propped open and I pulled my bedding onto the floor near it, where there was the faintest wisp of a breeze. The hotel's explanation was that there was simply not sufficient electric power for the system to run efficiently—a painful reminder of how backward the Polish economy was and how far it had to go.

On July 10 our visit began in earnest, coupling the protocol of a formal ceremonial state visit with a more private side: discussions with Jaruzelski and Walesa on the best next steps for Poland's evolution into a non-Communist state with a market economy, and encouraging the two sides to work together. The official day began with wreath-laying, both at the tomb of the unknown soldier and at Umschlagplatz, a memorial commemorating the suffering of Polish Jews in World War II. Those events, and the motorcades to them, were relatively sparsely attended by the citizens of Warsaw. I was disappointed with the absence of masses of enthusiastic Poles cheering the President, especially as I remembered the frenzied mob which packed the square in 1972 when President Nixon laid a wreath. At that time, the advance team had Nixon's limousine split from the motorcade in the middle of the square and turn directly into the crowd. It prompted an outpouring of enthusiasm which could easily have turned into a real riot.

Intellectually, I understood the difference between then and now. In 1972, the people had virtually no way to express their hatred of their government. When a legitimate opportunity did occur, such as the Nixon visit, they took full advantage of it to vent their anger against the system. Now, however, events were moving so swiftly in a positive direction that there was little anger to display. Therefore, the crowds were simply "normal."

GEORGE BUSH

I thought about my 1987 trip as we drove to pay what was billed as a courtesy call on Jaruzelski in his residual capacity as head of state. On my previous visit, he and I had some interesting talks, and I was looking forward to seeing him. I had found him to be much more reasonable and thoughtful than I had expected, charming and with a sense of humor. I was particularly impressed with his patriotism. Of course, I was disturbed by his dictatorial rule, and by the fact that he had imprisoned so many Poles for simply speaking out for freedom and democracy. Nevertheless, I saw a man caught between his love for his country and the subservience to the Soviet Union demanded of him by geopolitical realities. On my earlier visit he had repeated the official line that Solidarity was effectively dead. He wanted me to believe that the changes in the wind would not be radical, nor would they challenge Moscow's established political order. I also got the impression, however, that he felt the United States, in so vocally supporting the cause both of Solidarity and of change, was somehow slighting the strides already made by Poland. Now, two years later, Jaruzelski and I engaged in equally open discussion. When we arrived at Belwedere Palace, what was scheduled to be a ten-minute cup of coffee turned into a conversation lasting two hours.

Jaruzelski opened his heart and asked me what role I thought he should now play. He told me of his reluctance to run for president and his desire to avoid a political tug-of-war that Poland did not need. He did not think Solidarity would provide enough support for his election, and he worried about the humiliation of being defeated. I told him his refusal to run might inadvertently lead to serious instability and I urged him to reconsider. It was ironic: Here was an American president trying to persuade a senior Communist leader to run for office. But I felt that Jaruzelski's experience was the best hope for a smooth transition in Poland.

Jaruzelski believed that Poland needed a coalition government, with a Communist prime minister and an opposition deputy prime minister. The problem was that any government had to undertake tough economic measures, and this was particularly difficult for Solidarity, which was both a labor union and a political party. Organized labor in the United States controlled about 20 percent of the work force, he pointed out, but in Poland it was 80 percent. It was difficult to engineer competition under those conditions. "Free enterprise and the private sector are sick," he said. Solidarity was demanding that farmers get three times more for dairy products than the store price.

"Solidarity must realize all this must change," I said.

"The leadership knows it but is afraid of losing its constituency," he replied. "The West can help, because in this period in which Poland needs severe austerity, pressure is needed from the outside to adopt the reforms." They had to move to prevent economic collapse; then they could stabilize the economy. Restructuring, the final stage, could itself take ten years. He had written a letter to the G-7 outlining Poland's problems and hoped I would raise the issues in Paris.

I told Jaruzelski I would mention some of these problems with Walesa when I saw him the next day, and would talk to the G-7 about what could be done for Poland. I explained the package we brought with us and would announce that afternoon at the Sejm. I said I was aware some in Poland were asking for $10 billion in assistance. This would be wasted without fundamental reform first.

Jaruzelski agreed. "It is important that you remind Polish workers to keep their feet on the ground and to work hard," he said. "It is not enough to simply admire American riches." He wanted me to know that the Polish people were coming together. He respected Walesa, and said the labor leader was becoming a full partner in seeking solutions to Poland's problems. It was therefore a sensitive matter for him to be seen criticizing Solidarity in his conversations.

"I am aware of this," I nodded. "This is a delicate period, and it is important not to lose ground on the tremendous Polish accomplishments." I told him I believed the US system was best, but might not be transferable. "We will support reform whatever form it takes."

"There is a belief that Europe supports Gorbachev more than the United States does because the Europeans see the benefits of stability," he said. He told me that our conversation had convinced him otherwise and he would say so to Gorbachev. He added that Gorbachev hoped to see me soon.

I asked him whether a meeting with Gorbachev would be valuable even without an arms control agreement. He replied that I was a better judge of that. "But it should be remembered that Reykjavik looked like a lost cause initially but turned out well because the two sides' positions drew closer together," he said.

I said we would do nothing to make the course of reform in the Soviet

Union more difficult. "Americans and Russians are similar in their flamboyance," he replied after a pause. "Gorbachev told me that people look at perestroika and see mobs plus ethnic problems. The French, for instance, give perestroika little chance. But reform has already made a big difference and there have been involuntary changes already that make it impossible to reverse the course."

This remarkable meeting was followed by an equally remarkable luncheon at the residence of American ambassador John R. Davis, Jr. A seasoned Foreign Service officer, Davis was well respected by the diverse group of guests—some forty Communist, Solidarity, and Catholic leaders. It was literally the first time they had sat down together at a social gathering—the jailers and the jailed at the same table. Solidarity spokesman Janusz Onyszkiewicz, who clinked champagne glasses with Jaruzelski, observed that if one took into account that a year before he had been in prison, this was indeed quite a change.

It was still very hot, and I suggested that we remove our coats, an idea greeted with enthusiasm. When Jaruzelski arrived, he hesitated to take off his coat, but after vanishing into another room he reappeared without it. During the toasts he confessed to me that he had removed his suspenders as well and was afraid to give too long a speech for fear his trousers would fall down.

BRENT SCOWCROFT

The toasts captured the moment. "Your challenge is to rise above the mistrust, to bring the Polish people together for a common purpose," President Bush told his guests. Jaruzelski, surprised to be asked to give a toast, said, "I consider it significant that it is here at the residence of the US ambassador we could meet in such pluralistic company." Bronislaw Geremek, who headed the Solidarity caucus in the Sejm, spoke optimistically:

> "Poland is still divided, but it is possible that what is taking place right now is actually taking place throughout the country. . . . Even this very beginning tells us of what Poland stands for now. First of all and above all, we seek understanding for what is happening in our country. The future of Polish reforms depends on Poles alone. We do not expect that they will be carried at someone else's cost or by others' hands."

It was a dramatic scene and a graphic demonstration of the role the United States was playing as midwife at a critical moment in the strained but peaceful evolution of Eastern Europe from autocracy to pluralism.

Following the luncheon, the President addressed the National Assembly, the first time an American chief executive had spoken there. It was an uplifting speech. Poland was the country where the Cold War had begun fifty years before, and its people could now help to bring the division of Europe to an end. He echoed the promises of Hamtramck and outlined the steps the United States would now take in response to the progress of reform in Poland. Our limited proposals for economic support were received with predictably restrained enthusiasm. In the end, the Poles were generally gracious, recognizing both that no one was likely to do their hard work for them and that the political support demonstrated by the President was of more fundamental and long-term value than a few more dollars. The members of the assembly were enthusiastic, however, and chanted for him the traditional Polish cheer, *sto lat:* "One hundred years, one hundred years, let him live, live for us," something Jaruzelski later said no other foreign leader had received—not De Gaulle, not Khrushchev, not Brezhnev.

At the state dinner, I sat next to General Kiszczak. I found him to be practical and understanding about the rapid transformation taking place. He supported the move toward an open democracy, and spoke frankly his feelings about the speed and the manner of achieving it. He agreed with Solidarity that the Communists should fill the presidency, that a complete shift to Solidarity could put too great a strain on the political structure. I think he felt he understood the opposition better than did Jaruzelski, having negotiated the roundtable accords with them. Nevertheless, he spoke with conviction about the importance of persuading Jaruzelski to change his mind about running. I came away from this conversation feeling much better about the maturity of the players and the prospects for making this difficult transition work successfully.

GEORGE BUSH

The next day, July 11, we traveled to Gdańsk for a lunch and a speech, a journey which fulfilled our every expectation and gave me an opportunity to get to know Walesa better. Lech Walesa exudes an infectious enthusiasm. The minute I met him on my previous trip, I liked him. He has a twinkle in his eye, and smiles and laughs readily. I remember how, in 1987, he had brazenly ignored the Polish security guards stationed around the guest house where I was staying, and marched up to my motorcade as it was about to leave for Paderewski Square. He climbed in my limousine, and we drove downtown together. I was looking forward to seeing this gutsy man again.

The day's events began with a luncheon for Barbara and me given by Lech and Danuta Walesa in their modest home on the outskirts of Gdańsk. Lech told us that in this small house they had raised a large family. The house lacked a lot of the modern appliances and furnishings that most American families take for granted, but it was clearly a warm home. The press were pushing for photos, so we strolled out into the Walesas' garden, Lech pointing with pride to his plants and vines. There was something down to earth and natural about this true hero of Poland living so close to his roots, living, like any union member, within his means, devoid of all extravagance and glamour.

The meal was the ultimate in intimacy, with only the four of us, but the Walesas had organized a five- or six-course luncheon, complete with silverware, fancy food, and several wines. Stylish waiters borrowed from a nearby hotel did the serving. Danuta looked a little uncomfortable throughout the luncheon. She is quiet and shy anyway, and she seemed a bit overwhelmed by all this catered grandeur in her home.

Lech spoke effusively, and he appeared a bit uncertain and unrealistic in his requests of us. He said Poland would not ask for $10 billion, as the press had reported, but he wanted the banks to come in and make loans up to that amount. Poland would pay back every cent. He handed me a paper that showed requests to the World Bank, the International Monetary Fund, and elsewhere. He was confident that the banks and private partnership would take care of the country's needs. I wondered whether he understood all of the details of what he was showing me. I had the feeling that this proud man did not want his country, hat in hand, asking for money from us.

Walesa told me the Poles knew they had to work, but he insisted they could not wait for reforms before they received help. He wanted the West to buy shares in Poland's future. He was proposing a plan to put all enterprises on the auction block—even Polish farms, which he thought American farmers might want to buy. It was an ambitious plan. "My back is to the wall," he joked. "If I fail, I'll have to think where I can look for asylum."

Walesa believed only Kiszczak could be president and he would back him. "It's not what I liked, not what I wished, but I will do it," he promised. He thought Jaruzelski was a better choice but would not run. Everything hung on the economy. He predicted that without major American help there would be strikes and Jaruzelski would have to send in troops to put them down. He felt that the General was not being treated justly by many in the opposition. "What is happening today is wrong to Jaruzelski," he declared. There were few true Communists, he said. "The rest, including Jaruzelski, are 'radishes'—red only on the outside." He added that many people thought they had scores to settle with the general. "They underestimate him," he said.

Walesa wanted to channel aid directly to Solidarity. "We should slow down political evolution so that economic reform can catch up," he said, warning that if the Poles failed there would be a second Tiananmen in the middle of Europe. I gently asked about him about Solidarity's demands. He told me that the union was pragmatic and understood it would not have its way on some tough issues. I was not so certain, although I did not say so. Poland's economic problems were daunting, and I was concerned that Solidarity did not grasp what it would take to overcome them. Some of their demands, such as a five-year maternity leave, were so far-reaching that no government could fill them and undertake economic reforms at the same time.

Following lunch, Barbara and I rode with Walesa to the Lenin Shipyard, where I was to speak. As we drew near the site, Walesa looked overcome by the size of the crowd. "Oh my God, Oh my God," he kept saying in English. He said it was the largest crowd he'd ever seen.

I spoke in front of the Solidarity Workers monument to an animated throng which packed and overflowed the square. It is impossible to properly describe the excitement. There were thousands lining the street going into town, and estimates of up to 250,000 in the square. It was an emotional moment, with grown men and women crying. There were all kinds of signs of affection for the United States: flags, handwritten signs welcoming me, and expressing friendship between the United States and Poland, and everywhere the "V" sign.

In the speech I referred to Poland's struggle in World War II, only to be plunged into the sorrow of the Cold War. "Your time has come," I said. "It is Poland's time of possibilities. It is Poland's time of destiny, a time when dreams can live again." America would stand with them as they rediscovered a new land, a land of their own making, a Poland strong and proud. I was, heart and soul, emotionally involved as I spoke. I thought of past brutalities in Poland, of Walesa's courage, and of Polish pride. The crowd was very much in the mood and would have cheered anything. They alternated between chanting "President Bush, President Bush" and "Lech Walesa, Lech Walesa."

At the end of that day I had the heady sense that I was witnessing history being made on the spot, as the leaders from the regime and Solidarity came together. What I felt most was the warmth of the people I spoke to, from Solidarity and from the government. It was a miracle how far Poland had come since I had been there two years before. I was convinced that the people's desire for freedom was powerful and irreversible, and that the country would not willingly revert to Soviet domination. But I wondered uneasily whether the Soviets might try to stop the changes in Poland after all, fearful that Poland would slip entirely from their grasp.

Thinking back on this visit a few years later, and on those talks with the Polish leadership, I believe that Jaruzelski and other senior Communists, still in important positions, were very special leaders—Polish patriots and not simply party ideologues. Jaruzelski was particularly complex, and yet clear-headed. On the one hand, he symbolized the military crackdown of 1981 and the old order; on the other, he appeared deeply to want what was best for Poland, even if that meant dismantling parts of Polish socialism. I knew he counted Gorbachev as a friend and that he felt a certain loyalty to him. However, somewhere along the line he concluded that Poland could, and must, be free from Soviet domination. His friendship with Gorbachev clearly had an influence in making this goal more than simple hope. I think he believed, by mid-1989, that the Soviets would not intervene and that he now had the leeway he never had before to put his country on a new path.

BRENT SCOWCROFT

The Polish visit fully met our objectives. We had unmistakably demonstrated our support for the process of reform, had done it in a way which gave heart to the Poles without things getting out of hand, and had avoided provoking a backlash. Not bad. While we left Poland with its constitutional crisis still unresolved, we did not realize then the influence the President's separate conversations with Jaruzelski and Walesa had in bringing the sides together and moving them forward. Shortly after our departure, indications of the success of his talks began to manifest themselves. On July 14, Walesa declared he would support any candidate put forward by the Communist Party, emphasizing that the president should be elected only from the Communist-led governing coalition because of the delicate political situation. Walesa's statement was followed by an endorsement of Jaruzelski by the Peasant Party. With his election prospects dramatically improving, more positive statements began to emanate from the Jaruzelski camp.

For us, it was on to Hungary on July 11. Just as George Bush had been the first American vice president to visit Hungary six years earlier, he would now become the first American president to do so. The difference in mood between Poland and Hungary, to outward appearances, was dramatic. Poland, while hopeful, had been cautious and apprehensive. The Poles seemed to be concentrated more on the current problems of living and less on the promise of a brighter future. In Hungary there was a feeling of ebullience and expectation which was quite infectious. No Solidarity existed, of course, but there was considerable intellectual ferment within the Communist Party itself. I had the sense, from the spirit of Budapest, that this was a society which could manage the hard transition ahead. In one aspect, however, the mood of the two countries seemed similar. Both appeared determined to make drastic change as calmly and orderly as possible. Gone were the provocations of earlier periods, which virtually dared intervention from Moscow.

While Hungary was not as far along the path of political transition as Poland, change was in the air. Hard-liner Károly Grosz was still general secretary of the Communist Party, but he was now surrounded by three other leaders, one of whom was elevated to the newly created position of president. Grosz was obviously being eased away from the levers of power. A Party congress was scheduled for October, when substantial changes were anticipated. On June 16, 250,000 had gathered in Budapest for the reburial of Imre Nagy, the prime minister during the 1956 uprising who had been executed in 1958.

We arrived in Budapest during a summer thunderstorm, which delayed Air Force One's landing. President Bush was scheduled to make some arrival remarks in Kossuth Square, in the center of the city, and the crowd there stood in the downpour while our airplane circled above. The people were drenched, but their enthusiasm was undampened. They gave the President an enthusiastic welcome and even waited patiently while President Bruno Straub, unwilling to accommodate his introduction to the delay and the rain, stolidly plowed through all fifteen minutes of his prepared remarks.

When Straub finally droned to a conclusion, President Bush stepped up to the microphone, waved off an umbrella, and proceeded to tear up his speech, in full view of all. The crowd went wild. He then delivered a few extemporaneous remarks praising Hungary's reform-minded leadership. As he was finishing his brief comments, the evening sun began to break through the dark clouds, seeming to add its own soft rays to the warmth of the occasion. Noticing an elderly woman who was standing near the podium, soaked to the skin, the President took off his raincoat and put it around her shoulders. As the crowd roared its approval, he plunged into its midst, shaking hands and shouting good wishes. It was an incredible scene, one I will never forget. The empathy between him and the crowd was total.

GEORGE BUSH

To tell the truth, the coat belonged to a Secret Service agent who had insisted I put it on. When I saw the grandmotherly figure standing there looking cold with nothing to protect her, I forgot that it was borrowed.

After we returned to the car, Barbara scolded me for giving away some-one else's coat. We laughed, but I went hang-dog to the generous Secret Service agent to explain what I had done with his coat, which I later replaced.

BRENT SCOWCROFT

The next day, July 12, was a full one for President Bush. There were meetings with the Communist leadership, followed by a speech and more meetings, this time with opposition leaders. He called on Party President Rezsó Nyers, General Secretary Károly Grosz, and Prime Minister Mi-klós Németh. Later in the day he met with Presidium member Imre Pozsgay, leader of the Party's reform wing, who was the first to say pub-licly that the 1956 "counterrevolution" was in fact an uprising. With the exception of Grosz, what was most noteworthy about these men was the way they were all looking forward, not back. There was no indication of regret, of nostalgia for the past. Pozsgay said he hoped for a Hungary that would be a liberal constitutional state. One of the most dramatic moments came when Nemeth presented President Bush with a plaque containing a piece of the barbed wire from the border fence between Hungary and Austria—a literal piece of the Iron Curtain.

In the afternoon, the President addressed an intent but quiet audience at Karl Marx University. The task of a university is to promote unfettered competition of ideas, he told them, and that had been the spirit guiding one of the school's great teachers—Imre Nagy:

> "As his funeral proceeded in Heroes Square a few weeks ago, the rising voice of Hungary was heard reciting the 'Szozat.'* And in this somber ceremony the world saw more than a dignified act, an act of recon-ciliation: We witnessed an act of truth. It is on this foundation of truth, more solid than stone, that Hungarians have begun to build a new future. A generation waited to honor Imre Nagy's courage; may a hundred generations remember it."

Hungary was again becoming a beacon of light in European culture, and on its border with Austria it was removing the ugly symbol of Europe's division. "For the first time, the Iron Curtain has begun to part. And Hungary, your great country, is leading the way."

President Bush offered the partnership of the United States to help pro-mote lasting change in Hungary, and outlined proposals for aid. Among other measures, he announced Hungarian access to the Generalized

---

*"Szozat" is a Hungarian poem set to music, and similar in importance to "America the Beautiful."

System of Preferences (GSP), a $25 million private enterprise fund (similar to the $100 million for Poland), $5 million for a regional environmental center, a series of US-Hungarian exchange programs, and a US cultural center in Budapest. As soon as the parliament passed a government-recommended bill giving Hungarians the freedom to emigrate, he would make Hungary the first nation freed from the restrictions of the Jackson-Vanik Amendment, thus granting permanent most-favored-nation (MFN) status.* He also said he would send Peace Corps workers to Hungary to teach English. These would be the first Peace Corps volunteers to any communist country or in Europe. Hungary was in much better economic shape than Poland, and the audience did not seem to react to what I saw as the paucity of the assistance we could offer.

This was beyond a doubt the best speech of the trip, in both content and delivery, but the complete silence of the audience made me wonder. At the conclusion, however, the President got a standing ovation, and we subsequently learned that it was not customary to applaud during a presentation.

Following the speech, the President went to the American embassy, where he met with leaders of the opposition groups and parties, who were now free to operate. I was struck by the contrast between these aging leaders, some of whom had held the same position in their parties when they had been banned in 1947–48, and the progressive thinkers in the ranks of the Communists. A number of these men were setting forth the same tired old positions which had made it so easy for the Communists to set them aside when they took power at the beginning of the Cold War.

As we flew from Budapest to Paris, I reflected on the new Europe being born. Different as were the peoples, and the paths of reform they were following, there was something fundamental taking place, something I was becoming convinced would not be denied. Reform now seemed to be determined, deliberate, and without the bitterness or thirst for revenge which might trigger renewed repression. I had no idea what a short timetable lay ahead, but I was enormously encouraged by what we had seen.

We were now headed to our last extended stop. It was President Bush's first G-7 summit, and we wanted to focus attention on Eastern Europe

---

*Annual renewal of MFN trade status was required for non-market economies by the Jackson-Vanik Amendment of 1973. Jackson-Vanik never applied to Poland, because it had MFN status before that legislation was passed.

and the changes we had seen there firsthand. We hoped to convince our partners to bear some of the economic burden for those countries— after all, the G-7 summits were created to address just such problems. It might be difficult to shift emphasis to Eastern Europe, for summit discussions usually revolved around subjects researched and negotiated by staffs many months in advance. Furthermore, asserting American leadership, and our agenda, would have to be handled with consider- able subtlety. President Mitterrand was the chairman and he had his own ideas for this conference, which had a higher profile than usual. He had scheduled the summit to follow immediately his celebration of the two- hundredth anniversary of the French Revolution, to which he had invited a large number of developing-country heads of state, many of them mem- bers of the French Community. We had some concern that Mitterrand might attempt to overlap the two groups in such a way as to be able to pursue one of his long-held objectives—a North-South conference between the developed and developing worlds.

We opposed such a meeting, for we believed that the South would inevitably demand, in inflammatory Marxist-Leninist-inspired rhetoric, "reparations" for years of colonial "exploitation," possibly assisted by the left-leaning governing parties of some northern countries. Although we were concerned about the plight of the poorer nations, we preferred bilateral discussions on aid for these countries. To avoid the possibility of such a meeting, we originally considered scheduling our arrival only on the morning of the Economic Summit. However, the President was unwilling to risk affronting Mitterrand by failing to show up for the cli- mactic Bastille Day celebrations. Discussions with French officials made clear our position and, fortified with assurances against the possibility of a North-South meeting, we agreed to spend the entire day of July 14 in Paris.

BRENT SCOWCROFT

At the gigantic Bastille Day military parade on July 14, Mitterrand put on display what seemed to be every variety of military unit and every type of equipment extant in the French armed forces. It looked like a Soviet May Day parade, exhibiting the untarnished grandeur of France. The show was clearly designed to emphasize to his Third World guests that France was still a world-class military power. The reviewing stand faced directly down the Champs-Élysées, up which the military units marched, splitting directly in front of the stand. The parade was interminably long, but very impressive. Mitterrand's understandable pride was something to behold.

At the end of this extravaganza, Mitterrand summoned his motor-cade, climbed into his limousine, and departed, leaving his guests still seated in the reviewing stand. A glaring problem became evident almost immediately—no one had been told the order of departure. There were approximately twenty-five heads of state, each with a motorcade. The consequence was an unbelievable traffic jam, as the staffs of each country attempted—simultaneously—to gather up their leader and depart in a mad scramble. It was chaos at its best.

The three-day Economic Summit, which began that afternoon, was remarkably free of controversy, so much so that the leaders decided to conclude early, eliminating the final dinner. While the largest portion of the communiqué was devoted to environmental matters, President Bush managed to place Eastern Europe, with the magnitude both of its changes and its economic distress, at the center of the summit. We relaxed Poland's payment schedule on its foreign debt and created a con-ference to develop and coordinate Western aid to Poland and Hungary. It was a significant achievement and owed much to Jim Baker's negotiat-ing skills. In order to obtain this agreement, which we badly needed in order to augment our own slight assistance to Eastern Europe, Baker offered to let the European Community be the organizing institution. Thus appeared another in the eye-glazing tangle of international organi-zations, the Group of 24 (G-24). It turned out not to be one of the most productive of its type, but it served the purpose for Poland and Hungary.

A coordinated response to the events at Tiananmen was also on the agenda, and there was considerable sentiment toward imposing severe sanctions on the Chinese. The President believed China should pay a price for mistreating its citizens, but he argued that the stability of the US-Chinese relationship was too important to world peace to sever it completely, as the measures would have required. After considerable dis-cussion, during which several colleagues argued for extreme measures, the President, supported by Japanese prime minister Sosuke Uno, man-aged to restrict the sanctions to a reasonable and proportionate response. We urged the World Bank to withhold new loans to China, warned that China risked international isolation with its repression, and pledged to shelter Chinese students abroad as long as was necessary. Ironically, European ardor soon cooled and it was not long before the United States was virtually the only nation with any sanctions still operating.

GEORGE BUSH

This summit was noteworthy for another development: it marked the beginning of Soviet (or Russian) involvement. Gorbachev sent a letter to

Mitterrand appealing for closer East-West cooperation on global economic issues and declaring the Soviet Union's interest in participating in the global economy. Although it was not specifically a request to join the Economic Summits, there was no mistaking the intent. Gorbachev wanted both the prestige of membership as well as Western help in repairing his economy. I was wary about whether it was yet the moment to include the Soviet Union in these meetings. G-7 summits were about coordinating the efforts of free market economies. In my view, Soviet reforms were not far enough along or sweeping enough to include the USSR as a full partner. All the G-7 leaders agreed that the reply should be positive but noncommittal.

BRENT SCOWCROFT

It was not a dramatic summit, but a satisfying one. We put Eastern Europe at the top of the agenda and managed to avoid several potential problem areas. Nevertheless, there was some press grousing that, unlike his predecessors, the President had not dominated the discussions, but had accepted ideas from his colleagues. It was beginning to appear to me that the press definitely was not receptive to his collegial style. The reporters seemed to thrive on flamboyance and fireworks, rather than on friendly persuasion and cooperation—and results. President Bush's leadership style facilitated the acceptance of substance, and our friends and allies appreciated a cooperative rather than an imperious approach. I was frustrated—my feeling tempered by the fact that the skepticism and criticism were not universal and that some correspondents (obviously, to me, the most discerning) gave us full credit for a successful conference.

There was one other important development during our stay in Paris. On Sunday, July 16, as President Bush, Jim Baker, and I sat on the steps of the terrace at the embassy overlooking the garden and chatted about the trip in general terms, the President raised the issue of a meeting with Gorbachev. He simply said that the time had come to meet with him, and put it in that way he has when his mind is made up. Neither Baker nor I remonstrated with him. Baker had never been as negative as I about an early Gorbachev meeting, and I no longer felt so strongly about it. We now had our East European strategy well launched, and there was always the danger of miscalculation if we had no direct gauge of Gorbachev's current thinking. Perhaps we might be able to develop some way to choreograph a session which would avoid at least some of the pitfalls of a summit without specific agreements to conclude.

GEORGE BUSH

I had been mulling over a meeting with Gorbachev for a few weeks. On June 18 I had recorded in my journal:

> I'm thinking in the back of my mind what we should do about meeting with Gorbachev. I want to do it; but I don't want to get it bogged down on arms control, and I don't want the meeting to be judged by arms control. I would like to find some cataclysmic world event that we could [work on] together with the Soviets; or helping in some major international catastrophe; or something that shows cooperation and gives me and Gorbachev a chance to talk quietly, though not raising the expectations that we're going to solve the strategic arms problem in one high-level meeting.

As my trip to Europe drew to a close, I realized that to put off a meeting with Gorbachev was becoming dangerous. Too much was happening in the East—I had seen it myself—and if the superpowers did not begin to manage events, those very events could destabilize Eastern Europe and Soviet-American relations. We still did not know how much change Gorbachev would allow in the region, and I saw that the Eastern Europeans themselves would try to push matters as far as they could. The Western European leaders were also urging a meeting. In light of Gorbachev's letter to the G-7, I knew the pressure would mount, but I believed we could pull off informal talks without raising expectations too high. I wanted the same kind of forthright, honest exchange of views with Gorbachev that I had had with Jaruzelski, with the Hungarian leaders, and, indeed, with the Western Europeans.

I was moved by the hope I saw in Eastern Europe. While the trip had accomplished what I hoped it would—underscoring the importance of the region to us; reminding the Europeans of the better future offered by the West and thus offsetting Gorbachev's rival message which proposed disarmament first, as a prelude to ending the Cold War; and encouraging movement toward democracy and economic freedom—I came away with a great deal more. I saw how much was at stake for Eastern Europeans, and how delicate the situation there still was. We could not take progress in these states for granted. I had visited only the two countries furthest along—there were stirrings across the rest of the region, in places with governments less interested in better lives for their people than in retaining power for themselves. We had stepped carefully in Poland and Hungary and had avoided aggravating the Soviets, whose military presence still loomed there. It was a good start. But I understood that the pressure on Gorbachev from hard-liners to intervene would grow, as these once reliable allies began to pull further away and the Soviet security buffer against the West eroded. The dangers were ahead, and I would have to respond with even greater care as the Eastern Europeans pushed their own way to the future. We could not let the people down—there could still be more Tiananmens.

CHAPTER 6

Hope and Revolution

GEORGE BUSH

As we flew home from Paris, I sketched out my letter to Gorbachev suggesting a meeting. "I want to do it without thousands of assistants hovering over our shoulders," I wrote, "without the ever-present briefing papers and certainly without the press yelling at us every 5 minutes about 'who's winning' . . . " Up to this point, I explained, I had felt that a meeting would have to produce major agreements so as not to disappoint a watching world. "Now my thinking is changing."

"Perhaps it was my visit to Poland and Hungary or perhaps it is what I heard about your recent visits to France and Germany," I continued. "Whatever the cause—I just want to reduce the chances there could be misunderstandings between us. I want to get our relationship on a more personal basis." I offered an informal, no-agenda visit. "In my view, it would be best to avoid the word 'summit,' which is, at best, overworked and, at worst, a word whose connotation is one of a momentous happening." He could come to Camp David or to Kennebunkport. I was open to other arrangements, and would also understand if he simply felt awkward about such an informal meeting and declined to take me up on it.

BRENT SCOWCROFT

We gave the President's letter to Marshal Sergei Akhromeyev during his visit at the end of July to discuss arms control. Akhromeyev, the former chief of the Soviet General Staff, had retired from active service in December 1988 and was now Gorbachev's principal military advisor, with close and easy access to him. We thought he was a foolproof way to ensure absolute secrecy for a most sensitive communication, although some at the State Department were upset over bypassing normal channels. I had breakfast with the Marshal and we had one of the most fascinating conversations I have ever engaged in on the fundamentals of arms control and the strategic objectives of each side. He was candid and open.

GEORGE BUSH

Akhromeyev was an effective messenger. Within a few days came a response, delivered by Alexander Bessmertnykh, who had been minister counselor and chargé d'affaires at the Soviet embassy in Washington in the 1970s, and was now Eduard Shevardnadze's first deputy. Bessmert-nykh made the trip specifically to discuss my proposal and told me Gor-bachev welcomed a meeting as early as September. Gorbachev liked the format I had suggested and had a sweeping conversation in mind. But when Bessmertnykh and I began to consider a possible location, it soon became apparent that this would be a problem.

BRENT SCOWCROFT

Several places were suggested, from Alaska to Spain, but none proved mutually acceptable, for either scheduling or protocol reasons. We tried everything we could think of, over a period of weeks, and I was about ready to give up—and beginning to wonder whether the Soviets really wanted a meeting—when Gorbachev announced he was making a state visit to Italy at the end of November. We started to mull over the possi-bilities that trip might offer. The President's brother, William "Bucky" Bush, had just been to Malta and had spoken highly of it. I mentioned the Roosevelt-Churchill shipboard meeting at sea off Newfoundland in 1942 as a precedent. The President liked the idea of a conference at sea because it would preclude large numbers of press and staff and avoid cumbersome protocol events. Gorbachev had to adjust the arrange-ments of his own trip in order to hold the talks over a weekend, but he was willing to do that. His only request was that the two Presidents jointly approach the Maltese and that there be no helicopters involved— apparently because he hated flying in them. Because of the setting, and the desire to keep protocol to a minimum, Barbara Bush would not join us.

We had postponed high-level contacts with the Soviets until we had reviewed our goals and strategy and readjusted our positions, especially on strategic arms control. An exception had been Baker's trip to Moscow in May. With a surprised Baker standing by his side, Gorbachev had announced new Soviet proposals for cuts in short-range nuclear forces. His one-upmanship, coming as it did alongside his propaganda effort in Western Europe, timed to create and exploit divisions in NATO, had only kept us suspicious of his motives and dubious about his genuine desire for better relations. Our reviews complete, we began overtures to the Soviets on strategic nuclear arms with a June 20 letter from the President outlining our positions, but received no reply until September.

There were other problems to sort out with Moscow. On regional questions, where the United States and the Soviet Union had been confronting each other for years, the two countries had made little progress. As the President had declared in his Texas A&M speech, Moscow had to move beyond rhetoric and demonstrate the substance of the "new thinking" in Soviet foreign policy. We considered regional issues a good place to test Soviet sincerity, because their behavior in the Third World seemed mired in the Cold War. By the end of the summer, Moscow was pouring aid into several sensitive countries, including Afghanistan and Nicaragua, at a virtually unprecedented rate. They were also adhering rigidly to hard-line positions which all but precluded reaching agreement. It appeared that they believed we either were indifferent or unwilling—or unable—to impose costs on the over-all US-Soviet relationship in response to their actions. In some cases, Soviet clients seemed to be in stronger positions than they had been several months earlier. Moscow may have concluded that increased investment of their scarce resources in selected areas would bring big returns.

In February, the Soviets had withdrawn their troops from Afghanistan, but six months later we were no closer to resolving the problem of the Kabul regime, still led by the Soviet puppet Mohammad Najibullah. At the time of the withdrawal, conventional wisdom was that the Najibullah government would collapse within a matter of weeks. Instead, it had regained strength. Things had gone so well for the Soviets that they were again insisting on including Najibullah in a coalition government. To us he was the symbol of what was wrong in Afghanistan, and the US-backed Mujahedin had made clear that they would not stop fighting until he was gone. For our part, we could not agree simply to cut off arms supplies if there was no political settlement. That would only lock in a military imbalance strongly in favor of Najibullah and an unacceptable political status quo, setting the stage for further fighting. Neither were we prepared to permit the Soviets a major geopolitical victory. We needed a long-term solution to Afghanistan to end the fighting and restore a free government.

The biggest thorn in US-Soviet relations remained Central America, where the Soviets still supported their client Nicaragua and, through it and Cuba, the guerrillas in El Salvador. President Bush had scarcely ever communicated with Gorbachev without bringing up Central America or

Cuba, or both, and we had made a point of pushing him for progress on Nicaragua. The Soviets argued that the main obstacle to a settlement was the lack of an agreement to disband the US-supported Contras. While, as Shevardnadze insisted, the Soviets may have ceased supplying weapons, the Cubans and East Germans had stepped in to replace them. When challenged, the Soviets complained that Castro was beyond their control.

We also had inherited a battle with Congress over Central America, one which had tied the hands of the Reagan Administration policy there. This had been a topic of review during the transition, and both Baker and Scowcroft agreed that it was time for a truce with Congress. Our plan was to call for democratic elections in Nicaragua, which we hoped not only could dislodge the primary troublemaking regime on the mainland, but also would force Gorbachev to follow through on his pledge to champion democracy or show his true colors.

BRENT SCOWCROFT

Soviet recalcitrance in the Third World deepened my reservations about Gorbachev. The few positive regional changes which had occurred seemed to me to stem more from Soviet failures than from a general change of attitude about regional superpower competition. The withdrawal of troops from Afghanistan, for example, was a clear case of overextension. When it was obvious they could not prevail they decided to cut their losses. What was not evident was whether their appetite also had been dampened. In places such as Angola and Namibia, I believed that Moscow now judged its efforts too costly for any likely return. Instead of changing, Soviet priorities seemed only to narrow. Regional issues would remain a lingering irritant throughout the rest of the life of the Soviet Union, through three summits and many foreign minister meetings. If there was to be positive movement in Soviet policy, it appeared it would have to originate closer to home, under the leverage of political and economic pressures in Eastern Europe and the Soviet Union itself.

Changes in Eastern Europe over the summer continued with stunning speed, and we followed them closely but quietly: We could accomplish more by saying less. We championed self-determination, carefully avoiding rhetoric or the appearance of interference, which could only rankle the Soviets at a time when we hoped they would acquiesce in the positive evolution they had helped foster.

On the day we returned from Paris, July 18, Jaruzelski announced that he would resume his candidacy for president. The next day, he was elected by the National Assembly, but it required the abstention of several Solidarity members to give him the majority needed. It was an ironic situation. Jaruzelski, long the oppressor of Solidarity, had been seen by the West as one of the staunchest Communists in Poland. Here he was chosen, with the support of many of those he had previously jailed, in a genuinely free vote.

Jaruzelski's election cleared a major hurdle in the Polish transition process, and it was apparent to me that President Bush's discussions with all the parties during his visit were instrumental in achieving this breakthrough. The General had been persuaded that his participation was essential, and Solidarity that Jaruzelski would be the principal guarantee of political stability. But even with our persuasiveness, Jaruzelski's past and the discomfort, on both sides, with the notion of coexistence, made the election a squeaker.

The next step in Poland was to replace the caretaker government of Prime Minister Mieczyslaw Rakowski. Under the roundtable agreement, Solidarity was to remain in opposition and a Communist-led government would run the country. The dramatic election results had raised questions about that arrangement, with the Communists seeking Solidarity participation (to share the responsibility of coping with the economic crisis), and Solidarity split on the issue. Most of the Solidarity moderates did not want to share in a government over which they would have no control, and the most active anti-communists believed that the election results were a mandate for Solidarity to form the government itself.

Reportedly telling Solidarity that the Soviet Union, East Germany, and Czechoslovakia would oppose the naming of a member of the union as prime minister, Jaruzelski nominated General Kiszczak and called for a coalition government. Solidarity declared it would wait until it could form a government itself. Kiszczak was elected prime minister on August 2, but after two weeks of effort he was unable to put together a cabinet. The parliamentary allies of the Communists, the Peasant Party and the Democratic Alliance, refused to cooperate and, on August 16, Lech Walesa announced he would assemble a cabinet "under his direction" and under the Solidarity banner.

This was a bold move, going far beyond the bounds of the roundtable agreement, and it presented Jaruzelski with a difficult problem. He had either to accept this acceleration of the transition timetable or dissolve the legislature and call for new elections. Without the roundtable constraints, elections would be a disaster for the Communists, resulting in even faster change. After Walesa affirmed that Poland would remain in the Warsaw Pact and that the Communists would be given the ministries of Defense and Interior, Jaruzelski opted for the lesser of two evils. Kiszczak resigned, and Solidarity was asked to form a government.

BRENT SCOWCROFT

Although we were privately overjoyed with these developments, we tempered our jubilation. Moscow still had large forces in Eastern Europe and we did not want to embarrass the Soviets with Polish freedom at stake. Our public posture was therefore very restrained. We had Marlin Fitzwater say only that the President "would encourage" the formation of a non-Communist government.

Whether or not reassured by the US response, the Soviets reacted quite placidly. Yevgeny Primakov, a close advisor to Gorbachev, declared that the makeup of the Polish government was a matter to be decided entirely by Poland, but that a coalition of Solidarity and two small non-Communist parties was reasonable. Indeed, when the Polish Communists balked at participating in a Solidarity-led government, Gorbachev phoned Rakowski. While the contents of the call were not divulged, the Communists began to cooperate. This was perhaps the most telling indication to date of the change in Soviet attitudes toward the evolution gathering steam in Eastern Europe. At Walesa's suggestion, Jaruzelski nominated Tadeusz Mazowiecki, who had helped in the creation of Solidarity in 1980, as the new prime minister. He was elected on August 24 with only four negative votes. It was a giant step away from four decades of Communist rule.

GEORGE BUSH

Jaruzelski had demonstrated considerable political skill in these maneuverings. He had hung back as a reluctant warrior until exactly the right moment. Then he showed great political judgment in getting support from key Solidarity leaders. All along the way he had to properly assess the Soviet role, figuring just how much leeway Poland actually had in breaking ranks. I think that this chapter in his life led many Poles, who had previously detested him, to think more favorably of this complicated man. In Poland today, although many remember only the brutality of his Communist stewardship, most are forgiving of the past, recognizing the dilemma he faced and giving him final credit for his role in steering Poland away from total Soviet domination.*

*In 1996, Walesa, then out of office, came to visit Barbara and me in Kennebunkport. I asked him about Jaruzelski. He was very magnanimous, stating that, in spite of the crackdowns of the past, history would overall be very kind to the general.

Meanwhile, Hungary also was pursuing its own roundtable process for reform of elections and government structure. On September 18, the sides reached partial agreement on the transition to a multiparty parliamentary democracy. On October 7, the Communist Party voted to dissolve itself and reconstitute as the Hungarian Socialist Party. The move proved devastating, for few members signed up for the new party. The political process there was now wide open.

BRENT SCOWCROFT

With the political situation in Poland and Hungary now moving smoothly, our attention turned to economic assistance. Two battles developed. One was within our Administration over the still unresolved fundamentals of aid policy. The other was with Congress over the amount and its source. Our budget difficulties had not eased over the summer, but there was a new twist. Congress, now fully aware of the dramatic transformation taking place in Eastern Europe, cognizant of the political power of Americans with roots in those countries, and not so concerned about the budget deficit, was prepared to appropriate large sums of money, especially for Poland. It was uncomfortable to have to argue against more funding than we were requesting when the need for additional resources was plainly apparent.

We eventually fashioned a new aid package, in addition to the one the President had taken with him to Poland. The G-24 had agreed to provide $120 million of emergency food aid, to which we added another $50 million. To avoid the painful process of searching for money within the Administration so late in the fiscal year, we pledged funds from the following year's budget, which started October 1. On September 15, we announced a further $50 million in longer-term, non-emergency, food aid to Poland. Assistance to Hungary was even less generous. Three days later, Secretary of Commerce Robert Mosbacher announced that Hungary would receive permanent Most Favored Nation status, and Overseas Private Investment Corporation (OPIC) guarantees would be extended to American investments there.

Senate majority leader George Mitchell denounced the Polish aid package as insufficient and indicative of an Administration "almost nostalgic about the Cold War." Baker called the criticism politically motivated. "When the President of the United States is rocking along with a 70 percent approval rating on his handling of foreign policy, and if I were the leader of the opposition party, I might have something similar to say." Baker's comment raised my own discomfort level. We were in a very difficult position. If this historic evolution away from the clutches of the

Soviet Union and Leninism failed because of our deference to bureaucratic accounting practices, history would never forgive us and we would never forgive ourselves. So, while I agreed with Baker that Mitchell's attack was motivated by partisanship, I also believed we should be doing more.

On September 20, the Senate Foreign Relations Committee increased the pressure by approving a $1.2-billion three-year aid package to Poland and Hungary—by a straight party-line vote, after all but one of the Republican members walked out in protest over this interference in Administration foreign policy. The committee said it would pay for the package by taking funds from the Defense Department's research and development budget—violating the agreement which prohibited transfers between the aid and the defense budgets. Congress seemed determined to provide more money than we requested, and it would be extremely awkward if the President had to veto Polish assistance. The question was what could we do about it.

Within the Administration the acrimonious battle reopened over whether we should send aid to Poland at all. State and NSC wanted to commit to an increased program and try to induce the IMF and the World Bank to make substantial investments. The President was scheduled to address the annual joint meeting of the Fund and the Bank on September 27, which would have been a great time to lay out such an ambitious proposal. Treasury, however, was still adamantly opposed to doing anything until Poland adopted economic reforms. The Office of Management and Budget, while not so obstructionist, insisted that any funds provided had to be fully offset. I do not recall any enthusiasm on its part for finding a way around the problem or locating suitable offsets.

Polish deputy prime minister and finance minister Leszek Balcerowicz visited me the day before the President's speech, to outline his needs and a tough economic reform program. Balcerowicz presented what he considered a minimum package—$500 million to cover a payments deficit in the fourth quarter and $1 billion for a currency stabilization fund. His program seemed to meet any reasonable preconditions for aid, but it was too late to include a response in the President's address the next day, and we still could not agree upon aid policy. The most we could come up with was a statement that "we must do more" and "for its part, the United States intends to be out in front of this effort." The audience did not erupt with applause.

Despite the Polish plan, Treasury and OMB remained reluctant. Treasury did not want to move until the IMF and World Bank had approved loans to support the plan. OMB contended that funds for any new loans had to come from the foreign assistance account and thus be taken from another country's allocation. In exasperation, the President overruled OMB and Treasury, and decided we would seek to find aid for Poland from the international community rather than rely so heavily on scarce assistance from the US alone. We settled on an agreement to back a $1-billion stabilization fund for Poland, of which the United States would contribute $200 million—to be delayed until Polish negotiations with the IMF were completed. The remainder would come from Europe, especially Germany. Congress took the program seriously and kept its budget promise: While the eventual compromise was higher than the President's proposals, the earlier, much larger figures approved were scaled back.

The challenges to Soviet authority in Eastern Europe that summer now began to spread to the Soviet Union itself. Long-suppressed nationalism welled to the surface. Together with the worsening economic situation, it formed Gorbachev's most serious political challenge to date. In the Baltics, emboldened nationalists were moving from support of perestroika and plans for economic autonomy toward demands for independence. Estonia had already declared its sovereignty the previous November and reaffirmed the act on May 18. Lithuania adopted similar legislation the same day, while the Latvians followed on July 29. During a press conference about the Baltics on August 18, Alexander Yakovlev, a principal Gorbachev advisor, as a demonstration of glasnost, condemned the 1939 pact between Hitler and Stalin which had led to the annexation of these states, but he went on to assert that Moscow still considered the republics an integral part of the Union and would resist any attempt to separate them. Yakovlev's statement aggravated passions, and the dam holding back Baltic nationalism began to crack. Four days later, the Lithuanian parliament declared the Soviet annexation illegal. Nationalists in all three republics began to push in earnest for independence.

The Soviet reaction to Baltic nationalism was far different from its approach to liberalization in Eastern Europe. The Central Committee of the Communist Party denounced the accelerating campaign for independence and, in sharp contrast to his call to the Polish Communist Party boss only a week or so earlier, Gorbachev phoned the Party chief in Lithuania to warn that the three republics "must not think about secession." The difference was understandable. In Poland and Eastern Europe, the issue thus far had been reform of the existing regimes. More fundamental Soviet security interests, such as the cohesiveness of the Warsaw Pact, were not yet in question. The independence ferment in the Baltics, however, posed what the Soviets saw as a mortal threat to the integrity of the Union itself, and they were unable to view it with anything approaching equanimity.

For the United States as well, the Baltics were different. They symbolized for us the worst in the treachery and perfidy of the Kremlin. We had never recognized their incorporation into the Soviet Union in 1940 and there was no way we could react in a "normal" way to events which might, at long last, vindicate the long vigil we had held on their behalf. There was as well a powerful lobby, of conservatives in general and Baltic-Americans in particular, which was anxious to discomfit the Soviets on this issue. They wanted not just freedom for the Baltics, but freedom *now*. The result was a special sensitivity on the part of both Washington and Moscow as to what was happening in the Baltics. It was the area where we were inclined to apply the most pressure and display the least understanding and where the Soviets were the most paranoid and least willing to accommodate.

The broader domestic crisis in the Soviet Union also began to mount, due in no small part to Gorbachev's strategies for political and economic reform. To force change at the local and republic level, Gorbachev threatened and ordered real elections to put pressure on recalcitrant Party officials. He deliberately encouraged the people to confront entrenched Communist Party leaders and officials, whom he blamed for the problems the country was facing. At the same time, he began to bypass the Party, which was resisting his changes, turning to the government hierarchy to implement his reforms. He was concentrating power in his own hands and those of a few advisors. It was a risky approach, for Gorbachev was undermining the Party's local authority and legitimacy as well its ability to maintain order.

BRENT SCOWCROFT

In early September, the question arose whether the President should see one of Gorbachev's most vociferous critics—Boris Yeltsin—when he came to Washington as part of an eight-day speaking tour. Yeltsin's trip was one of high visibility. He was a flamboyant figure, whose personal habits, especially his drinking, led to colorful press stories. Dissatisfied with the pace and scope of reform, he was also taking advantage of every opportunity to blast Gorbachev, including some personal attacks, in the course of his interviews on morning television shows. Gorbachev cannot have been pleased with Yeltsin's performance in the United States, yet that was not grounds for not seeing him. He was obviously a popular opposition figure in Russia on the verge of becoming a key influence in

Soviet affairs, which warranted some kind of recognition—but what? Did he merit being received at the White House and, if so, in what manner? We had to be careful not to let him use a visit as ammunition against Gorbachev.

One of my responsibilities was to recommend to the President which foreign political visitors he should see. There were two important considerations. The first was to evaluate the effect in the home country, and on the visitor, of receiving or not receiving him or her in the White House. The other was not to waste the President's time, perhaps the most important asset we had. The President and I had worked out a sliding scale of importance for receiving visitors at the White House. At the top was a scheduled visit with the President himself. Next was a visit with me, as a part of which I would take the visitor down the hall to "drop in" briefly on the President. Slightly less prestigious was one with me, during which the President would "drop by" to greet the visitor, giving him total control over how long he spent with the guest. The lowest rung, other than not getting into the White House at all, was simply a meeting with me. In addition to these gradations, there was the very useful option of having the visitor meet with Vice President Quayle. There were other nuances as well. There were three entrances by which the visitor could arrive and leave. Top-level people came through the diplomatic entrance. Those to whom we wanted the press to have access were brought to the West Lobby. Guests not on the President's formal schedule whom we did not wish the press to see were brought to the West Basement entrance.

Yeltsin was not an easy call. I had in the back of my mind the visit of Soviet dissident Alexander Solzhenitsyn during the Ford Administration. On foreign policy grounds, there was no reason for Ford to meet with Solzhenitsyn—he was an émigré, an official outcast at home, and no head of government had seen him during his recent tour through Europe. All that said, Ford's initial refusal of a meeting was a domestic disaster. He was accused of kowtowing to Brezhnev and not supporting freedom and human rights in the USSR. The situation with Yeltsin had some of the same emotional content. It was a difficult case, but President Bush certainly did not need a domestic brouhaha.

GEORGE BUSH

I wanted to see Yeltsin. He supported the kinds of fundamental change in the Soviet Union we hoped for. The Soviets had long received all sorts of Americans running for president, so they had to be understanding about our willingness to meet with their opposition, especially those who backed perestroika. I wanted to hear his point of view on the changes in the Soviet Union. In the end, I decided on a "drop-by" in Brent's office.

BRENT SCOWCROFT

On September 12, Yeltsin, running about a half hour late, arrived at the West Basement entrance, where he was met by Condi Rice. He refused to get out of the car unless he was assured that he would be seeing the President. She told him that his appointment was with me. Yeltsin was distinctly unhappy. After a brief exchange, Condi said that if he did not plan to keep his appointment with me, he might as well go back to his hotel. Having lost his bluff, Yeltsin then followed her up the stairs to my office.

I began our discussion by asking him why he had come to the United States. A somewhat dour Yeltsin plunged into a long monologue outlining a ten-point program through which the US could assist Soviet economic reform, merging that into his ideas on how the Soviet Union should be managed. The President's arrival interrupted Yeltsin's presentation in midstream, but he brightened visibly, becoming ever more expansive. The drop-by lasted only a few minutes, during which President Bush told Yeltsin he considered that he had a positive relationship with Gorbachev and reaffirmed his support for his reforms. Shortly after the President left, Vice President Quayle dropped by for a photo-op and a brief discussion. We finished our conversation following his departure and, after about an hour, Yeltsin left.

We had brought Yeltsin into the West Basement entrance to avoid encounters with the press. As he drove off up West Executive Avenue, however, he must have spotted some reporters on the lawn where they televise their stand-ups from the White House. Yeltsin stopped his car and burst out, immediately attracting attention. He was soon surrounded by reporters and proceeded to give an impromptu press conference. It was not the quiet, uneventful conclusion to the visit we had hoped, but no harm was done.

In late September, Eduard Shevardnadze arrived in the United States. Except at those times when the United States wanted to send a disapproving signal to Moscow, it was standard procedure for the Soviet foreign minister, on the occasion of his address to the fall session of the General Assembly, to come to Washington to see the President. We had proposed a meeting in New York, where the President would himself address the UN General Assembly on a global treaty to ban chemical weapons. The Soviets instead asked that it be in the Oval Office, and they went to great lengths to give it visibility. It seemed that Moscow wanted to show that the US-Soviet relationship was being managed well and to divert attention from its own problems at home.

Shevardnadze had met with Baker three times since the Administration took office, but this would be his first talk with President Bush. It would give us an opportunity to get a better sense of Gorbachev's progress in reforms, as well as a chance to convey directly our support for them. We particularly wanted to signal Shevardnadze that we understood the ups and downs of reform and were not overreacting to the gloomy picture of perestroika painted in the press.

We were also interested in what he had to say about the spreading nationalism in the Soviet Union. He was arriving two days after an important Central Committee plenum on that subject. Continuing conflict between Azerbaijan and Armenia had led to massive, incapacitating strikes and the imposition of martial law to stem the tide of ethnic violence. The unrest was now reaching Ukraine, with miners' strikes and demonstrations. The actions of the plenum, however, did not seem to demonstrate that Gorbachev yet understood the gravity of the nationalist challenge. While he did call for a radical transformation of the Soviet federation to provide greater autonomy for the republics, the plenum reinforced the central authority of Moscow. Gorbachev declared that perestroika could only be delivered by and through the Communist Party. The result was a clear retreat from his emphasis on democratization and multiplicity of political forms and a strong reaffirmation of the inviolability of Party unity.

BRENT SCOWCROFT

Shevardnadze came to the White House on September 21, and delivered a letter from Gorbachev responding to the President's arms control proposals. He outlined a number of promising concessions, and reported that the Soviets wanted to speed up work on a convention banning chemical weapons. It appeared they intended to move forward on arms control and were prepared to make some modifications to get the ball rolling. At the same time, when the President raised the outstanding problems on regional issues, Shevardnadze dodged them. It looked to me as if arms control was Gorbachev's preferred focus in US-Soviet relations and that, despite political difficulties, he still had the capacity to force tough decisions out of the bureaucracy. It may also have demonstrated that he thought things were going relatively well for the Soviet Union in the Third World and he had no particular need for, nor interest in, a dialogue with us on the subject.

The meeting with Shevardnadze was fascinating for another reason. He gave us a graphic description of the internal situation in the Soviet Union, the first time any of us other than Baker had heard such a first-hand account. It seemed to me a frank and honest appraisal and was certainly not cheering. According to his account, the Soviets' problems were serious and growing. His candor was refreshing, because it was so un-Soviet. I felt that it really did reflect a different outlook from the decades of Potemkin village–like behavior which was more or less standard for a Soviet foreign minister.

By late summer, the turmoil in Eastern Europe reached high tide and now swept into East Germany—the keystone of the Warsaw Pact and the Soviet Union's most reliable ally. There the example of Gorbachev stood in sharp contrast to the Stalinist government of Erich Honecker, whose stubborn refusal to recognize or accommodate the changing situation now provoked a crisis. In response to repression and economic deprivation, East Germans began to take advantage of their August vacations and freer travel to flee their country. Visas were not required to visit Poland, Hungary, and Czechoslovakia, and, in perhaps the most dramatic evidence yet of the upheaval spreading through the region, East Germans in large numbers were showing up at West German embassies in those countries, and at the mission in East Germany itself, asking for asylum.

A new and easier avenue of escape had also opened. When Hungary began in May to remove the barriers along its border with Austria, it provided "vacationing" East Germans an opportunity to slip across the border to that country and then to West Germany. The Hungarian government was soon in an awkward position: whether to block the emigration or look the other way. After considerable hesitation and vain attempts to get the two Germanies to work out a solution to the emigration problem, on September 10 Hungary opened its border with Austria and more than 10,000 East Germans streamed across. Budapest had openly broken ranks with its East German comrades, and the recriminations were swift and bitter. East Berlin accused Hungary of violating treaties and the basic interests of East Germany. The Hungarians replied that they had no other choice under the Helsinki Accords, which further galled the East Germans. Soviet foreign ministry spokesman Gennady Gerasimov would say only that Hungary had taken "an unexpected step and a very unusual one," and that this episode, while of some concern, did not affect the Soviet Union directly.

BRENT SCOWCROFT

The Hungarian move posed an exquisite dilemma for East Germany. The exodus of its citizens, as in 1961 when the Berlin Wall went up in response to a similar outflow, was a public humiliation for the regime, which prided itself on the highest standard of living in the Warsaw Pact.

To close off all escape could lead to a domestic explosion. Yet to reform the system was to undermine the basic premise for a separate East German state—without socialism there was no longer continued justification for two Germanies. It begged the question of reunification.

Coming after the formation of a non-Communist government in Poland, and with both actions taking place with the acquiescence of the Soviet Union, Hungary's opening of its border revealed and widened the gulf within the Warsaw Pact between the liberalizing countries and the entrenched hard-line regimes of East Germany, Romania, and Czechoslovakia. Our reaction was one of guarded optimism. It was possible the Pact could no longer function as a cohesive military alliance. We were witnessing changes that looked irreversible and which might forever alter the character of the threat to NATO—and even the future of Europe.

After a period of blustery outrage, the Honecker regime allowed the release to West Germany of those escapees who sought refuge in West German embassies in Berlin, Warsaw, and Prague. But as soon as the embassies were emptied, they filled up again and, on October 3, East Germany in effect closed its borders—on the eve of Warsaw Pact celebrations of the German Democratic Republic's fortieth anniversary on October 7, with Gorbachev in attendance. The spectacle of East Germans scrambling to escape in the midst of what had long been planned as a triumphal event was perhaps more humiliation than the regime could stomach. Honecker was obviously hoping that Gorbachev's visit would serve to buttress and breathe hope into a faltering regime. At the same time, in something of a paradox, dissenters in East Germany generally looked upon Gorbachev as their hero who would force perestroika on a Stalinist holdout.

BRENT SCOWCROFT

How Gorbachev comported himself in East Berlin would send strong signals, not only in East Germany but also throughout Eastern Europe. Would he step aside from a regime which epitomized much of what he was attempting to change inside the Soviet Union, or would he swallow his principles in an effort to shore up the rapidly weakening walls of his western empire? In Gorbachev's mind, it is true, the alternatives may not have appeared this stark. He was trying to get rid of the Honeckers in his own political system, so the East German leader was certainly not a figure he found sympathetic. That he could behave as he would in a similar situation inside the Soviet Union may have seemed reasonable, because I believe he misunderstood the wholly artificial nature of the Communist governments in Eastern Europe: it was not possible simply to remove the hard-liners and replace them with liberal Communists such as himself.

As things panned out, Gorbachev tried to do a bit of both. He avoided direct criticism of Honecker, restricting himself to statements that the socialist societies had to face the need for change. What Honecker needed to restore control, however, was a ringing endorsement. Gorbachev's tepid comments instead had the effect of undermining him. I thought that Honecker's troubles were likely to deepen.

The East German dissenters seized on the Gorbachev visit to focus attention on their demands for change. There were recurrent angry demonstrations in Dresden and Leipzig, of increasing size and determination, accompanied by violence. Most ironic was the fact that the protesters were chanting, "Gorby! Gorby! Gorby!" The protesters seemed to smell blood, and there was a new and, for the Honecker regime, ominous verse added to the litany. While the problem thus far had been East Germans fleeing the country, the protesters' chant now changed to "We're staying here!" The clear implication was that, rather than escaping the oppression, large numbers of East Germans were determined to force reform. Violence was not used against the demonstrators, but Honecker made veiled threats. In a meeting with Chinese deputy prime minister Yao Yilin, he compared the protesters to those in China (who had also taken advantage of a Gorbachev visit) and darkly hinted they could face a similar response.

On October 18, Honecker was forced to resign and was replaced by Egon Krenz, a Honecker protégé. But the demonstrations grew larger and the flood of departing East Germans continued. On October 31, Krenz traveled to Moscow to consult with Gorbachev, and on his return shook up the East German leadership, removing members of the Politburo most closely associated with Honecker. He also indicated that some liberalization of the right to travel would be granted, although he appealed to East Germans to remain in their country. Again, the move had no discernible impact. The day after the announcement, 500,000 demonstrated, the largest number ever, while others continued to pour across the border into Czechoslovakia. On November 7, the entire East German cabinet resigned. The next day, Hans Modrow, a Party reformist, was appointed prime minister.

BRENT SCOWCROFT

I was coming to the conclusion that the situation had passed the point of no return. Discontent had spread so widely that repression had ceased to be an option for the regime. I now doubted that the situation could be stabilized. Helmut Kohl was increasingly nervous. The influx of East Germans was creating strains in the Federal Republic, where they automatically received aid as German citizens. It was possible the GDR would collapse into violent chaos into which West Germany might be drawn. Then there were the Soviets. East Germany would not be easily given up. If there was any place the Soviets might be tempted to intervene, this was it.

GEORGE BUSH

DIARY, NOVEMBER 8

I keep hearing the critics saying we're not doing enough on Eastern Europe; here the changes are dramatically coming our way, and if any one event—Poland, Hungary, or East Germany—had taken place, people would say, this is great. But it's all moving fast— moving our way—and you've got a bunch of critics jumping around saying we ought to be doing more. What they mean is, double spending. It doesn't matter what, just send money, and I think it's crazy. And if we mishandle it, and get way out looking like [promoting dissent is] an American project, you would invite crackdown, and . . . that could result in bloodshed.

On November 9, East Germany announced it was relaxing its border-control policy on all its frontiers with West Germany. The announcement, through a bureaucratic oversight, did not exclude Berlin—which was usually given a special status. Crowds began to build along the infamous Wall dividing the city, demanding that the border guards open the checkpoints to West Berlin. After some hesitation on the grounds that they had no instructions, the guards gave in to the press of people and allowed free passage. In that brief moment, the Wall fell.

GEORGE BUSH

I was at my desk about mid-afternoon when an excited Brent came in and told me there were reports that the Wall had been opened. We went into the study off the Oval Office and turned on the television to live coverage of jubilant crowds in Berlin. A few moments later, Marlin Fitzwater arrived with a fistful of wire service stories. He suggested I make a statement to the press. Although I was elated over what appeared to have happened, I was wary about offering hasty comments. The reports were still unconfirmed, so I did not want to jump in before we really knew the details. More important, I knew we had to be careful how we portrayed our response to the good news. I had to anticipate Gorbachev's reaction—and that of his opposition. As Brent pointed out, this was not the time to gloat about what many in the West would interpret as a defeat for Gorbachev.

Marlin suggested we call a brief and impromptu press conference right there in the office. It sounded much better than a formal briefing, which I thought would set the wrong tone. Soon, the White House press pool was crowding into the Oval Office, cameras, lights, and tape recorders in hand. As I sat down at my desk, reporters pushed up against it, among them Lesley Stahl, who was practically at the side of my chair.

It was an awkward and uncomfortable conference. The press wanted me to give a summation of the historic moment. Of course, I was thankful about the events in Berlin, but as I answered questions my mind kept racing over a possible Soviet crackdown, turning all the happiness to tragedy. My answers were cautious. I tried to explain that we were handling the event in a way that would not goad the Soviets. Lesley, poised over me, remarked that "this is a sort of great victory for our side in the big East-West battle, but you don't seem elated. I'm wondering if you're thinking of the problems."

"I am not an emotional kind of guy," I said.

"Well, how elated are you?" she demanded.

"I'm very pleased," I replied evenly.

I was bombarded with criticism over the perceptions this exchange created. Stahl and others took it to mean that I either did not grasp the significance of what had happened, or perhaps did not care. Yet nothing could be further from the truth. I keenly understood what the Berliners we saw dancing in the street felt. I had been to the Wall as vice president, and stood there with Kohl and with West Berlin mayor Richard von Weizsäcker. They had pointed out to me where young East Germans had been shot as they tried to cross to freedom in the West, and described the horrors in detail. I had also been to the town of Moedelreuth, through the heart of which ran the border fence between the two Germanies. I knew that at last those divided families might be reunited, and that these people could now come and go and enjoy the freedom we took for granted. But if we wanted to see all this happen, we had to be careful not to upset the process just as it began. A wrong move could destroy the joy we were witnessing. Senator George Mitchell, Congressman Dick Gephardt, and other Democrats soon suggested that I go to Berlin to "dance" on the Wall. This was pure foolishness. Kohl later told me how outrageously stupid such a move on my part would have been. It would have poured gasoline on the embers, an open provocation to the Soviet military to act.

In fact, the Soviet reaction to the opening of the Wall was one of outright alarm. On the day the Wall opened, Gorbachev sent messages to Kohl warning him to stop talking of reunification, and cabled me urging that I not overreact. He worried that the demonstrations might get out of control, with "unforeseen consequences," and he asked for understanding. This was the first time Gorbachev had clearly indicated genuine anxiety about events in Eastern Europe. Heretofore he had seemed relaxed, even blasé, about the accelerating movement in the region away from communism and Soviet control. It was as if he suddenly realized the serious implications of what was going on. As I read that cable I again thought of the posturing by many members of Congress.

DIARY, NOVEMBER 10

We get a message from Gorbachev yesterday urging that we not overreact . . . I think Kohl and the other leaders know we're being restrained . . . Moscow warns me in the same letter about getting this talk of reunification out of hand. It causes them real problems, but what I've been saying is, this is a matter for self-determination, and a matter for the German people, and I don't think he could object to that.

The big question I ask myself is, how do we capitalize on these changes? And what does the Soviet Union have to do before we make dramatic changes in our defense structure? The bureaucracy answer will be, do nothing big, and wait to see what happens. But I don't want to miss an opportunity . . . The budget process is crunching defense, but I'm telling our people that we must challenge the defense system, and go back to demand new studies, so we can see what bold [arms control] proposals can really benefit mankind and yet keep the West secure. As the changes happen, I'm absolutely convinced that there will be declining support for defense [expenditures] all around Europe.

A few days later, I wrote Gorbachev that I shared his concern that public safety and order be maintained, and told him the three Western allies had been cooperating with the Germans to help ensure this remained the case. However, I could not accept his view that Kohl was trying to use the events to stir up emotions. "As I see it," I said, "the FRG leadership has acted with the utmost responsibility, emphasizing the importance of a deliberate step-by-step approach to change in the GDR and the need to avoid destabilizing the situation in Europe." I remarked that I thought Gorbachev's own commitment to reform in the USSR had played a decisive role in encouraging Soviet allies to embark on a similar path. "We have no intention of seeking unilateral advantage from the current process of change in the GDR and in other Warsaw Pact countries, nor is it our wish to destabilize the situation," I assured him. "We continue to stand by all our commitments in the Helsinki Final Act, in particular to the principles of peaceful change and self-determination. From your own statements, I trust that you do the same."

Kohl, fresh from the heady events in Berlin, called me the afternoon after the Wall fell to describe the scene there. "It is like witnessing an enormous fair," he said with enthusiasm. "The frontiers are absolutely open." He speculated, or perhaps hoped, that people now might simply go back and forth rather than flee to the West. Free movement would work only if the GDR implemented reforms. He had his doubts. "Krenz will carry out reforms but I think there are limits. . . . I could imagine that this will continue for a few weeks—and that for a few weeks people will wait to see if the reforms come . . . [but] if there is no light at the end of the tunnel they will run away from the GDR in great numbers." Such an eventuality would be a "catastrophe for economic development," he warned. Good people were leaving—doctors, lawyers, specialists—who could not be replaced. "Over two hundred and thirty thousand people have already arrived, mostly young ones with an average age between twenty-five and thirty. They can earn more here." An exuberant Kohl added that "without the United States this day would not have been possible. Tell your people that."

BRENT SCOWCROFT

Overnight, the single most important symbol of the Iron Curtain had been struck down. It dramatically marked a turning point in the revolutions of Eastern Europe. Hitherto, the transitions had been achieved through collaboration between reform-minded communist governments and their people, as had been the case in Poland and Hungary. But in East Germany the wave of popular demand for change had slammed into one of the most immovable regimes of the Warsaw Pact and overwhelmed it. The East German government tottered and struggled to cling to power in the emerging political chaos. The revolutions had now crossed the line from surging to overpowering. With the fall of the Wall, suddenly anything was possible, even the dream none of us thought we would see in our lifetimes: a Europe whole and free.

CHAPTER 7

Ends and Beginnings

The remaining Communist regimes toppled with numbing speed, but it was almost anticlimactic after the shock produced by the fall of the Berlin Wall—and individually they seemed almost lost in the emerging whirlwind of events in the last weeks of the year. On November 10, the day the Wall fell, Todor Zhivkov, president and Communist Party leader of Bulgaria, announced his resignation after thirty-five years of Stalinist rule. His departure came as a surprise, with little of the unrest taking place elsewhere preceding it. This most docile and compliant follower of Soviet leadership was now out of step with Moscow. Perhaps Zhivkov hoped to leave with dignity rather than being forced out like Kadar and Honecker. Whatever the reasons, his departure left only two hard-liners still in power: Milos Jakes in Czechoslovakia and Nicolae Ceausescu in Romania.

Czechoslovakia was the most directly affected by the decline of communist authority in East Germany. The repressive Jakes regime was the ideological soulmate of Honecker's in resisting change and watched with horror the developments in the GDR. But the Czech people experienced the exodus of fleeing East Germans firsthand—the main route to the West lay through their country. They watched and befriended the escapees and, while difficult to measure, the exodus must have had a powerful impact upon them.

Compared to Poland, the Czech resistance movement had been small and somewhat hesitant. It was largely seen as an ineffectual group of intellectuals nostalgic for a return of the Prague Spring of 1968, isolated from the workers and youth who were essential to making revolution a reality. But there had also been something of an unwritten compact between the government and the Czech people: a degree of material prosperity in exchange for political passivity. That "understanding" had been only grudgingly accepted, and a series of developments began to galvanize the Czechs.

The emergence of the playwright Vaclav Havel as a heroic and pivotal figure for the opposition was an important turning point. When, as a result of disturbances in January, the government decided to make an example of him through arrest, trial, and imprisonment, it instead revealed Havel as a charismatic leader. In a way, he became the Czech Lech Walesa, symbolizing—and vocalizing in unparalleled fashion—the hopes of his people. This peaceable and quiet man soon became a rallying figure for the entire population. Yet the changing attitude of the Soviet Union was also emboldening the people to challenge the existing order. The Jakes regime, on the other hand, was appalled by Soviet support for a non-communist government in Poland and its failure to stand by Honecker.

The course of events in Czechoslovakia over the summer and fall was relatively placid. There was a small demonstration on August 21. Reinforced by the success of demonstrations in East Germany in getting rid of Honecker, however, the dissidents mounted a more serious effort on October 28, the anniversary of the founding of the republic in 1918. The authorities detained Havel and other dissident leaders, closed off Wenceslas Square for half the day, and dispersed the more than 10,000 demonstrators. But the crowning blow to the regime's credibility occurred on November 3, when Alexander Dubcek was interviewed favorably on Soviet television, his first such appearance since he had been deposed in 1968. It was suddenly clear that Jakes' days in power were numbered.

Coincidentally, the day after Dubcek's interview, East Germany reopened the border with Czechoslovakia and East Germans once again began arriving. The break in the Berlin Wall and the departure of Zhivkov inspired further, and growing, rallies in Wenceslas Square, beginning on November 12 with one of about 10,000 and building within a week to over 200,000. On November 24, Havel made a dramatic joint appearance in the square with Dubcek. A national two-hour strike on November 27 forced the regime to consent to a coalition government, which, with a non-communist majority, was sworn in on December 10. The "Velvet Revolution" had succeeded.

GEORGE BUSH

The stunning upheavals in East Germany, Bulgaria, and Czechoslovakia made it all the more fortunate that Gorbachev and I were to meet in early December. In the weeks beforehand, I began to prepare myself with numerous intense and sometimes exhausting briefings. Brent offered me about twenty topics to choose from: I took them all. I wanted to be prepared for everything. I found the CIA experts particularly helpful, if pessimistic. One analysis paper concluded that Gorbachev's economic reforms were doomed to failure, and that his political changes were beginning to cause problems he might not be able to control. It argued that the reforms were strong enough to disrupt the Soviet system, but yet not strong enough to give the Soviet people the benefits of a market economy. Based on those conclusions, some people in the NSC began to speculate that Gorbachev might be headed for a crisis which could force him to crack down in the Soviet Union to maintain order, or might even force him out of power.

BRENT SCOWCROFT

Everyone in the Administration seemed to agree that Gorbachev's chances of comprehensive reform were not good, but we were divided over what "comprehensive reform" might mean to him. Baker appeared to me the most optimistic concerning his sincerity about reform. He may have been influenced by his relationship with Shevardnadze, who we all thought came closest to being an apostle for fundamental change. I still believed Gorbachev remained a communist, perhaps not completely wedded to the notion of inevitable conflict between the two systems, but quite prepared to take advantage of us whenever the opportunity arose. He was moving in our direction, but for his own reasons. As long as he continued to do so he deserved our support, especially because, in my judgment, Soviet conservatives did not fear he was trying to overthrow the system. He was therefore the one most able to keep them on board as he moved "left."

Larry Eagleburger pragmatically pointed out that Gorbachev deserved credit for his recognition of how awful the system had become and for his courage to pursue far-reaching change. The argument about whether or not we should be supporting him he found academic and sterile. Gorbachev was the head of the Soviet Union. As a practical matter, there was no alternative to working with him. Bob Gates was more pessimistic. He thought that a reformed communist system—with democracy and a market economy—was a dubious prospect and that Gorbachev's efforts to create one would be easily reversed.

Dick Cheney was negative. He believed that it was premature to relax Cold War–style pressure. The Soviet system was in trouble and we ought to continue the hard-line policies which had brought us and it to this point. Why give up what appeared to be a winning hand? Colin Powell, now chairman of the Joint Chiefs of Staff, was difficult to pigeonhole. He loyally sought to avoid taking positions contrary to Cheney, but where there was daylight between them, Powell was to be found on the moderate side of Cheney. Vice President Quayle was the most conservative of all. He came close to the notion that what was going on in the USSR was little more than a ploy to lull us into thinking the danger was over and we could dismantle our security structure. These differing perspectives were seldom articulated as such, and never in the stark terms in which I have described them. They appeared most frequently in the course of debate on the merits of specific points of policy.

GEORGE BUSH

I was more optimistic than Brent or Gates about Gorbachev's chances for political survival and his intentions for reform. At the same time, I shared some of their concerns, and those of the CIA and the NSC staff. I worried that we were dealing with a ticking time bomb. We could not see what inside pressures were building against Gorbachev and his programs. We were getting hints from Moscow that one of Gorbachev's objectives at Malta was to gain some sort of "understanding" for his situation and for the measures he might take to crack down. I could not give him that, and if I did, it would have a lasting historical, political, and moral price.

I also knew I had to push Gorbachev at Malta to stop meddling in Central America. Incidents at the end of November, such as the crash-landing in El Salvador of a Nicaraguan plane filled with Soviet ground-to-air missiles and other weapons and munitions, did not help matters. A further sour note was the Soviet shipment of MIG-29 fighters to Cuba. This was an interceptor aircraft which could be configured to deliver nuclear weapons. I had no reason to think there were any nuclear arms in Cuba; nevertheless, I was unhappy, both with the fact and with the timing.

BRENT SCOWCROFT

These incidents kept alive suspicions that we were still facing, fundamentally, a Brezhnev system with a humanitarian paint job. I did not ascribe the MIG deployment personally to Gorbachev, but it was difficult to imagine he did not know of it. It was the kind of gratuitously offensive move the "old Soviet system" would have made, and with no visible need to do it, at least at this sensitive juncture. But the move had no significant military impact and I did not believe we should indulge our annoyance by a response which could put in jeopardy more important matters.

GEORGE BUSH

Coincidentally, an added benefit of the talks with Gorbachev was that they offered us a good reason to meet again with the Chinese leadership—on the grounds of briefing them afterward—and perhaps reopen our dialogue. The impasse with China was still on my mind, and I was frustrated that we had made little progress since Brent's trip to Beijing back in June. I had written another letter to Deng on my return flight from Europe in July. I hoped I could appeal to him to budge, for some kind of opening. I told Deng that Brent had related his reference to the proverb about tying a knot. "Herein lies our major dilemma," I wrote. "You feel we 'tied the knot' by our actions . . . We feel that those actions taken against peacefully demonstrating (non-violent) students and the nationwide crackdown against those simply speaking for reform 'tied the knot.'

> . . . I have great respect for China's long-standing position about nonintervention in its internal affairs.
>
> Because of that, I also understand that I risk straining our friendship when I make suggestions about what might be done now. But the US-China relationship, which we have both worked so hard to strengthen, demands the candor with which only a friend can speak.
>
> If some way can be found to close the chapter on the students whose actions were those of peaceful demonstrators, that would help enormously . . . If forgiveness could be granted the students and, yes, to their teachers, this would go a long way to restoring worldwide confidence. Such a move could well lead to improved relations with many countries. For example, it would give me the opportunity to make a statement supporting your decision. Also, if it would be helpful to China, I could then publicly dispatch a high-level emissary to Beijing, thus signaling to the world that our country was prepared to work back towards more normal relations.
>
> You see, rightly or wrongly, it was the students who captured the imagination of so many people around the world. They are young and, like students everywhere, they are idealistic . . .
>
> I am drafting this letter to you from 37,000 feet in the air on my way back to the USA from Poland, Hungary, France, and the Netherlands. Talk of economic reform is everywhere in Poland and Hungary. Others are finding, as China has, that incentive works, that joint ventures are good, and that standards of living can be improved through economic reform.
>
> I hope you still feel that economic contacts with the West are good. In spite of a US Congress that continues to try to compel me to cut off economic ties with China, I will continue to do my best to keep the boat from rocking too much. . . .

You have seen it all—you've been up and down. Now I ask you to look with me to the future. . . . We can both do more for world peace and for the welfare of our own people if we can get the relationship back on track. I have given you my unsolicited advice. If there is to be a period of darkness, so be it; but let us try to light some candles.

On August 11, Deng replied with a polite letter. China was sovereign, he told me, and was acting in accordance with its laws to put down the "rebellion." He hoped for improved relations, but he demanded that we "stop permitting the criminals in the United States [meaning the Chinese dissidents and students here] to carry out their activities against the Chinese Government." He reminded us that sanctions were still in place, and that there were other "incidents of interference." The Chinese were unmoved, and the situation remained unchanged for months.

Later that fall, I discussed China with Richard Nixon a few days after his return from a visit there.

DIARY, NOVEMBER 5
Nixon came to dinner at the Residence tonight. . . . Interesting on China—he feels we ought to make some move towards the Chinese. He lectured the Chinese pretty clearly when he was [there], and gave them a realistic view of how things were in [this] country. He thinks the best thing to do is to send Brady over there. I'm not sure. I still think that we ought to put it in the context of my meeting with Gorbachev, and making clear to China that we're not overlooking their views or their positions . . . [Representative] Solarz and others have [introduced] resolutions wanting to crack down more on China, but I cannot accept that. The matter got out of hand, and they made some terrible mistakes. [The Chinese are] trying to blame us; but we've got to keep moving, and somehow, we've got to get the relationship back on track. It's in our strategic interest; it's in our cultural interest; it's in our commercial interest . . .

Based on what I heard from Nixon, I wrote another letter to Deng suggesting that I send an emissary to Beijing after Malta, to debrief him on the discussions with Gorbachev. American attitudes in the Congress, in the public at large, and particularly in the press remained emotional and severely negative. If there was some way to start on the road back before there was serious and lasting damage to the relationship, we should try.

At about this time Henry Kissinger also went to China and returned with a letter from Deng, which he gave to me at the White House on

November 13. It spelled out a possible "package solution." Fang Lizhi and his wife, still holed up in the US compound, would be allowed to leave China, but Deng wanted both sides to make serious efforts to reach agreement on cooperative ventures in the near future, and suggested that the US should extend an invitation for General Secretary Jiang Zemin to visit the US in the first half of 1990. Like Nixon, Kissinger believed that the Chinese were ready for serious discussions and we should send someone to Beijing. It was reassuring that Nixon and Kissinger had returned from their separate trips to China with the same analysis of the situation.

BRENT SCOWCROFT

On November 15, the new Chinese ambassador, Zhu Qizhen, arrived at the White House to deliver his credentials. We met twice that day, and I explained our notion of sending a team back to explore the possibility of developing a "road map" which would lead us back from the brink on which we had been poised since June. Zhu handed me a reply to the President's letter. Deng welcomed another personal envoy and a debriefing on Malta. The President wrote back that he was agreeable to a visit from Jiang Zemin in 1990, but just when and where would have to wait until the Fang situation was resolved. "I am trying hard to untie my part of the knot, but please help by having China do its part."

Our refusal to cast China completely into outer darkness had outraged many in the Congress. On November 16, the Senate passed a bill to impose further sanctions, including bans on arms sales, US satellite exports and police equipment, an end to nuclear cooperation, no further liberalization of export controls, and a suspension of OPIC insurance. After some last-minute negotiations, we managed to get language included that permitted the President to lift sanctions if he thought it was in the national interest, and with that proviso he signed it. There was a far less cooperative spirit, however, over a bill to allow Chinese students in the United States to extend their visas until their government cleaned up its human rights behavior. We had already decided to let that happen, but very quietly through the Justice Department. We were certain that such confrontational legislation would result in China shutting down the student exchange program, which would be a real tragedy. The exposure of Chinese students to American values was one of the great hopes for future internal change in China. We also objected to the Congress legislating on an issue which was an Executive prerogative. Nevertheless, on November 19, the Pelosi bill passed the House 403–0 and the next day in the Senate by unanimous voice vote—veto-proof margins.

GEORGE BUSH

DIARY

It's November 29th, and we're all set to go to Malta tomorrow, but now comes the China Pelosi bill . . . I've already done most of this by executive order, but now Congress wants me to sign a bill. China made clear that if I sign such a bill, all the student exchanges would be cut off by them. I [will veto] the bill, even though it passed both Houses unanimously . . . People are editorializing against it; but I will put out a strong statement saying people will not be returned against their will, etc., though I'll still catch some hell from the libs and from the conservatives. It's probably the toughest call I've had to make, but we're going to be blasted. It isn't easy. There are several other vetoes we may have to undertake; but you've just got to call them the way you see them.

I vetoed the bill the next day, and braced for a veto-override fight.

In the final run-up to Malta, I made a point of consulting all our NATO allies, including Iceland and Luxembourg and the other smaller countries, to learn what they wanted to see in my talks with Gorbachev.

DIARY, NOVEMBER 25

Margaret Thatcher comes to Camp David [yesterday] and we had a good visit [but] she did not want to see any defense cuts at all of any kind . . . I explained that the pressures are on budget-wise; but the thing that really got me was that I couldn't . . . convince her that we've got to do less in the way of defense spending . . . Colin Powell and Cheney [agree with me], but she is rigid as she can be on this. Today, I called Lubbers, Gonzalez, Martens, and they all were saying, "stick with NATO—don't press for the dissolution of the Warsaw Pact"; but they aren't as rigid as saying, no deals [at Malta] of any kind on defense.

In the end, however, Margaret sent me a nice telegram pledging her full support in very comforting words.

I also had a long talk with Brian Mulroney over dinner on November 29 about his conversations with Gorbachev in Moscow. Brian said that Gorbachev wanted to establish trust with me at Malta. He was expecting no miracles or solutions, nor was he expecting offers of aid. He simply wanted to get to know me better and to convey his objectives and rationales. I told Brian I would try to convince Gorbachev that we wanted to work with him.

Finally, there was the question of how to brief the allies afterward. François Mitterrand had invited me to stop in southern France on my way home. While I wanted to see him, I felt that this would lead other countries to ask for individual meetings, and I simply did not have the time to dart around Europe. Instead, we hit upon the idea of asking Manfred Wörner to set up a NATO summit at which we could brief all the members together.

BRENT SCOWCROFT

The press speculated about a Gorbachev "surprise" along the lines of what had happened to Reagan at the Reykjavik summit in 1986 and to Baker in Moscow in May. The possibility concerned some of us. We discussed how to guard against it and how we might respond. We decided that if we were confronted by a proposal we had not analyzed, the President would thank Gorbachev and simply tell him we would carry it back to Washington, study it, and give him a response. Then Baker came up with the idea of taking the initiative ourselves and trying to put Gorbachev on the defensive. His notion was to create a package of initiatives on every subject and make that President Bush's initial presentation. The President liked the idea, feeling that, among other things, it would still those critics who continued to accuse us of drift and a lack of direction. We drew up a package of seventeen separate proposals.

I was not particularly receptive to Baker's idea, which I thought unprofessional at best and corny at worst. My concept of the President's initial presentation was that it should be philosophical, a "big picture" of how he viewed the world, the roles of the United States and the Soviet Union in it, and the perils and opportunities before us. That would establish an appropriate framework for more detailed discussions—although it would also, admittedly, leave ample opportunity for Gorbachev to try to seize control of the meeting.

The night we flew to Malta proved to be a complicated one. We departed Andrews Air Force Base about seven o'clock in the evening on November 30. After dinner, everyone had pretty well settled down to make the best of what would be a very short night. Sununu and I were about the only ones still moving about when the radio operator came back and said I had a call from Bob Gates. Gates told me it looked as if a military coup attempt was underway in the Philippines. He had called a gathering of the Deputies Committee but there were some hiccups. Vice President Quayle wanted to turn it into an NSC meeting. Cheney was at home and refused to come to the White House, on the grounds that the Vice President was not in the chain of command and such a meeting could not validly take place. Eagleburger had gone to the meeting.

The gathering debated a request for help from President Cory Aquino. The rebels had taken control of an air base and were threatening to bomb the presidential palace. The recommendation of the group, suggested by Powell, was to position US fighter aircraft aloft over the runway of the rebel base in an attempt to dissuade rebel aircraft from taking off. I liked the idea, because it would respond to Aquino's request while running little risk of involving us in the fighting.

Baker was sound asleep and I decided not to wake him unless the President had a problem with the concept. There was no reason for everyone to be exhausted the next morning. By this time I was also juggling calls from Quayle and Cheney, with Gates phoning every few minutes to try to interpret for me what the other two were up to. I had my hands full trying to placate everyone, so I asked Sununu to wake the President, explain the proposal and ask for approval, which he promptly obtained.

It was a tempest in a teapot, though with regard to the chain of command Cheney's position was correct. What this brief crisis showed me was that the system worked even under the most unusual circumstances. I was worried that the modest step we took on positioning aircraft would not be sufficient and things might get much more complicated to manage. But the action was precisely what was required to snuff out the uprising, and we accomplished our goal without having to fire a shot.

GEORGE BUSH

We arrived at Malta at about ten o'clock in the morning in a light rain, and after a brief meeting with Malta's prime minister Fenech Adami and a visit to the USS *Forrestal*, we boarded the cruiser USS *Belknap*—the flagship of the Sixth Fleet—in Valletta harbor.* Anchored about a mile away was the Soviet cruiser *Slava*, while the large Soviet cruise ship *Maxim Gorky* was berthed at the dock itself, and thus was in the most

---

*[BRENT SCOWCROFT] Our host aboard the *Forrestal* was Admiral Jonathan Howe, commander in chief, Allied Forces Southern Europe. I had first met Jon when I joined the NSC staff in 1972, where he was a lieutenant commander working directly for Henry Kissinger. He had done a superb job there, and went on through a series of key military and political-military assignments to rise to the highest ranks of the Navy. When the President nominated Bob Gates to become director of Central Intelligence, I asked Jon to replace him as my deputy.

protected position of the three ships involved in the talks. I was bunked aboard the *Belknap*, where I took over the comfortable cabin of our host, Admiral Jonathon D. Williams. As we settled on board, I managed to squeeze in some time to fish off the fantail of the ship. I caught nothing, but I did get one nibble.

Gales had been starting up outside, but when I went to bed the first night there was a gentle lull and I could hear the sea lapping at the hull. The weather got worse as the next day and night wore on. The heavy pounding seas disrupted much of the schedule and even forced us to cancel one of the meetings. Gorbachev, who was staying on the *Maxim Gorky*, did not want to venture out to the *Slava*, where the first meeting was scheduled. Instead, we went to the *Maxim Gorky*. Getting into the launch was a challenge, for the swells made footing difficult.

The *Maxim Gorky* was beautiful, with huge plate-glass windows. Recently refurbished, it had been brought in for the purpose of housing the Soviet delegation and staff. Gorbachev met me on a landing at the top of the stairs outside the salon. He had arrived late the night before and looked tired, but he was smiling. He was dressed in a dark-blue pinstripe suit, cream-white shirt, and red tie. His hair was grayer than I remembered from the year before. With him were Shevardnadze, Yakovlev, Bessmertnykh, and Anatoly Chernyaev, as well as a host of advisors— Valentin Falin, former ambassador Dobrynin, Akhromeyev, Viktor Karpov, current Soviet ambassador Yuri Dubinin, press secretary Gennady Gerasimov, and others. As Gorbachev introduced everyone in his large group, I realized I had met all the participants before.

BRENT SCOWCROFT

Like the President, I knew every one of them. Even so, the atmosphere, while friendly, was not relaxed. There was a feeling of anticipatory tension in the salon as we greeted one another across a long table. As host on the ship, Gorbachev opened with a formal welcome and invited the President to make the initial presentation. The President was taut as he began to speak, clearly nervous about the import of what was happening. He began to loosen up as he went along.

GEORGE BUSH

I set out my initiatives and proposed a summit for some time at the end of June. I turned to the obstacles to improving trade. "I want to waive Jackson-Vanik, which prohibits MFN [Most Favored Nation status]," I said. "Two things have to happen. [First] you are changing your emigration law and expect it to be completed early next year. [Second] our law requires a trade agreement before MFN can be granted. Let's begin trade negotiations immediately. I will push the American side to move. I want it done. If that word is not out to the top people in our administration— and I think it is—I will see to it. I would like to wrap up an agreement by the 1990 summit. . . ." I spelled out some troublesome problems. One was human rights and divided Soviet families, part living in the United States. As I spoke, Jim Baker handed Gorbachev a list of outstanding cases. Gorbachev observed that the US embassy had not been able to cope with the flood of those who wanted to emigrate. He promised to pursue the matter.

I raised Central America, the most contentious issue between our countries. I explained how the leaders there were pressing me to ask him to get Castro to stop exporting revolution into these democracies. "This is the single most disruptive factor in a relationship that is going in the right direction," I said. "It is not just the right wing in the United States. Concerns run deeper than that. I know it is sensitive for you, but in the US some ask: 'How can [the Soviets] put all this money into Cuba and still want [agricultural] credits?' . . . Nicaragua promised Mr. Shevard- nadze not to ship arms. [The Sandinistas] owe you an explanation." The solution, I added, was honest elections and a transfer of power.

"Arms control," I continued. "I want to get rid of chemical weapons. I mean it." I offered a suggestion, with a concession on our part. If the Soviets would agree to a chemical warfare initiative that I had set out in my September UN speech, I was prepared to halt our chemical weap- ons modernization program as soon as a global ban was in force. I also wanted a CFE treaty signed in 1990 and more steam put behind a START agreement. I spelled out changes we were prepared to make in our bargaining positions to get things moving. I asked him to make pub- lic the details of their military budget, Soviet forces in general, and weap- ons production figures the way the United States does. "As a former CIA man, I hope you got these from the KGB before our meeting."

"They say you are not publishing everything," said Gorbachev with a faint smile.

"I hope you can do this as a trust-building measure," I said. I con- cluded with a list of other areas where we could cooperate, such as envi- ronmental issues and science and student exchanges. "This is the end of my non-agenda," I joked.

BRENT SCOWCROFT

The Baker plan had worked. Whatever Gorbachev had originally in mind for his initial comments remains a mystery, for the President had obviously upset his game plan. He appeared nonplussed after having been buried in the avalanche of US proposals. He recovered fairly quickly and made a creditable presentation, but any fears we had of emerging from this initial exchange on the defensive were laid to rest.

GEORGE BUSH

Gorbachev paused before answering me. "This has been interesting," he said slowly. "It shows the Bush Administration has already decided what to do." He read aloud his own notes outlining his view of the world, written in a small orange notebook. "I believe it is important for both of us to evaluate the period of the Cold War. You cannot rewrite history. What happened, happened. That is the privilege of history. But it is our privilege, even duty, to examine what happened. . . . Today, all of us feel we are at a historic watershed. We have to address completely new problems, ones we did not anticipate or expect to become so acute. Now the question is whether we should approach these problems as in the past." He argued that some in the United States believed that the old policies had been right, that all we needed to do was gather the fruit. "But I know you do not agree with this," he said. "I know you have heard experts give their views, but what you have said today shows President Bush has his own understanding, which is consistent with the challenges of our times."

He outlined the new world he saw evolving—a multipolar world with an integrated Europe, a strong Japan and China. India too was becoming more dynamic. He could imagine new and enormous issues would come into play, all related to competition over limited resources. "We in the Soviet Union have been thinking about this for some time. The United States and the USSR are doomed to cooperate for a long time, but we have to abandon the images of an enemy."

Gorbachev said he was not suggesting a US-Soviet condominium, only describing reality. "I do not call into question our allied responsibility or previous patterns of cooperation," he said. "But there must be patterns of cooperation to take account of new realities." It was dangerous for either side to ignore or neglect the other's interests. "The United States has not entirely abandoned old approaches. I cannot say we have entirely abandoned ours. Sometimes we feel the United States wants to teach, to put pressure on others. We are aware of that. I want to hear your response, because this is how we will build bridges across rivers rather than parallel them. . . ."

"I hope you have noticed that as dynamic change has accelerated in recent months," I replied, "we have not responded with flamboyance or arrogance that would complicate Soviet relations. What I am saying may be self-serving. I have been called cautious or timid. I *am* cautious,

but not timid. But I have conducted myself in ways not to complicate your life. That's why I have not jumped up and down on the Berlin
Wall."

"Yes, we have seen that, and appreciate that," said Gorbachev. "We
have some concern on one thing: your actions on the Philippines." As for
Central America, the question of arms shipments was a misunderstanding. "If we promise something to you, we always want to keep our
pledges or you will not have trust in our relationship. We want to convince you that we are not engaged in political games. We pledged we
would not supply arms to Nicaragua and we are not." After the aircraft
crashed, he said, they had called the Nicaraguans and the Cubans. Both
said they had nothing to do with this incident. "But we will keep our
word," he promised.

"There is political pluralism in Nicaragua," he continued. "It has
nothing to do with Marxism. It is ridiculous to speak of the Sandinistas as
Marxists. The roots of the current situation in Nicaragua are economic
and historical. I don't see why Nicaragua is so unacceptable to you. They
will have a new government after elections. Let the UN and Latin
America monitor the election. Frankly, we are not that much concerned
with them. As for Cuba, Castro emerged without any assistance from
us. . . . No one can really give orders to Castro, absolutely no one. Castro
has his own views of perestroika, saying what he thinks." Gorbachev
laughed. "But we need mutual understanding. We don't want bridge-
heads in Cuba and Central America. We don't need that. You must be
convinced of that."

I was very pleased with this first session. With the large cast of charac-
ters present, it was something quite different from the small agenda-less
meetings I had planned. Our presentation had been well thought out,
however, particularly by Jim and Brent, and it had been well received.
Still, I think Gorbachev was relieved when we spoke in private about
noon. At this session, only Brent, our interpreter, and I met with Gorbachev, Chernyayev, and their interpreter.

Gorbachev made a strong pitch for me to talk to Castro. "My talks in
Cuba weren't simple," he said. "Castro expressed caution about our
policy [of reforms]—I explained our aims were good . . . He asked me, in
effect, to help normalize US-Cuban relations . . . I say this for the first
time in the most private way," said Gorbachev.

"Let's put all our cards on the table about Castro," I replied. "Our
allies can't see why we care about Central America. It just isn't a gut issue
for them. For the political left in the United States, it isn't a gut issue. But
for the fledgling democracies in Latin America and the US right, it *is* a

gut issue. Castro is like a sea anchor, as you move forward and as the Western Hemisphere moves toward democracy."

Gorbachev had said the Sandinistas had nothing to do with Marxism. "I am inclined to agree with you—I didn't use to think so," I said. "But I am convinced they are exporting revolution. They are sending weapons. I don't care what they have told you, they are supporting the FMLN [the leftist insurgent forces in El Salvador]. I am now convinced there is a new shipment of helicopters going from the Soviet Union to Nicaragua." I told him I saw the solution as a verifiable election and for Daniel Ortega not to try to cling to power regardless of the results. As for the US, "If it is a free election, we will abide by the results," I assured him. The only other issue in Central America was Panama, where Manuel Noriega remained a problem for us. I confided that we were preparing solid indictments against him.*

"Let me tell you how your steps are perceived in the Soviet Union," said Gorbachev briskly. "People ask, is there no barrier to US action in independent countries? The United States passes judgment and executes that judgment."

I raised the Philippines, which Gorbachev had referred to in the previous meeting and which I thought was a cut-and-dried example of positive US involvement. "There is a disparate group in the military [led by Colonel Honasan]," I said. "Democratically elected President Aquino asked for help to prevent the palace from being bombed by these rebels. It never occurred to me this would cause problems in the Soviet Union, though I probably would have done it anyway."

"In the Soviet Union, some are saying the Brezhnev Doctrine is being replaced by the Bush Doctrine," said Gorbachev forcefully. I reminded him that the Philippines was a democracy asking for help against rebel thugs.

"I agree she is a democrat," said Gorbachev. "It depends on the context. In Eastern Europe there are governments legitimately elected which are now being replaced. The question is, in the struggles in Eastern Europe, [what if] someone asks for Soviet troops to intervene? All is now interrelated. Some now are saying we are not performing our duty to our friends. But we have not been asked."

"In Eastern Europe, change is peaceful and encouraged by you," I answered. "In the Philippines, there is a colonel trying to shoot his way into power."

---

*The eventual military operation to restore democracy in Panama did not take place until December 26.

Gorbachev nodded. "Peaceful change is the way," he said. "Our position is non-interference. The process of change can be painful. Colonels can be found everywhere to do these jobs."

He changed the topic to Eastern Europe and Germany, and said he had three points to make. First, "the direction of change in the Soviet Union and Eastern Europe is such as to bring us closer—that is important." Second, he disliked it when some US politicians said the unity of Europe should be on the basis of Western values. "We have been accused of the export of ideology," he added. "That is what is now being proposed by some—not you." Finally, "Mr. Kohl is in too much of a hurry on the German question. That is not good."

Gorbachev speculated that Kohl's recent pronouncements* were motivated by some "pre-election game." He suggested that we "should let Kohl know that his approach could damage things." There were also unanswered questions. "For example, would a united Germany be outside alliances or within NATO? An answer is premature and we shouldn't push it—we should let it run its natural course. You and I are not responsible for the division of Germany. Let history decide what will happen. We need an understanding on this."

I told Gorbachev I thought Kohl felt an enormous emotional response to what had happened. "There is some politics to his program and some emotional outpouring," I acknowledged. "I think he knows the problems of his allies—after they support the right of the German people to reunite, they have some private reservations about reunification."

"Yes, I know," Gorbachev responded, "and they let me know. Unlike they—and you—I am saying there are two states, mandated by history. So let history decide the outcome. Kohl assured me he will abide by understandings we made in Bonn [in May]. Now he says he wants to talk on the phone—and Genscher is coming. I think this is an area for particular prudence."

I nodded. "We will do nothing to recklessly try to speed up reunification," I said. "When you talk to Kohl, I think you will see he agrees . . . I will be 'timid'—that is how Senator Mitchell describes my refusal to jump up and down on the Wall. This is no time for grandstanding or steps that look good but could prove reckless."

"The time we live in is one of great responsibility—great opportunity but great responsibility," said Gorbachev.

---

*On November 28, fueling talk of eventual reunification in the aftermath of the fall of the Wall, Kohl had announced a plan for closer association between the two Germanies.

BRENT SCOWCROFT

After about four and a half hours on the *Maxim Gorky*, we headed back to the *Belknap*. The weather had turned for the worse. The swells, even in the harbor, were enormous and the wind was howling. We had great difficulty getting aboard the ship and made it only because of the great skill of the crew of the Admiral's barge. The swells would take the barge up or down fifteen feet in a second, and transferring to the *Belknap*'s landing platform was quite a trick. The barge smashed the starboard platform to pieces, but we finally managed to get off onto the port platform. The crew worried that the barge would wreck that platform as well, and if it had, there would have been no way on or off the ship until the seas calmed down—helicopters were out of the question.

By nightfall, the ship was rolling like mad. The storm prevented any of our people then ashore from getting to the ship, and we ourselves could not leave, even though we were riding at anchor. Gorbachev could not reach the *Belknap* for dinner that evening, so we ate a marvelous meal meant for him—swordfish, lobster, and so forth. Here were the two superpower leaders only hundreds of yards apart, and they could not dine together. The storm cut us off from the rest of the world, and even though the talks were going reasonably well—when we could meet—we had no idea how they were being received.

GEORGE BUSH

I walked the deck and spoke with the enlisted men way up on the bow, with spray and rain driving down. The roll of the ship reminded me of my days aboard my old carrier the USS *San Jacinto*, and weathering some storms in the Pacific. One of the men warned me not to stand by one of the bow anchor chains, and pointed out that it had been chocked down. If it snapped it might well take my leg off. The seas were so bad the ship had to drop its stern anchor, but it added to the excitement. I went back through the walkway toward the stern and through the enlisted men's mess, where they were about to see a movie. Some of the sailors had cameras and asked to pose with me for pictures, which was fun. I looked into the Chief Petty Officers' quarters, where I saw triple-decker bunks, and I thought back to the double bunks on the USS *Finback*, the submarine that rescued me after I was shot down in 1944. It all came back—the steep ladders, the hatches, the faucets that turned off automatically—and here I was in the Commander of the Sixth Fleet's shower. And it worked great.

BRENT SCOWCROFT

We were truly isolated. I tried to communicate with Washington, with only modest success. The radio personnel were very helpful, but the equipment did not seem to me to be state of the art. I said a small prayer that no crisis would explode that night. Fortunately, the only one which developed was with the press.

Marlin Fitzwater was on board and had been scheduled to give a joint press conference with Gerasimov, but there was no way he could go ashore. He radioed Roman Popadiuk, our deputy press secretary as well as senior NSC director for public relations, who was on shore, to try to cancel the briefing, which would obviously be one-sided.* It was too late. Gerasimov was already singing the praises of Gorbachev. Margaret Tutweiler, State's spokeswoman, was reporting a similar situation. Marlin tried valiantly to radio Roman our version of the day's events. Roman managed to piece together the picture, and he and Margaret did their best to counter the impressions being peddled by their Soviet colleagues.

GEORGE BUSH

The storm had eased by the next morning and we were able to resume our schedule. Gorbachev still could not be persuaded to venture out to the *Slava*, so we went back to the *Maxim Gorky*. He was very jovial and once again direct—another relaxed meeting. Gorbachev could be tough, but he had a good sense of humor. I felt we were on the same wavelength as we talked.

"I want to say to you and the United States that the Soviet Union will under no circumstances start a war—that is very important," Gorbachev told me. "The Soviet Union is ready no longer to regard the United States as an adversary and is ready to state that our relationship is cooperative." It was time to think beyond the arms race. He complained that while the Soviet Union had switched to a defensive military doctrine, the United States and NATO had not yet changed their doctrine. As he finished his remarks, Gorbachev handed me a colorful map depicting US bases and fleets around the world. "I'm not sure if something is obsolete or if there have been additions," he joked. "The Sixth Fleet [which included the ships we used for the talks] is moving."

---

*Roman was an NSC staffer I had retained from Colin Powell and he had served marvelously in this dual capacity. Marlin and I agreed to continue it. Roman's instincts with the press were excellent and his reputation with them was very good. When he left in 1992 to become the first US ambassador to Ukraine, we replaced him with Walter Kansteiner, my senior director for Africa, who slid easily into Roman's capacious shoes.

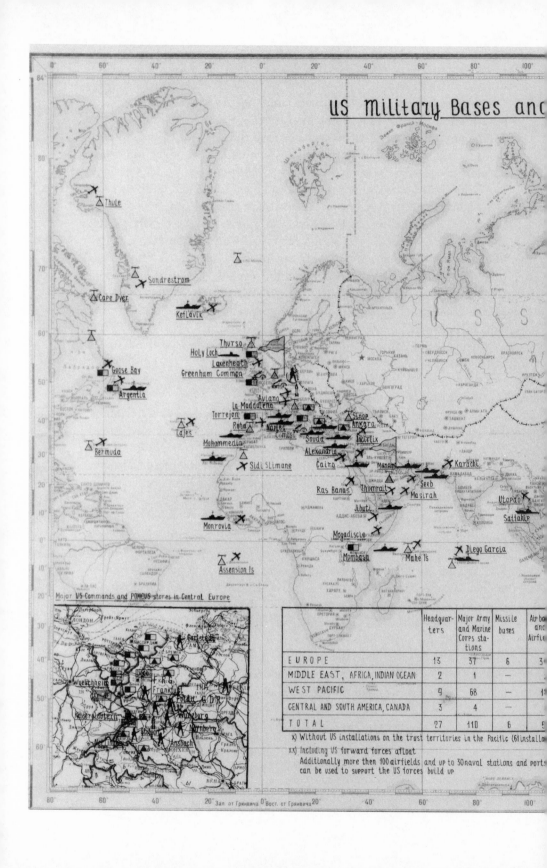

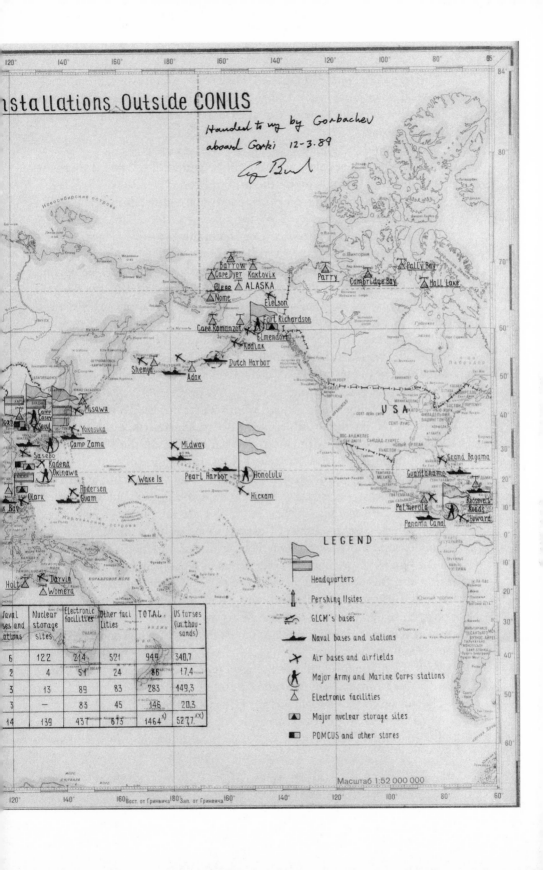

"Where is the *Slava*?" I laughed. His map was impressive, but not persuasive. For instance, they had marked the Panama Canal with a blue flag. "What does the Panama Canal have to do with encircling the Soviet Union?" I asked.

"Never mind the Panama Canal," he said, grinning.

"Why don't we see how accurate this is and we'll tell you if there are any problems," I said, handing the map to Brent.

I turned the discussion to Europe. "You are closer [to events], but I want to comment," I said. ". . . We cannot be asked to disapprove of German reunification. I realize that this is a highly sensitive subject and we have tried to conduct ourselves with restraint." I added that we were well aware of the Helsinki language about borders. "How do you see beyond the status quo?" Gorbachev replied that he believed all of Europe would draw closer together. "Our viewpoint, shared by all Europeans—even in nuances [by] Kohl—[is] that we should do everything within the Helsinki context," he said. We had to improve stability and make sure we did not ruin the instruments that had maintained the balance in Europe. He suggested that in the future the Warsaw Pact and NATO should have more a political than a military nature.

At the following one-on-one, I went straight for the Baltics and asked Gorbachev about the possible use of force. He described the problems he was facing, especially the interlaced nationalities of the Soviet Union. He had been ready to deal with the Baltics through greater autonomy, he said. But if they went for separatism, "that would be dramatic. I must not create a danger to perestroika. The Soviet peoples would not understand. We have lived together for fifty years. We are integrated." He pointed out that there were millions of Russians living in the Baltics. Half of the residents of Estonia were Russian, he said, and over half of the population of Latvia. "Our country is that way, and separatism brings out strong feelings in the people." There had been a "calming down," said Gorbachev, "but there are still problems. This is a sensitive issue for us. I hope you understand our position. This would bring all sorts of terrible fires. If the United States has no understanding it would spoil relations more than anything else."

"But if you use force [in the Baltics]—you don't want to—that would create a firestorm," I interjected. I pointed out that the United States would have to respond to any use of force by the Soviets there.

"We want all to get equal treatment," responded Gorbachev. "If we removed our MVD* troops from Nagarno-Karabakh,† we would have

*These were forces from the Interior Ministry.
†An area within Azerbaijan having a rebellious Armenian majority.

[localized civil] war. We are committed to a democratic process and we hope you understand."

BRENT SCOWCROFT

At this point Raisa Gorbachev entered to greet us and the formal discussion stopped. I came away from this exchange convinced that Gorbachev understood clearly what a neuralgic issue the Baltics were for us and, while his language was a bit elliptical in places, that he would restrict himself to non-coercive measures to deal with them.

GEORGE BUSH

We had covered a wide array of subjects with Gorbachev and, in spite of the differences, I thought we had a lot of common ground. Because we had to cancel one of the meetings, and had spoken so thoroughly on a few issues, we had not gotten to everything on the agenda. Gorbachev proposed, and I agreed, to let Baker and Shevardnadze continue discussions—basically giving them free rein. More important was Malta's positive effect upon my personal relationship with Gorbachev, which I thought was symbolized in our joint press conference—the first ever in US-Soviet relations. The talks had shown a friendly openness between us and a genuine willingness to listen to each other's proposals. Perhaps the growing trust helped him accept and promote changes in Eastern Europe, less worried that we would take advantage of the situation. All of this could only help further European security as we tackled new challenges there.

BRENT SCOWCROFT

The Malta meeting worked far better than I had hoped. No agreements were negotiated or signed, but it did renew the impetus to move ahead on START and CFE and toward an interim agreement on chemical weapons. President Bush expanded bilateral economic relations and offered steps to normalize trade through the prospective granting of MFN. The key accomplishment was the exchange on almost every topic of mutual interest, which made clear the attitudes of each on a whole series of issues. This gave us a much more reliable indicator of the perils and opportunities we faced. Additionally, the concerns which had led me for months to oppose a summit were not realized. There was no scorekeeping in the press about who won or lost. Perhaps because we had delayed for so long, perhaps because of the President's personality and grasp of the issues, perhaps because we had gone on the offensive with the President's opening statement, or for none of these, Gorbachev did not try to play "one-upmanship" or to paint the results in falsely glowing colors. We left for Brussels, and the NATO summit arranged to brief the allies, confident that we had established a good, solid foundation on which to build the relationship.

Soon after Malta, Larry Eagleburger and I returned to Beijing to brief the Chinese leadership on the talks and to explore the possibility of developing a "road map" toward better relations. Unlike our earlier trip, there was no need to make this a secret operation. We did, however, hope to keep it at a very low profile, since it was bound to be controversial. It was here that we—I—made a mess of it. We did not want to give advance notice of the trip because of the danger that Congress would demand an explanation of what we were about and why. We had absolutely no certainty that anything positive would result from the visit, and controversy in Washington at its very beginning would not enhance the prospects for success.

The problems began with our departure. To arrive in Beijing in mid-afternoon, as the Chinese had requested, required us to depart from Andrews Air Force Base at two thirty in the morning. Therein lay the dilemma. To inform the press in the middle of the night would make it appear we were trying to hide the trip. On the other hand, delaying the announcement until we reached China would also put it in the middle of the night, Washington time. I opted to wait until Beijing. Bad choice. But by far the most negative aspect was the television coverage. CNN happened to be in Beijing at the time, and the Chinese proposed extensive media attention. That was the last thing we had in mind, and after some discussion we agreed that camera crews would be permitted only at the initial meeting and at the outset of the session with the Chinese leadership. Following that script, there were cameras at the protocol meeting immediately on our arrival at the state guest house. However, as the ritual toasts began at the end of the welcoming dinner given by the foreign minister, the television crews reappeared. It was an awkward situation for me. I could go through with the ceremony and be seen as toasting those the press was labeling "the butchers of Tiananmen Square," or refuse to toast and put in jeopardy the whole purpose of the trip. I chose the former and became, to my deep chagrin, an instant celebrity—in the most negative sense of that term. I have no excuse, although none in the press saw fit to mention the highly critical comments in my toast about the Tiananmen events.

The Chinese took our visit seriously, and over the next days we met with the entire leadership for what became very frank discussions about our differences. On the day of our arrival I met twice with Foreign Minister Qian Qichen. Our first meeting was tough, with each side putting forth its complaints about the other. I spelled out in detail what had been covered at Malta, and he seemed deeply interested in how the two leaders had spoken of the end of the Cold War. He asked me to describe the differences in the President's and Gorbachev's positions on the possibility of German reunification, and what my own thoughts were on Gorbachev and the Soviet Union. The second meeting with Qian was a private one. We hammered out the terms of a "road map" of reciprocal moves to take us gradually but steadily toward normalization. At the end of this process was the vague notion of a visit to the United States by General Secretary Jiang Zemin. The plan was set out in general rather than explicit terms, giving each side some flexibility in its actions. But the Chinese linked releasing Fang to the lifting of sanctions—something to which we could not agree. The sanctions were in response to Tiananmen. Fang was a separate issue.

The following morning we met with Premier Li Peng. Li wanted my evaluation of the general situation after Malta and I repeated much of what I had told Qian about Malta and Gorbachev, as well as Germany. I pointed out that the Soviets, while they were undertaking economic changes, were also making military cutbacks, apparently in an effort to shift resources from the military to the civilian economy. These had a military effect upon NATO—and upon China.

Li Peng did not share the opinion that there was no longer a threat to NATO and the United States. "I believe with all the changes that the threat will still be there, so you can't depend on any particular person. . . . It is our view that the economy is the base, while politics is the manifestation. Without economic stability you cannot enjoy political stability for a long time." Similarly, weak diplomacy reflected the internal affairs of a country. For this reason he was not surprised by events in Eastern Europe and the Soviet Union. "You see, when China was in the Cultural Revolution we had a similar case—that is, chaos emerged in just a few days' time," he said. "Had we not adopted the resolute measures on June 4 [meaning at Tiananmen], the present situation in China would be even more turbulent today." While he did not deny there was an opposition in China, this was due to lapses in the Party's work and forces hostile to socialism. "But they are not in the mainstream in China," he confidently assured me, "and they cannot develop into the mainstream. So similar events as in Eastern Europe will not occur in China."

He told me China was ready to improve relations. "We can understand your repeated explanation of the difficulties faced by President Bush," he said. "But on the other hand, the Chinese government and leadership are also faced with difficulties and are under some restraints. We are ready and not reluctant to solve the problem of Fang Lizhi because this question has also caused a lot of trouble for us . . . President Bush on the one hand vetoed the Pelosi bill, but on the other hand has taken some administrative measures which are in essence the same as the legislation. So the Chinese people find it difficult to understand this. The US may think this is drastic action, but to China it is like old wine in a new bottle." It was expensive for China to send students to the US, and it had to justify the program to its people. Therefore they would have to issue a strong response to the President's statements on the matter after we left, but would do nothing while we were there.

When we met with Jiang Zemin later that morning, he cut to the point. He understood that President Bush was taking measures to try to improve the current situation between our countries. Both the US and China were proceeding on the basis of their own interests, he told me, as had been the case when President Nixon came here on his first visit to reestablish those relations. "Events have come a long way since 1972, and at that time our leader, Zhou Enlai, was still alive and he had a very important principle: to find common interest—or as the Chinese say, 'We should find the common ground while reserving our minor differences.' " We should not let ideology come between us.

After Jiang, we saw Deng Xiaoping, whose daughter and aide, Deng Rong, acted as interpreter. Deng was direct. He understood that both sides had to justify their actions to their peoples. The United States should not antagonize China, he said, but China did not consider the United States as a rival either. Since 1972 they had done nothing to hurt the interests or feelings of the United States. "Naturally, there have been some incidents in a technical sense, but not in a political sense," he added. "Since 1972, the international situation has enjoyed stability and in this regard the excellent development of Sino-US relations played a major role. It has carried great weight. I am not clear about the possible outcome of the present turmoil in Eastern Europe, but I believe Sino-US cooperation will be very important for peace. If a solution could be found, then Jiang should come to the United States to symbolize the end of the dispute. He added that he was in retirement and did not intend to interfere in the work of the new leadership—he was speaking as a friend.

At lunch, Qian Qichen gave us his appraisal of the Soviet situation. Gorbachev wanted to maintain East-West stability, he said, but could not continue his internal balance between economic and political reforms. The Soviets did not grasp the economy very well and Gorbachev often did not grasp what he was asking of it. Qian predicted the collapsing economy and the nationalities problems would result in turmoil. "I have not seen Gorbachev taking any measures," he added. The Chinese and Soviets had been talking about new areas of cooperation. "Gorbachev has called on the Chinese side to provide consumer necessities," he told us. ". . . [W]e can provide consumer goods and they will pay back in raw materials. They also want loans. We were quite taken aback when they first raised this. We have agreed to extend some money to them."

Our last meeting was also with Qian that afternoon. This time Eagleburger led off with some tough comments about the "package solution" the Chinese had presented the day before. "As the diplomat on this trip, let me be undiplomatic," he said. "My impression is that you and we are engaged in a kabuki dance. . . . We are circling each other, waiting for the other to move." While we had not given our final word on the proposal, it would not work as it was structured, largely because the linkage between sanctions and the release of Fang Lizhi was so direct that at home we could not politically manage it. The safe release of Fang would have the greatest impact of all the actions the Chinese might take and would make the rest of the package easier to accomplish. We were prepared to set the issue of Fang aside and, after the atmosphere in our relations improved, come back to it. "Fang is not necessarily the sine qua non to improving the atmosphere and undoing the damage collectively done over the last months."

He underlined the moves we had already taken, especially the President's politically costly veto of the Pelosi bill. "I raise them to demonstrate that the President is trying to improve the atmosphere." He added that if, as the Premier had said that morning, the Chinese government made clear its unhappiness with the President's administrative measures regarding the Chinese students in the United States after we went home, the impact there would undo whatever we had done in coming to China. As Larry spoke there was nervous laughter from the Chinese.

Eagleburger also raised the reports we were hearing—to which Congress had access, he pointed out—that Chinese officials were talking of sales of ballistic missiles to the Middle East. The Foreign Ministry had denied this on November 23, but it would help if the statement were reaffirmed, with some indication that surface-to-surface missiles would not be sold to regions of particular instability. We were hoping for small moves such as these on their part to demonstrate that it was wise to begin improving relations—steps to show Congress there was some movement. These were measures both sides could take without either appearing to prevail over the other. He suggested that we let Ambassador Lilley and their designee work out the details on when and how Fang might leave.

Qian outlined the first steps on the road ahead. Both sides would agree on a package solution, and we should avoid the appearance of winners and losers. Vice Minister Liu and Lilley should meet to discuss the details on Fang. "These negotiations can begin without waiting for a response to the package." As for Li Peng's remarks about the President's measures regarding students in the United States, this was a misunderstanding on the American side. The Chinese government could not justify the action by not reacting, but it had already done so. There would be nothing further. At the same time, China would send no more graduate students to the United States. On the missiles, China's position was clear and the United States was aware of it.

I considered the trip productive. There would be much good faith required by both sides to permit us to follow the road map successfully, but without such faith even the most rigidly laid out set of reciprocal steps would not have worked. Implementation of the plan began auspiciously enough with some small gestures. The Chinese accepted the Peace Corps, accredited a Voice of America correspondent, gave assurances on stopping missile sales, lifted martial law, and began to release people detained after Tiananmen. For our part, we fought to preserve the President's veto of the Pelosi bill.

As we reviewed the situation following the veto on November 30, the prospects could hardly have looked worse. There was not the ghost of a chance to sustain the veto in the House; our only hope was the Senate. And what a slim hope. Our initial count as we geared up for the battle revealed only five votes we could be sure of out of the thirty-four needed to sustain the veto. Probably no other fight with the Senate during the Administration was so bitterly contested and against such long odds. It was not a struggle along strictly partisan lines, but we got not a single Democratic vote. One measure of our difficulty was the fact that California Republican senator Pete Wilson left a sickbed to fly back to Washington to vote against us. In a final push, the President invited Republican senators to breakfast at the White House to make his case in person. The vote was uncertain right up to the end. The House voted 390–25 on January 24 to override. On January 25, our efforts in the Senate finally prevailed, 62–37, three more than the minimum required to sustain the veto.

After the Chinese had released only a handful of dissidents, however, it became apparent the entire, slow process was grinding to a halt—and we had no significant steps to point to in order to justify any normalization of our strained relations. The Chinese did not explain, and we could only speculate about the cause of their about-face. It is my sense that one of the most dramatic upheavals in Eastern Europe—the fall of Nicolae Ceausescu—was the main reason.

Despite harsh repression and serious economic difficulties in Romania, Ceausescu seemed singularly unaffected by the swirling winds coursing through neighboring capitals. For years he had made a ritual of distancing himself from Soviet policy, and he was even more caustic in his denunciations of glasnost and the events taking place in Poland, Hungary, and East Germany. Even after the ominous example of Honecker's fall, he brazenly continued to use the harshest measures to suppress dissent. Protests in Timişoara against the expulsion of a pastor of the Hungarian Reformed Church were crushed with ferocity on December 17. This time, however, the result was a national uprising—which military units began to join. It was the first such defection in Eastern Europe and struck at the foundations of the Romanian regime. Ceausescu hurried back from a visit to Iran to deal with the chaos. Addressing a huge crowd on December 21, he was booed off the balcony. The next day, the National Salvation Front proclaimed itself a provisional government. Then, in perhaps the culminating symbolic act of the end of the communist domination of Eastern Europe, the Romanians did what many had not dared imagine: They executed the Ceausescus, on Christmas Day.

BRENT SCOWCROFT

When Ceausescu was toppled, I believe the Chinese leaders panicked. It had appeared to me that they had taken great comfort from his apparent impregnability. They had referred to him frequently in our conversations and seemed to take him as proof that communism could survive the current liberal onslaught. When that proved not to be the case, they may have concluded that they had been right at Tiananmen, that any gesture of moderation would be simply too dangerous, and their only chance of survival was to be absolutely inflexible. Not only was this turn of events very disappointing, but it also made our domestic task much more difficult.

The image of the Ceausescus lying dead in the snow is the most haunting from the revolutions of Eastern Europe, a grim warning of the consequences of repression at the hands of the repressed. It was a sobering moment, reminding us that the revolutions of 1989 had been won with minimal bloodshed—something we never dared take for granted.

GEORGE BUSH

I was stunned and thrilled by the pace of events that fall. What generations of Eastern Europeans had pushed for—and risked their lives for so many times—had finally happened: freedom. I felt our patient approach of gentle encouragement had paid off, even if we could not take as active a hand as I wanted. I had been under constant criticism for being too cautious, perhaps because I was subdued in my reaction to events. This was deliberate, and based on my reading of the postwar history of Eastern Europe. During my trip to Poland and Hungary, I had been careful not to use language so inflammatory it would encourage people to do something reckless, something that would invite Soviet retaliation and lose everything we were working for. Instead, I kept up pressure for positive, incremental change. At the same time, I wanted it clearly understood—by Moscow and the East European countries—that we stood firmly on freedom's side and would not back down. Our detractors were rarely specific about what we were jeopardizing by our caution. In retrospect, given Gorbachev's priorities, it is not likely that a faster pace would have proved hazardous, but neither is it clear that it would have produced additional benefits.

I think we followed the right course from the outset, even if we had no way of anticipating what was to happen in the Soviet bloc. We had chosen to switch our focus from Moscow to Central and Eastern Europe in part to test the limits of Gorbachev's commitment to reform, openness, and "new thinking" in foreign policy. It was fortunate that we began the Administration with this change. By concentrating on Eastern Europe and delaying engaging the Soviets on arms control, we were able to pick up immediately on the promising developments in Poland. We were in on the ground floor and could encourage and take full advantage of the wave of liberalism as it moved through the region.

BRENT SCOWCROFT

It would be gratifying to say that our Eastern European policy—altered from support of those states most rebellious toward the Soviet Union to backing moves for greater freedom—had been among the catalysts of the changes. It was not. But our policy did provide solid encouragement and allowed us to react properly to events. Their speed and scope heightened a sense of euphoria in the West, and the President had to guard against crossing the line from championing the quest for freedom and self-determination to portraying the changes as victories in the Cold War struggle—thus provoking confrontation. For this reason, our policy evolved, perhaps even unconsciously, from quietly supporting the transformations to cultivating Soviet acquiescence, even collaboration, in them. The Cold War was not over; there was much left to resolve with the Soviets before I would be comfortable saying they were no longer adversaries, but a giant step forward had been taken.

Our biggest single problem with respect to Eastern Europe, aside from trying to gauge the limits of Soviet tolerance, was the lack of funds for aid. Did it make any difference? In the short term, probably not. Thanks to the President's trip to the region, the reformers had no doubts about our position and our commitment to their success, and their own exuberance seemed to compensate for the lack of material support. Over the longer term, however, it may have made a difference. Had the United States been able to provide the reformers with the means to demonstrate to their people that the new changes would in fact result in visible improvements in the material conditions of their lives, they might have received firmer allegiance to the painful process of reform. As it has developed, reform sometimes has become increasingly equated with chaos and disorder rather than economic progress, with the result that reformers have occasionally been replaced by neo-communists promising order and stability.

The revolutions in Eastern and Central Europe had only begun a transformation of the geopolitical landscape. As the climactic event in the breathtaking rush of the region toward freedom, the fall of the Berlin Wall symbolized the remarkable drama taking place in Central and Eastern Europe. Its disappearance immediately pushed to center stage the question of German reunification, which had been but a suggestive whisper in the shadows, and—ultimately—the future of Europe.

CHAPTER 8

A German Question

GEORGE BUSH

German reunification had very personal meaning to me.* During my trips to West Germany as vice president I had seen firsthand what the division of Germany had done to its people. Perhaps the defining moment came in February 1983, when Barbara and I, accompanied by then–Defense Minister Manfred Wörner, visited the small town of Moedelreuth in Bavaria, straddling the border between the two Germanies. It symbolized for me the significance of reunification as much as the Berlin Wall did.

It was a windy, snowy, and cold day, and we were bundled up in heavy coats as military helicopters flew us to the border. Like Berlin—in fact, it was nicknamed "Little Berlin"—Moedelreuth was divided into east and west: the tall, barbed wire–topped border fence ran right through the middle of the town. Grim-faced troops in drab uniforms patrolled the eastern side of the fence. It was constructed so that the steel mesh attached

---

*The terms "reunification" and "unification" are weighted with different implications and content for Germans and non-Germans alike. "Reunification" implies the joining together of the territories which made up much of the pre–World War II German state. The term in this sense has overtones of restoration of a previously existing political entity, which raised questions about German borders. "Unification" implies that the two postwar German states would create a new Germany with a new and distinct identity. The difference in preference for one term or the other is more than technical. It often underscores strong emotions and beliefs about continuity with the whole of the German past (good and bad), closure for the time of the Third Reich and the World War II and their places in history, and the conviction that modern Germany is politically and socially distinct from its "predecessor." In practice, and among all the countries and principals involved, the terms have been used interchangeably, although sometimes with an eye to the distinctions. We have preserved the original terms where they occur in quotations. Elsewhere, we use "reunification" to mean the end of the division of Germany as it became a symbol of the Cold War, not the restoration of a previous political identity. Whichever is preferred, the historical and cultural continuity of the German people remains, despite political and geographic changes.

to its cement posts faced east, not west, making it clear that the East German government had built it to keep their citizens in, not to keep the West out. The eastern side was also skirted in places with minefields and deep ditches to prevent people and vehicles from reaching it. Our soldiers pointed out East German guards, who followed our party through binoculars, and photographed us from tall concrete-and-steel guard towers with searchlights and reflective glass. I sensed the intimidation and fear they must have instilled in their own people. I knew they had orders to shoot any of their countrymen who tried to scale this fence and flee to freedom.

I could see the East German part of Moedelreuth through the fence as we walked through the snow along the border. Its traditional German houses were kept uniformly painted and tidy, although I was told the town was only partially occupied. The buildings were outwardly well maintained as a show of East German prosperity—a false front covering the shabbiness and decay of the town. Even the lights of the empty houses were turned on for the sake of appearance. It was a sad contrast to the warmth, color, and activity of the Western part of this farming community, one not so different from many I had visited in the American heartland.

I already felt an abhorrence for the German Democratic Republic before this trip. In my CIA days I had seen that East Germany was among the very worst offenders when it came to training terrorists or destabilizing countries. They were perhaps the most aggressive of all in the spying business and would stop at nothing to further their ends. It was the East Germans to whom the Soviets turned to carry out a lot of the ugliest missions. They were the chief bully of the East bloc.

Moedelreuth brought home to me the personal tragedies and costs of a divided country, and of the Cold War, in a way reports and photographs could not. Parents and children, brothers and sisters—Germans all—could look through the fence and, just a few feet away, see their relatives, but there could be no contact. Throughout the Germanies, many families like these had been separated for decades, perhaps with occasional visits as tensions between the two states eased. It was stark, chilling, and a sad reminder of the realities of the Cold War for people on both sides of the front line of the Iron Curtain.

This was the first time Barbara and I had met Manfred Wörner, and we got to know him well on the trip. Not long after we began the flight back to Bonn, a heavy snowstorm blew up, making it impossible for our pilots to see and forcing our helicopters to land at a small and rather isolated airstrip. There we sat in a cold waiting room while we figured out how to get to Bonn. Manfred began trying to make arrangements for ground transportation. I asked whether a train might be available. The next thing I knew, he, Barbara, and I were driving down to the railroad station together.

At the station we found a local train waiting, one which stopped at every small town on its route. We boarded a car which had been cleared for us and, as this was the eve of West German elections, Manfred, in great campaign style, leaned out of the window into the freezing air and began shaking hands with people—which he repeated at each stop. Happily, I found that the Germans had put several cases of marvelous beer on the train for us. We had a relaxed ride back to Bonn, and a wonderful chance to talk. On that day we became good friends.

I was delighted when later Manfred was chosen to head NATO. He was a staunch supporter of US participation in Europe, and a good and wise man. I would turn to him often during the Administration, on the future of NATO as well as German reunification. Ours was a close friendship, and his premature death of cancer in 1994 was a tragedy. Brian Mulroney and I together spoke with him over the telephone only four days before he died. I felt I had lost someone very close to me, a man I greatly respected.

The fall of the Berlin Wall marked the beginning of the dramatic and final chapter in the transformation of Europe—the unification of the two German states. At the end of World War II, Germany had been divided into zones of occupation among the four victorious Allied Powers: the United States, Great Britain, France, and the Soviet Union. Though meant as a temporary measure until a final settlement on Germany (and a peace treaty) could be reached, the occupation zones became two separate political states as the Cold War rivalries hardened. The two Germanies were in the odd position of being treated both as parts of an occupied whole and as separate member states of rival alliance blocs. For these reasons, ending the separation was significant: it would mark the conclusion of a division struck at Yalta between onetime allies in a bitter war and sealed in a hostile peace. It would mean the end both of World War II and of the Cold War, the closing of the postwar era.

For many Germans on both sides of the fence, the division was a deeply emotional matter. Since 1945, neither state had had complete control—sovereignty—over its own affairs. Special Allied rights remained in effect, and, as the unique status of Berlin as an occupied and divided city starkly underscored, foreign troops were more than simply invited peacetime allies. Germany, East and West, had been, at least at first, "singularized," treated as distinct from other countries, marked as politically suspect after two world wars, militarism, and Nazism. Its brief experiment with democracy after World War I had ended in failure and the resurgence of authoritarianism. Since World War II, Germans had questioned and rejected this militant nationalist past, embracing democracy (in the West at least) and building a constructive peace with their neighbors.

Some West Germans accepted the division as a reassuring measure that would prevent the reemergence of old tendencies and problems. Certainly the possibility of reunification seemed distant and unreal, even if the West German Basic Law* committed the government to seeking it. In the 1970s, West Germany under the (Social Democratic) SPD chancellor Willy Brandt had initiated *Ostpolitik*—developing closer ties to East Germany. It was a policy which tacitly recognized the existence of separate German states with different political and economic identities, and extended needed West German economic help to East Germany (in fact, as was eventually revealed, propping it up). But many Germans still viewed eventual unification—reunification—the restoration of a single German people, as a desirable if unlikely goal. For these people, the flow of East German émigrés over the summer and fall of 1989, culminating in the opening of the Berlin Wall, brought a heightened sense of anticipation that reunification was a possibility after all.

Disagreement within the ruling coalition in West Germany, as well with as the opposition parties, seemed to reflect domestic German differences over the prospect of reunification. While both Helmut Kohl and Hans-Dietrich Genscher understood the economic and political causes of the influx of East Germans, and the need for immediate reforms in the GDR if the pressure on West Germany was to ease, each appeared to have a different solution in mind. Kohl, perhaps moved by the plight of the émigrés and sensing a historic moment, spoke of more openness, closer ties, and eventual unity. He went so far as to declare reunification "back on the international agenda" in August. Genscher, on the other hand, appeared more reluctant to see a solution to the problem cast in terms of a nationalist German unity. He wanted any closer association between the Germanies to occur within an increasing European integration. For their part, the Social Democrats and the Greens simply opposed reunification on ideological grounds, also rejecting a "nationalistic" Germany but in some cases hoping for future harmony with a reformed socialist East Germany.

*Analogous to a constitution, which was to be put off until a reunited Germany could adopt one.

In general, the rest of Europe was leery, even fearful, of reunification. The notion of the return of a powerful Germany to the center of European politics stirred strong emotions about the unresolved "German Question." Not the least were bitter memories among Germany's neighbors and former adversaries of two world wars, such as France, Britain, and the smaller countries along its borders. Even five decades after its outbreak, the last German war of aggression had not faded from the minds of many. Could a united Germany be trusted? For Poland, reunification stoked doubts over its own old, but not forgotten, security concerns. At the end of World War II, large portions of eastern Germany had been given to Poland in compensation for territory it was forced to cede to the Soviet Union. Would a united Germany demand the return of these lands? After all, they historically had been part of Germany for centuries, although their German populations had been evicted after the war.

As in Western Europe, much of Moscow's uneasiness derived from past problems with Germany—some going back centuries. Most recently, Nazi Germany had inflicted huge casualties and destruction on the Soviet Union, in combat and in occupied areas. For many of the senior leadership, the scars of that war were still fresh. Eduard Shevardnadze lost a brother at Brest during the first days of the German invasion in 1941. Gorbachev's father also had fought, and three of his uncles had died. Both Gorbachev and Shevardnadze would refer often to the importance of the sacrifices of the war, and of the victory, to the Soviet people. A more immediate Soviet concern, however, was whether German reunification would destroy the foundations of their current security structures.

The strategic ramifications of German reunification were understandable causes for Soviet trepidation. While the Soviet Union could adapt to changes in Poland or Hungary, perhaps even in the Baltics, the disappearance of East Germany from close Soviet orbit was another matter. Since the GDR was the keystone of the Warsaw Pact, its loss—and, worse, its potential absorption into NATO—would be fatal to postwar Soviet military strategy and tantamount to a shift in the tectonic plates of the alliances themselves. East Germany was *the* prize of World War II, the Soviet Union's most reliable military ally, and an important economic partner. Losing it, and accepting that loss, would mean acknowledging the end of Soviet power in Eastern Europe and the complete erosion of Moscow's security buffer of satellite states, the very core of its security planning.

The reaction in the Administration to the prospect of German unification was markedly different from that of the Europeans and the Soviet Union. While the United States had fought Hitler, we had not experienced the devastation inflicted by his armies. We had long regarded the division of Germany largely from the pragmatic perspective of the Cold War and the geopolitical reality of the existence of two separate German states, rather than through a prism of fear. We also tended to view the policy implications of our phrase "ending the division of Europe" as separate and distinct from the question of one or two Germanies. The fact is that American administrations had, for so many years, simply paid rhetorical obeisance to the eventuality of German reunification that it had virtually ceased to have any real operational policy meaning.

However one had looked at the possibility of change in Eastern Europe, German reunification was never near the top of the list of realistic expectations. East Germany was perhaps the last state to come to mind when considering the possibility of political liberalization. Thus, at the beginning of 1989, reunification seemed to us as distant a prospect as it had been for the previous forty years.

GEORGE BUSH

In the opening months of the Administration, I had given little thought to reunification. I was no expert on the country, but I did see West Germany as a critical friend and ally. I had a great deal of respect for the Federal Republic and for the long-standing and vital American-German ties, which I was determined to do my part to make better.

I was, of course, mindful of Germany's history of aggression, but I knew the country had done a lot to live down its Nazi past, to compensate for the horrors it had inflicted on Jews and others across Europe. I felt that the Germans had made amends and that they hated the brutal chapters in their past just as much as the rest of Europe did. I did not believe that all present-day Germans should have to pay forever for what some of their countrymen had done in the past. The Germany of the 1980s had earned its place as a productive democracy.

While Thatcher, Mitterrand, and others feared that Germany might cause more trouble and tragedy, I did not. I did not belittle those fears but, as reunification moved on, I tried to help other leaders understand my view that this new Germany would be different. I also felt strongly that the United States ought to follow through on our past pledges of support for German unity when the time came. However complicated or risky the process might be, the pursuit of reunification was something for the Germans themselves to decide.

I must confess I did not feel that strongly about whether we should push the matter either. If the NSC or State Department had argued it was a bad idea, I certainly would have been receptive. I was not about to impose my own view on this highly controversial matter. I simply had a comfort level with it that others did not yet have, just as I was more comfortable with trying to do more in terms of arms control with the Soviet Union than, say, was the Defense Department. Because I was not afraid of reunification, I probably set a different tone for the Administration on the issue than it might otherwise have had.

BRENT SCOWCROFT

In fact, President Bush was the first in the Administration to back reunification unequivocally, as well as the first Western leader—a point Kohl never forgot. I do not remember a specific moment at which it was clear he had made a firm decision on the matter. His views on German self-determination emerged in a gradual process of occasional remarks to each of us, or in answers to questions posed by the press over time. By firmly supporting this right and by minimizing fears of a united Germany, the President probably made it harder for the Europeans to vocalize too boldly their own concerns and their barely disguised opposition. More important, his leadership and personal diplomacy emerged as key factors in preparing the way for German unity amid the larger questions of the transformation of Europe, issues such as security and changes in the strategic balance between East and West.

There had been some discussion of German reunification during the strategic reviews at the outset of the Administration. The NSC and State teams disagreed sharply over how to lay out the issue of the future of Germany. The NSC argued that we should be paying closer attention to the FRG—placing it at the center of our European policy—and to ending the division of Germany if we were ever really to put the Cold War behind us. State countered that discussion of reunification was, at least at that juncture, premature. No one else was talking about it, certainly not the Germans. The status quo was the basis of postwar stability and peace in Europe. Why disrupt the situation with unnecessary talk of reunification? The conclusion was that we would not open the issue but would continue the ritual incantations of support for reunification of Germany in freedom and by peaceful means. With minor grumbling, both sides accepted that watery formulation.

In truth, I was skeptical about the wisdom of pursuing German reunification and, in that sense, was probably closer to the State position than that of my own staff. No one outside the Germanies, especially among our European allies, basically liked the idea. Besides, what was wrong with a divided Germany as long as the situation was stable? The very process of unification could be extremely destabilizing, and could even lead to conflict. It was, of course, not possible to be rhetorically opposed to unification, but there seemed to me little reason at this point to put the issue on the active agenda.

As the émigré crisis in Germany mounted over the summer and autumn of 1989, and with the fall of Honecker in October, my views began to change. They had been based on the belief that it was best to let sleeping dogs lie. But the dogs were awakening, and that stance appeared no longer to fit the situation. I still believed we should be very cautious, however, and generally take our cue from Kohl, who was much more familiar than we with the pace and direction of changing moods in West Germany. The dramatic, if almost accidental, opening of the Wall revealed that even this approach was already being overtaken by greater events.

In November, the East German government continued its efforts to stem its political and economic crisis, striving for a respite in which to reorganize, but its actions seemed only to increase popular pressure. Premier Egon Krenz hoped for financial aid from West Germany to help stop the increasing flood of emigration and to proceed with socialist-style reforms. On November 8, Kohl announced his willingness to extend such aid, but only if East Germany undertook the deep economic and political reforms it so badly needed. Without them, he said, the money would be wasted. On November 11, Krenz told Kohl that reunification was out of the question, but indicated that the East German government was prepared to make radical reforms.

On November 13, however, at the Socialist Unity Party (SED, the official name of the East German Communist party) plenum, an impatient *Volkskammer* (the East German parliament) dropped Krenz as premier (although he remained general secretary of the Party, chairman of the Council of Ministers, and head of state) in favor of Hans Modrow. Modrow quickly formed a government which for the first time included non-communists. Like Krenz, he too set about trying to stabilize the political situation. On November 17, he announced a package of specific changes, including political reform, but, determined to preserve a separate and socialist East German state, he rejected reunification. Instead, he presented an alternative solution for closer inter-German ties, short of a formal single state, which he called "cooperative coexistence." It was built on a treaty community which simply carried forward past agreements between the two German states.

GEORGE BUSH

The same day Modrow announced his proposal, Helmut Kohl assured me he would do nothing to destabilize the situation in the GDR. He had had a long conversation with Gorbachev. As he had to Krenz six days earlier, Kohl bluntly warned the Soviet leader that without reform as in Poland and Hungary "the system will fall."

"In spite of Congressional posturing, the United States will stay calm and support reforms in just the way you talk about," I said, with Senator Mitchell and Congressman Gephardt in mind.* "We will not be making exhortations about reunification or setting any timetables. We will not exacerbate the problem by having the President of the United States posturing on the Berlin Wall." That same day I asked Brian Mulroney, who was about to meet with Gorbachev in Moscow, to convey to him the same message.

I also spoke with Margaret Thatcher. She focused on the European Community meeting on Germany called by François Mitterrand and scheduled for the following day, apparently in the hope that it might help to dampen talk of unification. Margaret seemed to feel that it was time to pull in the reins on the subject. "After the East Germans started coming out, there was too much euphoria, too many efforts to try to see into a crystal ball," she said. "There was too much of German reunification." Gorbachev should be our main concern, for none of this would have been possible without him. "Destabilize him and we lose the possibility of democracy in the Soviet Union," she warned.

BRENT SCOWCROFT

Like Thatcher, we recognized that the loss of East Germany might exacerbate political problems in the Soviet Union, causing a conservative backlash and jeopardizing Gorbachev's reforms and perhaps even his hold on power. Thus far he had accepted the changes in Eastern Europe and had overcome resistance to them among his military and the Party. Our question was whether he would, or could, sustain the loss of East Germany on top of everything else. We anticipated that the reflexive reaction of the opposition would be to fight reunification tooth and nail to protect the remnants of the Soviet security bulwark in Eastern Europe. Thus, by mid-November, our thinking on Germany was cast in terms of how it would affect the continued progress of reform throughout Eastern Europe and the Soviet Union. Our focus was on advocating East German self-determination, as Kohl was doing, rather than pushing

*See Chapter 6, p. 149.

reunification as a goal and planning how to get there. We intended to follow Kohl's lead, support him, and say nothing that would aggravate the situation.

GEORGE BUSH

As with any difficult policy question, I wanted to get outside views. On November 13, Henry Kissinger joined Brent, Jim, and me for dinner in the Residence. Although we met principally to discuss his recent trip to China,* the conversation inevitably turned to the dramatic events in Berlin. Unlike the controversial proposals he had put forth in our January meeting, this time his thoughts were similar to, and helped mold and reinforce, our own. He believed German reunification was inevitable because there was fundamentally no longer a basis for a separate East German state.

In Kissinger's view, Gorbachev must know that East Germany was no longer viable, and he (Kissinger) outlined two possible Soviet options. The first would be to get the two Germanies out of NATO and the Warsaw Pact. A neutral Germany could be controlled by the threat of nuclear weapons, and Eastern Europe could be kept in line through fear of a united Germany. The other option would be to attempt to get both alliances disbanded. Kissinger emphasized that, in his judgment, the United States could not appear to be—to the Germans—the obstacle to unification. I listened carefully. I respected Kissinger's special insight into the problem and his knowledge of Germany.

I had opportunities to hear European attitudes on Germany as part of consultations with our allies before my Malta talks with Gorbachev. Genscher visited Washington on November 21 and I asked him whether he felt the rapidity of change in Eastern Europe would result in an instant demand in Germany for reunification. "We know that in the long run this is for the German people to decide, based on self-determination," I said. "But will reunification move faster than any of us think?"

"No one can foresee," answered Genscher. "Last night, two hundred thousand in Leipzig shouted 'one nation' again and again. So things are changing. When the GDR establishes a democracy, the better for the whole of Europe." The events in the GDR were part of a greater European framework, he said. "It is important for all to know that we will stick to our obligations in NATO and the European Community. We do not want a special course for Germany, but we do not want self-determination everywhere except in Germany. . . . But all of this must

*See pages 157–58 in Chapter 7.

be done in a way that does not alarm the Soviet Union. That is why we must stick to our current borders. That is a condition of the building of a stable structure in Europe. . . ."

My November 24 meeting at Camp David with Margaret Thatcher also focused on Malta, but it was a chance to listen to her views on Germany in more detail. Like Genscher, Margaret emphasized encouraging democracy in the East as the way to stabilize the situation, and she particularly worried that talk of reunification or changing borders would only frighten the Soviets.

"The overriding objective is to get democracy throughout Eastern Europe," she told me. "We have won the battle of ideas after tough times as we kept NATO strong." But it would take time, for democracy was not just setting up elections. "It's a political way of life," Margaret observed wisely. "Only then is it irreversible." She added that such change could take place only in an environment of stability. "That means NATO and the Warsaw Pact stay. NATO should stay anyway. Had NATO been there in the 1930s, there never would have been a World War II. We cannot open the border issue now. It could undermine Gorbachev. Then look at Central Europe: there are massive problems with borders throughout the area. . . .* Focus on democracy now."

Margaret argued that Germany's fate was larger than a matter of self-determination. The borders issue, the role of the four powers in Berlin, the inviolability of frontiers, all widened the problem. She pointed to the Baltics. "We decided not to pursue these at the moment because it would undermine Gorbachev's larger efforts . . . ," she reminded me.

She pulled a map out of the large handbag she always carried with her. She traced the old 1937 German borders and the territories now in Poland which were marked upon it. "Look at Germany," she said. "Reunification means Gorbachev is lost. He loses the integrity of the Warsaw Pact. A unified Germany would be a country of eighty million in the middle of Europe, one with a strong balance of trade. We can't keep it from eventually happening if they want it. But for now, concentrate on democracy. That will solve some of the basic problems and will not raise the fears later that will be aroused now."

Thatcher's lack of sympathy for and even distrust of reunification was obvious from this conversation and the one on November 17, and was probably rooted deeply in Britain's stormy past relationship with Germany. Britain had long attempted to play keeper of the continental

---

*Virtually every Eastern European country had unresolved border disputes with its neighbors.

balance of power, ensuring that no single state came to dominate Europe. It had fought Napoleonic France, Imperial Germany, and the Third Reich for ever higher stakes at ever higher costs, and its economic and political influence had diminished as a result of the two world wars. Since 1945, Britain had approached the German problem through developing closer ties with West Germany and by depending on NATO and its special relationship with the United States to balance any potential German threat. Reunification raised serious questions for the future. Was Germany reformed or would it seek to dominate Europe again, if only economically? West Germany was already the engine of the European Community. A united Germany would overshadow Europe, and accepting it meant conceding European preeminence to Bonn.

GEORGE BUSH

While I did not agree with Margaret's concern about the implications of a united Germany, to some degree I did share her worry about the adverse political effect reunification could have on Gorbachev. However, I thought we could manage these issues in a way that would obviate most of her concerns. I believed that the United States, with its strong bilateral relationship with Germany and its standing with the Soviets, could be the catalyst for a peaceful resolution to the problem.

BRENT SCOWCROFT

I was not as optimistic as the President about the outcome and I had some lingering sympathy for Thatcher's position. She had her eyes on some very important priorities. The changes which had already taken place in Europe were breathtaking in their scope, and managing their consequences would take the best efforts of all to prevent dangerous instabilities from developing. To add to this already unsettling brew the potentially most destabilizing issue of all—German unification—could be asking for trouble.

Continuing his pre-Malta consultations, President Bush spoke with Dutch prime minister Ruud Lubbers on November 25, and with Italian prime minister Giulio Andreotti on November 30. They echoed Thatcher's concerns. "We should not be talking about national boundaries, which should be respected," Lubbers told him. "We should also avoid talk about the German problem." Andreotti had similar views. He had just met with Gorbachev, who had insisted that the Helsinki platform be followed,*

---

*The Helsinki Final Act of 1975.

which specified that borders could not be changed except by peaceful means and mutual consent. Mitterrand, reinforced by Thatcher's remarks, had obviously gotten what he sought at the EC meeting on November 18. The prevailing mood was definitely negative.

But Andreotti was also reacting to Kohl's move of November 28, one designed to accelerate the agenda. On that date he had unveiled a ten-point plan to address the future of inter-German relations. It did not specify negotiations for reunification itself but reforms and treaties to improve ties between the states. Presumably, it was also aimed at alleviating the emigration problem (over 130,000 East Germans crossed to West Germany in November alone) and, perhaps, stimulating greater interest in unification on the part of the East German population.

Kohl's program was full of goodwill and promises. He again offered aid to East Germany—if fundamental political and economic reforms were made, including free elections and an end to the SED's monopoly on power. Echoing Modrow but moving beyond him, Kohl proposed a treaty community to work out inter-German issues, to be followed, after East German elections, by a confederal structure and, eventually, a federal system for all Germany. Finally, perhaps in a nod to Genscher, the process would evolve in the context of "all-European development." There would be gradual progress toward reunification, both internationally and between the two Germanies, but he set no timetable for it. Kohl's surprise proposal rippled across the Germanies, Europe, and beyond, sparking irritated criticism—partly because it was only ten days since the Paris EC meeting, at which Kohl had assured his colleagues that there should be no discussion of changing borders.

GEORGE BUSH

Afraid of leaks, or perhaps of being talked out of it, Kohl informed none of the NATO allies—including us—of the speech beforehand. This was probably the main source of the criticism. He kept Genscher in the dark as well, and told him only that afternoon. I was surprised, but not too worried. He couldn't pursue reunification on his own, and I doubted he would want to alienate his closest ally. I was certain he would consult us before going further—he needed us. Kohl did have a text delivered to me as the speech was given in Bonn, and he sent a lengthy message, couched as a discussion of Malta. It was clear he wanted to be sure that Gorbachev and I did not come to our own agreement on Germany's future, as had Stalin and Roosevelt in the closing months of World War II.

BRENT SCOWCROFT

I was concerned by Kohl's unexpected announcement. I thought we had been close to him, had consulted with him every step of the way, and deserved his confidence. If he was prepared to go off on his own whenever he worried that we might object, we had very little influence. Suppose, for example, it came to the point that he decided he could get unification only by trading it for neutrality? We were a long way from anything like that, but Kohl's unilateral move did not, for me, necessarily bode well for the future.

GEORGE BUSH

The morning after his speech, I called Helmut, who described the situation in the GDR. The East German people, he said, were "shocked and disappointed at the corruption" that they were beginning to discover as they gained greater access to government records. "In a nutshell, things have changed a great deal. Therefore it is important that the reform process keep going." Kohl confidently predicted free elections in the GDR by the autumn of 1990 or the beginning of 1991. "I believe the process has reached a stage that makes it irreversible. One reason is that they cannot avoid a mass exodus if they do not reform."

Kohl also explained the meaning of his ten-point program, dividing it into three parts. "First, we must act with reason and caution. Everything in Central Europe and Germany will have enormous impact. For me personally, this means everything I do will be coordinated with our American friends. The second point is the will of the [East German] people, what they desire. Public reporting on the news gives a distorted picture. It will become clear after the elections. It will be the same as in Poland. If there are genuine elections, they will throw out all in the government. Third, it will be a long-term process. They [the GDR] will remain in the Pact, and we in NATO. The security dimensions are of great importance. . . ."

He hastened to assure me that he was aware of his responsibilities. He promised to consult not only with us, but also with the EC. "A week from now, in Strasbourg [at an EC summit], I will see to it that we make progress with respect to the Economic and Monetary Union. I think it is a great mistake on Maggie's part to think that this is a time for caution. It is an iron law that there will be no going alone in German policy. It is our responsibility that we are anchored in a general whole."

BRENT SCOWCROFT

Two things struck me about this conversation, one at the time and one in retrospect. The first was that Kohl over and over again expressed his solidarity with the United States and the allies and pledged that there would be no going it alone—only one day after he had, in fact, "gone it alone." Second, even at this point he envisaged a process which was likely to extend over a number of years: "They will remain in the Pact and we in NATO." He was certainly not yet out in front of the process as it was developing.

GEORGE BUSH

Brian Mulroney gave me his impressions of Gorbachev's attitude toward the German situation over dinner on November 29, also part of our pre-Malta consultations. At Moscow he had relayed my message that I would not posture on the Wall. He told me that Gorbachev was concerned that Kohl was trying to make "end runs" around the allies. His sense of Gorbachev's view was that "the Germans could forget about reunification." Brian had noticed what he called the Russian "hatred for the Germans." He had told Gorbachev that to understand Kohl he had to understand that the Chancellor was appealing to his electorate. Gorbachev responded that he understood, but there would be no reunification. "People have died eating unripened fruit," he warned. There might one day be reunification, Gorbachev had said, but, in effect, "not in my lifetime." If the Germans wanted progress toward reunification, they should not prematurely put it on the table.

In the Soviet Union, Shevardnadze responded to Kohl's plan by complaining that the acceleration of events was causing confusion, warning that it could lead to "unforeseen consequences," and labeling it a "diktat" from Bonn. East Berlin was equally unenthusiastic. It rejected outright the suggestion of unity that might compromise an independent and socialist East Germany, despite Kohl's inclusion of Modrow's community of treaties in his ten points. While the East Germans would eagerly accept aid from Bonn, they objected to what they saw as meddling in their affairs.

BRENT SCOWCROFT

Kohl's ten points provided a basic approach to cooperation and possible reunification for the two Germanies, but from our perspective they ignored the international and security aspects, especially a united Germany's relationship to NATO and the issue of boundaries. It was important that Germany remain firmly within the alliance, not just because it was important to anchor that nation to the West and to assuage the fears of its neighbors, but also because it was crucial to NATO. Germany is the geographic center of the alliance and its second largest economy and military power. A Germany outside NATO would "gut" the alliance. Its membership was also important to the United States for practical reasons. Without Germany and our bases there, our military presence in NATO, and in Europe, would be difficult if not impossible to maintain.

We had been considering the international context of German reunification for several weeks, and Jim Baker and the State Department had drawn up four principles to frame our own approach to the issue. To be acceptable to the United States, unification must: respect the principle of self-determination no matter what the Germans chose; be consistent with Germany's membership in NATO and the EC; be gradual and peaceful and regard the interests of other Europeans; respect the principles of Helsinki regarding the inviolability of existing borders and allow the possibility of peaceful change. I thought the principles focused squarely on the issues Kohl had omitted. They supported him completely, however, as well as reunification. And they backed a slow, gradual process, which would ease British, French, and Soviet concerns. Baker outlined them in response to questions at a press conference on November 29, but we planned to introduce them formally in the President's speech on December 3, when he briefed the allies after Malta.

My own attitude was now evolving under the influence of two developments. The first was the steady deterioration of the situation in the GDR. The chances it could reach and sustain some sort of stability as a separate entity seemed to be increasingly remote. If an equilibrium with two Germanies could not be maintained, unification then became the most attractive—indeed the only—feasible approach to the crisis. The other factor was the disposition of the President. In our conversations he was increasingly outspoken in support of Kohl and unification. It appeared he had firmly made up his mind.

In December, popular pressures on the East German government to make good on its promises of reform continued unrelentingly. The people were pushing for free elections, and on December 1 the *Volkskammer* ended the Communists' monopoly on power. On December 3, the Politburo resigned and the government began to arrest many former officials amid charges of corruption and abuse of power. On December 6, Krenz quit as head of state. Despite these changes, unrest was growing— citizens attacked government buildings to seize records, which many feared would be destroyed to cover up evidence of wrongdoing. Soviet military installations were also attacked, alarming the Soviets enough to order their forces to take measures to protect themselves as necessary. We worried that the incidents could escalate to actions against the troops themselves. That, among other possible provocations, could trigger a violent Soviet response—and an international crisis. On December 9, a beleaguered East German Communist Party congress, meeting to decide what steps to take to placate the populace, predictably backed confederation between two independent and sovereign Germanies.

GEORGE BUSH

At Malta, in early December, Gorbachev and I had only a brief discussion of Germany, but we did exchange attitudes and perspectives, mainly against the background of events throughout Eastern Europe. Leaving Malta, I flew to Brussels to brief our allies. I felt it was important to reassure them there was to be no US-Soviet condominium, no Yalta-style deal on Eastern Europe.

The evening I arrived in Brussels, over a dinner at the elegant Château Stuyvenberg, I finally had a chance for the talk Kohl and I had promised each other since late summer. We were accompanied by Brent and Sununu on the American side and Horst Teltschik and Walter Neuer for the West Germans.

I laid out for Helmut my support for German reunification, but warned him that Gorbachev thought that he was in too much of a hurry and that Moscow opposed his ten-point plan. Helmut filled me in on the latest developments in Germany.

"Can I tell you what happened today in the GDR?" asked Kohl eagerly, leaning forward, his eyes bright. "Everyone has resigned. There is a crisis supposedly in just running the government. The people want to know about special privileges being given to the leaders. That is only the beginning. In Rostock people broke into a factory and found arms there. They will want to know where the arms were going." He had told Gorbachev no one wanted events in East Germany to get out of control, which is why he had proposed his plan in the first place, but with no timetable. Gorbachev had said he would not stand in the way of free elections. "He has abandoned the old leadership," said Kohl confidently.

He thanked me for my "calm reception" of his program, and declared that European integration and NATO alliance membership were essential to the future Germany. "We are part of Europe and continue as part of the EC," he said flatly. He always carefully consulted with Mitterrand on such matters. "Ten points is *not* an alternative to what we are doing in the West." What his neighbors were really afraid of was that the Germans might drift to the East (meaning develop closer ties to

Moscow at the expense of the West)—which was nonsense—as well as the rapid development of Germany, faster than the rest of Western Europe. "Frankly, sixty-two million prosperous Germans are difficult to tolerate—add seventeen million more and they have big problems," he admitted.

Kohl speculated about what might happen next. After free elections in the GDR, the next step would be confederation between two independent states. The third phase, federation—a single state—would be realized "only in years, perhaps five," and would occur only with the agreement of Germany's neighbors. It could be stretched out, but he could not say that it would never happen.

I told Helmut that a way through the issue had to be found that did not alarm Gorbachev, yet kept the West together. "Gorbachev's problem is uncertainty," I said. "I don't want to say he went ballistic about it—he was just uneasy. We need a formulation that doesn't scare him, but moves forward."

"That's one reason I will do nothing to disturb the smooth running course," Kohl responded in reassuring tones. "[Helsinki] says borders *can* be changed by peaceful means. I don't want to put Gorbachev in a corner. I need to meet with him. I don't want to create difficulties. Newspapers write such nonsense!" Even Kissinger, he said, mentioned unification in two years. That was not possible. The economic imbalance between the Germanies was too great.

I think Kohl was hoping for the earliest possible reunification, but he wanted to do or say nothing that would imperil it. He was acutely aware of the problems Gorbachev was facing over the changes in Eastern Europe and now in East Germany. He did not want to exacerbate the situation. In addition, he recognized the European sensitivity to a huge, unified, and economically powerful Germany in their midst. For these reasons he was still walking lightly. I probably conveyed to Kohl that I had no objections to reunification, and in a sense gave him a green light. I don't think I ever contemplated cautioning him about going too fast. As I had told Gorbachev, and both Kohl and Genscher, self-determination was the key, and no one could object to it.

BRENT SCOWCROFT

In my view, this meeting with Kohl marked a turning point. There seemed a perfect conjunction of the minds on reunification, and the atmosphere of comradeship in a great venture was palpable to me. The easygoing discussion seemed to give Kohl the confidence, almost visible to me at the time, that he had the President behind him. Kohl, in his memoir of reunification, also points to this meeting as an important moment.

GEORGE BUSH

On the following morning I briefed the allies on Malta and in the afternoon I gave an address on "the future shape of Europe and the new Atlanticism." I reminded the other NATO leaders that

> "the alliance was established . . . to provide the basis for precisely the extraordinary evolution which is occurring in Eastern Europe today. . . . The task before us is to consolidate the fruits of this peaceful revolution and provide the architecture for continued peaceful change. . . . Our governments committed themselves again in May to seek an end to the painful division of Europe. We have never accepted this division. The people of every nation have the right to determine their own way of life in freedom."

I spelled out our four principles which should guide reunification, to which we had added that it should occur with "due regard for the legal role and responsibilities of the allied powers." I hoped this would help reassure Britain and France as well as the Soviet Union that their concerns would be addressed. I called for NATO to make the promotion of greater freedom in the East a basic element of the alliance, recalling that it was formed as a political structure, a foundation it should build upon for the future.

BRENT SCOWCROFT

After President Bush finished, Kohl spoke up, generously saying that no one could have done a better job of summarizing the alliance approach. He added that the President's remarks should be held as the final word of the alliance on the subject and called for immediate adjournment. After an awkward silence, Prime Minister Andreotti spoke up, warning that self-determination, if taken too far, could get out of hand and cause trouble. What if tomorrow the Baltics asserted their sovereignty? Furious, Kohl shot back that Andreotti might not share that view if the Tiber divided his country. Following this heated exchange, Lubbers backed the US approach. Thatcher said she shared Andreotti's concerns, and wanted to study the proposal more carefully. The other leaders generally supported the US framework.

While the Germans were greatly pleased, Thatcher was not happy. She agreed that a united Germany should be part of NATO, but she objected

to the idea that it should be accompanied by "an increasingly integrated European Community," a concept she was known to dislike.

Thatcher later wrote that she realized her options for slowing reunification were narrowing "once it was decided that East Germany could join the European Community without detailed negotiation [meaning through West Germany's own membership] . . . there was little we could do to slow down reunification via the Community's institutions." She hoped that the Four Powers framework would allow her some leverage, but she understood that, "with the United States—and soon the Soviets too—ceasing to regard this as anything more than a talking shop for discussion of the details of reunification" there was little chance Britain could influence the process there either. She renewed her effort to rally the French to a joint effort to stop or at least slow down the Germans, privately meeting with Mitterrand twice at the Strasbourg EC summit on December 8, and then again in January. The two could not decide on a course of action.* Mitterrand and Kohl also met at Strasbourg. Mitterrand asked his German colleague whether reunification was now more important to Bonn than European integration. Kohl avoided answering directly.

GEORGE BUSH

On December 16, I met with Mitterrand on the Caribbean island of Saint Martin, the reciprocal visit to his stay at Kennebunkport in May. As with Gorbachev, we spoke little about Germany, but François did emphasize that what happened in Germany must be linked with NATO and the EC. It seemed to me that, in contrast to the efforts within the French bureaucracy, he was resigned to eventual German unity. He urged we all approach the matter as friends. "We should show understanding over what the Germans wish. There is not much we can do because we are not going to war against Germany." But he cautioned against events in Germany moving too fast, fearing it would cause a crisis at a time when the West was winning hands down. Instead, we had to address arms control, EC integration, European monetary union, and US-EC cooperation all at the same time in order to create a new Europe. "Otherwise," he warned, "we will be back in 1913 and we could lose everything. We are friends of Germany. They can't take our advice amiss."

Since World War II, France and West Germany had overcome the hostility of the past and had become partners in Europe. Mitterrand and

*See *The Downing Street Years* (HarperCollins, 1993), p. 796.

Kohl themselves were friends. Nevertheless, German reunification raised complicated questions about the future for the French, ones with uncertain and uneasy answers. France and Germany had been the chief rivals for the domination of continental European affairs since the first unification of Germany in 1871, forged in the aftermath of French defeat in the Franco-Prussian War. Since then Germany had invaded twice more and had occupied much of France from 1940 to 1944. A divided Germany was not unwelcome. Paris had worked to manage West Germany through close economic and political ties (France had become West Germany's principal trading partner) and partnership in NATO. What effect would a united Germany have on Europe and what did that mean for France? Could it "control" such a state as it had its western part?

The Soviets, meanwhile, were anxious to find ways to direct any talk of reunification into entities they could still influence. On November 30, Gorbachev had proposed Helsinki II and a CSCE summit to discuss the matter in the broad context of changes in Eastern Europe. The French and British showed some interest in the suggestion, as did Genscher. Kohl was cool to it. Within the Administration, State was open to the notion, but the NSC was opposed to injecting German reunification into a CSCE summit, which should be convened *only* to seal a CFE treaty. Besides, the consensus requirements of CSCE would allow opponents of reunification to block it. Fortunately, Gorbachev did not press the idea.

The Soviets next turned to the Allied Four Powers structures. On December 8 they called for a Four Power meeting in Berlin, the first since 1971. Once again, the British and French responded with some enthusiasm and appeared nearly as eager as the Soviets to remind the Germans of their Four Power prerogatives. Our inclination was to decline outright: such Yalta-style intervention in the situation violated German self-determination and was exactly what we were trying to avoid. The Soviets, however, insisted that there could be violence in the GDR, in which case they "would be obliged to use force." We were sufficiently concerned about what they might do that we were not prepared to be obdurate about a meeting. We consented to one, but insisted that discussion be limited to Berlin Four Power rights and similar existing agreements— reunification was not to be on the agenda. The now-defused meeting took place on December 10 and no damage was done. Moscow tried several more times to divert discussion of the topic to a Four Power conference, but we were able to deflect each attempt.

On December 19, Shevardnadze laid out a new Soviet position in a speech to the European Parliament. He warned against changing the reality of two German states, yet he seemed prepared to support some kind of confederation—if certain matters were addressed. He listed seven broad questions, along with follow-up on each. What were the guarantees that German unity would not create a threat to the national security of other states and to peace in Europe? Would unified Germany be willing to recognize the existing borders in Europe and renounce any territorial claims whatsoever? What place would unified Germany take in the alliance structures of Europe? "For one cannot seriously think the status of the GDR will change while the status of the FRG will remain as it was." What would be its military doctrine, and would it be prepared to take steps toward demilitarization, to adopt a neutral status and radically restructure its economic and other ties with Eastern Europe? Would Allied troops remain on German soil? How would it fit into the Helsinki process? Finally, how prepared were the German states to consider the interests of other European states and, on a collective basis, to seek mutually acceptable solutions for all issues and problems which might arise, including a European peace settlement?

BRENT SCOWCROFT

Shevardnadze was underscoring Moscow's primary concern: reunification, if it came, must not compromise Soviet security. He was also hinting at the kind of outcome the Kremlin might accept: a united Germany either out of NATO or disarmed and neutralized. While we shared some of his concerns—such as German guarantees of their borders and their commitment to consult with their European neighbors as we collectively solved the problems surrounding reunification—changes in alliance membership and potential German neutrality were another matter.

GEORGE BUSH

Although at the time I did not focus too closely on this speech and the questions posed, they were the kind of concerns I knew the factions within the Soviet leadership must be wrestling with among themselves. We had to take their worries seriously and respond to them. Gorbachev had already acquiesced to so much change elsewhere in Eastern Europe, over the objections of conservatives in the military and the Party. It was possible that the unification of Germany, if not handled properly, could go beyond what they were prepared to accept.

I knew that if we were to see progress on reunification, it would be our role to work with Moscow as an equal on the issue, to show Gorbachev that without a doubt we understood the enormous problems that a united

Germany could cause the Soviet Union. While it was important that we keep up pressure on the Soviets for progress on the problems surrounding reunification, including Four Power responsibilities, we shouldn't press so hard that they would react negatively. If events went terribly wrong, and there was violence, we were the ones who would have to do something about it.

CHAPTER 9

A Careful Dance

BRENT SCOWCROFT

As 1990 began, we were cautiously optimistic. We looked back on a year filled with breathtaking, historic changes in Eastern Europe and saw ourselves on the threshold of opportunity. Perhaps we could achieve a fundamental shift in the strategic balance. Communist power was decaying, altering the assumptions which had underlain US-Soviet relations for decades. The President's frank talks with Gorbachev at Malta had boosted our relationship with the Soviet Union and had begun to put all this on the table. It seemed a good start.

Our policy objectives for the new year were pragmatic: to follow up on the progress at Malta and prepare the ground for a late spring summit in Washington. In practical terms, this meant further work on arms control, regional questions, and economic ties. There was also our unilateral agenda to pursue. We wanted to encourage the further withdrawal of Soviet troops from Eastern Europe. This would entail careful negotiations for conventional-force reductions, which were already in progress in Vienna. Then there was Germany. We would have to try to overcome resistance in order to solve the problems surrounding reunification and move the process forward.

These plans were tempered by the reality of domestic Soviet politics, for we could not be certain how long the window of opportunity would remain open. With such promise in the air and so much work remaining, it was in our interest to do what we could to prolong the tenure of Gorbachev and the Soviet reformers, men who through perestroika and glasnost had set these changes in motion. We believed that the Soviets would be anxious to keep improving relations, for foreign policy failures would only worsen Gorbachev's political troubles at home. We had to move quickly and carefully to make the most of the favorable climate before

Gorbachev left, or was forced from, the scene. We sensed we were run-ning against a clock, but we did not know how much time was left.

1990 promised to be another difficult year for Gorbachev. Problems were mounting, including challenges to the Party monopoly on power, as well as doubts about the ability of the command economy to adapt to the fundamental changes facing it. Beyond the events in Eastern Europe and Germany, nationalism within the Soviet Union exacerbated its security problems and threatened its political stability. Azerbaijan and Armenia were fighting among themselves, and the Baltics were pushing to leave the Union. The situation was also sensitive in economically important Ukraine, where there were strikes and secessionist rumblings. These upheavals could be Gorbachev's undoing, for the Russian population seemed to be beginning to view him as ineffective and indecisive in deal-ing with the turmoil. At the same time, his hesitation to use force led many nationalist ethnic groups to regard him as their best hope of reach-ing their own goal—independence.

Of the internal turbulence, the states which most concerned us, and which would most affect the US-Soviet relationship in the coming months, were the Baltics. Their national aspirations symbolized the self-determination we supported throughout Eastern Europe and Germany.

The Baltics were an emotional issue for us. They were different from any other Soviet republic or Eastern European state. Notwithstanding their incorporation into the Soviet Union in 1940 (which we had never recognized), we had allowed them to maintain diplomatic legations in Washington representing the old states. Feelings ran high within our Baltic-American population, putting well-organized and vocal political pressure on the Administration and Congress to provide active support for independence. We thought we had arrived at a kind of informal un-derstanding with Gorbachev at Malta on the issue, and President Bush had explained that we had limits on what we could tolerate. Gorbachev seemed to understand that it was important he exercise great restraint and not resort to force.

Baltic nationalists had continued to challenge Soviet authority over the summer of 1989 and into the winter. In December, the Lithuanian Communist Party had split from the national Party in Moscow. On Janu-ary 11, Gorbachev made a heavily publicized trip to Vilnius to try to convince the government and the people to turn aside from the indepen-dence route. It was the first time a Soviet leader had visited Lithuania. Amid substantial international TV coverage, he valiantly and conspicu-ously plunged into hostile crowds to appeal for unity. In one of his most visible efforts at personal diplomacy, he struck out completely. The international aura of Gorbachev, the can-do manager and leader, was tarnished. As he returned empty-handed to Moscow, new troubles erupted elsewhere. Anti-Armenian riots broke out in the Azerbaijan capital, Baku, with violence spreading through that republic and Armenia. Within a few days over thirty people were dead. By January 14, both republics were mobilizing troops. Moscow sent in Interior Ministry forces, but they proved inadequate. On January 20, Gorbachev dispatched Defense Minister Dmitri Yazov to Azerbaijan. Yazov ordered regular army troops into Baku to try to separate the factions and occupy the city. Bitter fighting took place and some reports put the dead at several hundred.

BRENT SCOWCROFT

We strongly supported self-determination as a matter of principle, as we were doing regarding German reunification. As a practical point, however, we were aware of Gorbachev's vulnerability to the political threat posed by nationalism. The people within the Party who most strongly opposed him on this issue were not those we would wish to see replacing him. Gorbachev's own political fortunes notwithstanding, Shevardnadze reiterated over and over that, should the Soviets use force, it would mean the destruction of perestroika. But we all believed there was some point at which Gorbachev would send troops, if only to save his position. If that meant the end of perestroika, we would lose the principal advantage of Gorbachev's presence.

GEORGE BUSH

I felt caught between my desire to back self-determination and the reality of the situation. If we exhorted change, our rhetoric might produce a military backlash and set back the cause of freedom throughout the Soviet Union rather than move it forward—and we could do nothing to stop what we had helped set in motion. I tried to find a balance, speaking out for dialogue and perestroika, but my caution prompted criticism. I took a great deal of flak in the press, from leaders in the US Baltic communities, and from "experts," that I was too accommodating, accepting Gorbachev's "new thinking" and reforms at face value. I was acutely aware of the dangers, but my experience with Gorbachev at Malta, and Baker's excellent relationship with Shevardnadze, made me confident that Gorbachev was sincere in his efforts to match his words with actions.

I was eager to follow up on the Malta talks. Arms control—which would be the heart of the summit Gorbachev and I had agreed would take place before the end of June—was especially important. In December and January, I again began to push within the Administration for bolder proposals on strategic-arms and conventional-force reductions. It takes a long time to close deals, and I was frustrated with the growing pessimism among my arms-control team as to whether we could get START finished in time for the summit, and worried that Congress, pointing to the changes in Eastern Europe, would legislate premature cuts in conventional forces below levels I thought wise.

BRENT SCOWCROFT

The President made clear that he wanted to take charge of the agenda and try to shape events rather than be shaped by them. His approach could hardly have been farther from his public image of caution. There were rumors that the Soviets were about to make fresh proposals for additional conventional reductions and the President wanted to announce a new US position in his State of the Union address on January 31. He asked me to set up NSC discussions on the matter.

I led off in the first meeting in the Cabinet Room on January 4. The question on START, I explained, was whether we should stick to the now three-year-old proposal we had inherited and get it signed as fast as possible, or modify it to reflect recent developments. Add-ons would slow it down and potentially interfere with strategic programs in the defense budget. Moreover, the Soviets might get upset and could derail things. Baker, Cheney, and I were split on the answer. Cheney argued that the Soviets had not changed. "We should take what's on the table and run," he said. "It defines the state of the relationship and there is a political dynamic involved in getting the agreement." We'd have enough trouble resolving the remaining issues as it was without adding new modifications. "Let's resolve the issues and get the deal. We can do the rest in START II." I pointed out that there were reasons to modify START I, such as budget constraints on our existing programs and the fact that the Soviets were deploying new systems. The Soviets would soon see that Congress was going to cut our defense anyway, and we'd have no leverage to stop them. Baker agreed with Cheney. "We've gone too far to reopen START I now," he said. "We should have done it earlier. Political dynamics are more important than the strategic [issues]." Powell supported Dick and Jim.

The President did not see why people were so pessimistic about getting a treaty in the next six months. "What's stopping us?" he asked. "The Soviets are open, let's talk to them. I'm worried that the world is in change, demonstrable change. The Congress is going to take this and screw us up. This is the opportunity to get something from the Soviets."

The discussion turned to conventional forces, where the question was similar and related to the changes in Europe. "Do we proceed as is or do we make an additional proposal on personnel?" I asked. I suggested we approach our allies and urge we negotiate a bilateral cut to 200,000. This would also get ahead of the Congress so as to be able to sustain the troop level we wanted. "Then we would go to the Soviets and propose a simple deal of going to two hundred thousand," I said. "Nothing else would be added."

Again, the President and I were in the minority. Baker's position was "don't rock the boat"—stick with what we had. We could talk quietly to the alliance leaders about a bottom line of 200,000 in follow-on negotiations. It was obvious he was after a successful negotiation and wanted no complications that might slow down agreement.

Cheney reminded us that he had to calm fears among our allies over uncertainty about US troop reductions. "The East Europeans, the Soviets, the West Europeans all want us to [keep troops there]. Everybody but the Congress," he said. He added that the intelligence community was saying the Warsaw Pact was now irrelevant, that it no longer had any offensive capability. "This only gives us a bigger problem on the Hill," Dick warned.

The President was getting irritated with the reluctance to revise our proposals. "Isn't this good news?" he asked. "So we sit here with two hundred seventy-five thousand troops, and no reaction to Soviet actions. The world is changing and we're going to change with it . . . Why do we always need the same number of troops and bombs? We should test the Soviets. Ask them to do something we think they'll never do [make asymmetrical cuts]. Otherwise we'll pass up the opportunity, be cut unilaterally by the Congress, and get nothing for it. We shouldn't be seen as begrudging change but acting boldly. We have an enormous opportunity to do something dramatically different."

The discussion resumed on January 16. The battle lines remained unchanged and the debate had more of an edge to it. The President was getting impatient. Why couldn't he get a proposal? He kept reminding us that we had to find something to advance our security and our political interests simultaneously. "Why is going to two hundred thousand so complicated?" Cheney made plain his attitude toward arms control: "Arms control is in the way of arms reduction. The Soviets have big problems. At the same time it's hard for us to get out of Europe. Why negotiate for further reductions? It just creates problems for the allies," he argued, to which Herres* added, "Arms control can't keep up with the political process." By this point somewhat exasperated, the President

*Air Force General Robert Herres, vice chairman of the Joint Chiefs of Staff.

tartly observed, "That's what I am trying to fix." Tempers were rising. When Baker repeated that the proposal would complicate relations with our allies, I rejoined, "Why not find out instead of pontificating about it?" As the meeting wound down, the President asked how we could shape a proposal if we didn't know what the allies thought. I urged that we sound out our allies on further cuts. If we did not reach agreement, we would not move ahead. "But give the allies the option and we get ahead of both the Congress and the allies."

By the time of our decision meeting on January 22, the situation had changed significantly. In the interim, I had asked Jim Woolsey* to chat with his German counterpart to ascertain how the Germans might react to additional cuts. Woolsey reported a positive response. He added that the East Europeans were urging greater reductions in Warsaw Pact forces in order to get Soviet troops out of the region, which was our main goal anyway. They were concerned that the higher levels would be used by the Soviets as an excuse not to draw down. Powell, who had just returned from Europe, believed that the Germans would support further cuts, although it might take a call to Kohl from the President, while the British would oppose and the French would be uneasy. There was great nervousness in Europe—East and West—about a Germany without US and Soviet troops, but, he said, all were expecting levels significantly lower than current levels.

That was the news the President had been hoping for. "This would be a big step along the lines of Brent's proposal," he said. Cheney read the tea leaves. "I can feel the sand easing out of my position," he remarked. He agreed we should be working to get the Soviet military out of Eastern Europe, but he was worried about "linkage"—efforts to reduce US and Soviet forces to equal levels in Europe, and that the size of any reduction on one side had to be matched by the other side. This was also called "parallelism" and "symmetry." We wanted to break this cycle, not only because we hoped to keep US forces in Central Europe (the "central zone," which meant Germany) while the Soviets withdrew, but because we had forces elsewhere on the continent that we didn't want to be counted in the same totals. Cheney acknowledged that he and Powell would have a problem with Congress regardless of what levels were set. "It's hard for us to argue against the proposal if the allies feel the way they do," he added. We discussed how to break the linkage between US and Soviet levels and what totals we should seek. The group eventually settled on 195,000 for the central zone, excluding another 30,000 US

*Our CFE negotiator in Vienna.

troops elsewhere in Western Europe. This would put the Soviets at 195,000 and us at 225,000.

This decision, and the process by which it was made, was typical of the way national security issues were worked through in the Bush Administration—strong men, expressing their views forcefully, under a President who joined the debate but sought to draw out the various arguments, not stifle them. Underlying it all was a sense of camaraderie that kept the discussion within bounds. When the President made the decision, debate ended immediately and attention turned to executing it.

The President observed that the next step was to get someone to explain to Thatcher, Kohl, and Mitterrand what we had in mind. Since he wanted to include the new CFE proposal in his State of the Union address on January 31, we had little time in which to do the necessary alliance consultations. The Eagleburger-Gates team had done the trick before, so he told "Tweedledum and Tweedledee" to saddle up again. The President called his foreign colleagues to pave the way for them.

GEORGE BUSH

On January 26, I phoned Helmut Kohl, who liked our proposal. He thought Thatcher would have problems with it, but Mitterrand would probably agree, if sufficiently consulted. "You know my old assessment," he joked. "Salute the flag of the FRG once, but the tricolor three times." I spoke with Mitterrand the next morning. He was interested, but deliberate in his reply. "But this approach [withdrawing troops] should not be confused with the neutralization of Germany, which is the Soviet objective," he said simply.

"Yes, of course," I replied. I asked if he was more worried now about the neutralization of Germany than when we had last talked. "I think there is a drive to reunification which the West Germans want and the East Germans are not resisting very much," Mitterrand replied carefully. "If, by the end of the year, we have elected parliaments on both sides that have [reunification] as their program, then there could be a great popular movement in favor of ridding Germany of all foreign troops and nuclear weapons. That is the only risk, and it is a major one. But I think it can be contained. I think your decision to go ahead with a hundred and ninety-five thousand is a good one, provided it is accompanied by a speech in which this idea is set forth. We cannot allow the neutralization of Germany."

When I called Margaret, she cut to the point, immediately demonstrating her grasp of the nuances involved. "Are you talking only about stationed troop levels in Europe?" she asked. "So the Soviets will fulfill their obligation of withdrawing from Eastern Europe by taking these troops behind or in front of the Urals?" She had long worried about the Soviets removing their troops from Eastern Europe but leaving them fully mobilized west of the Ural mountains. I explained we were talking about demobilization, not simply moving them. She seemed interested in the possibilities. "Fewer stationed troops in Eastern Europe might be helpful to the Soviets back in the Soviet Union," she observed.

Margaret folded our CFE proposal, reunification, and German neutrality into the larger terms of their strategic effect on NATO. "What worries me," she said, "is that it looks like we're being hustled, with piecemeal changes retiring [sic] fast from the NATO position without any political assessment of the new position we find ourselves in, especially in light of the political possibilities for German reunification. I have a telegram that says Kohl now wants reunification to occur by 1994. We should have a political assessment of the situation in Central Europe, with German reunification, and the effect on NATO strategy, and not piecemeal decisions on the withdrawal of troops. . . ."

She explained that she was discussing the political situation and what it meant to NATO with her foreign and defense secretaries. "We have our pledge to NATO with significant troops, and we have this [anti-] nuclear [problem] in Germany," she said. ". . . I don't want to be accused of proceeding without a fundamental assessment *between us*—only our two countries can do this without it leaking—without looking at our over-all defense strategy." Foreign Secretary Douglas Hurd was due to meet with us in Washington that same day, and she told me Hurd would detail her thinking.

I agreed with her argument, but reminded her there had been enormous changes since we had set the old CFE numbers. We had to take advantage of the situation, and I was convinced that meant decreased troop levels. We were simply reducing our forces to a point that could be politically sustained in Congress and still be supported by our allies in Europe. "There are a lot of weirdos [in Congress] who have all sorts of crazy ideas," I said. "Many of them do not want any of our troops in Europe at all. I'm proposing a level that will reduce the Soviet threat, lower our defense requirements, but not cause the alliance to unravel because of the important questions you raise." She agreed to see Eagleburger and Gates to discuss the matter.

It was clear Margaret still feared the worst from reunification and, like Mitterrand, worried that the Germans might "go neutral" and refuse to permit stationing nuclear weapons on their soil. She undoubtedly had in mind the wave of anti-nuclear protests that had swept across Germany when the alliance agreed to station intermediate-range nuclear missiles there. She would need a lot of convincing. For my part, it seemed pretty clear reunification was on its way and we had to work with it. By the end of January, with the inability of the East German government to regain control of its affairs, I had accepted it as inevitable and welcomed it. Furthermore, I trusted Kohl not to lead the Germans down a special, separate path.

BRENT SCOWCROFT

I believed Thatcher was motivated by two primary considerations. The first was that it was unlikely that fundamental change in the strategic challenge was taking place and we therefore should not modify tried-and-true defense policies as if it were. The second reflected her strategic cast of mind. She did not think we should be dealing with issues like reunification and CFE on separate tracks when everything we faced was interrelated. We should instead sit down together and map out a comprehensive strategy before making decisions on discrete elements of the current scene. There was great merit in her position. We had interconnected all the elements of a strategy for ourselves, and to some extent bilaterally with the British, but it was difficult to do multilaterally in the alliance. Thatcher's comment about our two countries working out a strategic assessment together may have been a move to shore up the special relationship. It never occurred to me at the time, however, that this was necessary. I doubt that there had been many periods when the relationship between the US and Britain was more open, intuitively close, and productive.

I was less sanguine than the President that reunification was inevitable or that it would take place in a satisfactory manner. It was still possible the Soviets would conclude that a united Germany was intolerable and oppose it, by force if necessary. Or they would successfully impose conditions on its taking place which would render it unacceptable to us. There was much other practical work to be done as well. The four wartime Allies had residual legal rights and responsibilities that had to be resolved. We also had to look to the question of European political and security order after the Cold War and unification. We had a great deal of sophisticated diplomacy ahead of us.

We launched Eagleburger and Gates on their missionary circuit on January 28, with London as the first—and most difficult—stop. Thatcher greeted them at 10 Downing Street, inviting them to "take their accustomed chairs." At the end of a long and searching conversation, in which Thatcher manifested a daunting familiarity with US deployments in Europe, it became apparent that, while not happy, she would acquiesce in what we wished to do. As this staunch ally cordially bade the two emissaries goodbye, she said they would always be welcome there, "but never again on this subject." The other stops were uneventful, and the team returned with consensus support from our allies.

GEORGE BUSH

With the allies on board, I called Gorbachev on January 31 to fill him in on the proposal, which I planned to announce in the State of the Union address that evening. Once again I told him that the United States intended to keep a substantial military presence in Europe. "I hope you recognize that the US presence makes a helpful and important contribution to European stability," I said, echoing the point I had made at Malta. "The main thing is that we want to conclude the CFE agreement. I do not want this new proposal to delay our negotiations in any way. But my experts think it is possible to accommodate this change and have an agreement that is a little more in line with current conditions."

Gorbachev said he shared my approach. "As I understand it, your proposal envisions a new and lower ceiling," he said thoughtfully. "You have emphasized that the United States will maintain its military presence in Europe after the negotiations are complete. If I understand you, this is regardless of what the Soviet Union does." I confirmed that it was.

"We'll give it some thought," said Gorbachev. "But let me say that we will need to talk about the central zone of Europe and other zones. We'll need to talk not just about US and Soviet forces but other forces. Baker and Shevardnadze will have a lot to do. You and I need to talk too. You can expect our cooperation — our constructive cooperation. And you can be assured that my response means that I am happy that we are keeping in touch [in order] to look at the most important problems today. I fully expect you will get more detailed answers from me or when Baker is in Moscow." Jim was due in Moscow at the beginning of February.

February and March brought new upheavals in the Soviet Union, with major institutional changes to the Soviet political structure, and elections to city councils and the parliaments of Russia, Byelorussia, and Ukraine. On February 4, there was a huge demonstration in Moscow in support of democracy, with up to 300,000 taking part. The next day, at a Central Committee plenum, Gorbachev challenged the Communist Party to give up one-party control of the country in favor of a multiparty system and "democratic socialism." He called for additional economic reforms, a reduction in the size of the Central Committee, and a new, Western-style presidency. In effect, he was asking the Party to surrender absolute control. On February 7, just as Baker was arriving in Moscow for his talks with Shevardnadze, the Party assented, after bitter and divisive debate. On February 12, the presidium of the Supreme Soviet called for a special session of the Congress of People's Deputies, for the purpose of increasing the powers of the presidency. Two weeks later came another large pro-democracy demonstration in Moscow, with up to 100,000 people, and there were reports that Army and KGB troops had surrounded the city. On February 27, the Supreme Soviet voted to institute the more powerful presidency Gorbachev wanted. The Congress of People's Deputies approved the legislation on March 13, and also formally nullified Article 6 of the Soviet constitution, which had enshrined the Party's role in governing the country.

To add to the Party's reverses at the center, elections on March 19 brought humiliation locally. In Lithuania, the nationalist Popular Front won overwhelmingly, and Communist candidates were also defeated elsewhere. Boris Yeltsin, running for the Russian parliament, was victorious in Moscow. Nationalism was on the march, and the danger signals for Gorbachev had to be obvious. The elections would embolden the secessionist movements, especially in the Baltics, where the opposition candidates had done so well.

GEORGE BUSH

On March 7, Jim Baker brought a telegram from Jack Matlock in Moscow reporting on a conversation with Shevardnadze and forwarding a message from Gorbachev. Shevardnadze had said that the situation in Lithuania was now "critical." He warned of a possible military takeover, and of a general deterioration in the republics. Shevardnadze was worried about Gorbachev's political situation, and asked for our understanding. I was concerned, very concerned. We could not be in a position of opposing an independent Lithuania. On the other hand, if we pledged support the minute it declared independence, that might cause Gorbachev to fall, or the Soviet military to act on its own. If there was violence, realistically there was not a thing the United States could do about it, and we would have blood on our own hands for encouraging the Lithuanians to bite off more than they could chew. It was a worrisome picture.

Shevardnadze proved to be prophetic. On March 11, the Lithuanian Supreme Soviet proclaimed the restoration of the Lithuanian republic, electing Vytautas Landsbergis president. Gorbachev condemned the declaration as "illegitimate and invalid," and warned that there would be no negotiations. He vowed to maintain the political and territorial integrity of the Soviet Union and threatened military measures. The Congress of People's Deputies endorsed his position that there would be no recognition of Lithuanian independence. With this backing, Gorbachev, on March 16, the day after the Congress had reelected him president, issued an ultimatum to Landsbergis to revoke the declaration by March 19. He attempted to cow the Lithuanians with a show of force. Aircraft were sent in "on maneuvers," flying low over the rooftops of the capital and dropping propaganda leaflets.

GEORGE BUSH

These measures threatened the so far peaceful changes in Lithuania, and I feared they could be the forerunner of a crackdown that would set back not only US relations with the Soviet Union, but all of Europe's as well. I asked the NSC to prepare a list of options we might explore in case I decided we had to respond, although I did not want to raise military intervention. We did talk about canceling official visits and the summit (or at least delaying it), hoping it would not come to that.

BRENT SCOWCROFT

Pressure from the Congress, the press, and Baltic Americans to recognize Lithuania became very heavy. Even Senator Nancy Kassebaum, a good friend and the soul of reasonableness, phoned to urge that we take some action on recognition. At the other extreme was some very reckless Congressional posturing, a flagrant example of which was Senator Al D'Amato's provocative trip to the Lithuanian border. Congressional demands for recognition of Lithuania reached something of a peak on March 21, when a resolution calling for recognition, sponsored by Jesse Helms, reached the floor of the Senate. Fortunately, the mood was not as emotional as we had feared and the initiative failed, 59 to 36.

No one was more desirous of seeing the Baltics independent than we. We could have climbed on the bandwagon, recognized the Landsbergis government, and called for Lithuanian independence. It would have felt good and would have ended the barrage of criticism. Many critics said, then and now, that we did not recognize the new Lithuanian government because we were more interested in supporting Gorbachev than independence for the Baltic States. That criticism misses the central fact in this sensitive situation. The reality was that the only way the Baltic States could achieve lasting independence was with the acquiescence of the Kremlin. Our task was to bring Moscow to that point. The very worst way to do that was to confront and threaten the Soviets. Not only would we lose, but also the Baltics, Soviet reform, and possibly German reunification. As the President observed over and over, what could we do if the Soviets sent in tanks after we recognized the government? I knew we were right, but it was tough being denounced by the "feel good" crowd.

Gorbachev's March 19 ultimatum deadline passed without resolution of the crisis. The next day, Shevardnadze assured Baker at a meeting in Windhoek, Namibia, where they were attending a celebration of that country's independence, that the Soviets would not employ force but would rely on dialogue. He believed that Lithuania had gotten caught up in the euphoria of independence and had lost sight of the consequences: The Baltics were dependent on the rest of the Union for energy and raw materials. "[T]hey get a lot from us," he told Baker. "And they can't simply go it alone." Baker cautioned that if the Soviets did use coercion it would seriously affect relations. Shevardnadze responded that Gorbachev was under pressure from the military to crack down.

BRENT SCOWCROFT

That same day, I met with Soviet ambassador Dubinin in my office and delivered much the same message. It appeared that our freedom of maneuver was rapidly becoming restricted and, if the situation deteriorated further, rhetoric alone might not be sufficient to prevent an uncontrollable explosion in Lithuania.

Senator Edward Kennedy and former JCS chairman Admiral William Crowe each went to Moscow in March. Gorbachev told Kennedy that the Lithuanian decision to vote for independence was "a palace coup d'état." When Kennedy asked whether he rejected the use of force, Gorbachev pledged not to resort to force unless violence threatened the lives of others. Crowe met separately with Gorbachev and his advisor Marshal Sergei Akhromeyev, reporting on his talks through a cable from Matlock. When he saw the Marshal, who was a friend, he found him depressed by the developments around him:

> Said the Lithuanians could do what they want, but the Soviet leadership would not allow a single republic to leave. He stressed that the population would not tolerate Gorbachev giving in to Lithuania's demands for sovereignty, and that if pushed to the limit, Moscow would crush Lithuania. He said the government hoped to avoid such action, choosing instead to drag out the process by using a variety of laws and procedures to buy time.

Crowe said his impression was that Akhromeyev was being continually overruled on decisions and had become tired and disillusioned. "Akhromeyev told Crowe that he had supported Gorbachev because he believed in what Gorbachev was doing," read the cable. "Nevertheless, Akhromeyev emphasized that he had not realized the extent of dissatisfaction within the USSR. He stressed that the country was not ready for all the changes underway, adding that there were limits. On the Party: Akhromeyev spoke at length about the declining fortunes of the Party, noting that 'we wrecked it ourselves.' . . . He said this had shattered his heart hundreds of times. He expressed hope that it might be possible to put the Party back together again, but insisted that the old Party is now gone."

BRENT SCOWCROFT

Baker's and Crowe's discussions were stark evidence of the widening division in the circle around Gorbachev. His friend and ally in reform, Shevardnadze, was determined that Lithuania would be handled through dialogue (although he still would not speak of their independence). Akhromeyev, the senior military leader in the Soviet Union, was equally determined that the Baltics would never be allowed to leave the Union. But the Marshal's frame of mind and sorrow over the events he was witnessing were surely not unique among the "traditionalist" military and Party leadership. It appeared that opposition to Gorbachev's changes was stiffening.

GEORGE BUSH

On March 28, Margaret Thatcher offered some additional insight into how this political pressure was affecting Gorbachev, based on a telephone conversation she had had with him that day. She was deeply worried that he was not talking about peaceful solutions in Lithuania. In fact, when she pressed him to rule out the use of force, he was evasive. She thought it possible he was exaggerating the seriousness of the situation, but it had not sounded so to her. Margaret said Gorbachev had been "lonesome," somber, pessimistic, and felt he was under attack. He had made the point that he was attempting to put the country under the "rule of law" and such changes should come through the constitution—not through the unilateral action of the Lithuanian leaders. She said it was clear he thought he was getting no cooperation or understanding from the Lithuanians, which narrowed his options, and that after his upcoming meeting with them in the new created Federation Council he might have to take action.

I met with Brent, Sununu, Gates, and Jim Baker and we decided that I should send messages to both Gorbachev and Landsbergis. I had already written a letter to Gorbachev on March 21 about a proposal to include a ban on MIRVed missiles in START, but it did not refer to Lithuania. In a new letter I tried to say to him privately what I could not say publicly without putting him on the spot and probably tying his hands:

> Believe me when I tell you that the United States has no desire to exploit the Lithuanian situation for advantage of any kind. While, as you know, the United States has never recognized the incorporation of the Baltic States into the USSR, and we support self-determination for them, we have taken great care in our public statements to avoid inflaming the situation and have not criticized the Soviet government...
>
> This measured posture has led to growing criticism in this country, including from Congress, the press and even members of my own party, people sincere—as am I—in their sympathy for Lithuania's desire for independence. This criticism is, in fact, beginning to reduce my own flexibility.
>
> You told Prime Minister Thatcher that your options are narrowing. I sense increasing pessimism on your part about a peaceful outcome. Mr. President, in the spirit of genuine respect and indeed friendship, may I state that any outcome not based on peaceful discussions and accommodation poses real risks to what you have achieved, and hope to achieve, not only in our relations but in your relations with other countries in the West. Both you and Minister Shevardnadze have said to Jim Baker and to me that the use of force would also be a serious setback to reform. I believe the use of coercion would have similar consequences for your efforts. Perestroika cannot be divisible. Imposed or military rule in Lithuania, the inevitable result of the use of force or intimidation, is simply inconsistent with democratization elsewhere.
>
> Taking this all into account, is it not possible to draw back from confrontation, ultimatums and demands, and return to a calm atmosphere in which reasoned discussion can proceed? In his recent conversation with Jim Baker, Eduard Shevardnadze seemed to accept the principle of referendum for dealing with nationality questions. Dr. Landsbergis has now publicly stated that he would be ready to consider a referendum. Does this offer some common ground? . . . We want to help defuse the current situation in the hope your interests and the aspirations of the Lithuanian people can be reconciled through discussions. I am informally and indirectly also urging Dr. Landsbergis to draw back from actions and demands that contribute to confrontation.

BRENT SCOWCROFT

We debated whether to send a letter to Landsbergis. If it leaked, it would imply that the President was trying to rein in the Lithuanians. Since the issue was so sensitive, we did not want to pass a written message through the Lithuanian legation in Washington. Instead, we asked Senator Dick Lugar, a seasoned diplomat and member of the Foreign Relations Committee, to communicate it to the Lithuanians.

On March 31, Gorbachev offered to begin a dialogue with Landsbergis if the Lithuanians repealed their declaration of independence. Landsbergis insisted this was impossible, although the parliament declared it was willing to enter into negotiations.

The April meetings with Shevardnadze in Washington gave us a chance to confront the Soviet foreign minister over the situation. They were not productive discussions. Shevardnadze was defensive, both in the Oval Office and with Baker. Baker felt the difference was almost night and day from their February meetings in Moscow, when the Soviet delegation had agreed to a series of arms control proposals. It appeared that, in the interim, the military had clamped down on arms control decisions, for Shevardnadze's team now backed away from their February agreements. Shevardnadze was almost apologetic, saying they were under attack for making too many concessions. "So please be aware that some of our positions reflect an awareness of our political pressures as well." As for Lithuania, Baker reported that a major sticking point appeared to be Landsbergis's refusal to accede to Gorbachev's demand that they hold a meeting in Moscow. In addition, Shevardnadze seemed angry that the actions of the Lithuanian Supreme Soviet on March 11 had "come overnight," without a referendum or vote. Baker asked whether the Soviets would be receptive to a "suspension" of independence. Shevardnadze was not willing to discuss it.

Shevardnadze delivered Gorbachev's response to the President's March 21 letter on arms control—and his more personal message a few days later. Gorbachev was confident that we could set ourselves far-reaching goals in arms control and expect to achieve them:

> In order to advance effectively along this path we have to attach particular importance to the atmosphere of our dialogue and the mutual willingness to avoid unnecessary complication and artificial problems. I appreciate your realistic approach to the development of Soviet-US dialogue, your desire to understand the other side, to consider its interests and problems. This is how I regard your private letter to me of March 29, 1990. I want to reiterate that we intend to continue to follow the course of radically reshaping Soviet society on the basis of democratization and glasnost, active and serious dialogue, and building a truly law-governed state. It goes without saying that all this presupposes respect for constitutional order and safeguarding the rights and security of all citizens of our country.

It was a positive response, speaking of dialogue, although it was non-committal about the use of force.

GEORGE BUSH

In our conversations at the White House on April 6, Shevardnadze attempted to explain some of his government's difficulties. He tried to put part of the blame on legal technicalities. "The problem is our state structure has a fundamental principle that is different from yours," he said. "We are a union of fifteen sovereign states." The legal process had fallen behind the political one. While the Soviet constitution contained the right of republics to secede, no mechanism was established for such secession. The laws they had since adopted had come after Lithuania took its steps. "I have said and I wish to reiterate that our main weapon is dialogue," he said. "With any state that is true but particularly with our own people. Perestroika and democracy, the right to self-determination, these are all part of our program. Dialogue must be open, candid, and frank with our people and with our leadership." The new presidency was set up to handle the problems. Gorbachev wanted him to tell me "that he will adhere to the principles he has stated." I told Shevardnadze that dialogue was the only way and that we were strongly sympathetic to the Lithuanians. Although we had not recognized Lithuania, we must support their self-determination.

I wanted to trust Gorbachev at his word that there would be no violence, but it was difficult to interpret the contradictions we were seeing. Who was calling the shots? Later, I tried to get Shevardnadze to speak frankly about how much pressure Gorbachev was really under from the military, but I was disappointed that he was not direct. He admitted there were difficulties within the Party and that people were severely criticizing Gorbachev and himself for not being decisive enough. At a recent Party plenum, the Soviet ambassador to Poland, who was also a Central Committee member, had attacked Gorbachev and the leadership for their policies in Eastern Europe. Shevardnadze recounted the debate. He had defended perestroika, declaring that without it the result would be either anarchy or dictatorship. Anarchy would destabilize the Soviet Union and Europe, and not only Europe. Dictatorship would lead to tragedy. Shevardnadze insisted that the Soviet Union was not yet at a critical stage.

The hard-line elements of the Party increased the pressure on Gorbachev, perhaps emboldened to speak up by popular criticism of the changes in Eastern Europe and events in the Baltics. On April 9, the Presidential Council, saying that Lithuania's response to Gorbachev's March 30 telegram was insufficient, threatened further economic, political, and "other" measures against Lithuania. It appeared that Gorbachev had decided he could not let Lithuania go. A series of warnings by him and stubborn rejections by Landsbergis culminated in a threat on April 13 to embargo oil and gas supplies within forty-eight hours unless Lithuania withdrew its declaration of independence. Except for electricity, Lithuania was virtually entirely dependent on outside energy sources and the cutoff would be quickly felt throughout the population. The deadline came and went without action.

GEORGE BUSH

I shared my concern with Margaret Thatcher on April 16 when we met in Bermuda. "Gorbachev is on the horns of a real dilemma," I told her. ". . . When Shevardnadze was in Washington he was quite different. . . . I asked him if Gorbachev was getting pressure from the right and he recoiled as if I had crossed the line. If Gorbachev doesn't get out of the Baltic dilemma, I can't do business with him. You and I are together on this, but it is getting more difficult. . . . We have come so far, but there is a danger we could slide back into the dark ages. . . ."

"Gorbachev has hardened up," agreed Margaret. The Soviet military was kicking up a terrible fuss. "They have been treated badly; they have to destroy decent weapons; their army is fragmenting along ethnic lines. The military is no longer on Gorbachev's side." This was also affecting Soviet policy on Germany, CFE, and START. "Gorbachev is a sensible politician, but he has been hardening his position over the last six weeks," she said. "This was unexpected, but it makes the case for [maintaining] NATO easier because it shows the danger of uncertainty, not only in Europe, but out of area* where robust forces are needed."

DIARY, APRIL 17

Big on the radar screen this morning is Lithuania . . . and the press is all demanding—what are you going to do? What are you going to do? They want us to ratchet up the pressure and announce a bunch of steps; yet if we did, the next criticism would be, well, why are you doing this when you have a whole bunch of other agenda items to worry about with the Soviet Union? . . . It's almost a no-win situation, and I keep hoping that Gorbachev will recognize the disaster this will bring him internationally.

I meet with Senate delegations, headed by George Mitchell, and they don't want to make any specific suggestions at all. They say,

---

*Meaning outside the geographical area of NATO's responsibility.

you're going to have to do something, but they won't say what *it* is, and that's right—the Congress has the luxury of doing that.

The question is, how do you preserve our relationship without condoning the very kind of behavior that the Soviets are involved in? We've got so much at stake that it affects the others in the world, and it affects us. Arms control comes to mind, but so does Afghanistan, Cuba, Angola, and many other regional questions. Then you have the natural wariness of the Germans, and the Poles, all of whom don't want to see a reversal of any kind with the Soviet Union. Then you have, in our country, the human rights groups, the right-wing, and others who seriously either detest or suspect Gorbachev, and want to go after him in the name of human rights.

On April 18, Baker told Shevardnadze that we would consider an embargo to be coercion, and warned it would injure US-Soviet relations. Shevardnadze reassured him that everything they had said in Washington and even before that was still in force. "We are deeply committed to using only political means in Lithuania—and there is no other choice." But he insisted that the Lithuanians would have to make the first move.

The next day, I met with Mitterrand at Key Largo. I recounted our conversations with Shevardnadze. "If they do cut off oil and gas, I must do something," I said. "I won't stop arms control negotiations, but one thing I could do would be to stop Most Favored Nation negotiations." I asked him what he thought we should do.

"We are in a terrible contradiction," he began. "Our interests are in keeping Gorbachev where he is, and in supporting Lithuanian independence." François urged that we try to negotiate to give him time to introduce changes. "Gorbachev has inherited an empire," he continued. "It is now in revolt. If the Ukraine starts to move, Gorbachev is gone; a military dictatorship would result." As for the Baltics, the French also had never recognized their incorporation into the Soviet Union and the Balts still maintained legations in Paris. He cautioned me about recognizing them. "It would be as if the United States sent an ambassador to Alsace."

I told François that what worried me was the Soviet military reacting on its own. "I think we must act in the interests of the Western world," he replied. ". . . We are building for the future. We are in a ten-mile stretch of road and we have gone only five hundred yards so far." If the Soviets went ahead and cut off all oil and gas, our response should be economic and nothing more, he advised. "I wouldn't threaten what I would not want to do. We cannot send troops." Mitterrand was at his thoughtful best and saw clearly what so many members of our Congress failed to see. The same day François and I met, the Soviets completed the gas and oil embargo cut-off.

DIARY, APRIL 20

The press is building up a lot of steam on me because there has been no moderation, and indeed, there is a crackdown. . . . They're turning back ships, and indeed, they've confirmed that gas and oil has been cut off, so we're not making headway. Baker has talked for a second time with Shevardnadze, Shevardnadze having said, judge us by what we do and not what we say. Baker says, "How could you have said that?" and he never acknowledged the question.

That evening, Brent, Jim, and I talked about our options, and our conversation turned to economic measures such as sanctions. I asked Jim to consult our allies on what they wanted to see, and decided to talk with the Congressional leadership the following week. That would buy us some time to work through a response.

BRENT SCOWCROFT

The President called an NSC meeting on Lithuania for the early evening of Monday, April 23. The participants gathered in the Cabinet Room included all of the economic team, such as Nicholas Brady, Secretary of Commerce Robert Mosbacher, Secretary of Agriculture Clayton Yeutter, and US Trade Representative Carla Hills. The President stressed that this was not to be a decision meeting, merely a discussion. I sketched out where we stood. There were three areas in which we could act. The first was security—arms control—negotiations, which I believed we should not suspend. The second was non-economic US-Soviet contacts and exchanges, which would make little difference. Third was economic, which would be broadly symmetrical to the economic coercion of Lithuania. "It would be hard to explain to Congress why we were negotiating economic agreements with Moscow that would help their economy at a time when they are using economic leverage to squeeze the Lithuanians," I said.

There were several ways to slice the economic agenda. One was to distinguish between the initiatives we had been working on before and since Malta, suspending those the President had discussed with Gorbachev, such as trade agreements and Most Favored Nation trading status. Another was to distinguish between commercial benefits and technical exchanges, the latter furthering our own goal of reform in the Soviet Union. We could also simply suspend initiatives which helped them more than us.

Baker urged that we have two goals: protect our overall relationship with the USSR and avoid a fight with our allies. He had consulted most of our allies around the world. The uniform reaction had been that we were on the right track and should take no action but to condemn the energy cut-off. The assembled advisors echoed this advice—none wanted any dramatic action. Baker and the economic team maintained that sanctions would be excessive unless Gorbachev resorted to violence.

I was somewhat taken back by the restrained attitude which dominated the meeting, although it was probably to be expected from the perspective of the economic agencies that were attending. They did not have to be concerned with the political and security problems or with the criticism that the President was "soft" on the Soviets. Yet neither of Baker's two goals dealt with our interests in Lithuania itself. I thought we should react more strongly, but not because of domestic pressure. Rather, Gorbachev was completely ignoring us and had violated every assurance he had given the President. He seemed to expect that the accommodation should be entirely on our side and I believed it was dangerous to let him get away with that. Responding with only a tiny slap on the wrist could come back to haunt us another time. But, given the attitude around the table, I decided that taking on the consensus would be a fruitless and time wasting exercise.

GEORGE BUSH

I was dissatisfied with this discussion since it did not point to action, and I wanted to take action. Our principal goal was to show support for the Lithuanians. While I still believed that the American people backed me on the way we were handling the situation, it was difficult to just sit on my hands. We did not want to give the Lithuanians the idea that we were ignoring their plight. We also could not suggest, however, that we would go to the barricades with them and then leave them hanging if the Soviets used force.

Selecting economic initiatives to suspend, short of sanctions, was attractive. It created incentives for the Soviets to lift the energy embargo without us resorting to threats which could make it difficult for Gorbachev to relent without losing face at high political cost. I decided we should halt our efforts to obtain a trade agreement and MFN until the Soviets began to work for a negotiated solution. I did not want to break off other contacts or cancel the summit.

DIARY, APRIL 24

We had a meeting with the joint leadership [of Congress], and I went through in detail my thinking on Lithuania and, to my pleasant surprise, they were strongly in favor of giving me flexibility and not moving dramatically out. Jesse Helms was an exception, wanting to recognize Lithuania, but Rostenkowski and others saw that my concerns about what would happen in Eastern Europe are valid. They favored our approach for dialogue and discussion trying to get the Soviets to move. They agreed that it should be in the economic field, so I have a little running room and time.

To complicate matters, Landsbergis, though a true patriot, turned out to be very difficult. That same day he complained that his country was the victim of another "Munich." I was furious. I could understand his disappointment, but I also wished he would realize that we were committed to Lithuanian independence. To accuse me of appeasement was outrageous. I didn't quite know what to do about it except get the message to him that it did not help matters, which I did in a press conference on April 25. The next day, Mitterrand and Kohl made public a letter to Landsbergis asking him to "suspend" Lithuania's declaration of independence and talk with Gorbachev, something Baker had raised with Shevardnadze. I thought it was a great idea and I encouraged them to do it. It might create some public pressure on Landsbergis to cooperate.

Before I acted, I intended to give Gorbachev fair warning, without a blast of publicity. I drafted a letter cautioning him about what I planned to do, that we could not go forward with MFN under the existing circumstances—a dialogue must begin. I wasn't sure whether circumstances would require stronger measures, or whether I would even send the letter, but I had a certain satisfaction from sitting at my typewriter that evening and hammering out five pages just to get it off my chest. A revised version went out on April 29:

> . . . I have given a lot of weight to your stated view that force would not be used and that eventual separation or self-determination is in the cards for Lithuania. The problem is we can no longer sit idly by, giving the impression that we are unconcerned about the aspirations to freedom of the people of Lithuania.
>
> I have often stated publicly, not only my desire to see perestroika succeed, but also to see you personally prevail. I still feel very strongly about that . . . On Tuesday I met with key leaders in our Congress and explained that I was not prepared to take action on this matter, though there is growing feeling in this country that my inaction delivers a serious blow to the aspirations of freedom loving people in Lithuania, and

indeed everywhere. This growing feeling, which I share, leads me to believe that there is no way we will be able to conclude our Trade Agreement, and thus MFN, unless dialogue with Lithuania begins. . . .

I have no choice but to identify with our strongly held convictions about Lithuania's self determination and the right to control its own destiny.

I look forward to seeing you at our upcoming meeting. I am determined to keep that meeting on track in spite of existing tensions. There is a lot at stake here.

As I waited for a reply, the Senate on May 1 voted 73–24 to withhold US trade benefits from Moscow until the embargo against Lithuania was lifted. Two days later came a chilly response from Gorbachev, hand-delivered by Ambassador Dubinin to Brent:

It seems to me that at Malta a fundamental mutual understanding was reached regarding the conduct vis-à-vis Lithuania. As I emphasized then, this kind of problem could only be resolved democratically, in a level-headed manner, and excluding any outside interference. I called your special attention to this latter point, noting that if you want to undermine the relationship, to worsen the attitude of our people to the United States, then you should encourage separatism. I also said we were counting on careful and thought-through actions by the US President in this extremely delicate area. You, Mr. President, expressed understanding of what I said. This created the foundation on which further actions should continue to be based.

Both your and our approach to the Lithuanian situation in the post-Malta period confirmed that this mutual understanding was indeed being implemented. . . . Are we now to understand you to have changed your view of the consequences of the negative steps in the area of Soviet-US trade and economic ties? Or is it that Washington is now prepared to go forward with that very escalation which no more than ten days ago was seen by the US side as unacceptable?

It was a disappointing reply. In my view, what was said at Malta had included an understanding that Gorbachev would not resort to coercion, and that was exactly what the energy embargo was. It was hardly part of a "democratic" solution, or the dialogue both Gorbachev and Shevardnadze had been promising. I had tried to be understanding toward both sides, but that did not mean we would look the other way when Moscow tried to intimidate and punish Lithuania. We had taken a measured, proportionate response in delaying progress on MFN and trade, and had not caved in to demands for sanctions, although our sympathies were with Lithuania. We were encouraging constructive dialogue, not separatism.

BRENT SCOWCROFT

Lithuanian prime minister Kazimiera Prunskiene was visiting the United States in early May, and she was invited to the White House for an informal meeting. It was a good way to demonstrate our support for Lithuania and for the prime minister, who was more judicious than the tempestuous and sometimes counterproductive Landsbergis. She was to arrive at the Northwest Gate, and we went into the Cabinet Room to await her. No prime minister. The heavy mechanical gate had broken halfway through its opening cycle and her limousine couldn't enter the grounds. She and her party had to walk from the gate to the West Lobby.

This unfortunate accident was maliciously described by some of the press as a deliberate move to humiliate Prunskiene. Nothing could have been further from the truth. We certainly did not wish to rain on our own parade. We had invited her in order to make a statement. As the first meeting between an American president and a Lithuanian prime minister since the annexation of the Baltics, it was a precedent-breaking event, and we intended it to be such. Our only concern was that it might be portrayed as recognition of the government's independence. For that reason, we did not allow the Lithuanian consul to accompany her to the Cabinet Room, and later explained in a press release that the President was meeting her not as prime minister of independent Lithuania but as a recognized and freely elected representative of the Lithuanian people.

GEORGE BUSH

Prunskiene was a strong, tough patriot and she had a broad grasp of the issues. I found her more reasonable to deal with than Landsbergis. She understood that the United States had long supported Lithuanian independence, and that it was a complex task to help her country while keeping in mind over-all US interests with the Soviet Union. The Kohl-Mitterrand letter opened some possibilities which might move things to a solution, she said, but the Lithuanians would need assurances: recognition of the continuity of Lithuanian independence, the legality of the current government, and the territorial inviolability of Lithuania. She argued that Western pressure on Gorbachev helped him resist the reactionaries, and thought he did not want to use force.

I wasn't as optimistic that a crackdown was so improbable. The military might yet intervene, and we had to be careful. ". . . I don't want to see Lithuania ground under the same boot that ground the children of Hungary into the dirt in 1956 by saying 'go to the barricades,' " I said. "They gave their lives—they were martyred—we weren't there; neither was Western Europe. We have to find a better way. It's hard for the people of

Lithuania to understand this, but that's what I'm trying to do." But this was not the only question, I said. I wanted Soviet troops out of Poland, and Vaclav Havel should have a chance to fulfill freedom for Czechoslovakia. "It's only the United States that can take a misstep and set back their chances. The world is crying out for arms control. . . . The Soviet Union still has a say in these matters. I cite this agenda not because I have a lessened view of Lithuanian independence, but because there is so much more at stake. . . . Does it make more sense to slap Gorbachev in public than to quietly make sure he understands our commitment? . . . One thing you must understand as you leave this office—the symbol of freedom. I am committed personally—and the Administration is committed—to Lithuanian freedom. We can argue about the methodology, but please understand what the heartbeat is."

A year which had opened with a feeling of cautious promise had sunk into foreboding uncertainty. The Soviet military was demanding that Gorbachev and Shevardnadze make no more concessions at home or abroad that might endanger the Soviet strategic position in Eastern Europe. We feared that if German reunification and the reformation of Eastern Europe as part of a free continent did not proceed now, we might soon be facing a new and hard-line Soviet government, one unwilling to make the kinds of compromises we needed. The situation in Lithuania cast a shadow over any settlement on Germany, and threatened the June summit.

CHAPTER 10

Toward Common Ground

BRENT SCOWCROFT

The easing of Cold War tensions threw open the fundamental assumptions on which the entire postwar security structures of Western Europe, and our own strategic planning, were based: a Soviet threat and a divided continent. The American military presence in Europe, in the form of NATO, had been predicated largely on the existence of that threat and the use of bases in West Germany. Suddenly, everything was open to reconsideration. What was the nature of future European security needs? What sort of security architecture might be needed? What was the future of NATO? What should be the relationship of a united Germany to NATO and would it permit us to station troops there?

We had to rethink the larger strategic picture of European security, of our role in it, and of superpower relations. The events underway across Europe were interrelated in their cause and effect and had to be considered in a collective context as well as individually. We were witnessing the sorts of changes usually only imposed by victors at the end of a major war. It was essential that we avoid another Versailles-type settlement, one which would leave Europe as divided and dissatisfied as it had been after the First World War—with tragic consequences. Our task was to develop a common vision of the outcome, the kind of post–Cold War Europe not only that we and our allies would want to see emerge, but also one in which the Soviets would recognize their own stake or which they would at least accept.

Our first requirement was to prevent yet another repetition of the turmoil which had beset Europe in the twentieth century. American isolationism had played its part in those tragedies. The lesson we drew from this bloody history was that the United States had to continue to play a significant role in European security, whatever developed with respect to the Soviet Union. The vehicle for that role must be NATO. The alliance was the only way the US could keep forces in Europe as a visible commitment to its security and stability. In addition, a united Germany as a full member of the alliance was key to our presence. Germany held our bases: If it left the alliance, it would be difficult if not impossible to retain American troops in Europe. We needed Helmut Kohl's commitment to keep Germany in the alliance and American troops on its soil. Together, these requirements gave us an enormous stake in the outcome of German reunification, apart from ending the division of Europe.

We had as well to revise NATO's mission, not only to convince the American people that continued sizable expenditures—not to mention military deployment—were still in the national interest, but also to demonstrate to Moscow that the alliance was no longer the menace they had preached to their people for forty years. President Bush had already raised the need for a new security architecture in his December address at the NATO summit, and Jim Baker had underscored its importance in Berlin a few days later. Baker had added that the new architecture would require new missions for NATO, the EC, and CSCE. His outline had been deliberately broad, underscoring a less threatening NATO for the Soviets and a greater emphasis on European structures to appeal to the French. He had touched on our primary requirement, however, that the United States preserve its link to European security. The outcome of reunification and the simultaneous changes in the security of arrangements in Europe must not only meet European and Soviet concerns but also address long-term American interests.

GEORGE BUSH

I knew it was up to the United States to respond to these questions and to shape the reunification process in a way that would avoid possible conflict now or in the future. With so much at stake, especially for our role in Europe, we would have to be deeply involved in the increasingly complicated diplomacy ahead. I wanted to set a constructive and collaborative tone, much as we had at the time of the opening of the Berlin Wall when we resisted the provocative calls for gestures and inflammatory rhetoric. Reunification and a new Europe, whole and free, should not come at the expense of other nations. It had to come with and through them—both East and West. We could not cast the changes around us in terms of winners and losers.

Shepherding reunification and the future architecture of European security in this way was a monumental undertaking. Because changes were unfolding so fast, we had little time for introspection. Fortunately, the tide of history in Germany and across Eastern Europe was in our direction. We had to push, guide, and manage, to the extent possible, the positive currents that were flowing.

For a brief moment in the last days of 1989, it had appeared as if East Germany might hold on. In an effort to broaden and strengthen the weak support for his government, Modrow began to work with a roundtable composed of the various political factions, an approach that had worked for the Poles. Most of the participants from outside the government had played a role in the October and November protests, but still favored a reformed GDR over unification. They advocated a system between free-market economics and communism—a middle ground. The roundtable soon agreed to set new parliamentary elections for May 1990, and even started to act as a parliament itself, leading the campaign against the hated Stasi secret police.

It was not to be, however. The Modrow government, full of old faces and locked into old habits, soon destroyed what little stability it had garnered. It was unable or unwilling to produce reforms that would overhaul the collapsed economy. Political reform had not materialized either, including responses to demands that the Stasi be disbanded. In early January, Modrow attempted to restore the authority of the Stasi by reorganizing it in a new guise and by staging "incidents," such as the defacing of Soviet war memorials, to which it was to respond. The flimsy credibility of the government now crumbled. The roundtable angrily protested and cooperation with the regime effectively ended, and with it the attempt to find a middle path.

On January 15, 1990, thousands of demonstrators flooded the streets of East Berlin and stormed the Stasi headquarters. By January 26, when President Bush spoke with him about our new CFE proposals, Helmut Kohl no longer believed that East Germany would or could reform itself. It was on the verge of total collapse.

GEORGE BUSH

A plainly tired Helmut related the latest developments. The East German government was having problems, but not because they did not want to make reforms, he said. "They just *cannot* do it right." While Havel had moral authority in Czechoslovakia, and Mazowiecki in Poland, Modrow now had hardly any influence among his people.

"I myself am pushing necessary reforms forward piece by piece," explained Kohl. "There is some success in the economic field, but things that should take one day take weeks. The result: The confidence of the population in the administration is catastrophic. People are leaving in the thousands, and the rest are sitting on packed suitcases. . . . Since January 1, forty-three thousand people have come over. In the long term, this is unsustainable. Those are good people, doctors, engineers, specialists. They cannot be replaced."

Kohl was to meet in February with Modrow in Switzerland to discuss how to bring order to the situation. "My job now is to stop destabilization in Central Europe," he said. "That is the matter I work on night and day." He asked me whether we might meet for a few hours, just the two of us. Perhaps at Camp David, as we had discussed in November. I was enthusiastic about the idea. I thought it was important that we sit down in just that sort of setting. We eventually set up a meeting for February 24.

Kohl was reluctant to work with an East German government unable to function and unwilling to reform. He also was not interested in the confederation plan to which Modrow was still clinging. After the attempted reassertion of Stasi authority in January, the West German parties had all concurred to stop further work on a community of treaties until East Germany held free elections, which Kohl hoped would oust the Communists and put the GDR on the path to confederation and, eventually, unification. For his part, Modrow realized that his government couldn't hold on to power for long and agreed with the roundtable on January 28 to move up the elections from May 6 to March 18. We expected that the earlier date would favor a Communist or Social Democratic victory.

BRENT SCOWCROFT

In Washington, we were beginning to realize that we had, along with everyone else, greatly underestimated the speed with which East Germany was disintegrating. The possibility of a careful, controllable "gradual, step-by-step" process, as Kohl had proposed and we had supported, seemed to be evaporating. If it was impossible to control the pace of unification, then the fastest movement toward it was perhaps becoming the best, or possibly the only, way to minimize chaos and unpredictability. It might also reduce the chances for opponents to derail the process. The rapidly changing situation called for strong US leadership if reunification was to occur on the terms we required.

Key to our efforts in the West had to be working closely with the West Germans to ensure they committed themselves to the outcome we hoped to see. The principles of our policy were simple. As the President had implied to Kohl at their December 3 meeting, we would back reunification, which would allow the West Germans to conduct their separate, "internal" diplomacy with East Germany without worrying about whether the United States would support them in the end. The weakness in this approach was that it was based on the assumption that Kohl maintained the same priorities regarding the "external," or international, aspects that we did. We hoped that the President's commitment to back Kohl would be our insurance that the Chancellor would insist on membership in NATO, and on retaining US forces. But there was always the danger he might feel compelled to strike a bargain with the Soviets: German neutrality in exchange for unification.

Again, we wanted all countries, especially the Soviet Union, to accept the external settlement and see themselves as having a stake in the emerging order of Europe. The strategy for reaching consensus among the parties would have to include resolving the practical sequence of basic reunification issues, how we determined what was handled, when, and with whom. Bob Blackwill, Philip Zelikow, Bob Hutchings, and Condi Rice—the NSC Soviet and European teams engaged in the process— drafted an outline of what we wanted a unified Germany to look like and how to get there. All Germany was to be in NATO, although perhaps no foreign troops would be on East German territory. Its borders would be those of West Germany and East Germany with Berlin absorbed into the unified whole, ending Allied Rights and any occupied status. Unification itself would be worked out and accomplished between the two Germanies. When that was done, the Germanies would present the results to the Four Powers for their blessing. I agreed with this approach, although the discussion of the unification process was short on details.

The State Department had a different idea. Concurring that the basic internal arrangements should be worked out between the two Germanies, Baker believed it was too dangerous to exclude everyone else from the external aspects of the process. Trying to freeze out the Soviets could result in separate Soviet–West German negotiations, with potentially disastrous results. State proposed, therefore, blending the negotiations between the two Germanies with a Four Power process—what would become known as the "Two-plus-Four." To mitigate the hazards of involving the Four Powers, he suggested that they agree ahead of time that the goal of the talks would be unification and that the Four Powers would be concerned only with the external, international aspects of unification.

I was dubious about State's proposal. I understood Jim's concerns about a "Germanies only" negotiation, but I was apprehensive about involving the Four Powers, given the mischief they could cause. It would let the Soviets work their opposition from inside the process. They might even be able to coopt the British and French, whose enthusiasm for unification was still nonexistent, into at least some delaying tactics. The least risky course, I believed, was to push inter-German negotiations as fast as we could, trying to protect them from interference and hoping things would move swiftly enough to present potential opposition with a *fait accompli*. At the same time, the outcome of the March elections would influence how rapidly the negotiations between the Germanies would proceed, and in what direction—federation or confederation.

Admittedly, it was a poor idea in principle to try to freeze Gorbachev out of the process. Cooption was preferable—if it was doable. That was what the Baker plan bet on. His conditions were that all six participants had to agree at the outset that the goal was unification, that the two Germanies were to deal with internal unification, and that East Germany had to have a freely elected government—which meant the negotiations would begin only after the elections. If those conditions were sincerely kept, Two-plus-Four would probably work. Jim, who would do most of the operational work to implement the strategy, was an outstanding negotiator. I was prepared to put aside my reservations about Baker discussing it with the allies, and went along with his approach.

Our next step was to create a unified Western position in support of reunification and a fully sovereign Germany without residual constraints on it. Western agreement that both reunification and membership in NATO were matters for the Germans to decide would make it more difficult for the Soviets to block either goal. At the same time, we would work with the Soviets to resolve the larger political and strategic questions, reassuring them that we would address their security concerns. The strategy would attempt to make it hard for Moscow to stop unification, and coax them to acquiesce in it.

GEORGE BUSH

The intensive campaign of personal diplomacy to sell our strategy among the allies began in earnest on January 29, with the arrival in Washington of British foreign secretary Douglas Hurd, on his first visit since replacing Geoffrey Howe. Hurd repeated Margaret Thatcher's position, which I knew from her conversation with me on CFE, expressing her reluctance to endorse unification on the grounds that it had not been carefully thought out in a larger, strategic context.*

*See Chapter 9, pages 211–12.

"She is reluctant to endorse reunification—a reluctant reunifier," Hurd told me as we sat in the Oval Office. "Not *against*, but reluctant. She sees things that need to be sorted out. Will Germany be part of NATO or not? Will East Germany be in the EC? What about Russian sensitivities? We need a framework in which these issues can be discussed." When, in other discussions, Baker told him of the Two-plus-Four plan, Hurd was interested, but he was inclined to accept the Soviet proposal for an early CSCE summit to discuss reunification, to which, he pointed out, the EC ministers had just agreed at a meeting in Dublin.

BRENT SCOWCROFT

The British interest in handling German unification at a CSCE summit was alarming. The large (thirty-five-member) and unwieldy all-Europe organization was not the place for such negotiations. If the Four Powers could disrupt reunification, CSCE, with its consensus procedures, allowed any country uneasy with the prospect of a large Germany much greater potential to stall or delay. A CSCE summit to ratify a reunification agreement could develop into a peace conference on Germany, opening up old wounds and unresolved disputes. Both Kohl and we opposed the notion of a formal peace treaty on Germany and the prospect of another "winner-loser" settlement.

Bonn, too, was beginning to think in operational terms about how to handle the practical international problems of reunification, especially the issue of NATO membership. On January 31, Genscher floated a unification proposal in a speech at the Tutzing Protestant Academy. He repeated his conviction that reunification must come within the integration of Europe, and that it must also mean guaranteeing the borders of Germany's neighbors. In addition, German membership in NATO and the EC must remain irrevocable. "We do not want a united neutralist Germany," he declared. Germany would remain in NATO, but East German territory would remain outside the alliance. He also proposed that both NATO and the Warsaw Pact be absorbed into a larger European security order resting on the EC and the CSCE. The CSCE would be strengthened, with new structures to be agreed upon at its summit later in the year.

BRENT SCOWCROFT

We had objections to some parts of the plan and also saw potentially disturbing omissions. Again, given the existing practical problems and the very nature of CSCE, there was no way we could accept that group absorbing NATO and its functions. Genscher had not made clear just what NATO's relationship to the territory of the GDR would be, and when, or even if, NATO was to pick up its defense. The role of the Bundeswehr (the West German armed forces) in the GDR was not covered, nor did he mention the future of US troops in Germany. Genscher's obvious detour around a Four Power role in reunification also was troubling, especially as he proposed that the Germanies would determine the extent of some sort of confederation and then take the matter to the CSCE for approval. We did not know whether this was Genscher's position alone, or if Kohl supported it.

A few days after the Hurd visit, on February 2, Genscher arrived in Washington for meetings with Baker. He explained his thinking behind the Tutzing proposal, emphasizing that the key was reassuring the Soviets that NATO territory would not be moved eastward. Baker accepted the formulation, perhaps not realizing the problems it created for NATO. This was an unfortunate "concession" to Genscher, one which could have created serious difficulties. Baker outlined the Two-plus-Four concept and Genscher reacted favorably, "as long as it was clear this was 'Two-plus-Four' and not 'Four-plus-Two' "—meaning that the allies would not dictate the outcome. Although Genscher had not committed himself formally, Baker felt he had obtained his support for the concept and his acquiescence that CSCE was not the place to negotiate Germany's future.

The coalition government in Bonn made foreign policy somewhat complicated—both for the Germans and for us. Genscher did not see eye-to-eye with Kohl on every issue, which meant that we occasionally had differing perspectives on what their policy really was. In addition, Genscher and Kohl sometimes did not inform each other of what each was doing or saying. Kohl had not told Genscher of his ten-point initiative in November, Genscher had neglected to reveal to Kohl his Tutzing proposals ahead of time, and, most recently, Kohl had not let Genscher know of Gorbachev's invitation to the Chancellor to visit Moscow in February. It was essential, therefore, that we also talk to the Chancellery in Bonn about our concept. As a way to sound out Kohl's views, Bob Blackwill and I took advantage of a conference in Munich on February 3 to see Horst Teltschik.

I first met Horst at a meeting in the latter part of the 1980s. It was only a brief encounter and I did not really feel I knew him when I assumed my responsibilities. It took me some time to get to know him in a comfortable way, especially since it was months before a direct phone line was installed. He was very sharp and direct, and more often than not could speak his chancellor's views with an easy assurance. I welcomed his cheery greeting on the phone—"Hello Brent, Horst here"—because our discussions were always productive, even when the result was not consensus. Teltschik was a strong supporter of the Chancellor's positions, which I felt he frequently had done much to shape. He was no fan of Genscher and was very helpful to me in understanding the nuances of difference between the chancellor and the foreign minister, and their significance.

Kohl was to meet with Gorbachev on February 11, and Baker was due in Moscow two days earlier. Horst told me Kohl planned to warn Gorbachev that a mass exodus of East Germans or actions by their parliament could force unification very quickly after the March elections. He would also make it clear there could be no question of German neutrality. We agreed that Kohl should be briefed on the Baker meeting before he saw Gorbachev.

Horst and I concurred that it was essential for our governments to cooperate in encouraging a quick pace if we were to achieve unification before its opponents had a chance to block it, but he still worried about Four Power intervention. I assured him that the US would not allow it. Likewise, we agreed we could not let any CSCE session turn into a peace conference. As I returned to Washington, I felt more confident that Bonn intended to work closely with us, and was backing the same "external" outcome we were.

Having outlined the idea of the Two-plus-Four process to the British and Germans and receiving positive reactions, though no firm commitments, on February 5 Baker undertook to sell it to the Soviets while in Moscow to discuss arms control. En route to a stop in Prague, Baker's plane landed at Shannon, Ireland, for refueling. There he met with French foreign minister Roland Dumas, who was in Ireland for an EC meeting. Dumas liked the plan and promised to raise it with Mitterrand.

In Moscow, Gorbachev was under attack from the Soviet right over a number of issues, an apparent "softening" on Germany among them. On February 1, after conferring with Gorbachev, Modrow had announced a new plan for a neutral confederation of the two Germanies, both keeping their governments, a plan which was publicly supported by the Soviets, and privately by Gorbachev in a letter to President Bush, as promoting a "gradual process" toward unity. The proposal was unacceptable to us and to Kohl, particularly because it called for a neutral, disarmed, and, at least for some time, only a confederal Germany. Nevertheless, the Soviets had now stated for the first time that they did not object to the principle of German unity, a development which upset Party reactionaries.

On February 7, Baker laid out the Two-plus-Four scenario for Shevardnadze, once again emphasizing that it was supposed to handle the diffi-cult international side of reunification and could begin only after the March elections. The US could not support Modrow's proposal for a neu-tral Germany. In fact, Baker argued, a neutral Germany would be more dangerous to the Soviets than one firmly embedded in NATO; it might seek nuclear weapons of its own. Baker repeated Genscher's formula of the status of the GDR: if Germany stayed in NATO there would be no movement of NATO's jurisdiction or forces eastward. NATO would evolve into a more political and less military alliance, something the President had already spoken about in December at the NATO meeting in Brussels.

Shevardnadze insisted that a united Germany must be neutral. He said he had nothing against unification, but he wanted certain guaran-tees for Soviet security. He urged Four Power talks to discuss a peace treaty, saying that what he feared was a resurgence of neo-Nazism on the political fringes, as well as the possibility of a remilitarized Ger-many. The Four Powers should slow things down. The British and French thought so too, although Shevardnadze acknowledged that events had already proceeded beyond that possibility. He backed the Modrow plan for a gradual process. Baker reiterated that Germany could not be neutralized or demilitarized: it had to be allowed to defend it-self. If the Soviet Union was worried about the potential military threat of unified Germany, might not keeping it in NATO be better from their perspective?

Baker broached Two-plus-Four to Gorbachev on February 9, with the preconditions necessary, including that the process could start only after the elections—to let the Germans make up their minds about reunification first. Gorbachev said he could accept the plan, as long as it relied on an international legal basis. He appeared to be less worried about a resurgence of German military power than did Shevardnadze. He told Baker he shared the American view that "there is nothing terrifying in the prospect of a unified Germany." However, he still had reservations about German membership in NATO.

Baker asked whether Gorbachev would rather have a Germany inde-pendent and outside of NATO or one tied to the alliance, with assurances "that there would be no extension of NATO's current jurisdiction east-ward." Gorbachev had not made up his mind on the matter, but he was against an enlargement of NATO. Baker reiterated that "there would be no extension of NATO's jurisdiction for forces of NATO one inch to the east." Gorbachev said he could see advantages to keeping US forces in Germany. He didn't want a replay of Versailles either, with Ger-many rearming. "What you have said to me about your approach and preference is very realistic," he said. ". . . But don't ask me to give you a bottom line right now."

BRENT SCOWCROFT

Baker's meeting with Gorbachev was important. Gorbachev not only had said he did not fear reunification, but also for the first time appeared flexible about how we might get there and what the outcome might look like. The discussions certainly paved the way for the Soviet leader's talks with Kohl and Genscher and very likely predisposed Gorbachev to be sympathetic. There was a great deal riding on Kohl's meeting and we needed to do everything we could to ensure its success. It was essential that whatever the Germans presented in Moscow was in step with our own position, and with what Baker had just heard from Gorbachev. In Munich, Teltschik had given me an outline of what Kohl planned to put before Gorbachev, which reduced our anxieties about the meeting. The President knew, however, that Kohl was under enormous pressure politically and personally, and that this was one of the most important foreign policy meetings the Chancellor would face. I suggested that he write to Kohl, giving him all the personal support he could and making clear to him our preferences concerning the future of a united Germany.

GEORGE BUSH

I assured Helmut that the United States still backed reunification. "If the events are moving faster than we expected," I wrote, "it just means that our common goal for all these years of German unity will be realized even sooner than we had hoped." When it came to the question of Four Power responsibilities, "I want you to understand that the United States will do nothing that would lead your countrymen to conclude that we will not respect their choice for their nation's future. In no event will we allow the Soviet Union to use their Four Power mechanism as an instrument to try to force you to create the kind of Germany Moscow might want, at the pace Moscow might prefer."

At the same time, I said again I wanted to see a unified Germany firmly within the Western alliance.

Naturally this is again something for the German people, and its elected representatives, to decide. So I was deeply gratified by your rejection of proposals for neutrality and your firm statement that a unified Germany would stay in the North Atlantic Alliance. In this connection I endorse the idea put forward that a component of a united Germany's membership in the Atlantic Alliance could be a special military status for what is now the territory of the GDR. We believe that such a commitment could be made compatible with the security of

Germany, as well as of its neighbors, in the context of substantial, perhaps ultimately total, Soviet troop withdrawals from Central and Eastern Europe. . . .

Even if, as we hope, the Soviet Union withdraws all its troops from Eastern Europe, it will still remain far and away the most powerful single military power in Europe. US troops in Germany, and elsewhere on the continent, backed by a credible deterrent, must in my view continue to help preserve the security of the West as long as our allies desire our military presence in Europe as part of the common defense. As our two countries journey together through this time of hope and promise, we can remain confident of our shared ability to defend the fruits of freedom. Nothing Mr. Gorbachev can say to Jim Baker or to you can change the fundamental fact of our deep and enduring partnership.

BRENT SCOWCROFT

In his letter, the President clarified our position on what the relationship to NATO should be of the East German portion of a united Germany. Adapting a suggestion that Manfred Wörner had used in a speech, he proposed that "a component of a united Germany's membership in the Atlantic Alliance could be a special military status for what is now the territory of the GDR." The proposal differed from Genscher's in that *all* of a united Germany would be inside NATO territory and jurisdiction and thus covered by NATO's security guarantee. The President explained that he expected this "special military status" would be accompanied by a substantial withdrawal of Soviet forces from Central and Eastern Europe. Since all of Germany would be in NATO, Soviet troops would have to be withdrawn from GDR territory. This was a critical correction to make in order to prevent Gorbachev from tying us in knots with the Genscher idea.

As Teltschik and I had arranged, Baker also sent Kohl a summary of his discussions with Gorbachev. Kohl thus embarked on his critical journey backed by the strongest possible guarantee of American support. We had done the most we could to encourage our preferred outcome. Despite our precautions, we were more than a little nervous. We had great faith in Kohl, but Gorbachev might decide to push hard. We could not rule out the possibility that Gorbachev could tempt—or threaten—him. Since Kohl did not call President Bush immediately following the meetings with Gorbachev to give the President a personal perspective, it was a relief to hear Kohl's press conference comments on the discussions:

General Secretary Gorbachev and I agree that it is the right of the German people alone to decide whether they want to live in one state.

General Secretary Gorbachev promised me in no uncertain terms that the Soviet Union will respect the Germans' decision to live in one state, and that it is up to the Germans themselves to determine the time of reunification and the way it will come about . . . [we] also agreed that the German question can only be solved on the basis of realities; that it must be embedded in the pan-European architecture [EC] and in the general process of East-West relations.

It had been a historic meeting. Gorbachev had accepted German reunification as a matter for the Germans to decide for themselves. There were strings, however. He made it clear that the external aspects were far from an exclusively German affair. He still was not prepared to accept German membership in NATO.

GEORGE BUSH

While Kohl met with Gorbachev in Moscow, NATO secretary general Manfred Wörner came to lunch at Camp David on February 10. He underscored the critical part he believed the United States had to play in assuring the future of NATO and in keeping Germany in the alliance. "This is a unique opportunity. This is a decisive moment," he said. "In weeks or in the next months, you personally will have to make decisions that can decide the future of Europe." There was only one critical issue: whether Germany would be neutral or remain in NATO. "The answer to this question will decide future decades of European history." He warned that if Germany were permitted to leave the alliance, the "old Pandora's box of competition and rivalry in Europe would be reopened." A neutral Germany of seventy-nine million people with the most powerful economy in Europe would be a considerable military power—and it might eventually want nuclear weapons.

A demilitarized Germany would repeat the mistake of the Versailles Treaty, he continued. "[It] would not be tied to any safe structure. The most natural reaction then would be for the British and French to try to control the new Germany. The Germans will react, forming their own alliances. We then would be repeating the game, with all its instability, that we witnessed in European politics at the beginning of the century. Potential instability in Eastern Europe will add even more competition and rivalry to the situation."

Manfred was frightened by such a vision. "We must avoid the classic German temptation: to float freely and bargain with both East and West," he said. "If I have one message, it is that you should not allow that to happen. That is your historic task." The Soviets were in a weak position. They could not prevent unification if the United States kept its clear line of support for the process.

Wörner believed Gorbachev would ultimately have to accept Germany in NATO. "If the Soviets correctly perceive their long-term security interests, how can they want German neutrality, given Moscow's historic memories?" he asked. "But in the short term, the Soviets may push for neutrality." He doubted that they had the means to prevent Germany from remaining a member of NATO. They had no leverage, even with their forces in the GDR. "You and Germany have to agree now on German unity within NATO and sell this to the Russians," he reminded us. "The Russians will have to accept it."

He was also adamant that Germany must be a *full* member of the alliance. "Just association with NATO will create temptations for Germany to make diplomatic deals with Russia," warned Manfred. "If Germany is out of the integrated NATO structure, the United States will be out of Europe. This will lead to great destabilization in Europe. If you leave now, you will be leaving at the decisive moment."

BRENT SCOWCROFT

I thought Wörner was brilliant in his analysis. Germany, and its membership in NATO, was at the center of many of the questions Europe faced about its future, and the President of the United States must assert leadership in finding the solutions, thereby setting the direction for Europe. When the time came, Manfred brought NATO along in a way which facilitated not only Gorbachev's acquiescence to German membership but also NATO's transition to a post–Cold War world. His untimely death in 1994 deprived the Atlantic community of a great strategist at a crucial time.

I was still uneasy with the Two-plus-Four formula. We had not discussed the issue in the National Security Council. That was probably my fault for not scheduling it, but I had thought that Baker was only taking soundings among the allies to see whether the concept might fly, not actually obtaining their consent. Now, suddenly, we were on the verge of finalizing the approach. I could not get out of my mind the possibility that Genscher was playing a game separate from Kohl and that Baker inadvertently was aiding and abetting Genscher.

Our only reasonable choice was to stand behind Kohl, but I was not sure that he fully supported Two-plus-Four. I feared he might think that it tied his hands. I knew from Teltschik both the Chancellor's hope for a free hand and some questions about Genscher's agenda. On February 12, Baker went to Ottawa to participate in a meeting of the NATO and Warsaw Pact foreign ministers on the Open Skies proposal. He would use that venue to try to nail down the Two-plus-Four formula among the six countries involved. I emphasized to him that the President did not want to interfere with Kohl's freedom of action. Baker, who clearly felt he had both Genscher and Kohl on board, asked Genscher to have Kohl call the President to tell him he supported our plan. Kohl did so on February 13, using the opportunity to describe his trip to Moscow.

GEORGE BUSH

Helmut thanked me for my help, as well as Jim's. "I do believe the letter you sent me before I left for Moscow will one day be considered one of the great documents in German-American history," he said very generously. He reported that he and Gorbachev had discussed Two-plus-Four, and he had also told Gorbachev again that the neutralization of Germany was out of the question. Kohl's impression was that the Soviets wanted to discuss the issue, but that we could win this point in negotiations. "The modalities will be important," he added, "but I do believe we can find a solution." I said our upcoming Camp David meeting would be very important in setting out a strategy—where to be more firm and where more flexible.

After some intensive negotiations in ad hoc meetings, the foreign ministers of the participants in what was soon to be the Two-plus-Four process made a joint statement in Ottawa announcing their intent to begin discussions on "the external aspects of the establishment of German unity, including the issues of security of the neighboring states." Preliminary discussions would start after the East German elections. The other NATO foreign ministers had been kept in total ignorance of the discussions until the announcement was released to the press. The result was an explosion of resentment and an acrimonious debate. At one point the Italian foreign minister angrily spoke for many when he observed that "we have worked together within the alliance for forty years." Genscher turned and with an icy glare bluntly told him: "You are not a part of the game." The meeting ended in the shock produced by that statement.

BRENT SCOWCROFT

Baker and Shevardnadze also reached agreement in Ottawa on a bilateral reduction of chemical weapons, to be formalized at the upcoming Washington summit, now scheduled for the end of May. CFE negotiations on further bilateral reductions in Europe were another topic. The Soviets wanted cuts to equal levels, but we wanted to break the symmetry of numbers between US and Soviet troops in Europe and favored unequal cuts. The Soviets would withdraw from Eastern Europe while we retained a troop presence on the continent. Baker clinched a deal for equal levels of 195,000 in Central Europe and an additional 30,000 for the United States outside that zone, for a total of 225,000. (The Soviets had no troops outside the zone.)

Baker called me to clear this proposition. It sounded like our proposal, so I got in touch with Cheney. He said the numbers were what Defense needed, but he was obviously uneasy about approving it on the spot on a Saturday night. I told him Baker was being pressed, and he finally said it was all right. I then cleared it with the President and phoned Baker to go ahead. In the haste, however, there had been a miscommunication. While there was no problem with the total number of troops allowed, it turned out that the sublimits (the 195,000 and 30,000) were also binding. This greatly reduced the flexibility of the Pentagon to move units around to deal with ad hoc situations. Not an insurmountable problem, but not a model way to make foreign policy. Integration and coordination of policy-making was my responsibility and I was not happy with such a messy outcome.

Baker had done a magnificent job of putting together a process (and negotiating concurrence with it) through which to manage German uni-fication. A giant step had been taken toward that goal. But this did not by any means signify that all the problems were settled. To the extent that my concerns about Two-plus-Four had any validity, the possibilities for obstruction were still very real. The Ottawa announcement did in-dicate a degree of consensus that reunification was rapidly on its way. However, there remained reason to think that the British and French would not be unhappy if the process could at least be drawn out and per-haps even that something short of a powerful, unified Germany might develop.

With respect to the Soviet Union, the situation was significantly more negative. Gorbachev had been quite accommodating to Baker and to Kohl. But whatever he himself may have been thinking, much of the Soviet hierarchy, from Shevardnadze on down, was far from reconciled to reunification. The Soviets and the East Germans still hoped to channel the process through a German confederation—thus retaining a powerful influence in German affairs. This would require a victory of the left, the Communists and Social Democrats, in the March GDR elections, an outcome that the polls were indicating. Failing victory, the leftists could still hope to force the Germans to choose between unity and NATO.

The Bonn coalition seemed to be struggling over just that question as it sorted out precisely how unification would be accomplished. There

were two possibilities under the Basic Law of the Federal Republic of Germany. The first, under Article 146, was that there would be all-German elections to select delegates to a constitutional assembly, which would then create an entirely new political state, form of government, laws, and constitution. The second option was Article 23, which allowed "other parts of Germany" to join the existing Federal Republic. This approach would call for East Germany to dissolve into its old *Länder*,* which, in turn, would be absorbed into the FRG, resulting in an enlarged FRG, its system intact. Article 146 would require a new state, perhaps via confederation, while Article 23 meant a direct takeover of the GDR.

Kohl (and we) strongly preferred Article 23, which avoided the possibility of changes to the West German system, especially if the SPD, east and west, won control of the constitutional assembly and sent the new Germany down a neutral (and possibly more socialist) path. This was a real danger. West German polls in mid-February indicated public support running at 58 percent for a united Germany outside of both alliances, and the expectation was that the East German SPD would win the March elections. Furthermore, the two SPD parties had announced that a future united Germany should belong to neither alliance. Kohl (soon followed by his allies among the East German parties) publicly backed Article 23, with unification preceded by a monetary and economic union (which was tantamount to absorbing the GDR into the existing FRG anyway, since it placed East Germany under the West German economic system). But there was serious division within the coalition about the preferability of all-German elections (a "third way," as Genscher was putting it).

At the same time, the relationship of East German territory to NATO was also under fierce debate in Bonn. Defense Minister Gerhard Stoltenberg was supporting full membership for all German territory, and Bundeswehr forces on East German soil. Genscher insisted that Moscow would agree to German unity only if the GDR were neutral and outside of NATO. On February 19, Kohl, trying to forge solidarity in the coalition over Article 23, and overriding the advice of both Stoltenberg and Teltschik, issued a joint statement with Genscher outlining a revised position on the GDR. While it dropped the idea that East German territory would not be in NATO, it declared that no NATO forces—including the Bundeswehr —would be stationed there. It was an unsatisfactory solution. The GDR would be demilitarized, and we still had not answered the question of how NATO would be responsible for this area, or how German

*Roughly the equivalent of US states.

membership could even function under these conditions. We hoped to address this question with Kohl at Camp David.

There was one additional, particularly vexing problem: the German-Polish border. Most Germans (including Genscher), other Europeans, and the Americans believed that the line formed by the Oder and Neisse rivers in eastern Germany, which had been part of the postwar occupation arrangements and was the *de facto* eastern border of postwar Germany, should be the *de jure* one. Kohl, however, insisted that only a unified German government could agree to any *de jure* change in the 1937 German borders, which had included substantial portions of what was now Poland. His ambiguous statements on this issue worried many who feared the behavior of a future Germany, lending support to the arguments of those concerned about unification, such as Margaret Thatcher.

For us, the border issue was complicated by the need to strengthen Kohl at home. The debate was seriously disrupting the Bonn coalition and testing the relationship between Kohl and Genscher. We were comfortable that Kohl's ultimate position on the border was identical to our own. We thought his primary motivation for evading a firm answer was to avoid alienating the large number of people expelled from the German areas of Poland after the war, most of whom were conservative (CDU and CSU) voters. The issue might become a campaign plank for the right-wing Republikaner Party in the upcoming FRG elections. Perhaps Kohl also had an eye on history and was reluctant to go down as the leader formally identified with giving up large territories which for centuries had been an integral part of the homeland. Since we wanted to bolster his position, we were prepared to defer to his judgment as to when he would officially resolve the border issue. He appeared to be speaking with a wink and a nod on the matter, but his current public position on this issue, and the disquiet it provoked among his fellow Europeans, caused us concern as well.

GEORGE BUSH

The Polish border and NATO membership were among the topics I planned to raise with Helmut at Camp David on February 24. In preparation, I called Thatcher and Mulroney on the morning of the visit. I tried to phone Mitterrand as well, but could not reach him.

Margaret made no secret of her concerns, notwithstanding the Two-plus-Four arrangement. She had been talking with Andreotti, Genscher, Stoltenberg, and Mazowiecki (Kohl was conspicuously absent from this list), all of whom, she said, accepted the fact that reunification was on its way, but who also were worried about the consequences and the uncertainty. She thought the agreement at Ottawa would help to allay some of the fears, but half of NATO was still annoyed at being excluded.

She pointed out that it was important to sort out a common alliance position. "There are not many options," she observed. "Helmut has been good on NATO, and on keeping your troops in Germany. There is the problem of East Germany. If all Communist troops leave the GDR, it would be an alarming development for Gorbachev. It would seem that the border of the alliance has moved closer to him." Genscher and she felt that if Soviet forces were allowed to remain for an indefinite transitory period, it would give Gorbachev some reassurance. "I fear that Gorbachev will feel isolated if all the reunification process goes the West's way. He's lost the Warsaw Pact to democratic governments . . ."

Margaret's fears of a united Germany, however, came ringing through. She darkly predicted that Germany would be "the Japan of Europe, but worse than Japan. Japan is an offshore power with an enormous trade surplus. Germany is in the heart of a continent of countries, most of which she has attacked and occupied. Germany has colossal wealth and trade surpluses. So we must include a bigger country, the Soviet Union [or] you, in the political area." She once again suggested that the time might be ripe to strengthen CSCE and use it for a wider, political framework. There were economic problems to sort out as well, especially those of admitting a new member (the GDR) to the EC, one with millions of citizens and no market economy experience.

Margaret raised the problem of putting eastern German territory in NATO. She opposed Stoltenberg's suggestion that West German forces could be stationed there; this too would be a problem for the Soviets. I asked what she thought of the proposal to demilitarize GDR territory, excluding Soviet troops as well. She doubted Gorbachev would go for it in the early stages. "NATO would be moving [east]. He's got to have some reassurance. That is the price for staying in NATO." I was not comfortable with the idea of Soviet forces remaining in the GDR. Although Mazowiecki wanted them to stay, I did not think the Polish people would support the idea for very long. But what I really wanted was a firm commitment from Kohl that the FRG would seek full membership in NATO for a united Germany. The problem of how to handle GDR territory was a sensitive political problem for Kohl. "That's why I just have a small group here for these talks," I said. "Genscher is not here; nor is their ambassador. It's just Brent and I and Jim Baker. We did this because we could have a better discussion on party problems . . . We have a lot at stake with the success of Helmut Kohl."

I asked Margaret what Mitterrand thought. "We talked," she said. "Privately, he is as fearful as we are. If we are not careful, the Germans will get in peace what Hitler couldn't get in the war. He is adamant on the Oder-Neisse line ... The French fear the domination of Germany. They fear the speed with which the FRG is pushing through to unification, and not addressing other questions first. We made a good start in Ottawa. . . . [But there] is great uncertainty, as people try to understand that there will be this great landlocked power that has quarreled with most people. It is not enough to anchor Germany in the EC—that might become Germany's new empire: the future empires will be economic empires."

BRENT SCOWCROFT

Thatcher had added remarkable sophistication to her position, but her concerns were still very evident and—to me—worrying. She disliked the notion of a giant Germany in the middle of Europe, and feared the political effect of reunification on Gorbachev. She skillfully used the Polish border issue to suggest that Germany had perhaps not changed after all, and she tied her concerns together in a way in which they reinforced each other.

While the tone of her views was much improved, I took little comfort from the content. Most of us in the Administration firmly opposed permitting Soviet forces to remain in East Germany. It could delay or prevent reunification. Certainly Cheney and I were against it, as was the President. Besides, we had been working hard to remove Soviet troops from Eastern Europe. Baker was perhaps the exception. He seemed willing to let them remain temporarily for tactical negotiating reasons, as a means to gain Moscow's support for a united Germany in NATO. I was also dismayed that Thatcher backed a demilitarized East Germany. Finally, her comment about strengthening CSCE made me uneasy. She seemed to have meant it in a useful way, but I had seen much evidence that the French might seek to use CSCE as a way to supplant NATO. That was an unacceptable notion, both because of the centrality of NATO to US strategy and because, to me, collective security, as typified by the League of Nations and United Nations, was, in the end, no security at all.

GEORGE BUSH

Brian Mulroney supported reunification but had some reservations. "I'm concerned personally that unification for Germany appears to be fueled not just by the legitimate desire of the two states to come together," he said, but "by the total collapse of the economy of one state and the economic strength of another . . . I told Genscher you're not really talking about a merger here; this is a takeover." He predicted that the real problems with unification would appear further down the road, in areas like the Common Market. "The Community was never designed with the possibility of having such a great European power in mind," he said. I saw these concerns as additional headaches to sort out, but I was not really worried about them.

I told Brian about the suggestion that we allow Soviet troops to stay in East Germany. "It gives me heartburn, though, if we suddenly, in an effort to get German stability, acquiesce in or advocate Soviet troops remaining in Germany," I said. "That is what we have been against all these years." Mulroney reacted strongly. "I don't see how, in fairness, we can accept that. The minimum price for German unity should be full German membership in NATO and full support in all the Western organizations and full support for American leadership of the alliance. I indicated to Genscher . . . and I will tell you: we are not renting our seat in Europe. We paid for it. If people want to know how Canada paid for its seat in Europe, they should check out the graves in Belgium and France . . . NATO got us this far. Solidarity in the alliance will get us further." Brian was right on target.

My objectives for the Camp David meetings with Kohl were simple: to coordinate the path to unification, keep Germany on the NATO reservation, and get a declaration on the Oder-Neisse line. It would be the first time a German chancellor had been to Camp David, and I was looking forward to showing Helmut around the place and putting our feet up for some relaxed talks.

February 24 dawned bleak, cloudy, and cold. The weather was even colder on the mountaintop and there was hard-crusted snow on the ground. An icy wind bit as Barbara and I, bundled up in gray anoraks, greeted Helmut and his wife, Hannelore, who arrived in the presidential helicopter. They were accompanied by Jim Baker (resplendent in red flannel shirt, cowboy boots, and hat) and Brent, who had met them at Dulles Airport. Barbara and I drove Helmut and Hannelore in golf carts to their cottage to freshen up.

The two-bedroom "cabins" at Camp David, though not elaborate, are very comfortable. Each cottage has a wood-burning fireplace and, as the Kohls arrived, welcoming smoke was curling out of the chimneys. We told the Kohls that casual clothes were the order of the day and that the agenda and schedule of meetings and activities could be rearranged in any way to suit them. I always hated it when jet-lagged visitors were expected to stay awake and be sharp at rigidly scheduled meetings. After a lively lunch at Laurel cottage, the social center of the camp, we moved to the large wood-paneled living room.

Helmut described events in East Germany and how he saw German unity unfolding. "The developments are so dramatic I can hardly believe it," he exclaimed, his eyes lighting up. "Communism in the GDR has collapsed like a house of cards." The Modrow government had effectively disintegrated in January, and its leader had no idea how to create confidence in it again. "Between January first and today, an entire city's worth of people left the GDR," said Helmut with a sweep of his hand. "We must persuade these people to stay. Productivity in the East is in sharp decline. Everyone wants to be paid in deutsche marks. Shortages are increasing. The corruption trials of former GDR officials are having disastrous consequences. Of the fifteen most important officials in the GDR a year ago, ten are in prison. That used to be the leadership. . . . In the rest of the country the corruption is just as bad.

"Three weeks ago the situation was such that I concluded we had to do something different," Kohl continued. "We had to change our program. So now we need monetary union." He knew that after the election the East German government would ask Bonn to pour money into state enterprises. He would have to say no, the situation was too serious simply to throw money at programs. Greater action on industrial development was needed. "Their telephone system doesn't work; the railroads are a disaster; and the environment is a mess, including two dangerous nuclear reactors—worse than the design of the one at Chernobyl. The situation is just as disastrous, so I must act quickly. I must insist that we move to a market economy immediately after the elections." This was the first I had heard of his ambitious plans in any detail.

Kohl downplayed the problem of the Polish border. "The border question is not serious," he declared with a confident smile. "Among friends I can be honest. In the FRG today eighty-five to ninety percent of the population are in favor of the Oder-Neisse border. The vast majority knows that this will be the border. The man who built Camp David, Mr. Roosevelt, will never be popular in Germany. The Poles were pushed west and the Germans were expelled. This was a reaction to Nazi crimes, but the Germans who were affected were innocent—this was twelve to fourteen million people. One third of the 1937 Reich was cut off. In 1945, two million German civilians were killed fleeing from Eastern Europe. We have to deal with this psychological problem in my country."

Kohl said the issue was to reassure the Poles about the 1,000-kilometer border, but that they had to understand the decision must come from a treaty ratified by an all-German parliament. He insisted that he and the FRG could not act for a united Germany, but acknowledged he would have to work to meet the expectations of the Poles. "The problem is that the Poles may demand reparations," he said. "I would find that unacceptable. We have already paid one hundred and fifty billion deutsche marks to Poland, Israel, and individuals. We won't pay more, fifty years after the war."

Instead of including the Poles in the Two-plus-Four talks, as Warsaw and others were suggesting, Kohl proposed a different tack. "If we coordinate between the US and the FRG, we *might* solve the issue vis-à-vis Poland, not through participation, but through consultation. . . . I'd like to help Mazowiecki, but 'Two-plus-Five' is not doable. We should stick with Two-plus-Four, but with a consultative mechanism for Poland. Gorbachev is not interested in the Oder-Neisse issue; he just doesn't want Poland to open up the question of its eastern border. There are old Polish cities in the USSR." In short, Helmut was proposing that the United States mediate.

He assured me again that Germany did not want neutrality. "A united Germany will be a member of NATO," he insisted, thumping the arm of the chair for emphasis. "One needs precise definition for Germany's NATO membership, however. We will also need a transition period. NATO units, including Bundeswehr forces dedicated to NATO, cannot be stationed on East German soil." At the same time, he did not want the Soviets to keep their troops in East Germany indefinitely because this would compromise German sovereignty.

He then floated a disturbing idea. "If West Germany is a member of NATO, should it be done in the way we are handling France?" he asked.* "What about German military integration of the new Germany? Is this a good idea? But we do not want any special military status for all Germany, as occurred after 1918. That is why NATO is so important." Kohl added that we also had to begin to think about US nuclear forces in Germany and how these weapons would be seen in Eastern Europe.

I was quick to respond. One France in the alliance, with its special arrangements, was enough for me. "The concept of Germany being in NATO is absolutely crucial," I reminded him. I added that sometimes he forgot to consult with our smaller NATO partners, and that Genscher's comment to the Italians at Ottawa had not helped matters. He acknowledged the problem and was trying to mend fences with Andreotti and the others. "I'll do the same thing with François Mitterrand at some time," he said. "He has been holding firm. Most of the French people are on our

---

*France is a member of NATO but does not participate in its military structures.

side, but the French political class is against us." Denmark, Norway, and the Netherlands were still problems. "Margaret Thatcher: I can't do anything about her. I can't understand her. The Empire declined [while] fighting Germany—she thinks the UK paid this enormous price, and here comes Germany again."

"We don't look at it that way," I replied. "We don't fear the ghosts of the past; Margaret does. But you and we must bend backwards to consult, recognizing our unique role in history." I told him I had called Margaret that day to listen to her views.

"In the FRG there is anger among Germans because we have been reliable partners for over forty years," complained Helmut. "Why doesn't that help?" I told him the United States could and would help. When he said Germany would stay in NATO with full membership, that reassured others. He would also have to address the Polish border—and US nuclear weapons in Germany, which I felt were an essential part of our presence there. Without those weapons in Germany it would be hard to persuade others in Europe to keep them. Furthermore, our public saw the nuclear deterrent as protection for our troops. If we lost the weapons, domestic support for keeping troops in Europe would erode.

Kohl replied that he wanted the United States in Europe, and not only its military presence. "I want to eradicate the concept of a Fortress Europe." Jim pointed out that NATO was the *raison d'être* for keeping US forces in Europe. "We couldn't have US forces in Europe on the soil of a non–full member of NATO," he reminded Kohl. Helmut speculated that convincing the Soviets about membership might "end up as a matter of cash. They need money." I told him I wanted perestroika to succeed and a good US-Soviet summit to give Gorbachev a boost at home. However, "the Soviets are not in a position to dictate Germany's relationship with NATO. What worries me is talk that Germany must not stay in NATO. To hell with that! We prevailed, they didn't. We can't let the Soviets clutch victory from the jaws of defeat."

Kohl urged that the United States speak with the Soviets outside the Two-plus-Four about full German membership in NATO. "That way [they] will understand that there is total US-FRG agreement without any games," he said. "The Soviets will be more willing to tell you their real price tag for their agreement." Moscow would want something in return. "You've got deep pockets," I joked.

I suggested a bracing walk around the Camp David perimeter to clear heads after the heavy dialogue. Helmut declared himself an enthusiastic walker. We set out at a good pace, following the pathway which runs along the fence around the compound. His joy in the outdoors was evident, but he was visibly tired from his long trip from Europe. The wind had died down, but there was a chilly late afternoon breeze. Helmut did well until we reached a long, steep incline. Partway up the hill, there developed substantial doubt that he would make it to the top. Huffing and puffing mightily, the jet-lagged Chancellor struggled to the summit. We immediately dubbed the incline "The Helmut Kohl Memorial Hill."

After breakfast the next morning, we attended a church service in Camp David's lovely new chapel, which always had great appeal for the Bush family. The Navy and Marine personnel on the base would come with their families. The twelve-member choir was made up of enlisted people, officers, and their spouses. A Navy chaplain performed the simple, moving service. On this particular day it had added meaning as, side by side with the German Chancellor, we asked God's blessing on our work. Familiar hymns were selected, and Helmut and his group sang along in German.

Following church, we renewed our discussions. Helmut wanted to know when we would get down to business on Two-plus-Four. The two Germanies would not negotiate until after the election. "We cannot negotiate with the Modrow government," he said. "It has no status." Baker reminded him that the allies were getting nervous about consultations, and explained that we were thinking about discussions between the US, Britain, France, and West Germany before negotiating with Moscow. "[That] would help dampen British and French anxieties as well as those of other NATO allies, especially if we let NATO know about these discussions."

"Let's make damn sure we don't leave our allies out, as if we are carving up Europe," I said. I asked when he thought reunification would finally come about. Kohl could only guess: perhaps the end of the year. Parallel to the political process was monetary union, which also required a great deal of work. "I don't want a hectic pace, partly because of the fears of others. So German unity might be next year."

Kohl predicted that Gorbachev would fix his bottom line on Germany during the summit in Washington. "Gorbachev will wish to take a real decision with the President, in the context of major agreements and progress on arms control with the Americans," he said. "That would not be the Two-plus-Four, just Gorbachev and the President."

"Gorbachev has to be provided with face, with standing," I replied. "That's a key point."

"That supports my thesis," said Helmut. "He wants to deal with the other superpower. The central question is the membership of Germany in NATO. In the end, Gorbachev will make that concession to the President."

At the end of our discussion, Horst Teltschik raised the problem of the status of East German territory. He pointed out that we had to be careful not to use "jurisdiction" when referring to NATO and GDR territory, but use "forces" instead. There was a critical difference: "Jurisdiction" affected the underlying alliance responsibility (which we did not want to compromise), while the location of forces did not. Baker agreed. "I used the term 'jurisdiction' before I realized that it would impact upon Articles 4 and 5 of the North Atlantic Treaty," he admitted. Kohl suggested we say that publicly.

In our joint press conference, I spelled out our solidarity on NATO membership:

> ". . . We share a common belief that a unified Germany should remain a full member of the North Atlantic Treaty Organization, including participation in its military structure. We agreed that US military forces should remain stationed in the united Germany and elsewhere in Europe as a continuing guarantor of stability. The Chancellor and I are also in agreement that in a unified state the former territory of the GDR should have a special military status, that it [the area of the GDR] would take into account the legitimate security interests of all interested countries, including those of the Soviet Union."

BRENT SCOWCROFT

I thought the meetings had been a great success, not that everything was agreed on but because it truly solidified the relationship between the President and the Chancellor. There was a closeness and a camaraderie which I felt would help enormously as we began hurtling down the final stretch to unification. There were several things which particularly struck me. One was Kohl's description of East Germany as a basket case. East Germany had been the powerhouse of the Warsaw Pact. It was at the forefront of espionage, training terrorists, pouring arms into the hands of left-wing and anti-US regimes, and shoring up communist states with economic aid. How could we have been so far off the mark? Perhaps domestic decay was part of the price for this international aggressiveness.

I was pleased at the promptness and firmness with which the President knocked down the notion of a French-like German role in NATO. It wasn't clear to me whether Kohl was serious or simply testing the President to see how determined he was on the NATO issue. If it was the latter, he departed with no doubts whatsoever. The problem of East German territory remained, however.

I was disappointed that at the post-meeting press conference Kohl ducked the border issue. The first question posed was whether he considered the existing border final. He was more than a little disingenuous on the subject. "According to the legal situation in our country, it is a freely elected parliament—thus sovereign—of the people which has to decide this question," he replied. He could have dealt with it by proclaiming that, while only a united Germany could act *de jure* on the border, Bonn was solidly in support of the Oder-Neisse line. He was being coy because he was still angling for support from the West German right wing.

GEORGE BUSH

The day after the Camp David meetings, I called both Mitterrand and Thatcher. "On the border issue, I believe Kohl's silence is a mistake," said Mitterrand. "Helmut Kohl must be responsible for his actions and he should use diplomacy. He must recognize the Oder-Neisse line. However, for election reasons, I do not believe he will do it. . . . I have told Kohl he is making a serious mistake. It is a fact of life that Europeans will always be suspicious of Germany because of the war, although they may be vague in articulating this suspicion. The SPD could well win the March 18 elections. If so, it will be hard for Kohl to regain momentum, and it will be in his best interest to be open." He argued that Kohl missed the point that it should not be up to Germany to verify borders. "The victors should have a say, presumably the World War II victors. There must be absolute clarity on this position among the UK, France, and the United States."

He was furious about the way the French Army in Germany was being treated since talk of reunification had begun. "I instructed the French ambassador in Berlin to organize a parade and the Berliners asked that the parade be canceled!" Mitterrand wanted the position of the allies to be clear. "We are in Germany for the Western world, and for the protection of Germany. If we were just a conqueror and did not need to be in Germany, we wouldn't want to be like the Soviets in the GDR, hiding from the people. We speak of German unity, it is Two-plus-Four. When we speak of borders, it is Four-plus-Two. I want you to know my thoughts. I also want you to keep my position in mind with the FRG. . . . We must not subjugate our national strategic concerns for Helmut Kohl's domestic political concerns. All of this will go very fast. Let's not believe that the USSR has vanished from the scene." It was not a happy Mitterrand.

Thatcher was pleased with what Kohl was saying about NATO membership but was still annoyed on the Polish border matter. While I understood Mitterrand's reservations, and hers, I was confident of the outcome. I believed Kohl would deliver on recognition of the Oder-

Neisse line. I listened patiently to their fears and tried to remain sensitive to their concerns. I was not, however, about to be dissuaded from the course I felt sure was best.

On February 28, I phoned Gorbachev, who was not especially pleased with my description of the Camp David meeting. He was uneasy with Kohl's evasiveness on the border and unhappy with what was being said about the future of Germany in the context of European security. "You have said that you have a mutual understanding with Kohl. I must disappoint you—we do not yet have a common understanding with Chancellor Kohl," he said carefully. "You have said that no one should be concerned about these changes and about the threat of a united Germany. But then, if so, if you believe a united Germany would not be a threat, why do Western countries want to incorporate them into one alliance? If we find that this would negatively affect the Soviet Union, we would have to think long and hard about it." He was pleased, however, that I called him to tell him about the discussions, and asked me to continue to do so.

BRENT SCOWCROFT

Gorbachev's tone was friendly, but there was no mistaking the ominous character of the phrase "think long and hard about it." He was not on board the Bush-Kohl train. Taken together with Mitterrand's somewhat surprising outburst—given the closeness of the Franco-German relationship—it was a sobering aftermath to the heady weekend with Kohl. It was far from obvious to me that we could do much to relieve the underlying anxiety these calls revealed, although a forthcoming Kohl statement on the border would certainly have improved the atmosphere.

The East German elections were now approaching, and all of us were nervous about the outcome. Based on experience up to that point in Eastern Europe, the East Germans would probably dump the Communists. However, given the "socialization" of the GDR, it was reasonable to expect that the bulk of the vote would cluster around the Social Democrats. Indeed, that was the broadly held expectation among observers both in Europe and the United States. Late polls, for example, were giving the SPD-East 44 percent against only 20 percent for the CDU-East. I did not indulge in the luxury of anticipating a Christian Democratic victory.

GEORGE BUSH

Helmut called me on the eve of the election, modestly optimistic. He hoped the result would bring a "reasonable coalition," and a new government by Easter at the latest; then work on monetary union could begin. He promised that no matter what happened, there would be no *fait accompli* on reunification. The Poles should be consulted in all areas that affected them. He promised again that the East and West German parliaments would make declarations about entering into obligations, and that an all-German government would immediately conclude an internationally binding treaty. He wanted, however, to end talk of a Two-plus-Four discussion on the matter taking place in Warsaw. "If this happened, we could go to 'Yalta' right away. I won't have that." I was meeting soon with Mazowiecki, and promised to discuss his thoughts with our top people before then.

If there were any remaining doubts that the collapse of the GDR, and the impatience of its people for political and economic freedom, had become the engine of reunification, the East German elections laid them to rest. With over 93 percent of the electorate voting, the CDU-led coalition, "Alliance for Germany," won 48 percent of the vote, with the Social Democrats polling only 22 percent and the PDS, the renamed Communist Party, taking 16 percent.

The outcome shocked all the parties involved. The results meant that Kohl's partners would control 193 of 400 seats in the East German legislature. At Kohl's urging, Lothar de Maizière, head of the East German CDU and the new premier, had committed himself during the campaign to rapid reunification via Article 23. Within days he announced full support for reunification and proposed July 1 as the date for monetary union. Negotiations between the two Germanies about economic and social union, to be followed by full political union, began immediately. The "two" had settled the internal aspects of reunification. Now it was our turn to handle the external, international, ones.

CHAPTER 11

The Face of a New Europe

The effect of the East German elections on the diplomacy surrounding the "external" aspects of reunification was dramatic. They definitively ended any Soviet hope to slow the drive for unification through an obedient East Germany. Instead, Moscow was confronted with an East German government which enthusiastically embraced speedy absorption into the Federal Republic. The Soviets were now politically isolated. Nevertheless, it was important that we continue to consult them and treat them as full partners, not simply present them with Western conditions for the outcome we wanted.

The importance of the elections was not lost on the Western allies either. In particular, the British recognized that reunification was now inevitable and, having accepted the fact, began to work in earnest toward the best possible outcome. Margaret Thatcher took an active role in our efforts to keep the Germans in NATO and to resolve the impact of reunification on the alliance. Solidarity was growing among the allies, denying the Soviets further opportunity to divide the West in the Two-plus-Four negotiations. The French and British began to warm to the Germans, no longer insisting that a peace treaty be included as part of a settlement. They also agreed to our plan to limit the scope of Two-plus-Four to Allied Rights and similar "singularization" questions, and prevent the Soviets from expanding the agenda.

GEORGE BUSH

I was surprised and pleased by the outcome of the election. Had the SPD won, I think the risks of a confederal Germany outside of NATO would have been much higher. Helmut Kohl personally had a great deal riding on the results as well. He was so tied to German unity that an SPD victory and delayed unity would probably have hurt his political fortunes in the upcoming West German elections. But Helmut had fought hard, helping to organize the efforts of the East German CDU. It had worked, and once again he had proved his skeptics wrong.

On March 20, I called Helmut to congratulate him. "You're a hell of a campaigner!" I told him. "It was a hard, tough time, but it was worth it," he said. "You have to bear in mind that these people are in a very difficult time. The last free elections were [over] fifty years ago. Since 1961, when the Wall went up, there have virtually been no communications with the world outside. . . . The workers voted for us. If we act reasonably, in five years or so the country will have a good economy. The results are very important for the NATO question as well. I will now find a totally different support than if the Left had won. So I am happy."

President Bush discussed with Kohl a remaining thorn in the side of Allied solidarity—the Polish border. It had become a rallying point for any government unhappy with the prospect of reunification. On March 8, after an intensive internal battle within the West German coalition, Kohl had presented a declaration to the Bundestag along the lines he had described to the President in their phone conversation just before the East German elections. The two Germanies would confirm the Polish border, but on condition that the Poles renounced reparations and respected the rights of the remaining German minority. A treaty affirming the border would be concluded after reunification. The Poles, however, were not so easily mollified. On March 9, Prime Minister Mazowiecki convinced Mitterrand to call publicly for a German-Polish treaty to be signed before unification. The situation was becoming serious. Mazowiecki was scheduled to visit Washington, and the President offered to mediate.

GEORGE BUSH

I explained to Helmut what I intended to tell Mazowiecki, and asked for his thoughts. "I will tell him what you have repeatedly assured me— and that I believe you—that the current GDR-Polish border should be the permanent German-Polish border," I said. I would also support Polish participation in the Two-plus-Four talks whenever matters pertaining to Poland would be discussed.

Helmut wanted the two German governments to write to Mazowiecki to reassure him. "Let me make a further remark, which I am not making publicly: I am ready and willing to agree on an eventual text with Mazowiecki." I asked him if I should mention this to the Polish leader. "If you think it would be useful, and if he does not make it public—and reassures you that he will not," replied Helmut.

BRENT SCOWCROFT

I was not sure it was a good idea to act on Kohl's apparent offer. Since the Poles would have a strong incentive to leak the news, we could end up in the middle of a public squabble between West Germany and Poland. I thought we should leave it to Kohl himself to decide when, and in what fashion, he might want to raise the issue directly with Mazowiecki.

GEORGE BUSH

I met with Mazowiecki at the White House on March 21. He thanked me for the joint statement Kohl and I had made at Camp David about including the Poles in the Two-plus-Four discussions. "The Polish people are paranoid about agreements being made over their heads," he told me. "It is crucial to us to ensure that our Western territories are not just a gift from Stalin—that they are guaranteed by all the powers, not just a unilateral act by one."

Mazowiecki repeated that he wanted a treaty written and initialed before unification and then signed by an all-German government as soon as one existed. I explained Kohl's political problems and strongly urged him to trust Kohl's word when he declared that the current border should be the permanent one. Mazowiecki told me of his high regard for Kohl—the problem was not the Chancellor but the position a united, and stronger, Germany might take. That was why he wanted assurances beforehand.

"Confidentially, what if I could get Kohl to agree with you on a text of a treaty now?" I asked. "Don't answer now, and please keep it confidential. If that would help move the process, I would try it." Mazowiecki indicated that his first reaction to the idea was positive, but that he would have to study it.

In fact, I had misunderstood Helmut's meaning when he made the offer to agree on a text. I thought he meant the text of an eventual German-Polish treaty. In a follow-up call, however, Horst Teltschik made it clear to Brent that Kohl was referring to the text of the common declaration for the two German parliaments to issue.

I spoke with Helmut on March 23 and explained what had happened. Kohl said that the misunderstanding was no big deal. I told him I had offered to approach him to ask if he would consider working out with Mazowiecki the text of a treaty. ". . . I asked him to keep it strictly confidential," I said. "It was presented as a George Bush idea with no reference to the idea that you and I had said anything about it." Kohl said we could further develop the idea. "Frankly, what you've proposed here is something he might recognize as something that's as far as Germany can go." He did not understand, however, why Mazowiecki did not simply pick up the telephone and call. "I would have told him that I wouldn't sign a treaty earlier," he declared. "No one will make me. But I do want to help him. If we have two German parliaments and two German governments saying this [acceptance of Oder-Neisse as the permanent border], it's not unreasonable to assume their positions will not change in two years."

BRENT SCOWCROFT

With these discussions, the border crisis was largely defused. The President's grasp of the problem and how to resolve it had proved on the mark. He jumped in the middle of the issue and brought both sides to an understanding. It turned out that his "misunderstanding" of Kohl's intent had moved a solution forward. He obtained Kohl's promise of assurances to Poland from both German states that the "key" text of the future treaty between the two states would be worked out.

The ironic part of the entire issue is that when the Federal Republic decided it would absorb East Germany by means of Article 23, which the de Maizière government in the East embraced, the border question became moot. A united Germany, which was simply an enlarged FRG with its existing laws, would still be bound by its old legal commitment to the Oder-Neisse line. But no one thought to link Article 23 to the resolution of the border. We had lost the forest for the trees.

The most important international issue remained—persuading the Soviet Union to accept a united Germany in NATO. If we were to have any chance of convincing them that this would not pose a threat, we would have to demonstrate how the character of the alliance itself was changing. There were already practical reasons for us to reexamine NATO's mission and strategies: the easing of tensions and the loosening of the Soviet hold over the Warsaw Pact. Reunification also complicated existing problems facing the alliance, such as the lingering question of modernizing short-range nuclear forces and negotiations over conventional force reductions.

By February we had begun to discuss seriously what future we wanted to see for NATO, and the President ordered a complete reassessment of our NATO strategy. We put together an interdepartmental group, the European Strategy Steering Group, headed by Bob Gates, to analyze the practical questions. Among the first issues tackled was short-range nuclear missiles. The allies had agreed at the NATO summit the previous year to begin new arms control negotiations on short-range nuclear forces after a conventional forces treaty was signed. Since then, the matter had quietly been put aside. As we asymmetrically reduced conventional forces, the importance of short-range forces as a means to offset Warsaw Pact superiority in numbers faded, and by early 1990 we began to worry that Congress would not fund modernization anyway. Canceling modernization was becoming feasible militarily and attractive politically. Formal consultations, however, might reignite German public debate over the future of the remaining missiles and make the issue grist for supporters of a neutral united Germany. We had to find a way to end the debate within the alliance quietly and to avoid Congress simply declaring that modernization was dead. The plan we devised was to cancel modernization before Congress acted and simultaneously offer new proposals for arms control talks on short-range forces after the ongoing conventional forces treaty was completed.

We had to figure out, as well, how the armed forces of a united Germany would fit into the new limits on conventional forces. We knew ceilings on German troops were of critical importance to the Soviets and that they wanted them set by treaty. Versailles, however, had imposed such "singularization" on the German military after World War I and it had been the cause of a great deal of resentment. While both the West Germans and the Americans could accept a ceiling on the Bundeswehr, we wanted it done in the context of limits placed on all national armies in both alliances.

All these issues affected the negotiations for reunification, especially NATO membership. For this reason, we wanted them resolved within the alliance as quickly as possible—which pointed to the need for another NATO summit sooner rather than later. In early April, Baker, Cheney, Scowcroft, and Powell suggested wrapping the cancellation of SNF modernization together with a proposal for a NATO summit in a presidential speech. It was an ambitious plan, since it would put additional pressures on us by raising expectations for a summit, which Manfred Wörner was already proposing.

It was essential to consult our principal allies about the future of NATO and the United States role in it, as well as to consolidate Western support for full German membership in the alliance. The first round of Two-plus-Four negotiations was scheduled for May 5 in Bonn, and the West should speak with one voice. We wanted to keep the agenda of these talks narrowly focused on Allied Rights and exclude any discussion of German membership in NATO and similar issues which should be left up to the Germans themselves. The President spoke with Genscher about some of these questions when he was in Washington on April 4 to consult with us prior to our discussions with Eduard

Shevardnadze.* We also set up meetings with Thatcher and Mitterrand for mid-April.

BRENT SCOWCROFT

There were lingering differences within the Bonn coalition over the nature of NATO membership. In a March 23 speech, just days after the East German elections, Genscher had speculated that NATO and the Warsaw Pact would both quickly wither away, implying it was acceptable to leave the GDR portion of a united Germany outside NATO and within a still ill-defined CSCE security structure. Kohl became so exasperated with his foreign minister that he reversed his previous position of solidarity with Genscher and publicly embraced the Stoltenberg formulation, that all Germany be in NATO and that German troops could be stationed in East German territory. In our April 4 talks, Genscher backed away from his position, speaking more positively about the future role of NATO and speculating that the Soviets might accept a united German membership if certain conditions were met. The change was encouraging, but Genscher's Foreign Ministry bureaucracy continued for some time to maintain that East Germany might remain outside NATO. Like Kohl, Genscher was also predicting that the upcoming Washington summit with Gorbachev would be crucial to settling the matter. As for Two-plus-Four, Genscher backed our narrow agenda.

When the President met with Thatcher in Bermuda on April 13, I was confident of British support. Our strategic and economic interests and goals around the globe had been similar for many decades, and I did not expect that our existing relationship with Britain would be changed by the end of the Cold War or reunification. Since the late 1940s, when, during the Truman Administration, the United States had first begun to assume Britain's traditional "balancing" role in Europe and around the globe, the British had looked to us to counter the Soviet threat, as well as add strength in their own voice in Europe and beyond. While we might have disagreements over new challenges, the thrust and spirit of our relations would probably remain much as it had been, especially if the Soviet Union eventually, after perestroika, became reinvigorated to play an active global role.

GEORGE BUSH

In Bermuda, I told Margaret of our intention to keep the agenda of Two-plus-Four narrow, and to consult closely before each meeting. She

*See Chapter 9.

readily agreed, but urged that we make sure these negotiations did not interfere with defense issues, which, like me, she preferred to see handled in other forums. I told her Manfred Wörner had suggested a summit, and spelled out what I thought a new NATO declaration could include, such as launching a reevaluation of our mission and strategy. She was enthusiastic. We both wanted to preserve NATO as the heart of the West's defenses and believed that the alliance could play a larger political role in the Atlantic community. She believed that in the future NATO would handle the defense responsibilities, while CSCE would be an East-West political forum, an opportunity for dialogue with Eastern Europeans. We went over the short-range nuclear forces dilemma, and I assured her that we remained committed to keeping the forces in Europe, but Congress would not vote money for the SNF modernization program. I wanted to announce its cancellation.

Margaret said that Kohl was absolutely firm, privately, on keeping conventional and nuclear forces on German soil, but we needed a public commitment from the Germans to maintain nuclear weapons there. "I accept that there will be no [modernization] because the Germans won't accept it." She complained that the Germans were "losing their appetite for defense . . . German politics is shifting more to the left than ours. But I am not so pessimistic that we might lose Germany. I think we can keep [it] in NATO, and Western conventional forces stationed there. I'm not sure about the nuclear forces." She felt that if we scheduled a NATO summit before the [all-] German elections it would help Helmut settle his commitment. "I do think a NATO summit is vital for public opinion," she said.

Margaret thought the Soviets would eventually see US forces in Germany as their guarantee of stability, as well as ours, but still argued that we should allow Soviet troops to remain for a transitional period—it would help Gorbachev with his military. "I don't agree," I replied. "I want the Soviets to go home."

BRENT SCOWCROFT

The President was to follow this meeting with similar talks with Mitterrand on April 19, at Key Largo. I felt that this could be a pivotal meeting if we were to revive the "spirit of Kennebunkport." US-French relations had deteriorated since the previous May, although not between the two presidents personally. I believed that the probable cause was differences over the substance of our respective visions for post–Cold War Europe and the US role in it.

While France had been a valued ally for generations, the bonds between us had not been as warm or consistent as those with Britain. France had long been ambivalent about the United States presence in Europe, seeing us in part as a rival and dominant outside voice in European affairs. During the Cold War, when the need for American forces as a counterbalance to the Soviet threat was strong, the French backed the US involvement in Europe and NATO, although their withdrawal from the integrated command structure, under De Gaulle in the sixties, had reflected their resentment of the American role. Now that the threat was receding, the French, I felt, were most likely to conclude that the need for a major US military presence would fade, and with it our voice in European affairs. This would offer the French an opportunity to strengthen their influence in Europe, based on a French-German entente dominated by France.

As German reunification appeared more and more inevitable, this French vision of a future Europe on its terms began to seem illusory, at least to me. A unified Germany would overshadow France and perhaps the EC as a whole. I had been hoping that Paris would recognize these changed realities and modify its strategy, perhaps turning toward the United States and NATO as a counterweight to an enlarged Germany. The French, however, seemed to be going in the opposite direction. They argued against NATO developing a common Western position for the CSCE summit, fought against NATO consultations on Two-plus-Four and the establishment of agreed positions among the Western allies, and objected to any attempt to expand NATO horizons. The United States seemed largely absent in longer-term French calculations about Europe. These appeared to be focused on the outlines of a Europe in which NATO would play a stagnant role, or even disappear, and the WEU (Western European Union), as the defense component of the EC, would gradually take over European security.

I hoped that the President could raise these issues with Mitterrand at Key Largo in the hope of stemming or reversing what I saw as the French negative drift. He mentioned many of these points in a letter to Mitterrand he sent on the eve of their discussions. It stressed the critical importance of a close US-French relationship to the stability of the emerging Europe and the President's determination that the United States remain deeply committed in Europe, including a significant military presence. Consultations in NATO on the Two-plus-Four were important, not to turn the alliance into a forum to provide guidance but to give the allies a sense of comfort about what was taking place. The President outlined our narrow agenda for the Two-plus-Four: "to end this legacy of war and restore full sovereignty to a peaceful, democratic, and united German state." We should try to give the Soviet Union a sense of assurance about its security concerns, but it should not be permitted to manipulate the Two-plus-Four process. The letter wound up with emphasis on strengthening NATO, enhancing its political role, and asserting that NATO, the EC, and CSCE were complementary, not competitive. It was a strong message, but one we hoped Mitterrand would see as reaching out to him in a collegial way.

GEORGE BUSH

As it turned out, the meeting at Key Largo was pleasant and non-confrontational. Our first session was just the four of us—Brent and I with François and Jacques Attali. There was no agenda, and most of the discussion focused on the future of NATO. Unification matters per se were discussed only briefly. As for the goals of Two-plus-Four, François was satisfied with the narrow agenda Margaret Thatcher and I had announced at Bermuda the week before. Concerned with Soviet anxieties on the matter, like Margaret, François thought there should be no NATO forces in East Germany.

In our discussion about NATO, I explained why it was important for the United States to stay in Europe. The question was how. "We are not seeking a thirteenth seat at the EC table," I said. "The CSCE cannot be a guarantor of security in Europe, but we do see an expanded role for NATO." Mitterrand observed that the role of NATO was already large. How could it be made larger? "It will be guaranteeing against instability," I said. "Its role will be different. The organization must be flexible."

"The risk of war has decreased," replied François. "The Soviet Union will have difficulty retaining its unity. The Eastern Europeans are no longer enemies. Nevertheless, a threat remains. Gorbachev may have to make certain dangerous postures if he is forced by necessity, so we must retain our security arrangements . . . The Soviet Union is not reassuring: a great power in a weakened condition is dangerous. The United States should have a say in all issues that affect the equilibrium in Europe." NATO was the organizational forum for the discussion of issues regarding European security and equilibrium.

François agreed that we could ensure complementarity among NATO, the EC, and CSCE, and suggested we organize regular ministerial contacts at the foreign minister level to discuss political issues. Such a scheme would not compete with the EC. "Europe is larger than the EC," he said. "Also, the East Europeans don't know where to go. They would have to come to an enlarged EC like beggars." It would take a generation to work all of this out completely, he said. ". . . People say that I do not want the United States in Europe any more; that is wholly wrong. I want the Americans to be a part of this." I told him we could not keep the United States in Europe if NATO did not adapt to a new role. Mitterrand proposed a NATO summit to discuss the matter—exactly what I had in mind.

BRENT SCOWCROFT

The meeting dealt satisfactorily with our key operational objectives. It brought us together for the immediate tasks ahead. But my concerns were not allayed. The thrust of Mitterrand's remarks was to keep NATO confined to its traditional role—defense against a massive Soviet attack on Western Europe. It was precisely what we did not want, and would surely result in the atrophy of the alliance. I left Key Largo even more convinced that the US and France had significantly differing views of the future of Europe and our role in it.

By the end of April, the West was more or less united on the objectives of Two-plus-Four and behind German membership in NATO. We now turned to the challenge of casting NATO's future and CSCE responsibilities in such a way as to convince the Soviets that there would be no future threat from them, or from a Germany in NATO. Since Gorbachev had appeared ambivalent about Germany's reunification and the issue of its NATO membership in his discussion with Baker in February, there was a possibility he could be open to persuasion if we could provide the right incentives.

On May 4, in a speech at Oklahoma State University, President Bush formally called for a NATO summit. It should launch a wide-ranging NATO strategy review for the transformed Europe of the 1990s. It should address four critical points: The role that NATO could play in Europe; the conventional forces the alliance would need and its goals for conventional arms control; the role of nuclear weapons based in Europe and Western objectives in new arms control negotiations; and finally, strengthening CSCE to reinforce NATO and protect democratic values in a Europe that was now whole and free. He also called for accelerated negotiations toward a CFE treaty and announced the cancellation of the SNF modernization program.

As we planned how to change NATO and provide incentives to the Soviet Union, Shevardnadze was considering what assurances Moscow would need. When he and Baker had met in Namibia just after the East German elections, they had discussed Germany.* While Two-plus-Four

*See Chapter 9, page 217.

helped meet some of their concerns, the Soviets had a basic problem. It was not who ran Germany now they worried about, it was the Germany of the future. Shevardnadze said they could not accept a unified Germany in NATO, but admitted that Germany could not be neutral either. Frankly, he said, "we don't know the answer to the problem." Baker went through the logic of anchoring Germany in NATO and the US presence there. Shevardnadze said he did not question the value of a US military presence now or in the future; in fact, Soviet forces in eastern Germany would undoubtedly be temporary. The problem, he said, was that US troops in Germany would be hard to guarantee; he doubted that in five or ten years the next generation of German leaders would want them.

But Admiral William Crowe had also raised the question of German membership in NATO with Sergei Akhromeyev when they had met in Moscow in March, and the Marshal's reaction was far harsher than the Soviet Foreign Minister's had been; the difference reflected the division among the senior leadership in Moscow. "Akhromeyev was quite vocal in his opposition," read Crowe's cable at the time. "[He] insisted that this was simply something the USSR could not accept; that this could not be sold to the people. He noted that all Soviet families have memories of the Germans from WWII and that this was a grass roots issue."

While Shevardnadze seemed more flexible than the Marshal when it came to Germany in NATO, he also appeared deeply worried about the future of Soviet reform and Gorbachev's hold on power, both of which could be profoundly affected by the outcome of reunification. Since February, Shevardnadze had found himself pinned down by the military and Party conservatives on reform and foreign policy, unable to develop any flexibility to strike a bargain with the West. In April, he delivered an incredible speech to a conference of Communist Party members at the foreign ministry. He blasted the single-mindedness of the Party and its obsession with holding on to power in Eastern Europe, declaring that its only purpose now should be to ensure the success of reform in the Soviet Union. Without reform, he warned, "dictatorship is possible." He called for a solution on Germany which would be "accepted by the Soviet people and . . . gives them confidence that there will be no new military threat" from German soil. "The Soviet Union must seek a new security framework for Europe using the CSCE," he declared.

At a meeting of the Two-plus-Four ministers in Bonn on May 4, Shevardnadze laid out a tough new Soviet position. Any treaty should settle Germany's alliance membership and the status of troops from all Four Powers. It would have to confirm all the Four Power occupation measures, and there would be regulations on German domestic politics to prevent any resurgence of Nazism. There could be no NATO membership; instead, the CSCE would be strengthened. The Poles would have to be included in discussions on the border, and Germany must renounce nuclear, biological, and chemical weapons.

Shevardnadze accepted Article 23 of the West German Basic Law as the means for unification, meaning that the Soviets were now resigned to the absorption of the GDR into West Germany, but he proposed that its internal and external aspects be "decoupled." Unification would progress, but the matter of the external settlement (the security questions, which were at the heart of the problems) would be postponed until a European security structure could be developed to replace the alliances. Four Power rights would remain after unification. In short, Shevardnadze called for the continued singularization of a united Germany—neutral and outside the alliance systems—one still under outside control. This was completely unacceptable to us—and Shevardnadze was the moderate voice in Moscow.

GEORGE BUSH

After the Bonn meeting, both we and the Germans concentrated on ways to soften the Soviet position. On May 17, Kohl came to Washington, where he gave me an update on the internal situation in Germany. "I am going to sign a treaty between the two Germanies next week," he said, referring to economic and monetary union. He thought it would take about fourteen months to implement, and predicted all-German elections by the middle of January 1991.

He seemed very worried about keeping Gorbachev in power during these crucial days of Two-plus-Four. He painted a dark picture of the Soviet economy and said he was looking for ways the United States and West Germany could help. He briefed me on a secret trip to Moscow Teltschik had made a few days before to offer economic aid. The Soviets had requested nearly $12 billion in credits from the West. Kohl predicted that Gorbachev would ask for similar assistance at the Washington summit. I told Helmut that the United States could not guarantee loans to the Soviets unless there was change in the Baltic situation. "My question is: do we want to help him or see someone else?" replied Kohl. "I think it is him."

Did his advisors think the Soviet military might take over? "Yes, but not with force," answered Kohl. "It would be a civilian group, but backed by the military. It is not a problem for us, but Poland and others will be upset." He thought Gorbachev himself probably didn't want to keep troops in the GDR, but that it was a domestic issue in the Soviet Union.

"It is not like the Stalin days," he said. "At home he must face public opinion. I think his meeting with you will be very important, not on substance but appearance. That is because he stands beside you as an equal. He has big problems. His East German allies say they want to be in NATO."

"We will treat him as an equal," I said firmly. "If only we could solve the Lithuanian problem. . . . We probably can't give him money. But we will address regional issues, arms control, and so forth. We don't want the summit to be a failure." Kohl offered to talk to Gorbachev ahead of time. "But this should be just between the two of us," he said. "My Cabinet doesn't know." As for Soviet troops in eastern Germany, he planned to let them remain for a limited period "if that is necessary."

"I am on a different wavelength," I said. "I know your position, but I think they should get out." I said I thought I could convince Gorbachev that US troops should stay in Germany, "but I must know that Germany would want US troops."

"What sort of NATO would it be, leaving US troops aside?" asked Kohl. If the Europeans allowed the Americans to leave, it would be a defeat for everyone. "Remember Wilson in 1919," he said.

As Bush and Kohl were meeting in Washington, Baker visited Moscow on May 16–19. We hoped to obtain some Soviet movement on Lithuania, Germany, and arms control, but there was little progress on any subject. It seemed the military was applying heavy pressure on Gorbachev and Shevardnadze. Shevardnadze even canceled one morning session, which we had hoped would help clear the way for progress in arms control—especially CFE. The Soviet leadership appeared stalemated within its own ranks.

When Baker saw Gorbachev, the Soviet President launched into a long lecture covering US relations, Eastern Europe, and German reunification. Gorbachev may have been uneasy about raising these questions directly with the President, especially financial aid. Perhaps he chose Baker to carry his message and to vent his frustrations. This may have been an occasion when the messenger, a close friend of the President, would reinforce the message. He revealed his thoughts in a way he rarely did to anyone, asking, "Why should we do this? What's in it for us?"

Gorbachev argued that Washington had not really made up its mind about the Soviet Union. He pointed to Eastern Europe. "Everything that's happening there we have discussed with you and we are acting in accord with what I said we would do," he lectured Baker. "But I have information that your policy is driven by trying to disassociate Eastern Europe from the Soviet Union. You know my attitude—if these countries seek to dis-associate themselves, if that's what they want, let them do so. That's okay. But not if they're being pushed in this regard."

Another example was Germany. "Your position on this I believe is con-tradictory . . . You've said to us that both Germanies want peace, they both want democracy, and, therefore, they pose no danger," Gorbachev continued. If this was so, why not let the Germans become a member of the Warsaw Pact? If we said that we can trust the Germans, that they have proved themselves, why, he asked, did we feel it necessary to include them in NATO? "So when you are talking about a united Ger-many and you say that if Germany is not in NATO, it would create prob-lems, what you are really saying is that you don't believe Germany can be trusted." If we had offered a realistic analysis of Germany's non-membership in NATO as a serious threat to the alliance's infrastructure, he could understand. "But if you *are* saying that, then there's a problem. Because you are saying you continue to need a bloc even when the other alliance is disappearing." The United States was saying that NATO was necessary for now, and for the future, because the Soviet Union still has large military forces. "But if that's the position you premise NATO on now, then I think that's really not consistent; I think it's contradictory [with] the principle we are trying to build our relationship on."

A united Germany in NATO would mean a very serious development in the strategic balance. "I think you have to ask what's going to be the next logical step for us," he warned. ". . . Well, one step might be for us to suspend all talks and think about how this development is going to affect our doctrine, how it's going to affect our forces, what effect it should have on our approach to the Vienna [CFE] talks. I say this not because I am playing games, not because I want to engage in a level of political squab-bling. I say it because I really believe this is a serious problem for us."

Gorbachev complained that the Soviet Union had shared with us their plans for perestroika. He doubted, however, that the United States was ready to build the kind of understanding needed to accomplish these ends. He suspected that instead of doing something, and sharing in the Soviet Union's problems, the US approach was really to let the Soviets go it alone, and if their problems got worse, it might even benefit the United States.

Baker tried to reassure Gorbachev that the last thing we wanted was instability in the Soviet Union. The United States was looking for no advantages, and was not engaged in political game-playing. As to not wishing to help the Soviet Union in its economic crisis, the situation was not so simple. It was difficult for the Administration to justify sending

This 1988 photograph on Governors Island was taken at the last official session between Ronald Reagan and Mikhail Gorbachev, and at the beginning of a new, important relationship—and friendship—between Gorbachev and President-elect George Bush. December 7, 1988.

President Bush and President François Mitterrand bond at Kennebunkport. The family home at Walker's Point is in the background. May 20, 1989.

The warm handshake and smiles belied the difficult discussions between Brent Scowcroft and Deng Xiaoping during the secret mission to Beijing of Scowcroft and Deputy Secretary of State Lawrence Eagleburger (far left), shortly after the harsh suppression of demonstrators at Tiananmen Square. July 2, 1989.

Responding to the roar of the massive crowd at the Gdańsk shipyard with Polish hero Lech Walesa. July 11, 1989.

François Mitterrand jokes with George Bush and Helmut Kohl during the G-7 summit meeting in Paris. July 16, 1989.

Prime Minister Margaret Thatcher enjoys Camp David's primary mode of transportation during her first visit with President Bush at the presidential retreat. Charles Powell looks on. November 24, 1989.

Chancellor Kohl warms up for his assault on "Helmut Kohl Memorial Hill" at Camp David. February 25, 1990.

A heavy discussion at Camp David during the 1990 summit. *Around the table, clockwise:* President Bush, Vice President Quayle, Brent Scowcroft, Foreign Minister Eduard Shevardnadze, President Gorbachev, Marshal Sergei Akhromeyev, Peter Afanasenko (interpreter), James Baker. June 2, 1990.

Discussing a particularly sensitive issue in private at Camp David. June 2, 1990.

A desperate attempt to win the "Scowcroft Award." June 26, 1990.

The White House press corps questions the President just prior to the beginning of the first National Security Council meeting after Iraq invaded Kuwait. On the right side of the table are (from left) Director of Central Intelligence William Webster, Acting Secretary of State Robert Kimmit, President Bush, Secretary of Defense Dick Cheney, OMB Director Richard Darman. Across the table are Brent Scowcroft, Chairman of the Joint Chiefs of Staff Colin Powell, and Secretary of Energy James Watkins. Helen Thomas, dean of the White House press corps, looks on from over Webster's shoulder. Cabinet Room, August 2, 1990.

With Brent Scowcroft standing by, the President confers with King Fahd of Saudi Arabia on how to respond to the Iraqi invasion of Kuwait. Aspen, Colorado, August 2, 1990.

The coalition begins to take shape on the deck at Walker's Point. *Left to right:* the Saudi foreign minister, Prince Saud al-Faisal, Richard Haass of the National Security Council, James Baker, President Bush, Deputy National Security Advisor Robert Gates, White House Chief of Staff John Sununu, and the Saudi ambassador to the United States, Prince Bandar. Kennebunkport, August 16, 1990.

Even during an international crisis, there's time to hear what's on the mind of grand-child Ellie LeBlond. Kennebunkport. August 26, 1990.

Condoleezza Rice, special assistant to the President and senior director for Soviet affairs, briefs the President and his senior advisors in Helsinki, Finland, before their meeting with Gorbachev. Clockwise from the President's left are: James Baker, John Sununu, Marlin Fitzwater (on sofa), Dennis Ross, and Brent Scowcroft. September 9, 1990.

Support by Congress was a key element in coping with Iraqi aggression. Joining President Bush and Brent Scowcroft for breakfast are Congressman Bob Michel (on the President's left) and Senator Bob Dole. Virginia Lampley, the NSC's congressional director, and John Sununu also participated. Private dining room, White House, November 13, 1990.

Trading stories with Czech President Václav Havel, hero of the "Velvet Revolution," in the music room at Hradcany Castle in Prague. November 17, 1990.

President Bush and King Fahd share a rare light moment during the serious deliberations in Jeddah, Saudi Arabia, on the Gulf crisis. November 21, 1990.

General Norman Schwarzkopf and the Commander-in-Chief tour the front. November 22, 1990.

The President with his coalition troops. November 22, 1990.

Fresh off the plane from Tel Aviv, Lawrence Eagleburger gives the President and Brent Scowcroft a rundown on the mood and concerns of the Israeli leadership on the eve of Desert Storm. January 14, 1991.

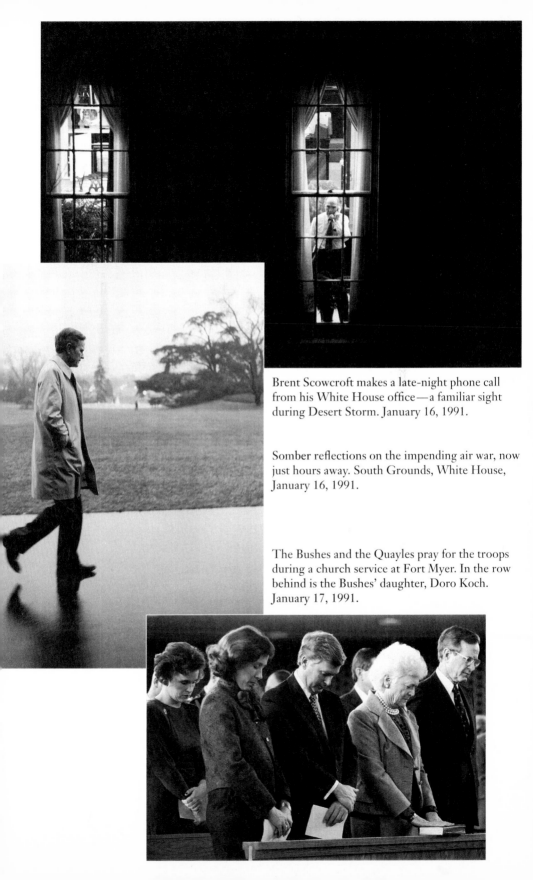

Brent Scowcroft makes a late-night phone call from his White House office—a familiar sight during Desert Storm. January 16, 1991.

Somber reflections on the impending air war, now just hours away. South Grounds, White House, January 16, 1991.

The Bushes and the Quayles pray for the troops during a church service at Fort Myer. In the row behind is the Bushes' daughter, Doro Koch. January 17, 1991.

A familiar scene in the Oval Office during Desert Storm: Brent Scowcroft presenting to the President the latest options. Looking on are (from left) Robert Gates, Marlin Fitzwater, John Sununu, and Vice President Quayle. February 12, 1991.

"No, no. That's *two* pepperoni, one sausage, and *no* broccoli." February 27, 1991.

The "Gang of 8" on the final day of the Gulf War. February 28, 1991.

Welcoming home the troops at Shaw Air Force Base in Sumter, South Carolina. Greeting the President are Captain "Spike" Thomas, who was shot down behind enemy lines, and Lieutenant "Neck" Dodson, who rescued him. March 17, 1991.

A surprised Brent Scowcroft receives the Medal of Freedom. July 3, 1991.

President Bush inspects a Soviet honor guard during the Moscow summit with Soviet Vice President Gennady Yanayev, who within a month would participate in a coup attempt against Gorbachev. August 1, 1991.

The President hears from Mikhail Gorbachev, who is in the Crimea, that he has been freed from the clutches of the coup plotters. Kennebunkport, August 21, 1991.

Ranger and Millie meet Boris Yeltsin on the White House South Lawn. June 6, 1992.

The initial levity will give way to difficult discussions at the G-7 meeting. *Clockwise from the President's left:* Italian Prime Minister Giulio Amato, Japanese Prime Minister Kiichi Miyazawa, EC Commission President Jacques Delors, British Prime Minister John Major, Canadian Prime Minister Brian Mulroney, President François Mitterrand (obscured), and Chancellor Helmut Kohl. Munich, Germany, July 6, 1992.

A final meeting with good friend Prime Minister John Major before leaving office. Camp David, December 19, 1992.

In his Camp David office, President Bush and Prime Minister Brian Mulroney watch an unrepentant Saddam Hussein. January 17, 1993.

our tax dollars when the Soviets themselves were still sending billions to help regimes such as Cuba.

Gorbachev objected, saying that the United States was putting a "dam" on Soviet efforts, and that other Western countries, particularly the Germans, had overcome their caution and saw possibilities for cooperation. If the United States wanted to mark time on economic matters, that would impose a cost on the relationship. "Our existing cooperative ties will be reduced as a result of that," he warned. "A process like that can be dangerous."

In what must have been a difficult moment for the leader of a proud people, especially in dealing with an adversary, Gorbachev said he would discuss the matter with President Bush, but that the Soviet Union required temporary financial support. "I think the best way to put it is that we need some oxygen," he said. "We are not asking for a gift. We are asking for a loan; we are asking for specifically targeted loans for specific purposes . . . What I will say to the President is that we're going to need fifteen to twenty billion dollars to tide us over." It was peanuts for the Soviet Union, he added, but because of the changes in the economy they could not muster such resources fast enough. He asked that Baker tell the President about the request. "If we reach agreement on arms reductions we will both save a substantial amount of resources and money," said Gorbachev. "[But] now we are in a special situation."

Baker returned to the Germans, saying we should let them choose their alliance membership. "We're not forcing Germany into NATO. But we do think it's important that Germany be part of NATO, not out of any fear of the Soviet Union but because we think that unless we find a way to truly anchor Germany in European institutions we will sow the seeds for history to repeat itself. If Germany was not anchored to the existing security institution, then we would have a powerful new entity in Europe concerned about developing its [own] security measures." It would be far easier for the Germans to renounce chemical, biological, and nuclear weapons if they were in NATO.

In an attempt to loosen Moscow's position, Baker presented the Soviets with nine "assurances." While these had all been offered already in various forms by both the Germans and ourselves, his staff had now put them in a comprehensive package:

1. The United States was committed to follow through on CFE negotiations for all of Europe.
2. The United States agreed to advance the SNF negotiations to begin once the CFE treaty was signed.

3. Germany would reaffirm its commitments neither to produce nor to possess nuclear, biological, or chemical weapons.
4. NATO would continue conducting a comprehensive strategy review of both conventional and nuclear-force requirements.
5. Extension of NATO forces to the former territory of the GDR would be delayed during a transition period.
6. The Germans agreed to a transition period for Soviet forces leaving the GDR.
7. Germany would make firm commitments regarding its borders, making clear that the territory of united Germany would comprise only the FRG, GDR, and Berlin.
8. The CSCE process would be strengthened, with a significant role for the Soviets in the new Europe.
9. Germany made it clear that it would seek to handle bilateral economic issues in a way that would support perestroika.

Baker added that a unified Germany in NATO would be a different Germany, and NATO itself would be different. The issue of "trusting" Germany was moot. Finally, if Germany did not want to be in NATO, it would not be.

Gorbachev asked what would happen if one day a unified Germany opted to leave NATO, which would undermine our ability to control it. "We won't have done anything in the interim period to try and shape the new system," argued Gorbachev. "Currently we have the Four Power Rights, the unification process—these give us means to do something. These give us a means to develop a new system, a new structure. Maybe a system based on demilitarization." He thought that perhaps we could document all the points Baker had made in a final settlement on Germany between the Four Powers and the Germans.

Baker asked if this final settlement would have to say that Germany would *not* have the right to remain in NATO. Gorbachev said yes. Was he talking about a neutral Germany? Gorbachev said he would call it non-aligned, and offered the example of the French arrangement with NATO. He added that if the Soviets were not able to persuade us to their point of view, "then I will say to the President that we want to enter NATO. After all, you said that NATO wasn't directed against us, you said it was a new Europe, so why shouldn't we apply?"

Baker said we could assume that Germany would want to be in NATO, because they were saying exactly that. The Soviets should not contemplate non-alignment as a condition for releasing our Four Power rights and responsibilities—that ran counter to the principles of Helsinki.

Would Gorbachev accept Germany having a free choice to remain a member of NATO? "As I have said to you frankly," he replied, "we cannot accept a unified Germany as a member of just NATO or the Warsaw Pact, because that's going to have a basic effect on the strategic balance in Europe and the world. You really should not leave us isolated at this crucial moment. We may have unusual moves to make."

BRENT SCOWCROFT

It was hard to tell whether Gorbachev meant what he was saying, or if he was simply voicing the conservatives' unhappiness for the sake of domestic consumption. Perhaps he was reacting to our differences over Lithuania. His cold warning in response to the President's letter on Lithuania had been delivered only two weeks before. As I look back on it years later, it is difficult to say how much of it was bluster and how much reality.

This period probably marked the high point of the pressure Gorbachev and Shevardnadze were facing from the conservatives and military, at least before the coup of August 1991. Indeed, as we have shown elsewhere, the picture from Moscow was not pretty. The Eastern European countries were flaking away from the Warsaw Pact at a rapid rate. And not only was the Pact falling apart, but also we were demanding that its linchpin, East Germany, join the Federal Republic and NATO. On top of all that, nationalism and ethnic divisiveness were on the rise within the Soviet Union itself. The conservatives wanted Gorbachev to put on the brakes—hard. Even Shevardnadze was showing his teeth, if more in sorrow than anger. It posed a serious dilemma for us. Gorbachev was unquestionably in danger.

The 1990 battle over renewing MFN for China came as we were concentrating on preparations for the Gorbachev summit. The President was obligated to make his annual determination on renewal by June 3. In order not to distract from the upcoming summit, or act too near the June 4 anniversary of Tiananmen, he announced his intention to renew on May 24. The reaction was immediate. Bills were introduced in both houses to overturn the decision. But while the accompanying rhetoric was strong, it was not, in the event, matched by action. In October, the House passed by very large majorities two measures—one a bill to revoke MFN status and the other to strongly condition any approval in 1991—but Congress adjourned before the Senate acted on either measure. MFN remained the occasion for most of the struggles with the Congress over China for the rest of the Administration.

GEORGE BUSH

The Democratic leadership in the Senate fought me tooth and nail on MFN for China. Senator Mitchell and others saw my support for China as something that could be very damaging to me politically. On vote after vote they stood against what I felt was best. The great irony is that when President Clinton—a relentless critic of our China policy in the 1992 campaign—proposed continuing MFN for China in his first term, the Democratic leadership reversed themselves 100 percent and supported him. So much for bipartisanship.

I spent a good part of May preparing for the Washington summit. I had reservations about meeting with Gorbachev while the Soviets were still blockading Lithuania, and I was being criticized at home that I was too accommodating to him by going forward with it. I knew the situation was not getting any better, but I wanted to take the risks and go ahead with the talks. Certainly, if the crisis got any worse, and if there was violence, we would cancel. But too much was at stake in our relationship, and for other countries, to allow the situation in Lithuania to torpedo the painful progress we had made in US-Soviet relations. We had to speak directly to each other.

I read briefing books up in Maine and sat through one session after another. I thought deeply about the state of our relationship with the Soviets. I didn't feel we had as many positive accomplishments as I had hoped. There was too much unfulfilled agenda between us, especially in arms control, as well as a host of regional issues, from Afghanistan to Angola. I also thought about the enormous problems facing Gorbachev. He was presiding over a rotten economy; the probable election of Yeltsin, his bitter enemy, as president of the Russian Federation;* and the struggle over the Baltics and other nationality problems. The man had accomplished an unbelievable amount and we should feel very lucky for that. Yet, who knew what would happen, whether he would be there the next day or the day after?

To make progress on the broad US-Soviet agenda and Germany, the Soviets, and Gorbachev, needed face and standing, although everything around them was falling to pieces—their empire and their economy, and now their union. I was trying to give them that standing and face without knuckling under or acquiescing in some of their wilder plans, or giving in on issues crucial to us. We couldn't hand them the $20 billion of financing they wanted unless they made deep economic reforms—and even

*Yeltsin was indeed elected on May 29, as Gorbachev was on his way to Canada and the United States.

then we didn't have the money. Also, we couldn't offer them the MFN status they wanted without emigration legislation and real progress in solving the Lithuanian crisis. They had to get negotiations started and lift the blockade. If they could do that, we might have a successful summit, something Gorbachev could take back to the Party congress in July. I certainly wanted to give him a boost if I could.

The Germans expected crucial movement on the Soviet position on NATO membership. I know Kohl and Genscher believed that Gorbachev would want to strike a deal with me—between the superpowers. Maybe they were right. This could be the time and place for a deal, but I was not so sure. Any concessions on his part might cause serious challenges to his authority at the Party congress. The analysts at my briefings were pessimistic about an agreement, pointing out that Gorbachev seemed to be delaying, hoping for more concessions from the Germans on issues such as the size of their armed forces. The Germans were also urging that we not back Gorbachev into a corner before the Party congress, and suggested we ought to use the talks to sound him out on the nine points Baker had raised in Moscow. Perhaps there were areas where he might be willing to move.

Mitterrand met with Gorbachev in Moscow on May 25, and the two of them talked primarily about Germany. François sent me a letter on the eve of the summit describing his impressions. "[Gorbachev's] hostility to the participation of a united Germany in NATO doesn't appear to me as being either fake or tactical," wrote François. "On this subject, he is both firm and determined. He even gives an indication that should he have to face a *fait accompli*, he would be compelled to alter his behavior on many issues, particularly on disarmament in Europe." He believed Gorbachev was still deeply worried about the change in the balance of power that would come about.

They had also discussed Lithuania. "Mr. Gorbachev is open to a dialogue, but is not ready to give up on the fundamentals," he said. "He keeps insisting that the Lithuanians renounce their vote of independence. . . . In brief, my impression is that Mikhail Gorbachev does not have much of a margin of maneuver left when it comes to the question of nationalities (Baltic states) or of the consequences of German unity. Regarding this last point, the calendar contemplated by Helmut Kohl will encounter, in my opinion, serious obstacles."

The day before Gorbachev was to arrive in Washington, Kohl called me, perhaps yet another sign that he expected the matter of German NATO membership to be settled at the summit.

"George, you can rely on our fullest support," he said. "One thing that is very important for Gorbachev to understand is that, irrespective of developments, we will stand side by side. And one sign of this coopera- tion is the link between us through the future membership of a united Germany in NATO without any limitations. You should make this clear to him, but in a friendly way, and also make it clear that this is the view I hold. There should be no doubt about that. A second point: we can find a sensible economic arrangement with him. He needs help very much. He should also know we have no intention of profiting from his weakness . . ."

"I don't expect much breakthrough," I said. "[But] we want him to come out feeling he has had a good summit even though there are no major breakthroughs. I think we can do it. We have a wide range of agreements to sign." I recalled Helmut's conversation with me earlier in the month when he predicted that Gorbachev would ask for aid at the summit, something he had raised with Baker in Moscow. "We have problems with that related to Lithuania. But I will take your advice. I don't want him to think we are taking advantage of him because of his weakness."

CHAPTER 12

Summit and Solutions

GEORGE BUSH

May 31 was a bright, hot day, and the arrival ceremony for Gorbachev was spectacular, set against the backdrop of the Washington Monument. The colorful ceremonial Revolutionary War uniforms of the Old Guard from Fort Myer stood out against the new green grass and leaves. A military band played and honor guards from each of the services dipped their flags as Gorbachev and I reviewed them, always a moving experience for me.

Gorbachev looked well and seemed confident as he greeted me with a smile and a strong handshake, not at all tired. He was a bit tense at first, and spoke very softly. He relaxed once we got to the Oval Office, and was almost jovial as we sat down on the white armchairs near the fireplace, under the Gilbert Stuart portrait of George Washington.

Our talk that morning was largely philosophical, the kind each of us had hoped to have at Malta. Gorbachev spoke of the need to free ourselves from old suspicions. We were at a watershed in history, he said. "You may or may not agree, but the confrontation we got into after World War II wasted our time and energy, while others—the former vanquished—were moving ahead." The world was changing in dramatic ways. The United States, despite its power, could not lead the world by itself and playing "cards" (such as China) against each other was not the way to go. There was a "regrouping" in the world, and US-Soviet relations were vital in this process. "The question is, can we cooperate?" he asked.

I listened carefully to his long and frank survey of the situation before us, writing notes to myself on each point. "There is significant change in US attitudes toward the Soviet Union, although there is an emerging suspicion," I replied, keeping in mind developments in Lithuania. I added that many Americans were probably not sufficiently sensitive, for example, to Soviet losses in World War II. "As we wrestle with arms control, not only have I become more sensitive to that issue, but all my people have as well," I continued. "I wanted to get that comment on the table before we get, inevitably, to Germany . . . We do not want winners and losers." Although the Soviets had problems, I wanted him to understand that as long as I was in office there would be no attempt to downgrade the position the Soviet Union rightly occupied. "You must believe my sincerity on this point as we get into detailed issues.

"You gave me that map at Malta with the blue flags," I continued. "I asked the CIA to see how accurate your intelligence was. They gave you high marks . . . I told Brent that we have to convince you that these flags don't mean we are trying to surround you, to encircle the Soviet Union. Some of it we can do by words; some must be by actions." Germany headed the list of difficult questions before us. "I understand you have hang-ups there which tie into the German problem. We don't want a Soviet Union that is threatened by any power. We may have very different ideas about the future of Germany. Will they return to their old ways, or have they learned and paid their dues? I am of the latter view." After forty years, Germany was different. I didn't want to single it out in a way which threatened to make history repeat itself.

I could not ignore Lithuania. "To the degree that we can see a commitment to your own principles of self-determination, we can cooperate," I said. "I have tried to conduct myself in a constrained way because I know you have big problems. But I am being hit both on my left and on my right by those who say that I am subordinating US dedication to principle."

As our rambling discussion ran on, Brent gave me an urgent look, pointed to his watch, and patiently reminded us that we had run into the time set aside for the plenary discussion with the staffs on each side. Gorbachev waved him off with a grin before wading back into an extensive description of the problems facing his country. "Let me take five minutes more," he said. "The phase of perestroika that we are now going through is probably decisive." Their political system had changed and they were in the process of reforming the federation. "The difficulties will be fundamental," he said. "Different republics may have different relationships, but our basic decision is for a market economy. . . . We are not yet ready for [it]. We have a centralized economy, and we must take account of this as we move."

"I see," I interjected. "But it's like being pregnant: You can't do it halfway."

"But neither can you have the baby in the first month," responded Gorbachev. "We need two years for the transition. . . . We hope to interact with you at this moment." He was hinting at financial help.

"We should talk about the practical end of it," I said, determined to remain noncommittal. "We have differences, but let's talk about them."

The discussion that morning was a good follow-up to Malta. The directness allowed both of us once again to put everything on the table. However, Gorbachev had run so far over the time allotted that we had to postpone the plenary so he could rush to a luncheon at the Soviet embassy.

We met again at four thirty that afternoon. In the Cabinet Room, with advisors and aides crowded around the long, polished wooden table, we spent two hours talking about Germany. I began with an elaborate presentation, discussing Soviet concerns about Germany, explaining again how we proposed dealing with them, and concluding that a united Germany inside NATO would be a stabilizing structure for Europe.

Gorbachev insisted that we address Europe and a united Germany at the same time. "One cannot be divorced from the other," he said. "Eastern Europe and the Soviet Union are changing in the direction of civilization and cooperation with other nations." This made dialogue possible about new security structures. He did not believe that a new Europe could be built without the United States, but warned that the USSR could not be isolated either. "If that happens, you will get a reaction," he said frankly. "As in hockey, these are the tough rules of the game. A fact. I hope I am making this clear."

He went through alternatives. "It is extremely important for us to make an agreement on Germany. The author is not important. It could be Baker and Shevardnadze [or] General Scowcroft and Akhromeyev. A solution is what is important," he said. Germany could be in both alliances or neither. Either would be acceptable to the Soviet Union, but a Germany only in NATO would unbalance Europe. There should be a long transition period, in which both alliances could become more political than military.

"We have a fundamental difference on Germany, driven by historical events," I said. "You are more suspicious of the intentions of a united Germany than we are. . . . I see Germany as a potential strong friend of the Soviet Union." Some in the West were more suspicious than I, but where we all agreed, in Western and Eastern Europe, was the danger of isolating or otherwise setting apart the Germans from other democratic countries. We didn't know what the Germans would decide. Germany was a democracy, and it could choose what it wanted. But, given history,

Germany in NATO—coupled with a stabilizing US presence through the alliance—was best for everyone. The answer to his concerns was to change the nature of NATO.

"We are in favor of the American presence in Europe," he said. "But you seem to link your presence to NATO, that Germany going out of NATO will be NATO's destruction and thus the end of the US presence." Perhaps a united Germany could have what he called "two anchors"—that is, participate in both alliances, with the FRG in NATO and Soviet forces in the old GDR, and some kind of agreement between the two alliances. He wanted to discuss these ideas in the Two-plus-Four (which was exactly what we did not want) and repeated his idea of a transition period. He added that we could let both alliances remain, and any country should be able to join either. "NATO is an open organization," he said. "Maybe we will join it too. . . ."

"I'm not sure Marshal Akhromeyev's former colleagues would like to be commanded by General Galvin," I joked.

I tried a new tack. I reminded Gorbachev that the Helsinki Final Act stated that all countries had the right to choose their alliances. To me, that meant Germany should be able to decide for itself what it wanted. Did he agree? To my astonishment, Gorbachev shrugged his shoulders and said, yes, that was correct.

The room suddenly became quiet. Akhromeyev and Valentin Falin looked at each other and squirmed in their seats. Bob Blackwill slipped me a note asking whether I thought I could get Gorbachev to say that again. I nodded to him. "I'm gratified that you and I seem to agree that nations can choose their own alliances," I said.

"Do you and I agree that a united Germany has the right to be non-aligned, or a member of NATO, in a final document?" asked Gorbachev.

"I agree with that, but the German public wants to be in NATO," I replied. "But if they want out of NATO, we will respect that. They are a democracy."

"I agree to say so publicly, that the United States and the USSR are in favor of seeing a united Germany, with a final settlement leaving it up to where a united Germany can choose," said Gorbachev.

"I would put it differently," I said. "We support a united Germany in NATO. If they don't want in, we will respect that."

"I agree," answered Gorbachev.

"With the second part?" I asked.

"With both parts," responded Gorbachev.

"Good," I said. "Can we have the ministers work on it?"

"Let them work on a transition period," said Gorbachev.

By this time, the dismay in the Soviet team was palpable. Akhromeyev's eyes flashed angrily as he gestured to Falin. They snapped back and forth in loud stage whispers in an agitated debate as Gorbachev spoke. It was an unbelievable scene, the likes of which none of us had ever seen before—virtually open rebellion against a Soviet leader. Then Shevardnadze tugged at Gorbachev's sleeve and whispered to him. Gorbachev indicated he wanted Falin to make a presentation. Falin launched into a lengthy filibuster on why Germany in NATO was unacceptable to the Soviet people, during which Shevardnadze kept gesticulating and whispering heatedly to Gorbachev. After a few minutes of this fascinating display, Gorbachev reentered the discussion. He now tried to back away from his previous statements by calling again for a lengthy transition period, concluding with the suggestion, "Let's let the foreign ministers pursue these issues."

It was an obvious ploy to get out from under the controversy he had created—but then came another incredible moment. Shevardnadze refused. "We can do that," he said, "but it is at the level of a President that such issues must be discussed." Clearly, he wasn't going to be the fall guy. Gorbachev lamely continued the discussion, trying to back away but never completely repudiating his earlier statements. Appearing completely frustrated, he hit the transition period one more time and then called again for the foreign ministers to continue the discussions. This time Shevardnadze gave in.

I am not sure why Gorbachev did what he did. Perhaps he realized that our position would prevail and this was the best way to manage it within his own team. In any event, it was an amazing performance.

BRENT SCOWCROFT

I could scarcely believe what I was witnessing, let alone figure out what to make of it. Gorbachev never did actually recant his apparent concession of our major point, but it was also obvious he had created a firestorm in his delegation and faced bitter opposition. The significance—and sensitivity—of what had happened was underscored by Shevardnadze refusing to rescue his boss. But the real question was where we stood at this point. This meeting marked the end of the discussions between Gorbachev and the President about Germany during the summit. We thought that, for the moment, we had gotten all we could from the Soviets on this subject.

GEORGE BUSH

We still had not spoken in much detail about the link between MFN, trade, and Lithuania. That evening, as we left the State dinner, Gorbachev buttonholed me in the hall. He told me that if we did not have a trade agreement, it would be a disaster. It would make or break the summit for him. He was very agitated, and almost acted as if he had not seen the letter I wrote him on the subject in April, something we had kept confidential. I didn't sleep too well afterward. I woke up very early thinking about a way to break the impasse, but I could do nothing unless the Soviets acted on Lithuania.

The next day Gorbachev had breakfast with some congressmen. When he and I met later that morning, he explained that he had told them how important a trade agreement was to him. I thought it was a smart move to meet with them so publicly and to lay out his case; it might help ease some of the opposition to MFN. He had said the Soviets looked on it as equal with START, he remarked. "These two were the principal pillars of the summit." In practical terms, an agreement would not cause much of an increase in real trade for years, he acknowledged, but it would let a serious business effort begin.

"What you said last night made a real impression on me," I replied. I read aloud the letter on the trade agreement I sent him, and explained again the political impact of Lithuania in the United States. "If a dialogue went on, and the blockade were lifted, the agreement would go through in a minute," I said. ". . . I understand why you can't have us in your internal affairs and I don't want to be. But it's a dilemma. . . . I know I can't get it through Congress in the present situation."

"We have each made our points," said Gorbachev wearily. "I can't force you to agree with my points. You have chosen the Baltics over me, and let's leave it at that."

"But what are the chances of getting talks going?" I persisted. "You have said you would do that." He replied that he preferred a dialogue with the Baltic nations within a constitutional framework, but was willing to talk outside it. They should go back to the original situation (i.e., before the declaration of independence) and discuss how to proceed from there. "We want a trade deal," I assured him. "I don't want to publicize any conditions because that makes it look like I'm dictating to you. But there is no point in sending up legislation and having the hell kicked out of it."

"Okay. I see you have given thought to this," conceded Gorbachev. "I see no way to work harder. We are without a trade deal today and have been without a trade deal for many years. . . ." I told him I wanted to work it out. "It is more my problem," he said with a shrug. "I have explained it to you and know it is in your hands. Let us say our concerns about the Baltics are as deep as yours. We want to find a solution because otherwise it would be a blow to perestroika. But life is not always under our control."

Immediately following the discussion we moved to the Cabinet Room for talks on arms control. Victor Karpov summarized the progress of the other talks so far and what documents had been prepared: one on START and a statement on future negotiations. There also was a statement on intentions on CFE based on the Ottawa accords.

After the meeting, I took Jim Baker aside. I had been thinking about the importance of a trade agreement for Gorbachev and, given his hesitation on Germany, I wanted to try to accommodate him. I knew he had to go home with something tangible. I asked Jim to try to get a compromise worked out.

The deal I suggested would have an open or publicized side, as well as a secret, stricter one. While we would sign the grain and trade agreements, we would not send the package to Congress until the Soviets completed the conditions we had publicly laid out for granting them MFN status: they had to pass legislation on emigration. The private, or secret, side was that we would not send the package up for approval until negotiations with the Lithuanians had begun and Moscow lifted the economic embargo. We could hand Gorbachev a tangible success in the form of a signed agreement with public stipulations that he had a chance of meeting, but we made sure the agreement would not be implemented until there was substantive progress on Lithuania. There would be no embarrassment for Gorbachev at home, and we would get the conditions we wanted. With these proposals in hand, Jim and Shevardnadze went back to the negotiating table.

As Baker and Shevardnadze talked, I called Kohl and gave him an account of my discussions with Gorbachev the day before. Helmut asked if Gorbachev said anything about economic aid. "Not yet," I said. "I think he'll hit me with that tomorrow at Camp David." I asked him if he had any problem saying that Germany, under Helsinki, has the right to choose whether it would belong to NATO. "Precisely," said Helmut. "We believe that. But we still have to change his mind. George, I think the economic side is more important."

Not long after this call, Jim came back with a trade agreement using the formula I had proposed. Our signing ceremony for the accords of the past two days was scheduled for five thirty that afternoon in the East Room. As Gorbachev and I met before we were to go in, he looked at me carefully and asked: "Do we have a deal?" I nodded. "Yes, we have a deal," I replied with a smile. Gorbachev beamed his relief.

Since no one had expected the trade agreement to be signed, we had to wait as someone dashed to the Commerce Department to fetch the documents. As we waited, the East Room became hot and uncomfortable under the blaze of television lights, the audience of dignitaries, negotiators, and press sweating and fanning themselves. Gorbachev turned to me and said he felt they would move faster than we believed on Lithuania. I hope so, I thought.

By the end of the second day Gorbachev was in an ebullient mood. He had obtained the trade agreement and had made progress on START, chemical weapons, and vowed to do better on CFE. We had not solved the German question, but I had not expected that we would reach a definitive conclusion. We also had not resolved Lithuania, but we had improved our mutual understanding. I had applied some leverage. I felt the personal contact had helped enormously. I thought he knew that I was not out to drive him against the wall, and that I was dealing in good faith.

I realized I would take some heat for the public side of the deal on Lithuania and MFN, which was all we could reveal. As expected, the press soon began to complain to Jim about selling out Lithuania. I knew, however, that everyone would calm down when it eventually came out that our agreement on trade and MFN was what encouraged the Soviets to work a deal with Lithuania. The criticism was frustrating, but we certainly did not wish to humiliate the Soviets by a public display of linkage between Lithuania and US trade.

We went up to Camp David Saturday for what I knew would be a big day. Gorbachev and I shared a helicopter, both of us, ironically, accompanied by military aides carrying the nuclear codes that allowed each of us to destroy the other's country. Yet we were sitting there talking about peace. During the flight Gorbachev seemed fascinated about real estate. He asked all sorts of questions as we flew over the Maryland suburbs and into the country. How do you buy and sell a house? Who lends the money? Who owns the house? What do you do when you have to leave? How much does this or that house cost?

As was my rule at Camp David, everything was to be casual, with an informal, flexible schedule. Gorbachev's aides said it was an achievement that I persuaded him to get out of his tie and jacket. He was relaxed and enthusiastic. The weather was perfect, with a warm sun and crystal-clear sky. We sat outdoors in the morning, the umbrella up over a glass table on the veranda outside the presidential cottage. A slight breeze played through the trees surrounding the six of us: me, Scowcroft, Baker, Akhromeyev, Shevardnadze, and Gorbachev.

The discussion exceeded my hopes and expectations. Gorbachev described the problems of reform in the Soviet Union, and the challenges posed by the nationalities. When he spoke of Yeltsin, he was irritated and dismissive. We covered a wide array of foreign policy issues—from Central America and Cuba to South Africa, Afghanistan, and Korea—but the most important aspect of our talks was the frank, rancor-free atmosphere. We developed a feeling of give and take; what we could do and what we could not do. Gorbachev understood that we wanted to cooperate, and I had the feeling that he did too. We even joked back and forth, including a couple of stories over which he roared with laughter. The jokes showed the degree of confidence we had reached, and how relaxed we had become. Gorbachev stayed energetic and fired up, and was agreeable to many of my suggestions.

The dinner that evening was memorable. Gorbachev had gone on a walk while I was taking a quick nap. Strolling past the horseshoe pit, he had picked up a shoe, thrown it, and hit a ringer on the first try. Talk about beginner's luck! Tim McBride, my assistant, retrieved the orange-colored horseshoe and had it put on a plaque with an inscription on it about the visit. I handed it to Gorbachev with an informal toast at the end of dinner. He was very emotional and choked up when he described what he felt about the new relationship between our countries and ourselves. Akhromeyev later told Brent that he too thought it was a new era. Coming from a veteran of the long years of the Cold War, this was change.

After supper, Gorbachev again took me aside, this time to ask whether Baker had talked to me about his discussions with Shevardnadze on financial questions. He explained that he did not want to raise the question of needing money from the United States in front of his own team. I told him Jim had mentioned it, but that there were still difficult political problems to overcome, problems he was aware of, such as aid to Cuba and progress on Germany. There also were issues of economic reform if they were to get credit. I said there could be private loans with guarantees from the government, but that these other matters had to be sorted out.

It was strange how in dealing with the Soviets we thought we knew a lot, but we really knew so little—and we were often pleasantly surprised. We had heard that Gorbachev did not like to fly in a helicopter, yet he seemed very comfortable in one, looking out the window and asking a lot of questions. If he was nervous, he didn't show it. We had also heard that Gorbachev did not like to relax, yet he told me how he loved to go outdoors and that he used to walk a lot. He would do fifteen-minute miles—which is a pretty good aerobic walk. Raisa told us he no longer had much time for exercise. He enjoyed walking on the wood chip paths at Camp David and we slogged through the woods as well. He asked about poison ivy, the ever-present nuisance. We talked about hunting, and he explained that he used to sport shoot. I asked him if he liked to shoot skeet, thinking I might take him to the superb range at Camp David, but I gathered he used only rifles, not shotguns.

BRENT SCOWCROFT

The easygoing atmosphere continued even as we got ready for the press conference the next morning. We had given the President's introductory statement to Ambassador Bessmertnykh the night before to test where we stood on Germany. It included the formulation, "We are in full agreement that the matter of alliance membership is—in accordance with the Helsinki Final Act—a matter for the Germans to decide." After the furor in the Soviet delegation over the issue the first day of the summit, I expected at least an objection to the language. To my surprise there wasn't a murmur. Gorbachev also did not demur when, at the conference itself, the President said that while the two of them did not agree that a united Germany should be a full member of NATO, they agreed that the question of alliance membership was, in accordance with Helsinki, a matter for the Germans to decide. We would have to see whether this acquiescence showed real flexibility in the Soviet position. While few picked up on the significance of these remarks at the press conference, it was an exciting moment. We cautiously hoped that Gorbachev was turning the corner on Germany.

GEORGE BUSH

As we flew back to the White House together, I asked Gorbachev to write out some autographs for each of our five kids, and he took the time to pen a full greeting to each of them. I sent one to his daughter, Irene. Gorbachev asked more questions about real estate. "Look in the newspaper tomorrow," I told him. "You'll see a lot of ads. If someone was selling a home, you get a real estate agent and he'll close the deal."

Gorbachev laughed. "There is a big difference," he joked. "In our country they'd find the real estate agent and shoot him!"

The helicopters touched down on the White House South Lawn and I took Gorbachev inside the Residence for a tour. I showed him the Lincoln bedroom and the copy of the Gettysburg Address and explained what it was about. Then we went to my upstairs office, where he saw my five-screen television set and my computer. I loved sharing the White House in this way with dignitaries, friends, and congressmen of both parties, many of whom had never been upstairs on the Residence floors. They all were moved by the history the rooms represented. It was everyone's house, and giving people a chance to see it was one act I could easily do.

In the Oval Office, I pointed out my daily schedule for that Monday and Gorbachev seemed impressed with its detail. He said he would have to get his office modernized—he didn't have that kind of thing. Then I showed him my block schedule for an entire month. He seemed positively amazed, so I gave it to him. He said he'd like to send his chief of staff over to work with John Sununu. That fall, John went to Moscow to help Gorbachev's staff modernize and streamline his office. As we wandered through the White House, Gorbachev invited me to come to Moscow and I immediately accepted.

It was these kinds of interactions which I thought made the summit an important success. Gorbachev and I were able to speak heart to heart, and bluntly, on literally any issue. We had brainstormed at Camp David about solutions, which we were not able to do at Malta. I think we parted as genuine friends, building on the personal rapport we had formed at the earlier talks. While we still needed to see the practical evidence of it (which came later in the month), we at least had a workable bargain in the works to get the Soviets to open a dialogue with the Lithuanians and back off the embargo.

BRENT SCOWCROFT

I too thought the summit had been a success. We had progress in arms control—directions for the negotiators. The atmosphere had been collaborative, and the talks between the two leaders gave me a sense that the Soviets wanted to work with us. But there were still problems. President Bush had made a major concession by keeping wraps on the linkage with Lithuania. Gorbachev went home with what he needed from the summit at the expense of the President, who had left himself open to charges of abandoning Lithuania. There was an air of uncertainty over Germany. Like Kohl, I had expected Gorbachev to want to solve the final reunification issues at the summit. His statement on the matter had been encouraging, as had the Soviet acquiescence in the President's summation at his press conference. Yet both had been ambiguous and inconclusive. There was still significant light between our positions.

The talks did help defuse the tensions about Germany and won some acceptance for the principle that alliance membership was a matter for the Germans to decide. Gorbachev never voiced opposition to the idea again, and both he and Shevardnadze began to call for the West to deliver on the "nine points," especially from the NATO summit. We had also won an agreement to speed up CFE negotiations. This would ensure that military reductions kept pace with and reinforced the rapid political change we were witnessing. We could not approach the final stages of German reunification without addressing the opposing force levels in Europe. The Germans and Soviets were already talking about ceilings on the Bundeswehr, but this was something we did not want to address without also setting the force levels of all the countries in the two alliances. It should be handled in the NATO summit, not the reunification talks.

GEORGE BUSH

On June 8, Kohl was back in Washington. We met twice, including a small dinner at the White House with Brent and Jim. Helmut speculated that Gorbachev now would probably push for economic aid. The Soviets were expecting the West to help them—with $20–25 billion to buy goods for consumption. Gorbachev was also approaching the Germans separately, however, asking for a loan of five billion deutsche marks to extend their credit line. "They said we could expect something in return," added Kohl. He thought Gorbachev was looking for a way to settle NATO membership. Gorbachev had asked what kinds of proposals NATO could make, and he floated the idea of a non-aggression pact between the two alliances. I was not enthusiastic, as I thought this would only prop up the Warsaw Pact at a time when it was on the verge of collapsing.

BRENT SCOWCROFT

Before the dinner meeting, a fascinating excursion, at least for me, took place. During the Chancellor's visit to Camp David in February, he, the President, and I had a long conversation over cocktails about military strategy and military leaders, comparing the United States and Germany. In the course of the chat, in which Kohl displayed catholic knowledge of the subject, he mentioned that he would like to visit Arlington Cemetery some time, and asked if I would be willing to accompany him. I naturally assented, but never imagined it would ever take place.

The day before Kohl was to arrive in June, however, I got a call asking if I would join him for a walk through the cemetery before dinner. I called the Arlington superintendent and arranged for a guide. The day was warm and clear, and by the time I met the Chancellor in the early afternoon, the temperature had climbed into the nineties, with humidity to match. I worried about Kohl, not a small man, under those taxing conditions and suggested restricting our visit to a motor tour. He would have none of it, and we set out across the lawn to visit the graves of some of America's outstanding military commanders. Our discussion, analyzing the traits, the successes, and the failures of the giants of the American military past and comparing them with the "greats" of German military history, was a truly memorable experience. Kohl's grasp of the subject was formidable and, even though military history was a hobby of mine, I was no match for him.

The weather eventually got the best of him, however, and, with rivers of perspiration pouring off him, he suggested a glass of iced tea. I panicked. Where could I take the chancellor of the Federal Republic of Germany, unannounced and with no advance security check, for an iced tea? I finally remembered a restaurant on the George Washington Parkway along the Potomac and we repaired there to cool off and continue our conversation.

GEORGE BUSH

On June 11, East German prime minister Lothar de Maizière came to the White House. This was an odd and fascinating session—the first, and last, meeting between an East German leader and an American president. Even more unusual, de Maizière had been the chairman of the Warsaw Pact meeting held only a few days before. While much of our own talk was fairly pro forma, he offered some interesting insights on Gorbachev and the dying alliance. Here was a US president getting debriefed on a Pact meeting by its chairman—amazing!

"Developments in the Warsaw Pact could [mean] that it won't survive very long," he told me. "The Hungarian and Czechoslovak representatives especially said that, following a transitional period, they don't want this alliance." It would be necessary to establish new structures to prevent these countries from re-creating the pact. He also spoke of the problems his people faced. "Forty years of socialism have changed the people," he observed sadly. "Defeat means a certain loss in life for many people. We need to recover souls and let them catch up."

He described his conversations with Gorbachev. "I felt he still assumes that the Soviet nationalities and people will have trouble accepting full German membership in NATO unless certain elements are added," he said. "For example, he has talked about a treaty [between the two alliances] for the continuing presence of Soviet troops in the GDR." During our discussion over lunch, I asked him whether he found Gorbachev confident. "I had the impression that he viewed the summit as very successful," said de Maizière. "He said it marked the transition from confrontation to partnership. In this context, he gave us a quite optimistic view, but that doesn't change his domestic problems. Hundreds of thousands are leaving the Party, which is fragmenting into groups. The Party congress in early July will be very important, because there is no integrative structure in the Soviet Union except the Party. . . ."

Our guarded optimism about resolving the last obstacles to German reunification was tempered at the Two-plus-Four meeting in East Ber-

lin on June 22. The Soviets suddenly appeared to dig in, showing a new and unexpected inflexibility. Shevardnadze introduced a tough draft interim settlement with unacceptable provisions. He raised the specter of a five-year period in which Germany would remain divided with its parts in the existing alliances. The troops of the Four Powers would stay until the end of the transition. There would be strict ceilings on the German armed forces—no more than 250,000. After the limits took effect, the forces of the Four Powers would be reduced to token numbers, and Western Allied troops would not be permitted in former East German territory. Four Power troops would be withdrawn from Berlin—although the Soviets would still retain a presence in eastern Germany. It was difficult to know what to make of Shevardnadze's plan, with its overtones of Versailles, coming as it did after Gorbachev's cooperative spirit in Washington and some positive remarks from Shevardnadze at a CSCE meeting in Copenhagen.

Baker seemed to think the Shevardnadze plan might be only window-dressing for Soviet domestic consumption, but it was strong stuff. It appeared that Soviet hard-liners had again yanked in the reins on Shevardnadze. We glimpsed as much when Baker confronted him, demanding to know what had changed since Washington and Copenhagen. Shevardnadze conceded that the document had been spurred by the domestic Soviet political situation. It was not their final position on Germany and much would depend on decisions at the NATO summit, and progress on CFE and CSCE. Shevardnadze believed that his country was approaching a political and economic crisis. It was essential that his government be able to point to changes in NATO to reassure the Soviet people that they no longer faced a threat from the alliance, or Germany, or the United States.

BRENT SCOWCROFT

It appeared to me that Shevardnadze had indeed offered some window-dressing. His private discussion with Baker seemed almost a call for help. He repeated at least four times that the declaration from the NATO summit would be critical to selling German sovereignty and NATO membership to the Soviet people. I took this very seriously. If we did not make bold moves at the summit to modify the alliance, we would fail to pass the public test the Soviets said was so crucial. We could not settle for rhetoric in place of solid substance.

The President had outlined his ambitious objectives for the NATO summit in May at Oklahoma State University. Since then, a small group in the Administration had been busy putting together the proposals he would make in July. By the end of June a short, twenty-two-paragraph declaration was ready. In it were initiatives to change NATO's relationship to the Warsaw Pact and its individual members, to alter its military deployments as well as its old doctrines, and to increase the stature of CSCE as a permanent structure.

The declaration proposed to transform the alliance in four areas: 1. It would emphasize its political mission, and develop cooperation and partnership with former adversaries. The alliance pledged never to be the first to use force, proposed a non-aggression pact with members of the Warsaw Pact (not with the Pact itself), and invited those governments to establish diplomatic missions at NATO headquarters in Brussels. 2. It called for changing the character of conventional defense by moving away from "forward defense" and relying increasingly on more mobile, truly multinational forces. The document also proposed follow-on conventional arms control negotiations (after the conclusion of a CFE treaty) further to limit offensive military manpower in Europe. 3. It announced a new NATO nuclear strategy, modifying "flexible response" to reduce reliance on nuclear weapons and make them "truly weapons of last resort." 4. It proposed strengthening the CSCE process by giving it a new mandate to promote democratic institutions, operational capacity in the area of conflict prevention, and, for the first time, an institutional structure through a new secretariat and other bodies.

While the declaration was primarily meant to help Moscow save face, it was too important a document to review with the allies in the usual way. Generally, the professional diplomats of each government assigned to NATO would pore over such drafts and work out a compromise package, nibbling at it extensively. With the shortage of time and the need to preserve the proposals, we decided we would bypass the usual bureaucratic procedures—including our own. There was a risk to this approach. If the allies balked, the summit could become deadlocked and fail. Members might also object to being presented for vote, without prior consultations, a complete, made-in-America package. To soften this impression, and win them over ahead of time, the President decided to go to the top, talking to his NATO counterparts ahead of time and then negotiating the US draft at the summit itself among only the foreign ministers and heads of state. He sent letters with the draft via special channels to Wörner, Kohl, Thatcher, Andreotti, and Mitterrand.

GEORGE BUSH

The reaction from the key allied leaders was predictably mixed, while their bureaucracies were furious at being left out of the process.

Kohl liked the proposals, and Wörner and Andreotti were enthusiastic. Thatcher was skeptical. She argued that we were abandoning the fundamentals of solid military strategy for the sake of "eye-catching propositions." She supported the idea of changing NATO's emphasis, but she wanted no part of altering the long-established strategy of flexible response. That policy kept open the possibility that NATO would use nuclear weapons first in the event of a Soviet conventional attack and thus help deter it. She saw the move to declare nuclear weapons "weapons of last resort" as undermining our short-range forces and as slipping us to a position of "no first use of nuclear weapons," leaving our conventional forces vulnerable. She thought the tone of the declaration would make people think that the Soviets no longer posed a threat. She also objected to the idea of Warsaw Pact liaisons, preferring CSCE and a Warsaw Pact–NATO joint declaration. She demanded an entirely new draft, to be prepared by the United States, Britain, France, West Germany, and Italy.

Mitterrand was more positive and supported most of the declaration. But he also shared Thatcher's concern over the "last resort" language on nuclear weapons, which he felt inconsistent with the concept of deterrence. He observed, however, that France was not part of NATO's military structures, and he would not try to tell us what strategies to adopt. The French also did not like the liaison idea, preferring that NATO remain dedicated to security problems. I sent François a cable responding to his objections, and again promised to talk through the matter in London.

I forwarded the proposal to the other NATO leaders on July 2, with a note explaining that the text would be discussed at the summit itself. In addition, I sent Thatcher a message on July 1, responding to her objections point by point and explaining the need for solidarity. We needed a bold proposal if it was to win over the Soviets to German membership in NATO. I turned down drafting a new document in favor of discussing the language when the leaders met.

At the London summit, after some skillful negotiating by Jim Baker among his counterparts, we reached a compromise final text close to the original draft. It strengthened the Warsaw Pact–NATO joint declaration, but kept it short of a non-aggression pact. It included the spirit of our proposal on nuclear weapons but linked it to an agreement on CFE, the problem Margaret was worried about. It watered down our proposal to express the pious hope that NATO would reach a state of affairs where its strategy would make the weapons "truly weapons of last resort." Flexible response was to be modified and the alliance pledged that it was "moving away" from forward defense. It was a landmark shift for the alliance.

On the way home from London, I sent Gorbachev a message explaining what had happened at the summit and detailing how the declaration addressed Soviet concerns.

> Working solely from a draft text I circulated to my NATO counterparts, we a few hours ago issued a declaration that promises the Alliance's transformation in every aspect of its work and especially of its relationship with the Soviet Union. As you read the NATO declaration, I want you to know that it was written with you importantly in mind, and I made the point strongly to my colleagues in London.
>
> . . . I hope today's NATO declaration will persuade you that NATO can and will serve the security interests of Europe as a whole.

The NATO declaration and my personal message to Gorbachev set the stage for what proved to be the final phase of the negotiations over German reunification. It offered the Soviets firm evidence of the West's genuine desire to change NATO. Our offer was on the table.

July 1990 was a decisive month for reunification. The economic and monetary union of the two Germanies took place on July 1, and the East German government in effect surrendered much of its control over internal affairs. The Germanies set about negotiating the second state treaty on political union on July 6, with the expectation that it would be finished by August and ratified in September. The crisis in the Baltics was also beginning to ease. On June 29, Lithuania suspended its declaration of independence, and Gorbachev lifted the blockade.

In the first week of July, as NATO gathered in London, the Twenty-eighth Congress of the Communist Party of the Soviet Union convened. Gorbachev and Shevardnadze battled the hard-liners over domestic reforms and foreign policy in one of the angriest congresses the Party had ever seen. After a bitter struggle, Gorbachev emerged triumphant. He was reelected general secretary by a three-to-one margin, his authority reaffirmed. We still feared that, following his comments at the Washington summit on a "transition," he might try to string out German reunification for as long as possible. But that did not happen.

On July 14, Kohl and Genscher flew to the Soviet Union for detailed talks, first in Moscow and then in the Caucasus at Gorbachev's home in Stavropol. Since the May 5 Two-plus-Four meeting, the Germans had been wooing the Soviets, trying to reassure them about NATO membership and proposing badly needed economic incentives. In mid-May Bonn offered to assume all GDR economic obligations to Moscow and provide a $3-billion credit as part of a package of agreements linked to German unity, assistance Gorbachev later said had come at just the right moment. The Germans would also pay the costs of Soviet troops in East Germany during the transition period. At a joint news conference at the conclusion of their talks, Gorbachev declared, "Whether we like it or not, the time will come when a united Germany will be in NATO, if that is its choice. Then, if that is the choice, to some degree and in some form, it can work together with the Soviet Union."

GEORGE BUSH

On July 17, I called Kohl, who filled me in on his discussions with Gorbachev. "He has managed to get through the hard work at the Party Congress," he said. "I think his success there gave him a push." Gorbachev acknowledged the importance of the NATO declaration. "As for central and eastern Europe, he seems to be preoccupied with the USSR and to have little interest in the situation of some of his colleagues."

Kohl described their talks on Germany. "The first point in his position was that he recognized there would be [all-]German elections by the end of the year," he recounted. "He also said that German sovereignty should be returned completely and unequivocally. I used your formula from Camp David that a sovereign country, under the CSCE, can decide for itself its alliances. And I explained that the Germans would vote unequivocally for NATO . . . I told him he had to exert strong pressure on his staff on this issue. He took that position as obvious.

"We then discussed the treaty between a unified Germany and the USSR on [withdrawing] troops. He accepted, although his staff had a different schedule, a period of three to four years. This was agreed between us. We also agreed that, pending the withdrawal of Soviet troops from the territory of the GDR, no NATO troops would be stationed there, although German troops not belonging to NATO could be there. After the withdrawal of Soviet troops in three to four years, only German NATO troops could be stationed there.

"One other interesting thing: We talked about German-US relations in our one-on-one. I told him this relationship was of great importance. And I told him that if the Soviets try to undermine it, this would affect German relations with the USSR. His reply will be of interest to you. He said they had learned a lesson that it was wrong to try to make the United States withdraw from Europe, and that they hadn't succeeded in this in the past. I touched on this repeatedly, and I think he was serious in his reply." Kohl said that his impression was of a man who knows himself well, and who has a sense of self-irony. "He has burned all his bridges behind him," he said. "He can't go back, and he must be successful."

The only question I had was the matter of parallel withdrawal of forces from Germany. Kohl said that this issue played no part whatsoever, nor did Gorbachev mention it. "I said I took for granted that US forces would remain in Germany," said Kohl. "He didn't refute this."

I called Gorbachev the same day to congratulate him and to brief him on the forthcoming G-7 discussions in Houston. Obviously we were pleased with his comments that a unified Germany has the right to choose its alliance membership. "This showed great statesmanship on your part, and we feel good about it," I said. "I hope we can make similar progress on CFE and START in the months ahead."

Gorbachev described the Party congress. "I believe that through reasons you understand the Communist Party remains a powerful political organization. Its position and actions will largely determine the course of events in our country. And it is only natural that, given the new situation and the period we are going through, the Communist Party has renounced its monopoly on power. New parties will be created." He was planning new relationships with the republics. "It was perhaps the most difficult and important period in my political life," he said. There was a lot yet to do, and he said he hoped he could count on our cooperation.

"I believe that without the meeting in Washington and at Camp David," he continued, "without the results of the NATO summit and the London declaration, without the major work in my conversation with Kohl and your talks with [him], without the activities of our foreign economic agencies, without this real political action it would have been difficult to arrive at the proximity in our points of view. We achieved all this because we understood each other's position. We tried to take into account each other's views. I consider the results of my conversation with Kohl to be quite positive." He hoped that Shevardnadze and Baker could build on this progress. "If these agreements are respected, we could achieve positive results."

BRENT SCOWCROFT

We were surprised and pleased at the swift change in the Soviet positions. Of course, questions still remained about NATO responsibility for GDR territory in light of the restrictions on its military presence there. Just what sort of commitment the German troop ceiling entailed and in what context, such as CFE, was still unclear. Nevertheless, these were details that would be nailed down in the run-up to the final Two-plus-Four settlement.

Some journalists termed the German-Soviet agreement "Stavrapallo," implying that, like the Rapallo Treaty in 1922, when the two outcast states had struck a bargain to cooperate, it was another bilateral deal struck over the heads of other powers. I disagree. If this had been a Stavrapallo, there would have been follow-up bilateral deals to cement it. Yet no Moscow-Berlin axis emerged. Kohl still looked westward and Gorbachev remained preoccupied with internal problems. Why then did he agree to a deal with Kohl in Stavropol and not with the President in Washington?

I think that Gorbachev had accepted the inevitability of early unification at least by the time of the March elections, but he had not come up with a reasonable alternative to NATO as a home for a united Germany. On May 31, he threw out the notions of dual alliance and a long transitional period, perhaps in the hopes we might bite. When we did not, he may have made his "concession" statement out of frustration or perhaps to test the waters with his colleagues. The consternation he caused within his team demonstrated both that his move was not in the plan and that it was premature, for he tried almost immediately to step back from it.

As a result, I believe Gorbachev concluded it was dangerous to move until he had dealt with the upcoming Party congress. To do that, he needed some ammunition from the NATO summit to argue that the alliance was no longer a threat. With that in hand, he triumphed at the congress and then felt free to let Germany go, which he did with Kohl at Stavropol. It was a far cry from a reprise of Rapallo.

With the breakthrough at Stavropol, the terms of German reunification were set. The third "ministerial" meeting of the Two-plus-Four was held in Paris on July 17, where agreement was reached on the Polish-German border as well as the outline of a final settlement. There was still a range of questions to sort through, and some serious technical problems to overcome. However, these were essentially details now that the main political process was settled.

The treaty itself was signed by the ministers of the six powers in Moscow on September 12. In it a united Germany was fixed as the FRG, GDR, and Berlin, and the Germans ratified the cession of the rest of their prewar territory. They renounced aggression, as well as nuclear, biological, and chemical weapons, committing themselves to the non-proliferation treaty West Germany had already signed. The Bundeswehr was limited to 370,000 troops and was to be reduced to that level within three to four years. That number was to be part of a general CFE agreement. The Soviets would withdraw their forces from the old GDR by the end of 1994, and, while they were still in Germany, only German units not connected to NATO would be stationed on former GDR territory. Allied troops could remain in Berlin as long as Soviet forces stayed in the east. Once the Soviets were gone, German NATO forces could be stationed in eastern Germany, but no nuclear weapons. Germany could join the alliances it chose and was fully sovereign. Finally, the Four Powers relinquished their rights and responsibilities. Formal German reunification took place on October 3, with the FRG simply absorbing the five now-reconstituted eastern *Länder* under Article 23 of the Basic Law.

GEORGE BUSH

In all, the Final Settlement came very close to our objectives. Germany was united and in NATO—although the eastern area would have a special status. For the United States, and ultimately for Europe, reunification was an astonishingly successful achievement. Was there an element of luck? Absolutely, considering how fortunate it was that the personalities involved could work as cooperatively as they did. But our sensitivity to legitimate German concerns, along with those of the French and British, as well as the Soviet stake in the outcome, kept the process alive and moving in the right direction. I am convinced that had the United States sat on the sidelines, the results might have been disastrous. Quite possibly the Germans and Soviets could have worked out a deal, with Germany united outside of NATO. Kohl and the German people are emotional about the US role, generously giving us credit for the successful reunification of Germany.

Reunification was an unparalleled, rapid set of events to which it was extremely difficult for many to adjust. At the outset, virtually all the players had very different perspectives on the consequences, value, or even threat of reunification for their national interests. Yet less than a year later we had accomplished the most profound change in European politics and security for many years, without confrontation, without a shot fired, and with all Europe still on the best and most peaceful of terms. There is probably no other time in history where events of such magnitude took place without conflict.

BRENT SCOWCROFT

For me, the Cold War ended when the Soviets accepted a united Germany in NATO. We had concluded the long process that had ended the superpower confrontation, set in motion during the Reagan Administration but secured on our watch. It had been facilitated by the President's political instinct for trusting Kohl and winning over our allies and the

Soviets. Much of the vital negotiations had been set and conducted at the highest levels. This was personal diplomacy in the finest sense of the term. Coalition-building, consensus, understanding, tolerance, and compromise had forged a new Europe, transformed and unified. There was no Versailles, no residual international bitterness. We had, perhaps, learned from the mistakes of the past. All had found their stake in the outcome. It was a shepherded victory for peace.

Because our focus was on Eastern Europe in 1989, the emerging prospect of unification that autumn had caught us almost completely by surprise. Our reaction was perforce ad hoc rather than strategic. All the wisdom on Germany—including that from Germans—was that unification remained a distant dream. As a result, we had not done comprehensive planning in advance and we had to scramble to get our act together. But even in the fall of 1989 the same was true of all our European allies and almost the entire German leadership.

It would have been useful had we been more open with our allies on the issue. We pursued it at length with the Soviets, but with our friends there were almost certainly too few occasions where frank discussions took place. More diligent dialogue with Germany's neighbors might have served at least to reduce their somewhat bitter feelings and fears. In the case of Poland, our efforts clearly helped allay their concerns. With respect to the United Kingdom and France, we may not have been as effective as we could have been.

One aspect of the process that was critical, and on which we could and did exercise real, perhaps decisive, influence, was whether a united Germany would remain in NATO. The outcome was not at all foreordained. Gorbachev started out unalterably opposed to unification itself, let alone to German membership in the alliance, and his thinking was far more generous than that of his colleagues. Our policy of refusing to exult over the course of events, first in Eastern Europe and then in Germany, or to talk in terms of victory for "us" and defeat for "them," helped to reassure him that we looked at events not as a zero-sum game but rather as one in which there were only winners. We worked very hard, not only bilaterally but also within NATO, to move alliance strategy away from the Soviet Union and toward post–Cold War objectives. This gave Gorbachev the opportunity to argue to his Politburo that NATO had been transformed and was no longer a threat.

The speed of unification was probably also a help in handling Gorbachev's objections. He appeared unable to come up with a better idea than what we were urging on him. He was failing in his efforts to keep the Germanies separated. His only remaining option, other than force, was to try to keep a united Germany neutral. Had he been insistent, he perhaps could have accomplished that, but an unattached Germany on the loose in Central Europe may have looked to him worse than one embedded in NATO.

Although unification was now complete, and Europe was healing, larger questions for the future remained open. United Germany in NATO had, for the moment, preserved our presence in Europe. We had moved ahead the transformation of NATO, establishing its direction to act as a political instrument of European stabilization rather than one of military confrontation. The Warsaw Pact was formally dissolved that summer. I believed that NATO alone would retain an important role in European security and stability, and the US with it.

How long would this last? The competition for political and economic leadership of Europe was now entering a new era, with new assumptions and participants. A heavyweight had emerged—Germany—and not everyone was sure what this would mean. A pessimistic Margaret Thatcher would later say that we had not attached Germany to Europe but Europe to Germany. François Mitterrand, on the other hand, still seemed confident that he could lead the Franco-German entente and through it maintain France's predominant influence in the EC. He also appeared to believe, or hope, that NATO would atrophy as the instrument of European security, with political stability increasingly supplied by the WEU/EC and CSCE. I think he envisioned that, eventually, an isolationist American public would demand US military withdrawal and the abdication of security leadership—to France. For our part, we believed that Germany would play a constructive role in the future of Europe and would support a stabilizing US presence there. It was up to us to continue to demonstrate the value of our role there through dynamic leadership of the alliance. But this was not unfinished old business; it was new business. Much of the way our role unfolded and evolved would depend on the developing cooperative relationship between the superpowers as they faced new, and unpredictable, challenges in the post–Cold War world.

CHAPTER 13

This Will Not Stand

GEORGE BUSH

At about 8:20 in the evening on Wednesday, August 1, 1990, a troubled Brent appeared at the basement White House Medical Office with Richard Haass, the NSC's Middle East expert, in tow. I was sitting on the edge of the exam table in a T-shirt getting a deep heat treatment to relieve my sore shoulders, the result of hitting a bucket's worth of golf balls earlier in the day. As I buttoned up my shirt, the three of us stepped out into the brightly lit hall. "Mr. President," Brent said gravely, "it looks very bad. Iraq may be about to invade Kuwait."

This was the first news I had heard confirming our worst fears. There had been scattered reports and rumors throughout the day that Iraq was shuffling troops around on its border with Kuwait. The NSC staff and our intelligence agencies were monitoring the situation, and Brent had kept me informed of developments. Tension between the two countries had been high for weeks, with a confrontation in OPEC over oil production and prices. This was stirred further by a long-standing Iraqi resentment of Kuwait due to territorial disputes. After an OPEC conference on July 25, and some regional diplomacy, the political crisis seemed to have eased. Reports began to grow of new military activity, however, although we could not confirm anything more definitive about Iraqi intentions than the movements themselves.

Richard now briefed me on the developing situation, and suggested that I phone Saddam Hussein to try to convince him not to attack. As we spoke, Brent took a call from Bob Kimmit of the State Department and learned that our embassy was reporting shooting in downtown Kuwait City. "So much for calling Saddam," I said, shaking my head. Brent and Richard left to find out more about what was happening.

I must confess that my mind that evening was on things other than

Iraq. We were in the midst of a recession and an ugly, partisan budget battle. Strained meetings with the congressional leadership were underway to find a compromise. There were other pressing foreign troubles catching my attention as well, such as a hostage-taking in Trinidad and a tragic civil war in Liberia, in which Americans were in danger.

About an hour later, Brent called. "It's clear," he said. "They're across the border." This was no longer a dispute accompanied by some melodramatic saber-rattling; this was outright aggression. Our intelligence had confirmed that Iraq had swept into Kuwait with a large number of troops. With his typical thoroughness, Brent had already set up a meeting to review the situation and to begin the recommendation process. It was the start of a critical, and often overlooked, role he was to play in what was to follow in the coming months. Much of the subsequent original planning and careful thought was done with him at my side, probably more than history will ever know.

I found it hard to believe that Saddam would invade. For a moment I thought, or hoped, that his move was intended to bring greater pressure on Kuwait and to force settlement of their disputes, and that he might withdraw, having made his point. I worried about the invasion's effect on other countries in the area, especially our vulnerable friend Saudi Arabia.

I asked Brent to set up an NSC meeting early the next day, before my departure for Aspen, Colorado, where I was scheduled to give a speech and to meet with Margaret Thatcher. A few minutes later, while the NSC staff consulted with State, I was on the phone with Tom Pickering, our UN Ambassador. While I was prepared to deal with this crisis unilaterally if necessary, I wanted the United Nations involved as part of our first response, starting with a strong condemnation of Iraq's attack on a fellow member. Decisive UN action would be important in rallying international opposition to the invasion and reversing it. I instructed Tom to work with the Kuwaitis and to do all he could to convene an emergency meeting of the Security Council.

Although I was optimistic, I was not yet sure what to expect from the UN. I was keenly aware that this would be the first post–Cold War test of the Security Council in crisis. I knew what had happened in the 1930s when a weak and leaderless League of Nations had failed to stand up to Japanese, Italian, and German aggression. The result was to encourage the ambitions of those regimes. The UN had been set up to correct the failings of the League, but the Cold War caused stalemate in the Security Council. Now, however, our improving relations with Moscow and our satisfactory ones with China offered the possibility that we could get their cooperation in forging international unity to oppose Iraq.

Soviet help in particular was key, first because they had veto power in the Security Council, but also because they could complete Iraq's political isolation. What we would be trying to accomplish ran counter to Moscow's traditional interests and policy in the region. The Soviet Union had long been a principal political and military sponsor of Iraq, selling Saddam Hussein Scud missiles and air defense systems, as well as tanks and other equipment. Moscow had close to two hundred military advisors there and a few thousand civilian technicians. My solid relationship with Gorbachev and Jim's with Shevardnadze promised goodwill, but how far they would (or could) go with us was still to be seen.

BRENT SCOWCROFT

I was in a nearby restaurant with a friend when, a little after seven o'clock, my pager buzzed. I excused myself to call the Situation Room and was told Richard Haass was asking that I return to the White House right away.

I had brought Richard into the NSC at the outset of the Administration. I had never worked with him, but had known him for several years, from his time at State and the Kennedy School at Harvard, from his writings, and from various conferences we had attended together. He had penetrating analytical ability, an innovative way of looking at issues, and he wrote well. He was also an indefatigable worker, which became a considerable blessing, inasmuch as the Persian Gulf crisis came on top of a full-time set of responsibilities. In addition, he had an incredible ability to turn out great prose under the most intense pressure.

When I arrived at the White House that evening, Richard had just returned from an interagency meeting. He filled me in on the latest gloomy intelligence reports, adding that the group believed President Bush should call Saddam immediately to urge restraint. It might already be too late, but we went to the Residence to tell the President what was happening. He took the news calmly and listened carefully to what details we could offer him. Following the call from Kimmit that the invasion was underway, I directed that the Deputies Committee be convened, which I would chair since Bob Gates was on vacation. I rushed home to check in on my wife and then returned to the Situation Room, where an interagency video conference had been set up for eleven that evening. The discussion that night lasted until well past two in the morning. We agreed to recommend some measures which could be taken quickly, such as moving forces, including sending a squadron of F-15s to Saudi Arabia, assuming Saudi approval. More important, we needed to freeze Iraqi and especially Kuwaiti assets in the United States—the latter was particularly urgent to accomplish before the Iraqis plundered them through the puppet government we learned they had set up. Boyden Gray, the White House Counsel, drew up Executive Orders to accomplish that, and, at four thirty in the morning I took them to the President for his signature.

The Persian Gulf had not been among our major concerns early in the Administration. Despite a number of sometimes exasperating differences with Iraq, developments in the region had begun to return to normal following the 1980–88 Iran-Iraq conflict and occupied the attention of our specialists rather than the policy-making team. Access to the Gulf, however, with its vast oil resources, was of intrinsically critical economic and security importance to the United States, and we had directed that one of the early strategic reviews (NSR-10) focus on it.

American policymakers had been concerned with the security and stability of the Gulf since the British had withdrawn from the region at the end of the 1960s. With the fall of the Shah, our first choice as the stabilizing force in the region, the United States turned to a policy of balancing off Iran and Iraq. This led the Reagan Administration to tilt toward Baghdad during the Iran-Iraq conflict, not out of preference for one of two reprehensible regimes, but because we wanted neither to win the war and were worried that Iraq would prove to be the weaker. After the war, the Reagan Administration set out to institutionalize this somewhat improved relationship with Iraq. It was an attempt to encourage acceptably moderate behavior on the part of Saddam Hussein. There was also the hope of securing a significant role for American business in what was assumed would be a substantial Iraqi reconstruction effort.

These objectives seemed to us reasonable and, pending the outcome of the policy review, we continued to pursue them. It was not easy. Saddam Hussein was a tough, ruthless, and even paranoid dictator with little exposure to, and deep suspicion of, the West. His regime's human rights record was abysmal and its history of harboring terrorists, even if its support for international terrorist organizations had been tempered during this period of improved relations, was well known and of considerable concern to us. There were also a number of security problems which complicated the relationship. Saddam had chemical and biological weapons programs and had used chemical weapons against the Iranians as well as the Kurds in his own country. Like his Iranian neighbors, he had been acquiring intermediate-range ballistic missiles, thus threatening ever-greater portions of the Middle East, including Israel. More ominous, we knew he was attempting to build a nuclear weapons capability, although our intelligence estimates on the amount of progress he had made varied widely.

The analysis in NSR-10 offered broad support for the Gulf policy of the

Reagan Administration. On October 2, 1989, President Bush issued a directive (NSD-26) which reaffirmed our strategic interests in the region and, with caveats conveying our concerns, generally confirmed the previous policy of engaging Iraq: "Normal relations between the United States and Iraq would serve our longer-term interests and promote stability in both the Gulf and the Middle East. The United States Government should propose economic and political incentives for Iraq to moderate its behavior and to increase our influence with Iraq." The problem was how to encourage Saddam Hussein to be at least a minimally responsible member of the international community and yet not accept or ignore his depredations.

The principal economic incentive we could offer was continuing the practice of providing Commodity Credit Corporation (CCC) credit guarantees to American exporters to encourage Iraq's importation of American grain.* In late 1989, we allocated $1 billion in such guarantees, with $500 million to be immediately available and the remainder subject to further review before release. In the Foreign Appropriations bill passed in November 1989, Congress specifically banned Export-Import bank programs for Iraq, and some members threatened to prohibit Iraq from receiving CCC credits as well. As of 1989, total US exports to Iraq were $1.3 billion, not much more than the total CCC aid available. US imports of Iraqi oil were expected to reach $2.5 billion for 1990. Loss of the CCC program would have nearly erased what little leverage we had with Iraq. In January 1990, Congress dropped CCC sanctions from pending bills. For its part, Baghdad made some modest positive gestures, such as indicating its willingness to pay compensation to the families of crew members killed on the USS *Stark*, which had been hit by an Iraqi anti-ship missile in 1987 during the Iran-Iraq war.

These steps were the most we were prepared to take, in view of Saddam's ambivalent behavior. We were making what we considered a good-faith effort toward better relations, but the results were not very promising. We continued to clash with Iraq on a variety of issues. For their human rights violations, we criticized them in the UN Human Rights Committee and in our annual report on the subject. We denounced Iraq's execution of the British journalist Farzad Bazoff on March 15, 1990. As we grew increasingly exasperated, some of the moderate Arab states, including Egypt, began to express concern that our relations with Iraq were becoming too confrontational.

*This Department of Agriculture program provided a degree of insurance for American exporters; it did not involve aid or the transfer of funds to Iraq.

BRENT SCOWCROFT

In early 1990, it gradually became apparent to me that Saddam had made an abrupt change in his policy toward the United States. The relative moderation he had adopted earlier, perhaps mostly to curry favor with us, was abandoned. His behavior became even less predictable. While he told our diplomats he sought improved relations with the West, especially the United States, he began to claim there was a conspiracy against him led by the United States, Israel, and Britain. It was my conclusion that, for whatever reason, Saddam had decided to drop his policy of getting along with the United States and, instead, to put himself at the forefront of the "rejectionists"—those states opposed to peace with, or even the very existence of, Israel. He joined their denunciations of the immigration of Soviet Jews to Israel and, at the beginning of April, threatened to incinerate that country if it attacked Iraq again, as it had in 1981, when it struck a nuclear facility. The threat created a major furor in the West. We dropped plans for providing the second $500 million in CCC credits and Congress started again to contemplate sanctions. If my analysis was correct, our current policy was no longer appropriate. Saddam was so notoriously mercurial, however, that I thought we should wait for further evidence before changing direction ourselves. There was minimal risk to such a course, because there was little remaining of our positive policy.

In addition to the strident anti-Israel rhetoric, there emerged disturbing signs that Iraq was still seeking to develop weapons of mass destruction. In March we uncovered and successfully blocked its attempt to procure—illegally—triggering devices which could be used for nuclear weapons. Together with the British, we investigated and blocked Iraqi efforts to procure parts for a long-barreled "super gun" artillery piece of vast range they were trying to build. Later, in July, we intercepted at dockside in New Jersey special tungsten furnaces which could be useful to their nuclear weapons program.

Saddam's increasing belligerence cast a pall over our Iraqi policy. The analysis that had led us to try to moderate his behavior still seemed the most valid approach, but we could no longer ignore the changes now taking place. We concluded we should send him an unambiguous message telling him what we wanted and expected: Unless there were clear changes in Iraq's international behavior, we would not continue to conduct business as usual. In other words, he was at a fork in the road, and if he made the wrong choice he risked making us his adversary.

This message was sent first through our ambassador in Baghdad,

April Glaspie, to Foreign Minister Tariq Aziz. In Washington, Larry Eagleburger had a similar conversation with the Iraqi ambassador. In addition,
we decided to make use of a bipartisan Senate group trip to the Middle
East, led by Republican minority leader Bob Dole and including Democrat Howard Metzenbaum, which was scheduled to visit Baghdad in
mid-April to meet with Saddam and evaluate the need for further sanctions. After their trip, Dole reported that Saddam was indeed convinced
that there was a conspiracy against Iraq, although the Iraqi leader seemed
pleased when Dole assured him President Bush was not plotting against
him. The conclusion of the Senate group was basically optimistic: stay
the course and keep the relationship open—sanctions would only lend
credence to Saddam's conspiracy theory. Through these approaches, the
Iraqis received a consistent message from us: we wanted regional stability and a constructive relationship, but Iraq's behavior presented major
obstacles.

Against this background of bewildering foreign policy moves, Saddam
also began to tangle with his Arab neighbors over oil. Oil exports constituted Iraq's principal source of foreign currency and represented almost
half its GNP. As with any member of OPEC, Baghdad's production and
price levels were set by agreement within the organization. The unity of
OPEC, and the willingness of members to observe their assigned prices
and production levels (and the consequent impact on world oil prices)
varied. In the past, the organization had shown periods of solidarity,
especially when prices were rising. In recent years, however, as more oil
flowed to market from sources outside OPEC and prices came under
pressure, members had increasingly broken ranks for political and economic reasons. As prices fell, it was tempting to overproduce and sell in
excess of the quotas in order to maintain revenue streams, further softening prices, to the dismay of other OPEC members who saw their own
revenues drop. Saddam, who desperately needed the income, began complaining bitterly about this practice, focusing his ire on Kuwait and the
United Arab Emirates (UAE).

Oil production was not the only source of friction between Iraq
and Kuwait. While Kuwait had been a major supporter of Iraq during the
Iran-Iraq War (along with Saudi Arabia, it had sold huge amounts of oil
drawn from the Neutral Zone on behalf of Iraq), their relations had been
strained in the past by several factors. There was a dispute over their
common boundary, which divided the rich Rumaila oil field. Iraq also
claimed islands off Kuwait, especially the large island of Būbiyān, which
controlled access to the major Iraqi port and naval base of Umm Qasr.
Kuwait had "lent" the island to Iraq for use during its war with Iran,

and Baghdad wanted to keep it. Added to these problems was the $30 billion debt Iraq still owed Kuwait for assistance during the war and for which Kuwait was demanding payment. It was a recipe for resentment.

In mid-July, Saddam sharpened the confrontation. On July 17, he accused Kuwait and the UAE of exceeding the OPEC production limits and driving down prices; he claimed that this had cost Iraq over $14 billion in lost revenue. He warned that Iraq would take "effective action to put things right" if they did not stop. Simultaneously, the Iraqi media launched a propaganda campaign against the two countries. Saddam formalized these threats with a bellicose letter delivered by Tariq Ariz to Arab League secretary general Klibi, charging that Kuwait's unwillingness to resolve the border problem, its refusal to cancel Iraq's huge debt, its oil policies, and its "theft" of oil from disputed fields, constituted "military aggression."

Kuwait sent representatives around the Arab world to give its side of the story and asked the Arab League to mediate the border dispute. Saddam increased the pressure, ordering two Republican Guards divisions to the border on July 19, and mobilizing additional troops. Kuwait immediately put its small forces on alert (although it did not request US help). The UAE, whose offshore oil rigs Baghdad had attacked during the Iran-Iraq war, followed suit on July 22, but they also asked us to send aerial tankers and participate in a joint military exercise. As a reminder of our important interests in the region, and as a sign of our displeasure with Iraqi bullying, we dispatched two tankers and a transport, which arrived on July 24. The Saudis put their own forces on alert July 23, but told us that, while they appreciated the US show of support, the matter was best resolved by the Arabs themselves.

We were uncertain of Saddam's objectives, in view of his repeated assurances and the opinions of such Arab leaders as Egyptian President Mubarak, Saudi King Fahd, and Jordan's King Hussein (all of whom were in contact with both sides), that there would be no attack. According to our ambassador in Kuwait, Nathaniel Howell, the Kuwaitis themselves were perplexed. To them this was no longer simply oil and borders but a bid for hegemony in the region: Who would play the leading role in OPEC and the Arab world? They saw parallels to the run-up to the Iran-Iraq war. We kept watch on Iraqi troop movements but, since there was as yet no logistical buildup near the border, we concluded the Iraqis were not planning an immediate major operation. Nevertheless, we decided it was imperative to escalate our warnings. We had no formal commitment to Kuwait or other states in the region, but our interests there had been declared in statements by every president since Eisenhower. The State

Department called in the Iraqi ambassador, reminding him that US actions during the Iran-Iraq War had demonstrated our commitment to the sovereignty and integrity of the Gulf States, and making clear that we would continue to defend our interests in the area. Ambassador Glaspie was directed to tell the Iraqi Foreign Ministry the same thing and, on a daily basis after July 20, she repeated our demand for clarification of Iraq's intentions.

The moderate Arab leaders scrambled to defuse the mounting crisis through telephone calls, envoys, and personal visits. Mubarak met with Tariq Aziz in Cairo on July 22, where they were joined by King Hussein the following day. Two days later, Mubarak flew to Baghdad, Kuwait, and Saudi Arabia in an attempt to mediate and proposed that the Arab League foreign ministers meet in Cairo. He cabled President Bush about his discussions. He had urged Saddam to contain the escalation and agree to solve the disputes through negotiation. "President Hussein was receptive and responsive," he wrote. Mubarak was "confident that accommodation can be worked out without delay," and asked that the United States avoid "any provocative action that is liable to add fuel to the fire and render the easing of tension more difficult. Announcements on joint military exercises in the Gulf and statements issued by outside powers should be measured to bring the parties closer together and not to deepen distrust among them." Prince Bandar bin-Sultan, the Saudi ambassador to Washington, told President Bush that the Arabs were pleased with Mubarak's talks with Iraq and Kuwait, and that Saudi Arabia approved of the way the United States was handing the situation.

On July 25, Saddam suddenly summoned Glaspie to the presidential palace. Fluent in Arabic, she arrived alone, without notetaker or interpreter. Afterwards, she sent a summary cable reporting her talks and indicating her belief that Saddam was worried. "He does not want to further antagonize us," she wrote. "With the UAE maneuvers, we have fully caught his attention, and that is good. I believe we would be well-advised to ease off on public criticism of Iraq until we see how the negotiations develop." Saddam complained that our joint maneuvers would only encourage the UAE and Kuwait to ignore conventional diplomacy. He theatrically warned that if Iraq was publicly humiliated by the United States, it would have no choice but to "respond," however illogical and self-destructive that might prove. Glaspie cabled:

> Although not quite explicit, Saddam's message to US seemed to be that he will make a major push to cooperate with Mubarak's diplomacy, but we must try to understand Kuwaiti/UAE "selfishness" is unbearable.

Ambassador made it clear that we can never excuse settlement of disputes by other than peaceful means.

In her longer, more complete report, Glaspie detailed the questions she had put to him in order to extract a clearer picture of Saddam's intentions:

> Is it not reasonable for us to be concerned when the president and the foreign minister both say publicly that the Kuwaiti actions are the equivalent of military aggression, and then learn that many units of the Republican Guard have been sent to the border? Is it not reasonable for us to ask, in the spirit of friendship, not confrontation, the simple question: What are your intentions?
>
> Saddam said that was indeed a reasonable question. He acknowledged that we should be concerned for regional peace, in fact it is our duty as a superpower. "But how can we make them (Kuwait and UAE) understand how deeply we are suffering?"

Glaspie described how Saddam left the room to take a call from Mubarak, who told him he had arranged for Kuwaiti and Iraqi delegations to meet in Riyadh, and that the Kuwaiti Crown Prince would subsequently come to Baghdad for negotiations. "I told Mubarak," said Saddam, that "nothing will happen until the meeting," and nothing will happen during or after the meeting if the Kuwaitis will at last "give us some hope."

GEORGE BUSH

Glaspie, a veteran diplomat in whom I had full confidence, has been much criticized for what happened in her meeting with Saddam. She was lied to by him, and she clearly spelled out that we could not condone settlement of disputes by other than peaceful means. It is a total misreading of this conversation to conclude that we were giving Saddam a green light to seize his neighbor. No one, especially Saddam Hussein, could doubt that the US had strong interests in the Gulf and did not condone aggression. Her statement "as you know, we don't take a stand on territorial disputes" (standard State Department language that we do not take positions on the merits of a boundary dispute, but expect it to be settled peacefully) has been grossly misconstrued as implying we would look the other way. I regret that Congress raked Glaspie over the coals.

As Glaspie spoke with Saddam in Baghdad, Arab diplomacy was operating at the crucial OPEC meeting in Geneva. There, Kuwait and the UAE accepted oil pricing arrangements which Iraq said were satisfactory. OPEC also set up committees to enforce compliance, which addressed one of Iraq's chief complaints. While it did not appear that Saddam would receive quick financial relief from his oil exports (the prices set were not quite as high as Iraq had demanded), he did get action from OPEC and promises that Kuwait and UAE would obey the new prices and quotas. The talks with Kuwait to which Baghdad had agreed were announced, and Mubarak declared that Saddam had personally told him Iraq had no intention of moving forces toward Kuwait. It appeared to us, and to the Arab leaders, that perhaps the worst of the crisis was past.

BRENT SCOWCROFT

The State Department and we in the NSC were encouraged by what we saw as some progress, both in Glaspie's conversation with Saddam and from the results of the OPEC meeting. Diplomacy seemed to be working, if slowly, and Arab leaders were optimistic. Iraqi rhetoric had been toned down and the media attacks abated. Glaspie was suggesting to us only that we not rock the boat yet, but let the negotiations proceed before we did anything. To lock in whatever we could of this improvement, the NSC and State staffs recommended a presidential cable to Saddam—a highly unusual step. We framed it to say that we were pleased with recent developments but also to warn against further belligerent actions. It reminded Saddam that we had interests in the region. We did not want a more "muscular" message before the talks began between Kuwait and Iraq, for this was not a time to posture and threaten. The Arab leaders were insisting that they had matters well in hand and that unilateral steps by the United States would only complicate matters. The cable was sent on July 28. King Hussein called the President the next day and said that the message had been "well received and nothing will happen."

Despite the new OPEC agreement on July 25, diplomatic warnings, and his assurances to the Arab leaders, Saddam continued to increase his troops on the Kuwaiti border. Our analysts had already determined by July 24 that he had sufficient forces and logistics "for all options." By July 31, those forces reached close to 100,000, nearly five times those of Kuwait. Was Saddam still trying to extort additional concessions from Kuwait, such as financial assistance, or did he want to ensure compliance by Kuwait and the UAE with the OPEC agreement? Would he try to seize the Rumaila oil field and Warbah and Būbiyān islands? There was also the chance that he might grab all of Kuwait. He now had forces on hand sufficient to overwhelm the Kuwaiti military within forty-eight hours.

Since Saddam was well on his way toward reaching his publicized objectives, it seemed unlikely that he would invade. He had obtained higher oil prices, the issue which seemed to have touched off the crisis in the first place, and Iraq's creditors would probably soon cancel major debts and pledge development assistance to help reconstruct its economy. For these reasons, his further moves appeared to be extortion, designed to extract additional economic and territorial concessions from Kuwait or perhaps resolve the border dispute on Iraqi terms.

On July 31, the two sides met in Jeddah, but the talks collapsed over Iraq's demands that Kuwait write off Iraqi debts and relinquish some territory. Tariq Aziz announced, however, that the meetings, mediated by Mubarak and King Fahd, would continue in Baghdad, and Iraqi Ambassador Mohammed Sadiq al-Mashat told Assistant Secretary of State John Kelly the same thing in Washington. The following night, Iraq invaded Kuwait.

BRENT SCOWCROFT

Our approach to averting conflict—to warn against belligerent behavior, to make clear we would stand by our friends, yet continue to offer good relations for good behavior—had failed. Would a "deterrent" policy, such as threatening to counter any Iraqi use of force, have been more effective? Since Saddam later was not dissuaded from his course by the presence of half a million troops arrayed directly against him, it is not likely. Not all wars are avoidable, and this was perhaps one of them. Saddam would have done what he did either way. If we had been more bellicose and he invaded (which probably would have been the case), then we would have been accused of provocation, a charge that would have greatly complicated the task of organizing the coalition which ultimately defeated him.

We had made no threats to intervene in large part because our Arab allies were telling us that would be counterproductive—not just in dealing with Iraq in the current crisis, but for the United States in the region. It was important that we listen closely to, and take seriously, their advice and not act unilaterally in the face of it. We needed Arab backing for whatever moves we might have to make. We almost certainly would forfeit improved US-Arab relations, and US credibility in the Middle East, if we acted against an Arab state without regional support. As it was, after the invasion the Arab coalition joined solidly with us, because it was clear we had done everything possible to avert conflict and Saddam was wholly at fault.

GEORGE BUSH

On the morning of August 2, Barbara and I were still in bed with the papers when Brent arrived just before 5:00. Visibly exhausted, he filled me in on the emerging details of the invasion and the discussions he'd had the night before. Iraq's official story was that it had moved in on the pretext that there had been a coup and that its "leaders," purporting to be the "legitimate" government in Kuwait, had requested their help. Our immediate options were limited. We had not yet officially been asked for help by the Kuwaitis or Saudis, but it was important to display promptly our support. I ordered our already alerted warships at the island of Diego Garcia in the Indian Ocean to head for the Persian Gulf. Our next requirement was to get air forces into the area. Brent explained that Bob Kimmit was already checking with the Saudis to obtain approval for sending an F-15 squadron. He handed me an Executive Order freezing the assets of Iraq and Kuwait in the United States. I signed it. At least we could take some economic measures.

After I showered, I headed for the Oval Office. At 6:30, Tom Pickering phoned to report on the UN Security Council's actions. Like Brent, he had been up all night working through the details of a resolution with the Kuwaitis and the other Council members. By morning, the Council had voted 14–0 in favor of UNSC Resolution 660, condemning Iraq's aggression, demanding that it withdraw its troops from Kuwait, and demanding that the dispute be resolved by negotiations. I was disappointed and concerned that Saudi Arabia's neighbor Yemen had abstained, probably in an effort to curry favor with Iraq. I knew President Ali Abdullah Saleh and didn't feel he would recklessly side with Saddam. Still, the UN action was good news. The Soviets had supported us, and that was step one in building opposition.

At about 7:00, Brent arrived in the Oval Office and at 7:30 Bill Webster and Hank Applebaum (the CIA briefer) appeared with a bundle of papers to give the daily CIA general briefing. During it, and with Brent on the line, I called Jim Baker, who was in Ulaanbaatar, Mongolia, on a side trip from an arms control meeting with Shevardnadze in Irkutsk. Jim had been warned of the ominous signs in the Gulf and had already spoken with Shevardnadze about the danger of an invasion. Shevardnadze said he believed, as we had earlier, that Saddam was simply "strong-arming" the Kuwaitis. With the news of the invasion, Jim had urged the Soviets to join an arms embargo of Iraq, and Shevardnadze departed for Moscow to consult with Gorbachev.

A little after 8:00, I joined Brent and the rest of the NSC in the Cabinet Room. In the "photo-op" just before our discussion began, I spoke briefly to reporters, who had been speculating wildly about what we were going to do. Among the forest of boom and hand-held microphones, I was careful in my remarks. I condemned the invasion and outlined the steps we had taken, as well as the fact that this was an exploratory meeting concerned with reviewing all options for defending our interests in the Gulf. Right off, Helen Thomas of UPI asked me whether I was considering intervention as one of those options.

I did not want my first public comments to threaten the use of American military might, so I said I was not contemplating intervention, and, even if I knew we were going to use force, I would not announce it in a press conference. The truth is, at that moment I had no idea what our options were. I did know for sure that the aggression had to be stopped, and Kuwait's sovereignty restored. We had a big job ahead of us in shaping opinion at home and abroad and could little afford bellicose mistakes at the start. What I hoped to convey was an open mind about how we might handle the situation until I learned all the facts.

BRENT SCOWCROFT

The President's comment that he was not contemplating intervention has been taken by some to indicate he was passive or indecisive about the notion of doing anything about the Iraqi invasion until Margaret Thatcher "put some stiffening in his spine" at their meeting later that day. Such speculation is wrong, although his choice of words was not felicitous. His language was picked with two thoughts in mind: First, don't say anything at this early point which would telegraph his thinking. Second, make clear that the NSC meeting was not a decision session but a discussion of the situation and options for reacting.

The NSC meeting was a bit chaotic. We really did not yet have a clear picture of what was happening on the ground, and the participants focused mainly on the economic impact of the invasion and what Saddam would do next. Webster outlined the extent of the invasion, and some of the responses from other countries. The Arab League had passed a resolution condemning Iraq, but there was no call for armed action. Moscow had still not said anything officially. NATO and Japan had called for Iraq's withdrawal. "The stock market in Tokyo is down; oil prices are increasing," said Webster. "The British have declared a grave threat to regional peace. It appears there was no military objective but Kuwait."

Bob Kimmit, sitting in for Baker and Eagleburger, spelled out the diplomatic steps we had already taken. State had called in the Iraqi ambassador, who claimed to know nothing more than what Baghdad had told the world. Diplomatic posts had all been briefed, and the Europeans were already working with us. No one was supporting Iraq. We had sent out cables asking others to join our economic measures. The British were in a cabinet meeting debating what to do. We were also asking the Soviets, French, Italians, and Chinese to stop arms shipments to Iraq. There were no reports of harm to any of the 3,800 American civilians and 130 embassy staff in Kuwait, or the 500 Americans and 42 embassy personnel in Baghdad.

Nicholas Brady pointed out that the source of Iraq's power was its oil. Without it, Baghdad would have no money to keep its military going. He proposed that we shut off Iraqi and Kuwaiti oil and ask other countries to make up the difference. Cheney added that if only economic and political sanctions were in effect, Iraq could become a major oil power overnight. "The rest of the world badly needs oil," said Dick. "They have little interest in poor Kuwait. It may be difficult to organize a good package of economic sanctions."

The discussion moved to the effects of cutting off oil, and then Colin Powell introduced our military options. "For several weeks the CINC [General Norman Schwarzkopf] and the [Joint Chiefs of Staff] have prepared military options should the need arise," he said. Schwarzkopf, Commander-in-Chief of Central Command (CENTCOM) and responsible for implementing any military response in the region, had been invited to the meeting as well. He now described what was at hand for air strikes, a naval bombardment of Iraq, when they could act, and also how quickly we could move forces to defend Saudi Arabia. While we had a few ships in the Gulf that could hit some targets within hours, it would take a few days to get a broader force prepared. We had F-15s and F-16s on standby and they could be deployed to defend Saudi Arabia. However, this would require that they be based there. So far, the Saudis had said no.

Schwarzkopf added that there was also a rehearsed plan for defending the Saudi oil region, using forces in the area, and he was confident we could blunt an Iraqi attack there. If we wanted an air campaign against Iraq itself, however, we would need far more forces and more time. We were facing over a million Iraqi troops. It would take about twenty days to deploy sufficient aircraft and carrier battle groups.

"Let's step back," said Scowcroft. "The most significant option economically is oil. . . . There are some things we can do: shut off the two pipelines [through Turkey and Saudi Arabia], tell tankers going into Kuwait to stop—in theory it's easy, but in practice it will be difficult. . . .

We should mount an embargo of Kuwaiti and Iraqi oil purchases." A long debate ensued over the effects of disrupting oil, and which countries would be affected. President Bush asked Brady to get an analysis on the issue and asked about international economic sanctions under Chapter VII of the UN Charter, which provides for mandatory observance by members. Pickering said we were ready to propose the matter at the UN. "International sanctions will give us security cover," said the President. "They will give some spine to Saudi Arabia and others to take difficult actions, like closing the pipeline."

Kimmit reported that State was reviewing the question of evacuating Americans from Kuwait and Baghdad. They had also discussed breaking off diplomatic relations, but decided against recommending it. The safety of American citizens was at stake, and we needed our officials in Baghdad to protect them.

President Bush suggested we ask Congress to pass resolutions imposing unilateral sanctions, commending the UN action, and supporting our responses. But we needed more information, he said. We didn't want to make statements committing us to anything until we understood the situation.

"Saudi Arabia and others will cut and run if we are weak," warned Cheney. Powell asked if we should declare that Saudi Arabia was a vital interest to the United States. "I think there is no choice," he said. "The question is how do you lay it out to the public."

"I agree," said the President, adding that we could not overlook getting the other major powers involved either. So far the reaction of the Soviets had been good. "We can get them to kick in," he said. "That is, no adventurism, but get them to agree to some action. US-Soviet relations are good, but we don't want to overlook the Soviet desire for access to warm water ports. We don't want to resurrect that. Maybe something positive like a joint statement." The next step was at the UN and the Security Council. "In New York we should press to put the heat on Saudi Arabia and the others. . . . Let's get [US] sanctions in place before noon."

BRENT SCOWCROFT

I was frankly appalled at the undertone of the discussion, which suggested resignation to the invasion and even adaptation to a *fait accompli*. There was a huge gap between those who saw what was happening as the major crisis of our time and those who treated it as the crisis *du jour*. The remarks tended to skip over the enormous stake the United States had in the situation, or the ramifications of the aggression on the emerging post–Cold War world. While some statements seemed to reflect the gravity of what had occurred, most tended to focus on the price of oil and the resultant upset in the Middle East. The tone implied that the crisis was halfway around the world and doing anything serious about it would just be too difficult. Later that morning, I spoke to President Bush of my concerns. I asked if, in the next meeting, I could depart from custom in NSC meetings and speak first, outlining the absolute intolerability of this invasion to US interests. He shared my concern and proposed that he himself make such an opening statement. I told him I thought that would stifle discussion, and we agreed I would go first.

Almost immediately after the NSC meeting we left for Colorado and what proved an unforgettable flight. The 707 usually used as Air Force One could not land at Aspen airport and, rather than waste time switching aircraft in Denver, the President decided to fly directly to Aspen on a small C-20 Gulfstream. He, John Sununu, and I crammed together in the small front compartment, knees practically touching, sharing the telephones, with papers strewn everywhere.

The President was scheduled to give a major address at Aspen, setting forth a new military strategy and force structure in response to the winding down of the Cold War. That speech now required a number of revisions. I frantically drafted changes and, in between the President's calls to Congressional and foreign leaders, checked them out with Washington, all the while trying to keep abreast of developments in the Gulf. It was in discussion on the changes in his speech that it became obvious to me that the President was prepared to use force to evict Saddam from Kuwait if it became necessary, although he did not explicitly say so.

GEORGE BUSH

I used the time aboard Air Force One to poll foreign leaders. I called Hosni Mubarak and King Hussein, who happened to be together in Alexandria, Egypt. Both were disturbed by the situation.

King Hussein told me he was just about to go to Saudi Arabia and Iraq. "I really implore you, sir, to keep calm," he said. "We want to deal with this in an Arab context, to find a way that gives us a foundation for a better future." I told the King that the world would not accept the status quo now, and that it was unacceptable to the United States. "I'm sure Saddam Hussein knows this, but you can tell him that from me." The King replied that Iraq was "determined to pull out as soon as possible, maybe in days," and promised to push for it.

Mubarak explained that they were trying hard to find a solution for withdrawal that would not "throw away" the Kuwaiti government. "George, give us two days to find a solution," he asked. I told him about the economic measures we had taken. "The only exception is, of course, if there are threats to Americans—that would be a whole new ballgame." Hosni supported sanctions (even though I had not specifically raised the issue). "I will talk to Saddam Hussein right now," he said. "I am also in contact with the Saudis."

"That is very important," I said. "Please tell Saddam Hussein that the United States is very concerned about this action. We are very concerned that other forces will be released—you know what that means, my friend. Tell Saddam that if you like." Hosni said he would, or this would be an even bigger disaster. "I'll pray for you," I said.

BRENT SCOWCROFT

I was wary of an "Arab solution," fearing that it might end up in a compromise with Saddam. It was a real dilemma. If we refused to give time for a possible Arab settlement, we could alienate our best friends when we needed them badly. But if we acquiesced, and the Arabs came out with a compromise, how could we reject it?

GEORGE BUSH

I got Baker on the line again in Mongolia and we went over our efforts with the Soviets. Simultaneously, Brent was hunched over another phone to the State Department's director of the Policy Planning Staff, Dennis Ross, who, with Bob Zoellick, was in Moscow with Shevardnadze. Jim said he would go back to Moscow to try to work out a joint statement (already being prepared by Ross and Zoellick) that would condemn Iraq's action and call for withdrawal from Kuwait.

I had a chance to talk with Margaret Thatcher in the living room of our ambassador to Great Britain, Henry Catto, who had a home in Aspen. Margaret and I saw the situation in remarkably similar ways, which I think was mutually reassuring. I told her about the US-Soviet statement we were working on, and that I had spoken to Mubarak and King Hussein. "Both were going to talk to Saddam and urged that we go slow—they needed time. I said we couldn't accept the status quo. It had to be withdrawal and the restoration of the Kuwaiti government." I added that I was moving a carrier battle group from Diego Garcia.

"If Iraq wins, no small state is safe," said Margaret. "They won't stop here. They see a chance to take a major share of oil. It's got to be stopped. We must do everything possible." She said she and her cabinet had been talking about trade sanctions, but this was something the whole world had to do. She wondered whether the Arabs would act and if the Saudis would close their pipeline. If they did, what would be the impact on the oil market? "The Saudis are *critical*, we can't do anything without them." She urged that by Monday we should go to the UN to ask for sanctions. "King Hussein was not helpful," she added. "He told me the Kuwaitis had it coming—they are not well liked. But he grudgingly agreed to weigh in with Saddam . . ." She wasn't sure where Syria and Iran stood.

I told her the Saudis could make up the difference for the Kuwaiti and Iraqi oil we cut off, and that Iran had been making some overtures. "One of my fears is that the Israelis might take some action," I said. "That's one thing which could unite the Arabs." Margaret thought it all came back to getting sanctions through the Security Council. "We must win this," she said. "Losing Saudi oil is a blow we couldn't take . . . We cannot give in to dictators. [And] we can't make an oil embargo work without a blockade."

At about two o'clock, Margaret and I stepped out to a patio for a press conference. We condemned Iraq's aggression and called for a peaceful solution, with the withdrawal of Iraqi forces and the restoration of the Kuwaiti leadership. She put her finger on the most important point— whether the nations of the world had the collective and effective will to implement the resolutions of the Security Council and compel with-drawal and restoration. It would be up to American leadership to make that happen.

I called King Fahd from the Cattos' bedroom later that afternoon, the phone perched on the bed and Brent hovering over my shoulder. Saudi Arabia would be indispensable to any military moves we might make, and might itself be in danger. At this point, we did not know whether Iraqi forces would stop at the Saudi border. It was an emotional call. The King was agitated and the interpreter struggled to keep up.

Fahd explained how he had tried to resolve Iraqi-Kuwaiti differences before Iraq struck and that both sides had expressed a willingness to talk. Saddam had even assured the Saudis that he "had no interest in attacking Kuwait." The King angrily added that Saddam had done the opposite "because he is conceited. He doesn't realize that the implications of his actions are upsetting the world order. He seems to think only of himself. He is following Hitler in creating world problems—with a difference: one was conceited and one is both conceited and crazy. I believe nothing will work with Saddam but the use of force."

He had reminded Saddam that during the Arab summit in Baghdad the Iraqi leader had suggested a nonaggression pact among the countries, agreeing not to intervene in one another's affairs. "My conversation with him today was strict and strong," the King said, "and I asked him to with-draw from Kuwait now, and that we would not consider any [imposed] regime representative of Kuwaiti public opinion or Arab public opinion."

Saddam had asked to hold talks with the Saudis, and the King speculated that something might be done to find a solution. "I told him that I hold him responsible for the safety of all people in Kuwait—Kuwaiti or not," he declared.

King Fahd said he was willing to meet with Saddam's envoy, who was due to arrive the next day, but Saddam would have to understand that Iraqi troops had to withdraw. "The only other solution is the use of force," he said severely. "Mr. President, this is a matter that is extremely serious and grave. It involves a principle that can't be approved or condoned by any reasonable principle or moral." Mubarak had proposed an Arab summit for the next day, which the King thought an excellent idea. "I hope these matters can be resolved peacefully," he said. "If not, Saddam must be taught a lesson he will not forget for the rest of his life—if he remains alive."

I asked whether the Kuwaiti royal family was safe, which he assured me was the case. (We subsequently learned that the Emir's younger brother had decided to stand and fight. He was shot on the steps of one of the palaces.) The Emir had barely five minutes to escape and the Foreign Minister was nearly captured. I then outlined what we were doing. I offered him an F-15 squadron, but he asked to discuss that option further.

King Fahd's hesitation rang alarm bells in my head. I began to worry that the Saudis might be considering compromise, that they might accept the new status quo on their northern border if there were guarantees from Iraq. There is a historical Arab propensity to try to work out "deals." Even though we knew the Saudis well, and trusted them, we could not be completely certain what course they would take. In these early hours of the crisis, with so much going on, I had to wonder if, under pressure, they might be inclined to strike some kind of behind-the-scenes arrangement with Saddam. I do not know if they even thought about it, but the King's reluctance to accept aircraft had me concerned. We couldn't have a solo US effort in the Middle East. We had to have our Arab allies with us, particularly those who were threatened the most—the Saudis.

BRENT SCOWCROFT

While we were in Colorado, I called Haass and asked him to draft an overview memo from me to the President as background for the next NSC meeting. In it we described a policy to contain Iraq, slow its development of both conventional and unconventional military capabilities, and effect its withdrawal from Kuwait. "The necessary instruments of such a policy," it read, "would be export controls, other economic sanctions, and enhanced military actions, both unilateral and with others." It warned that while it was proper at this point to emphasize diplomacy and sanctions, we had to anticipate that these might fall short and we would be faced with a choice between living with this new status quo or challenging Iraq directly, either with force or with actions (closing their pipelines, etc.) that were almost certain to lead to armed conflict. The memo summed up the stakes:

> I am aware as you are of just how costly and risky such a conflict would prove to be. But so too would be accepting this new status quo. We would be setting a terrible precedent—one that would only accelerate violent centrifugal tendencies—in this emerging "post Cold War" era. We would be encouraging a dangerous adversary in the Gulf at a time when the United States has provided a de facto commitment to Gulf stability—a commitment reinforced by our statements and military movements—that also raises the issue of US reliability in a most serious way. As if this were not enough, we must recognize too that Iraq has the capacity and the desire to complicate the peace process in the Middle East. We don't need to decide where to draw any lines just yet, but we do need to take steps—moving forces, pressing allies and reluctant Arabs, etc.—that would at least give us a real choice if current efforts fall short.

We arrived back in Washington very late that night. The next morning, before the NSC gathered again in the Cabinet Room, President Bush and I confirmed again that, after the intelligence briefing, I should speak first and remind everyone of the stakes. Eagleburger and Cheney would follow to reinforce solidarity for the larger group.

Despite rumors that Saddam had pledged to withdraw from Kuwait in a couple of days, Webster was not optimistic. Our intelligence was still sketchy, but what information we had was grim. Saddam was consolidating his hold on Kuwait. "All the intelligence shows he won't pull out," said Webster. "He will stay if not challenged within the next year. This will fundamentally alter the Persian Gulf region. He would be in an inequitable position, since he would control the second- and third-largest proven oil reserves with the fourth-largest army in the world. He would also have Kuwaiti financial assets, access to the Gulf, and the ability to pour money into his military. There is no apparent internal rival to Saddam. His ego cannot be satisfied; his ambition is to have ever more influence. Jordan and Yemen have tilted toward Iraq. Iran is militarily and economically weak, so it would not be an effective counter. . . . It

would not be a pretty picture. We don't expect the Arabs to confront Iraq, but instead to buy their way out."

". . . I detected a note at the end [of the previous NSC meeting] that we might have to acquiesce in an accommodation," said Scowcroft. "My personal judgment is that the stakes in this for the United States are such that to accommodate Iraq should not be a policy option."

Eagleburger added his support. "This is the first test of the postwar system," he said. "As the bipolar world is relaxed, it permits this, giving people more flexibility because they are not worried about the involvement of the superpowers. . . . Saddam Hussein now has greater flexibility because the Soviets are tangled up in domestic issues. If he succeeds, others may try the same thing." He believed that Saudi Arabia would be Saddam's next objective, and that over time he would control OPEC and oil prices. "If he succeeds, then he will target Israel."

Cheney was sober about both the gravity of the situation and the price of confronting it. "Initially, we should sort this out from our strategic interests in Saudi Arabia and oil," he said. "[Saddam] has clearly done what he has to do to dominate OPEC, the Gulf, and the Arab world. He is forty kilometers from Saudi Arabia and its oil production is only a couple of hundred kilometers away. If he doesn't take it physically, with his new wealth he will still have an impact and will be able to acquire new weapons. The problem will get worse, not better. Looking at the military possibilities and options," he added, "we should not underestimate the US military forces we would need to be prepared for a major conflict."

Eagleburger reported that Pickering was circulating a draft resolution on sanctions to the other permanent members of the Security Council. "The Soviets support it, the British and French want to discuss the details, the PRC is now not sure they won't support it." He was optimistic that we would succeed. The President asked about Iran. Eagleburger explained that it had condemned the invasion. The Kuwaitis and Iranians had been meeting. "According to the Kuwaiti ambassador here, Iran said to them, 'You tell us what you want and we will do it.' Kuwait said we want you to persuade Iraq to leave. After some delay Iran is now saying it will be supportive." He added that Syria asked us to push the Arab states. "In twenty-four hours there will be an Arab [League foreign minister meeting] in Cairo," he said. "Maybe they will agree."

Cheney gave an update on the military situation. He was concerned about the Saudi reluctance to agree to stationing our forces on their soil. "We need Saudi Arabia to agree to a presence," he urged. He asked that the President discuss the matter with King Fahd.

Powell briefed us on the forces required for contingencies. "There are two," he said. "The first, to deter further Iraqi action with Saudi Arabia, would require US forces on the ground. This is the most prudent option and we need to push it with Saudi Arabia so Saddam Hussein looks south and sees a US presence." The second was to deploy forces against the Iraqi troops in Kuwait, to defend Saudi Arabia or even strike against Iraq. "Looking at this option," said Powell, "this is harder than Panama and Libya. This would be the NFL, not a scrimmage. It would mean a major confrontation. Most US forces would be committed to sustain, not just for one or two days. He is a professional and a megalomaniac. But the ratio is weighted in his favor. They also are experienced after eight years of war."

"If we look at economic pressure, then we need to think how he will respond and look at the costs," Scowcroft pointed out. The question was not only what steps were needed to put sanctions in place, but also how to enforce them. Powell explained that the warships were already in place to interdict merchant vessels.

Scowcroft warned of the possibility that Saddam might use Americans as hostages. Eagleburger said that fourteen or fifteen US citizens were already in Iraqi custody, with reports of others being held in Kuwait. We could try to evacuate our people, but it would have to be done with the cooperation of Iraq. State had been working with other embassies to find a neutral ambassador willing to ask for all to leave. "It probably won't work," he added. They had warned the Iraqi foreign ministry not to harm Americans, and had called in the Iraqi ambassador. "He made no promises. Saddam is a tough son of a bitch. He recognizes this asset."

"We should tell Saddam this would be a new ballgame, and give him our bottom line," the President said. ". . . American deaths and hostages will not be tolerated."

BRENT SCOWCROFT

The tone of the NSC discussion was much better than the day before. We had established our case. Had the President taken his cue from the earlier meeting, our policy would have been vastly different, focusing on controlling the damage rather than reversing it. We wanted to act, but, as the discussions revealed, our immediate options, such as moving forces to the area and international sanctions as the President directed, were for the moment limited for practical and political reasons. Kuwait was so far away that it would take some time before enough troops were in place to do anything more than be a symbolic presence. Even putting those forces in place remained a question. We still had to convince the Saudis. For the moment we had to sit tight as Iraqi units continued to head south toward the Saudi border. All we could do was give Iraq a strong warning not to invade Saudi Arabia, which we did that day.

To help persuade the Saudis to accept US forces, we asked Ambassador Prince Bandar to come to the White House later that morning to discuss the situation. Son of the Saudi defense minister and King Fahd's favorite nephew, Bandar was Western-educated and a fighter pilot who had trained with the US Air Force. Most important, he was a troubleshooter for King Fahd, with the equivalent rank of minister in the Saudi government. The King frequently turned to him for advice. For these reasons, we knew he was a special conduit from us to Fahd.

Bandar came to my office a little after 11:00. After setting forth the serious military threat which we believed faced his country, I told him we were considering the offer of US forces to the kingdom, to assist in its defense. He seemed ill at ease and did not react with enthusiasm to the suggestion. Somewhat surprised at his equivocal posture, I asked him why he appeared to have a problem with an offer I thought was generous. His answer really set me back. He explained that the Saudis were not at all sure they wanted to be defended by the United States. The US, he said, did not exactly have a reputation in the region for reliability. He cited two examples to make his point.

In 1979, when the Shah was forced to flee Iran, the United States offered a squadron of F-15s to Saudi Arabia as a gesture of support and of warning to the Iranian radicals. The Saudis had immediately accepted. Then, as the aircraft were on their way, Washington had announced that they were unarmed. The second example he described was the US intervention in Lebanon in 1982–84. We sent the Marines into Beirut with great fanfare. Shortly after the terrible terrorist attack on the Marine barracks, the United States quietly loaded the Marines back on their ships and slipped away. Why should the King not be concerned that, if the going got tough, the United States would behave in the same manner once again?

I replied that we could debate the past, but I would prefer to get right to the point. President Bush had thought this issue through carefully, in full recognition of all the consequences. In light of that, I could give him a pledge that, if the troops were offered and accepted, we would stand with them to the end. Bandar said these assurances transformed the situation, but it would help if he was briefed on our defense plans. I consulted Cheney and sent Bandar over to the Pentagon, where he was shown CENTCOM's plan for responding to the Iraqi threat. This seemed to dispel the Prince's doubts about our resolve. The Saudis had previously planned to send a low-level technical team to Washington to discuss the situation and the best form of cooperation. Bandar now agreed that a senior US team should go to Saudi Arabia instead.

GEORGE BUSH

Early in the afternoon of August 3, I spoke with President Turgut Ozal of Turkey, who angrily said Saddam should "get his lesson." He had been on the phone with King Fahd an hour earlier, and was worried that the Saudis might not take action. "I told him that if the solution is that Iraq pulls back and Kuwait pays, that is not a solution but another Munich." I reminded him of Turkey's key geostrategic position and asked if he was willing to close down the pipeline from Iraq. He didn't respond, but said we needed more than an embargo. He suggested we get NATO together to discuss the situation. "We should not repeat the mistakes made at the beginning of World War II," he declared.

I also spoke with François Mitterrand, who concurred that we could not accept the status quo and that to do so would allow Saddam to secure his hegemony over the Arab world. If there was to be an oil blockade, he added, it had to succeed. If not, there would be tremendous loss of face to the West. We also had to be careful not to create solidarity against us in the Arab world. The key would be the Saudis. "If Saudi Arabia takes a courageous stand against the annexation of Kuwait, this would bring along others," he said. Helmut Kohl and Japanese prime minister Toshiki Kaifu, with whom I spoke later that day, agreed that we needed collective action.

BRENT SCOWCROFT

Later that day, Baker and Shevardnadze issued a joint declaration in Moscow condemning the Iraqi invasion. The statement was extremely important and surprised many, since it demonstrated that Iraq's principal backer would not support Saddam's aggression. It dramatically put the two superpowers on the same side of a major crisis for the first time since the Cold War began. While I had felt that a united Germany's membership in NATO marked the end of the Cold War, this was certainly further compelling evidence of it. The declaration translated into essential Soviet help at the UN in forming a solid bloc of support for resolutions against Saddam. We learned later that it masked political divisions within the Kremlin over chastising the Iraqis. While Gorbachev seemed to support the declaration, he steered clear of Shevardnadze's internal political battle to approve it. In the end, Shevardnadze had courageously gone out on a limb, taking personal responsibility for the statement.

At the August 4 NSC meeting at Camp David, we concentrated on military options. "Of course, much depends on what we decide are our goals," Cheney pointed out. Powell outlined the military situation and options. "What we will present is a longstanding plan refined over the last few weeks," he began. It would defend Saudi Arabia and lay the foundation for moving north into Kuwait. "It is difficult but doable," he added. "It will be enormously expensive to project and sustain a force of this size. It will require some reserve call-up."

There were two dimensions to the plan, he continued—deterrence and war fighting. "The sooner we can get an invitation from the Saudis the better," he said. "I believe the Iraqis would think twice before engaging us. We can get our air power in quickly. We can handle the Iraqi Air Force. We also have some naval forces that can be augmented. Ground forces can be introduced over the course of a month. All this would draw down our ability to act anywhere else in the world. The ultimate size of the force would be a hundred thousand men."

Schwarzkopf described what we were up against. "Iraq has over eleven hundred aircraft, but most are antiquated and they have almost no experience with using their airpower offensively," he explained. "Iraq is not ten feet tall, but is formidable. They have an army of nine hundred thousand men, sixty-three divisions, over fifty-seven hundred tanks. Once again we see a pattern of a large number of weapons but only a small number of high quality. They have no self-propelled artillery. One of our advantages is that they would have problems fighting over long distances. They have bigger forces but much lower quality than what we could field. Their aircraft could not reach the lower peninsula. It would be a short amount of time before we would gain air superiority. Their navy is insignificant. Very quickly we would gain control of the Gulf. They have dense SAM [surface-to-air] envelopes around key sites such as Baghdad. Overall, their strengths include numbers, experience, chemical weapons, and some modern arms. Their weaknesses are centralized command and control, a dependence on foreign spare parts, and a lack of offensive experience."

Schwarzkopf told us our major problem was distance. "Within one week, we could get five tactical fighter squadrons and carrier battle groups on the scene," he said. "We could double this over two weeks. We could also have a force slightly larger than a division in after two weeks. The overall plan would take seventeen weeks."

"We can have four hundred aircraft in the area in eleven days," added Lieutenant General Charles Horner, Schwarzkopf's air commander. "Our forces are on alert and ready to go."

What Schwarzkopf and Horner were suggesting relied on air power, at least in the short term. "The history of air campaigns suggests they are not terribly successful," observed Cheney. "Why would this one be different?"

"I am not an advocate of air power alone," replied Schwarzkopf. "But this is a target-rich environment. There is no cover in the desert. Their army has never operated under attack, and we have sophisticated munitions."

"I worry over one thing," said Scowcroft. "The Saudis are concerned about our seriousness. Ground forces are the best symbol of our commitment, but this plan is air-heavy."

"Bandar made a point that they were unhappy with our offer of one tactical fighter squadron, but they have no doubts now after hearing our briefing," put in Cheney.

"My worry is the lack of Saudi will and that they might bug out," said President Bush. "We need to ask them."

After the briefers left the room, the discussion turned to what to do next. Powell said he did not think Saddam wanted to mess with us. He believed we had to get Americans into Saudi Arabia, to show the flag. The President thought Powell was on the right track. "I'm inclined to feel that a small US military presence and an air option will do it," he said. "Iraq did badly versus Iran." Still, he was worried about the implications of attacking Baghdad, as the air option would require.

Baker, now back from Moscow, agreed. "Our using air against Baghdad could turn things against us unless it is done in conjunction with an Iraqi move into Saudi Arabia," he said.

"Our first objective is to keep Saddam out of Saudi Arabia," said the President. "Our second is to protect the Saudis against retaliation when we shut down Iraq's export capability. We have a problem if Saddam does not invade Saudi Arabia but holds on to Kuwait."

Cheney said we should start this only if we were prepared to see it through. "You must be prepared to defend Saudi Arabia and put the [Kuwaiti] royal family back," he said. "The problem is the American people might have a short tolerance for war." He added that it would all cost "one hell of a lot of money." Scowcroft felt that the American people would support intervention. Cheney was doubtful. "The oil mostly goes to Japan," he said. "We'll be seen as helping royal families. Their support may be short-lived." He urged that we must consider what we would do if Saddam did not attack Saudi Arabia. The President thought he might be underestimating world opposition. "Lots of people are calling him Hitler," he said.

"If we got a request from the Saudis, we should do more than simply show the flag," said Powell. "We may be able to do something along the lines of the Korean War model of a US-led multinational force," suggested Haass.

Baker wondered if we might lose international support if we blockaded Iraq. Scowcroft disagreed. "Closing shipping is no more than closing the pipeline," he said. The President suggested we try a blockade.

GEORGE BUSH

Our stakes and options now seemed clearer. I had a better feel for the military situation on the ground and the strategic implications of the invasion for the United States and for stability in the Gulf. I approved the plan, although we couldn't implement it until the Saudis agreed to accept our troops.

It was critical that King Fahd ask us to send forces before Iraq could attack Saudi Arabia. I understood that the Saudis would be under great internal and external pressure if US and Western troops were operating from their soil. Historically, Arab countries did not welcome US air or ground forces in the area. A naval task force such as a carrier was different—it was an accepted stabilizer of Gulf security since it was offshore and out of sight. But having planes and troops stationed on the ground was problematical.

I spoke with King Fahd on Saturday afternoon from Camp David to press for a decision to accept troops. He evaded the question and thanked me for our interest in Saudi affairs, and he kept referring to the team we were sending. We went back and forth for a few minutes like this, I pressing the King, he implying our team would discuss the matter.

"Good," I said, "but I want to know where you think matters stand on the ground. What are Iraq's statements on withdrawal? Will the Emir return? Are you worried about Iraq moving across your border? We worry about that very much."

"First," Fahd replied carefully, "the only solution must involve the return of the Emir to Kuwait. Second, there are no Iraqi troops near the Saudi border, but Saddam is not to be trusted. That is why it is important for a team to come as soon as possible to coordinate matters to prevent that from happening."

I tried to emphasize the gravity I saw in the situation, and the urgency. We couldn't wait any longer to deter an Iraqi move south and to pressure Saddam to withdraw and permit the return of the Kuwaiti government. "We must now begin taking the actions we described in detail to Bandar. And we can't wait until it is too late." I told Fahd that the Emir had asked us for military intervention, but by that time Iraqi troops had already occupied Kuwait City and there was nothing the United States could do. "It takes a long time to deploy troops," I said. "That is why I am worried about Saudi Arabia. . . ."

"It is probable that Iraq could attack, but then an invasion may not happen," said the King. He wanted the team to work on all contingencies, and thought we still had a few days to coordinate and make a tight, successful plan. "That's all we want."

"We will get the team underway," I said. "Another point I want to make here involves a word of honor. The security of Saudi Arabia is vital—basically fundamental—to US interests and really to the interests of the Western world. And I am determined that Saddam will not get away with all this infamy. When we work out a plan, once we are there, we will stay until we are asked to leave. You have my solemn word on this."

BRENT SCOWCROFT

Not long after President Bush had spoken to Fahd, Bandar entered my office. He had obviously discussed the situation with the King, and he agreed with the need for quick action. He now suggested I lead the team. The President thought that was fine, so I called Cheney and asked him to think about who should be on it from Defense. When Dick phoned back, he told me that he himself wanted to head the group, since the mission was basically Defense. I readily agreed, as did the President. There was one problem, however. If Cheney, a cabinet officer, went, it would inevitably become a high-profile mission; a Saudi rejection could trigger a crisis, in the sense that the inability of our two countries to cooperate would further encourage Saddam's aggression. If I went, I could go there quietly and if the Saudis decided not to cooperate, no one need ever know. I explained to Bandar that if Cheney went, we would have to know in advance that the King would approve and invite the deployment of US troops to the kingdom. Bandar blanched and hesitated, but he saw the logic of our position and the danger. He supported Cheney's heading the mission on the presumption that we were not talking about "if" we were deploying but "how" and what types of units would go, but said he had to clear it with the King. After a slight delay while he called the King, he agreed to the terms.

Saudi Arabia was not alone in its hesitation. Many of the Arab countries were anxious about what Saddam would do next. We were concerned that, out of fear, some of the moderates would accept the puppet regime Iraq had installed in Kuwait as a way to mollify Saddam. Unfortunately, one of the worst offenders was Jordan's King Hussein, a long-time ally of the United States, who had become almost a spokesman for his neighbor Iraq. We had to keep Baghdad from intimidating the other states. We also knew we had to be extremely sensitive to Arab perceptions of our intent in the Gulf. With our long and close association with Israel, we could not be seen as picking on an Arab country. Our efforts had to be made in coordination and consultation with the Arab world and with their full participation. This would take careful personal diplomacy on the part of the President and our highest officials. The first signs seemed promising, but the radicals who often influenced Arab popular opinion could easily decide to make big trouble, including mass demonstrations and a campaign of terrorism.

Sanctions, and the practical embargo of trade with Iraq, constituted an essential first step of the coordinated international response. Over the weekend of August 4–5, the President called the emir of Kuwait to update him and began to poll the allies to line up support for sanctions. The permanent members of the Security Council met the morning of August 5. Pickering reported that the UK and France strongly favored sanctions, but that the Soviets, though supportive, were still without instructions. China seemed to be leaning toward them, but claimed to be "impressed" by King Hussein's support for Iraq. Nevertheless, the Chinese did announce they would no longer sell arms to Iraq, which was an important show of support. Pickering was to table a resolution and try to get a vote on August 6.

Getting support for the sanctions was one thing, but making them stick — enforcing them — would be another. We were skeptical of them as a means for getting Saddam out of Kuwait. Too often there were "holes," when countries didn't comply with them, and we couldn't be sure what effect they would have on Iraq. We had to make sure nothing would be going in and out by sea — that would mean a naval blockade. Since Iraq is virtually a landlocked country, this posed a different, and more difficult, problem. We could not be sure that all of its neighbors would observe an embargo and, if they did not, its long borders might prove very porous. We were confident Turkey and Saudi Arabia would back sanctions. These were key countries. There were major pipelines for Iraqi oil through both and these had to be closed off. While it appeared that Syria would cooperate as well, Jordan and Iran remained uncertain.

GEORGE BUSH

On August 5, Brian Mulroney told me of a discussion he had with Turgut Ozal. Ozal was prepared to blockade all oil coming out of Iraq, but warned that there was another source through the Jordanian port at

Aqaba on the Red Sea. He added that Baghdad had sent an emissary to try to wean Turkey away from the West. The Iraqi had brazenly told Ozal that Baghdad had no intention of pulling out and planned to annex Kuwait. "The West is bluffing," he had said. Ozal believed that without Western action Iraq would probably invade the UAE and Saudi Arabia.

Ozal phoned me a couple of hours later with more details and concerns. The emissary had told him the Iraqis were forming a government in Kuwait, as well as a "people's army" of about 25,000. He had spoken to King Fahd, who would support an oil embargo but was waiting for UN action. Ozal urged that we get started with sanctions as soon as possible, after which he would close the pipeline. He warned that we would have to consider military action. "Saddam is more dangerous than Qaddafi," he said. "He must go. He killed a hundred and twenty officials who refused to fight. If the blockade is very effective, [his people] may overthrow him." The Iraqi emissary had boasted that they could live with a blockade, saying, "We are twenty million, we will fight to the end. . . ." Ozal wanted NATO to give a clear signal that the alliance would back him if Iraq attacked in retaliation for closing the pipeline. We tracked down NATO Secretary General Manfred Wörner, who was fishing in western Canada. He was confident that the alliance would back Ozal, and said he would come to Washington the following day to discuss it.

I flew down to Washington from Camp David on the afternoon of Sunday, August 5. Haass met me as I emerged from the helicopter on the South Lawn and brought me up to date on the latest developments. I walked up to the crowd of waiting reporters for a few informal remarks. Although over the weekend I had been thinking about the need to voice my determination to the American people, I had not decided when I should do it. At the moment, I just planned to fill everybody in on the diplomatic steps we were taking and the international reaction. I explained that none of our allies was willing to accept anything less than total Iraqi withdrawal from Kuwait, nor would they tolerate a puppet government. Then the questions started flying.

What we were willing to do about the puppet regime? Were we going to respond militarily? I simply said, "Just wait. Watch and learn." Everyone, of course, wanted to know what measures we would take ourselves to protect Americans in Kuwait, especially in view of Iraqi threats to close down foreign embassies. To this I answered:

> "I am not going to discuss what we're doing in terms of moving forces, anything of that nature. But I view it very seriously, not just that but any threat to any other countries, as well as I view very seriously

our determination to reverse this awful aggression. And please believe me, there are an awful lot of countries that are in total accord with what I've just said, and I salute them. They are staunch friends and allies, and we will be working with them all for collective action. This will not stand, this aggression against Kuwait."

Afterward, Colin Powell remarked that he felt I really had declared war on Iraq that Sunday. It was a widespread reaction. In retrospect, I don't know if I had yet determined that the use of force would be required. After all, the UN was still taking action and I hoped the matter could be ended peacefully with political and economic measures. It was still too early to make that call. On the other hand, I certainly felt that force *could* be necessary. I had decided that it was up to Saddam. I never wavered from the position that I would do whatever it took to remove Iraq from Kuwait.

CHAPTER 14

Shield and Sword

Late in the afternoon of August 5, the NSC gathered again around the long table in the Cabinet Room. Bill Webster reported that, owing to the state of Iraqi preparations and the uncertainty about Saddam's intentions, it would be difficult to provide additional warning of an attack on Saudi Arabia. Contrary to Saddam's claims that he was going to withdraw, we had evidence that Iraqi forces were massing on the Kuwaiti-Saudi border and that more appeared to be on the way. There were far more Iraqi troops involved than were needed simply to subdue Kuwait. "I was asked before what would be the earliest that Iraq could attack," said Webster. "The answer is now."

Colin Powell again briefed us on military deployments. Carrier battle groups were approaching the Gulf, but it would be a few days before they were in position. "Air forces are the most flexible," he said. "The first aircraft could actually arrive in twenty-four hours. Also, I can land Navy planes in Saudi Arabia in one day if all we want is some presence. As for ground forces, light forces can get there in a few days. But heavy forces would take three weeks to a month to arrive. Depending on what we hear from Dick Cheney (who, with Bob Gates and Undersecretary of Defense for Policy Paul Wolfowitz, had departed for Saudi Arabia that day) we can start moving naval air and light forces right away. We can also give the Saudis the additional F-15s we are holding."

"Now is the time to get the Saudis everything we have," urged Scowcroft.

President Bush thought we weren't in too bad shape, provided that none of our embassies was taken or that we weren't forced to liberate rather than defend Saudi Arabia. "The problem goes beyond our embassies," reminded Powell. "We are talking about thousands of Americans."

"Is there any plan for protecting our embassy in Iraq?" asked John Sununu.

"No," said Powell. "There is no 'Desert 1'* solution."

GEORGE BUSH

By Sunday evening, I was worried that the Iraqis would indeed move across the border into Saudi Arabia. With so many tanks heading south, it seemed incontrovertible that Saddam had such plans. Brent and I talked about the possibility of a swift Iraqi strike at the Saudi oil fields. Saddam could move into Dhahran and stop, saying, "Now what are you going to do?" This would be an enormously serious problem, for our objective then would necessarily be to free both it and Kuwait and we would have lost our best base of operations. In retrospect, if Saddam had wanted to make a go for Saudi Arabia he probably made a mistake in that he did not do it in this brief window—before my announcement that we would send forces. If he had, he would have had a free run. Saudi troops were not even at the border and Iraq had overwhelming superiority in numbers. Still, I was fairly confident that we could get some forces in place before Saddam struck. For the moment, I was more concerned that he would grab Americans as hostages—for that day Iraqi troops in Kuwait City began to round up American and British citizens and send them to Baghdad.

Late the next morning, Dick Cheney called me from Jeddah to say that King Fahd had accepted our plan and would permit US forces on Saudi soil. That afternoon, I gave Dick the order to alert and send the 82nd Airborne and to do the same with two tactical fighter squadrons. We would then begin a larger deployment.

Dick explained that the King wanted other nations to send forces as well and to show public support for Saudi Arabia, mentioning Morocco and Egypt. The Saudis had also said they would close the pipeline and increase their oil production to compensate for the embargo, turning over the money to Kuwait. I asked Dick to go on to Egypt to talk with Mubarak and encourage him to provide troops. Before he left the next day for Cairo, Dick met once more with Bandar and his father, Saudi defense minister Prince Sultan. They asked that we make no announcement of the invitation, or of any deployment, until our forces were on the ground in Saudi Arabia two days later and the world was presented with a *fait accompli.*

---

*The name for the abortive attempt to rescue the Tehran hostages in 1979.

Jim Baker was very concerned about delaying notification and the perception of secrecy among the press and public that our silence might create. He rightly pointed out that we needed to be ahead of public reports about the deployment. The promise of silence, however, was part of the way we had convinced the Saudis to invite us in the first place. I was less worried about congressional notification than keeping our word to the Saudis and getting our forces in place as safely as possible.

BRENT SCOWCROFT

Baker obviously remembered the serious problems created in the Reagan Administration by the absence of timely notification in the Iran-Contra case. But we had another important reason for staying silent, beyond the important fact that Cheney had given King Fahd our word. If we announced the deployment, as Baker urged, it would give Saddam approximately forty-eight hours to launch an attack before any US ground troops arrived.

GEORGE BUSH

Margaret Thatcher had stopped in Washington en route home from Aspen and was with me in the Oval Office when Cheney called. I confided to her what I was planning, provided the details of the deployment, and asked her to tell no one. Thatcher and I were joined by Manfred Wörner, who had just arrived from Canada, in the Rose Garden for a brief press statement about the UN Security Council vote on Resolution 661. After some intense lobbying by Baker and Tom Pickering, the council had voted 13–0 in favor of imposing economic sanctions on Iraq under Chapter VII of the Charter, with Cuba and Yemen abstaining. A question arose immediately, however, about whether the resolution permitted a blockade to enforce the sanctions. Margaret felt strongly that it did. She was right, although I hesitated to use the term "blockade" yet with the press. Our lawyers looked at the legal aspects of the issue. There was no doubt that, to be effective, the sanctions had to be enforced. But there was a problem about "blockade," which, in international law, is an act of war. Brent suggested we use the word "quarantine," as President Kennedy had in 1962 in response to the Cuban Missile Crisis.

I met separately with Manfred in the Oval Office later that afternoon. Armed help for Saudi Arabia would not be a NATO operation, but I wanted to work with him to enlist its support for collective action, especially to reassure Turkey that we would not leave it in the lurch. I asked him to convene a meeting of the North Atlantic Council the following week. He could also help the Western countries coordinate their military preparations for a multinational presence in the Gulf. These forces had to be in place quickly to help defend Saudi Arabia or Turkey if Iraq struck at them for cutting the oil pipelines (in fact, Ozal closed the pipeline through Turkey the same day as the UN Resolution).

That same day we had our first official contact with Saddam himself. He summoned our chargé in Baghdad, Joseph Wilson, and berated him. It was an infuriating confirmation of what Ozal and others had been saying about Saddam's defiance in the face of world opposition. Wilson cabled us the details. He had relayed our demand that Iraq withdraw from Kuwait. "You should refrain from being pushed into taking an action on wrong advice after which you will be embarrassed," Saddam had replied. "If what President Bush wants in fact is the preservation of US interests as he has described them, then escalation of tension and a military alternative is against these interests. I will tell you how you will be defeated. You are a superpower and I know you can hurt us, but you will lose the whole area. You will never bring us to our knees. You can destroy some of our economic and industrial base but the greater damage you cause, the greater the burden to you. In such a situation, we will not remain idle in the region."

Saddam boasted that Kuwait had become an appendage of Iraq. "Convey to President Bush that he should regard the Kuwaiti Emir and Crown Prince as history. . . . We will never leave Kuwait for someone else to take. We would never let Kuwait be an easy bite—even if the whole world were against us. We would fight on. . . . We know you are a superpower who can do great damage to us, but we will never capitulate."

He also claimed that Iraq would not attack Saudi Arabia, saying, "The Saudis are our brothers." The Saudis had helped them in the Iran-Iraq war, and had built the pipeline as well as extended grants, not loans, to Iraq.* As long as things did not change, he would do nothing. Wilson asked Saddam directly whether he would offer him "assurances that given the circumstances that exist on the ground today that you do not intend to take any military action against Saudi Arabia."

"You can take this assurance to Saudi Arabia first, then to everyone else in the region," said Saddam. "We will not attack any party that does not attack us."

---

*Conveniently omitting the fact that Kuwait had also done so. The Neutral Zone production was sold for the Iraqi account during the Iran-Iraq war.

BRENT SCOWCROFT

Saddam's warning that Iraq would "not remain idle in the region" was ominous. It sounded like a threat to turn out the radicals into the streets of the Arab world and mount terrorist attacks.

DIARY, AUGUST 6–7

I've never seen quite so much speculation. So many experts, so many people out there saying what I can or can't do. We've got friction inside. The economic side of the house feels excluded from the military options side; and yes, they are by my order . . . Economics are an important part of this but we are trying to curtail some of the information on a "need-to-know" basis.

One worrisome thing was when Baker went to call Shevardnadze [to] tell him we were going to put the troops in—he came up short on that. He felt that this would be difficult for them, etc., and how come we hadn't told him? He's going to have to report this to Gorbachev. Baker then said something about, well, maybe he could join in the blockade, and he noticeably picked up.

I think they want to be included, and they don't want to always be the last one to know. They want some standing, some face, and it's so important in the world . . . He's against what Iraq did. They disapproved of [the invasion] in the United Nations, but now if they see us go rushing in carrying the ball and they have no role, then they just look like bit players or unimportant.

BRENT SCOWCROFT

Baker's suggestion had been made on the spur of the moment. The rest of us were leery of Soviet military participation in coalition efforts. We had worked for decades to keep Soviet forces out of the Middle East and it was premature to invite them in. Cheney, Powell, and I opposed it, although a Soviet naval presence in the international flotilla was less objectionable. Baker thought having them in the coalition ground forces would be a major blow to Saddam. In the end, the Soviets sent a few ships to monitor the blockade but did not take an active role.

GEORGE BUSH

I was up most of the night of August 6–7 making calls. At two thirty in the morning I phoned François Mitterrand and told him we were sending troops. He supported both my decision and the idea of a NATO meeting, saying he understood Ozal's problem—Turkey was a member of NATO and we had to talk about the role of the alliance in the crisis. After I finished he said simply: "We will be there."

François often surprised me. There were allegations that the French might go their own way in responding to the invasion. However, every time I spoke to him we ended up in agreement and the worries leading to the call were dispelled. French-American differences arose between the bureaucracies and officials. At our level, working out dates for sending forces or starting combat, or coordinating command structures between our generals, François was always there, and we always stood together. I remain convinced that the best thing I ever did for US-French relations was to invite him to Kennebunkport in the spring of 1989. I still feel that the respect I tried to show him personally paid off in our diplomacy throughout the Administration, especially at times like this. Brent and his French counterpart Admiral Jacques Lanxade had a similar rapport. Brent was able to work closely with the Admiral so that when François and I spoke, a lot of the political difficulties had already been ironed out.

I began to follow up on King Fahd's request that we drum up troops from our allies in the region, and phoned Arab leaders asking them to receive Cheney, who now zigzagged across the region. I called Hosni Mubarak first, who agreed to see Dick and explained that he, like Ozal, was receiving an emissary from Iraq. He had sent a message to Saddam Hussein saying, "You are committing suicide," and was awaiting the Iraqi reply. I told Hosni I was disappointed with King Hussein, and he concurred. He thought Saddam had offered the King and Saleh of Yemen money and spoils. Hosni still hoped an Arab summit might resolve the crisis. King Hassan of Morocco also would see Cheney, and he appeared to be on the same wavelength as we were. He offered to help the Emir, explaining that there were already Moroccan volunteer troops.

When I spoke with Brian Mulroney, he filled me in on a conversation he had with Mubarak, who by then had already received the Iraqi emissary. The account was incredible, and showed just how cynical Saddam was about grabbing Kuwait.

"He said [the Iraqi] came in and announced that Kuwait has five hundred billion dollars they can put their hands on," said Brian. "The first thing they would do with that money would be to help Egypt. They were trying to tell Mubarak that there would be twenty billion for Egypt if Egypt supported Iraq. Mubarak said, 'We won't sell our principles.'" The Iraqi had said his countrymen were prepared to die. "They are most unreasonable," said Brian. "Mubarak has heard all sorts of rumors. He told the Iraqi he thought they would be driven out of Kuwait. The Iraqi response was that they would never accept that." Mubarak had said the UN resolution should be strictly executed, and that the Soviets agreed. Brian believed that Mubarak's views would provide "cover" for the other Arab states that wanted to join our growing coalition. "What clearly happened is that the Iraqis have just robbed the bank and will split it up with whoever will support them," he added.

Mubarak later told me that Saddam had indeed offered him a deal, one that he believed King Hussein and Saleh accepted. The idea was for the three of them to support the invasion in return for a certain percentage of Kuwait's oil and whatever Saddam managed to loot from the country's financial assets and treasures. Mubarak said he unambiguously turned down the offer. It was all part of Saddam's campaign to portray the issue as a matter of "haves" versus "have nots"—something the press picked up and played into—in his effort to win over the Arab world. King Hussein denies he was bought off this way.

Dick Cheney called me that afternoon from Cairo. He had told Murabak of the official Saudi request for military help—something we still had not released to other allies and the press. Hosni agreed to let the *Eisenhower* battle group go through the Suez Canal en route to the Gulf, and approved overflights of Egypt by our Air Force. He would also permit us to use Egyptian bases for refueling and transport, but wasn't eager to see combat missions flown from them. He remained noncommittal about joining a multinational force. He wanted an additional forty-eight hours, saying that a negotiated solution was not out of the question.

While we were trying to forge a collective response to Iraq's invasion, we also had to explain to the American people what we were doing. My impromptu remarks to the press on August 5 did not go far enough to make clear just why it was so important for us to stand up to Saddam. Two days later the need became urgent. Word started leaking out that we were sending troops and the media were showing our ships loading up. Furthermore, our first Air Force planes landed in Saudi Arabia that day. I had known that leaks would be inevitable with all the activity, but, in keeping with my promise to King Fahd, I wanted no official US comment until the last minute. I decided to make a television address the next day, August 8, at 9:00 am, once the first elements of the 82nd Airborne had arrived.

As I prepared my speech, I tightened up the language to strengthen the similarity I saw between the Persian Gulf and the situation in the Rhineland in the 1930s, when Hitler simply defied the Treaty of Versailles and marched in. This time I wanted no appeasement. Seated at my desk in the Oval Office before I went on the air, I felt a little nervous. I held out my hand to see if it was shaking. I was surrounded by technicians, cameramen, and aides, but I don't think anyone noticed. I was pleased when I saw it was still steady. I knew I was not nearly as good as Ronald Reagan in these situations, so I read through my copy a time or two.

Four simple principles guide our policy. First, we seek the immediate, unconditional, and complete withdrawal of all Iraqi forces from Kuwait. Second, Kuwait's legitimate government must be restored to replace the puppet regime. And third, my administration, as has been the case with every President since Franklin Roosevelt, is committed to the security and stability of the Gulf. And fourth, I am determined to protect the lives of American citizens abroad.

I also outlined the stakes of the situation, that Iraq already controlled the second largest reserves of oil in the world and had over a million men under arms. The United States imported nearly half the oil it consumed, leaving us economically vulnerable to Iraq's attempts to extend its hold on world oil reserves. Other nations, especially in the Third World, were even more dependent on imported oil.

We succeeded in the struggle for freedom in Europe because we and our allies remain stalwart. Keeping the peace in the Middle East will require no less. We're beginning a new era. This era can be full of promise, an age of freedom, a time of peace for all peoples. But if history teaches us anything, it is that we must resist aggression or it will destroy our freedoms.

That day I met with the Kuwaiti ambassador, who described to me his family's experience and how they had been threatened. His wife had decided to stay in Kuwait, and he was very nervous about her safety. He told us how the vaults had been looted of billions of dollars' worth of gold; how women had been raped; and that there was pillaging and plundering. (I also learned from Margaret Thatcher the next day that a stewardess from a British plane had been raped by Iraqi soldiers. The British protested and the Iraqis said one of the men had been shot.) I thought we should try to get the word out about Iraq's brutality, but despite these reports, the world did not seem to be really aware of what was happening in Kuwait, and this deeply disturbed me.

Throughout the rest of the day I worked the phones with our Arab allies, now reaching the other Gulf states. The year before, Mubarak had offered me some advice: touch base with these small countries whenever you can, just to acknowledge their importance to the United States, and it will make a difference with them. I had, and my wise friend Hosni had been absolutely right. We were now seeing some of the fruits of tending to these relationships. I talked to President Zayid ibn Sultan an-Nahayan of the UAE and Sultan Qabus bin Said of Oman, both for the first time during the crisis. Each promised to do everything he could to support a coalition against Saddam Hussein. Zayid welcomed US troops in the area and said that we must "stand side by side." He filled me in on the depredations Iraq was committing in Kuwait—which it had declared annexed that day.

Sultan Qabus was equally strong, saying, "Friends will not stand with hands tied behind." Oman was willing to provide what facilities we needed for our troops. Qabus had also been in touch with the Iranians, still an unknown for us. He gave us mixed news. According to the Sultan, the Iranians were not unhappy with what we were doing, and they were "eager" for spare parts and other things—they were not in a position to do more without them. However, he warned that the Iranians had also been talking with the Iraqis, who were ready to compromise on the differences between them. Apparently the Iraqis were trying to induce the Iranians to settle their old quarrel in order to move troops off their common border.

We were also gathering commitments from the Western allies. Britain had been quick to send naval and air forces to the Gulf, announcing the deployment the day after we had. Margaret called me on the morning of August 9, to inform me of her decision. Members of the Commonwealth intended to contribute, but wanted others alongside them. Late in the afternoon, I called Australian prime minister Bob Hawke, who without equivocation said he was solidly behind us and offered to send warships, but he wanted Canada to commit as well. I immediately phoned Brian Mulroney, who told me this helped him enormously in Canada. He indicated he would send aircraft and a small naval force—"but don't hold me to it," he added hastily. Just as I did in the United States, he still had a job to do selling it.

BRENT SCOWCROFT

Everyone wanted some sort of "cover" to protect themselves against any backlash. Ozal hoped his moves would be cloaked by NATO. Fahd did not wish to be the only Arab state opposing Iraq. Hawke didn't want to be the single Commonwealth country joining the coalition. Even we needed to demonstrate that this action was not a solo US effort against an Arab state. As countries individually joined up and sent forces, we gained momentum, but the interlocking nature of the requirements for the various members of the coalition illustrated the complicated task of putting it together as well as its inherent fragility. The welcome troop contributions themselves became a challenge to manage, and in the coming weeks and months CENTCOM scrambled to integrate new contingents, some quite small and others (such as the British or French) large, into their plans. The diversity symbolized international determination to reverse the invasion, but in practical terms the many smaller, specialized units sometimes left Schwarzkopf's planners scratching their heads.

GEORGE BUSH

During the first week or so of August a flap arose over whether I should go on vacation in Kennebunkport. I was aware that I might be criticized for leaving the White House and Washington with a crisis on my hands and be portrayed as a president frivolously at play, uncaring as we were deploying troops to the desert. But I was convinced that I should go to Maine and that the perception at home and, above all, abroad, of what the US president himself was doing was extremely important.

I remembered all too well the international and domestic perception of the Carter Administration during the Tehran hostage crisis. It had appeared that America's hands were tied, and that the attention of its president was controlled by thugs. I was absolutely determined that the American people would be spared this a second time. I wanted them, and Saddam Hussein, to see not only that the president had the situation under control, but also that he was unworried and confident. A relaxed George Bush was the best possible signal to send. Life had to go on as normally as possible, not just for the president but for the country as a whole. Saddam's threats, and the possibility of terrorism, scared many Americans that summer. Some were afraid to travel. When Barbara deliberately flew on a commercial airline, that was not just symbolism. The American recreation business was hurting. We had to show our people that the United States was still in charge and that they had nothing to fear.

In truth, a president is never truly on vacation and is never "away" from the office. His responsibilities follow him wherever he goes, day or night, and the office is wherever he happens to be. This is especially true in the modern presidency, where instant communications are easy and necessary. In the Cold War, as Brent knew first hand, a military aide is always hovering near the president with the "football" which contains the launch codes for our nuclear missiles. In helicopters, airplanes, cars, and boats (including the *Fidelity*) the president always has telephones at hand, and the distance from the person at the other end makes no difference. We had secure communications at our home on Walker's Point, and Brent could stay awake all night there just as well as in Washington. What we did was simply move shop from one location to the other.

Still, there was the continuing problem of public perception, and it was one we could have perhaps handled differently on a practical level. Up to this point we had a fairly good daily working relationship with the White House press corps. Suddenly that began to break down in the more private atmosphere of Kennebunkport. We had an arrangement where if we left the house to go out on the *Fidelity*, the press pool would have their own boat covering what I was doing and perhaps asking questions. Likewise, if I played golf, the pool would appear only at certain points on the course. The problem was that this ended up restricting press access and reporters might get only one shot at asking me questions that day. Inevitably, when I teed up at the first hole, one of their vantage points, frustrated reporters would begin shouting questions. Marlin Fitzwater was under great pressure. He would protest, explaining that this was just a photo opportunity and that they'd get a chance to ask questions later.

I flew up to Kennebunkport on August 10, and I was out fishing when Brent called from Washington with good news about the emergency Arab League summit in Cairo organized by Mubarak. It had been a chaotic session. The first reports we received had indicated that the Emir of Kuwait had stalked out, which we saw as a bad sign. However, we now learned that twelve of the twenty-one members had voted to send a pan-Arab force to defend Saudi Arabia.* Mubarak had prevailed. It was a very favorable result and put an umbrella over our troop movements. Saddam could no longer claim that the confrontation was only between Iraq and the United States. The news that Jordan had not backed Iraq was particularly welcome. Given my long friendship with King Hussein, I was gratified when he announced that Jordan would support the sanctions as well. It looked as if he might be turning the corner.

I called Mubarak at 5:30 in the morning on August 11 and thanked him for his help. Hosni said that everyone understood we had pushed diplomacy, and that it was making a difference in building Arab support. In retrospect, this is probably why the Arab world closed ranks with us — because they knew we had tried hard with Iraq before the invasion. Egyptian and Moroccan troops began to arrive in Saudi Arabia that same day, and with them stark evidence for Saddam that the Arab world too would stand up to him.

With Arab support solidifying, we turned to making the UN sanctions effective. Over lunch that afternoon, Baker briefed President Bush and Scowcroft on his trip to Turkey and the NATO meeting in Brussels on August 10. The alliance had condemned the invasion, backed our troop deployment, and endorsed action by other members as well, which already included naval commitments by France and Britain, and the use of their air bases by Italy, Spain, and Portugal. An international naval

*All six of the Gulf Cooperation Council states, as well as Egypt, Lebanon, Syria, Morocco, Somalia, and Djibouti, voted in favor. The only ones supporting Iraq were the PLO and Libya. Yemen and Algeria had abstained, while Jordan, Mauritania, and Sudan expressed "reservations," and Tunisia was not present.

flotilla would now be in place to enforce the sanctions, but there were still practical and legal questions surrounding a blockade. Did the resolution which imposed the sanctions permit us to use force to back them? This was no small matter, for if ships tried to ignore the embargo we would have to find some way to stop them. We were not eager to sink ships, and firing on them in peacetime would be a serious matter. We had to determine that the resolution gave us not only the authority to interdict shipping, but also the circumstances under which we could do so. On August 12 we finally received a letter from the Emir requesting that the US take action on behalf of Kuwait to enforce the UN sanctions in accordance with Article 51 of the UN Charter—which declares the right to individual and collective self-defense. In our view, this settled the matter of legality of interdiction, since we were acting at the request of the country the United Nations had set out to defend.

But there remained political problems to overcome. The following morning, we announced that US ships would begin enforcing the sanctions, effective August 16. Almost immediately, France, Canada, and the Soviet Union criticized the policy, arguing that no country could unilaterally implement a sanctions resolution. They preferred that we act under UN auspices. Britain, on the other hand, began to intercept and board ships before we even finished preparing instructions for the Navy. We still had a tough sell on the need to back sanctions with force.

It was a struggle to maintain the solidarity of a growing and diverse coalition. We were most worried about keeping the Arabs and the Soviets on board. The Arab members differed among themselves over how far they were prepared to help, some appearing ready to simply ride our coattails into battle, others standing tall alongside us. The Soviets seemed divided about their response to the invasion. On one side were the Arabists within the Foreign Ministry, led by Gorbachev's advisor Yevgeny Primakov and, together with the traditionalists—already entrenched in opposition to Gorbachev's foreign policy changes in Eastern Europe and Germany—angry with cutting off Iraq and against any use of force. On the other side, and leading the effort to back the coalition, was Shevardnadze, sometimes fighting almost alone. The task of coaxing Soviet support was never easy, as we debated first how to enforce sanctions, and then whether and how to use military action to eject Iraq from Kuwait.

Saddam was aware of the problems we faced in the coalition and he did his best to exploit them. He had tried to defuse Arab opposition to the occupation with a combination of intimidation and bribery, while contemptuously rejecting demands that he withdraw. He apparently believed that the West would not or could not kick him out, or that we lacked the will to overturn what he had done. But he misread his Arab neighbors and our determination to call his bluff—if that is what it was.

Failing to scare or bribe away the growing international solidarity, Saddam now tried to divide it any way he could. He knew the weak point was keeping an Arab-Western coalition together, and he used a combination of ploys aimed both at prying away individual Arab states and at rousing popular Arab feelings against the West and, above all, Israel. His campaign to win the support of particular Arab states was first couched in his "have-versus-have-not" propaganda, picked up by Jordan and the Western media, aimed at currying the sympathy of the more financially strapped Arab countries (no matter that Iraq was well endowed with oil and had squandered its revenues on military purchases and war). To this he added political pressure, attempting to stir up populations against their governments. Saddam frequently threatened to turn out radicals all around the region, predicting that they would topple leaders such as Mubarak. We worried about these possibilities, as well as threats of widespread terrorism, but little of it materialized.

Potentially, Saddam's most explosive ploy was his attempt to fan Arab-Israeli tensions. On August 10 he gave a speech declaring a "holy war" against the United States and Israel, and two days later he announced a cynical "peace initiative" in which he declared that the resolution of his invasion of Kuwait must be tied to what he called Israeli occupation of Arab lands. By exploiting Arab hostility toward Israel, Saddam tried to deflect Arab criticism away from his occupation of Kuwait and cast himself as the Arab leader against Israel. This would put popular pressure on individual governments not to oppose the invasion—perhaps splitting the coalition.

What Saddam was up to was clever, but fortunately he had little credibility in the Middle East. We rejected the Iraqi initiative as inappropriate "linkage," not compatible with the unconditional withdrawal we, his neighbors, and the UN were demanding. It became only one of Saddam's endless attempts to split the coalition. During the fall there were a number of other "peace initiatives" with such potential and we remained concerned that one of them might give him a shot at crippling the coalition and profiting in some way from his aggression.

GEORGE BUSH

Because of the Arab-Israeli tensions, throughout the crisis Israel remained very carefully placed outside the coalition. I knew we could not build a truly broad coalition, one that included many Arab nations, if Israel were part of it. The Israelis understood this point intellectually, although it was emotionally difficult for them to stand aside. In taking on Saddam Hussein diplomatically, and eventually militarily, we were tackling one of their principal enemies and probably their most hated adversary. Israel had been (and remains) a staunch friend and ally of the United States, and for the most part it cooperated, but from early in the crisis it made many demands of us for aid and information-sharing.

It appeared that Saddam might be able to exploit some gaps in the sanctions ring around Iraq. One potential problem was Iran. On August 15, he offered Tehran a peace settlement. Iraq withdrew from over a thousand square miles of Iranian territory, giving up everything it had won in their war. We were not sure whether Iran would now back off from pledges that it would respect the UN sanctions, for we had no reliable direct communication with Tehran. What was certain was that, at a minimum, Saddam was clearing the decks to concentrate on Kuwait and Saudi Arabia.

We were also concerned about Jordan. There was evidence that it was helping Saddam with more than propaganda: it appeared that Jordanian bankers were laundering money for Iraq, helping it evade financial sanctions, and that Amman was acting as a conduit for the delivery of Iraqi oil. We worried about arms shipments, and intelligence-sharing with Iraq, as well as the possibility that the Jordanians might help the Iraqi military operate the US-built Hawk anti-aircraft missile batteries they had captured from Kuwait, although there was no evidence they were doing so. On the other hand, we had made some slight progress with Jordan. It had not voted against a pan-Arab force, nor had it recognized Saddam's puppet regime in Kuwait. It rejected the acquisition of territory by force, and seemed willing (at least verbally) to back sanctions. We kept trying to find a way to break the link between Jordan and Iraq and reinvigorate the old, cooperative US-Jordanian relationship.

Iraq's hold on Jordan was explicable, if difficult for us. The country was economically dependent on Iraq, from which it imported 95 percent of its oil, with the cost charged against Baghdad's debt balance from the Iran-Iraq war. At the same time, Jordan was an important channel for Iraq's imports, about 45 percent of which went through Aqaba. This made Jordanian compliance with sanctions very important, but it also represented a hardship for the country's economy. There was also a serious political challenge. Jordan harbored large numbers of pro-Iraqi Palestinian refugees, making it vulnerable to unrest and instability. Their presence constituted a potential flashpoint for intervention either by Iraq or by Israel.

To wean King Hussein away from Iraq, we began to consider organizing international financial help as well as emergency Arab oil assistance, provided the King implemented the sanctions. Aid to Jordan and others affected by the embargoes and sanctions, such as Egypt and Turkey, would become a major policy effort in the coming weeks.

GEORGE BUSH

I had no desire to make things difficult for King Hussein, but I thought he went too far in his rhetoric. He was loudly opposed to allowing "foreign" forces on Arab soil and, almost alone, was still pushing for a negotiated Arab solution. He was blasting us in speeches and through the press, turning Jordanian public opinion against the United States. The King had in the past played a very positive role in the Middle East peace process, and these efforts to speak on behalf of Saddam Hussein surprised and disappointed me.

King Hussein saw Saddam on August 13, and he called me that evening to ask for an urgent meeting to discuss the situation. I invited him to Kennebunkport, where he arrived on August 16. The press was full of speculation about this sudden visit. The expectation was that he had some sort of message from Saddam, but he never mentioned one to me. It did appear he might be seeking to play a role as an intermediary, but I saw nothing to negotiate.

DIARY, AUGUST 16

. . . [The King] arrived by chopper at the point, and he and I went over to Mother's [bungalow] with Brent and his foreign minister. We talked very frankly about the differences. I kept trying to say that the friendship was intact. . . . He [pressed] for some middle ground that could solve the problem, and I kept saying, there isn't any—it's got to be withdrawal and restoration of the Kuwaiti regime. There cannot be any middle ground, because tomorrow, it will be somebody else's aggression.

We went over all the facts . . . that led to the invasion. . . . He wanted me to be sure to understand that he had tried very hard, and that he thought he could've gotten a deal if there had been some time. I made clear to him that when Saddam Hussein said he was going to get out of Kuwait and instead of that moved his forces south . . . a lot of us got very concerned about an invasion of Saudi Arabia. I also told him very frankly that . . . retaining Americans against their will was bad and unacceptable and that I was deadly serious. . . . Saddam Hussein shouldn't push us further by going against civilians.

Hussein refuses to admit that this is a madman. He talked about the "haves and the have-nots," and yet his minister was telling me at lunch that one of the big problems was they wanted higher oil prices so they could pay their bills and get their $16 billion production revenues. I said, you know who benefits [from] the lower oil prices around the world? It's the have-nots—not the haves . . . so he can't have it both ways it seems to me.

Not much came of the King's visit. It was not a bitter and mean meeting, but it was a disappointment—more of the same. He still wanted to persuade us that there should be an Arab solution. My position was that most of the Arabs were not on Saddam Hussein's side, and I wanted him to understand our resolve. I think he hoped to use the historic friendly ties between Jordan and the United States and our own friendship, which I valued, to get us to moderate or move a little.

Just after King Hussein left Walker's Point, Prince Saud, the foreign minister of Saudi Arabia, and Prince Bandar arrived. The contrast between Hussein and Saud could not have been sharper. Saud made it plain the Saudis wanted us to use force as early as possible, to go in and wipe out Iraq's forces in Kuwait. While I acknowledged it might come to that, I demurred, saying it was too early to contemplate such action.

In mid-August I became deeply concerned about the safety of US citizens in Kuwait. Iraqi troops had already started rounding up Americans and other foreigners and moving them to Iraq. On August 10, Saddam ordered all foreign embassies in Kuwait to close and send their personnel to their respective missions in Baghdad. We had no intention of complying: Kuwait was still a separate state, no matter what Saddam might claim, and the UK, France, and Canada agreed with us. Together we determined that we would keep our embassies in Kuwait in place as long as possible. My constant worry was that we would be presented with a hostage situation along the lines of the 1979 Tehran embassy crisis. My fears were soon confirmed.

DIARY, FRIDAY, AUGUST 17

9:45 at night Bob Gates calls me and said the speaker of the Iraqi parliament said they were going to detain foreigners until the . . . "aggression" against Iraq is contained. They would place them in various facilities and he mentioned near oil dumps or chemical plants—whatever—clearly putting them there so the facilities could not be bombed. Blatant hostage holding. Another blatant disregard of international law by a cruel and ruthless dictator. I cannot tolerate, nor will I, another Tehran. I am determined in that. It may cost American lives, but we cannot sacrifice American principle and American leadership.

The Security Council responded on August 18 with Resolution 664, which demanded that Iraq permit all detained foreigners to leave both Kuwait and Iraq. The next day Saddam offered to release the hostages provided the United States guaranteed—in writing—that its forces would be withdrawn from Saudi Arabia and the economic sanctions ended. In the face of the UN resolution, the Iraqis began to move foreigners to strategic sites.

Nothing angered me more than the cowardly use of human shields. It reinforced in my mind that Saddam had done more than simply attack Kuwait. Up to then, I had been reluctant to use the word "hostage" in public statements because I did not want to invite comparison to Tehran and lose the international focus on Kuwait, the real issue. But, as I said in a speech to veterans in Baltimore, there could be little doubt that whatever these innocent people were being called in Baghdad, they were, in fact, hostages. "I want there to be no misunderstanding," I warned. "I will hold the government of Iraq responsible for the safety and well-being of American citizens held against their will." I was angry enough to draft an ultimatum to Saddam using those same words:

> To the leaders of Iraq I will now make two clear points. [1] If any American is harmed you will pay a terrible price. [2] In moving citizens against their will you are violating the norms of your own religion, you are going against the age-old history of kindness to visitors, hospitality, and so my message "release all foreigners now, give them the right to come and go as they wish and as international law demands." And if you do not do this within ___ [sic] hours, if you do not comply with international law as decreed now by the UN, your forces will pay the price.

It was too early to send ultimatums, however, especially ones we could not yet carry out.

Saddam's hostage-taking only increased my resolve to resist permitting the invasion to stand. There would be no compromise, no bargaining for hostages, no trade-offs. It galled me when people played into Saddam's hands by trying to negotiate for the hostages. I was offended when former prime minister Edward Heath of Britain went to Iraq seeking the release of a handful of British nationals. I could understand some of the private groups and families making a stab at freeing people. But a former leader of one of our allies should have known better. The trip that irritated me most, however, was a high-profile effort undertaken later in the year by Oscar Wyatt, a Houston oil man who had made a ton of money dealing in Iraqi oil and who knew Saddam personally. Wyatt had not agreed from the outset with my standing up to Iraq, and he wasn't about to follow our policy on refusing to deal for hostages. I had known of Wyatt's prior connections with Baghdad, so I was not surprised by his public flouting of our policy. Accompanied by former treasury secretary John Connally, who was exploited to add prestige to his mission, Wyatt was cynically used by Saddam. He came home with some hostages only to hear the next day that the rest were being released. It wasn't surprising, however, that in December 1996, when the UN permitted a limited amount of Iraqi oil to be exported, a tanker chartered by Wyatt's Coastal Corporation carried the first shipment out.

Saddam was also increasing the pressure on us to shut down our embassy in Kuwait. On August 22, he threatened to close all embassies there by force and arrest any diplomatic personnel remaining after the 24th. In order to minimize the danger to our officials, we had decided to reduce their numbers to a minimum and get all the dependents out. After some difficulty with Baghdad, by August 23 we managed to evacuate most of the embassy. The next day we formally notified Iraq that we would not shut it down. Iraqi troops promptly surrounded the compound, along with the embassies of eight other countries which also refused to evacuate. They then began a long siege, trying to starve the remaining staff out. Our people had stockpiled canned food and filled a swimming pool full of water and, with strong morale, assured us that they could tough it out for some time.

BRENT SCOWCROFT

By late August, as Saddam was seizing innocent civilians, we also faced serious problems over enforcing the UN-mandated sanctions. The international controversy remained over whether the resolution had included authority to use force. The issue came to a head on August 18, when five outbound tankers, all low in the water with cargo and headed for Yemen, resisted being boarded or turned back, challenging the resolution. The question was, do we move unilaterally to stop them, or do we wait and try to get additional authority from the UN? President Bush wanted to let the Navy open fire. We had lengthy discussions with the British about it and of course Thatcher said go after the ships. I agreed completely that we had all the authority we needed. Declaring an embargo, as the Security Council had done, implied approval of measures to make it effective.

The French, on the other hand, while they saw the need to interdict, preferred explicit UN authorization to provide a basis in international law. We had a sharp internal debate over the matter. Gates, Cheney, and I were the hard-liners about this, urging that we act, even if it had to be unilaterally. Baker was insistent that we wait. He convinced the President we would lose the Soviets (who were still adamantly opposed to using force) and perhaps the chance for a positive vote in the Security Council on enforcement if we went ahead unilaterally.

GEORGE BUSH

I authorized Jim to call Shevardnadze to say we would briefly hold off military action to stop shipping, but we wanted the Soviets to support a new Security Council resolution on the matter. Shevardnadze thought the Soviets might still persuade Saddam to withdraw from Kuwait and asked for five days to negotiate. I was not enthusiastic about waiting. It would give the impression that we lacked the resolve to enforce the sanctions and, besides, the tankers in question would long since have made it to port. Nevertheless, Jim had convinced me that the additional effort for international cooperation made sense, and I wanted the Soviets totally on our side. I approved, but gave Moscow three days, until August 25, to convince the Iraqis to leave. In the meantime, the tankers went on to Aden, where the Yemenis did not, at least not right away, allow them to unload.

Margaret went along with this delay only reluctantly. I called her at about three in the morning her time—although I wasn't looking forward to it. Brent had already discussed the issue with Charles Powell about four times, and we knew how strongly she wanted to stop the ships. She insisted that if we let one go by it would set a precedent. I told her I had decided to delay and why. It was here, not earlier, as many have suggested, that she said, "Well, all right, George, but this is no time to go wobbly."

On August 24, Shevardnadze contacted Baker to say that the Iraqis were not cooperating and that the Soviets were now prepared to help put through a Security Council resolution. The next day, the council voted 13–0 (with Cuba and Yemen again abstaining) to pass Resolution 665, which specifically authorized "all appropriate measures" to enforce the naval blockade. Still, even with interdiction, we were genuinely pessimistic about the chances of the embargo being effective. It was true that Iraq was somewhat dependent on food imports, but there was intelligence evidence that the country had ample stocks of food and promising harvests. The hampering of industry through the reduced availability of spare parts, which we hoped would cripple Iraq's war machine, appeared not much more effective. The Iraqis had stockpiled enough to last years, and only a few plants were experiencing problems. It would take months before sanctions began to have much of an effect, even assuming there was no circumvention of them.

GEORGE BUSH

The more I thought about it at this juncture, I could not see how we were going to remove Saddam Hussein from Kuwait without using force. There was no specific event that put doubts in my mind; instead, it was the cumulative effect of my worries about the ability of Iraq to withstand economic and political pressure to withdraw from Kuwait, and whether waiting for the sanctions to work (if they did) risked too much. I wanted to find a path out of the stalemate, but I saw no way to move forward without some dramatic incident to justify immediate military action or unless something happened to Saddam Hussein personally. I was reluctant to speak publicly of using force. We were just beginning to get our warships in place and implement the blockade. I was not yet fully confident that we had the domestic or international backing to act.

These thoughts were in my mind when, on August 23, Brent and I went fishing for bluefish off Walker's Point. We had been so busy since the start of the crisis that this was the first opportunity for the two of us to unwind and talk. It was a beautiful, warm August day with a bright blue sky and a handful of clouds. Small swells lifted the *Fidelity* and waves lapped against its sleek blue racing hull, rocking it as we slowly trolled back and forth. There was a fresh ocean breeze, which tamed the heat. We were on the water about four hours under these ideal conditions and I put out a couple of lines, but the fish weren't biting. We soon became absorbed in a long, philosophical chat as we sat toward the stern of the boat with dark glasses and brimmed hats.

We talked about how the Gulf crisis might develop, whether Saddam would retreat without the use of force, and what it would take to eject him. I asked impatiently when we could strike. I wanted to know what we could do with our air power. How could we take out their air force and their armor; what did it take to really punish Iraq's military targets from the air? I thought the Defense Department overestimated Iraq's strength and resolve. Despite the size of their army, I just didn't see the Iraqis as being so tough. They had been unable to defeat Iran; they had never fought over long supply lines, or at any time when they did not control the air. Besides, some of our Arab coalition friends were telling me that

Iraq's military was overrated. Brent, far more knowledgeable and experienced than I was on these questions, was less certain that we could destroy Saddam's spread-out tanks and planes in one swoop. I feared he was right on this.

Not everyone in the Administration yet shared my feeling that it might be time to consider using force. From the beginning of the crisis, Baker was reluctant to contemplate it and believed strongly that diplomacy and sanctions should be given every chance to get the job done. He never backed away from any decision to use force or planning for it, but he advised pushing the diplomatic course first and giving sanctions more time. We all dreaded the loss of life that might come with military action, and I know that made Jim cautious. He worried, too, that we could get bogged down in another Vietnam, lose public support, and see the Bush presidency destroyed. He believed that force had to be a last resort, and his close contact with his coalition counterparts, especially in Western Europe and the Soviet Union, suggested to him that they were not yet ready to go to war. Jim probably remained hopeful longer than the rest of us that we could induce Saddam to give up without resorting to force.

I think Cheney recognized early that sooner or later it would come to force. Dick was probably ahead of his military on this. No good soldier wants to go to war and would prefer instead to see all other options exhausted. Dick led the way for the military, which I think is the model our Constitution envisioned: armed forces headed by civilians who were leading, not pushing, the military to understanding and fulfilling the missions set for them by the President. At the same time, our military never tried to avoid using force either, nor did they speak out against it. Colin Powell, ever the professional, wisely wanted to be sure that if we had to fight, we would do it right and not take half measures. He sought to ensure that there were sufficient troops for whatever option I wanted, and then the freedom of action to do the job once the political decision had been made. I was determined that our military would have both. I did not want to repeat the problems of the Vietnam War (or numerous wars throughout history), where the political leadership meddled with military operations. I would avoid micromanaging the military.

BRENT SCOWCROFT

Our conversation that day broadened to ruminations about being sure we handled the crisis in a way which reflected the nature of the transformed world we would face in the future. We were both struck with the thought that we were perhaps at a watershed of history. The Soviet Union was standing alongside us, not only in the United Nations, but also in condemning and taking action against Iraqi aggression. That cooperation represented fundamental change.

Heretofore, the eruption of an international crisis had almost automatically brought the United States and the Soviet Union down on opposite sides. If the attack on Kuwait marked the end of forty-odd years of such superpower confrontation, what vistas might open up? The Security Council could then perform the role envisioned for it by the UN framers. The United States and the Soviet Union could, in most cases, stand together against unprovoked interstate aggression.

Compared to the period we had just come through, the era ahead seemed like a new world order, and the phrase—not original—was used that morning to describe the possibilities before us. It has since been applied to a range of circumstances far different from our conception. We certainly had no expectation that we were entering a period of peace and tranquillity. Indeed, the outlines of a very messy world were already perceptible. The phrase, as we thought of it, applied only to a narrow aspect of conflict—aggression between states. A limited aspect of conflict, yes, but one which had been a chief ill of civilization since the beginning of recorded history. The term has subsequently been broadened beyond recognition, mostly to disparage its application. In retrospect, such an outcome was perhaps to be expected, but possibilities for dealing successfully with aggression between states in the current world still look promising.

By the end of August major elements of our response to Iraq's invasion of Kuwait were falling into place. We had used the United Nations to build a legal case for reversing the aggression. At the same time, we were putting together a military coalition to confront Iraq, with a multinational naval force to enforce sanctions. These were largely being complied with voluntarily. On the economic side, about half the oil lost in the embargo had been made up by the Saudis, Venezuelans, and others. We were also developing a strategy for compensating those countries most hurt by complying with the sanctions. All this was intended to keep Iraq isolated and deter it from further aggression until it either bowed under political and economic pressure or we had the military means and international political support to use force. But we also had to consider the grounds for eventual military action—if it came to that. Would we need specific provocation, or was reversing the invasion of Kuwait enough? There were plenty of legal grounds: the Security Council resolutions condemning and responding to the invasion, as well as Article 51 of the UN Charter (which provided for helping member states defend themselves), would give ample authority. There might be serious political problems, however, if we were perceived as launching an attack on Iraq without explicit UN endorsement.

In late August, Haass wrote up a possible plan he had developed with Bob Kimmit to rally support before formally introducing any resolution about force. It proposed to begin consulting first with our Arab allies and then with the permanent members of the Security Council. We would ask the council to act only if we knew in advance we had the backing of most of the Arab bloc and we were fairly certain we had the necessary votes. If at any point it became clear we could not succeed, we would back away from a UN mandate and cobble together an independent multinational effort built on friendly Arab and allied participation. The grounds for this would be the initial UN resolution condemning Iraq, the subsequent resolutions, and Article 51, along with a request from the Emir of Kuwait to intervene. In the end, if sanctions failed and it came to using force, Haass and Kimmit reminded us that our ability to rally the necessary political support, with or without UN endorsement, would be enhanced significantly if we were seen to have tried hard to make diplomacy work.

CHAPTER 15

A Delicate Balance

GEORGE BUSH

Public and congressional pressures affect policy-making and it is always difficult to choose wisely, weighing what is popular against what you believe to be right. At no time was this more true than over the next few weeks and months. The fall of 1990 was spent maintaining and strengthening our international coalition while building support at home and abroad for what we were doing—and what we might yet have to do. I hoped to avoid force until we had the domestic and international support to follow through with it to the end. I was comfortable and confident about handling the coalition. The domestic challenges were more complicated. Foreign policy and budget politics mingled, becoming charged with partisanship as the mid-term elections approached, and already soured relations with Congress grew bitter. This soon became one of the most frustrating periods of my presidency, as I tried both to strike a practical budget compromise and to build public understanding and backing for our evolving Gulf policy. It seemed to me that anything I wanted to do would be blocked by the Democratic leadership in Congress. I often thought how great it would be to work with a Congress in which both houses were not controlled by the opposition party.

I knew that there were some areas of genuine disagreement with members of Congress over policy, but I thought the budget and the Persian Gulf should not be among them. I wanted bipartisanship on these critical matters and I wanted consensus. At the same time, I understood I would not win over the last congressman, or the last American. I would face criticism no matter what I did and I decided to rely on my conviction about what was just and right to guide me.

At the outset of the crisis, public and congressional support for our immediate response to the invasion of Kuwait was strong and broad. Polls are an inexact measurement of public opinion, especially because they depend on how a question is put and the samples of the population researchers ask, but the results consistently showed that Americans generally backed our policy. My own numbers were at a high—76 percent according to one *New York Times*–CBS poll on August 22. While the support was gratifying, there were reservations. One criticism was that I had not adequately made the case to the public and the Congress as to the reason we had to get involved. Public opinion would not back for very long the large troop commitment we would need in the Gulf, let alone military action, without being given good justification. Some wanted me to deliver fireside chats to explain things, as Franklin Roosevelt had done. I am not good at that. I was convinced that the best way was to shape opinion not by rhetoric but by action.

I often felt that the magnitude of what was happening to Kuwait was not properly covered by the press, and therefore was not understood by the American public or members of Congress. This made communicating our interests all the more difficult. Over and over, Iraqi atrocities and stubborn criminal acts would pass by with little comment in the media. People seemed unmoved by the injustices we were witnessing, injustices in which I found even greater reason to resist Saddam. The inability of the television networks to cover these events due to Iraqi censorship was a major problem. I did try not only to explain what was at stake in my speeches and at press conferences, but also to keep Congress informed. On over twenty occasions during the course of the crisis I met with or briefed Congress, its leadership, and bipartisan groups, not counting meetings with individuals, beginning on August 28, even though Congress was in recess until after Labor Day.

There were those in Congress and the public who took exception to our goals. Some argued that we had no real national interest in restoring Kuwait's rulers. I found it very frustrating. "The Kuwaitis are rich," the reasoning went. "They're not democratic. We have no stake in the restoration of their rulers. The people of Kuwait should choose. We ought to call for UN-sponsored elections in Kuwait." As I recorded in my diary:

DIARY, SEPTEMBER 4

I worry that [Georgia senator] Sam Nunn has picked up on the compromise that some are offering—[that] there should be elections in Kuwait. . . . That stops short of the UN mandate and it plays right into the hands of King Hussein and some of the others who are frantically looking for an Arab solution and being basically critical of the US for being there. The rulers must be restored. Then what Kuwait does is their business. [And] what about [elections in] Iraq?

Besides its questions about our goals and interests, Congress demanded to know who else was going to put up money for Gulf defense efforts and how much. Our estimates of the costs ran into the tens of billions. Congress's concern reflected a widespread domestic feeling that we were doing the lion's share of work in responding to Saddam and were acting on behalf of the world's interests, not just our own. It was not an unreasonable position, especially in the middle of a budget battle.

While I believed the United States must be prepared to bear the brunt of the military burden, I thought it only just that other countries with interests at stake should contribute. Some countries had been quick to volunteer troops, but those who could not—or would not—might offer substantial financial commitments. We also had to find ways to bolster the coalition by offsetting the economic hardship upon not only those injured by the sanctions, such as Egypt and Turkey, but also Jordan and some Eastern European nations which depended on Iraqi or Kuwaiti oil. Burden-sharing among our allies when it came to defense matters was not a new idea and some measure of it had been in place for years. The Germans helped subsidize the upkeep of US troops on their soil. We also had agreements with both Japan and South Korea whereby these countries would help out with the local costs of our military forces.

Congress especially wanted to know about Japan's contribution. There was still a Japan-bashing mood around the country, which manifested itself in some of the questions at press conferences. I had talked to my friend Toshiki Kaifu on August 29, and he was as supportive as possible. He came through with a plan which would amount to a billion dollars for logistical support, not counting bilateral Japanese aid to Turkey, Egypt, and Jordan. This was later increased. Kaifu faced a difficult problem. He wanted to send non-lethal military help to the Gulf, but could not overcome his own domestic opposition.*

BRENT SCOWCROFT

Financial aid was the primary help Japan and Germany could offer the coalition. Both countries were constrained by their constitutions when it came to military action abroad. Much earlier, each had made efforts

*His government eventually fell over a proposal in the Diet to authorize Japanese peace-keeping troops.

to curb the militarism which had contributed to their aggressive foreign policies of the 1930s—and World War II. While these constitutional limits had been meant to prevent German or Japanese aggression, many now interpreted them more broadly, to include *any* deployment abroad—even peace-keeping activities. Both Kohl and Kaifu were under tremendous domestic pressure, with a vigor at times bordering on pacifism, not to allow their countries to take part either in enforcing the UN sanctions or in contributing troops to the coalition in Saudi Arabia.

At our August 30 NSC meeting, we decided to call on our allies and friends both to contribute economic aid and help defray our defense costs associated with the operation we were calling Desert Shield, through what subsequently was called the "tin cup" trip. President Bush prepared the way by phoning Thatcher and Mitterrand to inform them of our approach and then Kohl, Fahd, the Emir of Kuwait, and the President of the UAE, asking them to meet with our emissaries. We also decided to send a separate message to Gorbachev, encouraging him to help out the Eastern Europeans with their oil shortages. Baker and Brady soon headed out to Europe and Asia, tin cups in hand.

GEORGE BUSH

Egypt was in a particularly bad economic situation, with a heavy foreign debt which the embargo and reduced traffic through the Suez Canal would only worsen. If they did not find some relief there could be serious political problems in the country. I called Hosni Mubarak on September 1 to tell him I was going to recommend to Congress that Egypt's entire debt to the United States be forgiven. I knew it would be difficult to accomplish and that a chorus would rise in the Congress and elsewhere asking, what about Turkey, what about Greece? Mubarak was crucial to the entire Middle East peace process and the coalition. We had to find a way to help him out. A thirty-five-member Congressional delegation was due in Cairo in a couple of days, and I asked him not to tell them what I planned to do—I wanted to consult with Congress first—although he could raise the question of debt forgiveness with them.

We also talked about the effect of sanctions on Iraq. Hosni was convinced that Saddam was in a tight political corner and it was unlikely he would or could simply withdraw from Kuwait under economic pressure. After eight years of fighting, thousands of casualties, and the expenditure of $200 billion, Iraq had little to show for its war with Iran. He predicted that if Saddam withdrew, he would lose too much face. It would be suicide: his people would kill him. The foreign minister of Oman, Yusef bin Alawi, also insisted that Saddam would not bow under sanctions and argued for a military effort. I found these views discouraging.

Another debate emerged in August over whether I should go to Saudi Arabia in support of our troops. We had Americans waving goodbye to their loved ones at air bases and dockside and I thought it was important that the president show the flag. Besides, on my return it would give us a peg that we needed to speak to the nation about our commitment to the Gulf. I also wanted to tie in a visit to our Arab allies and demonstrate our appreciation of the courageous efforts they were making. I had first raised the idea in a note to Brent on August 10. It went over like a lead balloon. No one was in favor of it. Scowcroft, Sununu, and Baker all thought I should wait. They felt it could be counterproductive and worried that it would highlight the presence of US troops, playing into the hands of Iraqi propaganda. It could also provoke the radicals in the region. Mubarak discouraged me. King Fahd said I'd be welcome, and Prince Bandar even seemed to insist on it (and that I should go to Syria), but the word kept coming back that the Saudis were only showing Arab hospitality. So, reluctantly, I decided not to go. But I still wanted to *do* something diplomatically. In late August, I mentioned to Brent that perhaps we ought to think about a meeting with Gorbachev. Brent liked the idea (mainly, I believe, because I would not be headed for the Gulf) so we put it in train.

There were many good reasons to see Gorbachev. Above all, it would reinforce our message to Saddam that the United States and the Soviet Union were standing together in rock-solid opposition to the invasion. For these reasons, just having the meeting would itself be a major step. I was fairly certain Gorbachev would not agree to it if he thought we would have a heated argument over Iraq and, if our discussion was productive, it would only further isolate Iraq. I also felt it was important to acknowledge symbolically that the Soviets had a strong interest in the Gulf. They had been very sensitive about the potential use of force, which made it more pressing that I talk with Gorbachev sooner rather than later. I worried that some incident might arise to put a strain on the relationship before I had a chance to talk with him face to face.

I typed a letter to Gorbachev suggesting we get togther for a day in Finland or Switzerland, neutral ground so that it would not mix up the usual summit arrangements for meeting in each other's countries. In the spirit of our Camp David discussion in June, I wanted another opportunity to speak frankly and get things done. Jim passed the letter to the Soviet embassy on August 30, and Gorbachev agreed to meet on September 9 in Helsinki.

A major goal of the Helsinki talks would be to try to get Gorbachev to understand that we might have to resort to force if negotiations and sanctions did not work. I needed to convince him that the best way to create a new world order of Soviet-American cooperation against aggression was to support a strong response, which would have implications for the future of world peace. I wanted a tough joint statement on the matter—sending a powerful signal to Baghdad.

I did worry about Soviet talk concerning a comprehensive peace settlement and a Middle East peace conference which would include trying to solve the question of Israel's occupied territories—the very linkage of the Gulf crisis with the Arab-Israel confrontation we had been trying to avoid. Shevardnadze raised the idea with Baker, who pointed out that the UN itself is an international conference. Gorbachev had also alluded to it in a speech. We had to keep the Arab-Israeli peace process and Iraq separate, or the whole coalition with the Arabs might blow up.

BRENT SCOWCROFT

Jim Baker's staff, headed by Dennis Ross, prepared a joint statement declaring that the United States and the Soviet Union hoped for a peaceful solution, but that we were prepared to take additional measures should Saddam still refuse to withdraw from Kuwait. That was a good idea, but I thought Gorbachev would want to salvage everything he could for his former client state. Some sort of soft landing or compromise outcome would be optimal for him, and he was likely to do everything he could to preclude military action. I felt the statement would be a tough sell.

Gorbachev was probably very conflicted over his Iraq policy. Given the discouraging situation at home, standing by the side of the superpower United States might well be an image he eagerly sought. The danger was that he could appear just a small skiff towed along by the US dreadnought. There was also the prospect that three decades of Soviet policy toward Iraq were going down the drain, for which he might be blamed. To stand behind Iraq, on the other hand, in light of overwhelming world disapprobation, was not an attractive option. The result of his dilemma could be an attempt to straddle: stand strong beside the United States, but work diligently behind the scenes to protect Saddam and the Soviet investment.

GEORGE BUSH

On September 6, I spoke about the Helsinki meeting with Mitterrand, who had just been on the phone with Gorbachev. "He is very cautious about any movement toward open warfare, but he emphasized the need to maintain a common front regarding the Kuwait situation," he told me. "I found him in a very positive frame of mind. He said he had a very difficult visit with Aziz." François was concerned about the hostages, but said that situation should not alter our policy. "On the contrary," he declared, "this irritates us and strengthens our resolve . . . Saddam is making this more difficult." He thought it would help with Gorbachev if I emphasized solidarity. I asked him what he thought about military action to enforce the sanctions. François replied that it would be within the framework of UN Resolution 665. "If it is necessary to fire on an Iraqi vessel, it must be done," he said pragmatically. He didn't think it would be necessary. I hoped not.

The next day, Margaret Thatcher called and reported that the opposition Labour Party wanted an additional UN resolution. "I told them we already *have* the authority and don't need to go back to the UN," she said. "We may want another letter from the Emir, but we should not go back to the UN and risk a split vote, which would weaken our position. It took five days to get Resolution 665, and even then we couldn't get the word 'force' into the text."

That same day, before leaving for Finland, I went to the kick-off session for the budget negotiations out at Andrews Air Force Base. We seemed to be at an impasse and my frustration with Congress was rising.

DIARY, SEPTEMBER 7

I just hope that Iraq and the country's unity can now be parlayed into support for the budget agreement. I make a pitch to all the leaders around the table briefly and they all understand that I have to finish because I have to head off to Helsinki. Maybe this Helsinki trip with Gorbachev and the Iraq crisis will be the fulcrum that we need to lever a deal through the Congress. I sure hope so.

We had a lot of turbulence on the flight, so I didn't sleep much and was dead tired on Saturday when we arrived. But Finland was wonderful, and President Mauno Koivisto, an old friend, gave us a warm welcome. Jim Baker joined me fresh from a successful "tin cup" trip, in which he'd rounded up about $6 billion.

Gorbachev and I met the morning of September 9 in the presidential palace. He seemed relatively relaxed and even cheerful, despite the troubles facing him at home. It was a small group—just myself, Gorbachev, Brent, and Chernyayev. Jim met separately with Shevardnadze.

"I think there is an opportunity to have develop out of this tragedy a new world order," I told Gorbachev as we began. "But the bottom line . . . must be that Saddam Hussein cannot be allowed to profit from his aggression. I am not yet sure he knows that the United States is determined to prevail. I hope you will get word to him that we can't afford to fail in implementing the resolutions of the UN." I told him we had a strategy in place using sanctions that had a good chance of working. "I do not want this to escalate and I do not want to use force," I said. "But if he does not withdraw, he must know the status quo is unacceptable." I wanted to discuss the matter fully with Gorbachev so that if, in the end, the coalition had to resort to force, the Soviets would back us. "That may be difficult for you, but I would hope that you could do that," I said. "The press asked me if I would ask you to send forces. I said I had no such plans, but I tell you that if you so decide, I have no problems with that."* The United States did not plan to leave any substantial forces in the Gulf afterwards. "Any residual security presence to keep Saddam Hussein under control should be multilateral."

I pointed out that US tradition was to say the Soviets had no role to play in the Middle East. This policy had changed. "The world order I see coming out of this is US and Soviet cooperation to solve not only this but other problems in the Middle East," I said. "The closer we can be together today, the closer the new world order . . . I want to work with you as equal partners in dealing with this. I want to go to the American people tomorrow night to close the book on the Cold War and offer them the vision of this new world order in which we will cooperate." I handed him a color cartoon showing the two of us as boxers, our arms raised in victory over the Cold War dragon. He laughed. I asked if he would mind if we used first names in these small meetings. "Fine, George!" he said with a grin.

Gorbachev agreed that the crisis was a test of the transition the world was going through and the new US-Soviet relationship. "Without forgetting the scale of [it], I think that if we can't cope with this conflict, a new order can't come in," he said. "It may be that this crisis will be the stone on which we will stumble. Question is, can we act and think in a new way? If not, the results are serious. Without the meeting in Malta, without the new relationship, Eastern Europe and German unification could have been much worse. It would have turned into a horrible mess. We now find ourselves with a problem no less difficult." He told me that in Eastern Europe and Germany the main burden had been on the Soviet Union and they had to end old thinking. "In the Gulf, the United States is in a more difficult position," he said. "I understand that, perhaps more

*[BRENT SCOWCROFT] I winced as the President told Gorbachev he could accept Soviet forces in the coalition, although by this point it was pretty clear Gorbachev had no interest in sending any. It was a sign of the President's willingness to include the Soviets in more than just symbolic solidarity. For me, Soviet troops in the Middle East were something we should avoid if at all possible. Fortunately, Gorbachev never responded to the remark and the subject was dropped.

than our people. . . . Your people expect you to act decisively and win. Both our peoples expect quick results. . . . You should not doubt that our position is firm. We have condemned Iraqi aggression and supported the UN. We are as one here. But it was difficult for us at first because you decided to send forces and then told us."

"We weren't trying to do it behind your back," I said. "But I can accept that I should have called you and told you I was going to do it."

"But later on we were able to act shoulder to shoulder to mobilize the world community and that's a big achievement," said Gorbachev. "That has given a very different appearance to the forces and that is good. But there must be some kind of arrangement to manage this new order. You have taken the main burden of dealing with Iraqi aggression."

He offered his thinking on where the crisis stood. Saudi Arabia was now safe and Saddam Hussein had been contained, he said. The United States and the world community could boast of some achievements. Still, some things were not yet finished. Kuwait remained occupied, and Saddam would not leave easily. He knew we needed to act decisively, but a military solution was dangerous and unacceptable to the Soviet Union. How its troops were deployed showed that Iraq had no hostile intention toward Saudi Arabia. This meant that if Iraq did not attack Saudi Arabia or Israel, the United States would be the initiator of war. People would recall Afghanistan and Vietnam. Saddam was already a hero to many Arabs for standing up to the West, and he was not afraid of the US. "But we can't leave the situation as is," he said. "Primakov knows Saddam Hussein personally. All believe that backing Saddam Hussein into a corner is wrong. He must be allowed to save face."

He brought out a proposal. Saddam would release the hostages, withdraw from Kuwait, and restore the Kuwaiti government. In turn, the United States would promise it would not strike Iraq and we would reduce our forces, which would be replaced by an Arab peace-keeping force. An agreement for an international conference on the Middle East would follow. It was linkage. Gorbachev was convinced that Saddam would turn this proposal down, and when he did he would be unmasked, losing support among the Arabs. I thought Saddam would jump at the plan. He could use the link with the conference to cover his own aggression. "Any agreement on a plan which left the Kuwait issue open would be a major defeat for the collective action which has gotten us so far," I said. Saddam would get what he wanted. "He still has a nuclear program and can return to aggression as soon as the US leaves."

Gorbachev suggested we tinker with the plan, but argued that military action would appear as aggression. I objected, saying that Saddam was dismantling Kuwait. "I think this is why we should act quickly," urged

Gorbachev. "Force would destroy what we have achieved. If the current situation drags on without steps, we will have lost the initiative. Here we could say we are acting in a responsible way by suggesting ways to solve the problem."

I told him that whatever came out of our discussions could not be a US-Soviet plan. "That would look like a condominium of just the two of us trying to find a solution," I said. "But the idea is interesting and we must do some thinking. . . ." Gorbachev acknowledged that we could not act as if we alone were solving the problem. "But if we can do nothing, then why do we meet?" he asked. He suggested that we could say that we thought it was possible to find "a solution which would prevent even worse developments."

"I agree, except we should say 'look for,' " I said. "I'm not sure we can find such a plan . . . I would like to go the extra mile for peace, but we must not undermine the UN collective action."

"But if he gets nothing at all, if he is backed into a corner, it will be more costly for us all," countered Gorbachev. "We need to give him some daylight. Let's give the impression that he is not on his knees—though he would be because he would not succeed."

"If we had offered Hitler some way out, would it have succeeded?" I asked.

"Not the same situation."

"Only in personality."

"We have to choose," said Gorbachev with a shrug. "We don't have many options. I believe that you, who have achieved so much here, want to avoid a costly conflict with the possible destruction of oil. That would be a tremendous victory. . . . If we throw him a carrot, we will win, establish the role of international law [through the UN], our cooperation, and avoid serious conflict."

"I agree completely," I replied. "We must, though, have a way which does not incite future aggression. Much of what you propose does that." I said we would look at his plan carefully.

BRENT SCOWCROFT

I came out of the session filled with foreboding. Gorbachev's presentation had obviously been crafted by the pro-Iraqi bureaucracy—probably Yevgeny Primakov, who was the architect, or at least the protector, of traditional Soviet Middle East policy. It was further evidence of the battle between Shevardnadze and Primakov for Gorbachev, and it could not be happening at a worse time. It raised the specter of Moscow seeking a separate peace with Baghdad. We had to head that off. As we left the meeting, I suggested to the President that the Soviets had taken a major step backwards and were perhaps easing into the role of protector of Iraq. To me, "saving face" for Iraq, or a partial withdrawal, a promise not to attack, and, above all, linkage with the Arab-Israeli issue, would change the path we were on in fundamental ways.

At the lunch hosted by President Koivisto, I sat next to Marshal Akhromeyev. I had developed a great deal of respect for him as a result of our private breakfast the previous July. After chatting a bit about strategic arms control, I asked how things were going for him. He pointed at Gorbachev. "He is my leader," he said. "I am loyal to him and doing my best to help him. But I am confused." Akhromeyev told me he was a soldier and devoted patriot who had dedicated his life to the Soviet Union and the principles he had been taught it represented. Suddenly he was being told that everything for which he had stood and fought was wrong. The Soviet Union, its leaders, its actions, and motivation—had all been a lie. His world had been uprooted, his moral and national moorings destroyed. He no longer knew what to believe, what to defend. His children despised him and the system he represented.

It was a profound moment. I imagined where I myself would be, discovering that everything on which I had based my life since my days at West Point had been a charade. Less than a year later, Marshal Akhromeyev, the Soviet Union in ruins, committed suicide.

After lunch, and before the afternoon session with the Soviets, the President, Jim, John Sununu, John Kelly, Dennis Ross, Condi Rice, Richard Haass, and I discussed Gorbachev's proposal. As Baker recounted his meeting with Shevardnadze, it became apparent that his experience was far different from that of the President with Gorbachev. Shevardnadze also had raised the question of a Middle Eastern peace conference, one handling both the Iraqi invasion and the Palestinian problem. After a long discussion, Baker persuaded him that such a conference would hand Saddam a political victory. Instead, he proposed that our countries state our hope for a peaceful solution but, if Saddam refused to leave Kuwait, we were willing to take further measures as necessary along the lines of the Security Council resolution on naval interdiction. He showed Shevardnadze our draft statement. Shevardnadze liked the language and asked that his deputy, Sergei Tarasenko, and Ross work on it. In contrast, Gorbachev had made an impassioned presentation to the President, who had received an impression similar to mine—that Gorbachev was dug in on the matter, at least on linkage. We concluded that the best way to begin the plenary session to follow was to present reports of the two simultaneous meetings, beginning with that of the foreign ministers.

In the plenary, Baker outlined the discussion with Shevardnadze and reported that Ross and Tarasenko had now prepared a joint statement embodying it. President Bush suggested that we take a look at the statement. Gorbachev read the draft carefully, asked for some minor changes, and, in a move which absolutely astounded me, essentially said "okay." Gone, virtually without a trace, was the Gorbachev of the morning, defending his Iraqi client. It was, to me, an amazing—and exceedingly reassuring—turnabout. We had narrowly escaped a crisis.

In retrospect, it seems plausible to believe that Gorbachev was making a run at having it both ways. If he could have gotten us to go along with a formula which rewarded Saddam, he would have been a hero at home and in Iraq. When that failed, he had at least demonstrated to his Arabists that he had made a good faith effort. He then went on to his next best option, which was to sign on to our statement and get a joint press conference showing the two superpowers settling world issues. To have refused that and have the meeting break up in disagreement would have advanced none of his objectives.

The joint statement reaffirmed the August 3 declaration by Baker and Shevardnadze and our support for the UN resolutions. It called on Iraq to withdraw unconditionally from Kuwait, allow the restoration of Kuwait's rulers, and free all hostages. Iraq had to comply with the resolutions and return Kuwait to its former, pre-invasion status. We pledged to ensure compliance with the sanctions, recognizing that the UN resolution permitted, in humanitarian situations, the importation of food into Iraq and Kuwait. While we preferred to resolve the crisis peacefully, we were united against Iraq's aggression. "We are determined to see this crisis end, and if the current steps fail to end it," we warned, "we are prepared to consider additional ones consistent with the UN Charter. We must demonstrate beyond any doubt that aggression cannot and will not pay."

We concluded with language that sidestepped the linkage controversy. Once the objectives mandated by the Security Council resolutions had been reached, we would work with countries inside and outside the region to develop security structures and measures to promote peace and stability. "It is essential to work actively to resolve all remaining conflicts in the Middle East and Persian Gulf," we finished. "Both sides will continue to consult each other and initiate measures to pursue these broader objectives at the proper time."

GEORGE BUSH

I was pleased with the results of the talks. Even though Gorbachev was not yet prepared to contemplate military action, he had left that door open. We got the strong joint statement I wanted, declaring that the status quo accepting Iraqi aggression was unacceptable. We had, as well, headed off another attempt to link the crisis with Israel.

The next day, I learned from King Fahd that the Arab reaction was positive. He was convinced that Iraq was surrounded and would have to yield to pressure, optimistically predicting that this now would take only a couple of weeks longer. Remembering my discouraging conversation with Hosni Mubarak several days before, I asked him whether Saddam could withdraw and still remain in power in Iraq. The King replied that Saddam had no real choice, and that when he withdrew, it would be the end of him.

That same day, Iraq announced that it had drawn up a charge sheet against me in preparation for a "people's court" trial. The charges included: sending American troops to the Gulf region and occupying Muslim shrines in Saudi Arabia; threatening to attack Iraq and the Arab nation (shorthand for the entire Arab people); imposing economic measures against Iraq; issuing orders to the CIA to conspire against Saddam.

On hearing this fearful news, I wrote White House Counsel Boyden Gray a "Personal—Eyes Only" typewritten note which I instructed to be hand-delivered:

> Please get a visa and be ready to go to Baghdad to defend me on these four charges.
> I can beat the third "rap" by citing the UN.
> The same would apply to sending troops but be sure you are ready to present my case on the "shrines." I am innocent.
> They can never make rap #4 stick.
> I am not worried, but please call me after the first tribunal.
> Should they not permit you to leave, wire home; and we will have somebody temporarily hold down your job here.
> Many Thanks,
> [signed] GB

On September 11, I addressed a joint session of Congress to report on the Gulf situation and my talks with Gorbachev. I hoped to strengthen support for our approach to the crisis, and underscore the long-term importance of what we had accomplished at Helsinki.

DIARY, MORNING OF SEPTEMBER 11

Getting ready for the speech to the nation tonight, but a fourth of it, the budget part, can't be put to bed because the budgeteers met 'til 2:30.

It is said of me that I much prefer to work on international affairs. Well, I am fully engrossed in this international crisis, and I must say I enjoy working all the parts of it and I get into much more detail than I do on the domestic scene. So I think the answer is I do prefer this, but I see the budget deficit as very important—something essential to solve. I think the American people are fed up whenever they concentrate on this . . . The budgeteers were somewhat optimistic—Brady, Darman, and Sununu—this morning. They say that the Congress is worried about my [high] popularity ratings—the polls. You know how I feel about polls, dear diary. I think they come and go, and we can be up and down. And, yes, I am pleased with the amount of support that I'm getting, but I know it can change fast. This country gets into recession, we get down, and it will change real, real fast. So we ought not to crow, but if the strong numbers today can help us get a deal based on the fact that Congress does not want to be "bashed" in front of the whole country, so much the better. But inside, I don't feel over-confident or arrogant based on the polling numbers, at all. . . .

The speech that evening was warmly received, and I felt a charge of adrenaline as I addressed the crowded chamber. I recounted what Gorbachev and I had accomplished at Helsinki and spoke of the new relationship we were building with the Soviet Union, a new partnership. No longer could a dictator count on East-West confrontation to stymie concerted United Nations action against aggression.

We stand today at a unique and extraordinary moment. The crisis in the Persian Gulf, as grave as it is, also offers a rare opportunity to move toward an historic period of cooperation. Out of these troubled times, our fifth objective—a new world order—can emerge: a new era—free from the threat of terror, stronger in the pursuit of justice, and more secure in the quest for peace. An era in which the nations of the world, East and West, North and South, can prosper and live in harmony. A hundred generations have searched for this elusive path to peace, while a thousand wars raged across the span of human endeavor. Today that new world is struggling to be born, a world quite different from the one we've known. A world where the rule of law supplants the rule of the jungle. A world in which nations recognize the shared responsibility for freedom and justice. A world where the strong respect the rights of the weak.

The Gulf crisis was the first test of this new world we sought, and the stakes were high, I said. Had we not responded, and were we not to respond to the challenge, "it would be a signal to actual and potential despots around the world." America and the world had to defend common vital interests, I declared—and we would.

While I could not predict how long we would need to convince Iraq to withdraw from Kuwait, and sanctions would take time, we could not let the aggression stand. Our interest and role in the Gulf was not transitory. It predated Saddam and would outlast him. We had to deter future aggression, to assist in the self-defense of our friends, and to curb the spread of weapons of mass destruction.

> Let me also make clear that the United States has no quarrel with the Iraqi people. Our quarrel is with Iraq's dictator and with his aggression. Iraq will not be permitted to annex Kuwait. That's not a threat, that's not a boast, that's just the way it's going to be.

What pleased me most that evening was that there was strong support for the actions I had already taken (moving troops) and what I might yet have to do if there was provocation. As long as there was Congressional backing, I felt I had a good chance to prevail. Yet I saw confrontation brewing over the question of force.

I wanted to find a way to get Congress on board with an unmistakable show of that support for what we were doing, and what we might have to do. Early in September I had asked Boyden Gray to look into how Lyndon Johnson had handled Congress at the time of the Gulf of Tonkin Resolution in 1964. Johnson had worked hard to get individual members of Congress, and Congress itself, to go on record in support of what he was doing in Vietnam. He urged joint hearings of the committees on foreign relations and armed services in both Houses, and asked Congress to insist on roll calls so the record would be complete. In the end, he got a unanimous vote out of the House—414 to 0—and a Senate count of 88 to 2. I realized the Vietnam War was different, but his effort made a big impression on me, and I began to think about seeking a similar congressional vote of support.

DIARY, SEPTEMBER 13

We do not want to unleash a War Powers* debate [over the use of force], nor do most of the senators, so we're going to keep working the problem . . . My gut wonder is, how long will they be with us? How long will the Senate stay supportive, or the House? As long as the people are with us, I've got a good chance. But once

*See Chapter 16, pages 397–98.

there starts to be erosion, they're going to do what Lyndon Johnson said: they painted their asses white and ran with the antelopes. It's not all of them, of course . . .

Sunday night, the 14th . . . New polls are out: 57% support and 23% against—something like this. It used to be 7% opposed, and I worry, worry, worry about eroded support.

The President's September 21 meeting with the bipartisan leadership offered an opportunity to take the pulse of Congress. Speaker Tom Foley said there was a broad consensus of support so far in both parties and around the country, but it was too soon to talk about a military option. "You have to give sanctions a chance," he said. If there was provocation, that would be a different matter; we'd have to act and perhaps unilaterally. However, he believed it was important to have an international mandate before we did. "If we engage in hostilities," he warned, "the War Powers issue would resume." George Mitchell and Dick Gephardt concurred. "We've been supportive because your actions warranted it," said Mitchell. We should continue as we had. Claiborne Pell objected to any unilateral use of force. Republicans Bob Dole and Bob Michel each declared support for the existing policy. Jack Murtha did as well, but thought we were probably on a course toward war anyway. Sam Nunn declared that if it did come to war we should rely on air and sea power, not ground forces. Les Aspin agreed.

GEORGE BUSH

For the moment most members of Congress seemed to back our general approach, and grasped the stakes. Bob Dole was a particular asset from the outset, and a valuable source of wise advice about the mood in Congress and the country. But I felt strongly there was a certain thoughtlessness in the priorities of others. For example, we had problems helping Turkey, a NATO ally and a front-line state in the coalition against Saddam. Ozal was loyal in his support and he needed relief for trade on textiles, but Trent Lott and Jesse Helms were urging me not to veto a protectionist textile bill. Here was a staunch friend, standing by us against a tyrant, asking not for money and aid but only for an ability to trade with us on textiles. But nowhere did the problems of getting aid through Congress stand out more starkly than when we began to tackle the forgiveness of Egypt's debt and extensive military aid to Saudi Arabia.

BRENT SCOWCROFT

Inevitably, debt forgiveness was a sensitive issue with Congress. It had to be handled most carefully, with quiet groundwork laid with key congressmen. Despite the fact that the President had asked him not to say anything about Egyptian debt forgiveness, Mubarak unfortunately mentioned it in a way which became public—before we had consulted with Congress. The result was furious protest and resentment, which nearly scuttled our plans. I could understand how some in Congress would oppose debt forgiveness. It went over badly with constituents. At a time when many at home were struggling with school, farm, and FHA loans, people would ask why we didn't forgive these debts rather than those of foreign countries.

As we worked on financial support for Egypt, we also pushed for sending desperately needed military equipment to the Saudis. Iraq had a far larger military than did Saudi Arabia and enjoyed a qualitative advantage, in that the Saudis had no ammunition that could defeat Iraq's Soviet-made tanks. Getting material to them was a difficult task, especially since we were prohibited from selling certain special munitions to non-NATO countries. A further problem was a required thirty-day waiting period between congressional notification and actual shipment of the equipment. While the President could (and did) authorize the sale of the munitions using special authority under the Foreign Assistance Act, we still had to notify Congress in advance and explain why it was necessary.

On August 26, President Bush signed waivers to ship immediately 150 older tanks, 24 aircraft, and limited munitions. Congress did not object to this first emergency arms transfer, but it balked at the size of a second and much larger package in September, which included modern tanks and equipment. In total, the package amounted to about $17–20 billion. We believed it would send a signal to the Saudis, and to Saddam, about our commitment to the area beyond the current crisis. In addition, by building a stronger Saudi military, we were reducing the need for US forces in any future contingency. Following the complaints about the size of the second package, and consulting the contractors supplying the equipment, we broke it into two parts. The first was based on immediate Saudi need and the immediate availability of the arms. This would require us to curtail the normal thirty-day notification period for such assistance. The second part would contain the remainder. Some in Congress quickly kicked up a fuss over the arms package, as well as Egyptian debt relief, and tried to get something for Israel while we attempted to send emergency help to our Arab allies. Eventually the arms package went through on October 29, simply because Congress failed to pass a resolution of disapproval within thirty calendar days. Debt forgiveness legislation was approved the first week of November.

GEORGE BUSH

On September 14, the Iraqi troops besieging the embassies in Kuwait City raided several of the ambassadorial residences. They took away the US consul, as well as those of Britain, Ireland, Australia, Canada, and France. That day, the UN Security Council passed Resolution 667, which condemned Iraqi abuses of diplomatic missions. At the same time I was hearing stories about Iraq's treatment of Kuwait:

DIARY, SEPTEMBER 22

I've just read a horrible intelligence report on the brutal dismembering and dismantling of Kuwait. Shooting citizens when they are stopped in their cars. Exporting what little food there is. Brutalizing the homes. Dismantling the records. Indeed, making an oasis into a wasteland. They quote the Norwegian ambassador, a respected observer, who attested to the brutality and to the horrible intention of this dictator, Saddam Hussein. The problem is, unless something happens soon, there may not be a Kuwait—there may be no records—no one will know who Kuwaiti citizens are. There is evidence that he's trying to re-populate Kuwait with Iraqi stooges, so if there ever was a referendum, the vote would go against the [royal] family. He vows to never withdraw, and he vows that the family should never return. This just hardens my resolve. I am wondering if we need to speed up the timetable.

When he came to the White House on September 28, the Emir told me firsthand of the extent of the atrocities Iraqi troops were inflicting on his people, and this too had a deep effect on me.

It was during this period that I began to move from viewing Saddam's aggression exclusively as a dangerous strategic threat and an injustice to its reversal as a moral crusade. It was a conclusion I came to gradually through August and September. His disdain for international law, his misrepresentation of what had happened, his lies to his neighbors all contributed, but perhaps it was hearing of the destruction of life in Kuwait which sealed the matter. I became very emotional about the atrocities. They really gave urgency to my desire to do something active in response. I knew there was a danger I might overreact to what I heard and read. I'd tell myself to calm down, not to let these human rights abuses—bitter and ugly as they were, with medieval torture—cause me to do something hasty or make a foolish decision. Yet at some point it came through to me that this was not a matter of shades of gray, or of trying to see the other side's point of view. It was good versus evil, right versus wrong. I am sure the change strengthened my determination not to let the invasion stand and encouraged me to contemplate the use of force to reverse it. This was how I sorted it out in my mind, which made the choices before me clearer. It also made it a little easier to speak to the families of our troops and explain why their loved ones might have to sacrifice themselves. I was frustrated and impatient to resolve the crisis, hoping we could find reason to go in and settle the matter.

In the first weeks of the crisis, I happened to be reading a book on World War II by the British historian Martin Gilbert. I saw a direct analogy between what was occurring in Kuwait and what the Nazis had done, especially in Poland. This in no way diminished the evil crimes the Nazis inflicted upon helpless millions, or the suffering into which they plunged all Europe. The book recounted how the German Army swept through an area, followed closely by special units which would terrorize the population. I saw a chilling parallel with what the Iraqi occupiers were doing in Kuwait. I caught hell on this comparison of Saddam to Hitler, with critics accusing me of personalizing the crisis, but I still feel it was an appropriate one.

I did not have a personal grudge against Saddam Hussein, but I had a deep moral objection to what he had done and was doing. It was unprincipled, and we could not permit it to go on. My feeling at the time was to ask, "How do we get at this guy for what he is doing to the world?" I think you can be objective about moral judgment, and I think what he did can be morally condemned and lead one to the proper conclusion that it was a matter of good versus evil. Saddam had become the epitome of evil in taking hostages and in his treatment of the Kuwaiti people. He himself tried his best to personalize the crisis, pouring out rhetoric that portrayed our efforts to eject him from Kuwait as a matter of the United States picking on Iraq and the Arabs. I was equally determined to keep our efforts multilateral, and to emphasize that our policy was based on principle, not personalities.

As it began its Children's Summit and forty-fifth-anniversary celebrations in the fall, the United Nations became an active forum for policy statements on the Gulf. Every speech by political leaders to the General Assembly condemned Iraq, and some, including Shevardnadze's, reminded Saddam that the UN had the power to "suppress aggression" should the occupation of Kuwait continue. François Mitterrand used his address on September 24 to offer a peace plan which he said might begin a negotiation process for the region as a whole. While he added there could be no compromise as long as Iraq did not comply with the UN resolutions, he did make a point of calling for democratic choice for the Kuwaitis, demonstrating his unease about making the return of the Emir a condition.

Although Mitterrand's speech did not reveal any major gap between US and French policy, I did worry about his dislike for making the return of the al-Sabah family a prerequisite for Iraqi compliance. He had been stressing this theme in several statements in which he declared that the conditions for dialogue were withdrawal from Kuwait and release of hostages. Restoration of the legitimate government was conspicuously left out, yet this condition had been part of all the key Security Council resolutions. This turned out to be the one area where we differed, and the press zeroed in on it. I did not think we should impose democracy on the Kuwaitis—rather, it was something which had to grow from within. We could not allow a dictator to be the one to alter their domestic political structure. Above all, we could not give Saddam any measure of political gain from the invasion. Had we insisted on imposing democracy as part of the restoration of sovereignty, Saddam could portray himself as a catalyst for Kuwaiti political reform.

A few days after his UN speech, François sent me a letter explaining it. He emphasized France's position that UN resolutions were a non-negotiable precondition. "The position of France is without ambiguity: no détente or compromise can be envisaged with Saddam Hussein without the liberation of hostages and the withdrawal of Iraqi forces from Kuwait. . . ." France also backed "effective implementation" of the embargo. Mitterrand argued, however, for giving the Kuwaitis democracy. "France is carrying out a significant military effort, alongside its friends and particularly alongside the United States, in order to ensure the success of the embargo and to force Saddam Hussein to draw back," he wrote. "But I would not risk the death of one single French soldier if it was exclusively in order to restore an absolutist system. No country, other than the United States, has done as much as mine by way of sacrifice in order to assure the triumph of law in the Middle East. That gives us an additional reason for saying what we think." I responded with a letter urging that there should not be an appearance of differences between us, and Scowcroft sent a similar message to Admiral Lanxade. Fortunately, François ceased to make an issue of it, so that the matter had no practical effect on the coalition. Saddam, however, did try to exploit the apparent differences by releasing about 250 French hostages at the end of October, saying it was in response to the UN address.

October brought new strains on the coalition. It appeared that Soviet internal political problems were beginning to spill over into the crisis. On October 4–5, Primakov visited Baghdad, apparently carrying a message from Gorbachev. We were uneasy about the trip, especially when we learned that a furious Shevardnadze had not known of it ahead of time, nor exactly what message Primakov was supposed to convey. Shevardnadze promised Baker he would let us know the purpose of the mission as soon as he found out.* The Soviets were also reporting potential compromise or conditional offers from the Iraqis, deals we could not possibly accept. The proposals seemed to reflect a growing influence of the pro-Iraqi faction in the Soviet Foreign Ministry.

Shevardnadze soon reported that Primakov was sent as Gorbachev's personal envoy to try to extract the 5,000 or so Soviet technicians still trapped in Iraq, some of whom the Iraqis claimed were privy to military secrets they might pass to the coalition. Primakov evidently also protested the use of hostages as human shields. Shevardnadze told us Saddam had said that withdrawal of his troops would be possible "but not in conditions of the ultimatum: either a withdrawal, or a military strike on Iraq." Saddam threatened retaliation against all the oil fields of the Arabian peninsula if he was attacked. He wanted a political solution which would include coalition concessions enabling him to save face before his own people and the Arab world. Shevardnadze speculated that this meant settlement of the Palestinian problem and giving Iraq secure access to the Persian Gulf. Saddam was willing to withdraw from Kuwait in exchange for complete control of the Rumaila oil fields and two islands at the head of the Persian Gulf. Two days later, the President instructed Baker to announce that we rejected any territorial concessions.

GEORGE BUSH

Mikhail sent Primakov to Washington to brief me about his trip on October 19, and what I heard was discouraging. Primakov reported that Saddam was not being well informed by his inner circle and was hearing more about his support than about his political isolation. He also speculated that sanctions would still need five or six months to bite, but that these alone would not force Saddam out and could be counterproductive, encouraging him to strike at Israel. Saddam had said that if his choice was between leaving or being attacked, "I'd die before leaving . . . I'm prepared to die, but this battle is not confined to one country alone. I am a

---

*His deputy, Sergei Tarasenko, told us that Primakov was attempting to float a peace proposal of some sort and that Shevardnadze had objected but had been overruled.

realist. I know I must leave Kuwait, but I simply can't leave." Primakov had offered a proposal detailing what the coalition was willing to do after Saddam would withdraw from Kuwait. I cabled Gorbachev that I felt this violated the basic principles we laid out at Helsinki. "Rather than insisting on Saddam's unconditional withdrawal, this approach would offer him significant 'face savers' that he would inevitably present as a 'reward.' " The Primakov conversation reinforced my pessimism about finding any solution to the crisis short of the use of force. Even if the sanctions bit into Iraq, they didn't appear strong enough to get Saddam out of Kuwait.

BRENT SCOWCROFT

This was just one of several trips Primakov made that fall to Baghdad and other regional capitals to try to broker a settlement, working hard to pull a rabbit out of a hat for Soviet foreign policy. While Gorbachev appeared genuine when he told President Bush at Helsinki that it was for the United States to lead the international efforts against Iraq, and that the Soviet Union wished to cooperate, he was probably deeply sympathetic to Primakov's argument. His own political support at home was thin after giving up Eastern Europe and Germany. If the Soviets came out with Iraq intact, especially if they could get credit for brokering a deal between Washington and Baghdad, they stood to score a major diplomatic victory.

There were other challenges as well. On October 8, violent demonstrations erupted on the Temple Mount in Jerusalem and Israeli troops fired into the crowd, killing 21 Palestinians and injuring more than 150. The incident stirred anger in the Arab world, and we had to act quickly to control the reaction in the UN and avoid dividing the coalition. Coincidentally, there was already debate underway at the UN over a resolution introduced by Colombia, Cuba, Malaysia, and Yemen, urging members to move on the general Palestinian issue as decisively as they were on Iraq's invasion of Kuwait. The PLO representative now called on the Security Council to investigate the incident and pushed a resolution demanding the Council condemn the Israeli action as a "criminal act" and set up a mission to investigate both it and the general situation in Gaza and the West Bank that would recommend ways to protect Palestinians. We did not want to be put in the position of vetoing the resolution, or to appear uncaring about the loss of life in Jerusalem, reinforcing the perception that we were protecting Israel at the expense of the Arabs. In addition, the Iraqis were making noises about connecting the handling of the incident with resolution of the Gulf crisis.

The day after the incident, we introduced a resolution drafted with the British—and backed by the rest of the Permanent Five—that condemned Israel in less harsh language for using excessive force and called for a more restricted mission to the occupied territories. After some tough negotiations with the non-aligned sponsors of the other resolution, as well as discussion between the President and Mitterrand over the wording, we managed to win passage for a revised resolution on October 12. It called for the mission to submit a report on how the Palestinians could be protected, but affirmed that the principal responsibility for their protection rested with Israel as the occupying power under the Geneva Convention. Unfortunately, Israel angrily rebuffed the mission, causing more problems. The UN again condemned Israel for not cooperating.

With the introduction of the US-supported resolution, our relations with Israel hit a new low. Prime Minister Yitzhak Shamir and President Bush shot letters back and forth. The Jewish community in the United States was surprised, hurt, and furious. Their argument was that we had to be more understanding of Shamir. The death of the Palestinians in Jerusalem made that difficult.

GEORGE BUSH

The international storm over Temple Mount prompted speculation among the Washington pundits that the coalition was unraveling, just as relations with Congress were beginning to deteriorate. The budget battle dominated everything, dividing the Congress and the Administration, increasing tensions and unpleasantness. Although we managed to work out an agreement with the congressional leadership which included a firm cap on discretionary domestic spending, but also an increase in taxes, the House defeated it on October 5, sharpening personal animosities. I had signed one continuing resolution to keep the government open until that day, but I vetoed the next one, effectively shutting down everything for the Columbus Day weekend—although it did not affect the military. I signed another on October 9, promising to veto any others unless Congress passed an acceptable budget package by October 19. Yet there was positive legislation as well. On October 1, the House passed a non-binding resolution 380–29 supporting our objectives in the Gulf while urging me to continue to seek diplomatic solutions. The Senate quickly approved similar resolutions supporting the deployment of troops and our actions in the Gulf. The measures stopped short of backing military action, but it was the first time since the invasion that Congress had gone on record behind our troop deployment.

My 1988 convention rhetoric, "Read my lips, no new taxes," was strong language. That was my intention at the time. But in the fall of 1990, I had to decide between a compromise on taxes or literally to shut down the government. When I told Congress that everything was on the negotiating table (which would include tax increases), there was a fury of criticism. The upcoming November congressional elections made things more partisan, as the Democrats tried to exploit a dip in my support in the polls. The Washington media—right and left—had a field day with what they called the "disaster" I was causing the party, by "flip-flops" on issues and for breaking my word. The more conservative Republicans were calling it betrayal—no matter that anti-tax President Reagan had to raise revenues many times. Even the fact that we got a rock-solid guarantee from Congress against increasing government discretionary spending gave me no maneuvering room with my most vociferous critics. I was very disappointed that one of our top leaders in Congress, Newt Gingrich, very influential with the Republican right, at the last minute backed away from a compromise he had all but agreed to. Years later he told me that his decision was one of the most difficult he had made in his life. Maybe so, but it sure hurt me. His support could have eliminated the flak I took on the tax question and on my credibility.

As I look back, the effect of the budget deal was not economic but political. After a recession, which we were in when we made it, the economy recovered by the end of the first half of 1991, and, by the time the 1992 election rolled around, it was in robust growth. The problem for me was that the press refused to recognize the recovery and my political opponents were exceptionally good at reminding people I had broken my pledge on taxes. What they ignored was that we got a rigid spending cap that is, as of this writing, still in effect and has demonstrably held down discretionary spending. When I left the White House, the economy had grown 5.8 percent in the fourth quarter of 1992 and growth for the entire year was over 3 percent. "Read my lips" was rhetorical overkill. When push came to shove and our troops were moving overseas, we needed a fully functioning government. I simply had to hammer out a compromise to keep the government open, but I paid a terrible price.

As the struggle over the budget raged, the NSC core group met in the Situation Room on October 11 to hear from Powell and CENTCOM's Major General Robert Johnston what Schwarzkopf had in mind should we go on the offensive in the Gulf. They described an air campaign, the basic plans for which had already been laid out. When asked whether an air war might bring Iraq to its knees, or even to collapse, forcing Saddam to pull out of Kuwait, Powell was cautious. He warned that air power probably would not be enough; we would also have to use troops. We then listened to a plan for a ground campaign employing the troops already earmarked for the Gulf. It was basically a corps-sized frontal assault through the heart of the Iraqi strength straight up into Kuwait, with an initial goal of seizing the major road intersection north of Kuwait City.

BRENT SCOWCROFT

I was not happy with the briefing. It sounded unenthusiastic, delivered by people who didn't want to do the job. The option they presented us, an attack straight up through the center of the Iraqi army, seemed to me to be so counterintuitive that I could not stay silent. I asked why not an envelopment to the west and north around and behind the forces in Kuwait to cut them off. The briefer's answer was that they did not have enough fuel trucks for so extensive an operation and the tanks would run out of gas on the shoulder of the encirclement. In addition, they did not know whether the shifting sands of the western desert would support an armored operation. Therefore it was not feasible. I was appalled with the presentation and afterwards I called Cheney to say I thought we had to do better. Cheney shared my concern and sent the planners back to the drawing board.

GEORGE BUSH

The briefing made me realize we had a long way to go before the military was "gung ho" and felt we had the means to accomplish our mission expeditiously, without impossible loss of life. I still had a lot of unanswered questions, especially about how we might eventually initiate war. Considering how long it could take the sanctions to work, I thought responding to a provocation might be the most likely course.

DIARY, OCTOBER 12

Long visit at lunch with Sununu, Scowcroft and Baker. I am trying to figure how we handle the overall Iraq matter. Should we all convene a group at the top—heads of all the countries that are supporting in the Gulf—and make sure we are on the same wavelength when it comes to responding to provocation, or when it comes to using force without provocation? What do we do about declaring war, or getting congressional support? What do we do about the military? . . .

The thing that weighs on me is sending kids into battle and the lives being lost. Maybe it's from my own experience; maybe it's from the petty officer who was cut in half on the deck when I was standing a few feet away; or the number of pilots in my own squadron who were killed. . . . I think my wartime experience does condition me as commander-in-chief and makes me cautious, but it also makes me understand the importance of winning.

BRENT SCOWCROFT

It was my impression that somewhere in early to mid-October, President Bush came to the conclusion, consciously or unconsciously, that he had to do whatever was necessary to liberate Kuwait and the reality was that that meant using force. I began to detect in him a certain calmness. He seemed no longer wrestling with the issue of sending American boys to be killed—that awful decision that only a president can make. I think he had resolved that in his own mind and, therefore, the rest was general strategy and planning, not the terrible human decision he faced. I believe he had concluded that time was not on our side, that, as the problems with Israel and other "erosion" suggested, we could not keep the coalition together indefinitely.

GEORGE BUSH

Brent is probably correct. I don't know exactly when I became resigned to the fact that it would come to war. My diary reflects the frustration and impatience I felt:

DIARY, OCTOBER 17

A day of churning. Brent Scowcroft, my trusted friend, comes for dinner. We talk about how we get things moving, and what we do about the [question of] provocation [to justify the use of force]. The news is saying some members of Congress feel I might use a minor incident to go to war, and they may be right. We must get this over with. The longer it goes, the longer the erosion. I think we can draw the line in the sand— draw it in the sand in American life. There are eight people in the embassy and 40 non-diplomatic personnel, and I don't want them turned over to an uncertain fate.

The continuing Iraqi provocation at our besieged embassy offered a tempting solution to our problems. I was still very worried about it, although I was told the embassy could survive until mid-November. I did not want those people marched off in chains and staked out next to some military target. I feared Iraq would try to humiliate them, and the United States. I was determined to get the people out, but our military told me it could not be done with a raid. I also did not know how the United Nations, or our allies, would react to one.

DIARY, OCTOBER 17

As I look at our allies in the Gulf: the Brits are strong, and the French are French. Mitterrand himself has been great. [Their foreign ministry] is off wanting to compromise and get their own [agenda]. The rest of the Europeans do not want to use force. The GCC countries want us to kick Saddam [out] and do it fast—and that includes Egypt, incidentally. The Syrians probably are supportive. The Turks would be supportive. Then you have Jordan and other countries that are just wringing their hands and saying any use of force would be a total disaster.

I'm not sure where our own country is. But if they saw a clear provocation, and I think that would include unwillingness to permit us to get our [embassy] people out of Kuwait, they would be supportive of knocking the hell out of this guy. We can do it from the air. Our military is waffling and vacillating in terms of what we can do on the ground. They have changed the ground rules, but again, in fairness, the forces on the ground have changed too.

BRENT SCOWCROFT

The question of how we would initiate the use of force, should it come to that, remained. How could we act without it appearing as aggression on the part of the coalition? The President was coming to think that we should act once there was provocation—but could we do so without it? In the minds of some, obtaining a UN resolution, as we did to authorize the use of force to back the blockade, had set a precedent, suggesting we would need a similar resolution to use force to implement the original UN Resolution 660.

In addition, we had to set out our war aims if it came to military action. The over-all strategic political objectives were set out in the UN resolutions: principally, to eject Iraq from Kuwait and restore the Kuwaiti government. But beyond this were strategic military objectives for the coalition forces, and our own war aims—what outcome the United States wanted to see. These went hand-in-hand. Foremost among these was to reduce the Iraqi military as much as possible, starting with an air campaign. From a military standpoint, this would "soften them up" before any coalition ground campaign to push the Iraqi army out and liberate Kuwait. Destroying as much of the Iraqi military machine as possible would have other benefits as well. One was to reduce the threat Saddam posed to his neighbors. The trick here was to damage his offensive capability without weakening Iraq to the point that a vacuum was created, and destroying the balance between Iraq and Iran, further destabilizing the region for years. I asked the Deputies Committee to look into these questions and draw up some recommendations for our aims.

GEORGE BUSH

Margaret Thatcher was impatient to plan an early military action based on the existing resolutions. She rejected relying on provocation, which she thought would cause us to strike before we were ready. It was better to go to war on our terms. At the end of September, we had dinner with Brent and Charles Powell, his British counterpart, at the Waldorf-Astoria in New York during the opening of the UN General Assembly. Margaret and I talked about the coalition objectives, what planning the campaign would entail, and how to reduce the future threat from Iraq in the area. She argued that once we had the war planning sorted out we could worry about the politics and dates, and she remained leery of going back to the UN. "We risk amendments . . . ," she said. "I don't think we need an extra reason to go."

I told her I thought there would be a provocation, perhaps a terrorist act, before all our forces were in place and that we would have no choice but to respond—and we could then launch a huge air strike with everything we had. Because of the political pressure to let sanctions work, I did not want to name a date yet to carry out any planned action. Margaret reminded me that a military option would be there only a short time. We had to move during the cool months—November to March. If we waited for sanctions to work it would take us to the following November. She argued that we should not allow ourselves to be provoked. While she acknowledged that we would have to make some military response if Saddam did provoke us, she urged that we not let it prematurely trigger our whole plan.

At this point, Jim Baker arrived and I asked him to talk about our UN options when it came to force. "Unless we can show we have tried to stay within the international consensus, we risk losing public support for what we have to do," he reminded us. "We have to divide provocation from non-provocation. I think it is time to move [at the UN]; it is important to have consulted." Margaret was not persuaded, and insisted that if we went for a resolution we would raise doubts as to whether we could go forward without one. I still thought we could simply devastate Iraq's military and strategic facilities with all our air power after a provocation. But Brent warned that we might eventually have to follow through with ground troops to liberate Kuwait, and if we pounded from the air too soon, before our forces were ready, there could be public pressure to stop all fighting and turn opinion against ever launching a ground campaign. That might leave Saddam in Kuwait—and us without a military option.

BRENT SCOWCROFT

After that conversation, the British and US national security and military teams consulted in early October. Cheney saw Thatcher, and Charles Powell and I were in close touch. I sent Charles materials outlining the problem of the time frame for war. We would not be militarily prepared for attack probably until early December, assuming we continued our buildup. The window for military action would close soon after that. Late February ushered in a period of frequent bad weather in the region, and then came the Muslim holy month of Ramadan (March 17–April 14), followed by the Haj pilgrimage to the holy sites in Saudi Arabia. While there were various views about the acceptability of conflict during Ramadan, we did not consider it wise to test Arab tolerance. Following the Haj, the heat would become so oppressive that military operations would be all but precluded. These factors together led us to concentrate on a period no later than January or February.

GEORGE BUSH

On October 18, in the midst of the fallout from the Temple Mount incident, Margaret and I exchanged cables and a phone call about what to do next. In her first message, she said she was deeply concerned about how much longer we could hold the coalition together. She was convinced that we had to act by mid-February. "The Iraqis are clearly trying to avoid a provocation," she cabled. ". . . My own view is increasingly that once we have the necessary forces in place, we should go sooner rather than later. Otherwise we risk losing the support of Arab governments who will not understand delay and come to question our resolve. We shall also be confronted with further peace proposals, further incidents in the occupied territories and growing strain on the coalition against Iraq. Saddam Hussein has got to lose and be seen to lose."

I also sent her a cable in preparation for our phone conversation. I agreed we did not have the luxury of waiting for sanctions to work, but I believed it was better politically to work through the UN rather than act on our own. I was still thinking in terms of responding to provocation to give us the necessary cause. I told her I was figuring out how to free our embassy, and that I thought we should assert our right to protect our diplomatic missions. I outlined a plan in which we would attach a clause to a forthcoming UN resolution on Iraqi compensation for damages it caused saying we had the right to reprovision our embassies. This might be a flashpoint for military action if Iraq resisted.

While we certainly had the authority under the existing resolutions to act, there were political advantages to having a resolution which spelled out our right to take action, as well as potential risks to going to war without one. I assured her I would go back to the UN only if advance consultation revealed we could get what we wanted quickly and without unacceptable constraints. I added that we were thinking about having the resolution call for the secretary general to use his position to set a dead-line for Saddam to comply with existing resolutions. He would be given thirty or forty-five days to get Iraq out; if not, members would have a green light to use force. "I see two advantages to this approach: diplo-macy is only likely to work if Saddam sees we are serious," I said. "But if Saddam is not completely out and we must fight, I want to take away from people the argument that we did not give diplomacy a chance."

In our phone conversation, Margaret continued to oppose the idea of going back to the UN for anything and did not like the idea of going after our embassies in Kuwait because it put too many people at risk. There were still people in hiding and the missions in Baghdad to protect. For me, an Iraqi response, such as shooting down the helicopters we would use to rescue our diplomats, would be sufficient provocation to start an air war. Margaret countered that Iraq's brutality gave us general cause to go when we were ready. "We don't need more cause. Our embassies are there to protect our people. If we leave, aren't we deserting our people? But we need no more triggers for military action, and if you send helos in they could be shot down—they are sitting ducks."

"Our embassy must close anyway," I insisted. "We can't service our people inside. We are ready for the air campaign. We don't have unlim-ited time. This appeals to us to act on a moral basis and to act together." Margaret said she would think about it. "Your point is to do as much as we can." I said it was. "We can't get them all [the hostages]—especially those chained to factories, etc. Our people will be starved out soon. Why wait for that? If he shoots down a helo, we clobber him."

Later that evening Margaret cabled again. She could not support our proposal to amend the resolution on compensation with a "right to reprovision" our embassies. She thought Saddam Hussein would figure out what we were up to, and not only would we lose the advantage of surprise, we would also give him time to prepare retaliation against the other hostages. Besides, she did not think we were prepared to rescue the embassies. Much of the supplies and equipment had yet to arrive, and British forces were still disembarking over the next week or so, leaving them highly vulnerable.

We had not sorted out the grounds on which we would use force—or when. I was probably pretty impatient. I still staunchly believed that a provocation was all we needed, and that our overwhelming air power would smash Saddam's military threat and wipe out Iraq's nuclear, chemical, and biological weapons facilities. But Brent's point was good—that we had to be sure we could continue to get international political support to go in on the ground to kick Saddam out of Kuwait. Starting up the air campaign too early could cause us problems. There was still a lot of military, and political, preparation ahead of us before I would feel comfortable that I had the answers I needed.

CHAPTER 16

Holding the Course

GEORGE BUSH

After the budget battles of the preceding weeks, it was almost a relief when Congress adjourned on October 28 to prepare for the November elections. In the last two weeks of the campaign, I went around the country stumping for Republican candidates and speaking at fund-raisers. I wanted to keep the crisis out of the domestic political process as much as possible, and I made a point of emphasizing the bipartisan support for our efforts in the Gulf. Over and over I kept repeating Senator Arthur Vandenberg's adage that partisanship should stop at the water's edge. Yet there were occasional accusations by journalists such as David Hoffman that I was turning up the heat on Saddam to coincide with the elections to call people's attention away from the recent budget fight. I found this notion particularly infuriating. It implied that I was willing to play politics with the lives of our sons and daughters in the Gulf.

I got into hot water over my strong statements regarding the hostages, and these were the days of my frequent comparisons of Saddam to Hitler. I spoke out about our besieged embassy in Kuwait to make people understand that there was a real threat to decency and serious challenges to international law in the way the hostages were being treated. This led many to speculate that I would use them as a pretext for action. At one fund-raiser I said "I'd had it" with what was happening to our embassy, which was being starved. "And what am I going to do about it?" I asked. "Let's just wait and see. Because I have had it with that kind of treatment of Americans." I was angry because people had been so caught up in the budget mess they seemed to have forgotten about how bad the situation was. But I was not trying to prepare people for military action, only to remind them of what was occurring.

BRENT SCOWCROFT

It was clear that the President was becoming emotionally involved in the treatment of Kuwait. He was deeply sincere, but the impact of some of his rhetoric seemed a bit counterproductive, or at least it inflamed the press—who began to charge that the President was turning the crisis into a personal vendetta against Saddam—which amounted to the same thing. It was at this time that Bob Gates and I began the practice of one of us traveling with him on campaign trips. The primary purpose was to have someone at his side were a sudden crisis to arise in the Gulf or elsewhere. But, secondarily, it was to remind him about the occasional flights of rhetoric, which were getting him into trouble.

The adjournment of Congress on October 28 created a new problem. How were we to consult with and involve it when it recessed *sine die* and the new Congress was not due back until January 3? Congress had appointed a special eighteen-member team to consult with us. House Speaker Tom Foley and Senate majority leader George Mitchell asked for a special bipartisan leadership meeting to discuss the Gulf situation, because of the possibility of new developments—including military action—while Congress was out. We met the morning of October 30.

As we settled down to talk, Foley handed the President a letter signed by eighty-one Democratic members.* It was couched as an "expression of concern" about the role of Congress in the event of war in the Gulf. They asked him to select members from among them, in addition to the leadership, when consulting on developments. In it they outlined their worries:

> Recent reports and briefings indicate that the United States has shifted from a defensive to an offensive posture and that war may be imminent. We believe that the consequences would be catastrophic—resulting in the massive loss of lives, including 10,000–50,000 Americans. This could only be described as war. Under the US Constitution, only the Congress can declare war.
>
> We are emphatically opposed to any offensive military action. We believe that the UN-sponsored embargo must be given every opportunity to work and that all multinational, non-military means of resolving the situation must be pursued. If, after all peaceful means of resolving the conflict are exhausted, and the President believes that military action is warranted, then . . . he must seek a declaration of war from the Congress. . . . We firmly believe that consulting with this group in no way

*On October 9 a similar one had been signed by thirty-three Democrats.

replaces the President's constitutional obligation to seek a declaration of war before undertaking any offensive military action. We demand that the Administration not undertake any offensive military action without the full deliberation and declaration required by the Constitution.*

The President told the group that we were approaching a key juncture. Although compliance with sanctions was high, they did not seem to be having much effect; nor had Baghdad shown interest in doing anything other than weakening and dividing the coalition. Because the Iraqis had nearly doubled their forces in and near Kuwait since we began our own deployment, to make sure our military option remained credible we were also moving toward further augmentation of our forces in the Gulf and pushing our allies to do the same.

Foley outlined the fear in Congress that we were switching policies. "The reason for the extraordinary support you've received has been because you've used UN sanctions and an embargo," he said. "If there is any change, in the absence of severe provocation, support would change dramatically. The country and Congress are not prepared for offensive action." Mitchell agreed. He asked Baker about the basis for charges of mistreatment of the hostages, which Baker had mentioned in a speech the day before. He had told of people being used as human shields, forced to sleep on concrete, vermin-ridden floors with little food. The question reflected the worry among many present that we might use this situation as a provocation to act. Baker explained the details of what we had been hearing through released French citizens and others.

Mitchell and William Cohen countered that their briefings had indicated there were no worsening problems for the hostages. If it was otherwise, then they and the public were not being adequately informed. Cohen insisted that the hostages could not be the basis for offensive action. "You'll kill the individuals whose pain and suffering you are highlighting," he argued. Patrick Leahy also urged that we let sanctions do the job. "Patience is preferable to war," he said. "There is no consensus to attack in Kuwait." David Obey agreed. John Warner worried about the long-term effect of war in the region, especially on the Middle East peace process. Claiborne Pell wanted no use of force without Congress, and then only under a UN umbrella.

"I agree with my colleagues about the public mood," said Les Aspin.

---

*We decided not to respond to the specifics of the letter, and in early December Scowcroft wrote back saying that we would continue to consult with Congress.

"There's no question [the country has] moved away from a more hawk-ish position within the last month. The budget battle pushed Iraq off the front page. The crisis lacks freshness and outrage. The public is less confident that the government knows what it is doing." People were focused on domestic issues. If there was provocation, such as hostages killed, it would be different. Support for our objectives was still there, but unless Saddam played into our hands we should look to the UN.

Jack Murtha disagreed. "I don't think you have any alternative to the use of force," he said. "We forget Kuwait was invaded and oil prices have gone up. The longer this goes, the more the public will resent the use of force. I don't think we have the luxury of time. . . . We're seeing already exaggerated media attention on a few demonstrators. It will get more and more difficult for you to make decisions."

"You shouldn't make decisions based on public opinion," advised Bob Kasten. "The real question is whether time is on our side or the side of Saddam." The President pointed out that the allies were not in agree-ment as to how time would affect matters and, while he concurred that we could not make decisions on the basis of public opinion, it was important to have the support of the American people.

"It's been less than three months from the invasion," objected Mitchell. "It's less than two months since sanctions were put in place. No one expected them to work in a week. The case has not been made that sanc-tions have failed." Aspin pointed out that there was a difference between the sanctions technically working and having the political effect on Sad-dam we wanted them to. He could simply ride out their impact. "How long do you go before you have to decide the embargo is not politically working?" he asked. "Use of force questions will come up before then." The military decision time frame was between November 1 and December 1, while most of the public seemed to think the sanctions should be in place at least nine months before we took military action. The decision for force might come earlier than we thought.

"I want to plead with you personally before you take the country into war," said Foley. "Unless there is gross provocation, you won't have pub-lic support."

BRENT SCOWCROFT

That afternoon, just before four o'clock, with that unhelpful meet-ing as background, our core group met in the Situation Room to discuss whether to stick to sanctions or turn to force by a specific date if Iraq did not leave Kuwait and free the hostages.

My own view on the matter was laid out for the President in a memo to prepare him for the meeting:

> Our basic objective at this point ought to be to regain momentum and take the initiative away from Saddam. This requires a two-track strategy: on the diplomatic side, a renewed push for full and unconditional Iraqi withdrawal as called for by Security Council Resolution 660; on the military side, accelerated preparations that provide a real alternative should diplomacy fail. One way of implementing this strategy would be giving an ultimatum to Saddam demanding that he withdraw fully from Kuwait (and release all hostages while permitting the legitimate government to return) by a certain date. I would argue that the date certain should be around the end of the year, some five months since the attack and the imposition of sanctions.

I pointed out that this strategy could work only if we were backed at least by the regional members of the coalition. I thought we ought to tell them that the ideal approach was to get a new Security Council resolution authorizing all necessary means to achieve these objectives, but that we would be prepared to assemble an informal multinational effort (outside the UN) for the same purpose. Either way, we would aim to announce an ultimatum around the end of November to allow time for additional military preparations and to take care of the argument that we were not giving diplomacy a chance. "It would also allow us to take advantage of our Security Council presidency* should the UN route prove possible. It would also bring matters to a head before Iraq had much more time to work on its biological and nuclear weapons capability, dig in completely in Kuwait, or before we found ourselves heading into poor weather, Ramadan and the Hajj."

> I believe this general approach is preferable to sticking to sanctions. It does not appear that sanctions alone will accomplish what we seek in the foreseeable future. Meanwhile, the hostages remain hostage and Kuwait is being destroyed and resettled by others. The coalition shows signs of fraying at the edges because of disagreements over such issues as the use of force, the need for full Iraqi withdrawal, the restoration of the Sabahs, and the Palestinian issue.

Baker was already scheduled for a trip to touch base with our principal coalition partners to determine just how deep and broad was support for confronting Saddam. I suggested that he put three issues to them:

---

*The Security Council presidency rotates each month. The United States held it for November 1990.

Whether they supported the use of force, and test the waters for the possibility of a UN resolution authorizing it; what they would do if Israel responded militarily to an Iraqi attack (which would test the coalition); finally, whether they would allow our forces to strike at Iraq from their territory and were prepared to accept command arrangements that would place operational authority of their forces in US military hands. Jim's trip would be followed by talks with the Soviets and the other Security Council members.

The President opened the core group meeting. "The time has come to determine whether we continue to place most of our eggs in the sanctions basket, which would take a good deal more time as things now stand but would possibly avoid the risks and cost of war, or whether we raise the pressure on Saddam by pressing ahead on both the military and diplomatic tracks," he said. "I realize that if we do give Saddam some kind of a deadline, we are in effect committing ourselves to war. I also realize that by making such a threat and by preparing for it, we may also increase the odds that Saddam agrees to a peaceful solution. Indeed it may be necessary to push matters to the brink of war if we are to convince Saddam to compromise. But either way, I just want everyone to know that my commitment to seeing Saddam leave Kuwait unconditionally remains firm. . . ."

"The question is, are we at a break point in the situation in the Gulf?" said Scowcroft. "It seems to me we have three basic choices. First, we can ride out the sanctions and see what happens; second, we could plan on the use of force, which would involve aiming for a specific date, how we deal with the public, and whether we go for a UN Security Council authorization, developing our military strategy and tactics, and choosing a preferred date; and third, how do we react to a provocation or do we create a provocation that would permit military action—for example, our embassy in Kuwait City. Other questions involve congressional consultations and what we will need from our partners. In this connection we need to know whether they are willing to go with us, whether we need a provocation, whether they will go with or without the UN Security Council, whether we will have adequate command and control, whether they will provide forces . . . and who else we should consult with. We also need to think about how to handle Israel. How would the US respond to an attack [there]? Finally, if Saddam Hussein backs off now, do we require more [than the UN resolutions specify]?"

The President asked the basic question: were the sanctions working, and would they get the job done? "The question is: How long will it take to be able to say that we have given sanctions a chance?" replied Baker. "I believe sanctions will not get him out in a time frame we can accept."

"February to March," Cheney guessed. He summarized the military options. "We have a defensive force in place now," he began. "We can do an air campaign now, we can do a feint to the west now. But for a real offensive, we will need significant additional forces—three more divisions. So I recommend that we add to the force, if you want us to do anything other than option one [air attacks on strategic targets in Iraq]." Powell added that the planning was well advanced for more forces. "We could have an additional hundred and forty thousand people in place by 15 January," he said. "I also intend to send whatever else I can get in. We are talking about a major war against Iraq. I want to send in five or six carrier task forces."

"Since August there has been a big Iraqi build-up, and they have taken a lot of defensive measures," added Cheney. "They can do even more in the next two and a half months. . . ."

"Mr. President, you need to understand that if we go through this build-up, we will not be able to have a rotation policy of bringing up troops and relieving them," warned Powell. "We are at a fork in the road. We either have to rotate or build up." Scowcroft asked if we could implement parts of the plan, including a feint to the west, before February 1 and then move in the rest of our forces.

"Yes, we can do the air campaign and then just wait," answered Powell. "My view is that if you're going to do it, we should do it all and do it fast. Let's not string it out."

"An ultimatum, plus major force build-up, would make it clear we're serious," suggested Baker. "But I guess we shouldn't call it an ultimatum."

"Jim must persuade our coalition partners to lean into your [the President's] plan," said Scowcroft. The President asked what decisions needed to be made. "The troop augmentation and scenarios for Baker's trip," answered Scowcroft.

"I hope you will say yes to the troops, but let's hold on to such a decision until the Saudis say yes," said Baker to the President. "I will be in Saudi Arabia on Saturday [November 3]. Assuming there is no provocation, we should not use the forces before February 1. This would not be irrevocable, and we would get authorization to act."

"You mean we would forgo acting if we are not provoked or if we do not have congressional support?" asked Cheney. "Those are major decisions. We are giving up a lot. Finally, we are giving up a lot if we issue some sort of ultimatum. Saddam Hussein will then be able to improve his defenses. There will be erosion of support at home, and who knows what intervening events."

"If there is to be no UN action authorizing it, we will know this in November," said Baker. "The only time constraint is if we get a UN resolution."

"It is a major call to wait till February 1," warned Cheney.

"You want an earlier date, January 1?" the President asked.

"The forces won't be in place before 15 January," Powell reminded us. Baker suggested we think in terms of mid-January. "Our chances at the UN improve the longer the sanctions have a chance to work," he said.

"Defense should go ahead and move its forces," said the President, with a nod to Cheney and Powell. "What happens if Saddam Hussein bombs Israel tomorrow?"

"We attack first [in Kuwait]," answered Scowcroft.

"We will announce the troop build-up on Monday [November 5] if the Saudis say yes," said Baker.

"We will tell the press that our forces are continuing to move, but there have been no decisions," said President Bush. "Let's get questions written down for Baker, and the press line will be that troops continue to go in, and we're reviewing the situation."

BRENT SCOWCROFT

The decision taken that day was not that we would use force, only that we would continue a build-up for an offensive option. Powell simply needed to know whether President Bush planned to keep deploying troops. The existing pipeline was full. If we were going to stop at 250,000, which was our present commitment, the military had to know immediately so they could turn off the spigot. If Powell turned it off, and the President then decided to add more troops, it would tear the system apart. The President had already stated publicly that we would deploy sufficient forces to defend Saudi Arabia and keep our options open. To me, "keeping our options open" meant that if we wanted to move north we would have enough forces to do so. Saddam was increasing his forces in Kuwait by at least 200,000.

The timing of the decision to reinforce the troops was determined by practical military considerations, but the timing of the announcement of the increase was driven by political ones. The political experts wanted to delay announcement until after the congressional elections on November 6. I did not think it was necessary to say anything other than that the President was keeping his existing options open in the face of a continued Iraqi build-up. Cheney wanted to announce the decision immediately. As he pointed out, it would be too large a force to rotate, and too large an augmentation to keep quiet about. If he was to keep the pipeline open, Powell could not wait until after the election to give the order. He ordered the deployment and the troops and equipment began to move. This immediately triggered press stories before we had briefed Congress, which we planned to do the day after the elections.

We made the announcement on November 8, while Baker was overseas. He was furious when, in Moscow, the day before his meetings with Shevardnadze and Gorbachev, he heard the news. He launched into Haass, who was the NSC liaison on the trip, saying it was politically crazy. He fumed that it made it look as if we had already made up our minds to go on the offensive at a time when he was trying to drum up diplomatic support for our resolution. His anger surprised me, because he himself had proposed an announcement on November 5. Jim called the President and urged him to telephone the congressional leadership, as well as schedule a briefing for those who returned to Washington after the elections.

All in all, it was not a smooth operation, and the way it was carried out greatly exacerbated the negative reaction by many in the Congress.

GEORGE BUSH

The news of the troop increase, particularly its size, whipped up a new outcry in Congress and furious attacks on me that I had changed policy and decided to go to war without consultation. The chorus was still "let sanctions work." The pundits and congressmen on the morning talk shows and the op-eds averred that I was wrecking my presidency. Senator Pat Moynihan, chairman of the Senate subcommittee that watched the Gulf, a former UN ambassador, and a friend, was particularly angry and critical. In a TV interview on November 12 he argued that not only did we have to have UN and congressional approval to use force but also that we refused to consult and did not want a consensus. He did not feel Kuwait, and particularly its leadership, deserved to be liberated, depicting them as "those Kuwaitis who have taken over Sheraton Hotel in Taif and they're sitting there in their white robes and drinking coffee and urging us on to war." We later exchanged letters on some of these points, but it seemed to me he never thought what Iraq had done to Kuwait was worth fighting for, or even that Kuwait had the same rights to UN protection as other states. He called its existence an accident of history with boundaries drawn by the bureaucrats of the colonial powers.

DIARY, NOVEMBER 10

I telephoned Brent to say we've got to get our system of consultation [with Congress] down even if it's a perfunctory phone call from some staffer to members of Congress over the next two months. I'm ticked at Bill Broomfield saying we haven't consulted enough, pleased that Foley said that we consulted more than any other previous president. But we've got to prepare the Congress for any action that I might have to take and the more phone calls we make under the heading of consultation the better it is. I also suggested to Brent that we may want to show we are going the extra mile for peace. After we've announced we were sending these forces over, Aziz announces we ought to send diplomats. . . . One of the things I am thinking about is having a challenge—an invitation to Saddam Hussein to send [his foreign minister] here and then maybe having a meeting at the White House . . . just tell him that there is no room for compromise; that we are deadly serious; that we might well have to resort to military force. . . .

BRENT SCOWCROFT

Debate on the use of force was intensifying, but it would be inaccurate to say it developed into a struggle with Congress over policy in the Gulf as a whole. The issues were narrower; there was general agreement about the need to resist Iraqi aggression. Congress itself had passed resolutions soundly condemning the invasion and supporting the Administration's over-all policy up to this point. But the increase in troops brought subsidiary issues to the fore. Should force be used or should sanctions continue to be the main weapon against Saddam? And, if military action was to be considered, who—the president or the Congress—had the authority to order it? Congress itself was divided on these matters, and not only along party lines (although the Democratic leadership was nearly unanimous against the use of force).

The debate arose from the long-standing legal and constitutional scuffle over presidential prerogatives in foreign policy and Congress's power to declare war. This was a tension built into the structure of our system. While the Constitution provides that only Congress may declare war, it does not withhold authority from the president to use force as a tool of foreign policy. The War Powers Resolution, enacted in 1973 over a presidential veto, attempts to clarify responsibilities in two ways. It directs that the president "shall consult with Congress before introducing United States Armed Forces into hostilities or into situations where imminent involvement in hostilities is clearly indicated by the circumstances. . . ." Second, it requires that the president terminate conflict in sixty days and bring the troops home unless Congress specifically authorizes continuation of action. Every president has opposed this resolution as unconstitutional and many in Congress itself have been dissatisfied with it, some claiming that it was unworkable and some that it gave the president unlimited powers for those sixty days. Although we did explore options for the involvement of Congress, we never seriously contemplated invoking the War Powers Resolution.

We were confident that the Constitution was on our side when it came to the president's discretion to use force if necessary: If we sought congressional involvement, it would not be authority we were after, but support. In mid-November, after the election and our announcement of the troop augmentation, Senator Dick Lugar suggested that the President call what was now a lame-duck Congress back into session to take up a resolution specifically to back the use of force against Iraq. He believed this would settle the matter with a bipartisan show of support. While it seemed a good idea on paper, it was far from certain that the votes were there. If the resolution failed, it would undermine not only our credibility and our political leadership of the coalition, but also the international efforts to reverse the invasion.

There were other sources of discomfort within Congress, such as a lingering fear of a drawn-out foreign military entanglement—remnants of the "Vietnam syndrome." For some, there was also an honest difference of opinion, stemming from a different reading of what was at stake or how to handle Saddam, or from deeply felt abhorrence of the use of military force in (almost) any circumstance. At the same time, there was a strong dose of raw partisanship and unhealed wounds from the recent budget battle.

We were also running into increasing difficulty making our point understood about what was at stake. One criticism was that we had failed to explain why our troops were in the Saudi desert, why the United States had to lead the response to Iraq's aggression. Even supporters would tell the President that public backing would be there, but that we had to state our case more clearly. Too much of the reasoning, they argued, seemed abstract. In retrospect, I think our deepening involvement in the Gulf crisis was an important factor in the rise of resistance to our response. It was relatively easy to understand the need to defend Saudi Arabia and even to impose a quarantine on Iraq. The early explanations, however, were not sufficiently persuasive when it came to convincing critics of the need to build up our force rather than simply letting sanctions do the job.

GEORGE BUSH

I think part of our problem was that so much was happening away from public view, and few people outside the top echelon in the White House were paying attention to what was going on in Kuwait. Another obstacle was the perception of division within the Administration over our objectives. For example, at a press conference in Bermuda on November 13, Jim Baker attempted to explain the economic stakes of Iraq's invasion for the U.S. by saying the issue was "jobs, jobs, jobs." Immediately, the press jumped all over him, asking if that wasn't a different explanation of our stakes from my own. In fact, Jim was simply echoing what we had been saying about the economic impact of Saddam's control of so much of the world's oil supply—a point I myself had made in a speech in mid-August. There was no inconsistency.

BRENT SCOWCROFT

I thought Baker had made a mistake. I knew what he was trying to say, but the way he put it sounded like the whole dispute was simply commercialism. The press thought so as well, which was why they jumped on him. The import of his speech was that we couldn't possibly allow Iraq a stranglehold over the oil supplies of the industrialized democracies, but the way he phrased it—in exasperation, as I recall—demeaned that entire idea. It had to be phrased in terms of vital interests, which was the fact, and not commercialism, even if that was American jobs.

Baker's comment was an expression of the frustration we all felt from this apparent inability to communicate our view of the stakes involved. Our lack of success was certainly not due to a failure to speak out. I think there were two factors. The first was the implicit rejection by many in the opposition of our argument that national interests demanded increasingly heavy involvement. Explicitly rejecting this argument might not have been politic, but the same objective could be served simply by saying that the Administration had not adequately made its case. The second factor stemmed from the first. We tended to react to complaints by expanding the list of US interests, leading to charges that each of the principals had his own reasons and we really didn't have our act together. In a way, it was a tempest in a teapot, but it preoccupied us and our reaction to the charges tended to make the problem worse.

The core of our argument rested on long-held security and economic interests: preserving the balance of power in the Gulf, opposing unprovoked international aggression, and ensuring that no hostile regional power could hold hostage much of the world's oil supply. President Bush, appalled by the evidence of Iraqi atrocities, added the Hitler, holocaust, and morality arguments, and, as noted, Baker expanded the grounds to include American jobs.

As the crisis developed during the fall of 1990, another objective began to take form. It was rarely articulated to the public in specific terms, but it grew in importance to us as we developed our response to the invasion. In the first days of the crisis we had started self-consciously to view our actions as setting a precedent for the approaching post–Cold War world. Soviet cooperation in condemning the attack provided the initial impetus for this line of thinking, inasmuch as it opened the way for the Security Council to operate as its founders had envisioned. That, in turn, had led directly to our August discussions of a "new world order." From that point forward, we tried to operate in a manner that would help establish a pattern for the future. Our foundation was the premise that the United States henceforth would be obligated to lead the world community to an unprecedented degree, as demonstrated by the Iraqi crisis, and that we should attempt to pursue our national interests, wherever possible, within a framework of concert with our friends and the international community. This objective, however, remained distinctly secondary in our public explications of our purposes in the Gulf crisis.

On November 14, we met again with the bipartisan leadership to try to calm the outcry over the troop increase, and remind them of the stakes. The decision to augment our forces was not a decision to go to war, President Bush told them. "We have not crossed any Rubicon or point of no return . . ." He knew that many of them believed we should continue to give sanctions more time to work. We were, but the passage of time had economic and military costs. Saddam was reinforcing and digging in, as well as doing everything possible to improve his weapons of mass destruction. "In short, while we are waiting for sanctions to work, he's not standing still," he said. "And, of course, it's not possible to conclude as yet that sanctions will work as intended. . . ."

He would make every effort to consult closely with the Congress. "Consultations are a two-way street," he added. "I think it is only fair that I get to hear your specific ideas in private about the tough choices we face before people go out and take public stances. I'm entitled as President to your advice. Not what we can't do but what we can do." Public statements since the announcement of the increase were leading Saddam to conclude that we were divided and lacked staying power. "This in turn only weakens the prospects for the peaceful settlement we all want. I know public debate is a must, but I ask you not to lose sight of the impact of what you say." He read some clippings. "This is the wrong signal to send at this time."

Foley said that the President's decision to send additional troops had a major impact in the country. "It's believed that we now have sufficient force to conduct offensive operations, but there's no consensus to use those forces," he said. ". . . There's great concern if a decision is made unilaterally by you as President." He wanted a UN resolution on the issue and wanted it presented to Congress. "I caution patience—even if it takes a year or a year and a half. The American people support the current course and believe the coalition will stay together."

Mitchell argued that just two weeks earlier the President had said sanctions should be allowed to work. He demanded a report on their effect and prospects. He shared Foley's view that the President had to come to Congress for further authorization but did not believe it was time to do so. Cheney described for him the effects of the sanctions: We were confident we had shut off the flow of oil except a small amount out of Jordan. There was some smuggling of food through Jordan and Iran. "There are numerous efforts underway to try to circumvent sanctions," he said. "Some will probably succeed. It's anybody's guess if sanctions will work. The estimates are all over the lot. He hasn't blinked yet."

"We need to have frank talk about patience and how long we need to let sanctions work," said Bob Michel. Baker, back from his trip to our coalition partners, warned that time was not on our side. "We won't be able to sustain the coalition over a year, year and a half." Dick Gephardt countered that we would pay a high political price down the road if we used force. He preferred to wait the eighteen months or longer. "I urge you to keep working to keep the coalition together. I urge you to use the UN," he said. If it came to force, he wanted congressional consent.

Bob Dole was concerned about how Congress was handling consultations. "How do we have open debate without sending the wrong signal to Saddam?" he asked. "If we in Congress want to participate, then we owe our boys and the President support for policy."

"Three things have caused concern," said Les Aspin. "The announced increase in deployments is much bigger than we anticipated. Also, you announced no rotation policy. There were no assurances that Congress gets a vote if we use forces offensively. You're closing out options. It says to us, 'Next spring there will be a war.' It's created a climate that indicated decisions had been made. We need to have a consultation process as a decision is being made."

"The build-up and having no rotation is critical," agreed Sam Nunn. "It's reduced our flexibility and our options. I don't believe you frighten Saddam Hussein by building up ground forces. Air power is the way to go. I'm very concerned about sustaining four hundred thousand troops and how we deal with other crises if they arise."

"Public feeling is intensifying in opposition to your policy," insisted Claiborne Pell. Jesse Helms retorted that any erosion of support was being orchestrated—the President had consulted all along the way.

"I've supported everything you've done here to date," said David Boren. "I suggest you go back to troop rotation . . . Put talk of a special session to rest here and now. It would cause only more divisive debate, more constraint of presidential authority, and nothing would be worse. Go for closed session hearings." He argued that if there was any use of force it should only be targeting Saddam's nuclear, biological, and chemical capabilities with air strikes.

"Congress are supposed to be leaders," said Henry Hyde. "We should be carrying the message to the people." He thought a UN resolution would help Congress pass a ratifying resolution.

Jack Murtha reminded his colleagues that we had to have credible forces available. "I don't think we have a year," he said. "We need to make decisions based on weather and opportunity. You can't hold Congress, American people, and coalition together that long. Saddam Hussein can be toppled. . . . If we wait much longer, he'll have a nuclear device."

BRENT SCOWCROFT

This meeting made graphically clear what we were up against. There were stalwarts in the leadership—such as Dole, Murtha, Hyde, and Warner—but, by and large, there was no appetite for forceful action. Bitterness over our troop augmentation was still manifest. Judging from the comments around the table, it seemed to me the balance was no better than 30 percent willing to support force, at least in the near term. It was a chilling prospect. Hyde mentioned that a UN resolution would bolster our case, but it appeared dubious that even that would be sufficient to turn the tide. To go for a congressional resolution of support against such odds was daunting, to say the least. If we lost, we would be in an inordinately difficult position. A negative vote would dishearten the coalition, encourage Saddam Hussein, and create a domestic firestorm if we were to ignore it. And, should we seek UN approval, we would certainly put ourselves in a position where it would be almost impossible politically not to go to Congress. We had an unpalatable set of alternatives.

Baker's early November trip to drum up support for a UN resolution, as well to as sound out our coalition partners, was most encouraging. The ailing Emir Khalifah of Bahrain gave his backing, as did the Emir of Kuwait. King Fahd urged us to move soon and reassured us that Saudi

Arabia would do nothing if Iraq and Israel exchanged blows. Hosni Mubarak was equally positive, but uncertain whether he could further reinforce his troops. He was worried about domestic reaction to the prospect of fighting another Arab state and hesitated when we asked him to permit US aircraft to operate from Egypt.

In Ankara, Turgut Ozal still hoped that sanctions would do the trick, but he wanted a further UN resolution and agreed to think about sending an armored brigade to Saudi Arabia. Like Mubarak, he also hesitated when we asked to operate US aircraft from Turkish bases. While he had no problems with stationing planes there, he was uneasy about launching air strikes from them. This question of the use of Turkish bases, as well as flying over their airspace to attack Iraq, would be a sensitive issue in the coming months.

Baker described his discussions in Moscow as "extraordinary." Shevardnadze came close to the US position that a resolution should be passed in November and become operative six weeks later. He got Gorbachev on the phone and pushed him hard to go along with our general approach. He even went out to Gorbachev's dacha ahead of Baker to lobby him further. "Gorbachev is close but not there yet," cabled Baker. Gorbachev and Shevardnadze seemed to be acting on certain assumptions: first, that the United States and Soviet Union must stay together on the Gulf; second, that Saddam must unmistakably fail. They emphasized that his aggression must be reversed. Any hope for a new peaceful era depended on it, and on denying him victory—no matter how small. Both men, however, felt sanctions might yet work and that it was premature to play our last diplomatic card—one that left us no choice but to use force if it failed. While prepared to pursue more steps to build the pressure on Saddam, Gorbachev and Shevardnadze were, nevertheless, still ambivalent about a UN resolution specifically authorizing force, and said it was still too early. The Soviets wanted to look at all the options and would get back to us before the Paris CSCE meeting, scheduled for November 19, which the President had promised to attend once we had a CFE treaty to sign. Baker believed that, in the end, they would go along.

GEORGE BUSH

In a letter, Gorbachev proposed that we use two resolutions instead of just one. The first would warn Saddam that if he failed to withdraw by a certain time there would be a second resolution to authorize the use of all necessary means to fully implement the UN resolutions. In my reply, I agreed we had to demonstrate that we had explored fully our non-military options and that we had given sanctions a fair chance to work, but I felt the single resolution we were contemplating would do just that. While it would be passed that month, it would become operative only around the first of the year, having given sanctions five months to work. We also had the ten other resolutions to point to, all of which Saddam had rejected.

I thought a single resolution with a deadline offered some prospect of moving Saddam. "I am firmly convinced that the only way to achieve our end is, ironically, to convince Saddam that military action is imminent." I also pointed out that because the US would be in the chair of the Council only in November we ran the risk of getting just the first of Gorbachev's resolutions, not the second. We could be tied in procedural knots by our successors in the chair—Yemen, Zaire, and Zimbabwe. Furthermore, Saddam might simply pull back partially and try to manipulate world opinion to make sure we couldn't get a second resolution—or might believe that he could draw out the process long enough to break the coalition.

The upcoming trip to Paris for the CSCE meeting would give me a chance to sell Gorbachev on our resolution and see our Western European allies at a critical time. The Czechs were urging that I come to Prague as well. I had not visited them in 1989, but now they were members of the coalition. I also wanted to stop in newly unified Germany. I felt the Germans had been a bit "wobbly" in backing the coalition. Although they were pledging money, Kohl was deep in domestic political battles over the issue of deploying German forces abroad and, more important for our plans, support for the use of force. After Paris, I would fly to the Middle East for Thanksgiving with our troops and discussions with our Arab allies. I left Washington for Europe on November 16.

Czechoslovakia was a historic and moving visit—the first by an American president, and one I had been looking forward to since the Velvet Revolution the year before. I sat down with President Vaclav Havel on the morning of November 17, in the spectacular Hradcany Castle in Prague. I felt in awe of Havel. Here was a man who had been in jail only the year before. He had been beaten and driven to his knees, but had refused to give up. I found him to be a very modest, close-to-shy man, completely unpretentious and straightforward. I also felt humble as I stood beside Alexander Dubcek and addressed the Federal Assembly in Prague. I remembered Dubcek's role in the Prague Spring of 1968, and the brutal suppression of Czechoslovakia's bid for freedom then.

As it had in much of the rest of Eastern Europe, the embargo was affecting Czechoslovakia, where supplies of oil were limited. The country had been dependent on trade with the Soviet Union, which had been its principal provider of oil at concessionary prices. With the Soviet economic upheavals, supplies from that source had dwindled. Havel feared that the high world price of oil would, in turn, damage their fragile economy. He was also worried about destabilization once the country went to free market prices the following year. I offered to do what I could to help him obtain aid from the IMF and the World Bank.

I had said several times in various settings that I believed the Czechs knew better than anyone else what the Kuwaitis were going through. Now, at a joint press conference, Havel was direct. When asked by a reporter whether he agreed with my approach in the Gulf, he responded: "Czechoslovakia has made it clear on a number of occasions that it is necessary to resist evil, that it is necessary to resist aggression, because our own history has taught us ample lessons about the consequences of appeasement." Another journalist asked if he thought the Gulf was taking up too many of the resources that might be spent on the problems of Eastern Europe. Havel succinctly responded: "It is my opinion that all the resources that are expended on resisting aggression anywhere in the world are finally turned to the good of mankind." He had cut to the meat of it—this courageous man was speaking about the price of liberty.

Late that afternoon I spoke before an enormous crowd in Wenceslas Square to commemorate the end of communist rule and the Velvet Revolution, which had begun at the spot a year earlier. It was wall-to-wall people—we were told the crowd numbered around 750,000. I regretted that Havel and I were inside a Plexiglas cocoon, a measure dictated by the security people. We could not hear the crowd's reaction to our speeches, but even that did not detract from the moment. Afterward, Barbara and I waded into the crowd, shaking hands. We emerged atop another platform, where we joined the crowd in singing "We Shall Overcome." I saw exuberant faces all over Prague that day, and it reminded me that we must never take our democracy for granted. Everywhere we went, there were dense crowds of people, many waving small American flags and pouring out their love and respect for the United States.

In his native Rhineland, Helmut Kohl took us to see what he felt was the "soul" of Germany, the cathedral at Speyer, where so many German leaders of the past are buried. He treated Barbara, Brent, and me to a jovial lunch at his modest but comfortable home in Ludwigshafen. He served up tons of wurst and great sauerkraut, as well as a couple of wonderful wines. As we ate, he told me he wanted to send his own emissary to Saddam Hussein to underscore how serious we were. While Helmut reassured me that Germany was standing firmly with the coalition, he had also told the press we ought to carefully weigh the use of force against the

casualties and press on with a negotiated solution. It was a puzzling contradiction, but I did not take it as opposition to what we were proposing
to do, rather that it was more of a warning to Saddam. Nevertheless, his
message was ambiguous and potentially damaging for the coalition.

BRENT SCOWCROFT

Kohl, unintentionally I think, was being less than helpful, and his proposal to send an envoy to Saddam worried me. It seemed obvious that he
hoped to head off war in the Gulf because of the German elections.
These—the first for unified Germany—were just around the corner on
December 3. Earlier in the month, Willy Brandt, a leader of the opposition, had gone to Baghdad and returned with about 120 hostages, much
to Kohl's embarrassment. I concluded that he was trying to recover from
that and avoid stirring up anti-war feeling in the middle of a campaign.

GEORGE BUSH

That evening we flew from Ramstein to Paris, where I was to have dinner with François Mitterrand—barely an hour after our arrival at the US
embassy. I was looking forward to seeing him, and anxious to meet the
next day with Margaret Thatcher and then with Gorbachev. Gorbachev's
economic troubles were mounting and Thatcher was facing a political
battle, with a stiff challenge to her leadership of the Conservative Party.
Margaret was scheduled to be in Paris the very day of her crucial party
vote. The timing seemed odd to me, but I hoped her presence would give
her added stature with the Tories.

The day we arrived, Saddam announced he would free all foreign
hostages over a three-month period starting Christmas Day—provided
Iraq was not attacked in the meantime. It was a crude ploy to push any
military action into the holy month of Ramadan and perhaps beyond into
the bad weather season. I did not see the move as indicating any kind of
flexibility, only a cynical manipulation of the hostage families and an
effort to shift public opinion away from the use of force. I believed the
world community was as skeptical as I was about it. I knocked it down in
a press conference the next day.

At dinner at the Elysée Palace, Mitterrand and I talked about military
action and a use-of-force resolution with a deadline. We had used the
cover of the United Nations so far, I told him, and the additional measure
would show Saddam there was no other way out. "Such a resolution is
hard to draft," he replied, "but we will take part in the process and vote
for it if it is well drafted."

The next morning, Margaret Thatcher came to see me at the US ambassador's residence. We began to talk as we waited for word that breakfast was ready. After what seemed a long time, I asked one of the aides to find out where we should go to eat. A few minutes later, he returned, rather embarrassed: apparently no one had told the embassy domestic staff that this was a breakfast meeting, and no food had been prepared. We had a good laugh, and asked them to whip together whatever they could find in the kitchen. With toast and coffee in hand, we continued our discussion.

Margaret filled me in about her Tory leadership battle and then turned to the Gulf. "You asked for more forces," she said. "We will send another brigade and some minesweepers." We spoke about timing, and I told her I wanted the military to have whatever it needed. She was concerned that this meant pushing operations off even further. We discussed the hostages and our besieged embassies—ours were the last two holding out. Supplies were running low, and it was becoming difficult to protect the British and Americans still in hiding. Margaret reminded me that Iraq was demanding that the Kuwaiti nationals register with the occupying authorities by November 25. "It will be hard after that to shelter our people," she said. I told her I worried about the political environment if we tried to go ahead without a UN resolution along the lines I had proposed to her in October. A provocation would help—I was still considering a replenishment mission. Margaret argued that the hostages alone were enough reason to use force. "He has done terrible things," she said, but she was now willing to back a resolution. "The UN resolution will give you all you need." It would also provide warning to civilians.

The CSCE conference consisted of two long days of speeches—thirty-five of them—and what should have been a historic occasion was overshadowed by the threat of war. It was the leaders of those countries that had been brutalized by aggression in the past who understood the situation the best. Havel of Czechoslovakia, Mazowiecki of Poland, and Antall of Hungary spoke about what was at stake in resisting Saddam—all three had been in jail; all three knew firsthand about the crushing of sovereign nations. Others were wringing their hands, very much like many in our Congress. They wanted to tell me what not to do, not what I should do. Still, they were pleased that the United States was out in the lead. Unfortunately, their comments always seemed to come out in the press as being opposed to what we were doing, even though this was not what they were saying to each other or to me. We had been apprehensive about the possibility of mischievous resolutions on the Persian Gulf, but fortunately there were none.

While the conference was underway, the Iraqis made a new move to divide the coalition, announcing that they would free all German hostages immediately. It was, they said, "a message of encouragement to the people of Europe to take more independent actions and stand up against the arrogant position of the Americans." Saddam told his parliament it was because Kohl had made "helpful" statements. Helmut was embarrassed and apologetic about the development, assuring me that he had not compromised or negotiated with Saddam for their release. I told him I understood, but I knew that some in the press would have a field day, arguing that if only I were more "conciliatory" toward Iraq we could get our hostages out. The incident concerned me, particularly because it came a day after Helmut's suggestion that he send his own direct contact to Baghdad. Kohl seemed to be leaving the reservation, not only on his hostages, but on failing to recognize that we might need to use force. I hoped it was nothing more than pre-election jitters.

Before an informal dinner on November 19, Mikhail and I had a relaxed conversation over drinks at our embassy. We spoke about the situation in the Soviet Union, and I asked him about Yeltsin. "The mood supports stabilization, not rocking the boat," he said with irritation. The people resented separatists. "They ask: what prevents Gorbachev and Yeltsin from cooperating? The answer: Nothing. Objectively there is a need for cooperation. People are thinking, if you can't agree, go. . . . Why is he popular? Because he rejects everything and people say 'how true.' He just says everything is bad and blames the center. . . . He will be used and then thrown out—unless he can provoke the people because of existing tensions. He may be able to do that. I will include able people regardless of their ideology—even Yeltsin."

I turned to the Gulf. "I need your help," I said. "We need to get the UN to authorize force to convince Saddam Hussein to do what [it] demands. I can't think of any other way to convince him . . . I want you to know how strongly I feel. If we could do this together, it would send the right signal." I didn't need an answer right then. "I don't want to put you on the spot with your colleagues. If you can't go along I will still cooperate, but I had to tell you how strongly I felt."

Mikhail said he had given the matter a lot of thought. "Let me say it rests on just the two of us," he said. ". . . On some things, of course, we have different ideas, but on this we must be together. In my heart, as yours I am sure, the preference is to solve this without blood. It can all turn out very, very badly, worse than Vietnam. . . . After much thinking, I decided we need one resolution, but one which would combine your idea and mine. The first part would contain a deadline for an ultimatum. The second part would say 'all necessary measures' can be used. That should be adopted while you are still president of the Security Council." I asked him what time frame he had in mind for the ultimatum. He was thinking of mid-January.

Mikhail did not want an announcement yet for reasons of his own. With a large Muslim population in the Soviet Union, he hoped to pursue a peaceful course as long as possible and avoid a public threat of using force. He also wanted to speak with the Iraqis once more. But he recognized that the resolution was critical to me. Working late into the night, Shevardnadze and Baker hammered out the language for the draft resolution. They also put together a general statement on our discussions, which left out the resolution. My promise to delay our announcement on the resolution caused me some headaches—in particular because it allowed the press to label our meeting "chilly," although nothing could have been further from the truth. When the press pack concludes that a meeting has been "chilly"—a meeting they did not attend and one both sides have described as cordial—they stay with "chilly" and then speculate on what it means.

About twenty of us gathered for dinner, and we joked and told stories. Gorbachev and his defense minister, Dmitri Yazov, roared with laughter and had some of their own to contribute, including a few about Stalin. It was a relaxed and productive evening. Later, Gorbachev and I agreed that it had been the best meeting we ever had, even better than Camp David.

The next day there were still another fifteen speeches to go. As a courtesy to my fellow heads of government, I tried to stay at the table and, to stay awake, I took copious notes on the numerous candidates present vying for the International Scowcroft Award. There were some serious challenges—entire delegations sound asleep at the same time. I think Gorbachev and I remained present longer than anyone else. At one point he hurried over with his interpreter to report that he had just heard from Primakov. Saddam Hussein would agree to withdraw from Kuwait in exchange for access to the Gulf. When reminded there could be no conditions, Gorbachev appeared disappointed, but optimistic we could still persuade Saddam to leave peacefully.

In the afternoon, I met with Ozal, to whom I now felt close. He seemed prepared for conflict, and was confident that should war come, it would be a short one and our air power could do the trick. As we spoke, I took a call from Hosni Mubarak, who urged me to see Syria's president, Hafez al-Assad, on my way back from the Middle East. Hosni was not alone—all our Arab allies wanted me to meet with him. I asked where it could take place, suggesting perhaps Cyprus. Ozal's foreign minister had a problem with that, so we decided that it had to be either Geneva or somewhere in Turkey, and we kicked it back to Mubarak to pass along to Assad.

That evening, Margaret suffered her Conservative Party leadership defeat. She had steadfastly worked through the entire meeting that day, although she looked nervous and it was clear she had other things on her mind. She darted in and out to check on progress back in Britain. I left her at about five that afternoon, asking her if she had any word yet. She said it would be a couple of hours before she knew. I was saddened and surprised when I heard the news. Despite it, she courageously appeared for the dinner at Versailles, participating fully. Her downfall was amazing—so fast and almost unforeseen. While we had not been as close as she had been with Ronald Reagan, our relationship was excellent and it had grown steadily warmer over my time in office. I greatly respected and admired Margaret, and still do. She is a courageous woman of conviction. She had been a champion for democracy in the revolutions we had nourished, and a wise friend for the United States and myself. I valued her open and direct way of dealing with people, based on solid principles. It was a typical demonstration of Margaret's courage, and her determination that the coalition prevail, that in her "farewell" letter to me a few days later, on November 22, she added a note confirming that Britain was sending additional troops and warships.

I left Paris for Saudi Arabia, where I was joined by the four top congressional leaders I had invited along—Senators George Mitchell and Bob Dole, Speaker Tom Foley, and Congressman Bob Michel. Our arrival in Jeddah that evening was spectacular, with magnificent carpets laid out on the tarmac and a royal welcome led by the King himself. We were whisked into a lavishly appointed VIP lounge filled with the smell of marvelous incense. Afterwards, I met with the Emir of Kuwait at the Al-Hamra guest palace. He was concerned that the hostages would affect our willingness to use force, and I assured him they would not. I asked whether he thought Saddam would withdraw, now that we had so many troops in Saudi Arabia. He was pessimistic. He told me more about the cruel barbarities that were being committed in Kuwait and I suggested he speak out more about that tragic situation.

Barbara and I stayed in yet another of the King's beautiful marble guest palaces. It was tastefully decorated, with chandeliers everywhere, and heavily air-conditioned against the desert heat, even to the point of being icy. The King hosted a late state dinner for us—ten o'clock—which I was told was an early hour for him. It was an unbelievable meal. The only way to describe the amount of food was to say that if ever there was an occasion when tables groaned under a feast, this was it. I had never seen so much—and of nearly every conceivable type of food—and while such dinners usually lasted three or more hours, this one was less than an hour. Afterward, Fahd and I, along with Brent, Jim, John Sununu, and others, met for two hours across a table with inlaid green leather rectangles in front of each seat. The King recounted the situation at the time of the invasion and his fury over being deceived by Saddam's assurances he would not invade. I asked about Saddam's ploy to draw out the release of hostages into Ramadan, and he told me Saddam was misguided: wars had taken place in Ramadan; indeed, the Six Day War had been fought then. I cautioned the Saudis about statements from the Arab world. Assad had announced that his forces would not move from Saudi Arabia, and Mubarak declared that he was not willing to send his troops into Iraq. It gave the appearance that the Arab partners wanted the United States alone to fight Saddam Hussein. It was a terrible message to our troops and to the United States and made our task with Congress tough. It was close to two in the morning before we broke up. I came away once again impressed by the King and convinced he would stand by us as a friend and ally no matter what Iraq did.

Early the next morning, November 22, we flew to Dhahran for a memorable Thanksgiving Day. There is no way to describe properly our experience in the desert. We were greeted by General Norman Schwarzkopf, who was our guide for the remainder of the day. We began with a visit to a Military Airlift Command base in Dhahran, where Barbara and I waded through the crowd of enthusiastic young Air Force personnel, speaking to as many as we could. We shook hands, hugged people, and posed for pictures. From there we were whisked out into the desert to see the Army. We flew over miles and miles of empty desert. Occasionally I'd spot a herd of camels or a Bedouin tent. I wondered how anyone could eke out a living from such harsh surroundings. After another talk, and another plunge through the crowd, we got in the chow line for Thanksgiving dinner at long tables under a camouflage net. It was a thrill to eat with these courageous soldiers who were doing the heavy lifting of the coalition here at the front line.

From the Army's open-air mess hall we choppered to the helicopter carrier USS *Nassau*, which was out in international waters. There we joined a prayer service on the stern deck. It was crowded with sailors, and again I tried to talk to as many as I could and tell them how much I, and our country, appreciated what they were doing. From the *Nassau* we flew to a Marine desert position, where there were also Navy Seabees and British troops from the famed Desert Rats. I wasn't sure I could make it through my several short, off-the-cuff speeches without choking up, and my emotions did get to me on the MAC hanger and on the *Nassau* at the church service. The marines and sailors all looked so young, and I was thinking, "May God spare these lives if we have to fight."

An impressive Schwarzkopf, clad in desert fatigues and exuding the strength and confidence Americans would soon see and admire, briefed me on the battle plan. From the presentation, and what I was hearing back in Washington, the military seemed confident that any war would be a short one—far different from what many in Congress were saying. Norm made a point of thanking me for giving the military what it needed to get the job done. On this trip I became convinced we could knock out the Iraqis early; certainly he felt we would. The Arabs shared that confidence—King Fahd, Mubarak, and all the others we had spoken with over recent weeks. They all believed Saddam would "crater" quickly. Hosni was predicting it would be over in a matter of days. Nevertheless, while our Arab allies were convinced Iraq's army would simply run once the shooting started, we could not plan on it, and Norm didn't.

In Cairo the next day I met with Mubarak. As always, Hosni was direct, and friendly. I saw eye-to-eye with him on almost all of the issues. I mentioned that Assad was saying Syrian troops would not move out of Saudi Arabia, and Hosni told me Syria would be there. I also asked him whether Egyptian troops would go into Iraq. He said he'd do whatever was necessary.

That afternoon we flew to Geneva to meet with Assad. I found him engaging, but it was a tough discussion. In a long lecture, he blamed Israel for all the woes in the Middle East, including the Iran-Iraq war and even the invasion of Kuwait. He was dead-set against the Egyptian-Israeli peace process, and argued that since then everything in the Middle East had fallen apart. It was depressing, and we went round and round on it. He bristled a bit when I raised terrorism and human rights. I pointed out that it was important he not say that his troops would stay in Saudi Arabia if the coalition advanced into Kuwait. He looked a little uncomfortable. I explained that Mubarak had made a similar statement and had clarified it. He seemed interested and I asked him to talk to Hosni about it. While the meeting was not as productive as I wanted, it was essential to show that we would try any avenue for peace in the Middle East.

As we flew home, I felt resigned that we would not find a peaceful resolution to the crisis. We had given sanctions plenty of time to work, yet there was no sign they would cause Saddam to leave Kuwait. I doubted he would respond to the new UN resolution.

While we had been visiting our troops and allies, Baker, who left us soon after the President's arrival in Riyadh, was once again effectively working the diplomatic circuit to build support for the resolution among the remaining Security Council members—including pro-Iraq Yemen, Colombia (whose UN ambassador had spoken out against US policy), and a meeting with the Malaysian foreign minister in Los Angeles. Before the Paris CSCE discussions, he had already spoken with Chinese foreign minister Qian Qichen when both were in Cairo on November 6—Qian en route to Baghdad, Baker to consult with Mubarak on our plans. Qian had told Baker Beijing was still working for a peaceful solution and that the sanctions seemed to be taking a toll. He was noncommittal about backing the resolution, and wanted something in return. He tried to get Baker to promise that either he or the President would visit Beijing. Baker said that although we wouldn't hold it against the Chinese if they did not vote for the resolution, at least they should not stand in the way. Qian and Baker apparently agreed that Qian would come to Washington after the vote, to see the President if they gave a "yes" vote and Baker if it was an abstention. Baker had also obtained the support of temporary council members Ethiopia, Zaire, and Romania. Ivory Coast had indicated it would back us but, like the Soviets, was not ready to say so publicly. Thus, by the time Baker began this last push, we had nine votes in the council.

Not surprisingly, President Saleh of Yemen opposed the resolution and said so at the press conference with Baker after their meeting. The Colombians were evasive, looking for a compromise that would encourage Saddam to withdraw in exchange for a concession that let him save face. After an intervening phone call from President Bush, President Cesar Gaviria Trujillo told Baker that, in the end, they would find a way to vote with us. Baker's talk with Malaysian foreign minister Abu Hassan was also tough. Hassan was annoyed that Baker had asked him to come all the way to Los Angeles, but Jim was reluctant to travel to Asia for fear this would annoy the Chinese, since he would not stop in Beijing. Hassan argued that, while they were not opposed to punishing Saddam, Israel had to be punished for its treatment of the Palestinians in the occupied territories. The Malaysians wanted to give sanctions more time, and wanted no part of a resolution that might lead to throwing Iraq out of Kuwait by force. Hassan would promise only to study the resolution.

BRENT SCOWCROFT

In the midst of this careful diplomacy, former President Carter wrote the members of the Security Council asking them not to support the resolution. He argued that the costs in human life and the economic consequences, not to mention the permanent destabilization of the Middle East, were too high and unnecessary, "unless all peaceful resolution efforts are first exhausted." He called for the UN to mandate a "good faith" negotiation with the Iraqi leaders to consider their concerns, and to ask the Arabs to try to work out a peaceful solution, "without any restraint on their agenda." It was an unbelievable letter, asking the other members of the council to vote against his own country. We found out about it only when one of the recipients sent us a copy. Carter later acknowledged he had sent the letter, but claimed he had told President Bush what he was doing. He did send the President a similar one, but without mentioning he had also lobbied the President's foreign colleagues. It seemed to me that if there was ever a violation of the Logan Act prohibiting diplomacy by private citizens, this was it. President Bush was furious at this interference in the conduct of his foreign policy and the deliberate attempt to undermine it, but told me just to let it drop.

Baker made his final round of lobbying in New York on the eve of the vote itself. There he met with Shevardnadze and polished up the final language for the resolution, which originally called for a January 1 deadline. Gorbachev wanted to push the deadline to January 31—two months away. Mitterrand suggested we split the difference and go with January 15. As this was the date the military was using anyway, we agreed.

We were still not certain how the Chinese would vote and pursued some last-minute diplomacy. We did not want to push them so much that they became incensed and vetoed the resolution, but we did want to try to persuade them to support us. President Bush cabled Chinese president Yang Shangkun and Baker arranged for Qian to visit Washington the day after the vote, as the two of them had worked out. On November 29, Baker chaired the Security Council vote on Resolution 678. It was a resounding vote of support—12 in favor, Cuba and Yemen voting against, China abstaining. The resolution authorized "all member states cooperating with the government of Kuwait, unless Iraq on or before January 15 1991 fully implements [the resolutions], to use all necessary means to uphold and implement [all those resolutions] and restore international peace and security to the area." The deadline—six weeks hence—was set.*

*[BRENT SCOWCROFT] Baker had apparently forgotten to remind the Chinese that, since they had abstained, they would be seeing only him in Washington, not the President. When the foreign minister learned of this, he was furious. Their ambassador called me at three am to say the foreign minister would cancel his trip if he couldn't see the President. I was only dimly aware of the understanding about the arrangements, but we did not need an international crisis in the wake

GEORGE BUSH

By setting forth in plain language an authorization to use force to implement the earlier resolutions, and setting a deadline, the UN vote was a tremendous breakthrough. I was delighted. I knew other potential stumbling blocks lay ahead, but with passage of this resolution after a lot of very effective diplomacy by the whole team—particularly Baker and Tom Pickering—I felt a huge burden had been lifted from my shoulders. It eased some of the problems of coalition maintenance and resolved the debate about the need for provocation before we could act. Although we didn't realize it at the time, it also changed the debate with Congress, creating a context for the use of force which helped bring it aboard. The Security Council had voted to go to war.

---

of our UN success. I told the ambassador that Qian would see the President, whom I called at 6:00 am to explain what I had done. He agreed it was necessary, although it was certain to cause a ruckus in some quarters of Congress and the press. It did.

CHAPTER 17

Through a Cacophony

BRENT SCOWCROFT

While we had sought United Nations support from the outset of the crisis, it had been as part of our efforts to forge an international consensus, not because we thought we required its mandate. The UN provided an added cloak of political cover. Never did we think that without its blessing we could not or would not intervene. American (and world) interests were at stake and Kuwait had asked for help. In turn, we did not believe that additional authority beyond Article 51 of the UN Charter was required to enforce a blockade—though it was politically desirable. We sought that resolution in order to settle doubts and to keep the Soviets on board. By doing so, however, we had set an expectation that we should request authority again when it came to use force to implement the original resolutions. As with the vote to back the sanctions, the November UN resolution was a political measure intended to seal international solidarity and strengthen domestic US support by spelling out that we could use force and when. There could no longer be doubt in Saddam's mind—or anyone's—that the coalition had the will and means to go to war. But the carefully negotiated UN vote also called attention to whether, having asked the United Nations, we were obliged to seek similar authority from Congress. Once again we were faced with weighing the President's inherent power to use force against the political benefits of explicit support from Congress.

From the end of November into January, the debate with Congress intensified. The dispute was less about foreign and security policy goals in the Gulf than about domestic political and Constitutional questions. With the UN resolution behind us, the salient issue now was who could order the use of force. Central to the debate, carried out in the glare of camera lights on Capitol Hill and in the media, was how Congress should be consulted and whether we should call it back into special session to consider the matter.

At the end of November, Senator Sam Nunn opened televised hearings on our policy, posing questions on the use of sanctions and our military readiness. As chairman of the Armed Services Committee and a respected voice in Washington, he was not just another senator: He had great influence and authority on national security issues. Because of his stature, his position that we should stick to sanctions—a couple of years if necessary—attracted the support of many Democrats. The hearings rapidly became politically charged, as members and witnesses used the forum to voice their fears or as a soapbox for their agendas.

Nunn called a number of retired senior military officers and government officials to testify, including Henry Kissinger, Admiral William Crowe, and General David Jones, as well as former defense secretary James Schlesinger, former secretary of the navy James Webb, and former National Security Agency director William Odom. Crowe's appearance, given his recent service, was perhaps the most devastating. With the exception of Kissinger, all spoke out against the use of force. They argued variously that our military was not prepared for war, that casualties would be high, in the tens of thousands, that our aims were vague, and that sanctions should do the job. Schlesinger maintained that the impact of war on the region and the global economy would be enormous, and that as we had begun building our military presence in Saudi Arabia, public support had waned. Jones worried that the increase in troops would drive policy, causing us to go to war prematurely, as had happened to the European powers in 1914, and that the force was too large to rotate. Webb said that if we wanted an offensive option we ought to reinstate the draft and ask Congress for a declaration of war. Odom thought sanctions would eventually work and that we could wait. It would be worse to fight, incurring heavy casualties, and have to remain for years in Iraq (which he believed necessary to prevent regional collapse) than to sit tight in Saudi Arabia.

Kissinger's testimony was in stark contrast to most of the others. He argued that, while sanctions might eventually work, they would take far too long and by the time we could judge their success it would be too late for a military option. They would also be difficult to maintain, with heavy pressures to ease or lift them and withdraw our forces. For as long as possible, sanctions and the military option both had to be kept in place to be credible. But he predicted there would come a point when we would have to decide between them. The size of the deployment in Saudi Arabia, and the logistical and political efforts needed to keep it there, meant our time was limited. Eventually, we would no longer be able to sustain a military presence in sufficient size and we would have to choose between the consequences of withdrawal and those of military action.

Some of the caution, especially the arguments that the military was unready for war and that public support should be cultivated before-hand, seemed to reflect lingering memories of Vietnam. Outside of Kissinger, few seemed to note how little effect the sanctions appeared to be having, or that time might erode coalition solidarity. It also appeared that, while some committee members, such as John Warner, tried to keep the testimony focused on questions of readiness and military issues, others, such as Bill Cohen, attempted to lead the witnesses to the matter of whether Congress must be consulted before any use of force.

GEORGE BUSH

I thought the witness list had been "stacked" in favor of people who supported sanctions as the only option. Our chargé in Baghdad, Joe Wilson, later told me that the reaction in Iraq to Admiral Crowe's testimony in particular had been to encourage a belief that the US would never attack. My diary for late November reflects some of my irritation with Congress and the building pressures from critics:

NOVEMBER 28

The debate is raging now and Sam Nunn, I think running for president, is trying to decide how hard to push. Gephardt "breaks" with the President, saying "no use of force, sanctions must work." None of them seem concerned about the hostages, none of them share my anxiety about the Embassy . . . It's ironic, the isolationistic right lined with the [old] Kingman Brewster left [voicing the] Vietnam syndrome. Bob Kerrey, a true war hero in Vietnam and John Glenn, also a hero, "no force, no force."

. . . The final analysis: we will prevail. Saddam Hussein will get out of Kuwait, and the United States will have been the catalyst and the key in getting this done, and that is important. Our role as a world leader will once again be reaffirmed, but if we compromise and if we fail, we would be reduced to total impotence, and that is not going to happen. I don't care if I have one vote in the Congress. That will not happen . . . I want the Congress involved. The big debate goes on about the declaration of war, but the big thing is, we need them; we want them; and I'll continue to consult.

Over lunch on November 29 I talked with Tom Foley and Bob Michel about whether to call Congress back and ask for a resolution supporting the UN vote. Both strongly opposed a special session. They worried about an out-of-control House, thinking that lame duck members would be hurt and resentful after the election while newly elected people would feel left out. They also pointed out that it would be difficult to narrow the agenda of a session to consider only a Gulf resolution, and warned me that members would push all sorts of initiatives of their own. There could be veto override attempts and general chaos. My closest friend in the House, Democrat Sonny Montgomery, had similar worries. I met with the bipartisan leadership the next day and asked the same question.

One action I had been contemplating to help strengthen congressional and public support was direct contact with the Iraqis. I wanted to show that we were going the extra mile for peace and it would help quash some of the charges that I was contemplating war against someone we had not even tried to speak with. Since at least the early part of November I had been mulling over a high-level meeting where Saddam would be told exactly how determined we were—that there was no room for compromise, that unconditional, total withdrawal was the only answer. By the end of the month, encouraged that the UN resolution authorizing force might have given him the message at last, I had made up my mind to propose one. The only question was how.

One possibility was to ask Tariq Aziz to come to Washington; another, to meet with Saddam Hussein myself. I could also send a representative to Baghdad to deliver a personal message, perhaps Jim Baker, Brent, or Senator Dick Lugar. Jim worried that if someone else went to see Saddam it might undermine his work, suggesting he did not carry enough authority. My own concern was that in Saddam Hussein's case the talks would be too conspicuous; too much "face" would be involved. I was uncertain how public these meetings should be and how my message should be conveyed. It was possible that Aziz would not deliver the full message to Saddam. The evening after the UN vote, I decided I would propose both that Aziz come to Washington and that Jim go afterward to Baghdad.

BRENT SCOWCROFT

I was not enthusiastic about the idea because it reawakened the possibility of negotiations just when the UN had authorized the use of force, but President Bush had that look about him which told me he had made up his mind. He and I had already discussed the idea—several times— and I had pointed out that our closest allies might think he had gone soft.

But I did not press the case hard. There was strong logic to the argument that the stakes were so high that a serious effort at direct discussion was important. Besides, he was the one who faced the anguishing decision to send troops into battle. He needed to be comfortable in his own mind that, if it came to that, he had exhausted all feasible alternatives. We did make one mistake, however. He wanted to do it right away, without more argument, so Baker and I alone worked on his statement. Had we shown it to Richard Haass beforehand, he would certainly have pointed out the proximity between the dates we were proposing for the meetings and the expiration of the UN ultimatum, which would only invite delaying tactics down to the wire. On the morning of November 30, the President announced the invitation, spelling out his reasons and offering to meet in Washington with Aziz, along with our coalition's ambassadors, in the latter part of the week of December 10. He asked Saddam to receive Baker at a mutually convenient time between December 15 and January 15.

The reaction from the coalition allies to the announcement was sharp and, at best, mixed. We had not consulted with them ahead of time, so they were understandably surprised, not knowing if we were up to some secret deal or perhaps fearing a sell-out. The President called King Fahd, as well as Hosni Mubarak, Turgut Ozal, the Emir of Kuwait, and Britain's new prime minister, John Major, to explain the mission and assure them there would be no concessions. It was just an opportunity to lay out the facts for Saddam. While King Fahd himself was supportive, Prince Bandar was nervous and confused about the proposal. He asked worriedly, and pointedly, whether we were weakening. Baker reported that Bandar thought the King and the Arab allies, including Kuwait, were too polite to confront the President on this. They were also worried that Saddam might use the opportunity to withdraw with his military intact. Mubarak's reaction was more positive, and he called the idea of sending Baker to Baghdad a "good step." On the other hand, Ambassador Henry Catto cabled that the British government was "hopping mad" about the lack of consultation—especially since the announcement came just hours after Baker had had dinner with Foreign Secretary Douglas Hurd in New York.

BRENT SCOWCROFT

The downside internationally of inviting Tariq Aziz was instantly obvious and genuinely serious. It had shaken the coalition to its core, just as the UN resolution had seemingly cleared away the last hurdle to taking action. There was little we could do to reassure our allies, but the President tried hard. In the end it worked out, but we had a period of frantic efforts to calm a very restive coalition. The other negative was within our Administration team. Most were unaware that the President had anything so risky in mind. I had not spread the word because I hoped he could be dissuaded from carrying it out. Then we executed it by ourselves and thoughtlessly let the time for a meeting run right up to the expiration date of the ultimatum. We had some angry colleagues—who let us know it.

On the upside, there were two benefits. The first was the President's peace of mind, knowing he had taken extra steps for peace and avoided the charge that he was willing to send American troops into battle without having tried direct negotiations. The second was the reaction of surprised support in the United States. It blunted some of the damage caused by the Nunn hearings, and the Democrats who had staked out positions in opposition to war now found themselves in a quandary: how could they oppose a president who was supported by a powerful international coalition, and who now had reached out in such a dramatic way? The first sign of its effect came at a bipartisan congressional leadership meeting on November 30 in the Cabinet Room, where everyone seemed impressed by this obvious manifestation of the President's seriousness in trying to resolve the confrontation without force.

At the meeting, President Bush made a pitch for a resolution backing the UN vote—which avoided the problem of asking Congress for authorization yet demonstrated solidarity—and asked again whether there should be a special session to consider it. Tom Foley was wary, obviously hoping to give sanctions more time. While he acknowledged that we had been forthcoming, unless there was an emergency he preferred to wait until the new Congress in January. George Mitchell concurred. The President told them not to underestimate the signal a vote from Congress endorsing the UN resolution would send Saddam.

"The Constitution does provide for calling back just one house," Bob Dole reminded his colleagues. "We're missing an opportunity. We could expedite this process and have an agreement on a resolution in three hours—a resolution of peace, not war. We're abdicating our responsibility and seem to want to have it both ways . . . Let's send Saddam and his nine hundred thousand young men a message." It was not a time for partisan politics, he said. He hoped the President would call Congress back if Congress itself would not. "I'm inclined the way of Dole," said Bob Michel. "If we're going to do it, it must be bipartisan with a good vote."

Dick Gephardt said that if we were going to use force it should come only after we exhaust sanctions, and there could be disagreement on

what that meant. "Mr. President, you're being too nice," said Bob Kasten. "You've earned our support and should have a vote by House and Senate reaffirming the UN vote. People in Congress are anxious to go home, and sound bites are coming out of hearings selectively. The reading in Iraq is that there's dissension here, that this is Vietnam. The President has to ask for that vote. Limit it. You can get it in an afternoon."

Patrick Leahy said that if we had not been consulting there would be reason for a special session, but he wanted to give sanctions more time to work. "Then we'll back you with everything possible," he said. "You don't help yourself with debate in a special session." Claiborne Pell asked if there should be back-channel negotiations. "I'm perfectly prepared to 'jaw,' " said the President. "But the danger of concessions is an enormous price to pay for tomorrow. It's a dangerous precedent. The world is united. A country which rapes another doesn't deserve *anything*."

"No one is talking about backing out," said Nunn. "The question is do we dole out pain slow using sanctions or fast with war?" He still believed time was on our side. While he agreed that the threat of force was important, he was concerned that the size and logistics of our forces would start to dictate policy. "Open up the possibility of a policy of rotation; it would help rebuild consensus and give us time to let sanctions work," he said. "The size of our force and the no-rotation make a self-fulfilling prophecy."

"The immediate problem is that Saddam does not believe us," said Dick Lugar. "The potential for war is still here as long as he is. Seven times you've asked for help. It's inconceivable to me that Congress won't help. . . . The Constitutional structure calls for a debate."

GEORGE BUSH

The Senate Republican leadership wanted to go ahead and draft a resolution of support. They were worried that Republicans were being branded as the "war party," and hoped to push Democrats to take a stand by putting them in a position where the alternative was voting against the President in what was essentially a declaration of war. Dole was confident they could keep the agenda narrowed to a Gulf resolution and a positive vote. I had not yet made up my mind. With Congress divided on whether to call a special session—largely on party lines it appeared—and some threatening to introduce additional resolutions requiring me to seek their consent, I thought it might be better to do nothing than to have them trying to limit the power of the president. Somewhere along the line I'd have to veto such a resolution, sending the worst possible message to

Saddam about American resolve. If we could not limit the agenda of a special session and get a consensus in both houses, there was no point in asking for a vote yet.

The President's offer to exchange diplomats with Baghdad was followed by a month of Iraqi manipulation and diplomatic maneuvering, perhaps in the hopes of causing the coalition to divide or of exploiting pressure in the United States to give sanctions more time. Iraq indicated that it accepted the "idea of the invitation and a meeting," but offered no specifics. On December 4, Saddam announced he would allow all 3,300 Soviet citizens he had been detaining to leave and two days later, he said every foreigner would be permitted to go. The announcements were clearly timed to exploit the invitation to talk, and put additional pressure on the coalition to back off.

GEORGE BUSH

I learned of Saddam's statement releasing all the hostages in the course of a trip to South America, where I also received word that the State Department had announced that as soon as all of our people were out of Kuwait, the embassy would close. This was the first I had heard of the move and it bothered me. Since Saddam had been demanding that the embassy shut down, it could appear that we were making a concession just after the strong message delivered by the UN resolution and my own call for top-level meetings to warn Iraq of our resolve. Closing it also removed a potential provocation for the use of force, since we could no longer point to the need to relieve it and free those trapped inside. While I worried that the evacuation would be perceived as a sign of weakness, the US media played it as our attempt to clear the decks for further action. It probably did make a strike easier and I hoped it would be seen that way, but I was uneasy. Sure enough, I soon learned that back in political circles in Washington, and abroad among our allies, the announcement had been interpreted as a concession to Saddam. There were suggestions that the closing of the embassy, the proposed trip to Baghdad, and my invitation to Aziz all showed we were weakening.

Hostages began to pour out of Iraq on December 9, including 163 Americans. Ambassador to Kuwait Nathaniel Howell and the remaining four-member diplomatic staff left four days later. I met with a small group of the released Americans on December 13 at the White House and heard their stories of fear and horror in Kuwait. As I listened to them, and saw how little media coverage was being given to their experiences, I was angered, feeling that America didn't seem to care.

Having released the hostages, Saddam revived his ploys to link Kuwait with the Israeli-Palestinian problem and asked for a broader dialogue on the Middle East. We refused, repeating that talks would be confined to discussing Iraq's withdrawal. The Iraqis then began sparring with us over precise dates for talks, probably in an attempt to loosen the January 15 deadline. They proposed that Aziz arrive in Washington on December 17, and asked that he remain for three or four days, explaining that he wanted to talk to Congress and the press as well. We pictured all sorts of games with US politicians and the press, but we knew we could not deny him access to them. We accepted the date, but said he could stay only two days. We also asked for confirmation of the Baghdad meeting, and tried to correct our original scheduling mistake, offering dates to choose from up to January 3. Iraq replied by offering dates in mid-January. This was unacceptable: either Baker went before January 3, or the meeting was off. We toyed with the idea simply of receiving Aziz without a Baker trip, or even canceling his visit entirely, and then told the Iraqis that the Aziz meeting here was contingent on confirmation of one of the dates for Baghdad. They came back with a January date only three days shy of the UN deadline. Baker then suggested we show our flexibility and pin them to our time frame by offering fifteen possible dates between December 20 and January 3.

GEORGE BUSH

DIARY, DECEMBER 12

We get another cable from Iraq saying they're staying with their position on seeing Saddam on [January] 12. We've given him 15 different dates, and they can see John Connally in 10 minutes, or Ramsey Clark, or Muhammad Ali, but they can't see the Secretary of State. Tomorrow I may just decide to scrub this whole thing.

I was getting angry with Saddam's games, but I still wanted to exhaust all the possibilities. On December 14, I announced I had asked Jim to be available to go to Baghdad any time up to and including January 3. The next day Saddam canceled Aziz's trip to Washington—claiming that if all we wanted to do was repeat the UN resolutions there was no point in talking. For the next two weeks there was no further movement. Saddam's dance only reinforced my pessimism about a peaceful resolution to the crisis—although I would keep trying for one.

I was also still fighting Saddam's efforts to drive wedges in the coalition. On December 11, I met with Israeli prime minister Yitzhak Shamir for two hours in the Oval Office, and I tried to get some assurance from him that if Iraq attacked Israel he would let the United States respond. I thanked him for the low profile his country had been taking in the face of Saddam's endless threats. "If he attacks you, or if an attack becomes apparent, we have the capacity to obliterate his military structure . . . ," I told him. "A preemptive strike by Israel would be very bad. I know your position about responding to an attack and I respect it. But if we could consult first, our preference would be for Israel not to respond until you have seen our reply. We have common objectives and I would like to fulfill them." I wanted the coalition to stay together for a massive response.

Shamir said he supported all we were doing, and understood our difficulties. He pointed out, however, that if Iraq attacked Israel, the target would be civilians, which put his country in a difficult position. "I am encouraged by your words," he said, "but we will be obliged to defend ourselves and prevent continuation of such attacks. You say you will obliterate their capability, but you may miss some." I told him that if we saw rocket-fueling and so forth we would consult. Shamir replied that they were not thinking of a preemptive strike, but our militaries should share information anyway. "But if something should happen," he suggested, "we should try to consult beforehand, before something is launched." I assured him we were prepared to do that.

Through December the pundits were hard at work forecasting the darkest scenarios of a possible conflict. Estimates of casualties were tossed out and quoted almost haphazardly. Contrary to the reporting of columnist Robert Novak and others, who were citing numbers of 20,000 or more, military estimates were below 2,000. Former secretary of defense Robert McNamara predicted at least 30,000, while former senator George McGovern argued that the benefits of war did not offset a cost of up to 50,000 American lives, and painted a grisly toll in thousands of body parts.

Some columnists simply charged we were clueless. Rowland Evans and Novak were among the worst of the naysayers, proclaiming that Kuwait was a lost cause, that the other Arab states would never come to its aid, and later, that the coalition would collapse. Mark Shields insisted that we were deluding ourselves into thinking any war would be a short one, and that we were digging our own political graves. "This is an administration in trouble, it really is," he said. "It's bereft of ideas, it's bereft of direction. It is, right now in 1990—George Bush's administration is reminiscent of nothing so much as Jimmy Carter's in 1979." Joseph Sobran concurred: "You don't have to live in Washington to see that Mr. Bush is, politically speaking, destroying himself. And his party."

Some of the rhetoric was irresponsible posturing and opportunism,

with stances that switched as the crisis and war unfolded—free opinions
from a free press. Pat Buchanan was a good example on the isolationist
end. He predicted that war would split the Republican Party, polarize the
country, and poison its politics. But afterward he asked, "Did Saddam
think the American people would not rally around when the guns began
firing?" Another time it was, "The war against Iraq will be the last war of
Mr. Bush's New World Order. When this one is over, Americans will not
be looking around for new allied interests to defend, or new UN assignments to police the planet with US Marines." After the war, he said,
"Watching the American war machine, one is reminded of General Charles
de Gaulle's remark during the Cuban Missile Crisis: There is really only
one superpower."

GEORGE BUSH

While I knew that criticism came with the job, I worried that the barrage from Congress and the pundits sent all the wrong signals to Saddam
Hussein, with his selective information, and would only embolden him to
dig in and try to weather the sanctions. With our substantial coalition
forces in Saudi Arabia, he was now less likely to provoke us and he probably understood that we were serious (although until the first shot was
fired, I think he did not believe we would fight). But I felt he was bound
to wonder exactly what was going on and whether we had the will to do
what was necessary. I was less upset by those critics in the media and
Congress who had a consistent history of opposing the use of force than I
was with the others who were not offering constructive solutions but only
lecturing us. They had none of the responsibility or the worries that go
with a decision to take military action, yet they felt free to attack us. They
did not have to contend with the morale of the forces, the difficulty of
holding a coalition together, or the fact that time was running out. Above
all, they had no responsibility for the lives of our soldiers, sailors, and airmen. I tried to put individual congressmen on the spot by asking them
exactly what they'd do in my place, not what they wouldn't do. The usual
refrain was that we should give the sanctions time to work.

Yet there were strong and vocal supporters as well. In early December,
Democratic Representative Steve Solarz was key in organizing a bipartisan Committee for Peace and Security in the Gulf. It included Ann Lewis,
the former political director of the Democratic National Committee, former Reagan officials such as Richard Perle, Frank Carlucci, and Jeane
Kirkpatrick, and members of Congress such as John McCain, Dick Lugar,
Jack Murtha, Bob Torricelli. The group was a big help in giving the other
side of the issue. They argued that US interests were such that we should

do whatever was necessary, including the use of force, which they supported on the condition of consultation beforehand with Congress. Still, however valuable their help, it remained difficult to overcome the opposition from the press and many Democrats in Congress.

DIARY, DECEMBER 14

Finally we're getting some groups together to get out there and give the pitch. For too long, Sam Nunn, who they now joke about as "Neville," and George Mitchell and others dominated the scene. We still aren't out of the woods—the Congress still isn't on board—but the recent polls show the American people much more supportive than I thought they would've been.* I cannot say that I have made the determination to pull the trigger, but I can tell you . . . that if they aren't out by January 15th, I'm going to have to make that decision real fast. . . .

On December 18, I received an eighty-page Amnesty International report on human rights violations in Kuwait. It troubled me deeply and I encouraged others to read it. I sent copies to the coalition ambassadors as well as members of Congress. Amnesty International would deliver it to the Security Council. The report was full of descriptions of specific cases of abuse, documenting the accounts of the most horrible and systematic torture of Kuwaitis. There were gruesome accounts of mutilation and rape, as well as arbitrary executions. I read stories of Iraqi soldiers taking people from their homes and shooting them in front of their families, of people dragged from cars to be beaten and shot, of bodies tossed out into the streets, and of Iraqis withholding medical treatment from Kuwaitis and looting medical equipment. The document retold the story from the first days of the war of Iraqi soldiers removing babies from incubators at one of the hospitals and leaving them to die, now using the eyewitness accounts of the doctors and volunteers who had been there.

DIARY, THURSDAY, DECEMBER 20

We have a very emotional meeting, at least for me, with Bishop [Edmund] Browning.† He had just gotten back from Jordan and Iraq. He was appealing for peace, and he was pointing out to me

---

*On December 14, the *Los Angeles Times* reported that 61 percent in a poll supported our Gulf policy. NBC had a similar poll, citing 54 percent approval of a decision to go to war if Iraq had not withdrawn from Kuwait by January 15.

†Presiding Bishop of the Episcopal Church in America. He, among others, disregarded our opposition to travel to Iraq.

that everyone he encountered wanted peace. He felt that there was no way that he could possibly condone violence. . . . I put forward the Amnesty International report that had made such a profound impression on me, and asked him, now what do we do about peace? How do we handle it when these people are being raped? What would be the Bishop's position in World War II?

. . . I also met two delegations from Congress, including George Mitchell. The more I talk to these delegations, I'm convinced that I'm going to have to make the decision [alone], and I'm going to have to take the heat. I'm going to have to share credit with Congress and the world if it works quickly, [with] acceptable loss of life—whatever that is—and a quick defeat for Saddam; but if it drags out, not only will I take the blame, but I will probably have impeachment proceedings filed against me as Dan Inouye said. . . .

DECEMBER 22

I asked Bob Byrd, a week or so ago, to send me his view on what we ought to do in terms of consultations with Congress. He has written me a letter saying that I should try to get a declaration of war. It was a very thoughtful letter from a man who certainly knows the Senate, and has given a lot of thought to the tri-partite form of government. He feels we have not made the case for use of force, and he's in the mode that sanctions will get the job done.

What worries Bob Byrd the most, and this worries the American people and other members of Congress and indeed all of us, is a ground war where we get bogged down. He talks about "mounting casualties"; others call them "body bags." He points out that if there is a high death count on the Arab side, even in winning we'd lose. In fact, he says, "Even a quick knockout of Iraqi forces might well unleash a cascade of outcomes and reactions that would reduce our long-term ability, and influence events in that region." However, I think he's also underestimating the prestige that would go to the United States for being willing to stand up and support the United Nations resolutions fully, and I think he's underestimating the support we would get from many in the Arab world for getting this brutal dictator. I have it in my own mind that Saddam Hussein, in decline, will be like Ceausescu was in decline. There will be dancing in the streets, and they will say that he was brutal and a bully, and they will rejoice when he's gone—I'm confident of that—but I don't think Bob Byrd is.

I didn't quite know how to respond to Congress's hesitancy. I knew most senators and congressmen would be under pressure to support us if we went to war without them, but would be on the spot if I formally asked for a declaration or a resolution to back force. Some were still posturing for the press. Mitchell told me he would have no objection to eventually using force, but said it was still too soon. Nevertheless, when he was questioned by the press on December 23 he replied that he did not think a resolution to use force would pass, and he wouldn't vote for it—despite what he had told me. When he was put on the spot by reporters and asked whether he and other Democrats were deliberately undermining my position by questioning the need for war, he scoffed. If they didn't debate and question now, and it came to war, everyone would ask where he had been and why he had not said something. In contrast, other Democrats, such as Senators Joseph Liebermann and Charles Robb, seemed to understand the gravity of the situation and told me they were ready to support force.

The grumbling and hesitation within Congress were matched by restlessness within the coalition. The surprise announcement of the invitation to Aziz, which caused so much worry among some of our allies, sparked other diplomatic initiatives in December. There were indications that the French and the Italians, as well as the EC, might send separate missions to Baghdad. We were particularly concerned about the French. They had reacted coolly to the UN resolution, and began to distance themselves from it in public statements, though never quite breaking ranks with the coalition. Mitterrand was still reluctant to aid the restoration of the Emir's government. He had been helpful in much else regarding the Gulf—although the French still had not agreed to put their forces under US command—so we were optimistic about him. President Bush sent him a letter on December 7 asking him to reinforce the French troop contingent and not to set up parallel channels with Iraq. Mitterrand agreed to send reinforcements, but said he had not yet made up his mind whether to make direct contact with Iraq.

GEORGE BUSH

The British, on the other hand, seemed as resolute as ever. John Major arrived in Washington on December 21 for his first visit as prime minister. I had met him before and immediately liked him. We were supposed to fly up to Camp David as soon as he arrived, but the weather was "socked in" and the helicopters couldn't fly. Instead, we drove. While we waited for cars, I asked Brent if I should unload the full timetable and game plan for our military option on John, who, after all, had been in office only a short time. I wondered if it was better to speak in general terms now and save detailed plans for later. Brent strongly advised that I give John every bit of information we had right then. We all climbed in the car, Brent and Charles Powell in jump seats facing us and, as the motorcade sped toward the mountains through the dense fog and up the winding roads, I told John everything. We planned to commence offensive operations right after the deadline expired. "How about 0400 on the morning of the sixteenth?" I asked. "How does that grab you?" We had given no order yet to our military, nor had we discussed it with other government officials. This was a very "close hold."

It would have been perfectly understandable if John had said he would get back to me, that he had to talk to his cabinet or military, but he never flinched. He declared on the spot that the British would be with us all the way. I shall never forget that. He became the first foreign leader to know of our war plans, and the first outside our inner circle—fittingly so, given his dependability and unwavering support, and Margaret Thatcher's before him.

On December 20 came the startling news that Eduard Shevardnadze had resigned, followed by Gorbachev's revelation that his foreign minister had not even talked to him about it. I was alarmed by the development and what it might mean for the crisis, the coalition, and the superpower relationship as a whole. Shevardnadze had given no hint there was a problem when he visited us in Washington on December 12, nor had he breathed a word to Jim. This really surprised me, for I knew how close they were and what genuine respect and friendship they felt for each other. Their mutual confidence had been important in bringing Gorbachev to our side on Iraq. A few days later, on December 27, Gorbachev dispatched Alexander Bessmertnykh to deliver a letter about the resignation. Bessmertnykh told me Gorbachev was very upset and thought Shevardnadze was exhausted. He added that Gorbachev wanted to assure me that everything was unchanged in our relationship. He read the translated letter aloud. There was a tone of bitterness to it. Not just because the unexpected resignation was what he called an "act of disloyalty," but because Shevardnadze did it without consulting him. Gorbachev did not approve of the way he resigned, which appeared to him to be bowing to criticism. Nevertheless, Mikhail praised Shevardnadze's courage, contributions, and accomplishments as a reformer and leader. Sergei Tarasenko forwarded Baker a message from Shevardnadze about his resignation. He said he had a two-hour talk with Gorbachev, in which the latter refused his resignation. Shevardnadze had said it was final, and that he had made many sacrifices for perestroika. To stay would be moral suicide.

BRENT SCOWCROFT

We can still only speculate on the real reasons for Shevardnadze's resignation. In his memoir, he called it an act of "disagreement and protest, and simultaneously a warning." But Gorbachev was probably being a bit disingenuous when he said it was unprovoked and unwarranted. It seemed to us that he was at that moment in the course of a sharp turn to the right. Shevardnadze had already told us of his concern about Primakov's machinations regarding Saddam—which, as we were about to see, were intensifying.

I was shocked and concerned by Shevardnadze's departure. It took away the last voice of moderation close to Gorbachev, leaving him vulnerable to the conservatives, Primakov, and the Arabists. There was no telling what the implications would be for foreign policy. The increasingly strong statements and actions in the Baltics were clear indications that Gorbachev felt himself hostage, at least at the moment, to the military. Shevardnadze's warnings of dictatorship seemed almost bizarre at the time, and perhaps he was resigning in frustration because he appeared powerless to hold Gorbachev to a moderate course. He may also have been warning his fellow moderates that they needed to wake up to what was going on.

As we moved nearer to the possibility of war, there were several incidents which could be interpreted to suggest that at least some among our military were less than enthusiastic about the prospect. They occurred against the backdrop of the Vietnam conflict. There was considerable sentiment that the military had been ordered into Vietnam by the civilian leadership and then left holding the bag when the political climate shifted. Reinforced by the tragedy in Lebanon, this feeling was reflected by Secretary of Defense Caspar Weinberger in 1984 when he laid down several preconditions for the use of force, calling for public support amounting to a national crusade.

The initial plan for retaking Kuwait, briefed to President Bush in October, had not seemed designed by anyone eager to undertake the task. Similarly, the force requirements for a successful offense given to him at the end of October were so large that one could speculate they were set forth by a command hoping their size would change his mind about pursuing a military option. Any such concerns were offset by a meeting with the Joint Chiefs of Staff at Camp David on December 1, in which the tone was very positive. General Merrill McPeak gave an upbeat briefing on the effects of a thirty-day air campaign against Iraq, including projected losses: 150 aircraft lost, with half the pilots rescued, a quarter killed, the rest captured and probably paraded through the streets of Baghdad. He thought the bombing would destroy about half of the main Iraqi equipment on the ground.

On December 21, however, General Calvin Waller, the deputy commander in the Gulf, told the press the forces were not yet ready to do the job. That was followed by CENTCOM efforts to push back the date on which hostilities could begin. Wags pointed to President Lincoln's 1862 letter to General George McClellan asking that, if the General was not planning to use his army, could the President borrow it for a time?

GEORGE BUSH

On the morning of Christmas Eve, I met with Powell, Cheney, Scowcroft, and Gates at Camp David for an update. Cheney and Powell were just back from the Gulf, where they had investigated readiness in the wake of Waller's comments. I wanted to know how soon after the deadline we could begin the air strikes, and how long it might take for Saddam to run up the white flag. We reaffirmed our conviction that the earlier we could begin after January 15 the better—it would be close to the day I had mentioned to John Major.

We talked about whether the Arab forces would participate in a ground campaign if it came to that. The Egyptians and Syrians might hesitate to attack the Iraqis. How long would it take to disarm Iraqi troops left in Kuwait? What would we do then? Would we keep a military presence there, and how large and for how long? Would we leave equipment behind? What casualties could we expect? We also went over details such as when to close our embassy in Baghdad, and just how to break diplomatic relations. We spoke about a possible final démarche to Saddam that Jim would deliver. It would have to be a strong message, reminding Saddam that he was facing overwhelming odds and that he would be pounded.

BRENT SCOWCROFT

Some of these questions had been considered within the department staffs and the NSC. Earlier in the fall, I had asked the Deputies Committee, and my own NSC staff, to begin to review our war aims beyond what was set out in the UN resolutions.* The most important was to reduce

*See Chapter 15, pages 383–84.

Saddam's military might so that he would no longer pose a threat to the region, yet to do so in such a way that Iraq was secure from external threats and the balance with Iran was preserved. The subsequent committee discussions had centered on whether to extend air strikes beyond the Kuwait area of operations to Saddam's forces in Iraq. In the end, the recommendation was to focus on destroying Iraq's best-trained and best-equipped forces—the divisions of the elite Republican Guard— wherever we could find them. Since these troops were also the backbone of the regime, their destruction would further undermine Saddam's grip on power. Our Arab allies were convinced, and we began to assume, that dealing Saddam another battlefield defeat would shatter what support he had within the military, which probably would then topple him. Hitting the Republican Guard went to the heart of the problem.

The committee had also raised the question of making Saddam's removal an objective. The problem was, apart from targeting him personally (itself extremely difficult with air strikes, and assassination was not an option), we did not know how this might be achieved. We could not make it a formal goal of the coalition, since it was well beyond the bounds of the UN resolutions guiding us. It might also split the coalition. If the United States made it an objective unilaterally, and declared it as such, we would be in a difficult bind politically and operationally. We would be committing ourselves—alone—to removing one regime and installing another, and, if the Iraqis themselves did not take matters into their own hands, we would be facing an indefinite occupation of a hostile state and some dubious "nation-building." Realistically, if Saddam fell, it would not be a democracy emerging but another, perhaps less problematic, strongman. The best solution was to do as much damage as we could to his military, and wait for the Ba'ath regime to collapse. We would concentrate on liberating Kuwait and leaving the region as soon as possible—fulfilling our UN objectives and our promises to our Arab allies, and, we hoped, destroying Saddam's power base. Thus, these aims (and limits) were established well before the end of the year, and the committee's review eventually became the basis of the directive the President would sign in January, setting Desert Storm in motion.

GEORGE BUSH

DIARY, DECEMBER 24, CAMP DAVID

It's Christmas Eve, and you think of the families and loved ones apart. I read ten or fifteen letters, all of them saying "take care of my kid"; some saying "please don't shoot"; some saying "it's not worth dying for gasoline"; and on and on it goes; but the cry is "save my boy—save my boy." Then I sit here knowing that if there is no movement on Saddam's part, we have to go to war; but we're in a war, though . . . Kuwaiti families being devastated and scared, and even killed this very night. The principle has been set, and we cannot fail. . . .

I'm getting older, but does that make it easier to send someone's son to die? Or does that make it more difficult? All I know is that it's right. I know the consequences if we fail, and I know what will happen if we let the 15th slide by and we look wimpish, or unwilling to do what we must do.

I'm sitting here on Christmas Eve waiting for the caroling in our little church service. I keep thinking of the Gulf, and I see the faces of the young pilots I met when we first got to Dhahran—"let us go; let us do our job; we can do it"; and then the Marines and the Army guys—young, young, so very young. I think of the Iraqi babies, and yet, I think of the evil that is this man. He has to not only be checked, but punished, and then we worry about how we handle our relations with the Arab countries. . . .

They say I don't concentrate on domestic affairs, and I expect that charge is true; but how can you when you hold the life and death of a lot of young troops in your hand? . . .

I summed up my feelings in a letter to my children I wrote on December 31 from Camp David.

Dear George, Jeb, Neal, Marvin, Doro,
    I am writing this letter on the last day of 1990.
    First, I can't begin to tell you how great it was to have you here at Camp David. I loved the games (the Marines are still smarting over their 1 and 2 record), I loved Christmas Day, marred only by the absence of Sam and Ellie [daughter Doro's children]. I loved the movies—some of 'em—I loved the laughs. Most of all, I loved seeing you together. We are a family blessed; and this Christmas simply reinforced all that.
    I hope I didn't seem moody. I tried not to.
    When I came into this job, I vowed that I would never wring my hands and talk about the "loneliest job in the world" or wring my hands about the "pressures or the trials." Having said that, I *have* been concerned about what lies ahead. There is no "loneliness" though, because I am backed by a first-rate team of knowledgeable and committed people. No President has been more blessed in this regard.
    I have thought long and hard about what might have to be done. As

I write this letter at year's end, there is still some hope that Iraq's dictator will pull out of Kuwait. I vary on this. Sometimes I think he might, at others I think he is simply too unrealistic—too ignorant of what he might face. I have the peace of mind that comes from knowing that we have tried hard for peace. We have gone to the UN; we have formed a historic coalition. There have been diplomatic initiatives from country after country. And so, here we are a scant 16 days from a very important date—the date set by the UN for his total compliance with all UN resolutions, including getting out of Kuwait—totally.

I guess what I want you to know as a father is:

Every human life is precious. When the question is asked "How many lives are you willing to sacrifice"—it tears at my heart. The answer, of course, is none, none at all. We have waited to give sanctions a chance, we have moved a tremendous force so as to reduce the risk to every American soldier if force is to be used; but the question of loss of life still lingers and plagues the heart.

My mind goes back to history:

How many lives might have been saved if appeasement had given way to force earlier on in the late 30s or earliest 40s? How many Jews might have been spared the gas chambers, or how many Polish patriots might be alive today? I look at today's crisis as "good" vs. "evil." Yes, it is that clear.

I know my stance must cause you a little grief from time to time; and this hurts me; but here at "year's end" I just wanted you to know that I feel:

—every human life is precious.

—principle must be adhered to—Saddam cannot profit in any way at all from his aggression and from his brutalizing the people of Kuwait.

—and sometimes in life you have to act as you think best—you can't compromise, you can't give in, even if your critics are loud and numerous.

So, dear kids, batten down the hatches.

Senator Inouye of Hawaii told me: "Mr. President, do what you have to do. If it is quick and successful everyone can take the credit. If it is drawn out, then be prepared for some in Congress to file impeachment papers against you." That's what he said, and he's 100% correct.

And so I shall say a few more prayers, mainly for our kids in the Gulf, and I shall do what must be done, and I shall be strengthened every day by our family love which lifts me up every single day of my life. I am the luckiest Dad in the whole wide world.

I love you. Happy New Year and may God Bless every one of you and all in your family.

Devotedly,
Dad.

We closed the year with threats from Majority Leader Dick Gephardt and others that Congress might cut off funding if I went ahead without a congressional declaration of war. Over in the Gulf, the Iraqis invoked a curse on me and swore they would not leave Kuwait.

Brent and I talked a couple of times on December 31, and I told him I thought we should try once more for a meeting with Aziz or even Saddam. Mitterrand was pushing it for domestic political reasons, and I knew Jim wanted to try once more. But it also seemed to me a good way to persuade reluctant members of Congress that we had exhausted the diplomatic avenues, something we would need if we were to get the resolution through. Brent didn't feel either measure was necessary, but he didn't try to talk me out of them. He told me Jim suggested that we wait until January 3, when the window had closed, before making any further overture to Baghdad. I asked if there was any news about the date the military might be ready to go. He reported that Powell was saying it would be sometime between January 18 and 22. This was close to the deadline, but it seemed to be drifting further back. I told Brent we had to go in the January window.

DIARY, JANUARY I

I must confess that I woke up right about midnight wondering what 1991 would hold. . . . The more I think about the problem, the more convinced I am we're going to have to go down to the wire. . . . But it's tough when you have to consult so many allies and when you have to have so many things come together—the diplomatic front, third-party situations like Israel, how do you handle the Jordanians, keeping them from doing something? What [warning] do we give to Saddam Hussein? . . . How do we handle Congress? And I've about concluded that the way to do it is to talk, talk, talk over the next two weeks and then notify them under the War Powers Resolution—or put it this way, "consistent" with the War Powers Resolution.

The following morning, I gathered Brent, Jim, and John Sununu and explained that I wanted a last, one-shot meeting to get the message personally to Saddam about what he was up against, probably in Switzerland; the "home and home" arrangement was closed. We decided to announce it the next day, January 3, provided we could complete our consultations with the allies—there would be no surprises this time. To reassure them, I emphasized that the offer was still subject to the same conditions as our last proposal in December—no negotiations, no compromises, no attempts at face-saving, and no rewards for aggression.

DIARY, JANUARY 2

Baker calls me at 3:45 on the 2nd . . . and says "don't close the door on my going to Baghdad to meet Saddam Hussein," and I tell him I'm inclined to slam the door and leave it closed because this guy's jerking us around and this meeting will take the place of either of the home and home meetings. Jim seems unhappy about that, but he does seem to want very much to go to Baghdad and he has from the beginning. But I am disinclined. I think that given the reports that we are vacillating, we close the door now.

That evening I cabled the coalition allies to tell them of our plan, and early the next morning spoke with Major and Mitterrand. All were behind us.

The next day I announced the offer to send Jim to Geneva on January 7, 8, or 9, and that he would make the rounds again with our allies. It was a risk. Saddam could well use the meeting to announce a gimmicky plan with untold numbers of conditions attached, perhaps even pulling out some troops and taking his time to remove the rest while saying he wanted to talk. In retrospect, I think he must have interpreted the first "home and home" offer in November as a sign of weakness, not recognizing that it was made to show Congress and the European and US publics that we were willing to try for peace. When I followed up that offer with the proposal to meet in Geneva, he probably told his clique, "They are weak, they will not attack us, or why is Bush continuing to make peace feelers?" On January 4, Iraq accepted my proposal to send Jim to talk to Aziz and suggested January 9 in Geneva.

BRENT SCOWCROFT

I was very apprehensive. I could think of any number of deceptively attractive, purposely vague proposals and ploys Saddam could put forth which could result in severe strains on the coalition and accentuate divisions within the United States. There was absolutely no doubt that Jim Baker was a brilliant negotiator. But I also had no doubt that he would do everything possible to attain our demands by persuasion rather than force. The unhappy reality of the situation, from my perspective, was that an Iraqi withdrawal would leave us in a most difficult position. Saddam could pull his forces back just north of the border and leave them there, poised for attack. US forces, on the other hand, could not long remain in place. The force exceeded our capability to rotate it and, in any event, it would not be tolerable for the Saudis to have such a large foreign force indefinitely on their territory.

Meanwhile, members of the new Congress began to turn up the heat. On January 2, Representatives Richard Durbin and Charles Bennett, along with Senator Tom Harkin, announced plans to introduce a resolution requiring congressional approval before our troops fired a shot. We had two meetings with congressional leaders the next day, first with George Mitchell, Bob Dole, Foley, and Michel, followed by a conclave of the full bipartisan leadership. The President once again made his pitch for Congress to signal Saddam that we were united and resolute. There was no better way to do that than if they passed a resolution endorsing UNSCR 678.

The tone of Congress seemed to be changing. Foley now believed it would probably pass an authorization of the use of force, "but I can't tell you overwhelmingly." Congress would cancel its usual January recess and begin holding Monday, Wednesday, and Friday sessions, but there would be no regular business prior to January 23. He thought there would be competing resolutions as well.

The President said it would help if the measure could be put to an immediate vote—a long debate would be counterproductive. "You can't shut off debate or stifle it," Mitchell replied with irritation. "There are no limitations on amendments either. Pressler, D'Amato, and Harkin have already said they are offering some. I think a UN-type resolution would be close in the Senate, without a substantial majority. Several senators have said they won't give explicit authority. You might get a few more votes on specific authorization after the fifteenth. I'm reluctant to bring it up for these reasons. Pressure for debate and discussion is growing. I'd prefer to wait until Baker returns from Geneva." Dole advised that if we still could not get a consensus we should do nothing.

With the full leadership, the President explained where our diplomacy on the Gulf stood and outlined the purposes behind Baker's trip and his meeting with Aziz. The reaction was generally positive and some, such as Gephardt, applauded the extra diplomacy.

Bob Byrd said he did not intend to vote to support the UN-type resolution, preferring a declaration of war. But he did not believe that a declaration would pass. "[T]he American people are not ready," he insisted. "People are monstrously angry at the disgraceful contributions of our so-called friends Japan, Germany, and Saudi Arabia."

"There is no overwhelming fervor or wellspring in the country," added

Dante Fascell. "Fifty percent of the objective has been achieved. A resolution of support, even with the White House and the full leadership behind it, would still lose by a hundred twenty to a hundred twenty-five votes."

Sam Nunn was still backing sanctions. "I'm willing to use force after all other avenues are explored," he said. "Over half of the Iraqi GNP has been taken away. I believe that every month that goes by Saddam gets weaker. There is erosion of his economy and military capability."

"The real difference around the table is whether you use force sooner or later," said Lee Hamilton. "I personally go for later. I agree with Sam Nunn. Iraq is a country under great stress. Sanctions are working and we must exhaust all other possibilities."

We decided we would wait until Baker had met with Aziz before debate on a resolution would begin. Within hours, Foley and Mitchell both had their hands full reining in a few hot-headed members who tried to jump the gun with resolutions to prohibit military action without a declaration of war, and to force a debate, among them Dave Obey, Joe Kennedy, Brock Adams, and Tom Harkin. "We're all mixed up," remarked Bob Dole. "When we should have been debating we were on vacation. Now that we should be quiet we want to vote."

GEORGE BUSH

DIARY, JANUARY 4

For those who think I'm paranoid about the press, they ought to look at the ABC-Washington Post poll.* Last night it comes out with four tremendously supportive categories—80% think we ought to use force sooner rather than later; well over 2 to 1 think that the President's policy is correct; and on and on. Very succinct and summarized in the [White House] News Summary today. The Washington Post has a front-page story [on the Gulf]—no mention of it. They're the sponsors of the poll, and buried [on A19] at the back of the story [on Congress] are two of the categories, leaving out that 80% think sooner rather than later. And maybe they do say preliminary reports, but we'll have to see what they do with it finally. But it looks to me like they don't want to print the news they don't want to see read. Typical!

*According to the ABC–WP poll: 66% approved of how the President was handling the crisis. 29% disapproved. 70% thought the Congress should be giving the President more support (18% said they should not be giving more support). 65% said the US should go to war if necessary to force Iraq out of Kuwait (29% said no war). 82% say US should move quickly, within a month, if the January 15 deadline is not met (10% said wait 1–6 months).

On January 5, UN secretary general Javier Pérez de Cuéllar arrived at Camp David and asked what he might do to head off conflict. I tried to talk him out of another personal mission, which I thought would only offer Saddam hope that he could find another way out. I told Javier I thought we must insist on full implementation of every one of the UN resolutions. "If we compromise, we weaken the UN and our own credibility in building this new world order," I said. "I think Saddam Hussein doesn't believe force will be used—or if it is, he can produce a stalemate. I also think he misreads public opinion in the US. . . ."

"You have to exhaust all possible means for peace first," advised Javier. "Shouldn't you offer to send Baker to Baghdad? He [Saddam] will ask for time to study your letter and stall."

"Even more so if Baker goes to see him," I replied. "If nothing happens after the fifteenth, people will lose faith, the coalition begins to collapse, and our whole effort is in vain. The Security Council resolution is very clear and I think it is vital to implement that. If we agree Baker meets with him . . . we have undermined our efforts." He thought the most likely outcome of an additional trip to Baghdad beyond the meeting in Geneva would be Jim coming back empty-handed. He had seen the Iraqi ambassador to the United Nations the day before and had asked if there was anything to pass along to me. There was nothing. Javier observed that he was in a different position from that of Baker. "I almost have to do something before the fifteenth," he said. "I would present the resolutions to [Saddam]. But if *I* come back empty-handed, I could trigger a conflict."

"The bad side is you could be cover for his manipulations," I said. "The good is that this really would be the last mile." Javier did think it would come to that anyway, especially after the Iraqi ambassador had nothing to send on. He was thinking about going to Baghdad, but it would depend on what happened in Geneva.

We had hoped that the failure of the Secretary General's first mission to Saddam back in August would make it easier to talk him out of a repeat, but it was not to be. He had only the best of motives and he wanted very badly to be cooperative, but he had a reluctant but firm view of where his responsibilities lay. He also suggested another Security Council meeting prior to the January 15 deadline, but we saw no reason for it. We had done what we could at the United Nations. Later that day, I reworked the letter to Saddam that Baker would carry to Geneva, and signed a final version.

The following day I drafted a letter to Congress asking them to support the UN resolutions, and the use of all necessary means to eject Iraq from Kuwait, and faxed it to Brent for his comments. I was confident I did not need a resolution. The United States had used military force about two hundred times in its history and there had been only five declarations of war. But for the country's sake, and to show Saddam we were speaking as one voice, I wanted Congress on record, and before the deadline passed. We still did not have a draft resolution in hand, although individual congressmen were working on versions. The precise language would be critical. I wanted to avoid asking for "authorization," which implied Congress had the final say in what I believed was an executive decision. I also hoped to avoid turning this into a party-line vote, which meant the sponsoring names attached to it were important. There was a strong draft by conservative congressman Duncan Hunter which I could support, but we needed bipartisan backing. I asked Sonny Montgomery to have a word with Hunter, who understood the situation. We would try to keep its content, but work with a broader base of sponsors. I began a flurry of telephone consultations with members of Congress. Polls were saying support in Congress appeared split, but would probably pass a resolution by a thin majority. People were acknowledging, however, that this was becoming a political rather than legal issue. We also began strategy meetings with our legislative affairs people and members of Congress on how to push the resolution and arrange sponsorship.

On January 9, as the world watched, Baker met with Aziz in Geneva. He called the President twice, as soon as he could after each session: at 7:30 am, and then at about 1:00 pm. In the morning, Baker reported that Aziz had not come with anything unanticipated, but had launched into a long litany on Iraq's history with Kuwait. It was not clear if Aziz would or would not accept the letter to Saddam. Baker told him at the outset that he was not there to negotiate but communicate, at which time he had offered him the President's letter. It was in a sealed envelope, but Baker gave him a photocopy, which read in part:

> We stand today at the brink of war between Iraq and the world. This is a war which began with your invasion of Kuwait; this is a war that can only be ended by Iraq's full and unconditional compliance with UN Security Council Resolution 678 . . .
>
> We prefer a peaceful outcome. However, anything less than full compliance with UN Security Council Resolution 678 and its predecessors is unacceptable. There can be no reward for aggression. Nor will there be any negotiation. Principle cannot be compromised. However, by its full compliance, Iraq will gain the opportunity to rejoin the international community. More immediately, Iraq and the Iraqi military

establishment will escape destruction. But unless you withdraw from Kuwait completely and without condition, you will lose more than Kuwait. What is at stake here is not the future of Kuwait—it will be free, its government will be restored—but rather the future of Iraq. The choice is yours to make . . .

Iraq is already feeling the effects of the sanctions mandated by the United Nations. Should war come, it will be a far greater tragedy for you and your country. Let me state, too, that the United States will not tolerate the use of chemical or biological weapons or the destruction of Kuwait's oil fields and installations. The American people would demand the strongest possible response. Further, you will be held directly responsible for terrorist actions against any member of the coalition. You, the Ba'ath Party, and your country will pay a terrible price if you order unconscionable actions of this sort.

I write this letter not to threaten, but to inform. I do so with no sense of satisfaction, for the people of the United States have no quarrel with the people of Iraq. Mr. President, UN Security Council Resolution 678 establishes the period before January 15 of this year as a "pause of good will" so that this crisis may end without further violence. Whether this pause is used as intended, or merely becomes a prelude to further violence, is in your hands, and yours alone. I hope you weigh your choice carefully and choose wisely, for much will depend on it.

Aziz scanned the letter. Calling it nothing but "threats," he pushed it out into the middle of the table, where it remained. Baker went through his talking points, and warned that this would be a war Iraq could not win. Aziz replied that Iraq was not laboring under a false impression. They knew what they were up against. "We accept war," he said with confidence. Baker shot back that the United States was resolved on this and Aziz should not underestimate us—or the powers of the President. We could not control the bounds of a conflict once it began. He outlined what he thought would happen to Iraq if it came to war, but added that the Iraqis would not be attacked if they withdrew and fully complied with the UN resolutions. Aziz said they were insulted.

GEORGE BUSH

In the middle of a lunch meeting with the congressional leadership that afternoon, Patty Presock handed me a note that Jim was calling again. I picked up the phone at the table, and he briefed me on the second part of the discussions. He described it as "absolute total bullying," by Iraq, although Aziz had seemed a little nervous. "Anyway," said Jim, "it's over. Here's the way we left it: he invited himself to the United States and invited us to Baghdad. He said he was 'picking up the President's proposal to meet.' I said 'No! We gave you fifteen days—you said no. Now you're trying to manipulate the deadline. . . .' " In the end, Aziz refused to take the letter with him, leaving it on the table. The Iraqi embassy in Geneva also would not take it. I hoped that Aziz would at least tell Saddam the contents of the copy he had read.

DIARY, JANUARY 9

I guess Wednesday was one of the toughest days of my presidency—the tensest, waiting for Jim Baker to call. I work with the Congress, [at the same time] listening to the Aziz press conference. On the phone to Mitterrand, Mulroney, King Fahd, Bob Hawke of Australia—[still] talking to all four leaders of Congress . . .

The failure of the Baker-Aziz talk, I think, will help us with the Congress.

I called John Major on January 10 to fill him in on the talks in Geneva. Pérez de Cuéllar was going to Baghdad, but John was sanguine about the trip, thinking it might help keep the Europeans from making their own last-minute visits. He had just been to the Gulf himself. "The Arabs are all very robust," he told me. "They are angry with Saddam and ready to go . . . Mubarak was breathing fire. . . ." Troop morale was high. "They are ready, and most want to get underway."

BRENT SCOWCROFT

That day the resolutions were introduced on the floor of both houses, and the debate began. We expended enormous effort to ensure a favorable vote. Almost no members of Congress, except those about whom we were certain, went without multiple efforts to persuade him or her that the national interest lay in a positive vote. The President was on the phone constantly, and met with many members. Our vote count was perilously close, especially in the Senate, which was usually the more cooperative body. On this occasion, however, several powerful supportive and vocal Democratic members of the House, such as Aspin, Murtha, Solarz, and Torricelli, made prospects in the House more promising. Our initial focus, therefore, was to have the House vote first, providing positive momentum for the Senate. In that we were successful, but the outcome was in doubt until it became clear that enough Democratic senators (albeit a handful) had broken with the leadership to make a victory certain.

As Congress began its debate, there were more challenges within the coalition. French defense minister Chevenement was still pushing for the United States to make a "gesture" toward agreeing to an international conference on the Middle East. We feared that the Germans favored such linkage. Then, on January 11, the situation in Lithuania took a bad turn. Soviet troops surrounded the main printing plant in Vilnius and stormed some state defense centers. Gorbachev called President Bush at 8:00 am to discuss the situation, and to ask him to receive Bessmertnykh, who would carry a proposal on the Gulf. The President urged Gorbachev to refrain from more violence in Lithuania. He also agreed to see Bessmertnykh, although we wanted no part of the complicated proposal. The situation in Lithuania worsened over the following weekend. In a decision apparently made by local commanders, Soviet troops took the television station in Vilnius—thirteen were killed and dozens wounded. Baker sent a message to Shevardnadze (even though he had resigned, his successor had not yet been named) telling him that all the Western allies had indicated that the crackdown would hurt their willingness to offer aid to the Soviet Union. Even though Gorbachev denied ordering the storming of the television station, we could not help thinking that this was just what Shevardnadze had been predicting when he resigned three weeks earlier. It appeared Gorbachev was losing control. The reformers around him were bailing out or had been pushed aside. The crackdown could only complicate our relations with Moscow as we approached the Gulf deadline, but we tried hard to separate the two crises.

There were to be three resolutions for a vote on January 12 in each chamber. In the House the first would be Durbin-Bennett, which reaffirmed the right of Congress to declare war and stated that any offensive action taken against Iraq must first be approved by Congress. The second was Gephardt-Hamilton, which was a Sense of Congress resolution expressing continued support for economic sanctions. It also asserted that any offensive action taken against Iraq must first be authorized by Congress. The key vote would occur last. This was the bipartisan Michel-Solarz, a joint resolution which backed the use of force to achieve the objectives of the United Nations. This was the only one which required the President's signature; the other two were concurrent resolutions and were advisory. The Senate twin to Michel-Solarz was Dole-Warner. Mitchell and Nunn introduced a resolution challenging the President's authority to order an attack on Iraq by himself and the wisdom of doing so now.

In the following days, the debate in both houses was passionate, but not bitter. All preferred a peaceful settlement but most understood this was rapidly evaporating as an option. "I do believe that our best chance for peace and our best hopes for peace [are] to strengthen the President's hand in every way we can," said Dole. John Warner asked what the implications would be for our allies that had troops in the Gulf if Congress withheld its support. What would be the effect on our own soldiers?

"The President will have to come before the Congress under the Constitution, as he should," said Nunn. "He will have the backing of the United Nations, and I have said from day one of this debate that I think a war is justified . . . I don't think a war at this time is wise and I think there are alternatives." Arlen Specter argued that if the Congress "rebuked" the President and UN Resolution 678, "the credibility of the United States will be diminished, and it is this senator's view that the sanctions will fall apart. . . . I believe that we will be incapacitating the presidency as an institution in the future . . ."

"In the event of war, why should it be an American war, made up largely of American troops, American casualties, and American deaths?" asked Mitchell. "Just this morning I heard it said that there may be 'only' a few thousand American casualties. But for the families of those few thousand . . . the word will have no meaning. And the truly haunting question, which no one will ever be able to answer, will be: did they die unnecessarily? For if we go to war now, no one will ever know if sanctions would have worked if given a full and fair chance." Edward Kennedy put it more sharply: "There is still time to save the President from himself," he said. "And save thousands of American soldiers in the Persian Gulf from dying in the desert in a war whose cruelty will be exceeded only by the lack of any rational necessity for waging it." Daniel Patrick Moynihan still insisted that this was not an international crisis. "All that's happened is that one nasty little country invaded a littler but just as nasty country." Bob Kerrey urged that Congress tell Saddam that the United States would not declare war or initiate an attack "under the current circumstances."

Barbara Boxer quoted from predictions that there would be 15,000 American casualties. "If we keep reaching back to the old ways, it is gloom and doom for our society." She argued that the country was "about to be sucked into a war in the area of the world known for violence, known for terrorism, known for blood baths, known for atrocities. We will never be the same again."

"Are we supposed to go to war simply because one man—the President—makes a series of unilateral decisions that put us in a box—a box that makes that war, to a greater degree, inevitable?" asked John Kerry.

In the House, the debate was similar. "It is our very profound conviction that this is not a Democratic issue, it is not a Republican issue," said Solarz. "It is an American issue." Aspin urged that on the question of authorizing the President to use force, the right vote was yes, but "I believe there is little possibility of a bloodless victory."

"The only debate here in the Congress is over whether we slowly strangle Saddam with sanctions or immediately pursue a military solution," said Gephardt. "We say we can win without war, and the evidence is on our side."

On January 12, each house voted to support the joint resolution authorizing the use of force pursuant to the UN resolutions. The House passed Solarz-Michel 250–183, while in the Senate Republican Warner and Democrat Liebermann teamed up to secure passage of the Senate version with 52–47, the smallest margin ever to vote for war. The other resolutions were defeated.

GEORGE BUSH

Although all the Democratic leadership in both houses voted against, the count was better than I had expected. In the Senate ten Democrats* joined us on authorization, while among the Republicans only two, Hatfield and Grassley, voted against. It is interesting that, five years after this important vote, Sam Nunn admitted he had made a mistake in letting Mitchell and Boren talk him into voting no. I felt the heavy weight that I might be faced with impeachment lifted from my shoulders as I heard the results. In truth, even had Congress not passed the resolutions I would have acted and ordered our troops into combat. I know it would have caused an outcry, but it was the right thing to do. I was comfortable in my own mind that I had the constitutional authority. It had to be done.

With the resolutions at last in hand, at 6:00 pm on Sunday, January 13, our top defense and national security people met in the Residence for about an hour. Baker was still on his way back from briefing our coalition allies after Geneva. The mood was somber. There was a real difference in the air now—we were getting close to the wire. The first press reports were trickling in about Pérez de Cuéllar's mission to Baghdad the day before. It had failed. Now the news coverage was full of demonstrations, church services, and specials, all asking "Are we ready for war?" The antiwar demonstrations that had started many weeks be-

*Liebermann, Reid, Robb, Shelby, Heflin, Breaux, Bryan, Graham, Gore, and Johnston.

fore in Lafayette Square in front of the White House continued day and night, with drums beating incessantly.

We decided that the time of attack would be 3:00 am on January 17 Gulf time, 7:00 pm January 16 in Washington, and fine-tuned some of the major targeting problems we still faced regarding Iraq's power grids, electricity, bridges, and refineries. There was also the tricky question of overflights for our aircraft and missiles. This was a particularly sensitive issue with the Turks, who were not comfortable about some cruise missiles we wanted to fire across their territory. We eventually solved that by simply retargeting and not flying over Turkey.

GEORGE BUSH

I was still strangely calm. I kept saying to myself, Stay on track, do what you have to do, ask the right questions, make the proper changes, if you need to make them, and then be firm. We had to get rid of Saddam's nuclear and biological weapons capabilities. How would we notify our friends of the timing? How do we put the innocent on notice and how do we safeguard American embassies? Over and over I kept saying to Brent and the others, "Once we attack with this awesome air power, how do we end it? How does he surrender? He will, I know he will. He cannot prevail against it."

Later that evening I looked over speech material for my address to the nation on January 16, trying to capture the right phrases. I read through quotes by Robert Lowell, Thomas Paine, and others, but none captured quite how I was feeling. Before I went to bed, I turned on the television news and sat for a while. I watched as a father kissed his soldier son goodbye as he shipped out to the Gulf. The boy choked up and the dad gave him a hug. Memories of war flooded back. I remembered clearly when I went off to Chapel Hill, North Carolina, for pre-flight training on August 6, 1942. My dad accompanied me to New York's Penn Station. He too had given me a hug on the platform. I cried on the train; I had just turned eighteen. I didn't know one single soul and I was off for an experience into the unknown.

Monday, January 14, was filled with great tension, and I could feel it as I walked around the White House offices in the West Wing. All of us were anxiously thinking ahead, to the deadline before us and what would happen afterward. Over lunch with Dick Cheney, Brent, and General Merrill McPeak we went over the bombing campaign and talked about the worst cases we might face, with civilians killed and all the attendant horrors of bombs and missiles hitting the wrong targets. McPeak radiated confidence that the Air Force would carry out its mission with great precision and success. I was worried about American journalists in Baghdad. I was also concerned about innocent Iraqi kids, although the initial attack would be so early in the morning that most people would be at home in bed. McPeak and others assured me that the targeting was such that very few civilians would be killed, and I prayed they were correct.

That afternoon, we received word from French foreign minister Roland Dumas that Paris still wanted to make a last-minute attempt to persuade Saddam to withdraw, this time through another Security Council resolution. Dumas proposed once again that we tell the Iraqis that if they pulled out, we would agree to a conference on the Middle East. There were rumors that Mitterrand himself might go to Baghdad. It was linkage, even though they said it was not, and there was no way we could support the proposal, which the French soon dropped. It was now clear to me that it was going to be the United States alone that would have to pull the trigger.

At about six thirty the next morning, the day the UN deadline was to run out, I spoke briefly on the telephone with Jim, and then went for a solitary walk around the White House grounds before heading to the office at quarter to seven. I found myself thinking about how we would end the war after it began. In a quiet moment, I again dictated into my tape recorder:

> Quarter to 7—January 15—about to go to work. I have trouble with how this ends. Say the air attack is devastating and Saddam gets done in by his own people. How do they stop? How do we keep from having overkill? Most people don't see that as a scenario because they are convinced it will be long and drawn out with numerous body bags on the US side. But I want to be sure we are not in there pounding people. I think we need to watch and see when our military objectives are taken care of in Baghdad and Iraq . . .

At 10:30 in the morning, the NSC principals gathered again in the Oval Office to go over the final details for the beginning of the air campaign. We discussed the timing of the President's speech to the nation, which we decided would be broadcast about two hours after the air campaign began. We also reviewed the allies' notification times of the onset of the air strikes, which would depend on whether or not their forces were involved. Some, such as Mubarak, would be told at "H" hour; others, such as Mitterrand, Mulroney, Ozal, and Hawke, would get the word a little earlier, between half an hour and an hour ahead of time. John Major, whose

RAF would be alongside our own Air Force in the early strikes, would get twelve hours' notice. We decided that Baker would inform Bandar and Bessmertnykh, and Cheney would call Moshe Arens of Israel, at "H" minus one. We all agreed that the notifications to Congress required by the resolution would be sent essentially at "H" hour.

GEORGE BUSH

Even with this tight schedule I worried that a leak might alert the Iraqis and cost some of our pilots their lives. Brent handed me the National Security Directive authorizing the execution of Operation Desert Storm. Sitting in a wingback chair by the fireplace, I signed the document, but left the date and time blank. I told Cheney he could sign the actual execute order and convey it to General Schwarzkopf. I went back to the Residence at six thirty and watched the news.

DIARY, JANUARY 15

There is no way to describe the pressure. It's 9:45 the night of the 15th. Deadline runs out in two hours, 15 minutes . . . The reports from Baghdad are defiant. People marching in the streets—turning out. Yet their faces smile and they chant. And I think, oh God, save their lives. There's a kid that comes on television. I think it is an Asian child. It haunts me because it looks like an Iraqi child. And I say, pray to God, pray to God that we will be accurate and we will not hit that child.

The Pope wires in . . . It is beautiful. It is a beautiful, beautiful piece. Cardinal Law calls me, Bishop Browning called me. Halverson called me. Bob Schueller, Bill Bright, and many of the evangelicals. And of course, Billy Graham called in. Lafayette Square, in front of the White House, is full of candles and praying. I hope to God that they know we are praying . . .

At midnight, Washington time, the deadline for Iraq to withdraw from Kuwait ran out.

CHAPTER 18

Desert Storm

GEORGE BUSH

The day after the deadline passed was very strange, unlike any other I've experienced. Routine business had an unreal quality to it. At an education meeting I found that I could concentrate for only a few minutes. I would remember that our missiles and aircraft were being prepared to strike Baghdad, and in some cases might even be en route to their targets. Suddenly, everything else was trivial. Throughout the day, people kept coming up and saying, "God bless you." There was still anger in some members of Congress. Representative Henry Gonzalez, who had refused to vote on the resolution supporting the use of force, now filed a resolution of impeachment. Jim Baker and I ate lunch together in the Residence. He seemed to share my nervousness.

I had begun the notifications the afternoon before, with a call to John Major, and throughout the day continued to notify the other allies that we were about to go in. I also spoke with each of the former presidents, all of whom supported what we were about to do. This included Jimmy Carter, who was very gracious. I think he understood that we had made the last appeal with Aziz and had done what we could to avert war. Between 5:30 and 6:30, I phoned the congressional leaders and, after I finished, a feeling of uncomfortable expectation began to take hold as I waited until the bombs were to start falling at 7:00. Now it was in the hands of the military. At 6:40 Barbara, Billy Graham, and I sat in front of the television, watching as lights were blacked out all over Baghdad. We heard what sounded like gunfire and for a moment it looked as if we had struck early. I called Dick Cheney, who said it was probably just their own troops firing into the sky. At seven Cheney called again to say the first bombs had landed. I turned to the others and said, "They're right on schedule."

BRENT SCOWCROFT

I was sitting in my office with Richard Haass and Bob Gates watching CNN when the air campaign began. It was an eerie experience. There I was, with the time lines of the attack in my lap, simultaneously looking at the targets on television as they were struck. It was as if I were reading a script of a movie as it played out before my eyes. I was actually watching a war begin. At about 6:40 pm, Bernard Shaw of CNN, stationed in a hotel in downtown Baghdad, said there were reports of firing near the southern border. That would be the attack on the Iraqi warning radars, I thought. Right on time. Then I watched as the night sky over the city on the TV screen began to light up with anti-aircraft tracers—gunners firing at nothing out of nervousness. At precisely 7:00, the screen filled with bomb bursts.

GEORGE BUSH

A few minutes later, Marlin Fitzwater walked into the White House briefing room and read a short statement from me announcing that the liberation of Kuwait had begun and that I would speak to the nation at 9:00. As I prepared for the address, I was surprised to find I didn't feel nervous. I knew what I wanted to say, said it, and hoped it resonated. I learned later that I had addressed the largest U.S. television audience on record—79 percent of the sets were tuned in. At 10:00, just before I went to bed, Dick Cheney called me with the first reports from the Gulf. Fifty-six Navy planes went out, fifty-six came back. Some two hundred Air Force planes were also out and no sign of any of them missing. I felt a sense of relief and gratitude. I felt the need to pray.

That night of January 16–17 was another restless one. After tossing and turning for hours, I decided to get up. I took the dogs for a walk on the South Lawn at 5:00 am, and went to the Oval Office for a few minutes before going downstairs to the Situation Room. One American F-18 pilot had been lost, Lieutenant Commander Michael Scott Speicher, of Mayport, Florida, although Iraq was claiming fourteen. At 11:00 Barbara and I, joined by most of the cabinet and the Joint Chiefs, attended a service over in Arlington, Virginia, in Memorial Chapel at Fort Myer, where Billy Graham gave the sermon. We sang "God of Our Fathers" and "Amazing Grace." A soloist sang "God Bless America."

As the day progressed there was a general feeling of euphoria with the continued success of the air campaign and the light casualties. But just after seven that evening Brent called to tell me that the Iraqis had fired five Scud missiles into Israel—early in the morning of January 18 in Tel Aviv. The first reports were sketchy and confusing. We didn't know how bad the damage was, from where the missiles had been launched (we had targeted the fixed-site launchers in the earliest strikes), or even what types of warheads were on them. There were all kinds of rumors. First we heard that chemical weapons were used and that missiles had hit Lebanon. Then we learned that seven Scuds had been fired and that there had been very little damage, probably no one killed and no chemical weapons. There were also confusing reports over whether our Patriots had intercepted any of the missiles, or had even been fired. But the most important question was how the Israelis might react.

BRENT SCOWCROFT

The opening night of the air war had been a long one, but the first twenty-four hours of the fighting had gone exceedingly well. It was about seven o'clock and Bob Gates and I were preparing to go home when Marlin Fitzwater and Roman Popadiuk burst into my office with the first reports of the Scud strikes. The attack was a shrewd attempt to split the Arab allies from the coalition, either by directly provoking an Israeli military response or by gathering support among radical Arabs. I called Haass, Baker, and Cheney and asked them to come over. Cheney said that, in the midst of the air campaign, his proper place was at the National Military Command Center. I agreed, so we opened a direct line between us and I put him on a speaker phone. Larry Eagleburger arrived just after Baker and John Sununu came down the hall with Andy Card, Sununu's deputy. A few minutes later, Dick Darman appeared, followed shortly by the Vice President. All crowded into my office.

Cheney reported that Defense Minister Arens had called him immediately following the attack and asked that we ship a unit of Patriot air defense missiles as soon as possible. He had also asked us to make arrangements for an Israeli counterstrike.

I thought it would be almost impossible to keep the Israelis from retaliating, but we had to do it. Cheney said he doubted we could stop them and we could make a bad situation worse by trying. He suggested we let them go, go fast, and get it over with. Cheney's assessment caused dismay. Haass and I agreed it would be a serious mistake to let the Israelis strike back. To reach Iraq, their aircraft would have to cross Arab territory, either Syria, Jordan, or Saudi Arabia. I could not imagine that any of these countries would permit such a flagrant violation of their territory (assuming they detected it) without reacting militarily. If the Israelis went without permission, their most likely route was across Jordan. That they could cross over and back without detection was highly unlikely and, if the Jordanians did spot them, they almost certainly would attempt to intercept. That would bring Jordan into the conflict and change the entire calculus for the coalition. But there was one other obstacle to an Israeli strike which might help keep them out—a process whose technical term was "deconfliction." This meant providing identification codes and working out flight times and routes to avoid the possibility that the coalition might fire on Israeli aircraft. As long as we refused deconfliction, any Israeli attack would be seriously hazardous for them. The only other option was for Israel to retaliate in kind—using its Jericho surface-to-surface missiles. It was the least problematic of the possibilities, but it would mean Israeli participation in the war, which would still threaten the coalition.

As we debated, word came that at least some of the missiles had carried nerve gas. That altered the discussion. Eagleburger said that if Cheney was not right before, he almost certainly was now. He pointed out that if Israel struck back with missiles rather than aircraft it would avoid a requirement for our cooperation.

The first priority, we decided, was to mount a campaign to persuade the Israelis to hold off. Baker called the President to get his concurrence and to ask him to phone Shamir. The President asked that Baker make the call, but the White House operator could not get a line to Israel—they were all jammed by relatives phoning family there. Eagleburger immediately called Israeli ambassador Zalman Shoval to ask him to relay a message that the President was "devastated" by the attack and was requesting that, despite the provocation, Israel do nothing and let the United States respond.

Meanwhile, Cheney had managed to get through to Arens. As a way at least to buy time, if not dissuade them, he asked Arens to receive a US team to discuss how to respond. While Arens would not give a commitment not to attack, he did agree to receive a team. Finally, at 10:40 pm, Baker managed to get through to Shamir. By this time we had learned that the early reports were wrong. The Scuds had not carried gas and there were no casualties. From what Shamir said, it became obvious that Israel would restrain itself for the time being. Reassured, we asked Cheney not to push his plan for a technical team. We would operate on the basis of the Shamir, not the Arens, conversation. Thus, when Arens said publicly that Israel would retaliate, we considered it was meant for domestic ears.

This whirlwind evening became known as "Scud Thursday." No one had had any dinner, so we ordered in pizza and sandwiches to my office. That broke the tension and the evening descended almost into relieved levity as the seriousness of the crisis diminished. At one point, the usually staid Jim Baker was composing bawdy limericks. That evening also reinforced one lesson for me—never believe the first descriptions of a crisis.

Almost invariably, early reports are erroneous or garbled, and making decisions based on them could lead to serious mistakes. The difficulty is that there is nothing else to go on, and inaction is rarely a feasible option—one of the major problems of managing a crisis.

GEORGE BUSH

The next morning I had a long talk with Gorbachev, who was worried about escalation. His tone was somber as he tried to talk me into halting the air campaign. "The time is not simple for either of us," he said. Our doubts about Saddam had been proven right, and it had been necessary to use force, but it was time to try to shorten the war. Gorbachev insisted that we could now speak of Saddam's political defeat and that the coalition had already inflicted enormous damage on his military might and potential. "A fundamental victory has been scored," he said. "What is the purpose of further military action?" It would mean only more casualties among US forces—and Iraqi civilians.

Gorbachev revealed that the Soviet ambassador in Baghdad was about to see Saddam, and he had instructed him to ask whether Iraq would state it would leave Kuwait if we suspended further military action. If we agreed, he would make public his initiative. I told Mikhail that to stop now, after the attacks on Israel, would allow Saddam to claim victory, even make him a hero. Our Arab allies would certainly see victory for Saddam if his military was left intact. We would have to keep going until he withdrew on his own and under fire. I explained that we were trying to protect lives and went over just what targets we were trying to hit. Gorbachev argued that the air strikes had already brought the strategic results we wanted. He urged me to think of the long-term political problems. "We have demonstrated US-Soviet cooperation. Stop in time. Think of the casualties." I saw no evidence that Saddam was willing to comply with the UN resolutions, and, besides, he could withdraw in a minute if he wanted; we did not need to offer him anything. I had in mind the bombing pauses that Johnson and Nixon were pressured into calling during the Vietnam War. Instead of bringing peace, they gave the enemy a chance to regroup. I was determined not to repeat the mistake.

After a noon press conference, I spoke with Shamir, telling him of our efforts to root out the Scuds. "I hope you leave it to the coalition to act against Iraq," I said. I told him Cheney had assured me we could have the lead Patriot units to him in forty-eight hours. "We have worked so hard to get active participation of all coalition members," I added. "I would hate to see that jeopardized." He was pleasant but said Israel would probably have to respond. "We already know you are doing the utmost in destroying the Iraqi weapons," he said. "But please consider that we cannot take such an extreme position and then do nothing [meaning the Arens statement]. . . . We must do *something*." His cabinet would consider the issue within forty-eight hours. Shamir wanted to coordinate a response. He was asking us to "deconflict." I urged him to stay out and let us do the job, even though I knew it would be difficult for him.

DIARY, JANUARY 19

Fly to Camp David, plan for an early night and then all hell breaks loose about 1:30 [am] when Brent calls me and tells me that Israel has been hit again. They are going to retaliate. They want to send 100 planes across Saudi Arabia. [When we asked them,] the Saudis raise hell, and say that it is impossible. The [Israelis'] next choice is to overfly Jordan, either with the planes or with a bunch of helicopters and land people out in the desert to go search for the missile sites, [or use] missiles. That, of course, would bring Jordan tearing in. Whichever way they go, it hurts.

I talked to Shamir just after three in the morning. Flying over Saudi Arabia or Jordan to hit Iraq endangered everything we were trying to do. "I would like you to look at some other way than drawing in other countries," I said. "You were hit by missiles, and while I am not telling you what to do, maybe that could be an option for you. I just want to make one last appeal, recognizing how hard for you it is to wait. We are hitting those same targets that you would be going after." Shamir said he did not think Israel could continue to endure it much longer. "We have been attacked and are not doing anything," he said. "Our people don't understand. By our intimate relationship, we have to find a way to participate in this war. . . ."

I told him I understood, but that Israel couldn't do anything we weren't accomplishing already. Shamir asked if there was an alternative. I said that of the three bad options, retaliating with missiles would be the best. "Maybe some of the northern airfields could be targeted by your missiles and then this would make a good contribution to our efforts. . . . I have not discussed this with our military, but that would be a more proportional response to these horrible attacks on Israel. . . ." Shamir said he would consult with his colleagues and then let me know.

DIARY, JANUARY 19

Then this morning, Arens [said] that they are going to stand down—won't go tonight. I call Shamir in the middle of a briefing with Baker, Cheney, Scowcroft, Gates, Sununu, Quayle, and Powell and thank him. I tell him that we are going to send the Larry Eagleburger team with a couple [of] high-level defense people to see what we can do to help defend them better. We send some Patriot missiles [as Arens had requested] which are good against Scuds and he is grateful for that.

But, if tonight, the night of the 19th, the Iraqis hit Israel again, we've got a hell of a problem. Fortunately, the missiles aren't doing any damage. They are just scaring people—minimal damage. We own the skies—practically own the skies. Their SAMs are almost rendered inoperative. There is lot of anti-aircraft fire. But it doesn't seem to bother our people. There is a total, I believe, of 10 aircraft lost.

Fortunately, there were no Scud strikes that night.

BRENT SCOWCROFT

We sent Eagleburger and Paul Wolfowitz to hold the Israeli hand. Telephone calls were not going to do the trick and Larry was known as a particularly close friend. He arrived in time to welcome the Patriot team and the missiles, which was a happy coincidence. Immediately afterward, however, Shamir repeated that if the attacks continued, Israel would have to retaliate. Arens added that he didn't believe we were doing enough to destroy the Scud launchers. He wanted a direct link with Schwarzkopf, an Israeli team on one of our aircraft carriers, and, at a minimum, an Israeli general posted at Schwarzkopf's headquarters. Larry wisely rejected the demands.

I was incensed at Arens's charges. We had allocated a militarily disproportionate share of aircraft sorties to the Scud problem, as much as 30 percent of the total. Not only that, but we and the British were preparing to send special teams to the western desert of Iraq to hunt out the Scuds on the ground—an incredibly dangerous mission.

Eagleburger's trip turned out to be a brilliant move. It was probably the deciding factor in dissuading Shamir from retaliating. Shamir himself, however, deserves enormous credit for one of his finest moments. The Scud attacks continued, despite our efforts to root them out, and Shamir was under extremely heavy pressure from his "hawks" to retaliate. In exercising restraint, he was violating a cardinal Israeli rule: Do not leave terrorist attacks unpunished. Whatever other problems may have arisen between us and Shamir from time to time, on this occasion he showed himself a strong, stalwart ally.

GEORGE BUSH

The Scud attacks on Israel were alarming our allies as well. Helmut Kohl called a few days later to say he planned to send an emissary to Israel to show support. He also wanted me to know that if Saddam launched an attack against Turkey (which was unlikely), our NATO ally, Germany would be there and would fight.* "You have been able to count on Helmut Kohl up to now," he said. "And you will [continue to] be able to count on me, even if I face great [political] trouble." It was a courageous promise, since any German military action, even to defend Turkey, might well cost Kohl his job. I knew he wished he could do more.

DIARY, JANUARY 19

And now a kind of sophisticated argument starting up in the press quarters. How much is enough? What do we do next? How can we get out of it? How long will it take? Strong poll from ABC showing massive support for me, and certainly for the troops. Overwhelming [feeling] against the protests that are taking place in the country. I get some satisfaction from this. But the networks continue to play up the protests. I worry that it sends the wrong signals to the kids overseas.

BRENT SCOWCROFT

On January 20, Saddam began parading captured allied airmen on Baghdad television. They appeared to have been badly beaten and the Iraqis were holding them at potential targets. It was the same ploy he had tried before with the civilian hostages and once again we refused to allow it to interfere with what we had to do. He was also trying to manipulate the foreign media in Baghdad. The same day Iraq put the prisoners of war on television, the foreign ministry told all foreign journalists to leave Baghdad, but specifically asked Peter Arnett and CNN to stay. Saddam was apparently a frequent watcher of CNN, and Turgut Ozal at one point told the President that the Iraqi leader seemed to try to use it as a "tool"—which may be why they permitted it to remain when the others were thrown out. The Iraqis went to great lengths to take the CNN people to orchestrated events, where the journalists duly recorded whatever they were being told.

---

*The Germans, along with the Italians and Belgians, had finally sent aircraft to Turkey as part of a NATO Allied Command Europe (ACE) mobile force—the first ever deployed.

GEORGE BUSH

I was irritated by the argument that the media in general were only impartial observers, and that all this was only part of looking down at two warring parties. I questioned the logic of this position. These were people covering a war in which, as Americans, they had a stake. I had an awful feeling that they were hoping to prove the Pentagon wrong on something. While I knew the correspondents were trying to do their jobs, I thought the American people saw the selective emphasis in much of their reporting as prejudicial to US interests. I know I did.

The more I saw of Peter Arnett, the more I thought his reporting was one-sided and played into the hands of Iraq. In a February 11 interview in *Newsweek* he gave away his slant and hostility when he talked about "censorship" or "controlled news" under the Reagan White House, comparing it to the conditions he was working under in Iraq. I preferred the British approach to the problem (before they were kicked out). Their journalists would say, "I can't do this" or "please use your imagination," making very clear that the censorship was oppressive and that they were covering up a lot. CNN's occasional insert on the screen mentioning Iraqi censors was nothing compared to the images and propaganda they allowed Iraq to send over their airwaves. A controversial example was Arnett's coverage of the air strike on what the Iraqis insisted was a "baby formula" plant, which our intelligence indicated was actually a factory for the manufacture of biological weapons. This evolved into a lively dispute between Defense and CNN. Arnett stated emphatically that the Iraqis showed him that the plant was what they said it was.

BRENT SCOWCROFT

To commemorate the fifth anniversary of the air war, CNN broadcast a sort of retrospective. As part of the program, there was Arnett back in Baghdad at the bombed-out factory, even holding a bag of powdered milk. He reaffirmed his belief in the Iraqi description of the facility, adding that the UN Special Commission (UNSCOM)—the group assigned to ferret out Iraqi weapons of mass destruction—had never inspected the site and did not even have it on the list of suspect installations. The day after the broadcast, I received a call from Ambassador Rolf Ekeus, the executive chairman of UNSCOM. Ekeus, with whom I dealt frequently in the aftermath of the Gulf War, had seen the CNN program and wanted me to know that Arnett had misspoken. Not only had the site been inspected, it was, in fact, still on the commission's monitoring list because there was dual-use equipment located there. The suspicion was that the plant might have been used for filling biological munitions. The UN team had even discovered from Iraqi records that two engineers from the Technical Research Center, a component of the Military Industrial Corporation which manages Iraq's programs for weapons of mass destruction, had been assigned there in 1989 for a period of time. Ekeus said further inspections would take place when higher-priority missions (of potentially active sites) had been completed.

GEORGE BUSH

DIARY, JANUARY 24

. . . The 8th day of the war, sitting in the sauna at the end of the day and my voice lost, cold kind of coming back I guess — can't shake it, everybody's got the shivers. I worry about Brent Scowcroft. He's been up all night — many, many nights and I worry about him. I call the doctor and the doctor goes down and talks to him and says he's got a fever and the flu and the guy just won't go home and take care of himself.

. . . I get a report from Webster and Gates that the Iraqis have released a lot of oil in Kuwait and a tremendous slick [into the Gulf]. I think he said five times bigger than the Valdez spill. . . . He's also burning some more [oil-filled] trenches . . . I think this will outrage world opinion further — the burning — literally burned earth policy — scorched earth and now scorched sea policy. I worry about the Saudi desalination plant; I worry about marine life, etc.

I finally talked Brent into coming up to Camp David over the weekend of January 25–27, where we could spoil him enough to let him rest, relax, and catch up. He reluctantly arrived with his assistant Florence Gantt in tow and a mountain of paper. Instead of resting, he continued to work, and holed up with a secure phone and his feet up by the fire, although he did get a little more sleep than he would have in his White House office. Camp David's beauty and tranquillity were always relaxing, no matter how great the pressures outside.

Alexander Bessmertnykh was due in Washington on January 28 for his first visit as foreign minister. Although the Baltics were on the agenda, and he carried a letter from Gorbachev about them, most of the discussions were about the Gulf. In his conversations with Baker, Bessmertnykh was frank. The Soviets were furious about allied bombing in population centers, even though it was obvious we were picking targets carefully and had minimized civilian casualties. They also accused us of broadening the war beyond the UN resolutions when we struck at Baghdad instead of focusing on Iraq's military forces. Bessmertnykh suggested, as had Gorbachev after the first day of the air campaign, that it was time to look for political solutions with an eye toward the postwar situation in the Middle East. The Soviets were contemplating introducing another resolution in the Security Council calling for a pause in the bombing. This was unacceptable, for it would give the Iraqis a chance to catch their breath and rearm themselves, as well as an opportunity to build political momentum for a cease-fire that might allow Saddam to escape Kuwait with his military forces intact. As their first meeting closed, Bessmertnykh proposed that they conclude their talks with a joint statement, similar to the ones issued in Moscow in August and in Helsinki in September. Baker left the issue vague and asked him to come back with a draft.

GEORGE BUSH

I spent a portion of January 29 preparing for my State of the Union address, which I would deliver that evening. As I was in makeup in the basement of the White House, Brent hurried in with surprising and disturbing news. Bessmertnykh had just read to the press a joint US-Soviet statement which included a phrase saying we "continued to believe" that a cease-fire was possible if Saddam would make an "unequivocal commitment" to pull out from Kuwait, backed by immediate and concrete steps leading to full compliance with the Security Council resolutions.

BRENT SCOWCROFT

I learned about the joint statement in the worst possible way. Neither I nor the President was aware there was to be one. Bessmertnykh had come to Washington seeking it, but we did not want one, especially the kind the Soviets would prefer. It had been my understanding that Baker was going to try to hold him off, but, if something had to be done, it would be innocuous.

At about seven thirty that evening, I was giving a background briefing to the White House press corps on the foreign policy aspects of the State of the Union address. I had explained the comments the President would make on the war and was asked if we would agree to a cease-fire if Saddam promised to withdraw from Kuwait. When I replied in the negative, pointing out that unconditional withdrawal was the only acceptable avenue for Iraq, the questioner asked how I squared my answer with the statement by Baker and Bessmertnykh to the effect that a commitment to withdraw could produce a cease-fire. I was dumbfounded. I had no idea what Baker had actually said. I mumbled something about not having seen Baker's statement so I certainly could not comment on it, but I was stating the President's policy. "Was Baker out of line?" was the rejoinder. I simply reiterated I would have nothing more to say until I had seen his comments.

I was not happy. I had been completely blind-sided and wondered if our policy had been as well. My first requirement was to tell the President, so he would not be caught as I had been. I hated to clutter his mind just before so important an event, but he needed to be protected from possible embarrassment. When I told him what I knew, his face turned ashen even under the makeup. Then the anger—as sharp as I'd ever seen in him—started to rise. But the imperative of the moment was to get past the State of the Union address without a crisis over Iraq policy. Without knowing what Baker was up to, we agreed the right tactic was to say there had been no change in policy and simply brush it off. In the end that worked.

GEORGE BUSH

It was the first I had heard of the statement and I was furious. It implied that we would accept a cease-fire for Saddam's promise; that we were, in effect, prepared to take something less than the unconditional withdrawal we had been demanding since the invasion. To make matters worse, the statement also linked a cease-fire more closely to negotiations over the Palestinian question. If our announcement of the proposal for Baker and Aziz to meet had made our coalition partners uneasy, this was sure to panic them. When I arrived at Capitol Hill, the leadership started firing off questions, asking, "What's this new peace proposal?" We soon found that the statement had reverberated far and wide, and we scrambled to do some damage control. Fortunately, the ripples soon quieted and no serious damage was done. I knew Jim had not meant to "blind-side" me, and he apologized for not letting me know ahead of time.

On the day of the State of the Union and in the midst of the uproar over the Baker-Bessmertnykh statement, Iraq struck at the Saudi border town of Khafji. While not clear at the time, especially at the White House, the attack was not just a probe but apparently Saddam's attempt to draw us into what he hoped would be a bloody ground war. The attack was blunted, but the Marines suffered twelve killed—eleven of them to friendly fire. It was the first clash of ground forces and called attention to a looming issue: whether and when we might begin the ground campaign. The military imperative to use ground forces to eject Iraq from Kuwait was straightforward, and the President had long reached the decision that this was a necessary part of the war.

GEORGE BUSH

The argument, or "common wisdom," advanced among critics against committing to a ground war was, why play Saddam's game? Why allow his ground forces to inflict enormous casualties on the coalition? Why not let air power do the job? Their reasoning was lost upon me. Just why Saddam would want to face our superior forces and submit his own army to destruction, I didn't know. I did not believe that Iraq's army had the ability to inflict as much damage as Saddam, or our critics, seemed to think it could. Briefing after briefing had convinced me that we could do the job fast and with minimum coalition casualties. Besides, it was important to peace in the region that we do all we could to reduce the threat Iraq could pose in the future. Air power could do only so much.

I had no fear of making the decision to go. I was resigned to it. I knew there would be lives lost on both sides, too many, but I was convinced we would move fast, catch the Iraqis off guard, and have the job done in less than a week. I still worried about chemical weapons, and the accuracy of our assessment of Republican Guard strength after the bombing. The question before me then was really to choose when we would go—and for this I wanted to rely on the military as a guide. The answer depended entirely on their requirements: when the air campaign had done its job, and when the field command thought it was ready. From my perspective, these were both military calls, and when the military indicated it was ready I would give the order. I would allow them as much time as they needed—but not a minute more. I felt the urgency to get the war over with.

BRENT SCOWCROFT

I, too, was impatient to begin the ground campaign. I had never seriously entertained the idea that air power alone could do the job. It was a vital part of any military campaign, but we had typically overestimated its decisiveness—partly, I believe, out of wishful thinking. In the course of our discussions of military strategies the previous autumn, we had spoken of the role and length of an air campaign. We envisioned it as accomplishing the destruction of Iraqi air power and air defenses, command, control, and communication infrastructures, and the softening up of their military forces (such as the destruction of heavy equipment or shattering morale). These tasks had been estimated to require two to four weeks, after which we would move in on the ground to eject the Iraqi forces from Kuwait. The air campaign had already been considerably more effective than I had assumed it would be, yet the military seemed reluctant to begin ground operations, even though CENTCOM's own bombing assessments were optimistic (compared with those of the CIA), suggesting an earlier attack date. I thought it was time and we should act while we were riding a wave of military success and the coalition was still intact. There was no telling how long we could keep Israel out of the conflict. The press was beginning to question whether we had run out of targets and were bombing the rubble, speculation fed by Iraqi propaganda.

But Cheney and I also believed that a ground campaign would be necessary no matter what air power accomplished, because it was essential that we destroy Iraq's offensive capability. This was also a major objective, although it had not been feasible to list it openly as such while a peaceful solution to the crisis was possible. On the other hand, Baker was still hopeful that the air campaign might yet persuade Saddam to withdraw. If he did start to leave, Jim argued that we could not even contemplate a ground attack. To do so would cost us our support in world opinion. The President asked me to set up a core group meeting to discuss the matter.

We met January 31, although the discussion focused less on when to strike (which was put off) than to pose other questions. What would happen if Saddam Hussein stopped right then and left with his Republican Guard intact? What should we do about him personally? What if Iraq used chemical weapons? We had discussed this at our December 24 meeting at Camp David and had ruled out our own use of them, but if Iraq resorted to them, we would say our reaction would depend on circumstances and that we would hold Iraqi divisional commanders responsible and bring them to justice for war crimes. No one advanced the notion of using nuclear weapons, and the President rejected it even in retaliation for chemical or biological attacks. We deliberately avoided spoken or unspoken threats to use them on the grounds that it is bad practice to threaten something you have no intention of carrying out. Publicly, we left the matter ambiguous. There was no point in undermining the deterrence it might be offering.

GEORGE BUSH

As to dealing with Saddam personally, I worried he would emerge from the war weakened but as a "hero" still in charge. We discussed again whether to go after him. None of us minded if he was killed in the course of an air attack. Yet it was extremely difficult to target Saddam, who was known to move frequently and under tight security. We had had problems locating Noriega in Panama, a place we knew well. Saddam was far more elusive and better protected. The best we could do was strike command and control points where he may have been. There were several, and they were on our target list anyway. We later learned Saddam had been caught in one military convoy attacked by coalition aircraft but escaped unharmed.

DIARY, JANUARY 31

I just keep thinking the Iraqi people ought to take care of [him] with the Iraqi military. Seeing their troops [and] equipment getting destroyed—they've got to do something about it. I wish like hell that *we* could. . . . This is a war and if he gets hit with a bomb in his headquarters, too bad. But it seems to me that the more suffering the people of Iraq go through, the more likely it is that somebody will stand up and do that which should have been done a long time ago—take the guy out of there—either kick him out of the country or do something where he is no longer running things.

I firmly believed that we should not march into Baghdad. Our stated mission, as codified in UN resolutions, was a simple one—end the aggression, knock Iraq's forces out of Kuwait, and restore Kuwait's leaders. To occupy Iraq would instantly shatter our coalition, turning the whole Arab world against us, and make a broken tyrant into a latter-day Arab hero. It would have taken us way beyond the imprimatur of international law bestowed by the resolutions of the Security Council, assigning young soldiers to a fruitless hunt for a securely entrenched dictator and condemning them to fight in what would be an unwinnable urban guerrilla war. It could only plunge that part of the world into even greater instability and destroy the credibility we were working so hard to reestablish.

Should Saddam survive the war, I did think we could at least attempt to ensure that his military might was diminished or destroyed. This was behind my concern that he might withdraw from Kuwait before we had managed to grind down his armor and heavy equipment, and it underscored the need to launch a ground campaign to finish the job—and sooner rather than later. Our conditions for ending combat would be expanded, something we might be criticized for, but I did not see how we could leave Iraq's military intact.

February 1 was a moving and emotional day for me, with visits to three military bases to see the families of our service members in the Gulf. I began with Cherry Point Marine Corps Air Station, North Carolina. As we landed, I steeled myself for what I knew would be a wrenching experience. What I encountered was a very real demonstration of what war was doing to the families of those sent to the Gulf. Virtually all the young men were gone, and the crowds were mainly women, children, and older men. I did not trust myself not to choke up and break down as I spoke to them.

It was a cold morning, and the wind was blowing through the hangar where I was to speak. We had close to 85,000 Marines in the Gulf, some of whom had been among the casualties just days before at Khafji. While I was told that none of the wives before me were among those who lost their husbands, I kept thinking about the sacrifices already made. As I read my remarks, I said to myself, "Be strong, can't choke up." Still, I could feel the emotion rise in me as I saw some of the women with tears streaming down their faces. I tried looking away from them, for I found that if I gazed into the back of the audience or up at the press stand I was less apt to have a lump in my throat as I struggled through my speech. I also tried not to look long at the young kids, the teenage girls who were crying, the Marines saluting. It was the only way I could get through it.

After the speech we met with many of the wives. They were magnificent: strong and supportive and proud of their husbands. There was no self-pity. Each seemed to look me straight in the eye as if to say, "My husband knows why he is there—we support you." Some gave me letters, others pins and ribbons, and many of them asked for Barbara. I left Cherry Point inspired by what I saw. I was grateful for the courage and patriotism of our Marines and their families. As I got back onto Air Force One, I told the Marines nearby that I had come down there to strengthen the morale of the Corps, but instead it had worked the other way—they had boosted my morale.

Next was Seymour Johnson Air Force Base at Goldsboro, also in North Carolina, home of the 4th Tactical Fighter Wing and the 68th and 916th refueling units. There the emotion, and my reaction to it, was just as strong. Once again I tried to get through my text without breaking down. It is hard to do when they play "The Star-Spangled Banner" or when they salute you and hold up signs, or when you see a child mouthing the words "Bring my dad home safe."

I was scheduled to meet with two wives whose husbands were missing and two whose husbands were POWs. I felt bolstered by the courage of these four women, and the fact that they didn't cry. All the families I met said the same thing: my husband, my dad knows what he's doing there. He's doing what he has to do for his country. There wasn't one different voice raised and I didn't see one sign of protest anywhere or hear one complaint. Again, I felt emotionally drained but uplifted.

Our last stop was at Fort Stewart, Georgia, home of the 24th Infantry Division (mechanized), which was at the front line and one of the early units deployed—they had been there for five months. I had shared Thanksgiving with some of them a few weeks earlier. Now I was told of the send-off the division had received when it left back in August. The people of the surrounding towns had lined the streets, and even the nearby interstate highway, and cheered the soldiers as they passed through to the embarkation points. Once again I worked through my speech, and managed to spend some time with the families. As I left this last stop, my morale was sky-high. I was glad I had gone, grateful to have this sobering glimpse, beyond the Washington Beltway and the filter of the media, of what the war was doing to the families of the Americans who had put their lives on the line.

BRENT SCOWCROFT

That Sunday, February 3, our core group met again at the White House to discuss when we might go in with troops. The President was torn. He did not want to appear to be second-guessing the military experts. Still vivid in his mind was the image of Lyndon Johnson during Vietnam, hunched over aerial charts selecting individual targets for air strikes. On the other hand, the political situation was volatile and the coalition perhaps deteriorating. With our massive force now assembled, there seemed no obvious reason to continue to delay. More than two weeks had passed, and the air war appeared to have accomplished the objectives set for it; the President's anxiety—and mine—increased with each day. The propensity for our military to push off the date for the beginning of the ground war provided opportunities for Iraqi mischief-making and Soviet diplomatic initiatives.

GEORGE BUSH

At the meeting Powell explained that Schwarzkopf was anticipating at least another two weeks plus for the air campaign before a ground attack would begin. The news concerned me, for I thought this would give Saddam more time to wriggle out of his predicament with a cease-fire offer of some kind. We had to balance this danger against our own readiness and make a decision on when to go. Dick offered to go to Saudi Arabia with Colin and talk to Schwarzkopf. They could leave on Thursday, four days away. I immediately agreed.

DIARY, FEBRUARY 5

There's a big [propaganda] campaign being waged now . . . to show that we're . . . going after civilians . . . You hear [about the driver of a truck we hit who is] in Jordan in a hospital. [He] was going along this highway [in Iraq], under [the bridges of] which are hidden Scud missiles that are launching terror into Israel and the press seem to be very sympathetic or at least they report over and over again about the bombing on a truck that shouldn't be hauling that oil in the first place . . .

FEBRUARY 6

Press conference went well today, but I worry that they're chipping away, pounding, pounding away on the fact that civilians are being hurt and still support seems to be holding. . . . [A]ll of these things they're building up: the land mines, the flaming trenches, what they don't know is we're going around all those things. But anyway it's worst case, worst case, worst case. Half a million mines in the desert says ABC. One for every member of the coalition, and it shows how we plan to clear them out. What they don't understand as they present all these worst cases of our people going in the trenches, is that we're going to go around . . . and cut off the forces in Kuwait and let them figure out what to do. They'll [be] cut off from supplies and our forces will be able to handle a pounded Republican Guard [in] southern Iraq.

The next day Cheney joined Brent and me to talk about his trip. I told Dick I did not think we had much time and I hoped that Schwarzkopf was ready to go. But if the question was whether we should wait a month in order to make the military comfortable, or push them a month early in order to cut back the political risk from all the reports of bombings and coalition weakness, I'd err on the side of the military. Dick said he'd make clear what had to be done and why.

On February 9, I bounced my thoughts on the ground war off Dutch prime minister Ruud Lubbers—one of my closest friends among world leaders and someone whose wisdom I could count on and often tapped. I also wanted to ask him where the Europeans stood on a ground war. I confided I was worried about Saddam's propaganda campaign that we were targeting the civilian population, and outraged by the treatment of the POWs. Ruud didn't think the propaganda was having much effect, in the Netherlands at least, or in neighboring countries. "We Europeans hope that, although a ground attack may be needed, we go on as long as possible with the air campaign. Every day we diminish his ground potential is a good day, because it means he will be weakened further on. A ground attack will be divisive if people conclude that it was launched too early, so it is important to show we have gone the extra mile." I told him that the military question was how much good we were doing. At some point, the law of diminishing returns set in. "I don't think air power alone will do the job," he replied, "but from a political point of view it is better to start a ground attack later." It was an excellent point. "I guarantee we will not use ground power unless we are convinced it will be quick, with low allied casualties."

The political risks of a military delay, however, were becoming greater. On February 9, Gorbachev announced he was sending Primakov back to Iraq in the hopes of stopping the war. The Soviet embassy had contacted Baker that day with a preview. The Soviets were worried that "the logic of war," as they put it, would lead us to exceed the UN resolutions and cause greater civilian casualties. They were also concerned that Iraq's Scud missile attacks might yet escalate the war. Perhaps Gorbachev was only making noises for the sake of placating his Muslim constituency, for he would frequently remind us that what was happening was not far from his border. Still, we feared the Soviets were increasing their attempts to stop the fighting before Iraq had complied with the UN resolutions. Shevardnadze was gone, and there was no balance to the right-wing pressures on Gorbachev to intervene and save their old client—it was still possible that Moscow might bolt from the coalition. The proposal Primakov delivered to Saddam was little different from the one Gorbachev had pushed two days after the start of the bombing. Saddam would announce that he would withdraw from Kuwait and then the coalition might agree to a cease-fire. Fortunately, it went nowhere.

The day after Gorbachev's announcement, there were two meetings with Moshe Arens, another with Cheney and Powell in the mid-afternoon reporting on their trip to see Schwarzkopf, and a core group session. We tried hard to prevent the appearance that there was a connection between the two—that Cheney was reporting in and that we were trying to consult with the Israelis before making any decision. We scheduled the Cheney and core meetings in the Residence so the press would not make a connection.

GEORGE BUSH

Our meeting with Arens was difficult and unpleasant. Even though we were on the same side, we were still butting heads over how to respond to the Scud attacks. He was quite emotional, even angry, and made some claims about the damage that most of us thought were exaggerated, demanding that we coordinate retaliation. I was annoyed when he said Israel could do things we could not to destroy the Scuds in western Iraq, and irritated that the Israelis, or at least their hard-liners, seemed to offer so little thanks for what we were trying to accomplish for them.

That afternoon, Cheney briefed me on his trip to Saudi Arabia. The minute we got into the room, Dick told me that he, Powell, and

Schwarzkopf had agreed on a final concept of the operation. The military wanted to shoot for February 21—ten days hence—with a window of perhaps three days. Schwarzkopf did not want to get too rigidly pinned down on the date, so we agreed we would make clear to the others in the larger meeting to follow that it was not definite. I told the two of them we would have to know fairly soon, and definitely, so that I could notify our allies.

The plan, first outlined in December, was now firmly set. There would be a move around the west flank, the advantage being that much of our forces could swing wide of the main Iraqi force to cut them off and strike from the flank and rear. The rest would pin them down in the middle and on the right while some of the Marines would feint from the sea. The military were confident it could all be executed in just a few days, or at least that the Iraqi forces could be cut off in Kuwait, including the Republican Guard, preventing them from going north. Dick and Colin were very optimistic about getting this done with few casualties. The coalition air forces were making great headway in knocking out Iraq's armor, which was my concern. As Colin briefed me, he conveyed a quiet confidence that was contagious. He had always been willing to do what had to be done, but now I thought he was genuinely enthusiastic and felt this attack could be accomplished with minimum risk—although I asked myself what was minimum risk to a family whose son or daughter was killed. I left the discussion with an even greater feeling of surety that the campaign would be a swift success.

There were other pressing reasons to nail down the attack date. Late on the evening of February 12, we received alarming reports that the Air Force had struck a deep bunker of several floors in downtown Baghdad and hundreds of Iraqi civilians had been killed. We knew that the bunker was a command and control post for a section of Iraq's military intelligence, but we had no idea that civilians had been brought into the facility to use it as an air raid shelter. When I saw the bodies carried out of the bunker, the teenagers and the burned children, my heart ached. It hurt to see human suffering, no matter whose side it was on. As the media reports and TV pictures of the casualties began coming in, I asked Bill Webster what information we had on the bunker. He confirmed that all our reports had indicated it had been reserved for the intelligence service, but evidently the Iraqis had begun using other floors for civilians.*
In a disturbing discovery, Bill added that as of that day, the reports were

---

*A defector from the Iraqi intelligence service later confirmed that portions of the building were used by military technical sections.

that in the future *all* Iraq's military bunkers would be used as well by civilians. Evidently, Saddam planned to turn what appeared a tragedy into a policy. He saw the propaganda value of getting his people killed, so, although many of the bunkers were legitimate military targets, he deliberately placed civilians in them. I thought it was a brutal and depraved act. One immediate consequence to this tragedy was additional public questioning of the length of the air war—the implication being that we had run out of targets and were getting desperate. When would the war end? Another was a change in targets to avoid any possibility of repeating this human and public relations disaster.

BRENT SCOWCROFT

As we were meeting in Washington, Primakov was busy in Baghdad. On the night of February 13, we heard that he reported Saddam was willing to "cooperate" toward peace, but just what that meant was unclear. The following day we received a letter from Gorbachev, who explained that Primakov had told Saddam he had to withdraw. Primakov reported there had been some "encouraging" signs of movement. Evidently, Saddam had again shown interest in setting conditions for his troops to leave. Gorbachev was therefore inviting Tariq Aziz to come to Moscow for further talks. He asked for a halt in the bombing and carefully added that he hoped there would be no ground war while Aziz was in Moscow. All in all, nothing sounded new, or at least there was nothing closer to unconditional withdrawal. I thought Gorbachev asking for no ground operations during the Moscow talks was obviously meant to stall or spike the ground war.

I believed these attempts by Gorbachev to mediate were aimed primarily at salvaging some influence and bolstering his ever-weakening political strength at home. He was fighting for his political survival and was looking for a major foreign policy coup to burnish his reputation. Our efforts to discourage him were more in sorrow than in anger, and we tried hard to say no as gently as possible without causing him difficulty. It was a dilemma. Gorbachev had done so much to help us rally the international response to Iraq, and to isolate their former client, and we felt tremendous sympathy for him and his plight. Yet we could not let him interfere with our Gulf diplomacy or our operations at a critical moment.

GEORGE BUSH

Early on the morning of Friday, February 15, one of the White House staff came to our bedroom, where Barbara and I were reading the papers and drinking coffee, and reported he had heard there would be an announcement at 6:30 from Iraq. I turned on the TV and we anxiously waited as 6:30 came and went. Finally, an anchor cut in and reported that the Iraqis had announced they would comply with Resolution 660, including the withdrawal from Kuwait. Instead of feeling exhilarated, my heart sank.

I recorded my reaction as I listened:

> Now the question is, what comes next? But my emotion is not one of elation. We've got some unfinished business. How do we solve it? How do we now guarantee the future peace? I don't see how it will work with Saddam in power, and I am very, very wary. Cheney calls in, as does Baker—6:40—and I encourage them to keep going, keep moving; don't let anything change right now.

BRENT SCOWCROFT

We had prepared a detailed contingency plan for such overtures and had with our allies come up with a list of "tests" of the genuineness of Saddam's actions using military criteria. We never had to employ it because his maneuvers were transparent. Nevertheless, I was constantly concerned that he would make a proposal which would be hard to dismiss, one which would halt hostilities temporarily and leave him with his forces largely intact, even if he partially or fully withdrew from Kuwait. Once we stopped the fighting, it would be very difficult to get it going again if his proposals turned out to be a hoax or weren't carried out. The vague Iraqi announcement appeared to confirm my worst fears. Then over the wires came the full statement, as the President, Baker, and I, joined later by Sununu and Quayle, were sitting in the small study off the Oval Office. As each paragraph was printed out, there were more and more demands, including that we rebuild Iraq, that we withdraw all our forces from the Gulf, that the Israel question be solved and sanctions be imposed on it, that Lebanon be solved, and on and on. The conditions made it easy to say no. Marlin Fitzwater issued a quick statement to the press, pointing out that the "offer" fell short of the coalition's requirements. Furthermore, the statement had not been accompanied by any concrete action on the ground. During the morning we checked the reaction among the allies, none of whom seemed impressed. It has continued to baffle me that Saddam never made a plausible overture or proposal which might have allowed him to wriggle free. He could have tied us in knots.

GEORGE BUSH

I was scheduled to give a speech at about 10:00 in the Old Executive Office Building. I hurriedly added a response in my remarks. I called the statement nothing more than a cruel hoax by Saddam, "dashing the hopes of the people in Iraq and the world." I impulsively added what I called "another way for the bloodshed to end": to have the Iraqi people and the military put aside Saddam and rejoin the family of peace-loving nations. I was anxious to see how that played. There was some risk but perhaps the Iraqi people would respond. Almost every leader in the coalition had told me that in defeat Saddam would not be able to keep his hold on power. The words sparked a flurry of questions in the media about whether we had added a goal—toppling Saddam. We had not, although as I told the press again a couple of days later, quoting John Major, I wouldn't weep for him.

BRENT SCOWCROFT

This impulsive ad lib led, unfairly in my judgment, to charges that President Bush encouraged the Iraqi people to rise against Saddam and then failed to come to their aid when they did, at the end of the conflict. It is true that we hoped Saddam would be toppled. But we never thought that could be done by anyone outside the military and never tried to incite the general population. It is stretching the point to imagine that a routine speech in Washington would have gotten to the Iraqi malcontents and have been the motivation for the subsequent actions of the Shiites and Kurds.

GEORGE BUSH

The afternoon of February 15, I flew up to Kennebunkport for the Presidents' Day holiday weekend. That Sunday I talked to Dick Cheney, who reported that the military was still pinning down the date for the attack, but that it looked as though they would be ready to go before February 23.

DIARY, FEBRUARY 18

The meter is ticking. Gosh darn it, I wish Powell and Cheney were ready to go right now. But they aren't, and I'm not going to push them, even though these next few days are fraught with difficulty. Little turns of diplomatic mischief, but I will not order the military to go until they say they're ready. I talked to Scowcroft this morning [to] tell him I want to have a meeting with Cheney, Powell, Baker, and all our people at 4:30 in the Oval Office. He said fine. Maybe I can probe there to see how ready we are.

BRENT SCOWCROFT

That Monday was Presidents' Day, and the West Wing was deserted when we gathered in the Oval Office. It was a dank evening and the large room had become slightly chilly. The President decided to cheer things up with a fire, the logs for which were always laid in the fireplace. We sat down to begin the meeting when smoke suddenly started to pour into the room. An alarm screamed and the Secret Service burst into the room, guns drawn and poised for action. The President had forgotten to turn on the fan which helped the chimney to draw.

As we began again, a message came in from Gorbachev about his meeting with Aziz the day before, offering yet another plan. It was the same old stuff. The Iraqis would declare that they would withdraw; there would be a specific time frame to complete this, which would start the day after a cease-fire; and there would be no conditions other than troops not being attacked. Gorbachev had told them that any linkage was unacceptable but that, after withdrawal, there could be a new UN resolution and the Soviets would push the UN to deal with a whole range of questions, including Lebanon and Arab-Israeli issues. The Soviets were searching, with increasing desperation, for some way to head off a ground war. We, especially Baker and the President, did not want them to desert us, but neither could we be dissuaded from our goal. The problem was how to tell the Soviets politely why we could not accept their plan.

We discussed how to respond. If Saddam withdrew with most of his armed forces intact, we hadn't really won. There were other problems with the plan: no mention of restoring the royal family, or of fulfilling other resolutions such as reparations. We debated the idea of giving the Iraqis ninety-six hours to withdraw completely from Kuwait, which we felt was a "test" of immediacy. This meant they would have to go north immediately and leave their equipment behind, but there wasn't much enthusiasm for that option, which would have been difficult to monitor, let alone enforce. In the end, we sent Gorbachev an interim reply, thanking him, saying that hostilities would not cease and we were pleased he had informed us of the proposal.

Early the next morning, February 19, the President read and reread the letter from Gorbachev and resolved to stay the course. We gathered again in the Oval Office to discuss a more formal reply. We decided we would announce four criteria beyond the UN resolutions with which the Iraqis would have to comply to show their good faith: no cease-fire until the withdrawal was complete, no more launching of Scuds, no use of chemical weapons, and an immediate swap of POWs. The President outlined his objections, and our terms, in a letter to Gorbachev and thanked him for his efforts.

GEORGE BUSH

Over the next couple of days we waited for an answer to our counter-proposals. There was a lot of diplomacy on my part—with Mitterrand, Mulroney, Ozal, Mubarak—to keep the coalition informed about our letters to Gorbachev and solidly with us. Then there was a nervous lull. The peace ball was still in the air and I worried about a new spoiling action. To complicate matters, we had some intelligence that Aziz did not want to tell Saddam of our response. Finally, on the morning of February 21, Saddam gave a long televised speech, but I didn't hear anything that sounded like a new willingness to recognize reality, and no concessions, although there were some references to withdrawing from Kuwait. Mitterrand called at about two that afternoon and agreed there was no chance for negotiation.

That evening, as I was preparing to go to a play at Ford's Theater honoring the Tuskegee airmen, Gorbachev called again to report on further talks with Aziz. He seemed to feel there was a breakthrough. Iraq was willing to withdraw, but only after a cease-fire. He proposed that sanctions be lifted after two thirds of the troops were out. There was no mention of reparations, POWs, or what would happen with the rest of the Iraqi troops. This was not the unconditional withdrawal we required. I talked to Mikhail for about half an hour, scribbling down everything I could. I asked Bob Gates, who was standing in for Brent, to assemble everyone to debate the proposal and I went off to the play. I fidgeted throughout the performance. I kept thinking, how do we stop Saddam from snatching victory from the jaws of certain defeat?

BRENT SCOWCROFT

Cheney and I were both due at a dinner given by the Queen of Denmark. There was much work to be done before the President returned, so Dick and I agreed he would represent us at the dinner and I would get a response to Gorbachev drafted. Haass worked on an NSC version and Baker brought one in from State, both rejecting the proposal. It was quite a sartorial display we presented to the President when he returned to his office in the Residence. Cheney was in black tie, several of us in business suits, and Powell, who had come from home, in a turtleneck sweater. The meeting was all business. The President was not satisfied with either draft, feeling that the language was too hard-line. We hammered out a compromise, which put a deadline on the proposal and forced Saddam to demonstrate compliance, essentially an ultimatum. It was a way to keep from being nickeled and dimed to death. Rather than deal with each new run at us on a separate basis, we decided to set forth once and for all what it would take to make us desist. There was always the danger that Saddam would say okay. In my opinion we were at the point where it would be a disaster to take "yes" for an answer, but this was the best option available.

GEORGE BUSH

The next morning, February 22, I spoke to Mitterrand about the declaration. He suggested some minor changes, which we included, and proposed that all the allies issue it simultaneously. As we spoke, Gates handed me a report that the Iraqis were blowing up the entire Kuwaiti oil production system. "If there was ever a reason not to have a delay or wonder if they are acting in good faith, this report is one," I said to François. ". . . I don't know how this man can continue to talk peace through the Soviets and still be taking this kind of action." "I don't trust him one inch," he declared. ". . . Your document is a good one, subject to the few remarks I have made. France remains totally committed to moving in the same direction that you are."

President Bush tried to contact Gorbachev before making any announcement, but when he called at about 10:20, the Soviet leader was out. A half hour later, in the Rose Garden, he went ahead and read some brief remarks about our response and pledged a full statement with the specific terms we required. The language from Moscow had promised unconditional withdrawal, only to set forth a number of conditions. We had seen no evidence of goodwill on the other side, nothing to convince us that their words would be backed by actions. The Iraqis were conducting a scorched-earth policy in Kuwait. In addition, even as Aziz was negotiating in Moscow, Iraq had been launching more Scuds. The most important element in our terms was that Saddam would have until noon EST on February 23 (the next day) "to do what he must do: begin his immediate and unconditional withdrawal from Kuwait. We must hear publicly and authoritatively his acceptance of these terms."

Shortly after 11:00, Gorbachev phoned back, apologizing that he had been at a televised celebration honoring the Soviet military and could not leave to take the President's call. He had a refinement of his earlier proposal, and an account of his latest talk with Aziz. Since the President was already late for Lynn Martin's swearing-in ceremony as Secretary of Labor, he asked Baker to carry on the conversation until he could return.

It was a long call that morning, over an hour. Baker read Gorbachev the President's statement to the press. As he finished, the President returned to the Oval Office and took the phone.

GEORGE BUSH

"Do I understand that what we did in agreeing yesterday is not acceptable?" asked Mikhail. I said that was correct. He claimed that the situation had changed. He had spoken again with the Iraqis and they had agreed to withdraw immediately and unconditionally from Kuwait, beginning the day after a cease-fire. They'd be out in three weeks, after which the UN resolutions would be lifted. It was, I thought, neither immediate nor unconditional. There was still plenty of time for the Iraqis to continue the destruction of Kuwait. It was hardly a sign of good faith.

Gorbachev reacted strongly to our turning down the proposal. "What is the priority?" he asked, his voice rising with obvious irritation. "Are we trying for a political solution or to continue military operations to culminate in ground operations?" He hinted we were intentionally setting impossible demands for withdrawal in order to open the way for further military operations. It would be different if the United States objected to the terms of the political settlement. But, he said, on the basis of what the Soviets had been able to accomplish, and if it could be made into a joint US-Soviet approach we would turn over to the Security Council, we could find a solution.

I asked if Saddam had accepted the points he had put to him. Mikhail said they were still waiting for a reply. I thanked him for his efforts, but said I still did not trust Saddam and that what the Iraqis were asking was incompatible with the coalition goals. "Saddam is simply trying to save face and restore himself," I said. "He is taking advantage of the lull to destroy Kuwait. Get your intelligence people to show you photos of what the Iraqis are doing to the oil facilities."

I reminded Mikhail of the atrocities. "I still have not changed my views on the value of human life," I said. "I dread sending young men and women into combat. I know what I'm going to ask will put you in a difficult position. I will understand if you simply said, 'George, I cannot do it.' I want you to tell Aziz that the handwriting is on the wall. It is not just the United States; it is the rest of the coalition, and we must accomplish it with our proposal now. He has not responded to [yours]. We have waited and waited. We've been patient. We need an answer now. There are deadlines here and, after what he has done in Kuwait, we cannot yield. [Our] proposal is deadly serious. My request is that you support our position, after trying hard for a more reasonable position from your point of view but one that, for the reasons I have given, we cannot go along with now. If you can't support it, we would appreciate your not opposing it."

In the early afternoon, as we informed our allies of what was happening, Fitzwater read a more complete statement to the press outlining our terms in detail, all of which fell under the Security Council resolutions. Everything had to be back as it was before August 1, POWs released, and the cessation of all destructive actions against Kuwaiti citizens. In return, we promised not to fire on any retreating troops. The ball was back in Saddam's court.

About half an hour after the statement was made, we convened again in the Oval Office. Powell and Cheney briefed the President on what lay ahead. Scowcroft was not sure he should hear how grisly the battle might be. "We've got to spare you from some things," he said.

"I know," replied the President, "but this is not one of them."

Powell reported that the Iraqi Army was beginning to crack, and described again the ground operation. If necessary, the campaign could be delayed in twenty-four-hour blocks. "Norm and I would rather see the Iraqis walk out than be driven out," he said. "There will be costs. We will lose soldiers in substantial numbers at a time. It will be grisly. There will be pool reports of dead Americans. The battlefield will be confused. . . . It will be some time before we get any [accurate] reporting, requiring perhaps two or three days of real patience. If they pull out, there will be no contact. . . . There is a high probability of chemical attack. It involves an American attack on an Arab country. We will get more of their tanks and stockpiles by attacking, but the cost in lives and later problems is not worth it."

"Would you prefer a negotiated settlement?" the President asked.

"If it met our conditions totally, yes," answered Powell. "They will crack."

"If they crack under force, it is better than withdrawal," replied the President.

"But at what cost?" asked Powell.

BRENT SCOWCROFT

This was a telling exchange. Powell was rightly concerned, about both our troops and achieving our declared objectives. The air war had gone extremely well. Estimates indicated that Iraq's military capability had been reduced by at least 40 percent. If Saddam would evacuate Kuwait, our objectives would be largely achieved and without the need for land combat. The President, however, saw the dangers of an Iraqi withdrawal before its army had been destroyed. It would then remain a menace on the Kuwaiti border and in the region. Our forces were too large to rotate, and the Saudis would never tolerate a huge alien presence on their soil indefinitely to contain Saddam. We had to act now while we were mobilized and in place.

GEORGE BUSH

The ultimatum had set the timing for the ground campaign: we would strike at dawn the following morning in the Gulf. Since that would be 8:00 Saturday night, eastern time, I hoped to disclose the news as close to that time as we could. The military wanted to delay revealing their operations as long as possible for security reasons, to Sunday if possible. I didn't want to do anything to endanger the troops, but this was a decision that had to be announced by the White House; we simply could not launch the campaign and inform the country later. Not only did the American people have a right to know, but also every family member who had a loved one being ordered into battle. We settled on 10:00 Saturday evening. Of course, we had to work out the timing with the French and the British. Both Mitterrand and Major had reminded me that only they could order their respective forces into battle. I phoned the four Congressional leaders and asked them to take calls from Vice President Quayle and Sununu—who gave them a briefing on what we planned to do. That afternoon, February 22, I went up to Camp David for the weekend, taking Jim Baker along.

The night of February 22–23, Saddam made another attempt to stall, asking for discussion in the UN. It was too late for that. The next morning at 11:15, forty-five minutes shy of the deadline, Mikhail phoned with one last overture. His call came during a game of Wallyball with Baker, some Camp David Marines, and members of my staff. I took it in the locker room and stood there, sweating, a towel draped around my shoulders. Brent was also on the line, listening in from the White House. Mikhail said the Iraqis would now make a full, unconditional withdrawal—leaving Kuwait City in four days. Aziz had held a press conference to accept these conditions. Mikhail asked that we work together in the UN to resolve the matter. "Saddam has caved," he said.

"I can't let a deadline pass without action," I replied. "Hard as you have tried, there are still deadlines."

"Let's stay cool," he urged. "We are human beings. Saddam's fate has been determined. We need to attain our goals and prevent a tragic phase of conflict. Saddam wants to stall but we are not simpletons." He urged that we go to the Security Council. "I think Baker and Bessmertnykh can work it out," he added. "These are the words of a friend." He asked for more time, over the weekend, for negotiations. I thought Saddam was stalling to continue his scorched earth campaign to punish Kuwait. I carefully, firmly, and politely said that we could not change the deadline.

BRENT SCOWCROFT

Gorbachev was clearly desperate. None of his proposals had worked and this was his last chance. He tried everything and finally simply pleaded for a delay to give him one more chance to talk reason to Saddam. The President was patient and friendly but unyielding. This conversation had to be extraordinarily difficult for him.

GEORGE BUSH

At noon, the deadline passed. We had over 500,000 US troops standing by in the Gulf, and our Air Force had flown over 94,000 missions. That night at 8:00 pm Washington time, 4:00 am February 24 in Saudi Arabia, the ground campaign began. I informed the congressional leaders at 8:45, before leaving Camp David for the White House. Brent briefed me as we walked inside to the Oval Office, where I was to address the nation.

DIARY, FEBRUARY 23

The rumors I get before I make the announcement . . . are that 20,000 [civilians] were killed in Kuwait, and there was some rumor that the whole city of Kuwait—banking district and other areas— was on fire. This is no civilized human being piling on [destruction] at the last minute like this. I worry about chemical weapons, and I worry about some surprise weapon. There was a report the other day that if we had not taken out the nuclear facility, they would have had a nuclear bomb device by March of 1991, but I don't know whether it has been authenticated or not.

Regarding my emotions, I'm glad the decision has finally been made and implemented. I've got a deep concern about the families, the loss of lives, and am wondering how it will all end. For example, suppose they say they'll quit right now—what will we do? I'm determined to do what we have to do, and I'm convinced that we've taken the right step. I'm tired, very tired; but our team operated so I haven't felt lonely in this decision. I have felt that it is only the President that can make the decision, so that's why I want to be sure to be the one to make the announcement tonight—the first authoritative announcement. I will sit back, like every other American now, with apprehension and wonder how it's going, but not knowing. We arranged a little church service for tomorrow morning, and I'm looking forward to that. I hope he hasn't mistreated our prisoners more.

My address that evening was direct and to the point. The noon deadline had passed and Iraq had not withdrawn from Kuwait. Instead, Saddam had redoubled his efforts to completely destroy Kuwait and its people.

> I have therefore directed General Norman Schwarzkopf, in conjunction with coalition forces, to use all forces available, including ground forces, to eject the Iraqi army from Kuwait . . . The liberation of Kuwait has now entered its final phase.

I asked Americans to pause and say a prayer for our men and women in uniform.

The next morning, Sunday, February 24, Barbara and I attended a special 7:00 am service at St. John's, just across Lafayette Square from the White House. The historic Church of the Presidents was close to packed, with many of my White House staff and cabinet members attending. My assistant Patty Presock had called them after our friend Reverend John Harper had arranged this communion service, knowing that all of us would be in need of prayer.

The first situation reports were coming in as we listened to Reverend Harper's wonderful sermon. Dick Cheney quietly passed me a message on a folded piece of notepaper—"Norm says it's going very well!" After the service, I sat down in the sitting room in the Residence with Barbara, where Dick and Colin briefed me in more detail. Again I felt emotion well to the surface as they told how few casualties there were, and how quickly our troops were breaking through. Everything was going better than planned. The Marines had smashed through the Iraqi fortifications in southern Kuwait at 5:30 am and were on their way toward Kuwait City. The bulk of our coalition's troops were swinging around to the west in the desert to cut off the Iraqi army. Throughout the day, Dick and Colin kept me updated with the latest status reports of progress on the ground and casualties. As Colin told me, everyone was "up to their arms in prisoners." In our afternoon meeting, he reported that the Marines had reached Al Jabar airfield, thirty miles from Kuwait City. Both Marine divisions were now well into Kuwait, with only one Marine killed. They were moving fast, faster than planned. Our fears were being put to rest; the predictions of a bloodbath proved wrong. So now it was watch, wait, nervousness—and what comes next? But my emotions were in thankful pride of our troops, and sorrow. There was no elation in my heart.

Late the following morning, February 25, I spoke to Schwarzkopf, who told me that the Iraqi armored forces had now struck back at the Marines, but the casualties were still very slight. "Tomorrow or the next day we'll lock horns with them," he predicted. But the first heavy loss of American life came a bit later that day, when a Scud hit a US billet near Dhahran, killing 28 and wounding nearly 100. I watched the coverage of the devastation in frustration. The battlefield itself was claiming fewer lives than this one Scud fired in desperation. We had tried to pinpoint the launchers, but now one random missile had killed so many soldiers. I was angry, but I knew Saddam was going to pay a terrible price.

That afternoon I was at the gym in the Rayburn House Office Building, where I had just finished a game of paddle ball with Sonny Montgomery, when Brent called. There were reports of a Baghdad radio announcement that Saddam was withdrawing from Kuwait, as well as signs that columns of equipment were moving out. I tried to piece together what was happening from what he, Dick, and Jim could tell me about it, but we could confirm nothing. There was another announcement at about 6:30, just as I was about to sit down for dinner with Barbara and Brent, and soon the phone began to ring constantly. Apparently, the announcement said Aziz had contacted the Soviet ambassador in Baghdad and asked him to pass along a message to Gorbachev requesting that he get the UN to call a cease-fire. It also said that the Iraqi leadership had "stressed its acceptance to withdraw in accordance with UN Security Council Resolution 660 when it agreed to the Soviet peace proposal. In compliance with this decision, orders were issued to the armed forces for an organized withdrawal to the positions in which they were before the first of August, 1990." Saddam had declared victory and was trying to save as much of his army as he could.

At 8:00 pm we gathered in the Oval Office to discuss our response to the Iraqi announcement and what we still needed to accomplish to end the war on our terms. The Iraqi proposal remained unacceptable, since they still had not fulfilled all the UN resolutions or the coalition conditions, but apparently Saddam was beginning to withdraw, which complicated the situation. Thousands of Iraqi soldiers were surrendering, and others were heading north from Kuwait City in columns, but our troops had begun encountering Iraqi tank forces. The question was whether we should simply permit them to go or set new conditions to ensure that they left behind their heavy equipment.

Baker pointed out that requiring them to relinquish their armor exceeded the UN resolutions. The President remarked that it was a new ballgame and we were not bound by our earlier demands, but that we should spell out what the Iraqis had to do to end the war. Powell urged that we buy time to complete the job. "We can close the door [cutting them off] in two days," he said. There was no official Iraqi notification of compliance, anyway.

"We need the personal acceptance by Saddam Hussein of all the resolutions," Scowcroft said.

The President was worried about public reaction. "The pressure is going to be that as his people are going out, we're still shooting," he said. "I have to be interested in the security of our forces. They turned their guns on us in Khafji [where Iraqi tanks pretended to surrender, but turned and fired on the Marines]. There is a war on. The situation is different now."

Baker asked what would happen if Saddam now withdrew without accepting our list of requirements.

"We keep on fighting," replied Scowcroft.

Late that evening, Fitzwater offered our reply. We would continue to prosecute the war, and had heard nothing to change that. There was no evidence to suggest Saddam was withdrawing his troops, which were in fact still fighting. The Iraqis had declared that their forces would battle their way out of Kuwait, but we said we would not attack unarmed soldiers in retreat although we would consider retreating combat units as "movement of war." The only way Saddam could convince us of his seriousness would be "personally and publicly" to agree to the terms of our February 22 proposal, and fulfill the conditions of all the UN resolutions.

GEORGE BUSH

DIARY, FEBRUARY 25

It is my view that Saddam Hussein . . . is trying to put us in a box. He wants to get his troops out, perhaps, and then turn to us and say, what are [you] doing in Iraq, and turn world opinion against us . . . We have no evidence that they're quitting, but we're not going to let him bring victory out of the jaws of defeat. He's getting clobbered and we're about to have him cut off at Basra. . . . We must disarm the Republican Guard. . . . The problem is, if he has his forces out of Kuwait, we'll be the ones that are trespassing . . . with our [troops] in Iraq. So we're pinning our demands on all the UN resolutions being fulfilled. By that I mean reparations, and giving up any claim to Kuwait, etc.

It seems to me that we may get to a place where we have to choose between solidarity at the UN and ending this thing definitively. I am for the latter because our credibility is at stake. We don't want to have another draw, another Vietnam, a sloppy ending. I hope we can avoid it. The Soviets are now calling for a UN meeting tonight, but we are not going, having put this much into it and having lost life. We're not going to permit a sloppy ending where this guy emerges saving face. I'm not interested in his saving face and neither is the rest of the world. We may take some hits for having our forces in Iraq to stop this; but far worse than that would be if we lost credibility in some silly compromise. I'm not going to do it.

I felt terrible as I went to bed that Monday night. Down. Just as things were going smoothly, everything seemed to break loose again. It was frustrating. I was not about to let Saddam slip out of Kuwait without any accountability for what he had done, nor did I want to see an Iraqi "victory" by default, or even a draw. Either he gave in completely and publicly, which would be tantamount to surrender, or we would still have an opportunity to reduce any future threat by grinding his army down further.

The next morning, February 26, at 9:48 am, I spoke to the nation again, rejecting Saddam's latest proposal. Except for Gorbachev, who criticized our response, the coalition and the country seemed strongly supportive. The polls were astronomically high; I'd never seen anything quite like it. The people were together. Their view was we should not let Saddam get away. He had become a symbol of evil and something they could focus on.

About 7:00, Colin was on the phone with me again. "They're streaming out," he said. "They're tangled up on the bridges; the Iraqi Army is clearly withdrawing." Coalition forces were moving into the Euphrates valley to block whatever units were still organized on the road north. The weather had turned bad, the worst since the beginning of the crisis, and our planes were grounded so there was no air support for the ground troops. There were Marine units moving through the outskirts of Kuwait City, which, the Kuwaiti resistance was reporting, the Iraqis had fled. "Don't worry about the Republican Guard," he added. It was not clear whether they were staying in place or heading north, but either way very little armor was getting out of Kuwait. "They'll be out in a day," he said confidently.

DIARY, FEBRUARY 26

. . . We're surrounding their armor. We want the Egyptians and the Saudis to go into [Kuwait City] first, and I'm thinking, good God, isn't it exciting? Isn't it a marvelous thing that this little country will be liberated. . . . The big news, of course, is this high performance of our troops—the wonderful job they've done; the conviction that we're right and the others are wrong. We're doing something decent, and we're doing something good; and Vietnam will soon be behind us . . .

It's surprising how much I dwell on the end of the Vietnam syndrome. I felt the division in the country in the 60s and the 70s—I was in Congress. I remember speaking at Adelphi, and Yale was turning its back.* I remember the agony and the ugliness, and now it's together. We've got to find a clean end, and I keep saying, how do we end this thing? . . . You can't use the word surrender—the Arabs don't like that apparently. How do we quit? How do we get them to lay down their arms? How do we safeguard civilians? And how do we get on with our role with credibility, hoping to bring security to the Gulf?

In the course of the day, the Arab coalition forces entered Kuwait City, under a sky of dense black smoke from the burning oil wells, but the weather had cleared and coalition aircraft were intercepting Iraqi convoys headed north from the city. It looked as if we would trap or destroy the remains of Saddam's army in Kuwait, but he did not seem willing to capitulate. Eventually, I decided that it was our choice, not Saddam's: we would declare an end once I was sure we had met all our military objectives and fulfilled the UN resolutions.

BRENT SCOWCROFT

The tactical situation was changing very rapidly, and we did not have a clear picture of exactly what was happening on the ground. In an over-all sense, things were moving along according to plan, only more rapidly than anticipated. The door at Basra would be slammed shut within a day or two. What we did not know was that the plan to trap the Republican Guard in Kuwait was not working. The Marines had moved so rapidly up to Kuwait City that the Guard had not come down south to reinforce the Iraqi front lines. Consequently, most of those troops would not be caught by the encirclement.

Would it have made a difference had we known? I doubt it. We still would have relied heavily on the military judgment that the mission had

---

*There were student demonstrations during a commencement speech I gave at Adelphi. At a similar event at Yale, graduates turned their backs on the ceremonies awarding degrees. Both incidents disturbed me.

been accomplished. What might have happened is that the character of the Oval Office discussion on the final day would, at least, have been more complicated.

GEORGE BUSH

At 10:15 the next morning, February 27, Dick Cheney reported that the southern half of Kuwait was now free. Two of three Guard divisions in Kuwait had been destroyed. There were only five or six divisions still functioning out of the forty-two which had been in the theater. Cheney thought this would be the last day of operations—perhaps one more at most. Some of the allies were sensing an end to the fighting as well, although there was no pressure to finish it. Mitterrand called at about 10:40 am to say it would soon be time for diplomacy. It was time to talk about how we would end the war. I told him that we too were discussing when and how to end the war, but we would have to delay any cease-fire until the military situation was right.

BRENT SCOWCROFT

That afternoon, after a meeting with British foreign secretary Douglas Hurd, the President's advisors sat in the Oval Office for our daily discussions on the war. There was a sense of euphoria in the air. Ground operations had gone far better than the most optimistic of us had dared to hope—with respect to both successes achieved and casualties suffered. Powell described where our forces stood, and what had been achieved. He added that we were now in the endgame. I had come to a similar conclusion. I had received an estimate that there were probably only two or three Iraqi divisions in the combat theater which were still sufficiently organized to fight as units. The rest had lost essential cohesion or were just rabble trying to escape. Colin observed that the Basra "gate" would be completely closed at the latest by the end of the next day, cutting off the remaining Iraqi units. There seemed to be an unspoken consensus building that this was it. We had all become increasingly concerned over impressions being created in the press about the "highway of death" from Kuwait City to Basra.

In a very matter-of-fact way, the President asked whether it was time to stop. There was no dissent. Powell said we had better get the command views and reached for the direct secure line to General Schwarzkopf, which was in one of the front drawers of the President's desk. Schwarzkopf, having just conducted the "mother of all briefings," in which he had said, "We've accomplished our mission," replied he had no objections, but asked for time to consult with his commanders to make sure they could safely disengage their forces. Cheney and Powell were due on Capitol Hill for a briefing, so we agreed to reassemble when they returned.

We came together again at about 6:00 pm and called Schwarzkopf. His commanders had confirmed his conditional agreement. In what was probably too cute by half, we agreed to end hostilities at midnight, Washington time, for a ground war of exactly 100 hours.

GEORGE BUSH

Just after 9:00 pm I spoke to the country:

Kuwait is liberated. Iraq's army is defeated. Our military objectives are met. Kuwait is once more in the hands of Kuwaitis, in control of their own destiny. We share in their joy, a joy tempered only by our compassion for their ordeal. . . .

Seven months ago, America and the world drew a line in the sand. We declared that the aggression against Kuwait would not stand. And tonight, America and the world have kept their word.

This is not a time of euphoria, certainly not a time to gloat. But it is a time of pride: pride in our troops; pride in the friends who stood with us in the crisis; pride in our nation and the people whose strength and resolve made victory quick, decisive, and just . . .

No one country can claim this victory as its own. It was not only a victory for Kuwait but a victory for all the coalition partners. This is a victory for the United Nations, for all mankind, and for what is right.

At the time of the cease-fire, there were 79 US service members killed in action, 212 wounded in action, and 45 missing; 110,000 combat sorties had been flown in the campaign. I was (and am) proud of the way our military performed, very proud. Many of those who had served in the previous thirty years had been "beaten up" largely because of the way the Vietnam War had been fought. A generation of Americans had been acclaimed for refusing to serve. Those who did serve often returned home, not to gratitude and praise, but to ridicule—even while the draft-dodger and the protester were considered by many to be courageous, even heroic. Now this had been put to rest and American credibility restored.

DIARY, FEBRUARY 28

It's now early Thursday morning on the 28th. Still no feeling of euphoria. I think I know why it is. After my speech last night, Baghdad radio started broadcasting that we've been forced to capitulate. I see on the television that public opinion in Jordan and in the streets of Baghdad is that they have won. It is such a canard, so little, but it's what concerns me. It hasn't been a clean end—there is no battleship *Missouri* surrender. This is what's missing to make this akin to WWII, to separate Kuwait from Korea and Vietnam. . . .

The headlines are great—"We Win." The television accurately reflects the humiliation of Saddam Hussein and it drives the point home to the American people. But internationally, it's not there yet, at least in the Arab world that has been lined up with Saddam. He's got to go, and I hope those two airplanes that reported to the Baghdad airport carry him away. Obviously when the troops straggle home with no armor, beaten up, 50,000 . . . and maybe more dead, the people of Iraq will know. Their brothers and their sons will be missing, never to return.

Colin last night put it in perspective—this is historic and there's been nothing like this in history. Bob Gates told me this morning, one thing historic is, we stopped. We crushed their 43 divisions, but we stopped—we didn't just want to kill, and history will look on that kindly. (He also felt, very generously, that having been around four administrations, he'd never seen anything like this . . .)

Everyone seems to be giving me great credit, and yet, I don't look at it that way. I think our team has been absolutely superb and this is not a one-man job. I hope I've provided steady leadership; but on the other hand, I will confess that I have needed the strength that has come from Powell; Schwarzkopf, who is steady and dependable; loyal Dick Cheney; and the ability of Jim Baker. I don't like the criticism of him, because his diplomacy has been absolutely superb, and he has always come through with the tough language with getting the UN to do what's needed. The difficulty of the diplomacy has been underestimated and he's done it superbly. Then, of course, Brent Scowcroft . . . He takes the burden off of the President, tasks the bureaucracy, sorts out the differences, and never with credit for himself. He's always quiet but always there and always dependable.

CHAPTER 19

After the Storm

The end of effective Iraqi resistance came with a rapidity which surprised us all, and we were perhaps psychologically unprepared for the sudden transition from fighting to peacemaking. True to the guidelines we had established, when we had achieved our strategic objectives (ejecting Iraqi forces from Kuwait and eroding Saddam's threat to the region) we stopped the fighting. But the necessary limitations placed on our objectives, the fog of war, and the lack of a "battleship *Missouri*" surrender unfortunately left unresolved problems, and new ones arose.

We soon discovered that more of the Republican Guard survived the war than we had believed or anticipated. Owing to the unexpected swiftness of the Marine advance into Kuwait, the Guard reserves were not drawn south into the battle—and into the trap created by the western sweep around and behind Kuwait as we had planned. While we would have preferred to reduce further the threat Saddam posed to the region— and help undermine his hold on power—by destroying additional Guard divisions, in truth he didn't need those forces which escaped destruction in order to maintain internal control. He had more than twenty untouched divisions in other parts of Iraq. One more day would not have altered the strategic situation, but it would have made a substantial difference in human terms. We would have been castigated for slaughtering fleeing soldiers after our own mission was successfully completed.

We were disappointed that Saddam's defeat did not break his hold on power, as many of our Arab allies had predicted and we had come to expect. The abortive uprising of the Shi'ites in the south and the Kurds in the north did not spread to the Sunni population of central Iraq, and the Iraqi military remained loyal. Critics claim that we encouraged the separatist Shi'ites and Kurds to rebel and then reneged on a promise to aid them if they did so. President Bush repeatedly declared that the fate of Saddam Hussein was up to the Iraqi people. Occasionally, he indicated that removal of Saddam would be welcome, but for very practical reasons there was never a promise to aid an uprising. While we hoped that a popular revolt or coup would topple Saddam, neither the United States nor the countries of the region wished to see the breakup of the Iraqi state. We were concerned about the long-term balance of power at the head of the Gulf. Breaking up the Iraqi state would pose its own destabilizing problems. While Ozal put the priority on Saddam and had a more tolerant view of Kurds than other Turkish leaders before or since, Turkey—and Iran—objected to the suggestion of an independent Kurdish state. However admirable self-determination for the Kurds or Shi'ites might have been in principle, the practical aspects of this particular situation dictated the policy. For these reasons alone, the uprisings distressed us, but they also offered Saddam an opportunity to reassert himself and rally his army. Instead of toppling him as the cause of its humiliating defeat, the Iraqi military was put to work to suppress the rebellions. It was a serious disappointment.

Trying to eliminate Saddam, extending the ground war into an occupation of Iraq, would have violated our guideline about not changing objectives in midstream, engaging in "mission creep," and would have incurred incalculable human and political costs. Apprehending him was probably impossible. We had been unable to find Noriega in Panama, which we knew intimately. We would have been forced to occupy Baghdad and, in effect, rule Iraq. The coalition would instantly have collapsed, the Arabs deserting it in anger and other allies pulling out as well. Under those circumstances, there was no viable "exit strategy" we could see, violating another of our principles. Furthermore, we had been self-consciously trying to set a pattern for handling aggression in the post–Cold War world. Going in and occupying Iraq, thus unilaterally exceeding the United Nations' mandate, would have destroyed the precedent of international response to aggression that we hoped to establish. Had we gone the invasion route, the United States could conceivably still be an occupying power in a bitterly hostile land. It would have been a dramatically different—and perhaps barren—outcome.

We discussed at length the idea of forcing Saddam personally to accept the terms of Iraqi defeat at Safwan just north of the Kuwait–Iraq border—and thus the responsibility and political consequences for the humiliation of such a devastating defeat. In the end, we asked ourselves what we would do if he refused. We concluded that we would be left with two options: continue the conflict until he backed down, or retreat from our demands. The latter would have sent a disastrous signal. The former would have split our Arab colleagues from the coalition and, *de facto*, forced us to change our objectives. Given those unpalatable choices, we allowed Saddam to avoid personal surrender and permitted him to send one of his generals. Perhaps we could have devised a system of selected punishment, such as air strikes on different military units, which would have proved a viable third option, but we had fulfilled our well-defined mission; Safwan was waiting.

One other aspect of Safwan has occasioned debate: the decision to let Saddam use his helicopters. The Iraqis claimed they needed them as the only means of communication with the various parts of the war-ravaged country. Schwarzkopf was without instructions on the matter, and granted the request. Saddam almost immediately began using the helicopters as gunships to put down the uprisings. Scowcroft discussed the issue with Cheney, proposing that the authority to fly the helicopters be rescinded. Cheney and Powell felt this would appear to be undercutting Schwarzkopf, and the helicopters did not allow him to do much that he could not also do—albeit with greater effort—with artillery. Scowcroft did not pursue the issue and it was never taken to the President. In retrospect, since the helicopters were being used offensively, not for communications, Schwarzkopf would not have been undercut and, psychologically, it might have been salutary to have rapped the Iraqis on the knuckles at their first transgression.

As the conflict wound down, we felt a sense of urgency on the part of the coalition Arabs to get it over with and return to normal. This meant quickly withdrawing US forces to an absolute minimum. Earlier there had been some concern in Arab ranks that once they allowed US forces into the Middle East, we would be there to stay. Saddam's propaganda machine fanned these worries. Our prompt withdrawal helped cement our position with our Arab allies, who now trusted us far more than they ever had. We had come to their assistance in their time of need, asked nothing for ourselves, and left again when the job was done. Despite some criticism of our conduct of the war, the Israelis too had their faith in us solidified. We had shown our ability—and willingness—to intervene in the Middle East in a decisive way when our interests were challenged. We had also crippled the military capability of one of their most bitter enemies in the region. Our new credibility (coupled with Yasir Arafat's need to redeem his image after backing the wrong side in the war) had a quick and substantial payoff in the form of a Middle East peace conference the following year in Madrid.

The Gulf War had far greater significance to the emerging post–Cold War world than simply reversing Iraqi aggression and restoring Kuwait.

Its magnitude and significance impelled us from the outset to extend our strategic vision beyond the crisis to the kind of precedent we should lay down for the future. From an American foreign policy–making perspective, we sought to respond in a manner which would win broad domestic support and which could, as far as possible, be applied universally to other crises. In international terms, we tried to establish a model for the use of force. First and foremost was the principle that aggression cannot pay. In this respect, our short- and long-term objectives were indistinguishable. If we dealt properly with Iraq, that in itself should go a long way toward dissuading future would-be aggressors. We also believed that the United States should not go it alone, that a multilateral approach was better. This was, in part, a practical matter. Mounting an effective military counter to Iraq's invasion required the backing and bases of Saudi Arabia and other Arab states.

Building an international response led us immediately to the United Nations, which could provide a cloak of acceptability to our efforts and mobilize world opinion behind the principles we wished to project. Soviet support against Iraq provided us the opportunity to invigorate the powers of the Security Council and test how well it could contribute. We were, however, unsure of the council's usefulness in a new role of actively resisting aggression, and we opposed allowing the UN to organize and run a war. It was important to reach out to the rest of the world, but even more important to keep the strings of control tightly in our hands.

In our operations during the war itself, we were as well attempting to establish a pattern and precedent for the future. We had sought, and succeeded, to obtain the mandate of the world community to liberate Kuwait. Unilaterally going significantly beyond that mandate, we might have undermined the confidence of the United Nations to make future grants of such deadly authority.

The Gulf War became, in many ways, the bridge between the Cold War and post–Cold War eras. At the outset, the Baker-Shevardnadze press conference, when the United States and the Soviet Union stood together against Iraqi aggression, was epochal. It symbolized the changing US-Soviet relationship. Superpower cooperation opened vistas of a world where, unlike the previous four decades, the permanent members of the UN Security Council could move to deal with aggression in the manner intended by its framers.

But the war's impact on international relations went beyond breaking the diplomatic logjam in the United Nations. The United States had recognized and shouldered its peculiar responsibility for leadership in tackling international challenges, and won wide acceptance for this role around the globe. American political credibility and influence had sky-rocketed. We stood almost alone on the world stage in the Gulf Crisis, with the Soviets at best in sometimes reluctant support. Our military reputation grew as well. US military forces and equipment operated in superb fashion, whereas Soviet weapons, with which the Iraqis were largely equipped, did not reflect well on their maker. The result was that we emerged from the Gulf conflict into a very different world from that prior to the attack on Kuwait.

CHAPTER 20

A House Divides

BRENT SCOWCROFT

The Gulf War symbolized the hopeful new spirit which had developed between the United States and the Soviet Union over the preceding year. Certainly, in August 1990, when our countries stood together and denounced the Iraqi invasion, I was prepared to say the Cold War was over. The two nations had cooperated on a major overseas conflict for the first time since World War II—which to me confirmed that the world had truly changed. We could now consider the possibility of a new world order, one based on US-Soviet cooperation against unprovoked aggression.

While our planning focus in the spring of 1991 was on the problems and opportunities which emerged in the aftermath of Desert Storm, we were concerned as well about what was transpiring within the Soviet Union. Shevardnadze's angry resignation and the crackdown in the Baltics were indications of the growing political divisions within the country and its leadership.

In many respects, the relationship between Gorbachev and Shevardnadze, the complete story of which has yet to be told, reflected the turmoil inside the Soviet Union. Both were architects and advocates of glasnost, but each perhaps had different ideas about how that could be achieved or what a new system would, or should, look like.

Shevardnadze appeared the more committed to the principles of democracy and to the fundamental political change it required, seeking complete transformation rather than simply reform. Gorbachev's goal still seemed to be the preservation of the political structures and central authority of a renewed and revitalized, but still familiar, USSR. As time went on, however, and resistance to his reforms hardened, Gorbachev became more and more caught in the middle. He maneuvered between, and played off against each other, the reformers and the conservatives in an apparent attempt to remain in control of the process he had set in motion. His priority became, de facto, political self-preservation rather than pursuit of principled and thorough reform.

To me, Gorbachev's back-and-forth shifts arose more from tactical motives than from ideological ones. He seemed genuinely to want to press ahead, but he periodically bowed to pressures from within the Party and the military. For example, he understood the need for urgent structural change in the economy and spoke often about market reform programs, yet he either did not recognize or grasp the depth of the reforms required or was unwilling to take the political risks associated with them. As a result, despite the positive rhetoric, Soviet economic reform measures up to 1990 were generally superficial. In August 1990, Stanislav Shatalin, a Western-style free market economist and a close advisor to Gorbachev, outlined a "500-Day Plan," which he argued would quickly move the economy to a free market basis. Gorbachev more or less adopted the program rhetorically, fitting it into his presidential plan that October, but it was never implemented in practice. Whatever the merits of the Shatalin program as a crash course in capitalism, or shock therapy treatment for a moribund Soviet economy, Gorbachev balked.

Although he vocally agreed with Shevardnadze that the use of force would spell the end of perestroika, Gorbachev occasionally resorted to, or could not prevent the military from employing, physical repression when it came to preserving political order and the union itself. This had been true in Tbilisi, Georgia, in 1989 and in the Baltics in 1990 and early 1991. His maneuvers between reform and reaction become ever more frequent until, by the latter half of 1990, they seemed to become virtually an end in themselves—simply an increasingly harried effort to maintain the Union, and himself in power.

In contrast, Shevardnadze seemed to undergo a complete philosophical conversion to democracy and market reforms. Coming as he did from a Party mold and background similar to that of Gorbachev, it is not easy to account for his uncompromising commitment to change. Perhaps the differences reflected their personalities and choices when it came to placing conviction over pragmatism and weighing means against ends. Whenever we cautioned Shevardnadze against the use of force, he vehemently, and I believe sincerely, insisted that it should not even be considered an option—it would destroy perestroika itself. Compromise on issues of principle he appeared to think impossible. Gorbachev may have had a more "realist" view than his friend of what was possible in the political environment they faced—that only through patience and compromise could they achieve any practical and lasting reform.

Over the course of 1990, Shevardnadze emerged in our eyes as the leading forward-looking reformer in the Soviet government, battling the military and the entrenched right wing of the Party for the soul of Gorbachev. He struggled to keep Gorbachev on the path of a committed reformer. Time after time, it seemed to us that, as Gorbachev would show signs of straying or of a weakening resolve, Shevardnadze would intervene. From the arms control agreements in February, when he resolved nearly every important issue in dispute only to see those agreements nullified by the military by May, to his standing alone—abandoned by Gorbachev—with Baker to condemn the Iraqi invasion in August, Shevardnadze stubbornly fought to keep the Soviet Union on the course of reform.

While Shevardnadze had generally prevailed in arguments over Soviet policy in the Gulf in 1990, by late fall his task looked increasingly difficult. He had saved the day at Helsinki in September, even as Primakov tried to persuade Gorbachev that the United States was trying to negate the thirty years the Soviet Union had invested in Iraq. By the time of Primakov's trip to Iraq in October, however, Shevardnadze seemed to be losing some control over foreign affairs. At that time he gave us specific warnings through back channels that Primakov was doing his best to sabotage a cooperative Soviet approach. Gorbachev never altered his Gulf policy, but he was intrigued by and hopeful about Primakov's machinations. That was hardly surprising. Primakov was trying to preserve at least some of the enormous Soviet investment in Iraq and, at the same time, avoid a military conflict, something which Gorbachev certainly did not want. It appeared to us that by the end of the year Primakov had successfully undermined at least part of Shevardnadze's influence with Gorbachev.

Perhaps Shevardnadze resigned because he was discouraged by having to fight more and more alone, vulnerable to the right wing of the Party. He may have believed that he had finally lost Gorbachev, or feared the emergence of a dictatorship against or—most painfully—with Gorbachev. Without Shevardnadze to stiffen him, Gorbachev appeared even more irresolute and, in the Gulf, spurred by Primakov and others, redoubled his efforts to thwart US moves toward the use of force. The sharp contrast between what we saw as the remarkable progress in foreign policy in East-Central Europe and elsewhere in 1989 and 1990 and the retrenchment in 1991, we took as evidence of Shevardnadze's earlier steadying influence. Party opposition to reform, however, was also beginning to harden, and the pressures on Gorbachev to curb the republics were growing.

Early in 1991, even as Gorbachev looked for ways to avert first the air war and then the ground war against Iraq, Lithuania once again exploded into violence. Tensions between Vilnius and Moscow had simmered since Lithuania suspended its declaration of independence six months earlier. On January 2, Soviet troops seized public buildings in Latvia and Lithuania, signaling the start of a crackdown. These moves were compounded by a decision to send additional troops to other republics. We wanted to avoid any official statements by President Bush on the intervention for the sake of solidarity in the Gulf. We were only days away from the UN deadline, and Baker was to meet with Aziz in Geneva on January 9. A rift with Moscow now would only encourage Saddam to dig in his heels. Worse yet, it might bolster the hard-liners around Gorbachev and cause him to stop cooperating with us. But we could not let the intervention pass without comment. On January 8, Marlin Fitzwater read a statement during a press conference: we saw the deployment as escalating tensions, and were concerned that the decision to send military units into the Baltics, "which we view as provocative and counterproductive," would hurt the prospects for peaceful negotiations. President Bush spoke to Gorbachev three days later, urging dialogue.

On January 13, the situation plunged into tragedy. Troops fired on demonstrators in Vilnius, killing fifteen. After a sharp internal debate about whether he should do so, this time the President spoke out, condemning the violence. Gorbachev declared he knew nothing of the decision to use force until after the fact, and contended that a military and civilian cabal had ordered the attack without his knowledge.* Nevertheless, a week later, Soviet troops again fired on civilian demonstrators—this time in Riga, Latvia, where four were killed. Rather than being cowed by the crackdown, many of the other republics, including Russia, responded with sympathy for the Baltics, leaving no doubt that central Soviet authority was weakening. Leading the charge was Boris Yeltsin.

On the same day Soviet troops fired on the demonstrators in Vilnius, Yeltsin, as president of Russia, signed a mutual security pact with representatives from the three Baltic states. It was an act not only of support for Baltic aspirations, but also of defiance of Gorbachev and central Soviet authority. The pact called for each of the four republics to respect the others' sovereignty, to refrain from recognizing any non-elected government among them, and to come to one another's aid should the cen-

---

*[GEORGE BUSH] I believed him at the time, and still do. In 1995, at a conference I sponsored on the Cold War, Gorbachev reiterated this charge, adding that the group had tried after the fact to induce him to say he had given the order.

tral government use force against them. In addition, the presidents of the four republics issued a joint appeal to the UN for intervention. A few days later, Yeltsin demanded Gorbachev's resignation.

The crackdown, and Yeltsin's organizing of opposition, also had consequences for Gorbachev's plans to reforge support for central Soviet authority. He had proposed a new Union Treaty, with which he was trying to replace a Soviet Union based on coercion with one founded on a voluntary association. Following its ratification by all the republics, he planned a new Union constitution which would include mechanisms for secession and other problems. It appeared that Gorbachev had in mind movement from a highly centralized state to a federal, or even confederal, association. Six republics, however—Armenia, Estonia, Georgia, Latvia, Lithuania, and Moldavia—were emboldened to announce on February 6 that they would boycott the nationwide referendum on the treaty.

BRENT SCOWCROFT

The crackdown in the Baltics, coming as it did on the eve of the launching of the air war against Iraq, aroused my suspicions. I wondered if the timing might be designed to take advantage of our presumed reluctance to take harsh countermeasures at a time when we needed to maintain Soviet support in the Gulf. Whether or not that was a motivation, the authoritarian measures produced a debate in the Administration on exactly that point. This was a difficult moment for us, as we tried to balance the need for solidarity at a crucial moment in the Gulf conflict against our desire to respond to a domestic outcry—and our own outrage—over events in the Baltics. President Bush spoke out again on January 21, urging Soviet leaders to desist from force. At the same time, he sent Gorbachev a letter warning that we would freeze economic ties and would not support special associate membership for the Soviet Union in the IMF and World Bank if the violence in Lithuania continued. Gorbachev replied that he was acting only in order to avoid the outbreak of civil war.

We did not pay close attention to the personal battle between Gorbachev and Yeltsin as it played out over the Baltics. We viewed Yeltsin's actions and statements more as those of one republic president among several participating in a growing effort to wrest greater political and economic autonomy from the center. In fact, much of Yeltsin's struggle with the center seemed to be over control of the "Russian" portion of the Soviet economy, perhaps to consolidate his power base. Yet his challenge to Gorbachev was important not only because of their rivalry but also because Yeltsin was president of the core republic of the Union.

Historically, the Soviet Union and Russia had been virtually indistinguishable. Now Yeltsin for the first time was drawing a distinction and asserting Russian interests against the Soviet Union.

As in the old czarist empire, Russia and Russians formed the geographical and political heart of the republics and their imposed union. Russia was by far the largest republic in both territory and population— with close to 140 million people, over 80 percent of whom were ethnic Russians. As Gorbachev often pointed out, Russians also formed substantial minorities in some of the other republics. Russia was inextricably associated with the political system of the Soviet Union, as well as the dominance of the Communist Party over the republics and the nationalities they represented. What emerged in the 1920s as the Soviet Union was not only the child of the Russian Revolution and Civil War, but also a powerful echo of the old empire. In the throes of those upheavals, along with the post–World War I settlements, the empire had broken up, some of its nationalities asserting and briefly enjoying independence and sovereignty after centuries of Russian rule, only to be bloodily recaptured by revolutionary Russia in the name of international communism. Lenin and Stalin brutally imposed a union of republics— ostensibly a free association of socialist states each governed by its own one-party system, but all controlled by what was then still called the Russian Communist Party. They began a calculated and systematic campaign to remove or repress nationalism and national cultures— including the Russian—in the hope of establishing a broader, socialist identity.

BRENT SCOWCROFT

In retrospect, when Yeltsin started to reject the authority of the Union and the Party and to reassert Russian political and economic control over the republic's own affairs, he was attacking the very basis of the Soviet state, shaking its political structure to the roots. In withdrawing Russian support, Yeltsin, perhaps at this point unintentionally, may have helped remove the very means by which the other republics were forcefully bound to the Soviet center, emboldening them to pull further away. Without Russia, the ability of the center to enforce its will on the other republics would be cast into doubt—although ultimately much still hung on the loyalty of the military and KGB forces.

Gorbachev may not have recognized the depth of the smoldering resentment of national groups to Soviet authority, or the full threat of the nationalities problem to the survival of the Union. Apparently, he confidently (or naively) believed that they saw their economic and political futures wrapped in the Union and that the republics, and the nationalities they represented, would remain in the voluntary association set up under the new Union Treaty. He seemed convinced (or at least hoped) that, once reforms were introduced, resentment of the center would fade. Instead, nationalists found in Gorbachev's reforms an opportunity to challenge the center. In some ways, the United States may have made the same kind of mistake in reading the situation. For years we had tended to assume the Soviets had had more success in stamping out parochial nationalism than proved to be the case.

Moscow's political, economic, and social problems continued to multiply, and no leader was emerging with answers to any one of them, let alone a coherent program that addressed them all. The Soviet Union was, we thought, in a prerevolutionary condition. I summarized the situation in a March 7 memo to the President:

> There are any number of events, particularly during the next month, that could touch off a conflagration. Coal miners threaten to strike. . . . and the Communist party is preparing to force recalcitrant republics to participate in the all-Union referendum on March 17. The more visible and aggressive posture of the KGB, the police, and the army could spark violence at any time. The already dysfunctional economy is likely to get worse in the next few months and it is not clear how much longer Soviet citizens can muddle through and feed themselves. No one knows for sure where the army stands. . . . The situation in the Soviet Union is so bad that it is hard to believe that explosion can be avoided. . . .

It was the most difficult context in which to steer a steady course in US-Soviet relations. We had to sort out our priorities. We suggested three to the President: nail down what we had accomplished in the last two years; push cautiously ahead on the US-Soviet agenda, recognizing and accepting that progress was likely to be slow; avoid involvement in Soviet domestic political wars. After so much rapid progress, the window of opportunity appeared to be closing. It was time to consolidate our gains.*

---

*Late in March, Condi Rice left the White House to return to Stanford. Ed Hewett, one of the top-ranked scholars on the Soviet Union, replaced her. I knew Ed from many conferences and joint appearances, and his views were solid and balanced. My only hesitation was that he had always operated in the academic world of total independence. I was unsure of his ability to make the transition to the bureaucratic world of the White House and the give-and-take environment of the interagency process. I needn't have worried. Ed took immediately to his new circumstances, and his superb intellectual qualities were matched by an awesome bureaucratic competence. He was the perfect man for the job during the complicated final travails of the Soviet Union. Tragically, Ed was stricken with cancer, but he continued to work right up to the end, which came in January 1993.

Serious problems were arising in US-Soviet relations. The principal achievements in arms control over the previous two years were now in doubt. The Soviets—under intense pressure from their military—had precipitated a crisis in the implementation of the CFE treaty by claiming that large quantities of military equipment were exempt from ceilings on grounds that the equipment belonged to "naval infantry." They demanded renegotiation of what had earlier been agreed upon with the West. Significantly, every one of the CFE signatories (including the Soviet Union's own allies in the Warsaw Pact) opposed changes to the treaty. Soviet backtracking effectively stopped all arms control negotiations dead in the water. If we could not trust the Soviets on already concluded measures, there was no point in trying to hammer out future details on START. Gorbachev seemed unwilling or unable to sort out the problems over CFE, problems which were perhaps themselves indicative of the shift in the political alignment of forces in the Kremlin.

On the eve of the March 17 referendum on the new Union Treaty, and in the middle of a Russian miners strike and repression in the Baltics, Baker went to Moscow. He went chiefly to discuss the outstanding arms control issues, but he also met briefly with representatives from the Baltics. He cabled on March 17 that he found Gorbachev determined, but it was not at all certain he could ride out the crisis. The results of the referendum had been mixed for the Union and for Gorbachev, although he claimed victory. While nine republics had approved the treaty, the six others—Armenia, Estonia, Georgia, Latvia, Lithuania, and Moldavia—had boycotted the vote, as threatened. It had been a practical assertion of the political clout these republics had wrested from the center. In addition, Yeltsin was raising his political profile, and that of Russia, by attempting to intervene in the CFE controversy, criticizing the central government's call to revise the treaty. These were all open challenges to the authority of the center and Gorbachev.

GEORGE BUSH

DIARY, MARCH 17
My view is, you dance with who is on the dance floor—you don't try to influence this succession, and you especially don't do something that would [give the] blatant appearance [of encouraging] destabilization. We meet with the republic leaders but we don't overdo it. Jim meets with Shevardnadze . . . he [too] is not sure Gorbachev is going to make it . . . I'm wondering, where do we go and how do we get there?

Between the Baltics crackdown and these problems over CFE and the details of START, it looked increasingly likely that the summer talks with Gorbachev I had hoped to hold before the G-7 meeting would have to be postponed. I thought a summit would take some of the pressure off him at home. While we needed to get arms control straightened out, I would go in a minute if there was some way that he could announce that the Baltic states were being set free. Nothing would have done more for his standing in the West than if Gorbachev simply cut them loose. But I knew that was asking a great deal of him—I doubted he had the political strength and support to do it. I thought he had his hands full trying to stave off demands from the right wing of the Party for repression in Lithuania.

By late spring there were signs that Gorbachev was regaining a measure of control over the Party. He had again swung to the center-left and was trying to strike a new compromise with reformers and the republics. In early April, Prime Minister Valentin Pavlov announced a government anti-crisis reform package, intended to stabilize the economy, stanch the hemorrhage to independence of the republics—most recently Georgia's vote on March 31—and reassert central authority. Gorbachev called for the republic leaders to set aside their differences in ideologies, political platforms, and "individual passions" in favor of a unified effort to save the Soviet Union from anarchy. He also asked those republics that had passed the referendum to approve the Union Treaty.

A substantive indication of his change in course, and of the country's future, came on April 23, when Gorbachev met with reformers and the leaders of nine republics, including Yeltsin, at his dacha in the Moscow suburbs. There he succeeded in obtaining their agreement to cooperate to solve the country's economic and political problems, though at a price for himself and the center. The republics would now play a greater role in the Union's political decision-making. Furthermore, the treaty would be revised to formally permit secession. In exchange, the republics would honor their existing economic agreements with Moscow as the central authority and would enforce Soviet law and order within their boundaries.

Two days later, at an April 25 meeting of the Central Committee, Gorbachev fought off intense pressure from conservatives by threatening resignation as general secretary, a notion they hastily rejected on the spot. His reassertion of authority emerged in US–Soviet relations as well. President Bush received a letter from him in late March, indicating that the Soviets were prepared to make some concessions on the CFE impasse—not enough, but we took it as a good sign. We thought Gorbachev was making some headway with the military. In addition, on May 20, the Supreme Soviet finally enacted the emigration and travel legislation Gorbachev had promised at Camp David the previous year, removing the major impediment to increasing our trade contacts. As a result, the President was at last able, on June 3, to waive the Jackson-Vanik amendment to the 1974 Trade Act, thus giving the Soviet Union the same rights as most of our trading partners.

The agreement between Gorbachev and the nine republics marked the start of what some dubbed the "nine-plus-one" process. It was meant to include negotiations for a revised Union treaty, the signing of a new Soviet constitution, Union-wide elections, and the creation of a voluntary economic union, although the republics that wished to do so would be permitted to go it alone. The arrangement went surprisingly well, primarily because both Yeltsin and Gorbachev went out of their way to avoid confrontation and seek compromise. Just what had prompted the sudden change of heart between the two is unclear. Gorbachev avoided interfering in the Russian presidential election and, after Yeltsin's June 12 victory, even congratulated him. On June 17, seven of the republics agreed on a draft Union Treaty decentralizing many of the Union's powers.

Despite the restoration of a measure of stability, the accord between Gorbachev and the center on one side, and the republics, led by Russia, on the other, underscored that the days of the center's one-sided domination of the Union were probably over, and with it some of Gorbachev's own authority. It was impossible to predict how far and how quickly power might shift to the republics, and what the future role of the center—and Gorbachev—would be. The old order as we had known it for decades was disintegrating, but just what kind of Soviet Union was emerging? Were we looking at a change in regimes and leadership, or transformation of the structure and political system itself? There was no way of telling.

GEORGE BUSH

Whatever the course, however long the process took, and whatever its outcome, I wanted to see stable, and above all peaceful, change. I believed the key to this would be a politically strong Gorbachev and an effectively working central structure. The outcome depended on what Gorbachev was willing to do. If he hesitated at implementing the new agreement with the republics, the political disintegration of the Union might speed up and destabilize the country. At the same time, I wondered how the Party traditionalists, now grouped close to Gorbachev in the senior administration posts vacated by reformers over the winter, would react to the transfer of authority. If he appeared to compromise too much, it might provoke a coup—although there were no serious signs of one. I continued to worry about further violence inside the Soviet Union, and that we might be drawn into a conflict.

US–Soviet relations over the spring and early summer focused on arms control and the question of economic aid. In March, Gorbachev wrote me asking for $1.5 billion in grain credits under our agricultural programs. While I wanted to help, Soviet behavior over CFE and START, and the crackdown in the Baltics, made the case very difficult. I was also pessimistic about the Soviet economy and the commitment to the reforms needed to foster a market economy. I had seen no evidence that even basic economic changes were being implemented. There were other problems, such as poor creditworthiness. In my view, the Soviet Union suffered more from economic inefficiencies and poor priorities than from lack of money.

Economic aid would also be a major topic at the London G-7 economic summit in July. Gorbachev wanted to attend in order to seek immediate help, as well as support for full membership in the international financial institutions—the International Monetary Fund and the World Bank—which would give the Soviets greater access to financial assistance. The problem with both requests was much the same as in their bilateral pleas for help—little evidence of commitment to economic reforms, or of willingness to cut defense spending. Giving the Soviet Union full membership in the IMF would be difficult in any case. Membership required countries to contribute considerable capital to the fund, money we knew they did not have. I was prepared to support a "special associate" status for the Soviets, which would give them access to technical help to overhaul their economy and put market practices in place, but not full membership.

Whether the group should invite Gorbachev to London was another problem. If he came, we had to make sure the summit was a political success for him, but we did not want to commit ourselves to aid we could not offer—there were reports that he wanted $100 billion in aid pledges from the G-7. I had told Primakov we had to work it out so that Gorbachev did not ask for money and then go away empty-handed. Primakov assured me that Gorbachev would not come to London and push for a gigantic check.

Gorbachev's invitation was not up to me but to the group as a whole. Brian Mulroney had reservations and thought we should first consider carefully what was best for John Major, who was chairing the summit. Major felt we should invite Gorbachev, but in a special status, not as part of the main meeting. Eventually, we agreed to meet with him in a heads-of-government discussion outside the usual sessions.

BRENT SCOWCROFT

In the midst of our debates over the G-7 summit, and as we began for-mulating a Soviet aid package, there was a moment of alarm. On June 20, we received a message from Ambassador Matlock about a meeting he had just had with Gavril Popov, the reformist mayor of Moscow. During the course of the conversation at Spaso House, and fearful of KGB bugs, Popov had handed Matlock a note that Prime Minister Pavlov, KGB Chairman Vladimir Kryuchkov, Defense Minister Dmitri Yazov, and Chairman of the USSR Supreme Soviet Anatoly Lukyanov were engi-neering a coup to remove Gorbachev the next day. He urged us to warn Yeltsin, who was in Washington on his initial official visit since his victory on June 12 as the first directly elected president of Russia, and was scheduled to meet with President Bush that afternoon.

It was a puzzling report. We knew of a bid that Pavlov, one of the traditionalists, had made to the Supreme Soviet to shift some of Gor-bachev's powers to him, without Gorbachev's permission. There was to be a vote on that proposal in the next day or so. Was that the rumored coup or was there something else? Baker called in from Berlin, where he was meeting with Bessmertnykh. He had received a similar message from Matlock and wanted to tell Bessmertnykh about it. We agreed and decided as well that Matlock should inform Gorbachev, in case Bessmert-nykh could not get through in a way which would not alert the KGB. To make certain Matlock could reach him, we sent Gorbachev a message from the President through the Soviet embassy asking that he immedi-ately receive Matlock. Finally, we determined to discuss the whole issue with Yeltsin.

GEORGE BUSH

I saw Yeltsin at three o'clock that afternoon for about an hour—this time he came to the Oval Office. With all the well-publicized rivalry and difficulties between Yeltsin and Gorbachev over the past few months, I was concerned that he would once again take the opportunity to attack him. I was greatly relieved and surprised when instead he sang praises. I was impressed by him and pleased with the visit. He was engaging and fascinating, and his infectious laugh made him easy to like. In contrast to his previous trip, he seemed to have almost taken a page from Gor-bachev's book and arrived well-tailored and -pressed.

Almost at the very start, I passed on the message from Popov. I couched it as guardedly as I could. I wanted to be sure he didn't think we were involved in spreading misinformation.

"Look," I said. "I don't want to get into any internal affairs, but I'm just passing on to you the fact that Popov told Matlock in a handwritten note that Gorbachev would be overthrown tomorrow." I added that Popov indicated this would be the result of a conspiracy by Pavlov, Lukyanov, Yazov, and Kryuchkov. Yeltsin discounted the rumor entirely, saying there was no way it could happen. He suggested that we place a call to Gorbachev together. We tried to get through, but could not reach him. I hoped that Matlock had managed to pass the word to Mikhail about this strange rumor.

In the remainder of our talk that afternoon, Yeltsin said everything we wanted to hear when it came to reform, and he cast himself as Gorbachev's equal in political stature. Sensing that he was challenging the center's role as the main conduit of foreign policy for the Union and the member republics, I tried to strike a balance between support for this new president and for the center. I explained to him over and over again that we would treat him with respect, and wanted to do as much business as possible; but I could not undermine Gorbachev. Yeltsin said he understood and assured me he was on good terms with Gorbachev, who was, he said, fully in accord with what he was doing.

I asked Yeltsin about the internal situation and the pressures on Gorbachev. He replied by sketching out the last few months as he saw them. "Gorbachev is pressured by the military and the KGB and the party apparatus of the Communist Party, now joined by Pavlov," he began. "The situation in January, February, and March was particularly acute. Gorbachev hesitated and began to go back. Reforms were slowed. There was an offensive launched against glasnost. We had the events in Lithuania, in Georgia, South Ossetia. Please do not misunderstand the statement I made [calling for Gorbachev's resignation]. I said if Gorbachev goes back on reform, then he should step down. But in April came the consolidation of the democratic forces. Gorbachev understood he could not live without the left wing. He abandoned those positions of three months. That opened the way for the nine-plus-one agreement."

He assured me that Russia was firmly on the side of Gorbachev. "I cannot act without him," he flatly declared. "We can only act together. Gorbachev's departure and the arrival of some general would be tragic. People would take to the streets and there would be civil war. But I am not that pessimistic. That is only talk. In twenty-four hours I will be back home and I will know the situation firsthand. The Supreme Soviet cannot remove Gorbachev. Only the Congress of People's Deputies can do that, and they never would. Only a violation of the constitution would remove Gorbachev now. This cannot happen."

The next day, Gorbachev returned my call about the Popov message. Evidently he had tried to take my call the day before, but there had been some confusion. (He told me later he was furious my call had not been put through to him.) Matlock had met with him, and he was pleased that we had passed on the information. It was clear he felt confident and on top of the situation.

Mikhail told me of the attempt in the Supreme Soviet by reactionary deputies to create problems, referring to the proposal to transfer power from him to Pavlov. The Supreme Soviet had voted to end any discussion of the matter. "The people against me got a real thrashing from the other deputies today," he exclaimed enthusiastically. I wondered whether the incident had anything to do with the message Matlock had passed on to him, and explained how it came about. "George, I told the Ambassador to reassure you that this is a thousand percent impossible," said Mikhail.

"That's good," I replied. "I conveyed the message to Yeltsin at the specific request of Popov. And I did so, but I wanted you to understand that I was not trying to interfere in internal matters. But I felt it was important you be informed." Unfortunately, this was a slip-up. I had forgotten that Popov specifically asked Matlock that we not use his name in connection with the rumor. In fact, my talking points prepared for the call avoided mention of Popov, and simply referred to a "reliable person." We heard later that Gorbachev accused him of disloyalty for not having come to him directly with this information, and for some time Popov understandably remained angry with us that his name was raised.

BRENT SCOWCROFT

The question of what to do about, or rather for, the Soviet Union at the G-7 summit hung over our heads the rest of June and the beginning of July. The temptation among some of the G-7 would be to promise too much. There was already some quiet division in our ranks over what kind of help we should offer—ranging from more financial assistance to technical aid. While the individual G-7 leaders would probably come prepared to give Gorbachev a cautious, conditioned response with no promise of large amounts of financial assistance, we worried that when face to face with him, they might be inclined to do more. In our own view, if we put no conditions on aid, we would all waste resources and do nothing to encourage the Soviets to transition to a market economy.

GEORGE BUSH

My summit trip began with a visit to France on Bastille Day, July 14, where I briefly met with Mitterrand at Château Rambouillet. One reason I was anxious to make the stop was that I wanted to bestow our prestigious Legion of Merit on General Michel Roquejeoffre, the commander of French forces during Desert Storm, as a symbol of our gratitude to his country's tremendous contribution to the coalition. I arrived in London that evening, in time for cocktails and a delightful private dinner with John Major at Number 10—where I also bestowed the Legion of Merit on Sir Peter de la Billiere, who did a great job commanding the British forces in the Gulf.

In London most of the attention was on Gorbachev. He made only one reference to financial assistance during a presentation, when he said that if we could find $100 billion for a war, there ought to be some way to help the Soviet Union. I don't think he understood that the Gulf countries, Japan, and others, their very futures threatened by Iraq's aggression and grateful for our leadership role, had dug deeply to help defray the cost of the war.

Gorbachev had sent us ahead of time a detailed document outlining his economic and social reform programs, and he covered the major points again in his presentation—price liberalization, convertibility of the ruble—both of which he implied would need Western financial support although he never asked for it. He was vague on details, and the language still stressed a mixed economy and socialist goals, but he did commit himself to the broad principles that were necessary to construct a market-based economy, such as privatization. My feeling at the time was that Gorbachev and the Soviets were crawling before they walked. We were still concerned by their spending on defense and foreign aid to Cuba, and told Gorbachev so. He said the aid had been cut back, but the fact remained that they were propping up Castro.

For the most part, the joint meeting went well and without contention or confrontation. I did worry when some of the group put Gorbachev on the spot with a hail of detailed questions on his reform measures—delivered in lecturing tones. Jacques Delors, the head of the European Community, interrogated Gorbachev like a professor questioning a student. The implication was, if you don't pass, beware. Others, such as Brian Mulroney, made equally important points, but in a more collegial tone, without the lecture and the scolding. I was always careful to avoid the appearance of haranguing Gorbachev. I knew the enormous problems he was facing. He deserved to be treated as a peer and a friend.

In an intermission, I tried to explain to Mikhail that he shouldn't take the preachy approach personally. They simply had legitimate questions on economic issues that they wanted answered before they could support aid. He brushed it all off, saying he did not feel lectured. I was also irritated that some of the others (though not Major or Mulroney) tended to ignore Toshiki Kaifu when he spoke and almost treated the Japanese as outsiders. I felt that what Kaifu had to say made sense and was very helpful. It was a curious cultural gap that I've never been able to understand. This was not an isolated incident, and I often worried that a lack of courtesy to Japanese leaders not only was hurtful but also could prove counterproductive for the G-7—which needed Japanese cooperation. Incidentally, the Japanese put great stock in G-7 meetings, viewing them as perhaps the most important forum in which they participate.

The group responded to Gorbachev's plan with caution. We needed to see the reforms more fleshed out, and decided that the best option was offering practical technical assistance of the kind I had already proposed bilaterally—energy, defense conversion, agriculture, and food distribution. We also backed Special Associate status at the IMF and World Bank. Not much could be done for the Soviets from abroad, however, until they finalized their Union Treaty and sorted out the internal economic arrangements among the republics.

My own talks with Gorbachev on July 17 at Winfield House were warm. Just before the meeting, Bessmertnykh sent a message that he'd like to see Baker. Brent and I speculated that it was about ironing out some last differences on START—whether the Soviets could put into service new types of missiles. Our concern was less about the substance of the differences than about the perception that we had to yield to them. Here we were talking about peace and economic help to the Soviet Union, while it seemed to everyone that what the Soviets wanted to do was deploy new weapons aimed at us. I was prepared to explain this to Mikhail, but Jim came in to see me just before he arrived and said, "I think we have a deal." Brent agreed, looking at the language. They put in a call to the arms control experts to discuss the details as Gorbachev and I went through a photo-op getting ready to go into lunch. After we ate, I took Mikhail aside for a confidential talk, in the course of which Jim and Brent came in and flashed the thumbs up that we had an agreement on arms control. It was a momentous and exhilarating moment: we had just reached a historic agreement to reduce our arsenals by several thousand of the deadliest of our nuclear weapons.

The more I listened to Mikhail's presentations that day about the Soviet domestic situation, the more I saw how overwhelming his problems were, and how important it was for him to work out arrangements with the republics. I told him that Yeltsin had conducted himself well in his visit to the United States. Gorbachev replied that his problem was not with Yeltsin, but with the people around him. He did not trust Yeltsin's inner circle, feeling he had been lied to by some of them.

My mind raced back to Camp David, where he had voiced very different views about Yeltsin. I told Gorbachev that Yeltsin was advocating many of the things we wanted—cutting aid to Cuba, instant freedom for the Baltics. The one action Gorbachev could take that would help his cause most in the United States was granting independence to the Baltics. Mikhail replied that the machinery was there in the constitution and tried to explain again the complications of independence, about compensation and the economic interdependence of the republics with the rest of the Union. He was confident that the problem could be resolved, but stopped short of saying he would grant independence. In the course of the discussion, Gorbachev formally invited me to Moscow at the end of July, and I accepted.

When Gorbachev joined the other leaders at 10 Downing Street for a relaxed evening, he fit right in. He told jokes about himself, including one in which two Russians were complaining as they stood waiting in line to buy vodka. One declared impatiently that the line was too long and he was going to go and shoot Gorbachev, who was at the root of the shortages. After disappearing for a couple of hours, the man returned to his friend in line, who asked, "Well, did you shoot him?" The man shook his head, "No," he said, "the line over there was longer than this one." Gorbachev roared with laughter as he told it.

I left London on June 18 for a trip to Greece and Turkey (the first presidential visit there since Eisenhower). Turgut Ozal had called some weeks before and asked me to come to Istanbul, which I was eager to do. We expanded the trip to include Greece, our other NATO ally on the southern flank of Europe, where Prime Minister Konstantinos Mitsotakis invited me to his home on Crete. By the time I returned to Washington and a full domestic schedule, I was exhausted—and only a few days away from my trip to Moscow and another summit.

As we flew to Moscow, I read a report from Colin Powell detailing his impressions of the Soviet Union from a trip the week before, as part of a military exchange program. He described the deep disaffection which pervaded at least the upper reaches of the Soviet military. The report seemed to confirm our own judgments about how carefully we needed to proceed.

Powell laid out his observations about the military's support for

Gorbachev, reform, and the emerging relationship between the republics and the center:

> While supportive of Gorbachev, the senior military leaders are openly disdainful of the reformers. Soviet chief of the General Staff Mikhail Moiseyev was extremely vocal on the subject. He called Shevardnadze a "traitor" for leaving the Communist Party. (I don't know what he'll say if Gorbachev leaves.) The generals complained of having too many "presidents." One of the more infamous reformers, Major Lopatin (now a people's deputy) showed up to greet me in Vladivostok. Moiseyev was irate. . . . [At a banquet in Powell's honor, Lopatin tried to give a toast, but was cut off by the Pacific Fleet commander.] . . . Moiseyev told me he later had a one on one with him and squared him away. I asked if he treated all People's Deputies this way. He said, "You only need three qualifications to be elected a deputy: criticize the generals, criticize the government, and promise anything."

Powell also wrote that the Soviet military "detested the political pluralism that is now developing. They view it as a loss of order and control." They had vast amounts of new equipment, and were pampered. "The military infrastructure, from barracks to vacation sanatoriums, seems to be the only sector receiving any investment. We saw lots of new tanks—not one new bus." While Powell kept emphasizing that even a "trimmed down" Soviet military of 3.2 million was wasteful and now unnecessary, especially if they wanted to fix their economy and society, "Moiseyev and company did not agree. I sense they will fight any further reductions. I also believe further reductions are inevitable." Colin observed that General Moiseyev and his top officers were soldiers and bureaucrats trying to protect their institutions as best they could. "They are under political control and I don't see any guys on horseback taking over. I doubt that their conscripts would follow them anyway. Gorbachev has given them a lot to digest. It may be a while before Gorbachev or one of the other 'presidents' can force them to take another big bite, but they eventually will have to do it." Powell saw Moiseyev, with whom he had a good relationship, as "an honest soldier, not a visionary."

We arrived in Moscow close to 10:00 pm on July 29. I was met at the airport by Vice President Gennady Yanayev, who I had been told was something of a hard-liner and a cool character, but who could not have been more engaging and pleasant, with a good sense of humor. We had a short but stirring arrival ceremony, without speeches, meeting their "first team" and a review of an honor guard of fine-looking young troops. We took the thirty-minute ride into Moscow. A few people waved, and we turned on the parade lights of the car (which illuminate the interior and let people see clearly who is inside), giving Yanayev a taste of what it was like to campaign in the United States. It was hard to see out and we waved at lampposts a few times, giving us a good laugh.

The next day, I had separate meetings with Gorbachev and Yeltsin. I saw Gorbachev late in the morning in Saint Catherine Hall, an ornate reception room with chandeliers and gilt woodwork on the walls and ceiling. Mikhail, Chernyayev, Brent, and I talked for close to two hours across an ivory-colored table. Gorbachev was marvelous, and how he could stand up to all the pressures against him I simply did not know. At first I thought he still believed that there would be some windfall of Western money that would help bail out the Soviet economy—he seemed confident as he spoke—but it was soon clear that he was pragmatic and resigned to the fact that he would not get funds.

They had completed work on the Union Treaty, he told me. While a portion of the republics still opposed, two thirds to three quarters were in favor. The question now was when to sign it. Not all would sign at once. "The process will continue until Ukraine decides to sign. Then the next step is a new constitution, election of the president and Supreme Soviet, and the formation of a new government body." He was convinced that although there was still opposition to the changes throughout all sections of Soviet society, this was lessening. "Some are vociferous and our media pay attention. So we take account of it. But the process of cooperation with the republics is gaining momentum as well. The most difficult period will be the rest of 1991 and 1992. It is good that people begin to do more on their own." They were determined to accelerate privatization to let people get down to work. "But we have to learn from the experience of Eastern Europe, including East Germany." He added they understood they had to move faster in order to get the West's cooperation.

I wanted Mikhail to realize that we would support him as far as we could. I spoke about bilateral economic issues and possibilities of trade and cooperation. We needed to see visible progress, with US companies working with the Soviets. One success, one big project, could release billions of dollars of private investment. "But privately, what is it you really want?" I asked. "If you could just wave a magic wand?" He said he wanted to extricate the country from the transition to a market economy as soon as possible. From there we launched into what amounted to an informal brainstorming session of ideas to help out their hard-currency problems.

After lunch, Mikhail and I went into the Cathedral Square of the Kremlin, where he gave me a tour. We emerged into a bright, beautiful, sunny day, not at all hot. I peppered him with questions about everything.

He proudly pointed out the giant statue of Lenin, surrounded by well-kept flowers, as well as the huge Emperor's Cannon. The crush of the press, however, was overwhelming; we literally could only inch forward. The KGB agents had to bowl people over to keep our group moving. There were a few incidents, with staff members and press photographers pushed down, and a camera broken—but the "tank" rolled forward and Gorbachev himself told the shoving press people to get out of the way. There was a little edge to all this. I don't know why the photographers thought they had to stand fifteen feet in front of us, crunched together and surrounded by security people, snapping the same picture over and over again. The walk lasted all of perhaps fifteen minutes, since I had to hurry off to speak at the Moscow State Institute for International Relations.

After my speech I headed for the Presidium of the Supreme Soviet, and a meeting with Yeltsin. He had turned down an invitation to attend an expanded bilateral meeting with Gorbachev and two or three of the other republic presidents we had held earlier in the day, saying he refused to take part in a "faceless mass audience." In our separate meeting it was clear that his first priority was protecting the notion of Russia and the Soviet Union being treated as equals in their dealings with the United States. He informed me I was the first foreign leader he had received in his new position. I was later told that his new office in the Kremlin had once been used by Gorbachev himself. We talked about the problems the Union was facing, and the republics' drive for independence. I made a pitch about freedom for the Baltics, which he favored. He said he had urged Gorbachev the day before to move forward on them. But Yeltsin seemed worried about Ukraine's moves toward independence, which he feared would cripple the Union. "Ukraine must not leave the Soviet Union," he said emphatically. Without it would there would be a lopsided majority of non-Slavic republics.

That evening, as we stood in the receiving line in St. Vladimir's Hall before the state dinner, Yeltsin's wife, Naina, of whom Barbara and I were to become very fond when she later accompanied her husband to the United States, came through the line alone. Then, at the very end, after all the other guests had passed by, Yeltsin dramatically walked in. He attempted to escort Barbara to dinner, which would have been quite embarrassing to Gorbachev, but he was not successful. Gorbachev gathered up Barbara and we all walked in. Yeltsin also told Matlock that he wanted to give a toast at our "return" dinner at the embassy, and in every way tried to present himself as Gorbachev's equal.

The next day I laid a wreath at the Tomb of the Unknown Soldier at the Kremlin wall and then had breakfast with American and Soviet businessmen before driving to Gorbachev's suburban government dacha in Novo Ogaryevo. The three big dachas in the compound were marvelous, one of which was used by the Gorbachevs on weekends, although Raisa said they didn't get out there much. The one where we met was beautiful, with high ceilings, overstuffed furniture, grand bathrooms. Though without the artwork of the Kremlin, it was still very comfortable. We walked out around the gardens for about a quarter of a mile. The woods were full of deer and wild boar, but we were told no one was allowed to hunt there.

The relaxed meeting matched our Camp David talk the year before and lasted close to five hours. As at Camp David, we were casual. Gorbachev was dressed entirely in gray—shirt, sweater, slacks, and loafers. I had on a polo shirt. We sat outside on wicker chairs at a circular table, the dacha on one side of us and the woods on the other.

Gorbachev began with a lengthy monologue, during which I barely managed to squeeze in a comment. Once again he went over the domestic Soviet situation, and the roles of our two countries in a changing world. He said he wanted to keep the changes in the USSR moving along within the law, but without danger or chaos. New centers of power were developing. "No dogma will stop me," he exclaimed, underscoring a challenge he had made to the Central Committee a week before. "There will be no ideological constraint as we move ahead." He wanted to build a new economy that would structure social accord. "The leaders of the US can be our strictest judges," he said. He turned to regional issues. "Totalitarian, authoritarian regimes are leaving the scene," he continued. "We engendered this change." It was time to cooperate and no longer to seek advantage. He suggested that we continue in the spirit of our interaction on the Gulf War and Middle East.

At about 11:30, not long after the meeting started, Baker handed me a note reporting that six Lithuanian guards had been killed at a customs post near the Byelorussian border and others wounded. I immediately asked Mikhail what was happening. He visibly paled and sent Bessmertnykh to check on the situation. I hoped it was not true. A pall fell over the meeting. A few moments later, Bessmertnykh returned, leaned to Gorbachev's ear, and whispered. Mikhail explained that there had been a series of incidents—the death of a Byelorussian, an attack on an Army barracks, and now this. He said they had just learned there would be a joint investigation between Lithuania and the Byelorussians. Later Gorbachev took a great deal of heat over this incident, with many in the US blaming him personally. But I don't believe he played any role.

We resumed the discussions, but the ebullient spirit was gone. Gorbachev spoke of the problems he saw posed by self-determination and his desire for our cooperation on the matter, not only over the problems in Yugoslavia but also in the USSR. He attacked the separatist pressures the center faced, pointing to border disputes that were now cropping up across the republics. He repeated one of his favorite phrases, that "process" was what was important.

We returned to Moscow to sign the START treaty at St. Vladimir's Hall. I really did feel emotionally involved at the ceremony. For me this was more than ritual; it offered hope to young people all around the world that idealism was not dead. We were agreeing to true reductions in intercontinental ballistic missiles. In my remarks, I strayed from my prepared text. I ad-libbed Ronald Reagan's name, but Richard Burt and many others were extraordinarily helpful in negotiating this historic treaty, and I wish I could have credited them all individually.

BRENT SCOWCROFT

Despite the reports that the military was disgruntled, we didn't get the feeling that a takeover was imminent. There were some revealing moments, however. At the dinner President Bush gave for Gorbachev at Spaso House, I was seated at a table with Defense Minister Dmitri Yazov. Yazov was right out of central casting—a great bear of a man, with ham-like hands and a florid complexion hinting of a fondness for vodka. He was a man of relatively few words, obviously not at his best engaged in the niceties of diplomatic chit-chat. He was in a morose mood, complaining that everything was going our way while the Soviet military was deteriorating daily. No new equipment was coming in (although Powell had observed otherwise), young men were not responding to the draft, there was no housing for troops returning from Europe, and so on. I asked him why he was concerned any more about Soviet military readiness. What was the threat? He responded that NATO was the threat. NATO had always been a defensive alliance, I pointed out. To the extent that he had in the past been seriously worried about NATO, which I doubted, any offensive capability it might have had was now eliminated as a result of the reductions. He took little solace in that observation but, as the evening and the vodka wore on, I did eventually manage to get him to join me in a toast to NATO.

Little did we know, as we climbed aboard Air Force One, but this would be our final formal summit with Gorbachev. It had been a satisfying set of talks. We finally had put START I to bed, a large step on the road to rationalizing strategic nuclear forces in a new era. Gorbachev seemed upbeat, almost exuberant about his prospects for dealing with his domestic problems. The black cloud over the Baltics marred the proceedings, but we had established a good process and rapport for our bilateral summit dialogues and there seemed, on the whole, reason to see the glass as half full.

GEORGE BUSH

From Moscow on August 1, we flew down to Kiev for a quick visit to Ukraine and a meeting with Leonid Kravchuk, chairman of the Ukrainian Supreme Soviet. Once again, I was accompanied by Vice President Yanayev, who joined me aboard Air Force One—surely the highest-ranking Soviet official ever to do so. In the course of the summit events I had come to know him a little better and found he enjoyed fresh-water fishing. When I returned to the White House, I rummaged through the desk drawers in my Residence office, pulling out an assortment of fishing lures, largely for bass, that I felt might work for him. I often wondered, because of subsequent events, whether the lures ever found their way to him, or if he got to try them out.

Barbara and I were met by Kravchuk. As at the Moscow airport, we watched an impressive military ceremony. I couldn't get over the modified goose-step, with arms swinging, that the troops used. I'd seen it before at funerals in Moscow, but close up it was dramatic. In Moscow they had played the US and Soviet national anthems, but here they added the Ukrainian one as well. Emotional, warm crowds of thousands lined the streets along the way. After lunch I spoke to the Ukrainian Supreme Soviet.

BRENT SCOWCROFT

President Bush's address became instantly famous—infamous—as the "chicken Kiev" speech. In remarks dedicated largely to freedom, reform, democracy, and tolerance, there was the following passage:

> But freedom cannot survive if we let despots flourish or permit seemingly minor restrictions to multiply until they form chains, until they form shackles. Later today, I'll visit the monument at Babi Yar, a somber reminder, a solemn reminder of what happens when people fail to hold back the horrible tide of intolerance and tyranny. Yet freedom is not the same as independence. Americans will not support those who seek independence in order to replace a far-off tyranny with a local despotism. They will not aid those who promote a suicidal nationalism based upon ethnic hatred.
>
> We will support those who want to build democracy.

The press picked up on these words and accused the President of not supporting the aspirations of Ukrainians and others who sought freedom and self-determination. It was a plea, they charged, to keep the Soviet Union together. They got it wrong. The reference to local despotism was not directed specifically at Ukraine. It was aimed at a number of areas where an upsurge of intolerant nationalism threatened the outbreak of major violence. We were especially concerned about developments in Yugoslavia and in Moldavia and other Soviet republics. The speech was given in Kiev because it would obviously have been inappropriate in Moscow, and Ukraine was the only stop outside Russia where the issue was relevant. The ethnic makeup of Ukraine did, of course, contain potential for national strife. The subsequent history of Yugoslavia and several of the former Soviet republics certainly validated the warning the President expressed.

GEORGE BUSH

I was choked up when we went to the memorial at Babi Yar, where the Nazi occupiers had killed tens of thousands of Ukrainians, Jews, and others. Midway through my speech I faltered as I described the horrors of a day fifty years earlier when the Nazis had lined up their naked victims in front of a trench, their clothes saved for reuse by the SS for people back in Germany, and systematically shot more than 33,000 over thirty-six hours. The SS had played dance music over loudspeakers to drown out the screams. I was deeply moved by what I saw of this long suppressed and awful chapter in history memorialized there.

> Today we stand at Babi Yar and wrestle with awful truth. We marvel at the incredible extremes of human behavior. And we make solemn vows.
>
> We vow this sort of murder will never happen again.
>
> We vow never to let the forces of bigotry and hatred assert themselves without opposition.
>
> And we vow to ensure a future dedicated to freedom and individual liberty rather than to mob violence and tyranny.
>
> And we vow whenever our devotion to principle wanes, we will think of this place. We will remember that evil flourishes when good men and women refuse to defend virtue.

We honored those few survivors who were present, as well as those who had helped victims survive.

It had been a long July. By the time we arrived back in Washington late on August 1, I was looking forward to some rest in Kennebunkport when my vacation began five days later. Gorbachev, after announcing on August 2 that his new Union Treaty was now open for signing by the republics, also headed off for a vacation at a retreat in the Crimea. It was not to be much of a respite for either of us.

CHAPTER 21

Coup

BRENT SCOWCROFT

At about 11:30 pm on Sunday, August 18, I was lying in bed at the Nonantum Hotel in Kennebunkport, reading cables and listening to CNN. I had come up from Washington that day to spell Bob Gates, for what I hoped would be ten days or so of quiet and relative rest. As mentioned, experience taught me that crises mysteriously seemed to break out when the President was at Kennebunkport and the national security leadership dispersed.

I was only half listening to the TV and vaguely heard the announcer say there were reports that Gorbachev had resigned for reasons of health. Since we had seen him only a couple of weeks earlier apparently in the pink of condition, I shrugged off the comment but began to listen more carefully. In about fifteen minutes, there it was again. I called Gates in Washington and asked him to check it out. Then I phoned Roman Popadiuk, the deputy press secretary, who at that time had the duty at Kennebunkport. If something really had happened, we could not stay silent, so I asked him to come over.

It was then midnight. I awakened the President, told him what I had heard, and pointed out that, thus far, we had been able to turn up no confirming information. I thought we might have to put out some sort of statement and Roman and I would draft one. The President and I had been planning to play golf at 6:30 the next morning. We agreed that I would monitor the situation and call him at 5:30. I hoped we would know by then if anything serious had happened. We also had on our minds Hurricane Bob, which was forecast to blow through New England sometime the next day. We agreed this would be a bad time to be cut off from Washington if the hurricane turned out to be serious. The President felt strongly, however, that we shouldn't change the schedule and prematurely return to Washington, as it might risk heightening a sense of crisis or looming catastrophe. As we had the year before after Iraq invaded Kuwait, we could work just as well from Kennebunkport. We had all the best communications equipment and we could quickly get people up and back from Washington through Pease AFB if necessary.

GEORGE BUSH

Besides the coup rumors in July, which Gorbachev had dismissed, there had been some recent indication that the hard-liners in Moscow might be up to something. On Saturday morning, August 17, Bob Gates had joined me at breakfast where we went over the Presidential Daily Briefing. In it was a report that the prospective signing of the Union treaty meant that time was running out for the hard-liners and they might feel compelled to act. Bob thought the threat was serious, although we had no specific information on what might happen or when. The next day the plotters struck.

As the events of mid-August began to unfold, I kept a running account of my reaction to events in my tape-recorded diary:

DIARY, MONDAY, AUGUST 19

Brent called me and said there was a Tass report that Gorbachev had resigned for health reasons. I called the Situation Room, around 5:30, and they gave me the update that Gorbachev has been put out. Some of the news is that we've been taken by surprise. I mention this to Brent this morning, and he says "Yes, and so was Gorbachev." And that's about right. If they don't know how the hell could we know? . . . I keep wondering whether I should go back to Washington or not, but there's not much to do there, except look busy . . . I now feel that we took the right course with Gorbachev. Some will say no, but the one thing we worried about has been a right-wing coup, although in recent times I've become convinced that the moves towards democracy are irreversible. We'll have to wait now to see if that's true, see what the populace in the Soviet Union does. Will there be general strikes? Will there be resistance? Will the military use so much force and crack down so much that they won't permit any democratic moves to go forward?

BRENT SCOWCROFT

By 5:00 am Monday, there were few really concrete details, but there had been an announcement from Moscow that Gorbachev had been relieved of his authority and a "State Committee for the State of Emergency" set up, headed by Vice President Gennady Yanayev. The Committee included Prime Minister Valentin Pavlov, Defense Minister Dmitri Yazov, KGB chief Vladimir Kryuchkov, Oleg Baklanov (in charge of the military-industrial complex), Interior Minister Boris Pugo, and two lesser-known civilian figures: agricultural leader Valery Starodubtsev and A. I. Tizyakov, head of the national organization of factory directors. I called the President, learned he had talked to the Situation Room and was up to date. I raised the idea of a press conference. We were uncomfortable about the paucity of information, but decided it was important to say something. Our dilemma was we didn't know the current status of the coup. The President's inclination was to condemn it outright, but if it turned out to be successful, we would be forced to live with the new leaders, however repulsive their behavior. We decided he should be condemnatory without irrevocably burning his bridges. He also thought it would be a good idea to check with some of his foreign colleagues. We set the conference for 7:30 am, to make time for those calls.

GEORGE BUSH

My immediate response was to rely on some very active telephone diplomacy—depending on how events unfolded. It was not frantic, but rather to keep other countries informed of what we were doing, especially our allies but also those not normally on the front lines. My message was there would be no acceptance of the coup.

I spoke with John Major—mainly to begin to coordinate our responses. He had much the same information that I did, and neither of us knew what had become of Gorbachev. He agreed that Yanayev seemed to be a figurehead. A couple of minutes later I was on the phone with François Mitterrand. I explained that I planned to make a statement announcing we would continue to support the process of reform and openness. "But let's avoid statements about rearming," I added. François agreed. "Indeed," he said. "Let's not create a perception that all is lost. This coup could fail in a few days or months. It goes against the tide. It's hard to impose by force a regime on a changing nation. It won't work." He declared we should stick to our principles and asked if we were taken by surprise, too. "Yes," I said, echoing Brent's earlier comment to me, "but so was Gorbachev."

Our deputy chief of mission in Moscow, Jim Collins, who was in charge as he awaited the arrival of our newly appointed ambassador, Bob Strauss, said he had been to the Russian White House, heart of the government, but had not seen Yeltsin. He knew little more about the status of the coup than we did. I then phoned Helmut Kohl. "I hope," he said, "that the new rulers will be sensible enough to understand there can be no relapse into earlier policies." Whatever happened, all international agreements, and disarmament and arms control, must continue. The Soviets could get help only if they respected human rights. We all had a great respect for Gorbachev, he said. "As a German, I appreciate what he did for us."

BRENT SCOWCROFT

We had scheduled the press conference at the usual location, the lawn in front of the small house at Walker's Point which contained the President's office. Shortly before it was to begin, however, a pre-hurricane rain began to fall. Unfortunately, there was no adequate indoor briefing facility. We finally settled on a small room in the building occupied by the Secret Service. The press corps crammed into it, clothes wet and steaming from the rain.

The President explained that we had few details of the events, which he described as "extra-constitutional" and "disturbing." He praised Gorbachev and said he had been in touch with key foreign leaders. "Coups can fail," he said. We should remain open as to whether this one was going to succeed. He wanted to do or say nothing which would give approval to what was taking place. These very cautiously negative comments were followed, as soon as we ascertained that the coup had not yet been fully consummated, by a statement of sharp condemnation and opposition to the attempts of its leaders. It included, among other things, a declaration of support for Yeltsin's call for "restoration of the legally elected organs of power and the reaffirmation of the post of USSR President M.S. Gorbachev." It turned out that the President was the first foreign leader publicly to support Yeltsin, something the Russian president has often said he has never forgotten.

GEORGE BUSH

DIARY, AUGUST 19

[T]he questions for the most part were okay; [such as] "Why were you surprised?" There will be a lot of talking heads analyzing the policy, but in my view this *totally* vindicates our policy of trying to stay with Gorbachev. If we had pulled the rug out from under Gorbachev and swung towards Yeltsin you'd have seen a military crackdown far in excess of the ugliness that's taking place now. I'm convinced of that. I think what we must do is see that the progress made under Gorbachev is not turned around. I'm talking about Eastern Europe, I'm talking about the reunification of Germany, I'm talking about getting the troops out of the Pact countries, and the Warsaw Pact itself staying out of business. [Soviet] cooperation in the Middle East is vital of course, and we may not get it now, who knows?

I called Toshiki Kaifu just before 9:00 and had a longer conversation with Brian Mulroney a few minutes later. I confessed that we really didn't know much about the situation. "It's the hard-liners—Pugo, Kryuchkov, Yazov, Pavlov. We're not sure where Moiseyev is. The rumor is that he flew down to break the news to Gorbachev." I recounted my conversations with Yanayev when he had been my host in the Soviet Union just a few weeks before. "We were surprised like everybody else," I added. "The press is saying it was an intelligence failure." It was a typical charge. They expect every plot, scheme, or move, successful or unsuccessful, to be anticipated by "intelligence." At the same time, some reporters attack the very existence of intelligence services as somehow immoral or no longer needed.

"George," said Brian, "one point where you may get some criticism on behalf of all of us. They may say, well, if you people had been more generous in London, maybe this wouldn't have happened." He recalled a conversation at the G-7 meeting. "You may remember my turning at lunch to Helmut Kohl and saying to Helmut, who is closest to the situation . . . 'If a month from now, Gorbachev is overthrown and people are complaining that we haven't done enough, is what we're proposing the kind of thing we should do?' He said absolutely; there was no second-guessing the nature of the decision in London." Kohl had recently met with Gorbachev in Kiev, and he assured us that this was what Gorbachev needed and wanted.

I remembered the conversation. "I'll get hit for holding the country too close to Gorbachev," I said. "I'll point out it's a damn good thing because look at the changes that have taken place. And if we had tried to pull out the rug it would have happened sooner."

"Any doubt in your mind that he was overthrown because he was too close to us?" asked Brian.

"I don't think there's any doubt," I said. "It will be interesting to see what the new 'leaders' say. At first, they said he had health problems. Maybe that means that Gorbachev's fingernails wouldn't come out. Even more important is the economic chaos and disorder that goes with it and the economic drift. And I think, on the part of these guys, the down-grading of the Communist Party. These are hard-liners and they see the party that was their life's blood, the KGB, that has been the silent hand forever, undermined and threatened as well."

Brian asked if I thought there was any significance in the fact that the Union Treaty was to be signed in the next few days. He believed that Gorbachev coming back to sign it would be "the kiss of death" to the tra-ditionalists and that this may have precipitated the coup. I wasn't certain, but it was a good possibility. (Brent and I later agreed it was probably a contributing factor to the timing.) "Yeltsin is out there on top of a tank saying this coup must be reversed," I added. "You have to give him credit for enormous guts."

DIARY, AUGUST 19

I think of Gorbachev himself down in the Crimea on vacation. His sense of humor, his courage. I'm wondering what condition he's in, where he is, how he's being treated. I think of the old guard mili-tary, Yazov particularly, who was grumbling all the time at the meetings that we had in the Soviet Union. Drinking a lot, com-plaining at the table with John Sununu and others about how bad things were.

. . . The live CNN pictures are stark, bumper to bumper APCs [armored personnel carriers] parked in Moscow. Tanks moving down the streets. And then reports that the Kremlin has been blocked by a thousand people. There has been an official statement that they will honor their international agreements, [a question which has] caused angst and concern out of the Baltic states now. Landsbergis, who's been pushing Gorbachev the furthest, now hol-lering for support. That'll be hard to honor, just as it's hard to honor and support inside the rest of the Soviet Union, if by support you mean military. The extremists that wanted us to dump Gorbachev and deal with Yeltsin are now going to have some real rationalizing to do.

Yeltsin is calling for Gorbachev to be restored to office. Interest-ing. Our right wingers were saying forget Gorbachev, but he has represented a certain stability there, and now, even he, the more versatile and practical of the reformers, seems to be in the worst trouble. God knows what'll happen to the others. But obviously we must cast our support to the forces of reform. Gorbachev, Yeltsin, Shevardnadze, others all having told me quite recently that these changes are irreversible. The test is about to come.

In the course of the day we received a letter from Yanayev, via Soviet ambassador Viktor Komplektov, who gave it to Eagleburger and Gates in Washington. The plotters explained the "official" reasons for the coup:

> There has emerged a situation of uncontrollability with too many centers of power. All this cannot but cause widespread discontent of the population. There has also been a real threat of the country's disintegration, of a breakdown of the single economic space, and the single civil rights space, the single defense, and the single foreign policy. A normal life under these conditions is impossible. As a result of inter-ethnic clashes there has been bloodshed in many areas of the USSR. A disintegration of the USSR would have gravest concerns not only internally, but internationally as well.
>
> Under these circumstances we have no other choice but to take resolute measures in order to stop the slide towards catastrophe . . .

Yanayev claimed that the new regime would continue Gorbachev's reforms, and that international agreements remained in force.

DIARY, AUGUST 19

. . . I decided to bring Strauss back [to Washington], and [go down to] swear him in the Oval Office tomorrow and get him on his way. Jim Baker talks to him and is sending a plane to pick him up, [and Baker]. They'll get in tonight. And of course, during all of this we have a hurricane slamming in here. We had the Red Sox Roger Clemens, Matt Young, and others over here [who had come to play golf], and all of us trying to figure out how to evacuate the Walker's Point house—whether it is safe for Mother to stay.

Yeltsin's calling for a strike, and the thing we have to do is remain calm, stay in touch with our allies, and do what we can to reverse out this military takeover. Our options are few and far between of course.

At this point I worry about the Baltics. We're going to have cries to bring military help by Landsbergis. We hear that Estonia has been taken over by the Soviet military, that the radio and TV [are] now in the control of the Soviet military in Lithuania. And so we've got some big problems, that will have enormous impact here at home . . . The best thing at a time like this is calmness, firmness, adherence to principle. Do not get stampeded into some flamboyant statement. See where we can go . . .

We get on the phone on the way back [to Washington] on Air Force One to talk to John Major again. . . . Major is wondering whether we ought to have a NATO ministerial. My reservation on that is that it'll make it look like we're militarizing, that we are anticipating a military threat to the West. If NATO appears to be going to general quarters, we could have calls from the Baltic leaders (which might be coming in anyway) for us to support them with troops. This is the last damn thing we need, to get involved in that kind of a confrontation. Yeltsin wants us to go to the UN to announce support for the reforms and we can do a lot of that and we will.

Spanish Prime Minister Felipe Gonzales and others agreed that it was premature to speak of any military action, or even to foster such a step. When I spoke with Vaclav Havel and Lech Walesa, neither was worried about any physical danger to their countries, although Havel did compare the situation in the Soviet Union to that of the Czech Spring in 1968. Antall of Hungary added that this was simply proof that it had been a good idea to have acted in haste to get the Soviet troops out of his country. He was more nervous about Communist activity in Hungary than of a Soviet reoccupation.

DIARY, AUGUST 19

Strauss and Baker are flying back. They get back at ten tonight. I gun down the idea of having an overall cabinet meeting. I talked to Dan Quayle, who wonders what to do and I said he ought to stay where he is and get a little rest and I plan to go back to Maine tomorrow. I think it is a good thing I am coming back. Brent . . . talks to the press on the plane and they're wondering why is the President leaving? What's so urgent about it all? Kind of a needling press conference but nothing hostile at all.

I'm trying to figure out where the critics'll be hitting us. And it's hard to tell whether they'll be coming at me from the right. I don't think they can come at us from the left. By "right" I mean what are we going to do now about the Baltics? How are we going to guarantee their freedom? The Union Treaty was to have been signed tomorrow and that is what probably precipitated this takeover. The coup plotters have announced that they are going to do something about housing and energy and food—all the things that are of concern to the people . . . The question remains, how are they going to do it?

At about 3:00, we tried to reach the Kremlin by direct voice link, telling them I wanted to talk to Gorbachev, but could not get through.

Yeltsin is seen standing on top of a tank talking to people. Another question is where will the Soviet troops come down? Seventy percent of them support him in the election, the Russians. He's declared himself to be in charge of all functions of Russia now. How will that go down with the bad guys, the coup plotters?

. . . If I were to comment tonight I would say: "Mikhail, I hope you're well. I hope they've not mistreated you. You've led your country in a fantastically constructive way. You've been attacked from the right and from the left, but you deserve enormous credit. Now we don't know what the hell has happened to you, where you are, what condition you are in, but we were right to support you, I am proud we have supported you, and there will be a lot of talking heads on television telling us what's been wrong, but you have done what's right and strong and good for your country. I like you and I hope that you return to power, skeptical though I am of that. I'm not particularly close to your wife, but I think of her and your family. I liked Yanayev when I met him, and yet now I go back and see the clips of his adherence to communist doctrine and I agree with Antall of Hungary, who says he's a marionette controlled by puppeteers. I sit here the night that the force of nature clipped Kennebunkport, but not badly, and I see that the force of power politics has clipped you. If you are listening, Mikhail, don't listen to the extremes in this country. We support you, and we were right to support you.

As I sit here with all the best advice we can muster, I'm not sure that there's any chance that you, Mikhail, can come back. I hope that you never compromise enough that if you come back you'll be under a cloud. I hope that Yeltsin, who's calling for your return, stays firm, that he's not removed by the power of this ugly right-wing coup. I'm convinced we've been on the right track, but we'll wait and see how all that works out and in terms of world opinion.

We've got a lot of talking heads out now. Frank Gaffney, who seems to be on there all the time against our arms control policies, always sitting next to Pat Buchanan. He's on there tonight. They ask him if he wants military force and he says no, but he wants to give all the support we can to the reformers. Well, so do I. Bill Colby is on there with a very reasoned position. My problem is that, during Iraq a year ago, we knew what had to happen. What had to happen is Iraq had to get out of Kuwait. Here, I'm not sure what *has* to happen.

What I'd like to see is a return of Gorbachev, and a continuous movement for democracy. I'm not quite sure I see how to get there . . . This new crowd is hard-line and they're communists. Yanayev, there are some quotes on from him saying he's a hard-line communist, and he is. They see the demise of the Party and they see these reforms going against everything they've been taught to believe in, and they just can't adapt to it . . . My view is that the forces of democracy have been unleashed, they can't be set back, and so forward we've got to hope for and try to effect the return of Gorbachev and the forward movement of democracy as epitomized by the election of Yeltsin. But it isn't easy. It isn't easy at all. . . .

Enough for the night of the nineteenth. The hurricane's gone by. Mother and Bar and all are okay. The Soviet Union is in turmoil. Eastern Europe is worried. But life goes on. August nineteenth. A historic day.

The next day, before I swore in Bob Strauss at the White House, I placed a call to Boris Yeltsin, and much to my surprise I got him. I asked him what was going on.

"The situation is very complex," he replied. ". . . President Gorbachev is located in Foros in the Crimea. He is absolutely blocked, no way of reaching him. President [sic] Yanayev is using the pretext that Gorbachev is ill, but this is not yet confirmed. Essentially a committee of eight people has taken over the presidency and established a state of emergency in Russian territory and the Baltics. Troops have been brought up to Moscow, not only in the city, but in Moscow District and surrounding towns. And by issuing [these] decision[s], the group has exposed itself as no more than a right-wing junta. I appeared before the people and soldiers and I said that actions of the committee were unconstitutional, illegal, and have no force on Russian territory.

"The building of the Supreme Soviet and the office of the president is surrounded and I expect a storming at any moment. We have been here twenty-four hours. We won't leave. I have appealed to a hundred thousand people standing outside to defend the legally elected government.

"Basically, this is a right-wing coup; each member of the group is well known. They want to take over the democratically elected leadership of Russia, Leningrad, Moscow, and other cities. This morning I gave Lukyanov, Chairman of the Supreme Soviet, ten demands, the first of which is to meet with Gorbachev." Yeltsin asked that I too demand to speak on the phone with Gorbachev and to rally world leaders. He had announced a strike and practically all factories and plants were at a standstill. "We will continue demanding this until the committee is thrown out and tried in court. We are not losing any hope or faith unless they resort to the most extreme and bloody measures. Of course, a wounded animal is the most dangerous thing and we have no assurances that they won't resort to extreme measures." I told Yeltsin he had our full support for the return of Gorbachev and the legitimate government. I explained I had tried to call Gorbachev the day before but couldn't get through. However, I liked the idea of saying publicly that I wanted to talk to him.

"We have changes happening so fast that we should talk by the end of the day tomorrow," said Yeltsin. "Things are literally changing by the hour."

"I'm happy to do that," I said. "I hope the lines will not be cut off." I added that I was prepared to call Yanayev, but that I did not want to do anything to legitimize the regime.

"No, absolutely, you should not do that," said Yeltsin quickly. "An official call from you would legitimize them. We tried to send a group to the Crimea to meet with Gorbachev, but he is surrounded by three circles of armed guards and KGB."

"We'll keep trying to reach him," I replied. "We're not hopeful, but it legitimizes the Gorbachev regime."

BRENT SCOWCROFT

At the end of this call, or perhaps the one the next day, I recall Yeltsin saying he could hear the tanks moving at the end of the street and approaching the parliament building. He said that he had to go and that this might be the last time we heard from him. Of course the tanks were not storming the palace, but this bit of added drama was pure Yeltsin.

GEORGE BUSH

It was, as Yeltsin had said, a phenomenally complex situation. I was determined to handle it without getting us involved in a war, but standing by our principles of democracy and reform.

The next morning, Wednesday, August 21, I was on the phone again with Yeltsin. He sounded more confident, but he was not declaring victory. "We've spent the last two days sitting in the parliament building without leaving the premises," he began with an air of melodrama. "Mr. President, I want to tell you I had discussions with Kryuchkov and the military and the forces were stopped. Tens of thousands of people stopped them from storming the building." He explained that the Russian Supreme Soviet had unanimously decided to declare the coup attempt illegal and that it had no effect on Russian territory. They had backed all Yeltsin's decrees and actions as president of Russia. "They also gave me additional powers to see to it that if local authorities support the junta, they can be removed from office."

Yeltsin said that Kryuchkov had suggested they fly down to the Crimea to meet with Gorbachev. However, for safety reasons, the Russian Supreme Soviet would not allow him to go. Instead, Prime Minister Ivan Silayev and Vice President Alexander Rutskoi had been sent. Primakov and Vadim Bakatin were also on their way. "What I am trying to do is work with [Ukrainian President Leonid] Kravchuk to intercept them and have them land in Simferopol in the Crimea and not let them get to him first. Now there are three aircraft flying in that direction, trying to get there first.

"The danger of a siege remains as before. The group commander of the air assault troops refused to follow the orders of the Ministry of Defense and has decided to come over to the Russian side. Following my order, he has left Moscow with his forces and gone back to base. A group headed by my Deputy Prime Minister is located in the geographical center of Russia, so in the event that I am taken, Russian leadership will continue.

"Also last evening, Kravchuk and [Kazakhstan President] Nazarbayev reported that they too decided not to fulfill the decision by the junta. Tens of thousands of Muscovites continue to surround the RFSR [Russian Federated Soviet Republic] building. And, based on my order, all forces and tanks are moving out to the periphery of Moscow. However, there remain KGB [and] Spetznaz* forces not following my orders and capable of attack. This is the situation at this hour."

I asked Yeltsin whether Kravchuk would cooperate with him in preventing the five coup members from meeting with Gorbachev. He was not certain, but Kravchuk had said he would do everything possible. "However, those planes are jammed-packed with security forces. He promised that air traffic controllers in Ukraine would make them land in Simferopol and not where Gorbachev is. But I'm not sure because there are other technical problems."

"Can anyone in the USSR get in touch with Gorbachev?" I asked.

"No," he replied, "because even I have tried several times today. You need to have a special switching device. We are told by the operators that we can't get through even to any of his assistants. Either we can't get through or they are blocking us. Through Gorbachev's guards we have determined that he is quite healthy and determined not to sign any of the

*The Soviet army's elite special forces.

documents that would give his power to anyone. If we can't intercept the group in the Crimea we will attempt to intercept them when they return to Moscow. We are ready to do this. I can't give you the details about it over this phone."

I asked what had become of the other coup members. I kind of hoped that Moiseyev had broken away. Yeltsin told me that Lukyanov seemed to be backtracking, making it appear he had never been with the coup group in the first place, and he was fully supporting constitutional measures. The three leaders remaining in Moscow continued to manage the coup from here. "Pavlov is in bed in the hospital," he added.

"Is it a real sickness?" I asked.

"No, a 'diplomatic' sickness," replied Yeltsin.

I wondered whether Bessmertnykh, who was a career man, was back in his office. Yeltsin scoffed at this. "Yes," he said, "but he is maintaining quiet neutrality."

Was there was anything further we could do? Yeltsin said that other than publicizing their plight and offering moral support and statements, he did not see anything technical or otherwise that would help. The main task now was the August 26 session of the USSR Supreme Soviet. He would try to get a resolution passed saying that the committee's takeover was illegal. He was lobbying each of the deputies to guarantee such a vote. The coup plotters would then be outside of the law, and brought to trial. The other side, however, was also lobbying the deputies.

I asked about the situation in the Baltics, apparently a principal target of the coup leaders. Estonia had declared independence the day before and Latvia followed even as we were speaking. Yeltsin said that thirty Spetznaz aircraft were being sent there. "They are beginning to take over a number of sites and locations. What we're trying to do is lobby the commander of the Spetznaz forces to come over to our side and not send troops there. We are now holding discussions with him. If we convince him, he will withdraw his forces. He reports to Yazov, the minister of defense."

I promised we would continue to support him. "People throughout the world are supporting you, except Iraq, Libya, and Cuba," I said. "People are supporting you more than you can understand."

"I will do everything I can to save democracy in Russia and throughout the USSR," said Yeltsin dramatically.

Soon after, I checked in with John Major. He told me he had just been handed a note that TASS was reporting the Committee of Eight had been disbanded. We were not quite sure what it meant or who had given TASS the information. It was encouraging, but we did not wish to declare the coup over yet. I pointed out that we did not want to undermine Yeltsin, and we had to be careful of Gorbachev's position. Major judged that Yeltsin's future role had been strengthened and that Gorbachev might be in very difficult political straits. At least they were staying together, I told him. "Out of this we may have a very different-looking Soviet Union," I said.

DIARY, AUGUST 21

It's a stormy day in Maine. Brent and I sit in our living room. Back and forth on the calls. We get a call from Strauss who said that US had been asked to join in a mission of DCM level to go down to the Crimea to see Gorbachev . . . it's moot I think, because it doesn't look like the plane ever got off in order to go down there . . .

Another emotional day. I took [my friend] Johnny Morris and his guys . . . out on the boat—the *Fidelity*. We ripped through the choppy waters. And when I got back to the pier, John McGaw* said "You have a call from a chief of state." I [asked] "Who?" He said, well, they couldn't say on the phone. I got to the house, into the bedroom, took the call and it was Gorbachev.

BRENT SCOWCROFT

Since the outset of the crisis, I had asked the Signal (military) switchboard to try periodically to get through to Gorbachev. Finally, early Wednesday afternoon, unexpectedly, they did. We had to keep him hanging while we scrambled to find the President. While waiting, he conversed with the translator, Peter Afanasenko. "There is a God!" Gorbachev exclaimed. "I've been here four days in a fortress." Peter explained that we were getting the President. "We can wait," said Gorbachev. "You can't believe what it was like here. I was completely blocked."

GEORGE BUSH

As I picked up the phone, communications told me Gorbachev was on the line. "Oh my God, that's wonderful," I said. "Mikhail!"

"My dearest George. I am so happy to hear your voice again," said Gorbachev.

"My God, I'm glad to hear you. How are you doing?"

"Mr. President," replied Gorbachev, "the adventurers have not succeeded. I have been here four days. They tried to pressure me using every

---

*Head of my Secret Service detail, who later went on to run the Service itself.

method. They had me blocked by sea and land. My guards protected me, we withstood the challenge."

"Where are you now?" I asked.

"I'm in the Crimea. It's been only one hour since I have assumed presidential powers. I have maintained full contact with the republic leaders and handed over the Ministry of Defense to Moiseyev. He is to follow my orders only. Troops are to move out of the city or back to where they are normally based." He added that everything they had done to improve cooperation with the republics had paid off. "All of them had taken positions of principle. The greatest opponent of these illegal acts was Yeltsin." It had been a terrible tragedy, he said. "It showed that the adventurers won't succeed. The society is different now; things like this won't work."

I asked what had become of the plotters. "Some are coming [to see] me," he said. "I don't know what they are bearing in their hands. In the next two days I must make all these crucial decisions." He had already spoken with Yeltsin, the first call he had made. He thanked me for our support, and said he would be calling me once he was in Moscow and had sorted everything out. "We want to keep going ahead with you," said Mikhail. "We will not falter because of what has happened. One thing is that this was prevented by democracy. This is a guarantee for us. We will keep working in the country and out to keep cooperation going."

"Sounds like the same old Mikhail Gorbachev, full of life and confidence. Once you get back we'll talk about what to work on. . . ."

DIARY, AUGUST 21

All this brings home to me the importance of how the United States reacts. We could have overreacted and moved troops and scared the hell out of people. And we could have under-reacted by saying well we'll deal with whoever is there. But I think the advice I got was good. I think we found the proper balance. Certainly in this case we're getting enormous credit from the key players in the Soviet Union.

It's hard to know what will happen to the various participants. Yanayev is history I'm sure. There are rumors that Yazov is dead, [that] he's committed suicide. Rumors that Pugo and Kryuchkov are under arrest, and all in all it is a very murky situation still. . . .

Yeltsin called again that evening to update me further. He was at the House of the Supreme Soviet. Silayev and Rutskoi had brought Gorbachev back to Moscow, unharmed and in good health. So far Yazov,

Pavlov, and Kryuchkov had been taken into custody. Upon Yeltsin's orders, the attorney general of the Soviet Union had begun a case against all the plotters.

"I want to congratulate you with the fact that in our country democracy has won a great victory," said Yeltsin. "We must work together so that this will never repeat itself. Thank you very much for your tremendous help in the eyes of the whole world. I congratulate you myself and thank the American people."

"My friend, your stock is sky-high over here," I replied. "You displayed respect for the law and stood for democratic principles. Congratulations. You were the ones on the front lines, who stood in the barricades—all we did was support you. You brought back Gorbachev intact. You restored him to power. You have won a lot of friends around the world. We support and congratulate you on your courage and what you've done. If you will now accept some advice from a friend—get some rest, get some sleep."

I asked him about Moiseyev. Was he behaving? "No, he is not," said Yeltsin. "We are not holding him under guard. That is for President Gorbachev to decide. My orders were for Yazov, Pavlov, and Kryuchkov only."*

Before August 21 was over we were already under fire for our recent policy toward the Soviet Union—that we could have done more and might have forestalled the putsch. My diary that day and the next summed up my reaction:

> I can't describe the emotion I felt when we started to get hit from the right and the left. The left saying we should have put more money in and you wouldn't have had this—Gephardt. From the right, well you shouldn't have stayed so close to Gorbachev. . . . I think we walked the proper line. I think our policy has been vindicated. I think democracy has solidified itself. A cautious Gorbachev now has to worry less about the problems on his political right— military, KGB, etc. And maybe we can get a breakthrough on Cuba, Afghanistan, Baltics etc. . . .
>
> Why the coup took place had less to do with money. It is much more complicated than that. It has to do with Union, it has to do with power of the Army, it has to do with cutbacks, it has to do with

---

*Of the eight leaders, Pugo committed suicide before he could be arrested. The others were eventually pardoned under an amnesty law passed by the Russian parliament in February 1994.

.n arms control agenda that Yazov and company have had rammed down their throats. But for now it's very easy for some talking head to analyze things in a very simplistic manner. We are going to have problems with the Baltics . . . The best thing that Gorbachev could do [is release them]. I told him that when I was out in the dacha with him in Moscow. He now has less resistance from his right, obviously, the right having been beaten in the coup, and thus he ought to go ahead and get rid of the Baltic states, and [with] some program that compensates for the Soviet interests and sorts out the distribution systems and the dependency of the Balts in some formalistic way.

BRENT SCOWCROFT

A coup was something we had feared for some time, as resentment against Gorbachev continued to accumulate, both on domestic and on foreign policy issues. He had already faced several serious challenges to his authority and programs, both from the Party and the government. Occasionally he appeared cornered, but he had always shown great skill in outmaneuvering and facing down his challengers and detractors.

The scheduling of the signing of the Union Treaty might have been the precipitating event. The plotters may have calculated that if they allowed the Soviet Union to be so fundamentally altered, it would then be too late to turn things back. The evidence appears overwhelming that the coup cabal made its move in reaction to events, before it was really ready. After all, the plotters comprised the leadership of the organizations which had had the West trembling for forty years: the military, the security forces, and the Party. One can reasonably conclude that the plotters' reactive haste produced the Marx Brothers–like execution of the coup. Indeed, given who the perpetrators were, the incredible thing was that the coup did not succeed.

When Gorbachev later visited the President in 1992, he had a different theory. He said there had been a meeting of some of the leadership in the same suburban Moscow dacha where he had met with the President. He had been maneuvered into a certain room, obviously one containing listening devices. There he discussed a government shakeup he was planning, one which would have included the replacement of Pavlov and Kryuchkov. Hearing that, the cabal had reacted by accelerating its timetable.

In the end, it may be that the plotters simply felt that things were moving too fast and too far. Acting when Gorbachev was on vacation may have seemed a propitious time. Whatever explanation turns out to be the true story, critics who claim the coup could have been avoided had we given Gorbachev more aid that summer seem wide of the mark. Announcement of an influx of funds would almost certainly have added impetus to the cabal to act, before Gorbachev could reap any political benefit from additional financial support.

CHAPTER 22

Withering into History

BRENT SCOWCROFT

The failed coup accelerated the decline of central Soviet authority, particularly of the Communist Party, which was further discredited, and ultimately of Gorbachev. It also signaled the rise of the republics on the cue of an ascendant Yeltsin. The extent of its effect on relations between Gorbachev and Yeltsin themselves was made apparent when Yeltsin escorted Gorbachev to appear before the Russian Supreme Soviet on August 23. Yeltsin took advantage of every opportunity to humiliate Gorbachev and to make unmistakably clear who was now giving the orders. Gorbachev thanked Yeltsin for his support, heartfelt I am sure, but then was forced to read aloud from a report detailing the extent of backing for the coup within the Soviet government. But he contributed to his problems by making a lame attempt to defend communism during a press conference after his return to Moscow, still proclaiming that it could be transformed into a positive force. This performance showed how far out of touch he was with the current situation and revealed his true ideological colors as well. The signs were unmistakable. The Gorbachev era was over.

GEORGE BUSH

Although Yeltsin had very properly called for Gorbachev's return to power, I thought he was heavy-handed in the aftermath of the coup. I knew the two did not like each other, but at times Yeltsin treated a politically weakened Gorbachev with sheer disdain. He had won the day and was riding high. He could have been a little "kinder and gentler" as Gorbachev was pushed out of the picture. Nevertheless, the coup seemed to have made unlikely allies of these onetime political adversaries as they struggled to reassert control and prevent their opposition from reorganizing.

The events of the week after the coup were almost unbelievable. Understandably, there was a purge among the circle closest to Gorbachev, and not only among the direct conspirators. Just how many of these changes he chose to make and how many were at Yeltsin's insistence never became clear to me. Gorbachev appeared reluctant to punish some of the senior conspirators and had briefly retained Moiseyev. We soon heard that Yeltsin had forced him to fire this once-promising young general. I had admired and liked Moiseyev and was sorry to see him take part in the coup. I was less sorry about Yazov, whom I didn't find a sympathetic figure. I felt a deep sense of sadness, however, over Marshal Sergei Akhromeyev's suicide. Akhromeyev was somehow involved in supporting the coup, although he apparently played no direct role. He was an honorable and honest professional soldier, who had, as he had once told Brent, witnessed the destruction of everything he valued and worked for all his life. Other familiar faces were dismissed as well. Gorbachev removed Alexander Bessmertnykh for failing to oppose the coup. It was alleged that the Foreign Minister had sent out instructions to all embassies to support the action. He was replaced first by Boris Pankin, Soviet ambassador to Czechoslovakia, although Gorbachev finally persuaded Shevardnadze to return in November. Gorbachev also fired the entire Council of Ministers and ordered the KGB reorganized.

At the same time, he began to take measures against the Party leadership, which had in many cases supported the coup attempt. Some of this may have come from his desire to clean out the Party and reform it, but once again Yeltsin seemed to be pushing him. Yeltsin clamped down on his own, closing the Soviet Central Committee headquarters, banning Party papers, and even suspending the Russian Communist Party. On August 24, Gorbachev called to tell me he was resigning as general secretary (although he remained a member of the Party) and had ordered the government to seize Party property. When he announced this the next day, he also said the Central Committee should disband and urged that a new party be set up. A few days later, the Soviet parliament banned Communist Party activities. Despite these welcome developments, I thought there remained the potential for violent conflict. If Yeltsin or his supporters, tasting victory, brazenly rammed their new legislation and programs through the Soviet parliament and provoked enough of the now-cowed hard-liners to reorganize and lash out, there could be more trouble.

The republics took advantage of the turmoil to continue their drive to break free of the Soviet Union. Estonia and Latvia had declared their independence during the coup (Lithuania reaffirmed its 1990 declaration), and on August 24 the Ukrainian parliament, representing a fifth of

.ε Soviet population, voted for independence (subject to a December 1 referendum), a Ukrainian currency, and control over Soviet troops within its borders. The next day, Byelorussia also voted for independence. Gorbachev still refused to recognize the Baltics, insisting that only the Congress of People's Deputies could approve, but it was a losing situation. Russia did recognize them and Yeltsin urged that we move immediately as well.

For his political sake, and for US-Soviet relations, I hoped Gorbachev would grant the Baltics independence before we in the West acted. The longer he waited, the more likely it was that new tensions would build. I wanted to avoid the international and domestic political pressure on Gorbachev that immediate US recognition would bring, and the perception that he and his associates were acting under duress. I thought it should be said (and understood) in the Soviet Union, and in whatever it became, that we gave them time, a lot of time, to release the Baltics. I planned to use our influence behind the scenes to quietly work for the kind of change we and the whole world wished to see there. I also did not want the Soviet central leadership to feel backed up against a wall, or pushed into some final, grandstanding, military action. I was never certain about "rogue" hard-line elements inside the country, in the Party and security forces, especially if they felt there was nothing left to lose.

BRENT SCOWCROFT
The President had it right. We were under enormous pressure to recognize the Baltics and were severely criticized for not doing so immediately. That would have been the easy thing to do, and no one sought their liberation more than we. But we were striving for a permanent resolution of the issue. That could best be achieved only through voluntary Soviet recognition of Baltic independence. Otherwise, should the nationalist right ever come to power, they could more easily reverse the situation, claiming the USSR acted only under duress in a weakened condition. In other words, they could allege that the independence was not valid. By being patient for a few days until Moscow acted on its own volition, we prevented the possibility of anyone successfully asserting that claim.

GEORGE BUSH
I asked allied leaders for time before they acted, and then contacted Gorbachev, telling him we could not wait much longer. I cabled him that we would recognize the Baltics on August 30. He asked if we could wait until September 2, because the new Soviet State Council was to act on the matter that day. I agreed. It seemed to me much better to have

encouraged them to take the action, rather than to unilaterally recognize the Baltics, which everyone knew we were going to do anyway. That would only bludgeon Gorbachev one more time in the public arena, and add one more discordant note for an already weakened USSR.

DIARY

It's one o'clock, Kennebunkport time, September second, 1991. I'm sitting alone on our terrace. The last day of what has been a fantastic vacation, in spite of the turmoil in the Soviet Union. I'm alone out here. Finished a clam chowder luncheon, a little ham sandwich, a glass of sherry.

There are about forty seagulls sitting near me on the closer-in rocks. About ten, fifteen cormorants segregated, sitting on the end of the rock I use for fishing. It's perhaps the clearest September day I've ever seen here. My mind goes back to September second, 1944. Forty-seven years ago this very day I was shot down over the Bonin Islands. So much has happened, so very much—in my life and in the world.

Today I had a press conference. I recognized the Baltics. I called the presidents of Estonia and Latvia, having talked to Landsbergis of Lithuania a couple of days ago. I told them what we were going to do. I told them why we had waited a few days more. What I tried to do was use the power and prestige of the United States, not to posture, not to be the first on board, but to encourage Gorbachev to move faster on freeing the Baltics. Yesterday, he did make a statement to this effect and today there was a "ten and one" agreement discussed, where the various republics would be entitled to determine their own relationship with the center—all good as far as the Baltics go.

The fate of the Union was now up in the air. In the days following the coup, the Congress of People's Deputies met to consider its fallout. On September 5 it voted to "respect the declarations of sovereignty and acts of independence adopted by the republics," although full independence would be conditional on talks with the Soviet Union on the technicalities involved, the republics' signing of human rights conventions, and agreement to sign the nuclear non-proliferation treaty and join CSCE. The Congress backed a new confederal Union of Sovereign States, and set up a transitional government until the details and a treaty could be worked out. There would be a State Council of the presidents of the republics (at least those republics which decided to stay in the new political Union) d by the president of the USSR, which would act as the government coordinate common policies; an Inter-Republic Economic Committee, which would start work on an economic treaty not tied to the Union treaty; and a revised two-chamber Supreme Soviet. The new government would observe all existing treaties, nuclear weapons would be kept under a central command, and the Soviet military would also remain, although command (shaken up) would be shared by the central Soviet authority and the republics.

It was not yet certain just which republics would join a new Union, or what the end result would look like. On September 6, the new Soviet State Council approved independence for Estonia, Latvia, and Lithuania. None of these would probably choose to participate, nor would Georgia or Azerbaijan. Within weeks, all the republics except Russia, Kazakhstan, and Turkmenistan had voted for independence, although nearly all remained in the Soviet institutions and worked on a Union treaty.

At a cabinet meeting on September 4, the day after our return to Washington, we discussed how to respond to the upheaval, in particular on the economic front. President Bush did not consider it at all useful for the United States to pretend we could play a major role in determining the outcome of what was transpiring in the Soviet Union. He thought the Soviets—and the republics—would, and should, define their own future and that we ought to resist the temptation to react to or comment on each development. The momentum was clearly toward greater freedom. Demands or statements by the United States could be counterproductive, and galvanize opposition to the changes among the Soviet hard-liners.

GEORGE BUSH

The more I listened to the discussion in the Cabinet Room, the more I was convinced we simply did not know enough to design any detailed aid programs. We did not want the Soviets to starve, or to lack medicine. Yet, as far as I was concerned, the broad program of technical assistance that we set out at the G-7 meeting was still the best approach. We were already responding in two ways: I had announced that the United States would help alleviate probable food shortages that winter and would send experts to sort out what was needed. Second, we would be offering medical assistance through the end of 1992. We had to see what relationship survived between the republics and the center before we offered any major financial support. Kohl and Major suggested we consider how we each could reexamine and augment our existing bilateral economic relationship with the USSR—technical assistance—to help the nation cope with its immediate problems.

The next day there was a long NSC meeting over future strategy toward the Soviet Union, focusing on whether we should support a breakup, and arms control issues—we had a vested interest in what would become of the Soviet Union's nuclear forces.

President Bush observed that, with the Baltics free at last, and the rash of other independence declarations, it was a complex situation. There was also the problem of the future of the many small republics inside the Russian federation and other republics, as well as the ethnic enclaves across the Soviet Union. All of these were threatening to secede. No one here or there could even guess how that would work out. Furthermore, although Yeltsin was a hero, a genuine hero, how would he look a month from now? We should not act just for the sake of appearing busy.

Cheney called for a more "aggressive" approach. He argued that we had more leverage than we thought and if we simply reacted we could miss opportunities. "I assume these developments are far from over," he said. ". . . We could get an authoritarian regime still. I am concerned that a year or so from now, if it all goes sour, how we can answer why we didn't do more . . ." He suggested we pick up one of Bob Gates' ideas to establish consulates in all the republics, and said we should be looking at humanitarian assistance. "We ought to lead and shape the events." This, of course, would have been a thinly disguised effort to encourage the breakup of the USSR. Scowcroft countered that our aid program was premised on a strong center, as were those of the Europeans and the G-7 programs. "That's an example of old thinking," protested Cheney. Baker urged we continue to try to prop up the center. "We're thinking about how to deal with the republics," he said. ". . . [W]e ought to wait on the consulates and do what we can to strengthen the center. We need to consider how to react to the trend toward the independence of the republics."

"But what should we be doing now to engage Ukraine?" asked Cheney. "We are reacting." Scowcroft observed that Cheney's premise was that we would be dealing with fifteen or sixteen independent countries. "The voluntary breakup of the Soviet Union is in our interest," argued Cheney. "If it's a voluntary association, it will happen. If democracy fails, we're better off if they're small."

"The *peaceful* breakup of the Soviet Union is in our interest," corrected Baker. "We don't want another Yugoslavia."

The President asked whether we thought Ukraine would be in the new Union. "Out," predicted Cheney. "Should we encourage that publicly?" the President asked. Cheney thought not. "Our public point ought to be simply to discuss the events on the ground that we still desire to preserve and so forth."

croft asked Baker if he would support the Union if the alternative
bloodshed. "Peaceful change of borders is what we're interested in,
along the lines of Helsinki," answered Baker. "But if there's bloodshed
associated with the breakup, then should we oppose the breakup?"
asked Scowcroft. Baker thought we ought to relate to the republic lead-
erships as they existed, and go no further to encourage them.

"Shouldn't we wait for the new Union Treaty?" asked President Bush.

"Can you deal with a weak center?" put in Scowcroft. "Can the center
control the military if it has no other powers?" Cheney thought we could
do more if we knew that was the direction we wanted our policy to take.
Powell was less certain. "We want to see the dissolution of the old Soviet
Union," he said. "I am not sure that means fifteen republics walking
around. Some confederation is in our interest as well as seeking out
bilateral relationships."

There was also the problem of the fate and command and control of
nuclear weapons—spread across four republics—to consider should
the Soviet Union break up, a point Scowcroft raised. "I am comfortable
with where they are," said Powell. "Who has them is the more important
question. The Red Army has them now. If they move back to Russia, I am
not sure who will be in control."

"It is important not to alarm people on this," the President reminded
everyone. He wondered if there was anything we could do in defense to
save money in these conditions, and to take advantage of the changes.
Cheney said the Pentagon was beginning to reexamine all of its programs
and its strategy. One possibility was further cuts in short-range nuclear
systems, and perhaps going beyond the existing START agreement we
had just signed. Scowcroft suggested we look at nuclear testing, and
across the board at arms control. Powell added that we might consider
changing the alert levels of our strategic bombers. "A handful of such
proposals would put us on the offense," said President Bush. We had to
quiet those waters before the situation got any worse. He closed the
meeting by asking impatiently if there wasn't anything more ambitious
we could do.

GEORGE BUSH

In the coming months, the overriding debate within the Administration remained what we wanted to see emerge, and how best to make the
most of the greatly increased influence of the reformers while we could.
Was it better to have a number of independent republics, or to have a
weak center with some sort of federation, at least for economic purposes?
My own feeling was that, ideally, the best arrangement would be diffu-

sion, with many different states, none of which would have the awesome power of the Soviet Union. The republics, however, needed some relationship with one another through a "center," so they could get on with improving their economies. There should be some formal cooperation and coordination, since there was so much economic interdependence among the republics. The last thing we needed to see was barriers thrown up, or even economic warfare as one of them refused to sell or supply grain or energy to another.

I soon had a taste of the disaffection the republics felt for the Union, and the distance practical economic reform had yet to cover to make independence possible, when Leonid Kravchuk visited Washington in late September. So much had happened since I had seen him the month before in Kiev. Kravchuk, a long-time Soviet Communist Party official, explained that Ukraine wanted total independence. A December referendum was pending, to act on the independence vote in the Supreme Soviet, and it was possible that Kravchuk himself would soon be out of a job, although his support for Gorbachev during the coup had increased his standing with his people.

Kravchuk told me Ukrainians no longer believed the center could do anything other than foul up their lives. He asked for economic help and investment and wanted us to begin to deal directly with Ukraine in every way, bypassing Moscow. He did not seem to grasp the implications and complexities of what he was proposing. I pointed out that Ukraine still had to sort out its commercial and tax laws and set up arrangements with other republics. If they wanted investment, there had to be a climate in which people knew who they were dealing with and which simplified things for businesses operating in more than one republic.

BRENT SCOWCROFT

Although I had not stated it so bluntly at the NSC meeting, I believed we would be better off with a broken-up Soviet Union. Economically it was probably not the best solution, but I thought our primary security interest would best be served by breakup, thus fractionating the military threat we faced. However, I did not think this should be official US policy. Such a position would almost guarantee long-term hostility on the part of most Russians, who constituted the majority of the Soviet Union. We could actually do very little one way or the other to influence the outcome and, therefore, the downside of a public position favoring breakup seemed overwhelming.

The State Department, reflecting Baker's preoccupation with trying to influence a peaceful transition, did come up with some basic principles on

..idence that we wanted to see followed to avert violence and assure
own objectives were met. Jim discussed them with me and had
..nounced them the day before the NSC meeting. The "five principles"
were not unlike those we had devised on German reunification: self-
determination through democratic methods; respect for existing borders,
with any changes made through negotiation; respect for democracy and
the rule of law; human rights; and adherence to international law and
the USSR's existing treaty obligations. To these we later added a sixth—
central control over nuclear weapons, and safeguards against internal or
external proliferation. These principles notwithstanding, however, we
never really drafted a tight administration policy on the potential
breakup of the Union. This was partly because of the variety of perspectives, as well as the rapid movement of events and concern by some about
the diffusion of control over nuclear weapons that a breakup might
create.

On this latter point, I was perhaps the least worried. I thought there
was positive benefit in the breakup of command and control over strategic nuclear weapons in the Soviet Union to several republics. Anything
which would serve to dilute the size of an attack we might have to face
was, in my view, a benefit well worth the deterioration of unified control
over the weapons. The erosion of the center's authority, however, posed
some security dangers to be considered, especially the possibility of the
loss of physical control of the country's weapons of mass destruction. The
Union's nuclear weapons were concentrated in the territory of four
republics: Russia, Kazakhstan, Ukraine, and Belarus, not all of which
could give us comfort about their ability to handle or secure either weapons or fissionable materials. While the specific danger to the United
States was fairly remote, we did worry that these states could pose a host
of new security, control, and proliferation problems for one another as
well for themselves and those republics around them. Eventually, we (as
well as Gorbachev and Yeltsin) concluded that we would prefer to see the
weapons in the hands of just one entity, which had the stability and experience to secure them. In the end, the "one entity" became Russia, but
at this point in September we still considered a central government a
possibility.

As the President had indicated at the September 5 NSC meeting and
afterwards, he also wanted to reduce the number of nuclear weapons on
both sides even further than START stipulated. But we had to do this
while there were leaders in power, both in the Soviet Union and in any
successor states, who would work with us. His closing comments led to
a new round of arms control initiatives, both tactical and strategic.
Cheney's distaste for negotiated arms control, together with several

issues relating to tactical nuclear weapons, gave me an idea. Perhaps we could take advantage of the situation to solve a number of tactical nuclear weapons questions at the same time.

In Europe, for example, the unification of Germany rendered short-range nuclear weapons undesirable, since they would detonate on German territory. This had been the basis for Cheney's suggestion about reviewing the need for them. In Korea, and regarding the Navy's arsenal, there were other problems we could resolve. In connection with its efforts to engage North Korea, South Korea was suggesting the removal of the US nuclear weapons located there. We did not wish to make such a move solely in Korea, concerned that the North might take our actions as the beginning of a US withdrawal. The Navy's problem was different. A number of countries were reluctant to allow our warships carrying nuclear weapons into their ports. Navy policy was to neither to confirm nor deny the presence of the weapons, and this itself created problems, in particular with Japan and New Zealand. In addition, these were no longer the preferred weapon against submarines. The sum of all these issues led me to suggest that we unilaterally declare we were getting rid of all tactical nuclear weapons (except air-delivered ones).

President Bush and I discussed the possibility of such a sweeping initiative, as well as ideas about strategic ones, while sitting on the deck at Walker's Point. He was enthusiastic about the far-reaching nature of the idea and asked me to check with Cheney. Dick's initial reaction was skeptical but, after some discussion and modifications, such as not committing to destroy all withdrawn weapons, he signed on. With regard to strategic weapons, the focus of our proposals was the de-MIRVing of the ICBM force—some of the most destabilizing nuclear weapons in either arsenal and something the Soviets had previously rejected. Unlike the tactical reductions, however, the ICBM proposals would be sensible only if they were reciprocal, so they would have to be negotiated. We would also take our bomber force off alert. The result of these moves would not only be fewer nuclear weapons, but also a giant step toward increasing the stability of the forces which remained. Thus were initiated major new moves in arms control, moves of unprecedented size and character, designed in a way which made them more easily negotiated. These ideas became the heart of START II, signed in January 1993 just before we left office and ratified by the Senate in December 1995.

GEORGE BUSH

The Pentagon moved into high gear to respond to these initiatives, and Dick Cheney and Colin Powell (as well as the Chiefs of Staff) deserve great credit in producing a breakthrough in a very short time. By ber 27 we were ready to announce dramatic unilateral cuts. It was ,roadest and most comprehensive change in US nuclear strategy .ce the early 1950s, when we launched the containment strategy that saw us through the Cold War. I was looking forward to giving a speech spelling out these dramatic proposals, but I was a little worried about its impact in the United States. The proposals would be complicated to describe and perhaps too technical. We tried to get some clear language in the speech about what was happening. All the acronyms and jargon— SLCM, ALCM, etc.— didn't seem likely to register on most people, but apparently these did because the response to the final speech was great.

Our formal initiative included removing our strategic bombers from alert, the stand-down of all ICBMs we had already scheduled for deactivation under the terms of START I (which was not yet ratified), the halt and cancellation of a couple of missile programs, the withdrawal and destruction of our nuclear artillery shells, the removal of tactical nuclear warheads from our Navy's surface ships and submarines, as well as nuclear weapons used with our land-based naval aircraft. I called on the Soviets to do the same. I outlined our new strategic arms proposals and asked them to agree to permit only limited deployment of defenses for protection against limited ballistic missile strikes, whatever their source. Finally, I proposed discussions to explore cooperation on dismantling and destroying nuclear warheads, enhancing the physical security and safety of nuclear weapons, and nuclear command and control arrangements.

I phoned Gorbachev ahead of the speech, having sent him a letter with the details of the announcement, focusing on the proposals meant to ensure stability for the Soviet nuclear forces. Gorbachev reacted positively, although he could not yet tell me precisely what moves they would make in response. He asked if this was a unilateral move, which it was. The only sticking point was testing, and they would need to consult about this.

One feeling that came through in these telephone conversations, and other contacts between the governments, was that a real air of cooperation had developed. Perhaps it was how we had stood by Gorbachev and Yeltsin through the coup and had shown we wanted to see them succeed, or the ever closer relationship and trust that had grown up since Malta and Camp David. In any case, there was a genuine collaborative feeling. Mikhail seemed to want to solve the tough issues. We had seen some strong evidence of this when Jim Baker went to Moscow in early September. He spoke separately with both Yeltsin and Gorbachev, who were working together as best they could, and had engineered a deal for both the United States and the USSR to end all support to the combatants in

Afghanistan. Mikhail had also agreed to remove Soviet forces from Cuba, and announced it even before telling the Cubans. Both Gorbachev and Yeltsin backed central control of nuclear weapons—whatever became of the Union.

For the first time on an arms control initiative, I called Yeltsin, who immediately liked the proposal and promised to push the USSR to respond in kind, as we were asking in the initiative. I worried about signaling both Yeltsin and Gorbachev. We did not want to undermine Gorbachev, but neither did we want to neglect a rising Yeltsin—clearly the future lay with him. I thought arms control still came under Gorbachev's responsibility, and he was sensitive to the precedent I was setting, and to the political stature of Yeltsin I was recognizing. When I told him I was trying to call Yeltsin to brief him, and asked that he tell Yeltsin himself if I couldn't reach him, there was stony silence on the phone.

Gorbachev responded on October 5 with his own proposal, and he too called me ahead of time. He wanted to destroy tactical nuclear weapons on sea forces and was prepared to make further cuts in strategic weapons. The Soviets would also take their heavy bombers off alert and stockpile their weapons. He proposed a one-year moratorium on testing, and was ready to discuss a plan to reduce fissionable materials. In addition, the Soviets would reduce their army by 700,000. There were some differences in our positions, but on balance it was very positive and forthcoming. Mikhail told me he had spoken with Yeltsin, and indicated that Yeltsin was in agreement—which pleased me. He also reported that the twelve republics had drafted an agreement on economic union and there would be a new Union Treaty.

I discussed the economic treaty with Yeltsin on October 8. He said he hoped to work out the lingering problems in a meeting in Moscow scheduled for three days later. "We understand we have the least to gain; as a matter of fact, we might even lose something. But we'll sign it, because of the bigger political goal—to save the Union." He wanted to get all the other republics to sign the economic union treaty and then use that as a foundation for a formal political union. Yeltsin was working with Gorbachev on the arms control initiatives, and was suggesting even more radical cuts in Soviet forces since Russia had enormous military potential of its own. Eventually, on October 19, eight of the republics signed a vague Treaty on Economic Community of Sovereign States. Ukraine and Moldova would sign a few weeks later.

Through October, I prepared for the Middle East Peace Conference in Madrid at the end of the month, which we had asked the Soviets to

..sor. The conference was particularly gratifying to me because it
..one of the direct fruits of the Gulf War. Without the successful
..osecution of that conflict and our coalition-building with our Arab
allies, such a meeting would have been impossible. We hoped to take
advantage of the goodwill we had forged with our Arab allies to advance
regional peace and security. Much of our considerable collective energy
in 1991, especially on the part of Jim Baker, went into making this
process and the Madrid conference a success, as we worked to draw
together the still reluctant and uneasy players.

I looked forward to another opportunity to see Gorbachev in Madrid
and talk with him at length.

DIARY, OCTOBER 26

It is clear to me that things are an awful lot different regarding
Gorbachev and the Center than they were. He's growing weaker all
the time. I am anxious to see what his mood is. He's still important
in nuclear matters, but all the economic stuff—it looks to me like
the republics have been more and more exerting themselves. It will
be interesting to figure out his mood. I remember not so long ago
how he couldn't stand Yeltsin. How he, up at Camp David [in June
1990], made clear he didn't think Yeltsin was going anywhere. But,
now all that has changed. Reports recently that he might not be
around long. The briefing book indicates this may be my last meeting with him of this nature. Time marches on.

I met with Mikhail on October 29, the day before the conference, over
a luncheon at the Soviet ambassador's residence in Madrid, a boxy building on a hillside below the embassy. Gorbachev looked well. The smile
was there, but not with quite the same zip as before. He described internal developments in the Soviet Union and asked for aid. I knew this was
difficult for him. He said he needed $3.5 billion in new agricultural cred-
its and $1 billion as a grant in food assistance. It was difficult for me to
disappoint him. I told him we could only go for $1.5 billion in agricul-
tural credits. Our reports indicated that Soviet credit was in far worse
shape than we'd thought. Banks were near total collapse. Yet Gorbachev
contended that with all their resources they could pay off the loans. It
seemed he was out of touch with the pragmatic aspects of what he was
asking.

At one point I took Mikhail aside. "Look," I said. "I don't want to
undermine you with Yeltsin, but we need to know a little more what the
real relationship is." Yeltsin had just made a major speech on economic
reform in which he had not only outlined drastic measures—to eliminate

price controls, speed privatization of agriculture and some industry, and end foreign aid—but also warned the other republics that if they did not cooperate in creating a new Union Treaty, Russia would take its own path, with its own army and currency (for both of which Ukraine had already announced plans). Yeltsin made no mention of Gorbachev or the central government, but had warned that he planned to stop financing many of the ministries and agencies of the "former Union" as of November 1. Mikhail told me that the economic portion of what Yeltsin had said was positive, but the rest was worrisome. "He retreated on some issues in the Union Treaty," he said. "Still, I will give him support because he is pushing reform—as long as he doesn't go for separatism."

That evening we joined Prime Minister Felipe Gonzales at a dinner hosted by King Juan Carlos at Zarzuela Palace, his residence. The King warmly greeted me and I was pleased that our earlier visits at Tokyo (during Emperor Hirohito's funeral) and particularly at Camp David had broken the ice. I think highly of him. He is universally recognized as a great monarch, well respected in Spain and abroad for his key leadership in helping his country's transition to democracy after the Franco years.

Mikhail and Raisa soon arrived. At one point Raisa spoke of her days confined in the Crimea during the coup. I told her that Barbara (who could not attend) had tears in her eyes when she saw the picture of Raisa and her grandchild getting off the plane in Moscow. She had written Raisa a letter telling her how relieved she had been to learn they were safe. As we spoke, Raisa sounded genuinely fond of Barbara.

We sat on couches around a square glass-topped coffee table. The living room was extraordinarily comfortable. Personal pictures of the royal family covered the tables and lined the walls, along with more formal portraits and tapestries. We took several group photos, after which the Queen accompanied Raisa out of the room, leaving just the four of us for dinner.

I sat next to the King and across from Mikhail, whose mood was generally upbeat. He gave us a fascinating description of those fateful seventy-two hours in the Crimea. He said his own guards remained very loyal, but the head of his security unit "sold out" to the plotters and had given them access to him. He described making a videotaped statement to the outside world about his situation and to show that his health was excellent. He recorded four statements on a single tape, which they had then cut apart and rolled into tight wads, trying to figure out how to get them past their guards. I gathered the coup ended before the tapes were smuggled out. He had sent me one through Jim Baker in September when Jim had been to Moscow.

Mikhail reflected on how Khrushchev had been pushed from office in the early 1960s, on charges that he had been seeking too much power. He explained how, at a recent meeting with republic leaders, he had said "I don't need power," and wasn't looking for it. He had told them he wanted to preserve the Union, not power, and that if they wanted him out, he would resign. None of them took him up on the offer. The King at one point asked whether they were trying to clip his wings. Mikhail didn't think they could, or would, although he admitted some wanted to cut back the power of the center.

He felt confident that Ukraine would stay a part of the Union (I didn't contradict him, although I was thinking back to my talk with Kravchuk barely a month earlier). He pointed out the enormous "Russian problem" there, as well as in other republics. He did not sound very high on Kravchuk, whom he did not think would win the upcoming presidential election. In contrast, he was enthusiastic about Nursultan Nazarbayev, President of Kazahkstan, who had, he said, "a very good view of how the Union should work." As for Yeltsin, he told me he was going to continue to work with him, but I got the feeling that he simply couldn't stand him, although that may have been too strong.

The evening was a very good chance to visit with a man for whom I had high regard, with whom I felt a genuine friendship. As I reflected in my diary:

> His problems are enormous, and I'm wondering whether the predictions of some are true: "this will be the last meeting of President Bush and President Gorbachev. Things are moving too rapidly for Gorbachev, and he cannot remain the force he once was. Indeed, he will be almost a caretaker." If Gorbachev feels he's on a slippery slope, I must say he didn't show it in his talks. He made clear the problems were enormous, but he didn't show anxiety, and he didn't convey the feeling that he was washed up.

Our relations with Russia and Ukraine would be the critical issue as we grappled with responding to the dissolution of the Soviet Union. As November wore on, Yeltsin systematically began to assume powers from the USSR for Russia, to dissolve ties with the center, and to assert authority over economic, financial, and political matters. The Ukrainians were facing two decisions. The first was the referendum on independence. The second, if they selected independence, was membership in the new Union Gorbachev was proposing. The chances seemed good that they would vote for independence, which would raise the question of recognition. We had to be careful not to handle this so precipitously that

we encouraged the radical nationalists in Ukraine and in Russia—where there was considerable resistance to losing Ukraine and its twelve million ethnic Russians. The last thing we needed was confrontation between the two—perhaps an economic war where the Russians started charging Ukraine world prices for oil and the Ukrainians responding by cutting Russia off from their industrial goods and farm products.

Whether Ukraine would join a new Union (Gorbachev's optimism notwithstanding) was not certain, nor what kind of over-arching arrangement between the republics might be created. Gorbachev and the republic presidents were still arguing over structure: Gorbachev pushed for a union inside a single state; Yeltsin and the others backed a confederation of sovereign republics, although they differed about the tightness of such an organization. On November 14, the State Council agreed to a confederation of sovereign states, without a common constitution, and treaty-based. Once they consulted their parliaments, the treaty could be signed. It was a confusing situation. The treaty document, eventually made public, implied that each of the new states would have its own foreign policy and even its own military, although there would be a centralized armed forces, including nuclear arsenals. Just how the union was to work was vague. The treaty was to be signed at a State Council meeting on November 25, but during it Yeltsin announced that the Russian Supreme Soviet objected to parts of the document and wanted a delay—a call echoed by the other republic presidents. He also thought further work should wait until after the Ukrainian referendum on December 1. If a treaty was signed beforehand, it might influence the outcome against a union. Eventually, the presidents agreed to submit the treaty to their legislatures for approval and then meet again to sign it before the end of the year, sidestepping the problem until Ukraine made its choice. Gorbachev was forced to announce a delay.

GEORGE BUSH

On the day before the referendum, I called Mikhail to tell him that, as a democratic nation, we had to support the Ukrainian people whatever the outcome, but we wanted to do so in a way that encouraged a peaceful transition to a new order. It seemed to me that recognizing Ukraine would bring it back into the treaty process—removing any questions about their sovereignty. I added that I wanted to see certain arrangements made. Collective, central control of nuclear weapons, a non-nuclear Ukraine, respect for human rights and minorities, and the implementation of existing treaties such as START and CFE. I said we would be sending a special envoy to discuss the matter.

Mikhail was clearly not pleased with the news, unfortunately already leaked following my meeting with some Ukrainian-Americans, that we were giving serious consideration to recognizing Ukraine. "It appears that the United States is not only trying to influence events, but to interfere," he complained. He argued that even though the majority of the republics had declared independence, that did not prevent them from participating in the formation of a Union—he seemed to think that somehow Ukraine could be independent yet part of the Union.

It was obvious Gorbachev still believed the republics would remain freely in the Union. He urged me not to take any action that would push events in the "wrong" direction. He pointed out that if Ukraine left, the Russians living there, and other non-Ukrainians, would become citizens of a foreign country. Furthermore, Crimea (once part of Russia until Brezhnev gave it to Ukraine) threatened to "review its status" as part of Ukraine if the republic went for independence. Yeltsin was calling for a return of all Russian lands, including those in Kazakhstan, Ukraine, and elsewhere. "If this process unfolds," he warned, "it would be a catastrophe for Russia, Ukraine, and the rest of the world." I assured Mikhail that I wanted to cooperate, but that we welcomed independence to guard against radical elements in Russia and Ukraine. I was not trying to embarrass him or Yeltsin, nor mingle in their internal affairs. He told me of a meeting with the reformers, and that they had all agreed that political union was essential. "Without it," he warned once more, "the result would be a catastrophe for the Soviet Union, you, and the world."

I spoke with Yeltsin about forty-five minutes later, and went over the same points on Ukraine as I had with Gorbachev, and my worries about the stability of the Union. His view was quite different from Gorbachev's. He understood my concerns. He pointed out that only seven republics had yet signed up for the Union—five Islamic and two Slavic (Byelorussia—now renamed Belarus—and Russia). This concerned him, for it meant the two largest (and Russian) states would be outvoted.

"I will be very frank with you, as always," he said. "I believe that if Ukraine won't join . . . , then this will be a rather weak Union. I told Gorbachev today, and I said yesterday in a newspaper interview, that if Ukraine will not join the Union, then that is a problem for Russia." He believed that if Ukraine voted for independence it would not sign the new treaty. "I think the new Ukrainian president will not begin negotiations with Gorbachev, but will begin talks with Russia," he added. Because of the importance of Russian-Ukrainian relations, if the Ukrainians went for independence, then Russia would have to recognize Ukraine whether or not the new nation signed the Union Treaty. "Right away?" I asked. "Yes, we need to do it immediately," he said firmly. ". . . Gorbachev does not know this. He still thinks Ukraine will sign." Yeltsin added that he would meet with the new President of Ukraine in December to discuss the basis of the new relations. A top issue would be resolving the nuclear question.

He warned that if Russia did not recognize Ukraine, even with the conditions I had outlined to him and to Gorbachev, it would cause an uprising among the extremists. "But you are right," he said. "We cannot lose ties between Russia and Ukraine. I am now thinking very hard with a narrow circle of advisors on how to preserve the Union . . . Our relations with Ukraine are more significant than those with the central Asian republics, which we feed all the time." He asked that I not reveal the content of our discussion until the results of the referendum were published.

As I told Brian Mulroney that afternoon, I did not anticipate a long delay in US recognition of Ukraine, but I wanted to give it and Russia a chance to sort things out. While Gorbachev and Yeltsin differed on whether Ukraine would want to stay in the Union, I thought they would both eventually agree to independence.

Canada has a large ethnic Ukrainian population in the Western provinces and Brian was already under pressure to recognize Ukraine. "I'd like to do nothing harmful to Gorbachev," he confessed, "even though we all sense it's a lost cause regarding holding the Union together."

"It seems so," I agreed.

"It's almost a personal thing—to help Gorbachev," said Brian. "I feel almost the same way as I did when we had to deal with the Baltics. We don't want to do anything disruptive. It's a matter of semantics, of wording, but our approach is not far off from yours. We'll recognize or acknowledge the independence of Ukraine, then we'll negotiate the establishment of diplomatic relations."

"That's what we're going to do," I replied.

BRENT SCOWCROFT

Ukraine was key to creating a viable Union. Gorbachev somehow thought that Ukraine could vote for independence and still join the Union. Yeltsin did not agree. His comments about early recognition might have meant he was maneuvering to keep Ukraine out of the Union and thus cause it to fail. He was probably sensitive to the domestic Russian political ramifications of recognizing Ukraine and its large Russian population, but also of whether it was Ukraine or Russia that would drive the stake into the heart of the new confederation. Then he had to consider the long-term antagonism in Ukraine if Russia did not recognize its independence. For our part, we were in the middle of a very sensitive situation between Yeltsin and Gorbachev. We had heavy pressure from Ukrainian-Americans for instant recognition, but this could be seen as taking sides between the two and pronouncing on the fate of the Union.

When Ambassador Robert Strauss told Shevardnadze of our intentions, the Foreign Minister was darkly pessimistic. He had warned Strauss that there might be a harsh response from the military if Ukraine moved to independence. He had spoken the day before with the general who had organized the defense of the Russian White House during the August coup. The officer had warned that conservative elements in the military were still strong and were secretly organizing to act. Soviet troops remained in the independent Baltic states, but were extremely discontented. Similar problems could develop on an even larger scale in Ukraine. "These are desperate people," he concluded.

Shevardnadze also cautioned us not to rely on the leaders in many republics who were riding the wave of nationalism. In fact, he said, the Communist Party in Ukraine was one of the most conservative in the USSR, and its leaders had covertly supported the August coup. He contended that Kravchuk had actually known about the coup in advance but had done nothing to warn Gorbachev. Now the Party had united with separatist forces in the Ukraine to try to save itself.

GEORGE BUSH

On December 1, Ukrainians overwhelmingly backed independence— by 90 percent—and Kravchuk was elected with 62 percent of the vote. I called him on December 3, and congratulated him. He told me Yeltsin had already contacted him and had said Russia would recognize Ukraine. The two would be meeting on December 8 to coordinate policy, just as Yeltsin had said they would. I explained what we hoped to see take place, such as getting rid of nuclear weapons, adherence to the CSCE principles, taking care of their borders, and guaranteeing minority rights. We would be sending an envoy to discuss these issues.

On December 8, Yeltsin called to tell me about his meeting with Kravchuk and Stanislav Shushkevich, president of Belarus. In fact, he was still with them in the conference room at a hunting lodge near Brest.

"Today, a very important event took place in our country, and I wanted to inform you myself before you learned about it from the press," he said with flourish. He explained they had been meeting for two days and had agreed that "the system in place and the Union Treaty everyone is pushing us to sign does not satisfy us. And that is why we got together and literally a few minutes ago signed a joint agreement."

Yeltsin seemed to read aloud what sounded like a prepared statement, recounting the problems of the negotiations surrounding the Union treaty and those of the existing Soviet Union. He declared that the center's short-sighted policy had brought them to political and economic crisis. As a result, they had signed an accord. "This accord," he intoned, "consisting of sixteen articles, is basically a creation of a commonwealth or group of independent states." In short, Yeltsin had just told me that he—and the presidents of Ukraine and Belarus—had decided to dissolve the Soviet Union.

When he finished the prepared text, his tone changed. He explained that the accord included an article that opened the commonwealth to all former republics. The members would guarantee international obligations under agreements and treaties signed by the former Union, including foreign aid debt. "We are also for the unitary control of nuclear weapons and non-proliferation," he assured me. The document had already been signed by the leaders of the three republics present. He had just finished speaking to President Nazarbayev of Kazakhstan, who was in full agreement with their actions and planned to sign as soon as he could.

To me, the provisions sounded as though they'd been designed specifically to gain US support for what was being done, since they directly addressed the conditions for recognition we had laid out. I did not want to imply prematurely our approval or disapproval. "I see," I said simply.

"This is very serious," said Yeltsin. "These four states form ninety percent of the national product of the Soviet Union. This is an attempt, a step, to maintain a commonwealth, but to free us from the global center which has issued commands to us for over seventy years. This is a very serious step, and we hope, we are sure, we are certain, that this is the only way out of the critical situation we find ourselves in.

"Mr. President," he added. "I must tell you confidentially, President Gorbachev does not know these results. He knew we were to meet—in fact, I told him myself we would meet. Surely we will immediately send him the text of our accord, as certainly he will have to make decisions at his level. Mr. President, I was extremely, extremely frank with you today. We four states feel there is only one possible way out of this critical situation. We don't want to do anything secretly—we will give a statement immediately to the press. We are hoping for your understanding.

"Dear George," he said. "I am finished. This is extremely, extremely important. Because of the tradition between us, I couldn't even wait ten minutes to call you." I promised to read the accord as soon as he sent it to me and to respond quickly. I felt a little uncomfortable. "We will work with you and others as this develops," I said. "Of course, we hope that this whole evolution is a peaceful process." Sidestepping the question of American support for Yeltsin's implication, I added that we understood this must be sorted out by the participants, not by outside parties such as the United States. Yeltsin agreed, and confidently added that he was sure all the other republics would join them soon.

BRENT SCOWCROFT

Following the agreement on a Commonwealth of Independent States on December 8, Yeltsin worked assiduously to complete the dismantling of the USSR. In reality, he had begun this process when he appeared with Gorbachev before the Russian Supreme Soviet following the attempted coup. The target of these efforts appeared to be Gorbachev, rather than the Soviet Union per se. One wonders whether this had been a long-standing goal or whether Yeltsin simply seized an opportunity unexpectedly offered by the weakening of Gorbachev—and his own strengthening—as a result of the coup.

The importance of the scheduled Union Treaty vote in August as a trigger for the coup is perhaps substantiated by Yeltsin's own preoccupation with the Ukrainian vote on independence. He seemed determined to forestall Ukraine from joining Gorbachev's Union. Both for the coup cabal and for Yeltsin, the new Union was seen as a step which would have put the Soviet Union on a new footing and a new course—and therefore beyond reach.

It was painful to watch Yeltsin rip the Soviet Union brick by brick away from Gorbachev, and then transfer most of them to Russia. By the end, Gorbachev controlled little more than General Yevgeny Shaposhnikov, commander of the Soviet military, whose forces were dissolving into the former republics at a rapid rate. Perhaps Gorbachev's time had indeed come, but he deserved a less ignominious end.

GEORGE BUSH

Gorbachev was furious with Yeltsin's machinations, and the deliberate body blow to the collapsing Union. Both he and Yeltsin sparred as they tried to draw the military's support behind them.

DIARY, DECEMBER 8

Now we hear from Gorbachev saying that the whole deal by Yeltsin and the others is illegal. "We need a referendum, we need the people to speak." And, I find myself on this Monday night, worrying about military action. Where was the Army—they've been silent. What will happen? Can this get out of hand? Will Gorbachev resign? Will he try to fight back? Will Yeltsin have thought this out properly? It's tough—a very tough situation.

Five days later, Yeltsin called me again. The parliaments of Ukraine, Belarus, and Russia had each ratified the Commonwealth accords the day before, and the leaders of the five central Asian republics had decided to join and would sign the document on December 21 in Alma-Ata, in Kazakhstan. He added that Moldova and Armenia had indicated they would sign as well. "So the way it works is that on either December 20, 21, or 22 ten independent states will sign the accord together. In addition, I met with the Army general staff, the security forces, and the internal security forces. They all support our decision. Today all is very calm in Moscow." He was in daily contact with Gorbachev to ensure a smooth transition. "What will happen by the end of December, early January is that we will have a complete Commonwealth of Independent States and the structures of the center will cease to exist. We are treating Mikhail Sergeyevich Gorbachev with the greatest respect and warmly. It is up to him to decide his own fate." Nuclear weapons would be under a unified command. As for the rest of the forces, all that remained were the ground troops, since they considered their Navy and Air Force part of the strategic forces—except for Ukraine, which would have its own ground forces.

I asked him what he thought Gorbachev would do. Yeltsin said he had met with Mikhail the day before. "He is not averse to agreeing to the decision of the ten. He is taking reality into consideration. In accordance with the 1922 treaty, we can now say that the ten republics will sign the accord and that their decision is final. So, the central organs will simply cease to exist." In short, the Soviet Union would evaporate.

I was worried about the contempt with which Yeltsin seemed to be treating Gorbachev, who had done so much for the Soviet Union—and peace. I reminded Yeltsin we had worked closely with both him and with Gorbachev over the years as this had evolved. "We have a high regard for him and for Shevardnadze and the reformers, and history will show they did a great deal," I said. As these changes took place, I hoped it would be in a friendly manner. "I do guarantee, and I promise you personally, Mr. President," said Yeltsin, "that everything will happen in a good and decent way. We will treat Gorbachev and Shevardnadze with great respect. Everything will be calm and gradual with no radical measures."

I called Gorbachev that afternoon and told him we were not trying to influence events. "I am thinking of you professionally and personally," I said. "I wondered if you could shed light on what for us is a confusing situation." Gorbachev's fury was obvious. He spoke rapidly, recounting the events since November 25, when they had agreed on a draft Union treaty and the State Council, including Yeltsin, had signed a resolution. The treaty had gone to the republics for ratification, and then to the USSR Supreme Soviet. "Yeltsin participated at all stages in cooperating with me," he said angrily. "He changed course radically by turning up in Minsk. For two days, I had no contact with him . . . and this was an unexpected change for me." Gorbachev said he had done his best to keep the treaty process going, and everything had pointed to a positive outcome from the Russian parliament. "But all of a sudden Yeltsin made a change. In politics anything can happen, especially when one deals with such politicians." People were saying the process was at a dead end but he did not understand why. Everyone had agreed except Ukraine. "Okay, so Ukraine wanted to become independent," he said. "But it had indicated it could be part of the economic and defense treaty—that is what Kravchuk indicated to me and what he is indicating now by his actions. So what is different? Ukraine could have become part of the Union treaties." Events were now going in a different direction from the one he'd wanted, but he was pragmatic about what he seemed to feel was a betrayal at the hands of Yeltsin and Kravchuk. "We are politicians," he said. "We deal with realities and have to act accordingly."

Whatever happened, he wanted the process to move within the framework of the constitution. "I will abide by the decisions of the republics," he said. "The Minsk statement was published in an impromptu fashion and there are many things that are not clear. The country was a whole and now could break into pieces." He hoped the other republics would be involved, perhaps to counter the Russian and Ukrainian push to dismantle the old Union. Many legal questions were unclear, especially who was responsible for the foreign and security affairs of the USSR and its obligations. What would become of the Security Council seat at the UN? "All this looks like the work of amateurs," he complained.

I think Gorbachev was a bit stunned about what was happening to him personally, and as the president of the Soviet Union, the leader of a great country. His authority was slipping away. "They have refused my role," he said. "I understand this situation, even if I don't share the approach." He confirmed what Yeltsin had said about the armed forces, and that their nuclear weapons were under control. "How do I see my role in the future?" he asked. "If the Commonwealth is an amorphous organization with no mechanism for foreign policy and defense and economic interaction, then I do not see any role for myself. Now as I see the situation— and I think the Commonwealth was a mistake—we must have greater coordination among the republics; otherwise we will not get out of the situation, the mudslide we are in. . . ." Whether "greater coordination" meant a president, and a place for Gorbachev in all this, I don't know. Yeltsin had already methodically stripped the Union away from Gorbachev.

The end came swiftly. On December 21, at Alma-Ata, all the republics except the Baltics and Georgia signed the Declaration of Adherence to the Commonwealth of Independent States. There was nothing left of the USSR.

My friend Mikhail Gorbachev resigned as president of the Soviet Union on Christmas Day. That morning I received a message that he wanted to talk with me, a "final call," at 5:00 pm Moscow time, 10:00 am Washington time. I took the call at Camp David, where I was spending the holiday with my family.

He wished Barbara and me a Merry Christmas. He explained that he had sent me a letter as well, and that he wanted to reaffirm its content— that he valued what we had done together, first when I was vice president and then as president. He was not bitter about the collapse of the Soviet Union, or his own political fortunes, but he seemed drained and uncertain about the future of the country he loved.

"The debate in our Union on what kind of state to create took a different tack from what I thought right," he acknowledged. "But let me say that I will use my political authority and role to make sure that this new Commonwealth will be effective. I am pleased that already at Alma-Ata the leaders of the commonwealth worked out important nuclear and strategic agreements. I hope that in Minsk they will make decisions to assure a mechanism of cooperation among republics."

He was worried about the fate of what had been his country. "George, let me say something to you that I regard as very important. Of course, it is necessary to move to recognize all of these countries. But I would like you to bear in mind the importance for the future of the Commonwealth that the process of disintegration does not grow worse. So, helping the process of cooperation among the republics is our common duty. I would really like to emphasize this to you.

"Now, about Russia—this is the second most important emphasis in our conversation. I have here on my desk a decree of the president of the USSR on my resignation. I will also resign my duties as commander in chief and will transfer authority to use nuclear weapons to the president of the Russian Federation. So I am conducting affairs until the completion of the constitutional process. I can assure you that everything is under strict control. As soon as I announce my resignation, I will put these decrees into effect. There will be no disconnection. You can have a very quiet Christmas evening. Again, about Russia, let me say we should all do our best to support it. I will do this to support Russia. But our partners should do this too and should play a role to help and support it.

"As for me, I do not intend to hide in the *taiga*, in the woods. I will be active in political life. My main intention is to help all the processes here begun by perestroika and New Thinking in world affairs. Your people, the press here, have been asking me about my personal relationship with you. I want you to know at this historic time that I value greatly our cooperation together, our partnership and friendship. Our roles may change, but I want you to know that what we have developed together will not change. Raisa and I send to you and Barbara our best wishes."

"Mikhail," I replied. "Let me first say how grateful I am for this call. . . . We will stay involved, particularly with the Russian Republic, whose enormous problems could get worse this winter. I'm delighted to hear that you do not plan to hide in the woods and that you will stay involved politically and publicly. And I am totally confident that that will benefit the new Commonwealth.

"I've written you a letter that probably will be posted today, but in it I express my conviction that what you have done will live on in history and will be fully appreciated by historians. . . . Mikhail, on the personal side: I have noticed some very wonderfully strong statements about the relationship you have had with me, the relationship you have had also with Jim Baker, and, of course, I appreciate that very much because that's exactly the way I feel. You have found me up at Camp David, once again. We're here with Barbara and with three of our children's families. . . . The horseshoe pit where you threw that ringer is still in good shape, all of which reminds me that in my letter to you I say that I hope that our paths will cross soon again. You will be most welcome here. And, indeed, I would value your counsel after you have had a little time to sort things out. And perhaps we could do it right back up here at Camp David. But, in any event, that friendship you referred to—from my standpoint at least—is as strong as ever and it will be as strong as ever as these events unfold. No question about that.

"I will, of course, deal with respect—openly, forcefully, and hopefully progressively—with the leader of the Russian Republic and the leaders of these other republics. We will move forward with recognition and with great respect for the sovereignty that each republic has. We will be working with them on a wide array of issues just as we have been working productively with you in that direction. But none of that will interfere with my desire to stay in touch with you, to welcome suggestions from you as you assume whatever your new duties will be and furthermore to keep intact the friendship that Barbara and I value very, very much.

"And so at this special time of year and at this historic time, we salute you and thank you for what you have done for world peace. Thank you very much."

"Thank you, George," said Mikhail. "I was glad to hear all of this today. I am saying goodbye and shaking your hands. You have said to me many important things and I appreciate it."

"All the best to you, Mikhail."

"Goodbye."

After we hung up, I once more spoke into the small tape recorder into which I had confided so many thoughts over the course of the years:

> It was the voice of a good friend; it was the voice of a man to whom history will give enormous credit.
>
> There was something very moving about this phone call—a real historic note. I mentioned to him Camp David and wanting him back up here—the place where he threw the "ringer"—and I think he would like that; but this is the way I feel. I didn't want to get too maudlin or too emotional, but I literally felt like I was caught up in real history with a phone call like this. It was something important, some enormous turning point. God, we're lucky in this country—we have so many blessings.

BRENT SCOWCROFT

It was over. An event I had never imagined I would see in my lifetime had actually taken place. It left me feeling numb, disbelieving. It was not that I had not seen it coming. I had become accustomed, even somewhat inured, to watching a constantly embattled Gorbachev, but the signs of rapid deterioration since the attempted coup were unmistakable. No, the events themselves were creating a clear trend; it was rather the sheer incomprehensibility that such an epochal event could actually be occurring.

My initial reaction to the Soviet flag being lowered from the Kremlin for the last time was one of pride in our role in reaching this outcome. We had worked very hard to push the Soviet Union in this direction, at a pace which would not provoke an explosion in Moscow, much less a global conflagration, which was historically not an uncommon occurrence in the course of the death throes of great empires. We had done our part in crafting a beneficent outcome to this great drama, but the key actor in the final scenes was most certainly Gorbachev. He didn't plan or want it this way. He had started out to reshape the Soviet Union into a more efficient, more effective, more humane version of itself. He failed to understand that when he tried to force reform on a resistant system, his methods were pulling the threads right out of the fabric of that system. By the end, rather than reform the system, he had destroyed it.

For all his brilliance, Gorbachev appeared to have a fatal flaw. He seemed unable to make tough decisions and then stick with them. He had made a fine art of temporizing and trimming his sails. When he was personally under attack and had his back to the wall, as was more than once the case in the Supreme Soviet, he could fight back with great skill and resourcefulness. But when it came to selecting and enforcing a stern program of economic reform, Hamlet-like he shrank from the task. While I characterize his tendency to vacillate as a flaw, from our perspective it was very much a blessing. Had Gorbachev been possessed of the authoritarian and Stalin-like political will and determination of his predecessors, we might still be facing a Soviet Union. It would be one rejuvenated and reinvigorated, yet possessing at least some of the qualities which made it such a threat to the stability and security of the West.

It was a rare great moment in history. The end of an era of enormous and unrelenting hostility had come in an instant. And, most incredible of all, without a single shot being fired.

The final collapse of Soviet power and the dissolution of its empire brought to a close the greatest transformation of the international system since World War I and concluded nearly eight decades of upheaval and conflict. The world we had encountered in January 1989 had been defined by superpower rivalry. The Cold War struggle had shaped our assumptions about international and domestic politics, our institutions and processes, our armed forces and military strategy. In a blink of an eye, these were gone. We were suddenly in a unique position, without experience, without precedent, and standing alone at the height of power. It was, it is, an unparalleled situation in history, one which presents us with the rarest opportunity to shape the world and the deepest responsibility to do so wisely for the benefit of not just the United States but all nations.

GEORGE BUSH

I felt a tremendous charge as I watched the final breakup of the Soviet Union. I was pleased to watch freedom and self-determination prevail as one republic after another gained its independence. True, as Gorbachev told me in our last conversation, Russia and its neighbors still had far to go, but I had always been confident that, in the end, given the choice, the people of Central and Eastern Europe and the Soviet Union would put aside communism and opt for freedom. I remember the many uplifted bright faces in the crowds in Warsaw, Gdańsk, Prague, and Budapest, sensing that freedom was near. This was their victory. We all were winners, East and West. I think that was what made much of the process possible—that it did not come at the expense of anyone. I convinced Gorbachev that we were not trying to gain an advantage from the problems of the Soviet Union or its allies and that we sincerely wanted to see perestroika succeed. I could trust him, and I hope he knew he could trust me as we worked together to solve the international problems we confronted as our world changed. I think our relationship facilitated and smoothed matters at a critical time.

I was extraordinarily lucky to have had the privilege of serving as president during what turned out to be the closing years of the Cold War. The changes we participated in were the culmination of many years of effort by many people, both in the United States and elsewhere. We built on the careful planning and successes of Ronald Reagan and his

Administration, who in turn had carried on the work of their predecessors. From those who served in our military to those who planned and implemented policy across succeeding administrations, all had a hand in bringing the Cold War to a peaceful conclusion. The special roles of Gorbachev, Shevardnadze, and the other courageous reformers around them in bringing the Soviet Union back into the international family were crucial. Without them the Cold War would have dragged on and the fear of impending nuclear war would still be with us.

While we, of course, did not (and could not) anticipate what was about to happen as we came into office, I think our accomplishment or contribution was in how we guided and shaped the final critical events we have described here as they unfolded. Some tend to see the outcome of the revolutions in Eastern Europe, German reunification, or Desert Storm as inevitable; but nothing was a foregone conclusion. We set the right tone of gentle encouragement to the reformers in Eastern Europe, keeping the pressure on the communist governments to move toward greater freedom without pushing the Soviets against a wall and into a bloody crackdown. On Germany, working closely with Helmut Kohl, we managed to unite the allies behind unification and persuade the Soviets to accept a united Germany in a new NATO—probably the most important moment in the transformation of Europe. It brought an end to the division of Europe and showed that real peace, peace without fear, was at hand. In Desert Storm I hope we set positive precedents for future responses to international crises, forging coalitions, properly using the United Nations, and carefully cultivating support at home and abroad for US objectives. Above all, I hope we demonstrated that the United States will never tolerate aggression in international relations.

I am proud about what we accomplished and grateful for the wisdom, experience, and insight of the finest team I could want around me in the Administration. If there was ever a time when teamwork and camaraderie made a critical difference in policy-making, this was it. I remain convinced we had the right people in the right places at the right time. I was also fortunate to have so many wise friends among leaders elsewhere in the world—from Ottawa to Paris, Bonn, and London, and from Tokyo to Cairo, Ankara, and Riyadh—whose counsel I wanted and needed.

As I look to the future, I feel strongly about the role the United States should play in the new world before us. We have the political and economic influence and strength to pursue our own goals, but as the leading democracy and the beacon of liberty, and given our blessings of freedom, of resources, and of geography, we have a disproportionate responsibility to use that power in pursuit of a common good. We also have an obligation to lead. Yet our leadership does not rest solely on the economic strength and military muscle of a superpower: much of the world trusts and asks for our involvement. The United States is mostly perceived as benign, without territorial ambitions, uncomfortable with exercising our considerable power.

Among our most valuable contributions will be to engender predictability and stability in international relations, and we are the only power with the resources and reputation to act and be broadly accepted in this role. We need not, indeed should not, become embroiled in every upheaval, but we must help develop multilateral responses to them. We can unilaterally broker disputes, but we must act—wherever possible in concert with partners equally committed—when major aggression cannot be deterred, as in the Persian Gulf.

For these reasons, the importance of presidential leadership is probably greater now than ever. From a domestic perspective, the president must take seriously his constitutional role as the chief foreign policymaker, developing objectives and setting priorities, doing what is right for all even if it is unpopular, and then rallying the country. The challenge of presidential leadership in foreign affairs is not to listen to consensus, but to forge it at home and abroad. Nowhere is this leadership more critical than in creating a new domestic consensus for the American role in the world. There should be no question that we must face future challenges head on, without reverting to the isolationism and protectionism of the earlier part of the century. Our nation can no longer afford to retire selfishly behind its borders as soon as international conditions seemed to recede from crisis, to be brought out again only by the onrush of the next great upheaval. This was a pattern I was determined to break as we moved beyond the Cold War, and it is one we must continue to put behind us.

The present international scene, turbulent though it is, is about as much of a blank slate as history ever provides, and the importance of American engagement has never been higher. If the United States does not lead, there will be no leadership. It is our great challenge to learn from this bloodiest century in history. If we fail to live up to our responsibilities, if we shirk the role which only we can assume, if we retreat from our obligation to the world into indifference, we will, one day, pay the highest price once again for our neglect and shortsightedness.

PHOTOGRAPH CREDITS

Reagan, Gorbachev, and Bush at Governors Island: *Courtesy Ronald Reagan Library*

Bush and Mitterrand at Kennebunkport: *George Bush Presidential Library/Carol Powers*

Bush and Walesa in Gdańsk: *George Bush Presidential Library/David Valdez*

Mitterrand, Bush, and Kohl at the G-7 summit in Paris: *George Bush Presidential Library/Susan Biddle*

Thatcher and Bush at Camp David: *George Bush Presidential Library/Carol Powers*

Kohl and Bush at Camp David: *George Bush Presidential Library/Susan Biddle*

Discussion at Camp David during the 1990 summit: *George Bush Presidential Library/David Valdez*

Bush, Gorbachev, and interpreter: *George Bush Presidential Library/David Valdez*

Bid for the "Scowcroft Award": *George Bush Presidential Library/David Valdez*

Meeting with the White House press corps after the Iraqi invasion: *George Bush Presidential Library/Joyce Nalchayan*

Bush on the phone to King Fahd: *George Bush Presidential Library/Susan Biddle*

Meeting with the Saudis at Walker's Point: *George Bush Presidential Library/Susan Biddle*

Bush, Scowcroft, and Ellie: *George Bush Presidential Library/Susan Biddle*

Rice briefing in Helsinki: *George Bush Presidential Library/David Valdez*

Breakfast with Michel and Dole: *George Bush Presidential Library/David Valdez*

Bush and Havel: *George Bush Presidential Library/David Valdez*

Bush and Fahd: *George Bush Presidential Library/Susan Biddle*

Bush and Schwarzkopf: *George Bush Presidential Library/David Valdez*

Bush, Scowcroft, and Eagleburger: *George Bush Presidential Library/Susan Biddle*

Bush and the troops: *George Bush Presidential Library/Susan Biddle*

Bush walking alone: *George Bush Presidential Library/David Valdez*

Scowcroft on the phone: *George Bush Presidential Library/Steven Purcell*

The Bushes and the Quayles praying: *George Bush Presidential Library/David Valdez*

Oval Office meeting during Desert Storm: *George Bush Presidential Library/David Valdez*

Powell and Bush on the phone: *George Bush Presidential Library/David Valdez*

"The Gang of 8" meeting: *George Bush Presidential Library/David Valdez*

Bush with Thomas and Dodson: *George Bush Presidential Library/David Valdez*

Scowcroft receiving the Medal of Freedom: *George Bush Presidential Library/David Valdez*

Bush inspecting Soviet honor guard: *George Bush Presidential Library*

A NOTE ON THE TYPE

This book was set in Janson, a typeface long thought to
have been made by the Dutchman Anton Janson, who
was a practicing typefounder in Leipzig during the years
1668–1687. However, it has been conclusively demonstrated that these types are actually the work of Nicholas
Kis (1650–1702), a Hungarian, who most probably
learned his trade from the master Dutch typefounder
Dirk Voskens. The type is an excellent example of the
influential and sturdy Dutch types that prevailed in
England up to the time William Caslon (1692–1766)
developed his own incomparable designs from them.

Composed by Creative Graphics,
Allentown, Pennsylvania
Printed and bound by
R. R. Donnelley & Sons,
Harrisonburg, Virginia
Designed by Peter A. Andersen